# Football Psychology

Presenting an empirically underpinned synthesis of research and theory, while offering guidance for applied practitioners, this is the first book to comprehensively map the psychology of learning, playing, and coaching the world's favourite sport.

The book provides a complete analysis of key topics that capture the broad range of football psychology such as personality, motivation, cognition, and emotion; coaching and team essentials; psychological skills for performance enhancement; and developing players in youth football. Including contributions from a range of international researchers, each chapter provides a review of the relevant literature, key theories, real-world examples, and reflections on how knowledge can be applied in practice. Split into four sections, the book covers a diverse range of topics relevant not only to coaching and performance but also to personality development and health promotion.

Essential reading for any student, researcher, or professional in the area, the book is the most cutting-edge overview of how psychology can explain and improve the way football is both played and understood.

**Erkut Konter** has various degrees specializing in Sport Psychology and Football. He has more than 30 years' experience as a sport psychology consultant and football coach at national and international levels. He has a number of publications on football psychology and is currently at the Dokuz Eylül University, İzmir, Turkey.

**Jürgen Beckmann** is Professor and Chair of Sport Psychology at Technical University of Munich, Germany and Honorary Professor of the University of Queensland, Australia. He is a former president of the German Association of Sport Psychology. He has been consultant to numerous elite athletes and teams since 1987 including professional football teams of the German Bundesliga.

**Todd M. Loughead**, PhD, is Professor of Sport and Exercise Psychology in the Department of Kinesiology and Co-Director of the Sport Psychology and Physical Activity Research Collaborative at the University of Windsor, Canada. His current research interests are related primarily to group dynamics including athlete leadership, coaching, cohesion, and team-building. Outside of work, he enjoys coaching both football and ice hockey.

# Football Psychology

## From Theory to Practice

**Edited by Erkut Konter, Jürgen Beckmann, and Todd M. Loughead**

Routledge
Taylor & Francis Group

LONDON AND NEW YORK

First published 2019
by Routledge
2 Park Square, Milton Park, Abingdon, Oxon OX14 4RN

and by Routledge
52 Vanderbilt Avenue, New York, NY 10017

*Routledge is an imprint of the Taylor & Francis Group, an informa business*

© 2019 selection and editorial matter, Erkut Konter, Jürgen Beckmann and Todd M. Loughead; individual chapters, the contributors

*British Library Cataloguing-in-Publication Data*
A catalogue record for this book is available from the British Library

*Library of Congress Cataloging-in-Publication Data*
A catalog record has been requested for this book

ISBN: 978-1-138-28749-5 (hbk)
ISBN: 978-1-138-28751-8 (pbk)
ISBN: 978-1-315-26824-8 (ebk)

Typeset in Baskerville
by Wearset Ltd, Boldon, Tyne and Wear

MIX
Paper from
responsible sources
FSC
www.fsc.org   FSC™ C013985

Printed in the United Kingdom
by Henry Ling Limited

To my son Etkin Öge Konter. Thank you for giving me energy, courage, leadership power, psychological skills experiences, and most importantly happiness.

E. K.

To my wife Denise, my daughters Nicola and Lilian. Thank you for your sustained encouragement, support, and love.

J. B.

To my wife Krista, son Travis, and my late parents Lucy and Irvine Loughead. Thank you for your encouragement, support, and love.

T. L.

# Contents

# Contributors

## About the editors

**Erkut Konter** has a bachelor's degree in Physical Education and Sports specializing in Football. He also completed two master's degrees from England and Turkey in Sport Psychology examining state anxiety and performance in football. He received his PhD in the area of Counselling Psychology of Sport where he examined the relationship between psychological skills and performance in football. In addition, he pursued postdoctoral studies as a visiting scholar in the USA, where he investigated leadership power in sport and had the opportunity to coach children and adult football teams. Interestingly, he served as head coach for the Central Washington University football team which won a championship title in 2003. Dr Konter was nationally and internationally involved in various sports as a student, an athlete, a Physical Education teacher, a coach, and a sport psychology consultant. He is the former head of the Physical Education and Sports Department at Dokuz Eylül University, İzmir, Turkey. He is currently a full Professor Dr at the same university instructing various undergraduate and graduate classes that include Sport and Exercise Psychology, Motor Behaviour, Games Education, Football, and Futsal. He has published 12 books and more than 50 research publications, and a number of conference and congress presentations related to performance enhancement in sport psychology primarily in the areas of Leadership Power, Non-verbal Intelligence, Courage, and Psychological Skills. He holds a UEFA A Level Coaching Licence. Moreover, he has a number of experiences as a sport psychology consultant at amateur and professional, national and international levels including Olympic and premier league football teams.

**Jürgen Beckmann** is Professor and Chair of Sport Psychology at Technical University of Munich (TUM), Germany (since 2006). He was Dean of the TUM Department of Sport and Health Sciences from 2007 to 2013. In 2018 he was awarded an Honorary Professorship by the University of Queensland, Australia. Professor Beckmann was president of the German Association of Sport Psychology (ASP, 2005–2009), and editor in chief of the German *Journal of Sport Psychology* (1998–2000). Professor Beckmann has published 13 books and more than 160 peer-reviewed journal and chapter publications with more than 4,000 citations. A main focus of the TUM chair of sport psychology is translating research into interventions. Research areas covered are performance psychology, clinical psychology, and development and validation of assessment instruments. Recently, embodiment and green exercise have become major research topics. Professor

Beckmann has been consultant to numerous elite athletes and teams since 1987 (e.g. German National Team Alpine Skiing; German National Team Golf; German professional football teams in the Bundesliga).

**Todd M. Loughead** is Co-Director of the Sport Psychology and Physical Activity Research Collaborative at the University of Windsor, Canada. Dr Loughead's research uses a group dynamics perspective to examine human behaviour. Specifically, his interests are investigating athlete leadership and coaching, and how these two sources of leadership impact team functioning. As well, he is interested in athletes mentoring their peers and its associated benefits. He is also interested in team cohesion and how this contributes to an enhanced team environment. Dr Loughead consults with coaches, sport teams, and individual athletes that include local, provincial, Olympic, and professional teams/athletes. Dr Loughead is a member of the Canadian Sport Psychology Association (CSPA), Association of Applied Sport Psychology (AASP), Canadian Society for Psychomotor Learning and Sport Psychology (SCAPPS), and North American Society for the Psychology of Sport and Physical Activity (NASPSPA). Outside of work, he enjoys coaching both hockey and soccer.

## About the contributors

**Erwin Apitzsch** is an associate professor affiliated to Lund University, Sweden, and is a registered psychologist. He is the president of the Swedish Association for Behavioural and Social Research in Sport, SVEBI (1975–1985, 2017–). He is the editor in chief of the *Swedish Journal of Sport Research* (2012–) and was the secretary general of the European Federation of Sport Psychology (FEPSAC) (1983–2003). He was the international network coordinator for the Intensive Programme of the European Master's Degree in Exercise and Sport Psychology (2006–2014). Currently, he is a consultant to elite athletes and teams in Sweden and internationally.

**Itay Basevitch** is a senior lecturer in the Sport and Exercise Sciences programme and the course leader of the Coaching for Performance in Football degree at Anglia Ruskin University in the United Kingdom. He has vast experience working with athletes and teams as a sport psychology consultant and is a certified consultant through the Association for Applied Sport Psychology in the USA.

**Denise Beckmann-Waldenmayer** is a highly experienced psychologist, with a diploma in Psychology and several degrees in clinical therapy (family therapy, behavioural therapy, hypnosis). From 2006 to 2011 she was a research associate at the chair of sport psychology at Technical University of Munich, Germany. From 2012 she worked as a psychologist in several clinics (psychiatry and psychosomatic) before opening her own private psychological practice. She is listed as an expert for sport psychological training at the German Federal Institute of Sport Science (*BISp*) and since 2006 has been involved in sport psychological counselling for several German national teams (e.g. ice speed skating, pistol shooting, golf, biathlon). With a keen interest in supporting young players, she also developed the sport psychological framework for the youth academy of FC Bayern München and is also frequently asked to conduct parental coaching.

**José Lino O. Bueno** is Full Professor in Psychobiology at the University of São Paulo and Researcher at the National Council of Research (Brazil). He graduated in Philosophy and has a PhD in Experimental Psychology from the University of São Paulo. He was Fulbright Visiting Scholar at Duke University and did collaborative research at McMaster University, Cornell University, Tufts University, Université de Bourgogne, and Paris-Sud. He was President of the Brazilian Society of Psychology and Distinguished Visiting Scholar of the Southern Behavior Modification Society (USA).

**Lucas S. Capalbo** is a PhD candidate in Kinesiology specializing in the psycho-social aspects of sports at Michigan State University. He has worked, studied, and coached football in more than 10 countries. His vast exposure to different cultures has influenced his work as a scholar and coach. He investigates strategies to empower coaches to promote development and peace through sports, which he believes is a great platform for social growth.

**Alberto Cei**, psychologist and psychotherapist, teaches Sport Psychology and Psychology Applied to Football in the Department of Human Sciences and Promotion of the Quality of Life, at San Raffaele Roma Open University, Rome, Italy, and Psychology at the School of Sport of the Italian Olympic Committee. He attended the last 6 Summer Olympic Games working with athletes who won 12 Olympic medals. He has written 15 books in sport psychology and performance development. Alberto is the editorial manager of *International Journal of Sport Psychology*, and former European Federation of Sport Psychology (FEPSAC) treasurer.

**José L. Chamorro** has a doctorate in Sport Psychology, and he is a lecturer at the European University of Madrid, Spain. He is a member of the Research Group Society, Sport and JJOO as well as a member of the Research Group ACAFYDE at the University of Extremadura, Spain. His research interests are career transitions, dual career, motivation, and psycho-social variables that have an influence in sport. He is also a consultant to numerous athletes and teams.

**Tristan J. Coulter** is a lecturer of sport and exercise psychology at Queensland University of Technology, Australia (since 2015). Tristan sits on the Queensland State Committee of the Australian Psychological Society's College of Sport and Exercise Psychologists. He has consulted with numerous elite athletes and teams, since 2008 (e.g. England and Wales Cricket Board, Australian football teams) and is an early career academic with 11 publications, including several in the area of mental toughness in sport.

**George K. Doganis** is Professor of Social Psychology of Sport at Aristotle University of Thessaloniki, Greece. He was Chair of the Department of Physical Education and Sport Science (2008–2013), Founder and Director of the Sport Psychology Laboratory (1988–2013), and has about 45 publications with more than 800 citations. He provided consultation to a number of athletes in various sports. He taught sport psychology to UEFA national coaching certification (UEFA B', A', and Pro) for many years.

**Ashley M. Duguay** is a PhD candidate in the Department of Kinesiology at the University of Windsor, Canada. Through her research, she seeks to better understand athlete leadership in sports teams. She has received provincial and federal funding to support her research. She also works with athletes, coaches, and sports teams helping them achieve their performance goals.

**Daniel Ekvall** is Team Performance Psychologist for the Swedish men's National Team, Coach Educator at the Swedish FA, and Sport Psychology Consultant in the Swedish Premier League Club IFK Norrköping (since 2010). He studied Sport Psychology and Sport Pedagogy at Halmstad University, Sweden (1999–2003) and studied to be a CBT therapist at GIH, The Swedish School of Sport Science.

**Marije T. Elferink-Gemser** is an associate professor at the Center for Human Movement Sciences, University Medical Center Groningen, University of Groningen, The Netherlands. She has 75 publications indexed in the Web of Science with over 1,000 citations on the topic of talent development in sport. Her studies are characterized by their longitudinal design, focusing on multidimensional performance characteristics of both the youth athletes and their environment.

**Mirko Farina** is a British Academy postdoctoral fellow in the Department of Philosophy at King's College London. He is also a visiting scholar at the National Research University Higher School of Economics in Moscow. He holds a PhD in Cognitive Science from Macquarie University, an MPhil in Philosophy of Mind from the University of Edinburgh, and an MRes in Logic and Philosophy of Science from the University of Milan. His academic interests fall at the confluence of non-Cartesian cognitive science, philosophy of mind, philosophy of science, developmental neuroscience, sport psychology, and evolutionary biology.

**Edson Filho** is a lecturer in Sport and Exercise Psychology at the University of Central Lancashire. He has authored over 50 peer-reviewed manuscripts and book chapters in the field of Sport, Exercise, and Performance Psychology and has received numerous research fellowships and awards, including the American Psychological Association Dissertation Award. His work on expert performance has been funded by the Union of European Football Associations (UEFA), and featured in distinguished media outlets including BBC Latin America and Scientific American.

**Tomás García-Calvo** was a professor in the Faculty of Teacher Training at Autonomous University of Madrid, Spain (2002–2005), and has been professor in the Faculty of Sport Science at University of Extremadura, Spain since 2005. He has a master's degree in Sport Psychology (2002), a PhD in Sports Sciences (2006), and a UEFA Pro Licence (2001). Since 2000 he has been head coach in several football teams. He is a member of the Spanish Association of Sport Psychology (since 2005) and is Head of the Research Group BAPAS: Behavioral Analysis of Physical Activity and Sport, with more than 150 publications with about 2,000 citations. He is also the associate editor of several scientific journals.

**Zoltán Gáspár** is a physical education teacher at Eötvös Loránd University (since 2007) and a tennis coach in Budapest, Hungary (since 1996). He teaches numerous sports at the university: tennis, football, badminton, basketball in physical education courses as well as the theory of sports exercise. Working with adults, adolescents, and children (competition level) in a local club as a tennis coach gives him the opportunity to experience and understand the background and key issues of sports performance. Currently he is finishing his doctoral studies in Psychology at Eötvös Loránd University, Faculty of Education and Psychology, Doctoral School of Psychology.

**Inmaculada González-Ponce** is a postdoctoral researcher in the Faculty of Sport Science at the University of Extremadura, Spain. She has a master's degree in teacher training and in sport science research (2011), a PhD in Sports Sciences (2018), and has been a head coach in football teams since 2015. She has been a member of the Spanish Association of Sport Psychology since 2014. She is a member of the Research Group BAPAS: Behavioral Analysis of Physical Activity and Sport, with more than 100 publications with about 1,500 citations.

**Marios T. Goudas** is a professor of psychology of physical education and youth sport at the University of Thessaly, Greece. He has more than 100 publications in the area of motivation in youth sport with about 2,000 citations, and has consulted for youth soccer clubs.

**Daniel Gould** is Director of the Institute for the Study of Youth Sports and Professor in the Department of Kinesiology at the Michigan State University. Dan's current research focuses on how coaches teach life skills to young athletes and developing youth leaders through the sport captaincy experience. He has also been heavily involved in coaching education.

**Michelle Guerrero** is currently a postdoctoral fellow at the Children's Hospital of Eastern Ontario (Ottawa, Canada), working with the Healthy Active Living and Obesity (HALO) Research Group. Her primary research interests include studying environmental and psycho-social correlates and determinants of physical activity participation among children and youth (with and without physical disabilities).

**Henrik Gustafsson** is an associate professor at Karlstad University, Sweden and a visiting professor at Norwegian School of Sport Sciences, Norway. In addition, he works as a sport psychology consultant with the Swedish Olympic Committee (since 2010), and has worked with elite football teams. Dr Gustafsson's research is focused on burnout in athletes and coaches and the application of cognitive behaviour therapy in elite sport.

**Chris Harwood** is Chair of Sport Psychology at Loughborough University and in the Psychology Division for the British Association of Sport and Exercise Sciences (BASES). He is the former vice-president of the European Federation of Sport Psychology (FEPSAC) (2007–2011) and is an International Society of Sport Psychology (ISSP) Managing Council member (2017–2021). He is a fellow of BASES and the Association of Applied Sport Psychology (AASP) with over 100 publications and 3,000 citations. He is a Health and Care Professions Council Registered Sport Psychologist to youth and senior athletes, coaches, and parents including professional football academies.

**Jahan Heidari** is a research assistant and PhD candidate in the Unit of Sport Psychology at the Faculty of Sport Science, Ruhr University Bochum, Germany (since

2015). His research interests include the investigation of psychological underpinnings of recovery and stress in back pain development and chronification as well as recovery monitoring in elite sports. He also works as a sport psychology consultant in a youth academy of a professional German football club (since 2018).

**Bart Heuvingh** is an elite lifestyle developer at professional football club AZ Alkmaar on topics like mental training, nutrition, recovery, social media, and sleep. He is a public speaker about talent development in sport and the role of implicit theories of ability (mindset). He is the author of the book *Talent van morgen – Groeimindset als basis voor talentontwikkeling* about the role of growth mindset in talent development of athletes. He has an MSc in Human Movement Sciences (VU Amsterdam) and an MSc in Sport and Performance Psychology (UvA Amsterdam).

**Matt D. Hoffmann** is a postdoctoral fellow, jointly affiliated with the School of Arts and Social Sciences at Cape Breton University (Nova Scotia, Canada) and the School of Human Kinetics at the University of Ottawa (Ontario, Canada). He primarily investigates the nature and benefits of peer mentoring relationships between athletes, but he is also interested in the leadership practices of athletes and coaches across various age cohorts (e.g. youth, masters athletes). He has published in peer-reviewed journals such as *Psychology of Sport and Exercise* and *Measurement in Physical Education and Exercise Science*.

**Barbara C. H. Huijgen** is an assistant professor at the Center for Human Movement Sciences, University Medical Center Groningen, University of Groningen, The Netherlands. She has 25 publications indexed in the Web of Science with about 300 citations on the topic of talent development in sport. Her focus is on football and tennis research, characterized by focusing on multidimensional performance characteristics, and specifically on cognition.

**Laura Jonker** is a researcher at the Center for Human Movement Sciences, University Medical Center Groningen, University of Groningen, The Netherlands, a director at XOET, and an employee of Hypercube Business Innovation and also a former employee of the Dutch Football Association. She has about 500 citations on the topic of self-regulation in scientific journals. Her studies are characterized by their practical use for coaches, teachers, athletes, and students. She is a research consultant with a speciality in sport psychology for coaches and athletes in different types of sports, for professional football clubs and football associations since 2011.

**Michael Kellmann** is Head of the Unit of Sport Psychology at the Faculty of Sport Science, Ruhr University Bochum (Germany) and Honorary Professor at the School of Human Movement and Nutrition Sciences, University of Queensland (Australia). He is a member of several psychological associations and societies and has (co-)authored numerous books and articles concerning regeneration and recovery in elite athletes. His research focuses on different areas of regeneration and intervention in elite sports.

**Göran Kenttä** earned his PhD in Psychology at Stockholm University in 2001. The majority of his research has focused on elite sports with a stress–recovery perspective. He currently holds a research position in Stockholm at The Swedish

School of Sport and Health Sciences, and has been a director of the Coach Education Programme at the university; he is also the past president of the Swedish Sport Psychological Association. In addition, Göran currently holds a position at the Swedish Sport Federation as Head of Discipline in sport psychology and an adjunct professor position at Ottawa University.

**Tom King** is Lecturer in Sport and Performance Psychology at Glyndwr University (UK) and Assistant Sport and Performance Psychologist at a professional football academy, specializing in support for professional development phase players.

**Francisco M. Leo** has been a professor in the Faculty of Teacher Training at the University of Extremadura, Spain since 2014. He has a master's degree in High Performance Sport (2010), a PhD in Sports Sciences (2012), and a UEFA Pro Licence (2013). He is a member of the Spanish Association of Sport Psychology (since 2009) and an associate editor of the *Journal of Sport Psychology* (since 2018). He is a member of the Research Group BAPAS: Behavioral Analysis of Physical Activity and Sport, with more than 100 publications with about 1,500 citations.

**Fabian Loch** is a research assistant and PhD student in the Unit of Sport Psychology at the Faculty of Sport Science, Ruhr University Bochum (Germany) (since 2016). His research focuses on the investigation of mental recovery strategies in elite sports as well as recovery–stress monitoring in team sports.

**Clifford J. Mallett** is Professor of Sport Psychology and Coaching at The University of Queensland. He is also Honorary Professor of the Technical University of Munich in Germany. Professor Mallett has published more than 100 peer-reviewed papers and is Chair of Research for the International Council for Coaching Excellence (2013–2019), currently Associate Editor of the *International Sports Coaching Journal* (2013–2019), and former Associate Editor for the *International Journal of Sport and Exercise Psychology* (2009–2014). He is a former medal-winning Olympic coach in athletics and consults for international and national sports organizations and with several professional sport franchises in Australia.

**Krista Munroe-Chandler** is recognized for her work in the psychology of sport and exercise. She is a professor in the Faculty of Human Kinetics at the University of Windsor, Canada. Her research interests include imagery use by performers (sport, exercise, dance), as well as youth sport development. She works with able-bodied athletes as well as athletes with a disability of all ages, levels, and sports helping them achieve their personal performance goals.

**Christine Nash** is Head of the Institute for Sport, Physical Education and Health Sciences at the University of Edinburgh in Scotland and Honorary Professor, Institute for Advanced Study, Technical University of Munich. She is Programme Director for online MScs in Sport Coaching and Performance. She is a national swimming coach in the UK, actively involved in coach development around the globe and consultant to coaches and teams.

**Insa Nixdorf** is a research associate at the Chair of Sport Psychology at Technical University of Munich, Germany (since 2012), and won a research award from the German Association of Sport Psychology (ASP) for her thesis on depression in elite athletes (2012) and is a Laura-Bassi Award winner (2016). She successfully applied for and conducted research grants and applied projects on prevention of psychological disorders in athletes. She is trained in cognitive behavioural therapy and clinical hypnosis. She is listed as an expert for sport psychological training at the German Federal Institute of Sport Science (*BISp*) and is currently working for the German Swimming Association (DSV).

**Raphael Nixdorf** (formerly Raphael Frank) is a research associate at the Chair of Sport Psychology at Technical University of Munich, Germany (since 2012), and won a research award from the German Association of Sport Psychology (ASP) for his diploma-thesis on depression in elite athletes. He successfully applied for and conducted research grants and applied projects on prevention of psychological disorders in athletes. He is trained in cognitive behavioural therapy, clinical hypnosis, mindfulness, and listed as an expert for sport psychological training at the German Federal Institute of Sport Science (*BISp*).

**Kyle F. Paradis** obtained his PhD from the University of Western Ontario in the Psychology of Sport and Physical Activity. Dr Paradis has also been Postdoctoral Fellow and Adjunct Professor at Western University and the University of Windsor (Canada) teaching in the areas of sport and exercise psychology, sport sociology, and sport management. Dr Paradis' research interests include group dynamics and social/organizational psychology in sport. He has published several peer-reviewed articles examining various group processes in sport such as conflict, competition, cohesion, leadership, and team building. Dr Paradis has a particular passion for football and enjoys following all of the top professional leagues.

**Juan J. Pulido** is a postdoctoral researcher at the University of Extremadura (PO17012) – ACAFYDE Group and he collaborates with the PANO-SR Group (Physical Activity, Nutrition and Obesity – Self-Regulation) – Faculty of Human Kinetics, University of Lisbon. Research topics include motivation and physical activity in young athletes and sport-based interventions with coaches on motivational strategies. He is also a UEFA Pro Football Coach.

**Jean Rettig** is an adjunct faculty in higher education at Florida State University. She has authored several peer-reviewed manuscripts in the fields of higher education and sport psychology. She also serves as a research associate for the Alliance for PROS. Her research interests include higher education finance, student-athlete engagement, and student outcomes. Dr Rettig received her PhD degree from Florida State University and was a National Collegiate Athletic Association (NCAA) Division I student-athlete at Penn State University.

**David Sánchez-Oliva** has a doctorate in Sport Sciences, and he is currently postdoctoral researcher at the University of Cádiz, Spain. He is a member of the Research Group GALENO at the University of Cádiz as well as member of the Research Group ACAFYDE at the University of Extremadura. His research interests are motivation and physical activity in physical education and leisure-time physical activity, school-based interventions on multiple health behaviours, and teacher motivational strategies in physical education.

**Victor C. Souza** graduated in Psychology from the University of São Paulo (USP), and is a Master and PhD student of the Psychobiology Program of USP

(FFCLRP). He is a specialist in Sports Psychology via the Brazilian Federal Council of Psychology and a member of the Brazilian Sport Psychology Association (ABRAPESP). His research interests are mood states, sports performance, athlete leadership, and psychological interventions in sports.

**Karl Steptoe** is Sport and Performance Psychology Lead at Loughborough University (UK). He is a chartered member of the British Psychological Society (BPS) and a Health and Care Professions Council (HCPC) Registered Sport and Exercise Psychologist to athletes, teams, coaches, and parents including a UK professional football academy.

**Attila Szabó** is currently Professor of Psychology in the Institute of Health Promotion and Sport Sciences at Eötvös Loránd University in Budapest, Hungary. He completed his BSc in Psychobiology at Concordia University in Montreal, then obtained an MSc from the same University, and he got his PhD in Sciences of Physical Activity from the University of Montreal in 1993. Subsequently, he worked in the UK and was a British Association of Sport and Exercise Sciences (BASES) accredited researcher in Sport & Exercise Psychology (1999–2009). He has over 150 publications and 3,000 citations, and he is a Doctor of Science (DSc) of the Hungarian Academy of Sciences.

**Richard C. Thelwell** is Head of Department for Sport and Exercise Sciences, and Professor of Applied Sport Psychology at the University of Portsmouth, UK. In addition to having an extensive publication and invited presentation record, Professor Thelwell has extensive applied-practitioner experience in elite sport and is a Registered Practitioner Psychologist with the Health and Care Professions Council.

**Rasmus Tornberg** is a lecturer in Sport Psychology at Halmstad University, Coach Educator at the Swedish FA, and Team Performance Psychologist for the Swedish women's National Team. In addition, he has worked as a Sport Psychology Consultant for elite sport teams in football, ice hockey, and handball. He has a master's degree in Sport Psychology from Halmstad University (Sweden) (2001–2005) and did basic cognitive behavioural therapy training at GIH, The Swedish School of Sport Science.

**Chris Visscher** used to be Head of Department in the Center of Human Movement Studies, University Medical Center Groningen, University of Groningen, The Netherlands before his retirement. He has about 100 publications indexed in the Web of Science with about 1,500 citations on the topic of learning and performance, talent development, sport, and cognition.

**Christopher R. D. Wagstaff** is Principal Lecturer and Psychology Pathway Lead at University of Portsmouth (UK). He is a Chartered Psychologist, registered Practitioner Psychologist, and Associate Fellow of the British Psychological Society. He has published widely in the area of organizational sport psychology, with projects relating to emotions and attitudes, stress and well-being, organizational behaviour, and high performance environments. He is Editor for *Sport and Exercise Psychology Review* and Associate Editor for the *Journal of Applied Sport Psychology* and *Journal of Sport Psychology*.

**Paul M. Wright** is Presidential Engagement Professor and Lane/Zimmerman Endowed Chair in the Department of Kinesiology and Physical Education at Northern Illinois University (since 2011) in the United States. He has been Fulbright Scholar (2010), Erasmus Mundus Visiting Scholar (2014), and Honorary Professor at the University of Edinburgh (2017). He has more than 60 publications and funding from sources including the US Department of State (2013) and Robert Wood Johnson Foundation (2005). He is an internationally recognized expert on the Teaching Personal and Social Responsibility (TPSR) model.

# Foreword

Football, the most popular European team sport, is played by hundreds of millions of children and adults worldwide. In the past, football research has focused mainly on how to improve players' physical and technical abilities. Due to the fact that demands on elite players both on and off the pitch have become increasingly more complex, many teams are now working with sport psychologists in order to meet the players' multifaceted needs and to enhance their performance. It is, however, important that the sport psychological interventions conducted with players and teams are based on scientific evidence. Up until now this scientific evidence has been published mainly in scientific journals, making it hard for practitioners to access this knowledge.

The editors of this book, therefore, can only be congratulated for compiling this new and one of a kind collection of research specifically addressing the psychology of football. This book excellently covers a wide range of topics relevant for football practitioners involved with different performance and age levels. In four sections it covers topics such as personality, cognition, and emotion; coaching and coaches; psychological consulting and interventions; as well as a number of specific issues relevant to working with young players. Because of the game's popularity, football players are often under a lot of pressure and the book does not shy away from addressing critical issues like mental health problems, an issue that the European Federation of Sport Psychology (FEPSAC) also has tried to shed more light on with its recently published position statement, or the challenges of transitioning from junior and senior level. The chapters offer a wide variety of content spanning from case examples, reviews of relevant literature, theories and models, specific interventions, and reflections on lessons learned from applied practice in football. All chapters include sections on applied implications, future research directions, or reflections from the authors' own practice.

The editors have done an excellent job in bringing together the world's leading experts in the field who were all willing to share their most current knowledge on their respective topics. Thus, this book provides an excellent and international overview of sport psychological football research.

This book is an invaluable resource not only for sport psychologists working in football but also for other target groups such as coaches, scouts, football managers, and sport science students. It is a one of a kind knowledge resource that will contribute to positive player and team developments on and off the field. As President of FEPSAC, I am especially happy to see that this project has been led by two European plus one Canadian scientist and would like to see that this book makes a positive impact on the sport of football not only in Europe but worldwide.

Prof. Dr Anne-Marie Elbe
President of FEPSAC

# Acknowledgements

When trying to find relevant publications in the scientific field of football psychology extensive search of the Internet and other sources was needed. As a consequence the idea arose to pull together current research and research-based interventions in football psychology. Fortunately, we found a number of colleagues who were fascinated by the idea. It was even more fortunate that Routledge as one of the renowned publishers in sport science was also very fond of the idea. We first came together with George Russell of Routledge at the European Federation of Sport Psychology (FEPSAC) congress in Bern, Switzerland in 2015 to discuss the outline of the book. We have worked on this book since then.

The claim to assemble a comprehensive volume in football psychology covering all relevant areas was of course huge. Gradually, we found colleagues who were willing to contribute their expertise in scientific research and translating findings into applied work. Along the way and with the help of reviewers we shaped the contents of the book into its present form. We were very happy that the authors supported us by agreeing to review the chapters of other authors. The reviewing and the revising of the chapters was a laborious process but eventually very rewarding.

Without a number of people who supported us the book would not have come true. Of course, a major thanks must go to the authors without whom the book would not have been possible. We really appreciate the fundamental support of the Routledge team with George Russell, Ceri McLardy, and Alex Howard who were always ready to help and encourage when the editing process appeared to be slow. We would like to thank the teams at our universities, especially the Technical University of Munich (TUM) team with Petra Sollnberger, Simon Blaschke, and Florence Theil.

Furthermore, we thank our families for consistently supporting us to realize this book.

İzmir, Munich, and Windsor, August 2018
Erkut Konter, Jürgen Beckmann, and Todd M. Loughead

# Introduction

## Football psychology on route to becoming an integral part of football

*Erkut Konter, Jürgen Beckmann, and Todd M. Loughead*

Football or soccer is played by 250 million people in more than 200 countries making it the world's most popular sport (Strudwick, 2016). We know from FIFA that in 2007 the total number of football players registered with a club or team in the world was reported to be 38 million players, of which 34 million were male. Football appears to be so highly attractive worldwide because it is a fairly simple game and is economical to play. Sport psychology consultation became the norm in the 20th century, however, football lagged behind. This has changed over the last few decades. A 2018 Google Scholar search with the key words of 'soccer' and 'psychology' produced over 151,000 results. However, closer inspection of this search reveals that there is an increasing demand for optimizing psychological skills within the game of football. In the fast-paced, high-stakes modern game, mental skills are critical to making good decisions under pressure and coping with increasing demands on and off the pitch (Pain, 2016). Football psychology is a field of research that has been one of the fastest-growing areas in sport psychology over the past decade. This book attempts to bridge the gap between research and practice.

The book does not only address the performance of football players but encompasses a broader perspective that incorporates talent selection and development as well as the area of players' mental health that has started to receive increased attention. Furthermore, the perspective is taken beyond the player and the team considering the whole social system in which football is embedded. Other agents in this system are, of course, coaches but also officials, sponsors, and fans. Parents are of particular importance for young players. Only recently has research addressed the role of parents and how to improve their contribution through parental coaching. The book chapters are presented by researchers and practitioners focusing on football psychology with years of experience. This book could be the first international collection of the flourishing research and practice themes within the domain of football psychology.

Football psychology is interdisciplinary, multifaceted, and multidimensional in nature. The study of football psychology incorporates topics from different areas of psychology, such as clinical psychology, social psychology, personality and developmental psychology, health psychology, and the psychology of coaching all of which are relevant areas for football.

Over the past decades, the demands for football scientists and performance consultants has been growing (Strudwick, 2016). Mental processing is increasingly being perceived as a critical factor for success, the 'cutting edge' in football. Therefore, many football teams now routinely employ the services of a sport psychologist or sport psychology consultant mainly with the aim of improving team functioning and performance (Strudwick, 2016).

In addition to giving an overview on current topics and research findings in football psychology, this book also intends to help practitioners to understand the psychological and psycho-social processes in football. It presents the application of sport psychological research findings in football which has proven to support positive results in different aspects and levels of football.

As recent development in the field of football shows, providing psychological help and consultancy in relation to performance, team functioning, and health promotion has become an increasingly important issue to footballers, football coaches, managers, and administrators around the world. The demands placed on sport psychologists and consultants are increasing in football clubs, Olympic teams, and national squads. Specific football evidence-based knowledge is required.

The objective of the book is to provide such knowledge and cover advances in football psychology through contributions from various fields of sport psychology and psychology representing the cutting edge of current developments in research and practice. The general idea was to establish a go-to resource for sport psychologists working in football but also for coaches, scouts, football managers, and students of sport sciences.

Our book attempts to offer an empirically based synthesis of theory and research providing guidance for applied practitioners. Chapters include reviews of relevant literature, theories, and models, specific interventions illustrated in case examples, and reflections on lessons learned from applied practice in football.

The book contains 25 chapters which are structured into four parts. Part I addresses fundamental psychological factors which play a crucial role in sport performance: personality, motivation, cognition, and emotion. Part II deals with coaching essentials in football. Part III provides an overview of psychological skills for performance development, and Part IV focuses on developing young players in football. Within each chapter, the focus is on outlining relevant theoretical and conceptual issues, before providing a review of the most recent empirical research in the respective areas. All chapters include sections on applied implications, future research directions, or reflections from the authors' own practice.

The first chapter by Bueno and Souza addresses the relations of subjective states with motivational/emotional conditions and performance in football. It focuses on the importance of considering positive aspects of mood and its interaction with motivational aspects. The second chapter, by Coulter and Thelwell, focuses on the topic of 'mental toughness development in football'. This chapter provides readers with an overview of the key themes to understanding mental toughness in football. Specifically, it explores the different perspectives from which mental toughness has been addressed (e.g. from player, coach, parent, and refereeing standpoints). It also identifies some of the behaviours and situations in football associated with being 'mentally tough'. This initial groundwork provides the basis for considering how mental toughness might be developed in football. The third chapter, by Konter and Beckmann, concentrates on courage in football from a self-regulation perspective. The chapter examines courage in football at the amateur and professional levels as a multidimensional concept taking into account a number of individual, social, and performance variables considering courage as a self-regulation process.

The unifying role of player responsibility in football is addressed by Doganis, Goudas, and Wright in the fourth chapter. Player responsibility has largely been neglected in research on football. But it affects a range of behaviours, either individual or collective, related to training and team performance. The concept of responsibility is treated not primarily in relation to moral behaviour, but rather as a willingness to act responsibly, or the willingness to 'take full ownership' of one's behaviour, both in individual and collective settings within the football team. This is something frequently discussed in the context of team collapse when players should take responsibility on the pitch after momentum has been lost. The approach taken will illustrate that personal responsibility of players in football may be used as a unifying concept and could be used as a starting point for the development of interventions addressing these kinds of problems.

The fifth chapter, by Steptoe, King, and Harwood, deals with the subject of consistent psycho-social development of young footballers. The authors describe the implementation of the 5C's as a vehicle for interdisciplinary cohesion. The 5C's of Commitment, Communication, Concentration, Control, and Confidence (Harwood, 2008; Harwood, Barker, & Anderson, 2015) represent a framework that aims to increase awareness and development of motivational, interpersonal, and self-regulatory skills applicable to the football domain. The chapter considers the challenges associated with delivering consistent messages regarding player development within a multidisciplinary team and details the priorities given to coach, parent, and player intervention across foundation, youth, and professional phases of development.

Chapter 6 by Basevitch and Konter elaborates on decision making in football including non-verbal intelligence. Players consistently have to make decisions throughout a football game. On average, each team makes more than 500 actions per game (e.g. shots, passes, headers, dribbles; Luhtanen, Belinskij, Häyrinen, & Vänttinen, 2001). Each action is a consequence of a decision made by a player (Tenenbaum, 2003). Thus, decision making is one of the most important skills in football that has been studied extensively and has been shown to differentiate between high- and low-skill players, older and younger players, and between successful and less successful performances (Ward & Williams, 2003). Football involves many decision situations and players need non-verbal intelligence (non-verbal problem-solving skills) during the game in order to be successful.

Chapter 7 by Loughead, Duguay, and Hoffmann focuses on athlete leadership in football. Leadership and team dynamics are the cornerstones to helping athletes achieve individual and team success. The general objective of this chapter is to provide an overview of the most prevalent frameworks and research that have been used to understand athlete leadership in football.

Nash and Mallett deal with the question of what the effective football coaching is in Chapter 8. Coaches are typically judged by performance outcomes (wins/losses). However, the effectiveness of coaches is multifaceted and the actual performance depends on a number of factors including player and team development. The chapter also examines the role of coach education and development in facilitating effective coaching behaviours.

Chapter 9 by Erwin Apitzsch focuses on the aforementioned collective collapse or team collapse in football. The chapter provides practical applications, based on scientific results and proven experience, on how to improve communication and avoid collective collapse and emotional contagion within a team. In times of adversity, facing possible defeat, it is quite common to use derogative language towards teammates, sometimes accompanied by negative body language. Establishing positive communication, both verbal and non-verbal, appears to be a successful measure to prevent or settle team collapse.

In Chapter 10 Konter, Loughead, and Paradis address leadership power in football. The chapter highlights the basic concepts, theories, and research related to leadership power perceptions in football. In addition, the chapter deals with a number of questions regarding how leadership powers make leaders and coaches successful in football.

García-Calvo, Leo, and González-Ponce address coach justice and coach competence in football. The ability of a coach to be perceived as fair and competent by players can be very important in the functioning of a football team. This chapter provides both theoretical and applied explanations of justice factors (distributive, procedural, interpersonal, and informational) and competence components (physical training, motivational skills, character building, game strategies, and technical knowledge), and suggestions for team success and performance.

Chapter 12 by Gáspár and Szabó deals with an issue that was avoided for a long time but has become salient over the last couple of years: burnout in football coaching. Internal and external sources of stress are identified that lead to burnout in football coaches. The factors are integrated into an explanatory model for a better understanding of the phenomenon. This model also incorporates the consequences of burnout based on scientific evidence as well as on individual case studies.

A balance of stress and recovery is seen as a requirement to avoid burnout. In their chapter (Chapter 13) on recovery in football Heidari, Loch, and Kellmann indicate that high levels of performance in elite sports can only be maintained if athletes are sufficiently recovered. In effect, the exposition to challenging and exhausting activities needs to be followed by appropriate and individualized recovery in order to counterbalance stress and recovery and prevent a downward spiral of health and performance (Kellmann et al., 2018). Recovery seems to represent an essential element in the schedule of elite football players and teams.

In Chapter 14 Konter, Beckmann, and Mallett give an overview of psychological skills that are successfully applied in football. This chapter indicates that the most successful athletes consistently require and employ psychological skills to enhance performance. Psychological Skills Training (PST) is increasingly becoming accepted in modern football but a systematic integration of PST into football training and match routines is still the exception rather than the rule in many countries.

Stress in football is viewed from a clinical perspective in Chapter 15 by Wagstaff, Kenttä, and Thelwell. The authors indicate that stressors occur in a wide variety of competitive sports, including football. The main purpose of this chapter is to focus on elite-level players' experiences of stress and describe these within the theoretical framework of Acceptance Commitment Therapy (ACT).

In Chapter 16 Munroe-Chandler and Guerrero describe the applicability of imagery in football. All football players, regardless of age or skill, are capable of using imagery as a means to enhance cognitive, behavioural, and affective outcomes. Imagery can be referred to as creating or recreating experiences in one's mind. The authors discuss the uses of imagery in football including skill and strategy execution, goals, arousal regulation, and confidence.

Filho and Retting address self-confidence and collective efficacy in football in Chapter 17. The authors indicate that self-confidence is one of the major predictors of performance in football. Collective efficacy is also paramount as high-performing teams show greater group-level confidence compared to lower-performing teams. The authors review the antecedents, moderators, and outcome variables of self-confidence and collective efficacy in football.

Chapter 18 by Farina and Cei addresses concentration and self-talk in football. The authors discuss the extant literature concerning concentration and self-talk in term of ability to lead the mental processes (cognitive, emotional, and interpersonal) with the aim to select the information needed to perform the best. The chapter underlines the team mindset as an important aspect influencing the team concentration. Furthermore, it is shown that the influence of physical tiredness and the ability to maintain the correct focus on the match is the main issue for the winning mindset.

Applied behavioural analysis (ABA) in top-level football is presented by Tornberg, Gustafsson, and Ekvall in Chapter 19. The authors report that ABA is an important part of the Cognitive Behavioural Therapy (CBT) framework and offers a structured and effective way of working with elite football players' development and performance.

Only recently has the importance of including parents in the development of players been discussed. In Chapter 20 Beckmann-Waldenmayer points out that parents have multiple, indispensable roles and functions in the development of talents. The chapter indicates that in order to avoid negative impact and maximize positive effects for the talents, parental coaching should be designed to optimize parents' interactions within the systems. The author argues that family therapy provides a good framework in this context. Positive parental support leads to higher enjoyment of the sport and higher intrinsic motivation as well as better participation and a prevention of drop-out.

Chapter 21 by Beckmann and Beckmann-Waldenmayer proceeds in the same area with perspectives on talent development in football. The authors report that most German professional football clubs employ at least one sport psychologist in their youth academies and that sport psychology has become an integral part of talent development. The chapter describes how psychological assessment, fundamental training (relaxation techniques), and mental skills training are systematically implemented in youth football from the age of nine years on. In addition, the chapter proposes a systems approach to talent development from football coaching to 'life coaching'.

Chapter 22 by Jonker, Huijgen, Heuvingh, Elferink-Gemser, and Visscher is in the same realm, addressing how youth football players learn to succeed. Based on extensive research the authors report what kind of skills talented players should develop to be successful. Data on youth players from Dutch professional soccer academies are presented. Overall, the data show that those players who have a growth mindset score higher on aspects of executive functions, and on aspects of self-regulation of learning. The chapter advocates that a high level of executive functions and self-regulatory skills enhance talented players' development and increase their chance of signing a professional contract.

In Chapter 23 Gould and Capalbo go beyond traditional coaching approaches focusing on the development of football-related skills. These authors intend to help players develop life skills. The chapter addresses how football can be used to develop more encompassing life skills. The authors also identify and discuss barriers to life skills development in football.

Barriers are also an issue in Chapter 24 by Chamorro, Sánchez-Oliva, and Pulido. These authors address the transition from junior to elite football. The chapter reviews three different theoretical frameworks used to explore the transition to professional sport: (a) career development descriptive models, (b) career transitions explanation models, and (c) career transitions intervention models. The authors discuss the main conclusions from the research that has studied this transition and those factors that influence the performance and well-being of young elite footballers including the barriers and resources of transition in and off the field.

Only recently has depression become an issue in football. Young athletes, in particular, seem to be vulnerable to mental health issues. In Chapter 25 Nixdorf, Beckmann, and Nixdorf develop a perspective on preventing burnout and depression in youth football. The authors overview the current research on prevalence rates of depression, and discuss findings on causes and vulnerabilities leading to depression and burnout in adolescent football players. The chapter further elaborates vulnerabilities and approaches for treating and especially preventing burnout and depression. Finally, intervention programmes are described.

## References

Harwood, C. (2008). Developmental consulting in a professional football academy: The 5Cs coaching efficacy program. *The Sport Psychologist, 22*(1), 109–133.

Harwood, C. G., Barker, J. B., & Anderson, R. (2015). Psycho-social development in youth soccer players: Assessing the effectiveness of the 5Cs intervention program. *The Sport Psychologist, 29*(4), 319–334.

Kellmann, M., Bertollo, M., Bosquet, L., Brink, M., Coutts, A. J., Duffield, R., & Beckmann, J. (2018). Recovery and performance in sport: Consensus statement. *International Journal of Sports Physiology and Performance, 13*, 240–245. doi:10.1123/ijspp.2017-0759.

Luhtanen, P., Belinskij, A., Häyrinen, M., & Vänttinen, T. (2001). A comparative tournament analysis between the EURO 1996 and 2000 in soccer. *International Journal of Performance Analysis in Sport, 1*(1), 74–82.

Pain, M. (2016). Mental interventions. In T. Strudwick (Ed.), *Soccer science* (pp. 389–413). Champaign, IL: Human Kinetics.

Strudwick, T. (2016). *Soccer science.* Champaign, IL: Human Kinetics.

Tenenbaum, G. (2003). An integrated approach to decision making. In J. L. Starkes & K. A. Ericsson (Eds.), *Expert performance in sport: Advances in research on sport expertise* (pp. 191–218). Champaign, IL: Human Kinetics.

Ward, P., & Williams, A. M. (2003). Perceptual and cognitive skill development in soccer: The multidimensional nature of expert performance. *Journal of Sport and Exercise Psychology, 25*, 93–111.

# Part I

# Personality, motivation, cognition, and emotion

# 1 Mood states as motivational and emotional determinants of football performance

*José Lino O. Bueno and Victor C. Souza*

**Abstract**

This chapter will present the findings of several studies that have investigated the momentary mood states of Brazilian football players in pre-competition situations, emphasizing the role of psychological aspects that have been studied in the literature. The data were obtained by Engelmann's Present Mood States List, a Brazilian instrument to access subjective states. In these studies, mood states were related to variables such as playing position of the athletes, location of the competition, sequences of games and training sessions during the season, behavioural repertoire, and technical performance in the games. There is a common mood profile of football players in the moments before the game begins (interest, happiness, and hope); however, there are differences especially between defensive and forward players in different competitive contexts. Behavioural repertoire changes were related with pre-competitive mood states, revealing emotional and motivational components of the athletes' performance. Factors such as Fatigue, Interest, and Serenity varied during the sequences of games and training. Young Brazilian football players feel a high level of pressure for winning, showing relief after victories (more than happiness or pride) and humiliation and shame after defeats. The present chapter focuses on the importance of considering positive aspects of an athlete's mood and their interaction with emotional, motivational, and social aspects, expanding the understanding of the influence of psychological variables on human performance in sport. Practical implications, especially for coaches and sport psychologists, and future research directions are discussed.

FIFA World Cup 2014. Mineirão Stadium in Belo Horizonte. Semi-finals. Brazil vs Germany, giants of the world of football. Eight World Cup titles between them, five for Brazil and three for Germany.

The Brazilian nation was excited about the game. The Brazilian home team was supported by thousands of anxious yet hopeful fans. The team was missing some of their most important players, Neymar and their captain Thiago Silva. However, central defender David Luiz emerged as a leader during the tournament. The game started the same as any other but within half an hour, Brazil was already facing a substantial beating. Completely unheard of in FIFA history and to the shock of the Brazilian fans, Germany scored five goals within the first 27 minutes. It was a triumph for the German team, which hadn't won the World Cup since 1990 and had something to prove. From the start of the game to the 27th minute, it can be argued that five elements factored into Germany's five-goal lead: confidence, hope, and self-esteem of the winners, and anxiety and despair of the losers.

The Brazilian media highlighted several aspects related to performance, especially regarding the tactics of the game, in an attempt to find an explanation for their greatest defeat. On the contrary, very little was noted about the motivational and emotional aspects involved to help explain Germany's impressive win and the huge disparity in the teams' performance.

Naturally, the athletes' performance can be examined not only from a technical and tactical perspective, but also considering motivational factors, emotional responses, and social dynamics manifested over the course of the competition. Psychological dispositions such as humiliation, anger, fatigue, hope, empathy, limerence, disgust, interest, surprise, hunger, disregard, envy, openness, and serenity can all affect an athlete's performance on the field.

Measures of subjective states, or momentary mood states (Engelmann, 1978), assessed through verbal reports of the athletes, can describe these psychological conditions. The evaluation of momentary moods in the immediate pre-competition situation can reflect emotional, motivational, and social conditions that may be related to an athlete's behavioural repertories categories during a game.

## Overview of the chapter's objectives

This chapter will present the findings of several studies that have investigated the momentary mood states of Brazilian football players in pre-competition situations, emphasizing the role of psychological aspects that have been studied in the literature. In these studies (e.g. Dias-Silva, 2013; Nogueira, 2009; Picoli, 2016), mood states were related to variables such as playing position of the athletes, location of the competition, sequences of games and training sessions during the season, behavioural repertoire, and technical performance in the games. The present chapter will focus on the importance of considering positive aspects of an athlete's mood and their interaction with emotional, motivational, and social aspects, expanding the understanding of the influence of psychological variables on human performance in sport.

## Subjective states and motivational, emotional, and social conditions

When talking scientifically about motivation and emotion, there has been a great deal of controversy over the last few decades about the definitions of these concepts as well as the possible relationship between the underlying processes (e.g. Bindra, 1976; Cofer, 1972).

Cofer (1972) synthesized the most accepted notion of motivation, emphasizing the irrational components of the motivational concepts of human nature, which give energy to and control the vigour and efficiency of behaviours, as well as guiding behaviour for specific purposes. Emotions, like motivations, have an irrational character, and both are often treated very similarly. Emotions, however, are known for their open manifestations and are expressed by statements of how one feels.

The study of motivational and emotional conditions implies the notion of organization of action and subjective states. Bindra (1976) emphasized that both motivation and emotion have to do with the organization of action, which depends not only on the present conditions of the organism or on the characteristics of the stimuli, but on how these processes are structured in a central motivational state and constitute subjective states in humans. Lazarus (1998) paid attention to the fact that

> Whatever the person is momentarily experiencing, be it emotional or not, happens against a background of other psychological conflicts and states, even if these are tentatively pushed into the background. This background of latent emotionality is constantly lurking in the shadows and is undoubtedly the major influence on the immediate figure states, just as is the immediate stimulus.
>
> (p. 24)

Thus, studies that allow the description of momentary mood states through individual verbal reports can identify the variety of subjective states present in the individual that are more directly related to the motivational and emotional processes linked to an action (Engelmann, 2002).

Qualitative methods and descriptions of behavioural repertoire can give important support to the study of motivational, emotional, and social elements involved in an athlete's performance. For example, 'studying high-level performers may provide insights for other athletes, but detail and transparency is needed when classifying their competitive level' (Clancy, Herring, MacIntyre, & Campbell, 2016, p. 242). From a methodological point of view, the authors argued that qualitative methods can provide essential data for the understanding of the motivational phenomenon. Furthermore, they underscored the use of behavioural or physiological data and also proposed longitudinal investigations that would permit the expansion of knowledge on which to base future interventions.

Some theoretical models that take into account motivational and emotional aspects to explain behaviours and sports performance among high-performance athletes involve methods for measuring these states. These will now be discussed.

The use of psychological tests in sport provides relevant information that is useful for psychologists and coaches; however, several issues must be taken into consideration for effective application of the construct being evaluated, how to evaluate it, where to do it, when and why to do it. For a long time, psychology has made use of psychological tools that were not designed exclusively for sport evaluations. Moreover, it is worth noting that in the Brazilian context, it is common to see the use of such tools coming from other countries without validation or transcultural adaptation.

The starting point for the measurement of mood state is the choice of a theoretical model. Prapavessis (2000) carried out a critical review of the concept of mood states from the perspective of the Mental Health Model, which was conceptually based on the Profile of Mood States (POMS) proposed by McNair, Lorr, and Droppleman (1971; 1992). POMS has been applied to many sport studies around the world, generating adaptations of the instrument and validation in different contexts. In his own revision, Prapavessis made a critique of the iceberg profile that served as the graphic representation of optimal mood states for sport performance, in which the vigour mood would be above average, while the other five factors with a negative aspect would be below the population average. The author presented research results that contradicted this model (e.g. Daiss, LeUnes, & Nation, 1986, for football players; Durtschi & Weiss, 1986, for marathoners).

The Inverted-U Theory is another model that proposes that sport performance reaches an optimum baseline when the arousal level is moderate. When this level either increases or decreases, performance tends to decline just the same. In agreement with this theory, moderate anxiety states have been found to be related to good performance in some sports. Hanin (2000) suggested an alternative that relates to the Inverted-U Theory. However, this alternative emphasizes individual differences, with each athlete having an optimal functioning zone (Individual Zone of Optimal Functioning – IZOF). Hanin himself used the model in football and noticed differences in intra- and interindividual analysis, but not in analysis at the group level. The most successful players showed a higher deviation from non-optimal zones than less successful players in pre-competition situations just before an important tournament. According to Hanin (2000), the IZOF Model differs from other systems because its 'framework is conceptually broad and therefore not limited to specific instruments' (p. 88). Moreover, the author considered the methodology of IZOF to cover biopsycho-social elements such as cognitive, motivational, performance, and motor-behavioural factors.

The Circumplex Model in sport and exercise psychology developed by Ekkekakis (2000) maps affective response on two axes: activation (or arousal) and valence (pleasantness or hedonic value). Most studies use this model to discuss the benefits of physical activity on the psychological states of the participants, however; the concept can also be applied to any sport. The activation and valence dimensions result in the following four quadrants: pleasant/activated (energy/excitement), pleasant/inactivated (relaxation/calm), unpleasant/inactivated (boredom/fatigue), and unpleasant/activated (anxiety/tension).

The Present Mood State List (PMSL) proposed by Engelmann (1986; 2002) is a conceptual model of subjective states or moods assessed by verbal reports, which follows a research line initiated in North American psychology (e.g. Nowlis, 1970). The conceptualization of mood by Engelmann is similar to what is called the subjective state. Locutions (e.g. 'feeling conformed', 'being impatient') refer to these moods or subjective states. Verbal reports are written in the first person and refer to locutions of mood states (e.g. 'I feel a necessity', 'I am proud').

Engelmann (1986; 2002) elaborated the PMSL as an instrument to evaluate mood states, resulting from wide empirical research performed in Brazil. Engelmann's quantitative studies initially submitted thousands of participants to 370 locutions and asked them to evaluate each locution using 18 scales involving several elements (e.g. hedonic value and activation level). The results permitted the classification of these locutions and showed that these locutions could probabilistically give adequate access to subjective states, both emotional and non-emotional (Engelmann, 1978). Quantitative analysis of these data resulted in the selection of 40 locutions which are representative of the subjective states. The PMSL is the list of 40 verbal reports referring to these locutions. The list is presented to the participant, who must use scales in order to show the intensity of momentary mood or subjective state. This assessment translates possible conscious states at the moment when the instrument is implemented (Engelmann, 1978).

The notion of mood or subjective state employed by Nowlis (1970) and Engelmann (1986; 2002) represents fundamental patterns of functioning and orientation that affect a person's activity. The identification of mood states with the PMSL involves the direction of social orientation (self-orientation/orientation to others) and positive or negative subjective assessment in the present moment, representing motivational and emotional elements.

Engelmann (1978) also carried out factor analysis of the Brazilian data, obtaining 12 factors that take into account the hedonic value and activation level of each item. In order to facilitate the description and identification of the data, the authors who have used the PMSL in the sporting context (Picoli, 2016; Silva, 2017) have named the following factors from the representative locutions: I – Humiliation/Anger, II – Fatigue, III – Hope, IV – Limerence/Empathy, V – Physiological Response, VI – Repulsion, VII – Interest, VIII – Surprise, IX – Hunger, X – Disregard/Envy, XI – Receptivity, and XII – Serenity.

Different researchers have proposed that mood can best be understood either based on a number of specific dimensions or in broad, generic terms, and that the adequate choice of model or instrument usually depends upon the precise nature of the research question (Lane & Terry, 2000). An advantage of using the PMSL is that it is a larger and more complete list of positive and negative mood states than other instruments used in similar studies with athletes, such as the POMS and BRUMS (Brazilian translation of POMS; Rohlfs, Carvalho, Rotta, & Krebs, 2004, Rohlfs et al., 2008), amplifying the potential relationships of mood states with motivational, emotional, and social processes.

The first study using Engelmann's PMSL in a sporting context was conducted by Bueno and Di Bonifácio (2007), who evaluated changes in mood states in volleyball players during competitions. A total of 13 female players and 11 male players filled out the PMSL during the semi-final and final matches of their respective tournaments. The results revealed a common profile for both groups based on the high-intensity presence of locutions such as 'I feel a desire', 'I'm hopeful' (Factor III – Hope), 'I'm interested', and 'I'm reflecting' (Factor VII – Interest). Comparing the first game of the semi-finals and the last game of the finals, locutions such as 'I feel a necessity' and 'I'm proud' (Factor XI – Receptivity) as well as 'I feel calm' (Factor XII – Serenity) were present at higher intensities in the last game.

## Relationships between subjective states, motivational/ emotional conditions, and performance in Brazilian football

The results of research using the PMSL with Brazilian football athletes describe the presence and strength of different mood states and are discussed in terms of the possible relations with motivational, emotional, and social processes. These analyses involve contextual conditions. In some cases, analyses have related momentary mood states to changes in the behavioural repertoire of athletes during the game.

### *Mood states and players' positions*

Nogueira (2009) examined the mood states of football players before and after a game according to the respective position and function of each player. The PMSL was applied to groups of players aged 14–17 years. The participants were divided into defenders, midfielders, and forwards. The participating teams adopted the 4–4–2 diamond formation. Thus, the group of defenders was composed of right-backs, left-backs, fullbacks, and defensive midfielders. Right midfielders, left midfielders, and wide midfielders formed the midfielders group. The group of forwards consisted only of forwards. The position of goalkeeper was disregarded because of its high specificity and the low number of participants in the sample.

This study identified significant differences in the players' mood states before a competition considering the positions they played (Table 1.1).

The considered locutions had a mean intensity of 4 or more (on a scale of 1–5) for the six games. In the pre-competitive situation, the locutions 'I'm happy' (Factor I – Humiliation/Anger) and 'I'm hopeful' (Factor III – Hope) were present for all groups in all games. The locutions present in at least one game were 'I miss somebody' (Factor III – Hope), 'I'm interested' (Factor VII – Interest), 'I feel a necessity' (Factor XI – Receptivity), and 'I'm calm' (Factor XII – Serenity). These results indicate a common profile of mood states for all players and games in the pre-competitive situation, regardless of playing position. Locutions of Factor VI – Repulsion, and Factor X – Disregard/Envy were not present in any group.

A comparison of the intensity of locutions between the tactical positions of the players showed statistically significant differences in the pre-competition situation. Midfield players showed a higher intensity of the locution 'I'm embarrassed' (Factor I – Humiliation/Anger) than defenders and forward players. Midfield players also showed a higher intensity of the locution 'I miss somebody' (Factor III – Hope) than defenders did. In turn, defenders showed a higher intensity of the locution 'I accept something' (Factor XI – Receptivity) than forward players did.

At the same time, forward players showed a higher intensity of the locution 'I feel sexual attraction to somebody' (Factor IV – Limerence/Empathy) than defender

*Table 1.1* Significant differences among group positions (defender, midfielder, and forward) in the pre-game situation for each PMSL factor

| PMSL factor | Pre-game | | | Post-game | |
| --- | --- | --- | --- | --- | --- |
| | Position | | | Win | Defeat |
| | Defender | Midfielder | Forward | | |
| Humiliation/Anger | – | + | – | – | + |
| Fatigue | * | * | * | – | + |
| Hope | – | + | * | * | * |
| Limerence/Empathy | – | – | + | * | * |
| Physiological response | * | * | * | * | * |
| Repulsion | * | * | * | * | * |
| Interest | * | * | * | + | – |
| Surprise | * | * | * | – | + |
| Hunger | – | + | * | * | * |
| Disregard/Envy | * | * | * | * | * |
| Receptivity | + | * | – | * | * |
| Serenity | * | * | * | + | – |

Note
+ and – indicate a statistically significant higher level (+) or lower level (–) when comparing one group to another regarding each factor; * indicates no differences between groups. Significant differences exist between wins and defeats in the post-game situation for each PMSL factor: + and – indicate a statistically significant higher level (+) or lower level (–) when comparing winning to the defeat condition regarding each factor; * indicates no differences between conditions.

players did. The locutions of this factor reveal a subjective mood that is oriented towards another person and carries much higher hedonic value and activation than the other factors on the scale. Forward players showed a high activation level and orientation towards the other person in their mood state at the pre-competition moment.

The results were also analysed according to the match outcome. Only victory or defeat was considered, whereas draws were discarded. There were statistically significant differences between post-competitive moods after victories versus after defeats, regardless of the players' tactical positions. After victory, the intensity of several locutions was higher than in the defeat situation: 'I am happy' (Factor I – Humiliation/Anger), 'I feel relieved' (Factor VII – Interest), and 'I am resigned' (Factor XII – Serenity). After defeat, the intensity of the following locutions was higher than in the victory situation: 'I feel guilty', 'I am ashamed', and 'I feel sad' (Factor I – Humiliation/Anger), 'I feel something is weird' and 'I feel surprised' (Factor VIII – Surprise).

There were marginal results indicating a trend towards other mood states in the post-competitive moment due to defeat with locutions such as 'I feel humiliated' and 'I feel angry' (Factor I – Humiliation/Anger), contrary to the relief obtained after victory ('I feel relieved' – Factor VII – Interest). These results also confirm previous findings indicating that athletes show lower levels of depression and anger as well as higher levels of vigour after victories than after defeats (Jones & Sheffield, 2007). Brandão (2000) also described negative states reflecting stress during a competition. A comparison of pre-game and post-game results showed hope and interest moods before a game and surprise after a game only when the team was defeated, suggesting the effect of an unexpected result.

It is important to note that this defeat effect should be considered within the specific stage of a player's athletic training. Young players might face a competitive situation as an opportunity for recognition of their abilities and the beginning of a sporting career (Sanches & Rezende, 2010). For this reason, defeat can represent a stressful situation for players at the beginning of their developmental progression, affecting their self-esteem, motivation, and negative mood.

## Mood state and performance

Sport performance is a complex phenomenon requiring the consideration of several internal and external processes. Performance is expressed through physical and psychological conditions originating from environmental interactions to which the athlete is submitted (Kiss, Bohme, Mansoldo, Degaki, & Regazzini, 2004).

Dias-Silva (2013) developed a tool to evaluate the behavioural repertory of football players during a game. The behavioural category system was built in several stages. Initially, the athlete's behaviour was assessed during three football matches, considering the activities, actors, space, physical objects, and sequences of activities and events (Sherman & Webb, 1988). These behaviours were grouped by taking into account the elements of football found in the literature and in the observations. Fifteen broad and mutually exclusive categories were defined. The definitions of each behaviour and the construction of the categories were evaluated by three judges namely two coaches and one sport psychologist.

After the instrument was revised for adequacy and replication, it was possible to provide a final version including the following categories: Long balls forward,

Passes, Long passes, Ball possession, Moving to the ball, Moving far from the ball, Kicks, Defence actions, Faults, Reaction behaviours, Challenges to the referee, Social behaviour, Individualistic behaviour, Aggressive behaviour, and Staying in position.

Dias-Silva (2013) evaluated the mood states of 18 football players in a male football team in the U-17 category during three games. During the games, three cameras recorded the behaviours of one player in each position (defence, midfield, and forward), following each player individually during the whole game.

In a descriptive manner, the researchers related pre-competition mood states to player behaviour in each position during the game. For midfielders, the strong presence of the locution 'I am calm' (Factor XII – Serenity) was more related to 'Ball possession' behaviours and less related to 'Long ball forward' behaviours. When the locutions 'I miss somebody' (Factor III – Hope) and 'I'm liking someone' (Factor IV – Limerence/Empathy) were present for this position, there was a larger number of actions, including 'Moving to the ball' and 'Social behaviour'.

The defence and forward positions showed no clearly observable pattern between the strength of locutions and behaviours; however, some approximations may be suggested. The midfield players showed some mood states and behaviours similar to those of forward players, while their other mood states and behaviours were similar to those of defence players. When the locution 'I feel a desire' (Factor III – Hope) showed a high presence intensity for the midfield and forward positions, high behaviour frequencies of 'Kick' and 'Moving to the ball' were observed. The presence of the locution 'I'm taking care' (Factor III – Hope) was linked to a high number of behaviours such as defensive actions and to lower frequencies of 'Staying in position' for the midfield and defence players.

Using another analysis that took the game location into account, Silva (2013) noticed that no matter where the competition occurred (home or away), the players remained interested and hopeful. The locutions 'I'm hopeful' (Factor III – Hope) and 'I'm interested' (Factor VII – Interest) were present in all games, three of them at home and three away. However, the locution 'I'm calm' (Factor XII – Serenity) had high intensity presence for midfield players in home games. At the same time, the locution 'I feel sexual attraction to somebody' (Factor IV – Limerence/ Empathy) had a high intensity among forward players in away games. The games occurring away from home might have resulted in the necessity of high affiliation (McClelland, Atkinson, Clark, & Lowell, 1953), a motivational component that leads to greater intensity of this locution.

The numbers of fouls and referee challenges experienced by the players in away games were higher than at home games. This difference in behaviour can be related to the high-intensity presence of the locution 'I'm calm' (Factor XII – Serenity) at home games. These findings show that where the game is held has implications on behaviour.

### Mood states during the competitive season

Picoli (2016) examined the mood states of young football athletes over a sequence of games and training sessions, considering decaying processes and expectations during a competitive period. The participants were 18 male players under 15 years old playing a São Paulo state championship. The data were collected at three time points: immediately before the last training session, before the state championship game, and before the first training session after the game.

The PMSL results were analysed using the mean values of the presence of locutions for each factor, which were normalized to permit comparisons of factors with different numbers of locutions. Factors such as Fatigue, Interest, and Serenity varied during the sequences of games and training sessions. The strength of locutions regarding the Interest factor increased as proximity of the main event increased, while those regarding the Fatigue factor decreased. The Hope factor showed variation depending on the game's result and on the chance of classification of the team in playoffs.

No differences were found regarding the players' position on the field. A possible limitation of the study was due to the results of the team's games: the team lost all games during the studied competition period.

### Mood states in sports similar to football

Similar studies have been conducted with futsal and American football, which are sports with similar tactics and technical aspects to those of football. Souza (2014) related pre-competition mood states to the performance of high-level futsal players, as measured through a scout (Tourinho Filho, Soares, & Barbanti, 2010). In this study, the description of performance considered the quantity of technical action attempts but not their results. For example, the performance index was considered to be the quantity of passes attempted by a player during the game.

The goalkeepers' results showed that the high strength of the locution 'I'm tired' (Factor II – Fatigue) may be related to the 'Goals suffered' and that the low strength of the locution 'I am ashamed' (Factor I – Humiliation/Anger) may be related to high frequencies of the behavioural category 'Leave the goal line'. Also, outfield players showed high-intensity presence of the locution 'I'm hopeful' (Factor III – Hope) in the pre-competitive moment, which was related to the behavioural category of 'Dribble' attempts.

American football players were also examined by Silva (2017), who applied the PMSL to a Brazilian male team. Forty-four players, divided into defensive and offensive players, participated in the study, which was conducted during a national competition. The strengths of the locutions 'I'm hopeful' (Factor III – Hope), 'I'm interested' (Factor VII – Interest), and 'I'm feeling a necessity' (Factor XI – Receptivity) were higher for the defensive than for the offensive players.

## Practical implications

Knowing the factors that influence an athlete's emotions and reactions is critical for the development and application of behavioural strategies, which will reflect on his or her performance and well-being. In this context, the tactical positions of the players on the field might influence positive and negative mood states at the time immediately preceding the competitions. Players and coaches may work on the players' capacity to manage their own mood states, so that they can play their role in the game regardless of the environment, personal variables, or other factors that may interfere.

Studies also draw attention to how athletes experience emotional victories and defeats in competition. How they face the opportunity of competing and the game's result will determine an athlete's mood states, with the effects of defeats being most striking for football players' moods, reflecting, for example, components of emotional orientation towards goals and outcomes (Brandão, 2000; Jones & Sheffield, 2007; Nogueira, 2009).

The psychological consequences of a victory or defeat should be a concern for the coaching staff, mainly within the context of an athlete's development. In Brazil, for example, the pressure for results is constant and disproportionate within the context of men's football in youth teams. This pressure comes from the club itself, the manager and other people involved, and even from members of the family, who place the weight of the possibility of social rise on the shoulders of 14- or 15-year-old boys.

The presented data show that a significant victory provides more relief and conformity than pride and satisfaction. On the other hand, defeat leads to states of shame and humiliation. It is necessary for young athletes to develop psychological skills to deal with adverse situations and defeats. In addition, clubs, family, managers, and coaches need to consider the psychological consequences of the results of competitions for young athletes.

Since physical preparation, techniques, and tactics follow specific patterns according to playing position, the implications of the cited studies call attention to psychological interventions that take into account each athlete's function during the game. The anticipation of what might happen during the game might influence the athletes' mood states. On this basis, the sport psychologist and the coaching staff can provide interventions that consider these processes, which would therefore be more effective for the development of the particular athletes and the team as a whole.

Midfield players, for example, have high participation in the game in terms of the number of ball touches and ball possessions (Dias-Silva, 2013). Therefore, if they approach a game more open to personal relationships they might perform better in terms of technical and tactical executions due to motivational and emotional dispositions optimizing the interaction with their teammates.

The behavioural category system for football provides high-quality information about players' behaviour during the game. In order to enhance the effectiveness of the sport psychologist, it may be more important to have information about the athletes' social orientation and behaviour, rather than about the number of displacements and correct passes by a player during the game. Descriptions of behavioural patterns can improve understanding of the relationship between mood and motivational states.

Behaviour descriptions and the categorization of football players during a game can reveal a vast complexity of possible actions by a player during the 90 minutes of action. The athlete connects with his or her teammates, adversaries, referee, coach, and supporters and experiences a variety of emotions and situations during the game. Thus, the understanding of athletes' mood states can help when planning an intervention that will reflect not only the improvement of technical and tactical actions but the whole behavioural repertoire observed in the game.

Mood states also refer to the level of organism activation and to the positive or negative evaluation of the situation. They reflect how players deal with different situations they face during a game and how they tend to approach or avoid a particular situation according to their past experience and current perception of it. Therefore, it is important to obtain data about the orientation of the behaviour and the intensity of the athlete's efforts during the game.

## Conclusions and future research directions

### Intervention-based research designs

Environmental variables are the source of momentary mood changes to energy and behavioural orientation. The complexity and dynamism observed in a competitive context often require the athlete to have sufficient individual/mental resources to deal with the situation. Thus, the intervention of coaches or particularly of sport psychologists must be based on the understanding of mood variations during a competitive period, while considering aspects such as the match context and motivational aspects.

### Development of a new, specific scale for pre-competitive mood states

Athletes in the field carry with them a great emotional and motivational load induced by several types of economic, social, and even political pressures. For example, the success of a football player in the World Cup can result in the support of their particular sponsor, the national hero title, or affect the political image of their country. It is essential to understand how the athlete perceives the moments before the beginning of a competition, so that, along with other evaluations, it would be possible to predict the athlete's behaviour and performance on the pitch.

It is therefore necessary to develop a self scale that considers factors interfering with the athletes' behaviour, as a way of understanding them individually and as a group to predict the behaviours they exhibit during a game. This would permit the coach to make the best decisions about how to handle the athletes, not only regarding tactical issues but also the motivational and emotional elements present during the immediate pre-competition moments that the athletes would then take with them on to the pitch.

## Summary

- Scales of verbal reports containing a wide range of moods (including positive ones) draw the most complete profile of an athlete's present mood states. A limitation of this research field so far is that no quantitative comparisons exist between the presence of locutions of momentary mood states and empirical values, as measured by the use of motivational, emotional, or social scales.
- Football players have a common mood profile the moments before the game begins, in terms of interest, happiness, and hope.
- The profiles of athletes' mood states before a competition begins differ according to the position and role they play in the game: the emotional profile of defensive players differs from that of forwards.
- Young Brazilian football players feel a high level of pressure to win, and they show relief after victories (more than happiness or pride) and humiliation and shame after defeats.

- It is necessary to evaluate an athlete's mood during a competitive period to understand the impact of environmental variables such as the result of the previous game, the importance of the upcoming game, and the team's ranking in the championship.
- The performance of football players should be understood on the basis of their entire behavioural repertoire during a game, as it can reveal emotional and motivational components: the positive dimension of moods (Hope and Limerence/Empathy) is correlated with attack actions and social behaviours during the game.

## References

Bindra, D. (1976). *A theory of intelligent behaviour.* New York, NY: John Wiley and Sons.

Brandão, M. R. F. (2000). *Fatores de stress em jogadores de futebol professional* [Stress factors in professional football players] (Unpublished doctoral dissertation). University of Campinas, Campinas-SP, Brazil.

Bueno, J. L. O., & Di Bonifácio, M. A. (2007). Alterações de estados de ânimo presentes em atletas de voleibol, avaliados em fases do campeonato [Changes of present mood states in volleyball athletes, evaluated in phases of the championship]. *Psicologia em Estudo, 12*(1), 179–184. doi:10.13140/RG.2.1.4113.0648.

Clancy, R. B., Herring, M. P., MacIntyre, T. E., & Campbell, M. J. (2016). A review of competitive sport motivation research. *Psychology of Sport and Exercise, 27,* 232–242. https://doi.org/10.1016/j.psychsport.2016.09.003.

Cofer, C. N. (1972). *Motivation and emotion.* Glenview, IL: Scott, Foresman.

Daiss, S., LeUnes, A., & Nation, J. (1986). Mood and locus of control of a sample of college and professional football players. *Perceptual and Motor Skills, 63,* 733–734.

Dias-Silva, W. (2013). *Relação entre estados de ânimo momentâneo e desempenho em atletas de futebol de campo* [Relationship between momentary moods states in pre-competition and performance in elite soccer] (Unpublished master's thesis). Faculty of Philosophy, Sciences and Letters at Ribeirão Preto, University of São Paulo, São Paulo, Brazil.

Durtschi, S., & Weiss, M. (1986). Psychological characteristics of elite and non-elite marathon runners. In D. Landers (Ed.), *Sport and elite performers* (pp. 73–80). Champaign, IL: Human Kinetics.

Ekkekakis, P. (2000). Measuring affective responses to acute exercise the circular way: Development and validation of the Circumplex Affect Inventory. *Journal of Sport and Exercise Psychology, 22,* S36.

Engelmann, A. (1978). *Os estados subjetivos: uma tentativa de classificação de seus relatos verbais* [The subjective states: An attempt to classify their verbal reports]. São Paulo, Brazil: Ática.

Engelmann, A. (1986). Lep – uma lista, de origem brasileira, para medir a presença de estados de ânimo no momento em que está sendo respondida [Lep – A list, of Brazilian origin, to measure the presence of mood states at the moment of being answered]. *Ciência e Cultura, 38*(1), 121–146.

Engelmann, A. (2002). A new scale for evaluating hedonic precepts. In J. A. Da Silva, E. H. Matsushima, & N. P. Ribeiro Filho (Eds.), *Fechner day. Annual meeting of the International Society for Psychophysics* (pp. 191–196). Rio de Janeiro, Brazil: The International Society for Psychophysics.

Hanin, Y. L. (2000). *Emotions in sport.* Champaign, IL: Human Kinetics.

Jones, M., & Sheffield, D. (2007).The impact of game outcome on the well-being of athletes. *International Journal of Sport and Exercise Psychology, 5,* 54–65. doi:10.1080/1612197X.2008.96 71812.

Kiss, M. A. P. D., Bohme, M. T. S., Mansoldo, A. C., Degaki, E., & Regazzini, M. (2004). Desempenho e talento esportivo [Performance and sports talent]. *Revista Paulista de Educação Física, 18,* 89–100.

Lane, A. M., & Terry, P. C. (2000). The nature of mood: Development of a conceptual model with a focus on depression. *Journal of Applied Sport Psychology, 12,* 16–33. doi:10.1080/1041 3200008404211.

Lazarus, R. S. (1998). *Fifty years of the research and theory of R.S. Lazarus: An analysis of historical and perennial issues.* Mahwah, NJ: Lawrence Erlbaum Associates.

McClelland, D. C., Atkinson, J. W., Clark, R. A., & Lowell, E. L. (1953). *The achievement motivation.* New York, NY: Appleton-Century-Crofts.

McNair, D. M., Lorr, M., & Droppleman, L. F. (1971). *Manual for the profile of mood states.* San Diego, CA: Educational and Industrial Testing Services.

McNair, D. M., Lorr, M., & Droppleman, L. F. (1992). *Revised manual for the profile of mood states.* San Diego, CA: Educational and Industrial Testing Services.

Nogueira, J. E. (2009). *Alterações de estados de animo em atletas de futebol de campo, avaliados em* (Unpublished bachelor's thesis). Moura Lacerda University Centre, Ribeirão Preto, Brazil.

Nowlis, V. (1970). Mood: Behaviour and experience. In M. B. Arnold (Ed.), *Feelings and emotions – The Loyola symposium* (pp. 267–277). New York, NY: Academic Press.

Picoli, R. M. M. (2016). *Alterações dos estados de ânimo de jovens atletas de futebol em função do decurso temporal durante um período competitivo* [Youth soccer players' mood changes in function of time course during a competitive season] (Unpublished master's thesis). Faculty of Philosophy, Sciences and Letters at Ribeirão Preto, University of São Paulo, São Paulo, Brazil.

Prapavessis, H. (2000). The POMS and sports performance: A review. *Journal of Applied Sport Psychology, 12*(1), 34–48. doi:10.1080/10413200008404212.

Rohlfs, I. C. P. M., Carvalho, T., Rotta, T. M., & Krebs, R. J. (2004). Aplicação de instrumentos de avaliação de estados de humor na detecção da síndrome do excesso de treinamento [Application of mood assessment instruments for detection of overtraining syndrome]. *Revista Brasileira de Medicina do Esporte, 10*(2), 111–115.

Rohlfs, I. C. P. M., Rotta, T. M., Luft, C. D. B., Andrade, A., Krebs, R. J., & Carvalho, T. (2008). Brunel Mood Scale (BRUMS): An instrument for early detection of overtraining syndrome. *Revista Brasileira de Medicina do Esporte, 14*(3), 176–181.

Sanches, A. S., & Rezende, A. L. G. (2010). Avaliação da percepção das situações de estresse de jogadores de futebol em função da idade [Evaluation of the perception of soccer players' stress situations according to age]. *Revista Brasileira Ciência e Movimento, 18*(3), 43–50.

Sherman, R. R., & Webb, R. D. (1988). Education and grounded theory. In R. R. Sherman & R. B. Webb (Eds.), *Qualitative research in education: Focus and method* (pp. 123–140). London, England: Falmer Press.

Silva, R. C. (2013). *Relação entre estados de ânimo momentâneos e desempenho dentro e fora de casa em atletas de futebol* [Relation between momentary mood states and performance in football athletes in home and away matches] (Unpublished bachelor's thesis). Faculty of Philosophy, Sciences and Letters, Ribeirão Preto, University of São Paulo, São Paulo, Brazil.

Silva, R. C. (2017). *Ataque e defesa: A influência da posição nos estados de ânimo momentâneos em atletas de futebol americano de alto rendimento* [Offense and defence: The influence of position in momentary mood states in American football athletes] (Unpublished master's thesis). Faculty of Philosophy, Sciences and Letters at Ribeirão Preto, University of São Paulo, São Paulo, Brazil.

Souza, V. C. (2014). *Relações entre estados de ânimo pré-competitivos e desempenho de atletas de alto rendimento em jogos de futsal* [Relations between precompetitive mood states and performance in elite futsal] (Unpublished master's thesis). Faculty of Philosophy, Sciences and Letters at Ribeirão Preto, University of São Paulo, São Paulo, Brazil.

Tourinho Filho, H., Soares, B., & Barbanti, V. (2010). Análise do desempenho em quadra de jogadores de futsal: um estudo longitudinal [Analysis of the performance in futsal players' court: A longitudinal study]. *Revista Digital, Buenos Aires, 14*(141).

# 2 Mental toughness development in football

*Tristan J. Coulter and Richard C. Thelwell*

**Abstract**

This chapter examines the concept of mental toughness in football and provides comprehensive coverage of the extant literature in this area. Attention is specifically dedicated to a review of the mental toughness research to have been conducted in the game, to date. These studies include a focus on understanding the conceptual foundations of mental toughness in football across several populations, including academy and professional players, elite coaches and referees, and the parents of elite players. Building on these foundations, an overview of the existing interventions used to develop mental toughness are provided. These interventions range from the creation of challenging learning contexts to the implementation of traditional psychological skills training programmes. The chapter concludes by proposing a systematic and wider organisational strategy to develop mental toughness in the game, with particular attention given to the different stages of players' psycho-social development. It also calls for continued attention to be given to referees and an instigation of mental toughness development programmes for coaches, given the inherent stressors this group experiences. Lastly, based on the current state of research, several options for future mental toughness studies in football are proposed.

Since the turn of the millennium, mental toughness (MT) has become one of the most prevalent topics in the field of sport psychology (Gucciardi & Gordon, 2011). It is a concept that has caught the interest of many people invested in sport, where the goal has been to establish a better understanding of individuals who regularly perform to high personal levels, despite facing incidences of challenge, pressure, or adversity (Mahoney, Gucciardi, Ntoumanis, & Mallett, 2014). To develop this understanding, scholars have gathered perspectives of MT in sports such as tennis (e.g. Cowden, Anshel, & Fuller, 2014), cricket (e.g. Bull, Shambrook, James, & Brooks, 2005), swimming (Driska, Kamphoff, & Armentrout, 2012), and football (e.g. Thelwell, Weston, & Greenlees, 2005), the latter being of particular interest here. In doing so, opinions of MT have been collected from various cohorts, including Olympic champions, professional and amateur athletes, sport psychologists, coaches, and others associated with sport (e.g. parents). Overall, the main goal of these efforts has been to synthesise and refine what MT is and means in sport, and explore the mechanisms of how, and to what extent, it can be developed.

A recent review of extant research indicates a particular group of psychological attributes to comprise MT. These attributes are: generalised self-efficacy, buoyancy, success mindset, optimistic style, context knowledge, emotional regulation, and attention regulation (Gucciardi, Hanton, Gordon, Mallett, & Temby, 2015). In addition to its conceptual elements, there has also been a keen interest to study how MT develops. For example, studies involving athletes (e.g. Bull et al., 2005), coaches (e.g. Gucciardi, Gordon, Dimmock, & Mallett, 2009), parents (e.g. Mallett & Coulter, 2011), and sport psychologists (Weinberg, Freysinger, Mellano, & Brookhouse, 2016) have been conducted to identify the particular environments and strategies that best enable people to build up their MT. Taking stock of this research, Anthony, Gucciardi, and Gordon (2016) recently proposed a Bioecological Model of MT Development, based on their identification of four key themes from the (qualitative) development literature: *personal characteristics* (i.e. malleable skills or resources); *interactions with the environment* (e.g. positive coach–athlete relationships); *progressive development* (e.g. contextual experiences, such as a positive but tough practice environment, that promote MT); and *breadth of experience* (e.g. experiencing positive and negative critical incidents that facilitate personal growth). These themes suggest that MT develops as a result of interactions between personal and contextual factors. They also emphasise the importance of developing a certain coaching climate – one that is supportive, motivating, and challenging.

Currently, identifying the recurring properties and mechanisms of MT is an important conceptual and practical achievement. In this chapter, we focus on MT in football, which, to date, remains one of the most popular sports to be examined on the topic. It was Bill Beswick, an experienced mental skills coach, who first devoted a chapter to MT in his book, *Focused for Soccer: Develop a Winning Mental Approach.* Beswick (2001) described MT as one of the most important psychological characteristics of the elite footballer. He also identified four steps to developing MT, namely (i) developing a strong identity; (ii) becoming and staying motivated; (iii) establishing a disciplined work ethic; and (iv) developing self-control strategies. Like many early MT researchers, Beswick provides a subjective account of his experiences and observations of MT in the game. His views are appealing and correspond with some of the commonly identified MT attributes, reported earlier. However, these insights lack a rigorous grounding in the approach taken to understand and examine MT. Since 2005, several research teams have studied MT in football in a more methodical manner. These groups have tended to give attention to the elite end of the playing spectrum and focused almost exclusively on understanding MT in male populations. They have also examined MT and its development across several participant samples, including academy and professional players, elite coaches and referees, and parents. Overall, the goals of these endeavours have been guided by the following questions:

- What is MT?
- What are the situations and events that require MT in football?
- What cognitions do players (and referees) exhibit when they are being mentally tough?
- What behaviours convey MT in the game?
- What intervention strategies foster MT?

We will now review this collection of research and consider what the practical implications are for developing MT in the game. We begin by reflecting on early empirical studies of MT in football, followed by an overview of the investigations that have targeted MT at the academy and professional levels. We then devote a section to a recent pioneering study exploring MT behaviours in football and, subsequently, review the examination of MT and its development in elite referees. To finish, we offer a summary of key conceptual and practical observations to developing MT in football, and conclude with some future recommendations.

## Initial perspectives of MT in football

The first rigorous study to examine MT in football was conducted by Thelwell et al. (2005), who used football as a context to seek clarity of an earlier proposed definition of MT. They also wanted to identify football players' perceptions of key MT attributes. To achieve these aims, Thelwell et al. analysed the views of 6 male British footballers, who had all played at the international level, and then sought confirmation of their findings through a sample of 43 male professional players. Ten MT attributes were identified and ranked accordingly by the participants (see Table 2.1). Having total self-belief to achieve success, wanting the ball (e.g. despite poor form), and reacting positively, where stated as the three most important attributes of MT in the study. Interestingly, Thelwell et al. also reported how their participants had remarked on the importance of the environment in developing MT during the interviews. It was suggested that having to deal with certain challenges during a player's formative and early career years was important, in this regard. Such challenges included being dropped, being sent out on loan, and lacking suitable support structures (e.g. parental support; see Table 2.1).

Similar developmental experiences were later reported by Coulter et al. (2010), who triangulated perspectives of MT from a select group of elite male coaches and players, and the parents of players, participating in Australia's A-League. As part of this study, situations requiring MT in football were identified and then organised into general (e.g. being dropped), match-specific (e.g. goals being scored), and developmental categories (e.g. the transition to senior level football). Knowing the situations that demand MT in football is useful for several reasons. As an *educational tool*, they provide a clearer expectation about the challenges a footballer must deal with to be considered mentally tough. They provide coaches and practitioners with *opportunities to intervene* with players (e.g. using failure as a chance to improve). They also offer a platform for creating *training programmes and simulations* that develop MT.

In addition to reporting particular situations requiring MT, Coulter et al. (2010) identified 14 attributes of MT in football (see Table 2.1). Several attributes reflected earlier findings described by Thelwell et al. (e.g. self-belief, concentration, coping under pressure). Others added to the breadth of attributes to be linked to MT in the game (e.g. winning mentality and desire, physical toughness, emotional intelligence). In their study, Coulter et al. also explored perceived behaviours and cognitions exhibited by mentally tough players. Common behaviours of MT included playing with injury, repeatable high performances, and demanding the ball. MT cognitions broadly centred on motivational and instructional forms of self-talk that reinforced a player's self-belief, perseverance, perspective, and desire to succeed.

*Table 2.1* Research-identified attributes of, and potential situational experiences for developing, MT in football

| Study | MT attributes | Situations |
|---|---|---|
| Thelwell et al. (2005) | Ranked:<br>1 Having total self-belief at all times that you will achieve success<br>2 Wanting the ball at all times (when playing well and not so well)<br>3 Having the ability to react to situations positively<br>4 Having the ability to hang on and be calm under pressure<br>5 Knowing what it takes to grind yourself out of trouble<br>6 Having the ability to ignore distractions and remain focused<br>7 Controlling emotions throughout performance<br>8 Having a presence that affects opponents<br>9 Having everything outside of the game in control<br>10 Enjoying the pressure associated with performance | Being dropped/not considered for selection<br>Being selected when not expecting it<br>Lacking parent/school support<br>Having to gain respect from the manager<br>Being sent out on loan to another club<br>Training with the senior squad |
| Coulter, Mallett, and Gucciardi (2010) | Ranked:<br>1 Winning mentality and desire<br>2 Self-belief<br>3 Physical toughness<br>4 Work ethic<br>5 Resilience<br>6 Personal values<br>7 Concentration and focus<br>8 Performance awareness<br>9 Sport intelligence<br>10 Tough attitude<br>11 Coping under pressure<br>12 Competitive effort<br>13 Risk taker<br>14 Emotional intelligence and control | General:<br>Injury and rehabilitation<br>Being dropped<br>Preparation<br>Balancing commitments<br>Form<br>Media pressure<br>Distractions off the pitch<br>Playing overseas<br><br>Match-specific:<br>Goals<br>External pressures (environmental and playing conditions, match variables)<br>Internal pressures (coping with mistakes, fatigue/physical pain)<br><br>Developmental:<br>Early or late developer<br>Being away from home<br>Peer and social pressures<br>Stepping up to senior football |

| | | |
|---|---|---|
| Cook, Crust, Littlewood, Nesti, and Allen-Collinson (2014) | Competitiveness with self and others<br>• Commitment to excellence<br>• Motivation to achieve<br><br>Mindset<br>• Focus<br>• Confidence<br><br>Resilience<br>• Coping and rebounding after setbacks<br>• Perseverance<br>• Courage<br><br>Personal responsibility<br>• Independence<br>• Discipline and sacrifice | Loss of form<br>After being criticised<br>Playing with/recovering from injury (or being fatigued)<br>Watching other players progress<br>Positive transitions (e.g. breaking into the reserve team) |
| Diment (2014) | Not applicable | Internal:<br>Making an error<br>Being consistently beaten by your opponent<br>Getting a yellow card<br>Being injured<br>Coping with fatigue<br><br>External environment:<br>Responding to poor referee decisions<br>Intimated by opponent off the ball<br>Being criticised by others<br>Poor pitch or weather conditions<br>Being consistently fouled<br><br>External match:<br>Conceding or scoring a goal<br>Being ahead or behind on the scoreboard<br>Time periods (e.g. first/last 10 mins, +/−half-time)<br>Not being involved in the game (e.g. striker/GK)<br>Opposition changes tactics<br>You (or opponent) going down to 10 men |

*continued*

*Table 2.1* Continued

| Study | MT attributes | Situations |
|---|---|---|
| Slack, Maynard, Butt, and Olusoga (2013); Slack, Butt, Maynard, and Olusoga (2014) | Coping with pressure<br>Achievement striving<br>Resilience<br>High work ethic<br>Robust self-belief<br>Tough attitude<br>Sport intelligence | Competition-specific:<br>Pre-match:<br>Pre-match protocol<br>Refereeing a high-profile match<br>Refereeing a lower standard of football<br>During match:<br>Dealing with player and manager mindgames<br>Critical incidents and flashpoints<br>Tough decision-making<br>Post-match:<br>Media outlets scrutinising performance<br>Player/manager post-match criticisms<br>Performance evaluation of refereeing stakeholders<br><br>Off-field:<br>General elite refereeing situations:<br>Select group pressures<br>Schedule and travel demands<br>Transitioning to elite level football<br>Performance growth<br>Refereeing setbacks<br><br>General life:<br>Personal and professional sacrifices<br>Stress on family welfare<br>Maintaining a referee life balance |

## MT in youth players

With formative experiences being a potentially significant period for developing MT in football, as with other sports (e.g. Hardy, Bell, & Beattie, 2014), scholars have sought to examine how the concept develops in youth-aged populations and, in particular, those playing at the academy levels. Here, four MT studies are noteworthy, and three of them conducted with players and coaching/support staff from English Premier League (EPL) academies (the fourth was conducted in Spanish youth football; see Guillén and Santana, 2018). Two of these studies adopted the 4Cs model of MT, which is a popular framework in mainstream literature that conceptualises MT as a generic, trait-like concept, underpinned by four key attributes: challenge, commitment, control, and confidence (Clough, Earle, & Sewell, 2002). Using the 4Cs (and, specifically, the MTQ18 inventory), Crust, Nesti, and Littlewood (2010a) found no significant cross-sectional differences in MT across various age groups (U13s to U19s) in a single EPL academy. They also found no significant differences in MT between academy players who were either released or retained from the club. These findings led the authors to question the importance of the academy climate in developing player MT (although, by the authors' own admission, the precision of the MTQ18 may have influenced these outcomes). In a similar design, again using the MTQ18, the same research team tested (pre-post) the stability of MT in 21 male academy players across a 3-month interval (Crust, Nesti, & Littlewood, 2010b). The findings suggested support for the stability of MT, which, when operationalised through the 4Cs, questions the dynamic nature of the MT construct. Interestingly, their study also involved gathering observational data from two academy coaches, who were asked to rate each player on his MT. The findings identified substantial differences between the coaches' perceptions of the attributes and behaviours of the players' MT, in doing so, demonstrating (albeit on a very small scale) the idiosyncratic issues associated with what signifies MT in the game.

Taking a more grounded approach to understanding MT at the academy level, Cook et al. (2014) conducted an examination of MT, and its development, from the perspectives of eight senior coaches and support staff in an EPL academy. Using semi-structured interviews, Cook et al. identified four general dimensions of MT: (i) *competitiveness with self and others* (e.g. player commitment to excellence); (ii) *mindset* (e.g. showing high levels of confidence on the pitch); (iii) *resilience* (e.g. ability to cope with stress); and (iv) *personal responsibility* (e.g. regulating self-discipline).

To develop the four dimensions of MT, two main strategies were identified by the academy coaches. First, providing a *challenging* learning context was believed to be important for developing MT. For these participants, a challenging context involves creating a demanding coaching climate that sets and expects very high standards from players. For example, it is deemed to be one that pushes players physically (i.e. close to breaking point), exposes their weaknesses, stretches their capabilities, and uses criticism as a form of motivation. This approach assumes that, to create mentally tough footballers, it is necessary to be subjected to a harsh and intense training environment. However, taking this path raises several safeguarding issues. For instance, Owusu-Sekyere and Gervis (2016) reported that MT can become a façade for using questionable (i.e. unethical) coaching practices, where emotionally abusive behaviours (e.g. belittling, bullying, shouting) are acceptable strategies for developing MT. As such, the coaches in Cook et al.'s study also recognised the need for a sense of balance between exposing young players to tough training conditions, while providing them with appropriate *care and support* to ensure they can cope with the demands placed upon them. It was reported that ex-players are useful mentors, in this regard, because they can help share their experiences with younger players, normalise their setbacks, and provide them with useful ways to cope.

The second reported strategy to developing MT was to encourage player *independence and personal responsibility.* For example, purposely withholding support to players or helping them solve their own problems were identified as important ways to develop MT. Overall, while the findings illustrated that coaches associated MT development with a context exuding challenge, support, and autonomy, a key discovery by Cook et al. (2014) was the general lack of awareness the participants had for developing MT in the game – this despite MT being regarded as *the* most important psychological construct for a young player's career progression.

## MT development in senior-age footballers

Given the prominence of football in world sport, it may come as a surprise to many readers to learn that only one study currently exists that focuses on the development of MT at the senior/professional level. This study, by Miçooğulları and Ekmekçi (2017), entails the pre-post evaluation of a psychological skills training (PST) programme aimed at enhancing the MT of 26 male members (aged 18–33 years) of a Turkish Division III football team, the majority of whom (80%) had played at the professional level for over 10 years. The programme consisted of a 16-week – during season – intervention, involving the development of four mental skills: goal-setting, imagery, self-talk, and arousal control. For each skill, 12 sessions were conducted over a 4-week period, ranging between 35 and 45 minutes in duration, and included drills, group discussion topics, and homework tasks. In the study, MT was measured using the Sport MT Questionnaire (SMTQ; Sheard, Golby, & van Wersch, 2009) which defines MT through three factors – confidence, constancy, and control. The results suggested a positive intervention effect across each subscale of the SMTQ and total MT score, although it should be noted that no comparative control group was included in the study. Nevertheless, like other MT development studies (e.g. Fitzwater, Arthur, & Hardy, 2018), the research indicates that traditional PST packages may be useful to facilitate the development of MT at the senior level.

## MT behaviours in football

From a conceptual standpoint, much of the extant literature on MT has focused on the task of examining the core psychological attributes shared by mentally tough performers. Some scholars have emphasised the importance of behavioural outcomes as a potentially more profitable avenue of inquiry (e.g. Hardy et al., 2014). However, few studies reflect such an in-depth approach as that recently shown by Diment (2014), who provided a comprehensive behavioural analysis of MT in Danish football. In particular, Diment aimed to identify specific behaviours that represent MT in competitive matches, and proposed that doing so could form the basis for the development of a behavioural profiling tool to measure and train MT in the game.

Diment identified 28 behavioural categories of MT using video analysis from elite male and female matches. These categories incorporated general, offensive, defensive, and communicative actions, and positive (e.g. adaptive reaction following an error) and negative (e.g. anger directed towards the referee) behaviours associated with MT. The top 10 behavioural categories indicative of MT in football are reported in Table 2.2. These categories mostly relate to offensive acts of play (i.e. when a team is in possession of the ball). They also suggest a mentally tough player is someone who (i) is *highly involved in the match* at both a team (e.g. tactical and motivation communication) and individual (e.g. physical presence, clear movement, and communication to want the ball) level; (ii) understands *how the game is played*, and has the ability to act on this understanding; (iii) is *confident* in one's ability; and (iv) *responds positively* to incurred errors and setbacks. Overall, using a systematic approach that accounts for a range of ages, levels, and genders involved in football, from an applied perspective, an awareness of such behaviours is particularly useful. Specifically, when combined with the knowledge of perceived situations and events that require MT in football (see Table 2.1), these behaviours could inform the development of individualised (or team-based) training programmes that aim to encourage players to outwardly respond to such encounters in more adaptive and desired ways.

*Table 2.2* Top 10 behavioural categories of MT in football (see Diment, 2014)

| Category | Description |
| --- | --- |
| 1 Quick recovery after an error | A quick and productive reaction immediately after an error or loss of possession |
| 2 Wanting the ball – Movement | A clear change in speed or direction that displays a desire to want the ball, attract the ball to yourself, or be involved in the game when your team is in possession of the ball |
| 3 Motivation communication – Team | Verbal and non-verbal communication directed at teammates to encourage, or motivate, in order to influence the motivation level in the game |
| 4 Wanting the ball – Communication | Communication that displays a desire to want the ball, attract the ball to yourself, or be involved in the game |
| 5 Tactical communication – In play | Verbal and non-verbal communication directed at teammates to improve or enhance the tactical coordination or effectiveness of the team whilst the ball is in play |
| 6 Playing with 'confidence' | When in possession of the ball, having the confidence to take risks, to impact the game, and to use technical skills |
| 7 Enjoying the game | Actions that displays experiencing fun, enjoyment, or having a good time |
| 8 Tactical communication – Break in play | Verbal and non-verbal communication directed at teammates to improve or enhance the tactical coordination or effectiveness of the team during breaks in play |
| 9 Having a physical presence | Physical actions that display a physical strength or presence to opposition within the laws of the game |
| 10 Taking time on the ball | Playing the ball in a way that gives time and composure on the ball |

**Developing mentally tough referees**

Until now, this chapter has focused on the goal of understanding and developing MT in football players. However, more recent research has extended this inquiry to include referees. Leading the way in this area is a series of studies led by Slack and colleagues, who have explored MT and its development with referees in English football. Stemming from initial research (see Slack et al, 2013; Slack et al., 2014), this research team has provided grounds for the design and evaluation of a comprehensive MT education and training programme with this cohort (Slack, Maynard, Butt, & Olusoga, 2015). This programme consisted of four individual and two group-based intervention workshops designed to develop MT and enhance performance in three early career English Football League (EFL) referees. Specifically, Slack et al. (2015) incorporated a collection of situation-based stress inoculation training methods (e.g. pressurised role play, behavioural modelling techniques) and cognitive-behavioural techniques (e.g. reframing) into an 8-month (18 EFL match) MT development programme. The content of the four individual workshops, held during early (0–3 month) and middle (4–6 month) phases of the intervention process, involved many educational and role-play tasks geared at developing the participants' awareness of MT components. For example, several tasks placed an emphasis on educating the officials about the seven referee-specific MT attributes (e.g. exercises exploring what makes a confident football referee, video analysis of EPL referees displaying high work ethic; see Table 2.1). Some tasks involved the identification, ranking, and awareness training of adaptive behaviours adopted by EPL referees in on-field situations requiring MT (e.g. player vs player confrontations, manager reaction to a decision). Other tasks targeted developing an awareness of MT cognitions and the practice of effective self-regulatory strategies (e.g. rationalisation, refocusing techniques) used by mentally tough referees. Lastly, role-play activities involved exposing the participants to situations requiring MT in elite refereeing (e.g. simulated exercises of players reacting to a decision). Following the four individual workshops were two group-based workshops conducted during the latter (7–8 month) phase of the intervention programme. One group workshop stressed the importance of effectively dealing with off-field situations demanding MT. A major theme, here, involved participant awareness training about the sources and issues related to the football media, and the completion of role-play exercises to develop effective strategies to deal with media scrutiny. The second group workshop focused on the topic of referees successfully dealing with the required peer and coach assessment process of match day referee performances.

To gauge the impact of their intervention, Slack et al. (2015) collected data at multiple points during the course of the development programme. They used generalised (4Cs; MTQ48) and (self-designed) referee-specific measures of MT, and objective referee-assessment reports, as tools to measure the efficacy of their work. Their results highlighted that all three referees reported higher generalised MT scores during the intervention phase. Similarly, they showed high experimental effects across all components of referee-specific MT from baseline to late intervention. Lastly, all referees reported higher mean match-day assessor performance scores across all intervention phases compared to baseline. In their summary, Slack et al. (2015) paid special attention to the applied implications of their research. This included acknowledging the benefits of behavioural modelling techniques as a means for showing referees what MT looks like, thus, aiding the process of behavioural self-evaluation; the benefits of self and group reflective processes as an indicator of one's MT strengths and potential developmental areas, especially during times of high seasonal pressure (e.g. end of season); and the call for practitioners to consider evaluating MT in other performance and off-field areas that go beyond the mere focus on match-specific interests.

## Practical implications and next steps

The preceding commentary suggests the MT phenomena within a football context is a salient variable. What has emerged from the narrative is that MT is a multi-dimensional construct made up of a number of key components that are perceived to develop over an individual's career (Thelwell et al., 2005). Despite the conceptual questions that have existed in recent years, there appear to be common characteristics to what MT is in football. Basic themes include: achievement motivation, adaptive self-regulation, a thirst to compete, high levels of self-confidence, and high game intelligence. These themes underpin the abilities, conduct, and skills that footballers and referees exhibit, which are expressed through such things as their intense work ethic, desire to want the ball, focus, commitment, resilience, coping abilities, and presence on the pitch. We have also identified many situations that require MT in football and, equally, proposed mechanisms and strategies that may develop it (e.g. behavioural modelling, role play, self-regulatory cognitive strategies). Perhaps most interesting is the suggestion that MT can be an observable construct via behavioural presentation. Although questions remain as to the precise measurement of MT, there are several practical implications that can be taken from the knowledge thus far and these are generally within the realm of ensuring that key stakeholders in football (e.g. players, coaches, parents) are educated to what MT may constitute, especially given that it is not designed to be a vehicle for selection.

With the above in mind, it would seem reasonable to suggest that national organisations responsible for all facets of football development establish a blueprint to what they perceive MT to constitute (see Eubank, Nesti, & Littlewood, 2017). From this, a recommendation would be to integrate MT attributes and experiences throughout their development processes (e.g. coach-education, player welfare programmes, stakeholder training) to ensure that all significant parties have a common understanding of the construct. It is arguably the case that, at present, a structured, developmental approach to instilling MT characteristics is not evident and that a process aligned to that proposed by Harwood, Barker, and Anderson (2015), via a psycho-social development approach, or others (e.g. Slack et al., 2015), would be advantageous.

To explore this further, within the formative stages of their careers, an individual's focus should be on skill mastery, enjoyment, socialisation, and discipline. Supporting this, it would be advisable to expose individuals to a variety of situations and environments that affect the experiences necessary to promote the onset of MT development. Integral to this stage are coaches and parents. In particular, coaches have prominent roles in shaping the motivational environments that develop the foundational attributes of MT (Connaughton, Hanton, & Jones, 2010), while parents are considered the primary influence on upbringing, instilling hard work and discipline, and providing encouragement and support (Mallett & Coulter, 2011).

When in the middle to intermediate levels, individuals are likely to be engaged in a more disciplined and structured training regime where coaches can lead MT development initiatives. Specifically, coaches can facilitate MT development via the training environments that they create, and the ongoing exposure and challenges they present to players. Further, they are well-positioned to influence the prescription of individualised training programmes and psychological skill development that may be influenced via observing and learning from higher level performers, or role models to establish a mindset built on a belief of superiority and desire for success. Nevertheless, despite this position of influence, football coaches admit feeling ill-equipped to design and implement suitable MT development programmes. Hence, there is an opportunity to better educate and support coaches to effectively use behavioural, cognitive, and circumstantial strategies to develop MT in players. It might also include discussions about the potential dangers associated with this pursuit (e.g. overemphasising harsh, uncaring training environments).

When individuals move into the latter stage of development, which may also coincide with being at the elite level, the evidence suggests the development of MT to be facilitated by sport psychology support. Specifically, this can be achieved via advice and education on, for example, strategies to achieve success, controlling unhelpful thoughts, and handling competitive pressure, through to gaining knowledge from respected individuals via mentoring schemes. Should national organisations recognise the role that vicarious learning plays in the development of MT, the prevalence of such exposure and experiences will inevitably enhance individuals' capabilities to cope more positively in their performance environment.

To now, the focus of MT development has been largely player-centric, with some consideration to referee toughness. Moving forward, it would be prudent to consider the initiation of MT education programmes for coaches, with specific reference to their own toughness. It is well documented that coaches experience a myriad of challenges (see Olusoga & Thelwell, 2017 for a review) and this is no better illustrated by the recent work of Wagstaff and colleagues (Wagstaff, Gilmore, & Thelwell, 2016) where they reported the revolving door nature of football management and coaching, and the subsequent impact on organisational stability. Acknowledging that the average tenure for a manager in the English League was estimated at 1.55 years in 2013, it is plausible to suggest that such individuals would benefit from a mentally tough disposition. Whether such programmes develop mediated (e.g. coaching classes), unmediated (e.g. mentoring), or internal (e.g. reflection) learning contexts, one cannot deny the environmental, occupational, and performance challenges to which they are exposed daily.

To complement the attention to coach MT, we would also like to see the field extend its inquiry to other areas and cohorts of the game. For example, to date, few MT football studies have been conducted outside of the UK (exceptions include Coulter et al., 2010; Diment, 2014; Guillén & Santana, 2018; Miçooğullari & Ekmekçi, 2017), which limits the awareness of alternative perspectives and approaches to MT development adopted in other countries and cultures. Also, while there is an appeal to examine MT at the elite end of the playing continuum, there is also potential merit to seeing it investigated at other levels of the game. One interesting path could be to study MT in school or club level football. A MT development programme in these settings provides greater public reach. Similarly, it would provide an opportunity to examine the potential transferable effects of MT to other personal and social outcomes beyond sport (i.e. MT as a life skill; see Gould, Griffes, & Carson, 2011).

## Conclusion

In the current chapter, we have offered an up-to-date review of MT research in football. We have explored how prominent individuals believe MT can be developed, especially at elite player, academy, and referee levels. We have also provided thoughts about the key MT constructs in football, alongside suggestions for future research on its development. To close, it is clear MT is a salient concept in football psychology. Given its prevalence as a focal sport for conducting MT research, the game will likely feature as an important domain for advancing the conceptual and developmental knowledge-base on this topic in the years to come.

## References

Anthony, D. R., Gucciardi, D. F., & Gordon, S. (2016). A meta-study of qualitative research on mental toughness development. *International Review of Sport and Exercise Psychology*, 1–31. doi: 10.1080/1750984x.2016.1146787.

Beswick, B. (2001). *Focused for soccer: Develop a winning mental approach*. Champaign, IL: Human Kinetics.

Bull, S. J., Shambrook, C. J., James, W., & Brooks, J. E. (2005). Towards an understanding of mental toughness in elite English cricketers. *Journal of Applied Sport Psychology, 17*, 209–227. doi:10.1080/10413200591010085.

Clough, P. J., Earle, K., & Sewell, D. (2002). Mental toughness: The concept and its measurement. In I. Cockerill (Ed.), *Solutions in sport psychology* (pp. 32–43). London, England: Thomson Publishing.

Connaughton, D., Hanton, S., & Jones, G. (2010). The development and maintenance of mental toughness in the World's best performers. *The Sport Psychologist, 24*, 168–193. doi:10.1123/tsp. 24.2.168.

Cook, C., Crust, L., Littlewood, M., Nesti, M., & Allen-Collinson, J. (2014). 'What it takes': Perceptions of mental toughness and its development in an English Premier League Soccer Academy. *Qualitative Research in Sport, Exercise and Health, 6*, 329–347. doi:10.1080/2159676x. 2013.857708.

Coulter, T. J., Mallett, C. J., & Gucciardi, D. F. (2010). Understanding mental toughness in Australian soccer: Perceptions of players, parents, and coaches. *Journal of Sports Sciences, 28*, 699–716. doi:10.1080/02640411003734085.

Cowden, R. G., Anshel, M. H., & Fuller, D. K. (2014). Comparing athletes' and their coaches' perceptions of athletes' mental toughness among elite tennis players. *Journal of Sport Behavior, 37*(3), 221.

Crust, L., Nesti, M., & Littlewood, M. (2010a). A cross-sectional analysis of mental toughness in a professional football academy. *Athletic Insight Journal, 2*, 165–174.

Crust, L., Nesti, M., & Littlewood, M. (2010b). Player and coach ratings of mental toughness in a professional football academy. *Athletic Insight Journal, 2*, 239–250.

Diment, G. M. (2014). Mental toughness in soccer: A behavioral analysis. *Journal of Sport Behavior, 37*, 317–331.

Driska, A. P., Kamphoff, C., & Armentrout, S. M. (2012). Elite swimming coaches' perceptions of mental toughness. *The Sport Psychologist, 26*(2), 186–206.

Eubank, M., Nesti, M., & Littlewood, M. (2017). A culturally informed approach to mental toughness development in high performance sport. *International Journal of Sport Psychology*, *48*(3), 206–222.

Fitzwater, J. P. J., Arthur, C. A., & Hardy, L. (2018). 'The tough get tougher': Mental skills training with elite military recruits. *Sport, Exercise, and Performance Psychology*, *7*, 93–107. doi:10.1037/spy0000101.

Gould, D., Griffes, K., & Carson, S. (2011). Mental toughness as a life skill. In D. F. Gucciardi, & S. Gordon (Eds.), *Mental toughness in sport: Developments in theory and research* (pp. 163–186). Abingdon, England: Routledge.

Gucciardi, D. F., & Gordon, S. (2011). *Mental toughness in sport: Developments in theory and research*. Abingdon, England: Routledge.

Gucciardi, D. F., Gordon, S., Dimmock, J. A., & Mallett, C. J. (2009). Understanding the coach's role in the development of mental toughness: Perspectives of elite Australian football coaches. *Journal of Sports Sciences*, *27*(13), 1483–1496. doi:10.1080/02640410903150475.

Gucciardi, D. F., Hanton, S., Gordon, S., Mallett, C. J., & Temby, P. (2015). The concept of mental toughness: Tests of dimensionality, nomological network, and traitness. *Journal of Personality*, *83*, 26–44. doi:10.1111/jopy.12079.

Guillén, F., & Santana, J. (2018). Explorando la Fortaleza mental en jóvenes futbolistas de diferentes niveles de rendimiento [Exploring mental strength in young footballers of different performance levels]. *Revista Iberoamericana de Psicología del Ejercicio y el Deporte*, *13*, 297–303.

Hardy, L., Bell, J., & Beattie, S. (2014). A neuropsychological model of mentally tough behavior. *Journal of Personality*, *82*, 69–81. doi:10.1111/jopy.12034.

Harwood, C., Barker, J., & Anderson, R. (2015). Psychosocial development in youth soccer players: Assessing the effectiveness of the 5Cs intervention program. *The Sport Psychologist*, *29*, 319–334.

Mahoney, J. W., Gucciardi, D. F., Ntoumanis, N., & Mallett, C. J. (2014). The motivational antecedents of the development of mental toughness: A self-determination theory perspective. *International Review of Sport and Exercise Psychology*, *7*, 184–197. doi:10.1080/1750984X.2014.925951.

Mallett, C., & Coulter, T. (2011). Understanding and developing the will to win in sport: Perceptions of parents, coaches, and athletes. In D. Gucciardi, & S. Gordon (Eds.), *Mental toughness in sport: Developments in theory and research* (pp. 187–211). Oxford, England: Routledge.

Miçooğullari, B. O., & Ekmekçi, R. (2017). Evaluation of a psychological skill training program on mental toughness and psychological wellbeing for professional soccer players. *Universal Journal of Educational Research*, *5*, 2312–2319. doi:10.13189/ujer.2017.051222.

Olusoga, P., & Thelwell, R. (2017). Coach stress and associated impacts. In R. C. Thelwell, C. Harwood, & I. Greenlees (Eds.), *The psychology of sports coaching: Research and practice* (pp. 128–141). Oxford, England: Routledge.

Owusu-Sekyere, F., & Gervis, M. (2016). In the pursuit of mental toughness: Is creating mentally tough players a disguise for emotional abuse? *International Journal of Coaching Science*, *10*, 3–23.

Sheard, M., Golby, J., & van Wersch, A. (2009). Progress towards construct validation of the Sports Mental Toughness Questionnaire (SMTQ). *European Journal of Psychological Assessment*, *25*, 186–193. doi:10.1027/1015-5759.25.3.186.

Slack, L., Butt, J., Maynard, I., & Olusoga, P. (2014). Understanding mental toughness in elite football officiating: Perceptions of English Premier League referees. *Sport and Exercise Psychology Review*, *10*, 4–24.

Slack, L. A., Maynard, I. W., Butt, J., & Olusoga, P. (2013). Factors underpinning football officiating excellence: Perceptions of English Premier League referees. *Journal of Applied Sport Psychology*, *25*, 298–315. doi:10413200.2012.726935.

Slack, L. A., Maynard, I. W., Butt, J., & Olusoga, P. (2015). An evaluation of a mental toughness education and training program for early-career English Football League referees. *The Sport Psychologist, 29*, 237–257. doi:10.1123/tsp. 2014-0015.

Thelwell, R., Weston, N., & Greenlees, I. (2005). Defining and understanding mental toughness within soccer. *Journal of Applied Sport Psychology, 17*, 326–332. doi:10.1080/10413200 500313636.

Wagstaff, C. R. D., Gilmore, S., & Thelwell, R. C. (2016). When the show must go on: Investigating repeated organizational change in elite sport. *Journal of Change Management, 16*, 38–54. doi:10.1080/14697017.2015.1062793.

Weinberg, R., Freysinger, V., Mellano, K., & Brookhouse, E. (2016). Building mental toughness: Perceptions of sport psychologists. *The Sport Psychologist, 30*(3), 231–241. doi:10.1123/tsp. 2015-0090.

# 3 Courage in football

*Erkut Konter and Jürgen Beckmann*

**Abstract**

The chapter addresses a number of issues related to courage in football including conceptual definitions. Courage is frequently considered a major factor in sport performance. However, it has received little scientific attention in sport psychology. In this chapter, we address courage from a self-regulation perspective. Courage in football should allow players to initiate actions and persist at goal pursuit despite risk. Thus, courage as a self-regulation process refers to the ability to face danger, difficulty, uncertainty, or pain and overcome the fear to maintain the chosen course of action. In line with this, research identifies a number of variables influencing courage in football (e.g. self-confidence, determination, assertiveness, venturesomeness, coping with fear, as well as sacrificial or altruistic behaviour). In addition, the chapter attempts to outline a multidimensional sport (football) specific courage model. Initial assessment instruments and research findings are presented. In general, the research suggests that: (a) courage plays an important role in football performance, (b) learning to regulate one's affective reactions appears to be of high importance, (c) children and adolescents need to be given opportunities to develop courage-related self-regulation skills in football academies, (d) autonomy appears to be very important for courage development, (e) accordingly, giving players responsibility early on seems to have positive effects on the development of courage, (f) positive coaching in childhood and adolescence is important, (g) coaches and managers should learn more about courage, courageous personality, courage development, and its role in modern football.

Courage is valued universally across cultures (e.g. Dahlsgaard, Peterson, & Seligman, 2005). However, for a long time scientific psychology has not addressed courage. With the advent of positive psychology an increasing interest in the concept can be noted in recent years (Pury & Lopez, 2009). In sport, courage is frequently considered a major virtue (Konter & Toros, 2012). In spite of this, it has received little scientific attention in sport psychology (Corlett, 2002; Konter, Ng, & Bayansalduz, 2013). In this chapter we attempt to approach an understanding of the role of courage in football. Different dimensions of courage in football will be addressed. Also, studies on courage in football will be presented. In addition, implications for players and coaches as well as sport psychology practitioners will be discussed.

## Definitions of courage

Various authors have suggested a number of different definitions and concepts of courage. Courage and bravery have historically been primarily addressed as behaviour in high risk situations where life is at stake. Research has focused on the behaviour of military personnel and that of professionals in high-risk occupations such as fire fighters (Rachman, 1990). Only high-risk sports would fall into that category of behaviours. Even though athletes are made heroes in modern societies they are usually not risking life and limb in pursuit of social values which social scientists would refer to as 'heroism' (Becker & Eagly, 2004). 'Football heroes' may risk severe injuries but normally not their lives.

When addressing courage most researchers link it to taking action despite internal or external opposition (e.g. Lopez, O'Byrne, & Petersen, 2003). However, such a definition does not differentiate courage from what has been addressed in self-regulation research in general (e.g. Beckmann, 2001). What could be seen as the distinguishing feature in courage is overcoming fear. As Mark Twain (1894) put it 'Courage is resistance to fear, mastery of fear'. However, Mark Twain also stated that courage was not 'absence of fear'. If a person is completely fearless, s/he does not have to overcome the opposition caused by the fear. Thus, such a behaviour would not qualify as courageous. In fact, Pury, Kowalski, and Spearman (2007) found fear to be positively correlated with personal courage.

The perspectives of an actor and an observer may differ regarding courageous behaviour. An observer may rate a behaviour as extremely risky and thus infer courage if s/he sees a person act. The actor her/himself may perceive only low risk and not relate his acting to courage. Consequently, when speaking of courage, the subjective representation of the actor is crucial.

However, most research only took into account the observer perspective. Rate, Clarke, Lindsay, and Sternberg (2007) investigated the distinctive characteristics of courageous behaviour from the perspective of observers. From their research four defining features of what their participants believed to be courageous emerged: (1) wilfulness and intentionality, (2) mindful deliberation, (3) objective substantial risk to the actor, (4) a noble or worthy end. Acting despite fear was also frequently mentioned. Not surprisingly, fear was strongly correlated with risk to the actor. Kilmann, O'Hara, and Strauss (2010) point out that the involved risk must be assessed as reasonable and therefore the behaviour be considered as justifiable. A foolhardy action would not be considered courageous.

Three different types of courage are commonly distinguished. Traditionally a differentiation is made between (1) physical courage, i.e. facing physical risk and dangers, and (2) moral courage, i.e. standing up for moral principles in the face of social opposition. Recently, vital or psychological courage which involves overcoming internal struggles was added as a third form (Finfgeld, 1999; Putman, 2004).

Peterson and Seligman (2004) assume that that the universal virtue of courage is characterised by 'bravery' which refers to not avoiding threat, showing persistence, or finishing what one starts. They also postulate 'integrity' (acting authentically) and 'vigour' (approaching situations with energy) to be additional components of courage. Whereas empirical research has shown persistence, bravery, and integrity to be involved in courageous behaviour, vigour was not found to play an important role (Pury et al., 2007).

The above considerations acknowledge that fear may or may not be present to any significant degree for an act to be considered courageous. It becomes evident that there are two generally agreed upon components of courage; threat and worthy or important outcome. Similarly, Konter and Toros (2012, 2013), and Konter (2017) found a set of strengths present in sport courage including football. In addition, Konter (2013) defined sport courage as a 'natural and developed, interactional and perceptual concept between person and situation, and the task at hand that enables a person to move in competence, mastery, determination, assertiveness, venturesome and sacrificial (altruistic) behaviour on a voluntary basis and in danger(ous) circumstances' (p. 966). These strengths of courage in football should allow players to initiate and persist at goal pursuit despite risk.

## Courage as self-regulation

A proverb says that fear and courage are brothers. In 1094 AD Aristotle stated in his *Nicomachean Ethics* that courage is a means with regard to fear and confidence (Irwin, 2000). Thus, courage refers to the ability to face danger, difficulty, uncertainty, or pain and overcome the fear to maintain the chosen course of action. This is the problem that was addressed by will psychology in the early 20th century (Kuhl & Beckmann, 1985). It is the core element of today's self-regulation approaches (Beckmann, 2001).

Hannah, Sweeney, and Lester (2007) presented a model outlining the subjective experience of courage. They propose various positive psychological states and traits to reduce the level of fear experienced when facing risk. This self-regulation relies on the individual's implicit self. To create a courageous mindset the individual's core values and beliefs have to be linked to the action. Such a mindset involves bolstering of affirming normative and informational social forces. Access to the individual's implicit self is seen as necessary for effective self-regulation in many self-regulation theories (cf. Kuhl, 2000). This involvement of the implicit self is akin to Peterson and Seligman's (2004) courage component of integrity: access to one's own self which is related to autonomy and a personal commitment to an intention which involves assuming responsibility.

The next question to be addressed is which self-regulation problems have to be solved and what kinds of self-regulation strategies can be employed. Furthermore, particularly from a sport psychological perspective the question arises how these self-regulatory aspects of courage can be developed.

One of the major self-regulation problems is to initiate an action despite the opposing threat. This point is addressed by Sekerka and Bagozzi's (2007) model of moral courage. The model focuses on the internal influences, called 'the means', to initiate morally courageous actions. The 'means' are seen as being associated with an individual's internal processes regarding affects and expectations, as well as personal ends, such as applying moral standards. Individuals' experience of different emotions and how they think about competing pressures play an important role in this process. A decision to act (or not to act) is assumed to be additionally influenced by personal factors which are dependent on social forces such as social norms, perceived rewards or punishments, social pressure, and other situational and contextual factors. For the actual decision to act, several self-regulation variables are addressed by the model. Affect and cognitions influence the decision-making process in which choices are seen as self-controlled and consciously directed. Sekerka and Bagozzi's process model is akin to other self-regulation models such as Heckhausen's Rubicon Model of Action Phases (Beckmann & Gollwitzer, 1987; Heckhausen, 1991). In the Rubicon model phase 1 consists of deliberating motivation-relevant variables in an undistorted, reality-oriented mindset. From this motivational deliberation a want to act can emerge. The next step is to reach a firm commitment to the necessary action. According to self-regulation models a firm commitment is mandatory for initiation and maintenance of the action in the face of adversity (Beckmann, 1984). After a firm commitment has been made, the information processing changes. In the now volitional mindset information processing becomes realisation-oriented, favouring information that supports the maintenance of the action the person has committed her/himself to. The theory of action control (Kuhl, 2000; Kuhl & Beckmann, 1985; 1994) has specified a number of volitional processes supporting the initiation and persistence of an action in the face of adversity.

Regarding the question of the acquisition of courage, Hannah et al. (2007) suggested that intrapersonal attribution processes after successful courageous actions influence self-perceptions of courageousness. Thereby, they reinforce the courageous mindset promoting future courageous action. Research by Cavanagh and Moberg (1999) supports the assumption that these kinds of experiences will further develop courage. They suggest that courage can be considered a moral habit which is developed by practice. This is compatible with Bandura's (1977) concept of self-efficacy. Individuals are more likely to face a situation and attempt to cope with it if they have the expectancy to manage the challenge. This expectancy is based on their previous experience with such a challenge. In fact, there is empirical evidence that psychological variables related to self-efficacy such as hope, the ability to develop pathways to reach a desired goal, and one's perceived agency to reach those goals are correlated with courage (Kowalski et al., 2006; Pury et al., 2007; Snyder, 2002).

## Courage in sports

As stated above, courage is frequently conceptualised as a tool to overcome internal or external opposition and manage associated fear and stress. Such self-regulation requirements are given in many sports (Corlett, 2002). Not surprisingly, courage was mainly addressed in the area of extreme sports (Brymer & Oades, 2008).

Football is not a high-risk sport in terms of risking one's life. However, showing courage is commonly considered a major asset of football players (Konter, 2015a, 2017). Typically, courage is attributed to actions like playing a long pass across the pitch, shooting at the goal instead of passing the ball to a team member, engaging in a tackle against a seemingly invincible opponent, and taking responsibility for a free kick at the goal or shooting a penalty. Sometimes it may involve risking an injury; sometimes it may involve embarrassing oneself in the case of failure. The first is traditionally referred to as physical courage, the latter as moral courage (Putman, 2004).

Successful footballers seem to display many forms of courage. Footballers who performed their best breaking records, achieving their goals, and extending their limits had to take relatively high risks and were frequently challenged by strong opponents. They had to endure threatening, stressful situations in their career (Konter, 2013, 2015b). However, there is still a lack of knowledge on the self-regulation that is involved in such achievements. Furthermore, from a practical point of view, one would like to know how the courage-related self-regulation can be developed in young players. Other questions related to this are whether there is a courage personality trait? Does being a team member make a difference in terms of making courageous actions more or less likely? Is there something like team courage?

In the military context, Gee (1931) differentiated between 'individual versus collective bravery'. There are examples in football, where an assumed lack of collective or team courage results in a team collapse (e.g. Apitzsch, 2006). Hannah et al. (2007) postulate that positive social forces, such as interdependence, social identity, cohesion, and informational influence can promote courageous behaviour. Players as leaders on the pitch can have a significant impact upon a range of team-related factors including satisfaction, cohesion, and team dynamics. However, the mechanisms through which this impact occurs are still less well understood (Cotterill & Fransen, 2016). Individual courage of a leader on the pitch could be an asset that may turn a game around. Thus, team influence but also team values may influence courageous behaviour. Having observed courageous behaviour in team members is likely to instigate courageous behaviour by other team members (Nemeth & Chiles, 1988; Worline & Steen, 2004). Emphasising the positive value of courage, defining courage as a team or club asset (value) can also have positive effects on the pitch when a game is on the razor's edge.

## Theoretical models of sport courage

Woodard (2004) proposed a sequential conceptual model of courage which has much in common with Lazarus's (1966) Transtheoretical Model of coping with stress. According to Woodard, fear is a prerequisite for courage. Fear is seen as the result of a perception of vulnerability. Woodard (2004) assumes that fear is established through an evaluation of a threat as outweighing the personal resources of the individual. Independent of whether or not this evaluation is accurate it influences the individual's perception of the situation. Additionally, Woodard introduces assumptions that go beyond the Transtheoretical Model. First of all, the situation has to be perceived by the individual as meaningful or relevant. Furthermore, the individual will calculate if the benefits of engaging the threat without sufficient resources outweigh the potential costs. This will decide whether or not action will be considered. Woodard assumes that in a next step, managing the physiological reactions to fear is vital. According to this model, courageous behaviour happens essentially as a result of high perception of meaningfulness to react. Some conclusions could be drawn from Woodard's (2004) model of courage regarding football. According to the model courage would be required in football when the situational demands exceed the potential resources perception of the player. Next the player has to perceive meaningfulness of taking action. Thus, it would be crucial to create a team atmosphere that emphasises such a meaningfulness through a team philosophy and team building increasing coherence.

Nesti's (2016) 'Mode of Delivery in Applied Work' is a model that partly focuses on how to create a situation to make something like courageous behaviour more likely. The proposed mode of delivery progresses from less personal to more personal approaches. It involves instructions on how to increase motivation, build self-confidence, self-esteem, and how to face existential anxiety. The approach also involves more indirect forms of individual development, a mentoring of authentic learning or self-discovery of the essential components of integrity. It also focuses on promoting an individual's access to the identity/core of self which is crucial for self-regulation and thus courage as we discussed above. The suggested strategies involve mediating a mindful experience of virtues such as patience and courage as well as instigating paying attention to values such as honesty, integrity, and morality. However, these interventions can only work if they are in line with the overall value system of the club and the club management (cf. Worline & Steen, 2004). Nesti (2016) demands that we need to see the person alongside the athlete based on a philosophy of the person first, the athlete second which is in line with many approaches to positive coaching (see e.g. Gould & Capalbo, 2019, Chapter 23 in this book; Nash & Mallett, 2019, Chapter 8 in this book).

Konter (2013) suggested a model of sport courage which is based on a literature review and organised individual meetings with coaches, teachers, and university lecturers specialising in sports. His sport-specific courage model addresses the interactions between situational factors (e.g. risk, danger, fear at present), personal dispositions (e.g. personality traits, experience and knowledge of the athlete), type of sport-related factors (e.g. individual and team sports, contact and non-contact sports), and the specific problem situation (e.g. a decisive penalty kick at the last second of a football game, etc.). The suggested concept of sport courage is a dynamic and transformational process which is determined by an interaction of the above-mentioned factors.

## Assessment of sport courage

Recently, several measures of courage have been developed in positive psychology (e.g. Lopez et al., 2003; Woodard & Pury, 2007). But there are only very few measures of courage in sport psychology, particularly with regard to football. However, there are a couple of initial efforts to measure courage in sport including football addressing different age groups (children, adolescents, and adults) and competition levels (amateurs and professionals).

Konter and Ng (2012) developed the SCS-31 consisting of five factors emerging from factor analyses based on the data of 768 Turkish athletes from different individual and team sports. The resulting scales were labelled: Determination, Mastery, Assertiveness, Venturesome, and Self-Sacrificing Behaviour. The psychometric quality of the different scales is good to very good (Konter & Ng, 2012). Konter et al. (2013) adapted the SCS-31 to be used with 10 to 12 year old children. They obtained the same five-factor structure and similarly good psychometric quality measures as for the original version of the scale.

The SCS-31 was developed in Turkish (Konter & Ng, 2012), so its applicability to other cultural groups (e.g. the United States) could be seen as questionable due to possible different perceptions of courage in different cultures. Adaptation processes of the SCS-31 in different cultures are still going on (for example, the USA, Canada, Malaysia, China, and Croatia). Some of the research with these scales in football will be reported in what follows.

**Research on courage in football**

Using the courage in sport scale (SCS-31) in football Konter and Ng found that professional football players had significantly higher scores on the scale (especially regarding Mastery) than amateurs. Also, starters had significantly higher scores than substitutes regarding Mastery, Determination, and Assertiveness. Team captains were found to have significantly higher scores on the Assertiveness subscale than the other team members. These research findings suggest that courage as measured through the SCS-31 is related to performance as it appears that the more courageous footballers are more likely to become professionals, and be starters and team captains than those with lower scores on the scale.

Konter and Toros (2012) also investigated football players' courage in relation to their playing positions. Among professional players, stoppers and centre forwards had higher total SCS-31 scores than full backs, midfielders, and wing players. In general, right and left midfielders seem to have more Determination than other positions. These results were supported in another study by Konter (2017) – interestingly, in both studies goalkeepers had lower Mastery as well as Assertiveness scores than players in the above-mentioned positions. This might be related to unique position requirements of goalkeepers in football. One explanation for this finding is that goalkeeping is more reactive than proactive. Therefore, proactive or mixed proactive and reactive positions might involve more Mastery as for example in stoppers, left and right midfielders, and wingers.

Hidrus, Kuan, Konter, and Kueh (2017) examined the relationship between athletes' coping skills and their courage in football. This study revealed that there are significant relationships between SCS-31 and athletic coping skills as measured through the ACSI-28 (Smith, Schutz, Smoll, & Ptacek, 1995). Particularly, the results showed that footballers with higher levels of courage also had a higher ability to cope with stress as well as higher levels of confidence and achievement motivation.

Courage has been addressed from a self-regulation perspective according to which individuals need to find means to deal with an adverse, threatening situation. In sport psychology, such means are usually subsumed under psychological skills. Accordingly, Konter (2017) investigated the relationship between psychological skills to levels of courage. In this study ($n$=380) the SCS-31 and the revised version of the 'Soccer Psychological Skills Scale-16' (SPSS-16, Konter, 2009) were filled out by 380 amateur and professional male football players. The revised SPSS-12 consists of four scales (imagery, commitment, peaking under pressure, and coping with stress) with three items each. Analyses revealed significant positive correlations between the SPSS-12 and the SCS-31. Both scales were moderately and positively correlated between 0.274 and 0.487. In general, football players (both professionals and amateurs) with high overall SCS-31 scores had significantly higher scores on the four scales of the SPSS-12 than football players with low overall SCS-31 scores. Thus, this not surprisingly indicates that the football courage and the football psychological skills concepts seem to be related. But, low to medium correlations clearly indicate that there is some coincide, but courage is substantially different from the indicated concepts of football psychological skills.

In a study with 473 male amateur and professional football players aged 14 to 44 (M=18.40) with an average playing experience of 8.36 years Konter (2015a) investigated courage in relation to perception of risk taking, adventure, and injury.

In general, the results suggest that higher scores on the Mastery component of courage are related to being more adventurous. Furthermore, higher football courage seems to be related to the perception of success. The greater the level of courage in football, the higher the perception of success. Interestingly, footballers with higher scores on Mastery do not appear to be negatively influenced by negative referee decisions. The higher the perception of mastery, the less negative was the effect of negative referee decisions on performance. Thus, it could be concluded that the positive relationship of better performance and courage in football is mediated through adventurous behaviour, perception of success, and reduced irritability which are components of courage.

In a study with 411 amateur and professional male football players Konter (2015b) examined the relationship of courage and performance consistency under different conditions. When playing against strong opponents the players who were more confident revealed significantly higher points of Determination and Venturesome than players with less confidence. It seems that Determination and Venturesome are important determinants for performance consistency when playing against strong opponents. The results also showed players with higher courage to be less affected by spectator presence independent of whether the crowd was hostile or supportive.

Additionally, Konter (2015c) investigated the courage profile of male adolescent football players aged 13 to 17 (M=15.22). This study (*n*=413) provides some insights into the development of courage. If young players are given responsibility via being team captain they might become more assertive. However, it cannot be ruled out that more assertive players with higher performance consistency are more likely to become team captains. The results of this study also suggest that being injured could interfere with developing courage in football. It may be quite likely that young players who were injured may become more cautious after the injury and have problems dealing with the anxiety of another injury. As a negative side of having greater Determination, Assertiveness, Venturesome, courageous young players were found to have higher chances of receiving yellow and red cards.

An at first sight surprising finding by Konter (2015d) is that courageous players appear to have fewer chances of being selected for the national team than less courageous players in spite of their better and more consistent performance. One of the characteristics of courageous players is that they are not conforming to a large degree but stand up for their convictions even if that means opposition to the coach. Thus, the coach might perceive them as quarrelsome and hard to coach. There is currently little understanding of the importance of the psychological aspect of courage in coaches and officials. In general, selection of players is primarily based on physical, technical, and tactical skills.

Findings show that courageous players appear to be more injury prone (Konter & Toros, 2013). This could result from higher risk taking. Coaches might demand that their players should play it safe, stick to the game plan, tactics, and strategies, and carry out the positional demands assigned to them. This conflicts with the courageous player's basic orientation with a high degree of autonomy. If they are forced to stick to the coach's directions it might interfere with taking risks and creativity. Consequently, Konter (2015d) found the performance of the more determined, courageous footballers to be frequently negatively affected by problematic relationships with their coaches. But courageous players are especially needed when the going gets tough. As the concept of courage suggests, more courageous footballers (with higher Mastery and Assertiveness) appear to be positively motivated by negative events (such as bad referee decisions or being behind at half time). Therefore, courage is needed under negative or aversive conditions to maintain or increase performance. A courageous leader on the pitch may be needed to prevent team collapse and turn the game around (cf. Apitzsch, 2019, Chapter 9 in this book).

## Practical implications

The research findings presented above indicate that courage plays an important role in football performance. In conceptualising courage, we addressed a self-regulatory model that fits the commonly shared assumptions about the core elements in courage which are enduring and/or coping with threatening conditions, overcoming fear, and daring to perform risky behaviour. The empirical findings support this general self-regulation model as the correlation between courage and psychological skills is high. Therefore, when addressing the question of how to develop courage one can draw upon the existing literature on the development of self-regulatory skills. The literature shows that self-determined confrontation with challenging tasks, developing confidence in one's efficacy and mastery ability are important conditions for the development of self-regulation skills (Beckmann, Szymanski, Elbe, & Ehrlenspiel, 2006). Furthermore, learning to regulate one's affective reactions, especially to learn downregulating negative affect and upregulating positive affect appears to be of high importance (cf. Kuhl, 2000). Children and adolescents need to be given opportunities for such development. Autonomy appears to be very important in this regard (Deci & Ryan, 2013). Giving players responsibility early on is related to this and was shown to have positive effects on the development of courage (Konter, 2015a).

Thus, positive coaching in childhood and adolescence is important. The coaching should be personalised, and supporting self-determinant dealing with challenges (Beckmann & Nash, 2018). Specific, age-based programmes in football youth academies should address courage as part of personality development. For coaches to make use of the knowledge on players for team line-up, more research is needed to further clarify the relationship of courage to successful performance on the various positions on a football team.

## Conclusions and future research directions

Research on courage in football is still scarce. A major step forward was the development of measurement instruments to assess courage in football. The ideas on the development of courage in youth footballers should be further developed and evaluated. Psychological Skills Training as interventions for problem situations requiring courage such as the threat of a team collapse need to be developed based on existing skills. Perhaps most of all, coaches and managers should learn more about courage and its important role in modern football. Part of this is to better understand the personality of courageous players and learn to promote courageous behaviour instead of obstructing it.

# References

Apitzsch, E. (2006). Collective collapse in team sports: A theoretical approach. In F. Boen, B. de Cuyper, & J. Opdenacker (Eds.), *Current research topics in exercise and sport psychology in Europe* (pp. 35–46). Leuven, Belgium: LannooCampus.

Apitzsch, E. (2019). Collective collapse in football. In E. Konter, J. Beckmann, & T. M. Loughead (Eds.), *Football psychology: From theory to practice*. London, England: Routledge.

Bandura, A. (1977). Self-efficacy: Toward a unifying theory of behavioral change. *Psychological Review, 84*(2), 191–215.

Becker, S. W., & Eagly, A. H. (2004). The heroism of women and men. *American Psychologist, 59*, 163–178. doi:10.1037/0003-066X.59.3.163.

Beckmann, J. (1984). *Kognitive Dissonanz: Eine handlungstheoretische Perspektive* [Cognitive dissonance: An action control perspective]. Berlin, Heidelberg, Germany; New York, NY: Springer.

Beckmann, J. (2001). Self-regulation of athletic performance. In N. J. Smelser & P. B. Baltes (Eds.), *International encyclopedia of the social and behavioral sciences* (pp. 14947–14952). Amsterdam, The Netherlands: Elsevier.

Beckmann, J., & Gollwitzer, P. M. (1987). Deliberative vs. implemental states of mind: The issue of impartiality in pre- and postdecisional information processing. *Social Cognition, 5*, 259–279.

Beckmann, J., & Nash, C. (2018). *Sports coaching for lifelong development: A sustainable ambition?* Manuscript, Technical University of Munich.

Beckmann, J., Szymanski, B., Elbe, A., & Ehrlenspiel, F. (2006). *Chancen und Risiken: Vom Leben im Verbundsystem von Schule und Leistungssport* [Chances and risks: Living in a linked system of school and elite sports]. Cologne, Germany: Sportverlag Strauß.

Brymer, E., & Oades, L. G. (2008). Extreme sports: A positive transformation in courage and humility. *Journal of Humanistic Psychology*, 114–126. doi:10.1177/0022167808326199.

Cavanagh, G. F., & Moberg, D. J. (1999). The virtue of courage within the organization. In M. L. Pava & P. Primeaux (Eds.), *Research in ethical issues in organizations* (Vol. 1, pp. 1–25). Stamford, CT: JAI Press.

Corlett, J. (2002). Virtue lost: Courage in sport. In A. Hollowchak (Ed.), *Philosophy in sport* (pp. 454–465). Upper Saddle River, NJ: Prentice Hall.

Cotterill, S. T., & Fransen, K. (2016). Athlete leadership in sport teams: Current understanding and future directions. *International Review of Sport and Exercise Psychology, 9*(1), 116–133.

Dahlsgaard, K., Peterson, C., & Seligman, M. E. P. (2005). Shared virtue: The convergence of valued human strengths across culture and history. *Review of General Psychology, 9*(3), 203–213. http://dx.doi.org/10.1037/1089-2680.9.3.203.

Deci, E. E., & Ryan, R. (2013). The importance of autonomy for development and well-being. In B. W. Sokol, F. M. E. Grouzet, & U. Müller (Eds.), *Self-regulation and autonomy: Social and developmental dimensions of human conduct* (pp. 19–46). Cambridge, England: Cambridge University Press.

Finfgeld, D. L. (1999). Courage as a process of pushing beyond the struggle. *Qualitative Health Research, 9*(6), 803–814.

Gee, W. (1931). Rural-urban heroism in military action. *Social Forces, 10*, 102–111.

Gould, D., & Capalbo, L. (2019). Helping players develop life skills in football. In E. Konter, J. Beckmann, & T. M. Loughead (Eds.), *Football psychology: From theory to practice*. London, England: Routledge.

Hannah, S. T., Sweeney, P. J., & Lester, P. B. (2007). Toward a courageous mindset: The subjective act and experience of courage. *Journal of Positive Psychology, 2*(2), 129–135.

Heckhausen, H. (1991). *Motivation and action*. Berlin, Heidelberg, Germany: Springer.

Hidrus, A. B., Kuan, G., Konter, E., & Kueh, Y. C. (2017). Relationship between courage and coping among football players in Kelantan. 14th ISSP World Congress of Sport Psychology, 10–14 June, Seville, Spain.

Irwin, T. (2000). *Aristotle: Nicomachean ethics* (2nd ed.). Cambridge, England: Hackett Publishing.

Kilmann, R. H., O'Hara, L. A., & Strauss, J. P. (2010). Developing and validating a quantitative measure of organizational courage. *Journal of Business and Psychology, 25*(1), 15–23. doi:10.1007/s10869-009-9125-1.

Konter, E. (2009). Development of the Football Psychological Skills Scale-16 (SPSS-16). Proceedings of the 14th Personality, Motivation, Sport conference, National Sports Academy, Sofia, Bulgaria.

Konter, E. (2013). Towards multidimensional interactional model of sport courage. *Energy Education Science and Technology Part B: Social and Educational Studies, 5*(2), 957–968.

Konter, E. (2015a). Courage of association football players: Decision-making at risk. 14th European Congress of Sport Psychology, 14–19 July, Bern, Switzerland.

Konter, E. (2015b). Courage and football performance in the face of negative and positive circumstances. International Sport Sciences Research Congress-USBAK. 10–13 September, Çanakkale, Turkey.

Konter, E. (2015c). Courage profile of adolescent football players in relation to their selected individual variables. Third International Exercise and Sport Psychology Congress, 23–25 October, Marmara Üniversitesi, Anadolu Hisarı, İstanbul, Turkey.

Konter, E. (2015d). Courage profile of professional footballers in relation to selected individual, social and performance variables. National Sport Medicine Congress, 20–22 November, Swiss Otel, Ankara, Turkey.

Konter, E. (2017). Psychological skills of football players in relation to level of courage, individual and performance variables. 14th ISSP World Congress of Sport Psychology, 10–14 June, Seville, Spain.

Konter, E., & Ng, J. (2012). Development of sport courage scale. *Journal of Human Kinetics, 33*, 163–172. doi:10.2478/v10078-012-0055-z.

Konter, E., Ng, J., & Bayansalduz, M. (2013). Revised version of sport courage scale for children. *Energy Education Science and Technology Part B: Social and Educational Studies, 1*, 331–340.

Konter, E., & Toros, T. (2012). Courage of football players and their playing positions. *Energy Education Science and Technology Part B: Social and Educational Studies, 4*(4), 1997–2006.

Konter, E., & Toros, T. (2013). Courage and performance in football. *International Journal of Academic Research, 5*(4), 276–282. doi:10.7813/2075-4124.2013/5-4/B.42.

Kowalski, R. M., Pury, C. L. S., Sporrer, L., Hunter, E., Gorney, A., Baker, M., & Mitchell, T. (2006, November). *Courage and hope: Pathways to action.* Paper presented at the annual meeting of the Society of Southeastern Social Psychologists, Knoxville, TN.

Kuhl, J. (2000). A functional-design approach to motivation and self-regulation: The dynamics of personality systems interactions. In M. Boekaerts, P. R. Pintrich, & M. Zeidner (Eds.), *Handbook of self-regulation* (pp. 111–169). San Diego, CA: Academic Press.

Kuhl, J., & Beckmann, J. (Eds.) (1985). *Action control: From cognition to behavior.* Heidelberg, Berlin, Germany; New York, NY: Springer.

Kuhl, J., & Beckmann, J. (Eds.) (1994). *Volition and personality: Action and state orientation.* Seattle, WA: Hogrefe.

Lazarus, R. S. (1966). *Psychological stress and the coping process.* New York, NY: McGraw-Hill.

Lopez, S. J., O'Byrne, K. K., & Petersen, S. (2003). Profiling courage. In S. J. Lopez & C. R. Snyder (Eds.), *Positive psychological assessment: A handbook of models and measures* (pp. 185–197). Washington, DC: American Psychological Association.

Nash, C., & Mallett, C. J. (2019). Effective coaching in football. In E. Konter, J. Beckmann, & T. M. Loughead (Eds.), *Football psychology: From theory to practice.* London, England: Routledge.

Nemeth, C., & Chiles, C. (1988). Modelling courage: The role of dissent in fostering independence. *European Journal of Social Psychology, 18*(3), 275–280.

Nesti, M. (2016). Performance mind-set. In T. Strudwick (Ed.), *Soccer science* (pp. 415–430). Champaign, IL: Human Kinetics.

Peterson, C., & Seligman, M. E. P. (2004). *Character strengths and virtues: A handbook and classification*. New York, NY: Oxford University Press and Washington, DC: American Psychological Association.

Pury, C. L. S., Kowalski, R. M., & Spearman, J. (2007). Distinctions between general and personal courage. *The Journal of Positive Psychology, 2*(2), 99–114. doi:10.1080/17439760701 237962.

Pury, C. L. S., & Lopez, S. J. (2009). Courage. In S. J. Lopez & C. R. Snyder (Eds.), *Oxford handbook of positive psychology* (2nd ed., pp. 375–382). New York, NY: Oxford University Press.

Putman, D. (2004). *Psychological courage.* Lanham, MD: University Press of America.

Rachman, S. J. (1990). *Fear and courage* (2nd ed.). New York, NY: WH Freeman.

Rate, C. R., Clarke, J. A., Lindsay, D. R., & Sternberg, R. J. (2007). Implicit theories of courage. *The Journal of Positive Psychology, 2*(2), 80–98. doi:10.1080/17439760701228755.

Sekerka, L., E., & Bagozzi, R. P. (2007). Moral courage in the workplace: Moving to and from the desire and decision to act. *Business Ethics, 16*(2), 132–149.

Smith, E. R., Schutz, W. R., Smoll, L. F., & Ptacek, T. J. (1995). Development and validation of a multidimensional measure of sport-specific psychological skills: Athletic Coping Skills Inventory-28. *Journal of Sport and Exercise Psychology, 17*, 378–398.

Snyder, C. R. (2002). Hope theory: Rainbows in the mind. *Psychological Inquiry, 13*, 249–275.

Twain, M. (1894). *The tragedy of Pudd'nhead Wilson.* Hartford, CT: American Publishing Company.

Woodard, C. R. (2004). Hardiness and the concept of courage. *Consulting Psychology Journal: Practice and Research, 56*(3), 173–185. doi:10.1037/1065-9293.56.3.173.

Woodard, C. R., & Pury, C. L. S. (2007). The construct of courage: Categorization and measurement. *Consulting Psychology Journal: Practice and Research, 59*(2), 135–147. doi:10. 1037/1065-9293.59.2.135.

Worline, M. C., & Steen, T. A. (2004). Bravery. In C. Peterson & M. E. P. Seligman (Eds.), *Character strengths and virtues: A handbook and classification* (pp. 213–228). Washington, DC: American Psychological Association.

# 4 The unifying role of player responsibility in football

*George K. Doganis, Marios T. Goudas, and Paul M. Wright*

## Abstract

This chapter posits that the much-neglected concept of personal responsibility in football is a central one in explaining a range of player behaviours related to training and team performance. The concept of responsibility is treated not primarily in relation to moral behaviour, but rather as a willingness to act responsibly, or the willingness to 'take full ownership' of one's behaviour, both in individual and collective settings within the football team. Related motivational concepts are used to provide a tentative explanation of behaviours in football and their relevance to personal or individual responsibility and subsequent football performance. To this effect, insights offered by the Triangle Model of Responsibility, Personal Responsibility Orientation Theory, and the Teaching of Personal and Social Responsibility Model are highlighted. Further, responsibility in football is discussed in relation to concepts such as locus of control, causal attributions, and self-regulation. Next, manifestations of (or lack of) responsibility in football – such as in role development, leadership effectiveness, social loafing, and error correction – are discussed. The approach taken will illustrate that personal responsibility of players in football may be used as a unifying concept and as a starting point in developing a respective theory. Thereafter, subsequent procedures and training practices within football may be developed to enhance player responsibility on and off the pitch.

> Responsibility – true responsibility – requires that people act autonomously in relation to the world around, that they behave authentically on behalf of some general good.
>
> (Edward Deci)

The concept of personal responsibility constitutes a fundamental problem in both philosophy and psychology, as it involves the long-lasting debate of free will versus determinism in human behaviour. That is, how much of our behaviour is determined by the choices and decisions we freely make or how much our behaviour is determined by factors beyond our control. This issue has significant implications regarding the extent to which systematic interferences could influence and increase personal responsibility in any individual endeavour. This lengthy and long-lasting discussion is beyond the scope of the present chapter, but the position adopted is that of free will and this approach is consistent with the authors' disciplinary perspectives and practices, i.e. education and psychology, with a focus on personal agency and autonomy. While the present literature has mostly treated responsibility as a concept related to morality (good behaviour), this chapter argues that, as a construct, personal responsibility as applied to football may unify constitutively the findings of related studies in sport psychology. Moreover, responsibility may provide a framework for better understanding player behaviours and subsequently suggest appropriate approaches to coaches for the players' development. In order to cover the vast amount of related literature, it was necessary to be selective, concise, and compact. To this effect, after a short introduction to the topic, a conceptual analysis is followed by a short presentation of terms related to responsibility. Next, related theories and models are reviewed, alongside the factors assumed to affect responsibility. Finally, a brief summary of research and applications for academics, coaches, and athletes is presented.

## Significance of responsibility in football

The development of personal responsibility in athletes is considered to be one of the best ways coaches can enhance their motivation. Additionally, when a coach assists a player to develop personal responsibility and autonomy, s/he contributes to the player's personal development (Burton & Raedeke, 2008). Beswick (2016), reflecting on his consultation work in elite level football, argues that players should take responsibility for their attitudes and coaches should develop a winning attitude in their players by teaching them to take responsibility for their actions on and off the field. Failure to do so conveys a lack of trust in their players and denies them opportunities to mature.

Whitmore (2002) defines performance as 'the full expression of one's potential' (p. 97) and explains that the essence of coaching is developing each player's responsibility for and ownership of their performance. As a consequence, each player, by taking personal responsibility, should strive for team success during training sessions when the psychological development of each player and the team, as a whole, takes place. Additionally, a group of players can become a team only when they have a vision and a purpose, put 'we' before 'me', support each other, and take responsibility for their roles in the team (Beswick, 2016).

What differentiates competitive sport, in general, and football, in particular, is that participants are expected to perform well and win under pressure. Whether a player can cope by maintaining his/her attention and focus requires a high level of self-awareness and personal responsibility for managing thoughts, emotions, and responses that are counterproductive (Kyndt & Rowell, 2012). For coaches, good communication with players – rational rather than emotional responses and positive feedback – assists players in developing intrinsic motivation to improve and take ownership and responsibility of their game (Saxena, 2012). If coaches want their players to develop confidence, they should give them responsibility and involve them in decision-making (Weinberg & Gould, 2011). The absence of responsibility and challenge can lead to failure on the part of players to meet the demands of the team (Beswick, 2016).

## Conceptual analysis of responsibility

The construct of personal responsibility does not have a concise and generally accepted definition. In fact, a plethora of definitions may be found in various bodies of literature. This excess is partly due to the fact that, as a term, personal responsibility is used in a wide spectrum of domains ranging from philosophy to psychology, politics, law, education, and sport. In these domains, the concept is considered important in understanding individual or collective behaviour, because it undergirds the decisions made and actions taken in any of these arenas that impact the individual, others, and potentially society at large. The broad notion of responsibility is a common denominator across fields.

Lenk (2006) distinguishes between at least four dimensions of responsibility, namely: (i) *responsibility for actions and their results*, (ii) *task and role responsibility*, (iii) *universal moral responsibility*, (iv) *legal responsibility*. He identifies four elements of responsibility: someone (the bearer of responsibility) is responsible for something (actions, consequences, tasks, etc.), to somebody, in the face of an instance of judgement or potential sanctions, with regard to a prescriptive criterion (e.g. a rule), within the framework of a realm of relevant actions and responsibilities (Lenk, 2006, p. 29).

Long, Pantaleon, and Bruant (2008) described two main modalities constituting responsibility: *retrospective modality* (also known as retroactive modality) and *responsibility to others' modality*. The retrospective modality refers to the attributional dimension of responsibility and serves to justify and defend one's choices to prevent or minimize any sanctions. For example, a football player who is late for training may provide excuses to divest himself of responsibility. Responsibility to others has two forms. The first of these is termed either *functional or instrumental* responsibility. It can also be called contractual responsibility and, together, they refer to explicit contracts that describe the nature of the associations between people involved and which may be considered as a 'responsibility of results' (Long et al., 2008, p. 523). An example is a professional player's detailed contract with his club, where team norms and relationships among people are included. The second form of this modality is the *moral* one. This form is more subjective and manifests in response to situations and in interaction with others. An example is a player's commitment to respecting all refereeing decisions (Long et al., 2008).

Finally, Mergler (2007) defined personal responsibility as 'the ability to identify and regulate one's own thoughts, feelings and behaviour, along with a willingness to hold oneself accountable for the choices made and the social and personal outcomes generated from these choices' (p. 70). In her proposed model, Mergler considered responsibility as having four components, that is,

> 1) an awareness of, and control over, individual thoughts and feelings; 2) an awareness of, and control over, choices made regarding behaviour; 3) a willingness to be accountable for the behaviour enacted and the resulting outcome; 4) an awareness of, and concern for, the impact of one's behaviour upon others.
>
> (pp. 66–67)

The present chapter focuses on the concept of personal responsibility mainly as a willingness to act responsibly. However, it is often the case that individual behaviours in football take place within a social context. Hence, a player who is responsible is expected to also consider the impact of his/her behaviour on others within the team. From this perspective, two dimensions of responsibility proposed by Lenk (2006) – responsibility for actions and their results, and task and role responsibility – as well as the functional form of responsibility to others proposed by Long et al. (2008), are more applicable to this chapter.

## The unifying role of responsibility

This section will explore critical concepts related to responsibility in football, other sports, or domains other than sport, that have been used to understand people's tendency to either hold themselves accountable or attribute their performance to external factors. To this effect, selected concepts, such as *locus of control, need for achievement, attributions, self-regulation,* and *personal agency,* will be briefly presented. All these concepts share an element of intentional action toward a goal that is emanating from the self. Therefore, they can be considered conceptually close to two of the four dimensions of responsibility identified by Lenk (2006), namely, responsibility for actions and their results, and task and role responsibility.

Rotter (1966) proposed the concept of internal versus external control of reinforcement (later locus of control) to describe individuals' tendencies to believe that positive or negative reinforcements they receive are a result of their own behaviour or a result of luck or chance. For example, an adolescent football player with an external locus of control may believe that negative comments by his/her coach occur because the coach is not fond of him/her. An adolescent football player with an internal locus of control may perceive similar comments by his/her coach as constructive feedback that can help them understand and target opportunities to improve their performance through additional practice. Thus, footballers who have an internal locus of control assume a degree of personal responsibility for rewards and sanctions they receive.

The concept of achievement motive, first introduced by McClelland, Atkinson, Clark, and Lowell (1953), and outlined as a need to improve one's skills and do well against a standard of excellence, is also connected to the concept of personal responsibility. According to Schultheiss and Brunstein (2005), individuals with a high achievement motive tend to choose challenging tasks that provide direct personal control over the outcome and seek feedback about their performance. They also provide summarized evidence showing that achievement motivated individuals prefer to be personally responsible for their performance and, to this effect, they select tasks that are under their direct control (Schultheiss & Brunstein, 2005).

Weiner's (2005) causal attribution theory posits that people's cognitive reactions to events denoting success or failure determine their behavioural reactions to this event. These cognitive reactions, termed attributions, have three underlying properties: locus, stability, and controllability. Locus refers to the location of the cause being within or outside the actor. Stability refers to the duration of the cause. Finally, some thought causes can be controlled by the actor while others cannot. The locus of attributions is related to personal responsibility in that people who attribute success and, more importantly, failure to causes within themselves assume responsibility of their own actions and related outcomes. The locus, in conjunction with controllability, influences behavioural reactions. For example, a youngster who ascribes his/her failure to make the first team on his/her fellow players' superior ability (external and uncontrollable attribution) is more likely to decrease effort in comparison to an athlete who attributes such a failure to his/her lower efforts in training (internal and controllable attribution).

Personal agency, together with that of self-efficacy, are core concepts of Bandura's (1997) social-cognitive theory. Personal agency has been defined as the capacity to exercise control over one's thoughts, motivation, affect, and action. Individuals employ the control of these factors to achieve desired outcomes. 'Agency refers to acts done intentionally', said Bandura (1997, p. 3). The intentionality of agency attests for a resemblance with personal responsibility.

Finally, the concept of self-regulation is also related to personal responsibility. Early on, Kirschenbaum (1984) commented that 'the self-regulatory perspective applied to sport raises the question of how each athlete can take more responsibility for the quality of his or her participation and begin working to improve it' (p. 181). Self-regulated learning emphasizes the agentic role that learners have in the process of learning and refers to 'self-generated thoughts, feelings and actions that are planned and cyclically adapted to the attainment of personal goals' (Zimmerman, 2000, p. 14). Thus, a young footballer who regularly sets goals for training and monitors his/her performance in taking an active approach to improve him/herself and assumes responsibility for achievement.

## Theories and models of responsibility

### The Triangle Model of Responsibility

The Triangle Model of Responsibility (TMR) refers mainly to accountability that can be judged either by the actors of behaviours or by an external audience. According to the model's creators (Schlenker, Britt, Pennington, Murphy, & Doherty, 2004), responsibility is a necessary component of the process of holding people accountable for their conduct. 'Accountability refers to being answerable to audiences for performing up to certain prescribed standards thereby fulfilling obligations, duties, expectations and other charges' (Schlenker et al., 2004, p. 634). For example, a football player has certain obligations to fulfil, such as being on time for training or expectations to meet (e.g. producing best performances in games).

TMR identifies three elements of responsibility and outlines the linkages between them as related to perceptions of accountability. The three elements are: (i) *prescriptions that may guide the actor's behaviour in a particular situation*, (ii) *the specific situation or event*, and (iii) *the facets of the actor's identity that are relevant to the situation and the related prescriptions*. For example, a football player is about to score a goal with the goalkeeper of the other team out of action due to injury, and the referee not having stopped the game (anticipated event); the player has high aspirations for setting a goal record (identity facet); but an unwritten rule of conduct dictates that the game should stop on such an occasion (prescriptions). Schlenker et al. (2004) propose that 'responsibility is a direct function of the combined strength of the three linkages, as perceived by the individual who is making the judgment' (p. 638). Further, the strength of the linkages between the three elements has important effects for self-engagement. Thus, a football player who considers him/herself as an offensive player (identity facet), may not be committed when assigned a defensive role by his/her coach (prescriptions), while another player may provide excuses for bad performance relating to the prescriptions–event linkage such as, 'I wasn't sure what the coach wanted me to do'.

### The Personal Orientation Responsibility Model

The Personal Orientation Responsibility Model (Brockett & Hiemstra (1991) provides a framework for understanding the concept of self-direction in adult learning. However, this model may have important implications for sport and, in particular, for football, as continuous learning and improvement are at the heart of players' and teams' development. Brockett and Hiemstra (1991) state that self-directed learning 'refers to activities where primary responsibility for planning, carrying out, and evaluating a learning endeavour is assumed by the individual learner' (Brocket, 1983, p. 42, cited in Brockett & Hiemstra, 1991). From this definition, it is evident that personal responsibility is a central concept in this model. Brockett and Hiemstra (1991) describe responsibility as 'assuming ownership for their own thoughts and actions' (p. 6). Individuals possess different degrees of willingness to assume responsibility for their own learning and improvement. This degree of willingness affects two dimensions of self-directed learning identified by the model. The first dimension, termed *personal orientation*, refers to an individual's personal characteristics that predispose him/her towards taking responsibility for learning efforts. The second dimension, called the *process orientation*, refers to the instructional method the individual employs for learning, which may involve planning, implanting, and evaluating learning activities. Both dimensions influence self-directed learning; however, it is their interaction per se that determines effective learning, that is, an activity of construction, driven by the learner's agency, plus the monitoring and review of whether approaches and strategies are proving effective for the particular goals and context (Watkins, Lodge, Whalley, Wagner, & Carnell, 2002). As the level of both dimensions may vary across situations, effective learning is facilitated when there is a balance between one's level of self-direction and the degree that a particular situation provides for self-directed learning. For example, if a footballer is predisposed toward a high level of learning and improvement and the training sessions allow for self-direction, then the chances for improvement are high. Therefore, a challenge for coaches is to match the opportunities and emphasis for self-regulation provided in training, to the level of self-direction exhibited by the players.

### Hellison's model

Hellison's (2011) Teaching Personal and Social Responsibility (TPSR) Model, developed in sport and physical education settings, uses sport as a vehicle to teach generalizable life skills. Hellison wanted to capitalize on the appeal of sport to promote positive values and teach life lessons to youth from challenging backgrounds (Hellison, 2011). Although developed in the US, due to its practical appeal, TPSR has been successfully applied in multiple countries and cultural contexts as varied as Belize (Wright, Jacobs, Ressler & Jung, 2016), Greece (Hassandra & Goudas, 2010), South Korea (Lee, 2013), New Zealand (Gordon & Doyle, 2015), and Spain (Pozo, Grao-Cruces, & Perez-Ordas, 2016).

Hellison (2011) uses the terms 'personal responsibility' to refer to the ways players conduct themselves and 'social responsibility' to mean the ways these players treat each other. The practical value of TPSR rests in the way responsibility concepts are connected to concrete behaviours. For example, the first responsibility level is *respecting the rights and feelings of others.* Coaches can connect this to various behaviours, ranging from controlling one's temper when fouled to making a new player from a different culture feel included. Other responsibility levels and corresponding behavioural examples include *self-motivation* (e.g. giving best effort, focusing on improvement), *self-direction* (e.g. making good choices, working independently), and *caring* (e.g. leadership, helping others). By operationalizing responsibility-based concepts as specific life skills or competencies, Hellison's approach enables coaches to explicitly teach lessons about responsibility. For example, if a coach wants to help his/her players become better decision-makers, Hellison would encourage him/her to give players opportunities to make group and individual decisions (i.e. to practise those skills). In addition to empowering players to take on responsibilities in the programme, a key feature of the TPSR Model is helping players see the relevance of these life skills in other contexts. In promoting the fifth responsibility level in the model, *transfer,* coaches help players reflect on the relevance of skills such as leadership and responsible decision-making and to apply them in other contexts such as the classroom, neighbourhood, or home. Hellison advocates building time into lessons and practice sessions for such debriefing and reflection.

## Research and measurement of responsibility in sport

The bulk of empirical evidence and instrumentation related to the study of responsibility in sport revolves around Hellison's (2011) model (Pozo et al., 2016). Qualitative and quantitative studies indicate TPSR is effective in creating a positive, athlete-centred environment that is characterized by responsible behaviour (for reviews, see Hellison & Walsh, 2002; Pozo et al., 2016). Multiple studies demonstrate ratings of personal and social responsibility are positively correlated with ratings of enjoyment and intrinsic motivation in physical education and sport programmes (e.g. Li, Wright, Rukavina, & Pickering, 2008). Also, multiple quasi-experimental studies have shown significant increases in psycho-social factors such as self-efficacy for self-regulation, self-regulated learning, and sportsmanship in TPSR versus comparison groups (see review by Pozo et al., 2016). While the topic requires further exploration, several studies indicate that participants in TPSR programmes often transfer programme values and responsible behaviours to other settings (Hassandra & Goudas, 2010, Hellison & Walsh, 2002; Pozo et al., 2016).

Instrumentation for the assessment of responsibility in sport has mainly been developed for the evaluation of TPSR programmes. To this end, scholars have developed user-friendly assessments, such as checklists and rubrics (Hellison, 2011), as well as validated self-report scales (Li et al., 2008) and systematic observation tools (Escartí, Wright, Pascual, & Gutiérrez, 2015). In addition to their use as research instruments, these tools have proven useful in training teachers and coaches to use TPSR and in supporting implementation fidelity (Wright et al., 2016).

While current research and instrumentation provides a foundation for a more applied and conceptual understanding of personal responsibility, there are gaps to be addressed. Much of the existing research is based in physical education and multi-sport programmes. However, studies on responsibility in competitive football programmes are lacking. As most of the literature focuses on Hellison's (2011) model, future studies should examine other frameworks for responsibility in football. A strong programme of research can support the development of best practices for promoting player responsibility in the game.

## Implications

The implications derived from the use of the concept of personal or, in the case of football, player responsibility vary and recipients are academics, coaches, players, parents, officials, and other support staff. In the following paragraphs, some implications for coaches are shared as examples of the promising use of the concept and its association with other critical parameters related to football training and performance. These include (i) *team building practices and role development*, (ii) *players' attributional retraining*, (iii) *error correction during practices*, (iv) *loafing*, and (v) *leadership style*.

An effective way to promote team building is through *role taking*. Role clarity is a significant factor affecting the effectiveness of role assignment (Eys & Carron, 2001). Unless consistent and clear information regarding their roles is provided to team members, ambiguity arises, which may take the form of task and socio-emotional ambiguity. This has relevance to sport teams' development, such as football. The former (*task ambiguity*) refers to lack of information related to performance and consists of: (i) the exact expectations (scope of responsibility), (ii) what activities will accomplish these expectations (behavioural responsibilities), and (iii) the priorities to meet these expectations (hierarchy of responsibilities) considered to be rare in sport (Eys & Carron, 2001). The latter (*socio-emotional ambiguity*) refers to the lack of information related to the psychological consequences, such as when the individual fails to play his performance role in the team (e.g. insufficient justification provided by a coach for keeping a player on the bench).

The statement 'Excuses are the way we try to escape responsibility, although they seldom get us off the hook entirely' (French, 1991, p. 20) applies to the concept of attributions (i.e. to the reasons people give when attempting to explain an outcome). In football, after a negative result, this is commonly referred to as 'blame game'. Therefore, for football coaches, *attributional retraining* should be a priority and, to this effect, football players should develop a personal responsibility for both successful and unsuccessful endeavours, as is the case with elite performers (Hardy, Jones, & Gould, 1996). Coaches are advised to give emphasis in training their players to form proper attributions for both success and failure, that is, to attribute success to internal, controllable, stable, and global factors and their failures to internal, controllable, unstable, and universal factors. This will lead players to adopt a more responsible attitude and focus more on factors under their personal control. Regarding applying attributional retraining to teams effectively, persistence can be improved by teaching players to attribute negative outcomes to controllable factors (e.g. effort). One such attribution could refer to poor strategy employed during the game, an approach that should prevent players from losing their morale, in case of defeat, when attributions to lack of ability may arise (Anderson, 1983; Rees, Ingledew, & Hardy, 2005).

Performance *mistakes or errors* have been considered a 'natural part of the learning process in sport and form the stepping stones to success' (Burton & Raedeke,

2008, p. 23). The correction of such mistakes and errors in football is of central concern to coaches, who invest considerable time in promoting functional behaviour responses from their players, following error occurrence, either during training sessions or games. Focusing on the attributional perspective, the suggestion has been made that coaches should focus on the process of interpreting error occurrence by creating an atmosphere where participants take consistently personal responsibility and promote perception of task control after error occurrence. Eventually, 'players will develop a functional interpretation of handling their mistakes during task execution and dealing with them constructively' (Homsma, van Dyck, Gilder, Koopman, & Elfring, 2007, pp. 582–583).

*Loafing* refers to reduced effort exerted by individuals who participate in a collective task. When the identifiability of individual performance is absent in a team, diffusion of responsibility is prevalent; that is, on the one hand, performance of individuals decreases when players are not personally responsible for the team's performance. If, on the other hand, individual performances are assessed in terms of their contributions to the team, social loafing is less likely to occur (Hanson, 2006). Scholars suggest that one way to reduce loafing in football is to challenge players to examine their responsibility to the team and their unique contribution being communicated and recognized routinely (Weinberg & Gould, 2011).

Regarding *leadership*, autonomy-supportive coaches, in contrast to the controlling ones, are more likely to enhance the development of personal responsibility, through teaching players how to deal with increased autonomy (Ntoumanis & Mallett, 2014). For example, one such approach in football would be leading players to think about various options of the game and identify benefits and drawbacks of alternative strategies employed. These approaches will eventually lead players to enhance their sense of ownership of the overall outcome of the performance during competitions (Ntoumanis & Mallett, 2014). As an example from another team sport (basketball), reference is made to the Los Angeles Lakers' coach, Phil Jackson, who insisted on developing full coachability through increased self-management and acceptance of responsibility among his players (Beswick, 2016). In football, there are numerous cases of players and coaches who put great emphasis on self-management and full responsibility for learning and performance improvement during practice sessions (Beswick, 2016).

Hellison's (2011) TPSR model provides practical coaching strategies and structures that have proven effective in fostering a culture of responsibility in sport programmes. These may provide a starting point for developing and testing best practices specific to football. While such practices may support individual performance and team cohesion, it is important to remember that helping players develop responsibility should be more than a means to an end. Integrating such lessons supports their overall development as people, not just football players. By embracing this opportunity, coaches can instil values and teach skills that will serve their players well throughout their lives as they engage in societal roles and relationships that extend beyond the boundaries of the football pitch, yet require similar forms of personal responsibility.

## Conclusion

In conclusion, player responsibility in football has not been extensively studied, but may provide a framework for understanding and promoting a range of behaviours that can benefit the individual player and their team. The goal of this chapter was to examine the concept of responsibility as it applies to player behaviours and choices in the context of football. We highlighted the relationship between responsibility and a number of motivational constructs and existing models for developing responsibility in sport. Based on the potentially unifying role of player responsibility in football, we provided some suggestions of how this concept can be implemented in practice and further developed as a theory.

## References

Anderson, C. A. (1983). Motivational and performance deficits in interpersonal settings: The effect of attributional style. *Journal of Personality and Social Psychology, 45*, 1136–1147.

Bandura, A. (1997). *Self-efficacy. The exercise of control.* New York, NY: W. H. Freeman.

Beswick, B. (2016). *One goal: The mindset of winning soccer teams.* Champaign, IL: Human Kinetics.

Brockett, R. G., & Hiemstra, R. (1991). A conceptual framework for understanding self-direction in adult learning. In R. G. Brockett & R. Hiemstra, *Self-direction in adult learning: Perspectives on theory, research, and practice.* London, England; New York, NY: Routledge. Reproduced in the informal education archives: www.infed.org/archives/e-texts/hiemstra_self_direction.htm.

Burton, D., & Raedeke, T. D. (2008). *Sport psychology for coaches.* Champaign, IL: Human Kinetics.

Escartí, A., Wright, P. M., Pascual, C., & Gutiérrez, M. (2015). Tool for Assessing Responsibility-based Education (TARE) 2.0: Instrument revisions, inter-rater reliability, and correlations between observed teaching strategies and student behaviors. *Universal Journal of Psychology, 3*, 55–63.

Eys, M., & Carron, A. (2001). Role ambiguity, task cohesion, and task self-efficacy. *Small Group Research, 32*, 356–373.

French, P. (Ed.). (1991). *The spectrum of responsibility.* New York, NY: St. Martin's Press.

Gordon, B., & Doyle, S. (2015). Teaching personal and social responsibility and transfer of learning: Opportunities and challenges for teachers and coaches. *Journal of Teaching in Physical Education, 34*, 152–161.

Hanson, T. (2006). Focused baseball: Using sport psychology to improve baseball performance. In J. Dosil (Ed.), *The sport psychologist's handbook: A guide for sport-specific performance enhancement* (pp. 159–182). New York, NY: John Wiley & Sons.

Hardy, L., Jones, J. G., & Gould, D. (1996). *Understanding psychological preparation for sport: Theory and practice of elite performers.* New York, NY: John Wiley & Sons.

Hassandra, M., & Goudas, M. (2010). An evaluation of a physical education program for the development of students' responsibility. *Hellenic Journal of Psychology, 7*, 275–297.

Hellison, D. (2011). *Teaching personal and social responsibility through physical activity* (3rd ed.). Champaign, IL: Human Kinetics.

Hellison, D., & Walsh, D. (2002). Responsibility-based youth programs evaluation: Investigating the investigations. *Quest, 54*, 292–307.

Homsma, G. J., van Dyck, C., Gilder, D. de, Koopman, P. L., & Elfring, T. (2007). Overcoming errors: A closer look at the attributional mechanism. *Journal of Business and Psychology, 21*, 559–583.

Kirschenbaum, D. S. (1984). Self-regulation and sport psychology: Nurturing an emerging symbiosis. *Journal of Sport Psychology, 6*, 159–183.

Kyndt, T., & Rowell, S. (2012). *Achieving excellence in high performance sport: Experiences and skills behind the medals.* London, England: Bloomsbury.

Lee, O. (2013). Features of TPSR implementation and directions for model adaptation. *Korean Journal of Sport Pedagogy, 20,* 17–37.

Lenk, H. (2006). What is responsibility? *Philosophy Now, 56,* 29–32.

Li, W., Wright, P. M., Rukavina, P., & Pickering, M. (2008). Measuring students' perceptions of personal and social responsibility and its relationship to intrinsic motivation in urban physical education. *Journal of Teaching in Physical Education, 27,* 167–178.

Long, T., Pantaleon, N., & Bruant, G. (2008). Institutionalization versus self-regulation: A contextual analysis of responsibility among adolescent sportsmen. *Journal of Moral Education, 37,* 519–538.

McClelland, D. C., Atkinson, J. W., Clark, R. A., & Lowell, E. L. (1953). *The achievement motive.* New York, NY: Appleton-Century-Crofts.

Mergler, A. (2007). *Personal responsibility: The creation, implementation and evaluation of a school-based program.* Unpublished Doctoral Dissertation. Queensland University of Technology, Kelvin Grove, Australia.

Ntoumanis, N., & Mallett, C. (2014). Motivation in sport: A self-determination theory perspective. In A. G. Papaioannou & D. Hackfort (Eds.), *International perspectives on key issues in sport and exercise psychology. Routledge companion to sport and exercise psychology: Global perspectives and fundamental concepts* (pp. 67–82). London, England; New York, NY: Routledge.

Pozo, P., Grao-Cruces, A., & Perez-Ordas, R. (2016). Teaching personal and social responsibility model-based programmes in physical education: A systematic review. *European Physical Education Review, 22,* 1–20. doi:10.1177/1356336XI16664749.

Rees, T., Ingledew, D. K., & Hardy, L. (2005). Attribution in sport psychology: Seeking congruence between theory, research and practice. *Psychology of Sport and Exercise, 6,* 189–204. doi:10.1016/j.psychsport.2003.10.008.

Rotter, J. B. (1966). Generalized expectancies for internal versus external control of reinforcement. *Psychological Monographs: General and Applied, 80,* 1–28.

Saxena, A. (2012). *Soccer: Strategies for sustained coaching success.* Auckland, New Zealand; Vienna, Austria: Meyer & Meyer Sport.

Schlenker, B. R., Britt, T. W., Pennington, J., Murphy, R., & Doherty, K. (2004). The triangle model of responsibility. *Psychological Review, 101,* 632–652.

Schultheiss, O., & Brunstein, J. (2005). An implicit motive perspective on competence. In A. Elliot and C. S. Dweck (Eds.), *Handbook of competence and motivation* (pp. 31–51). New York, NY: The Guilford Press.

Watkins, C., Lodge, C., Whalley, C., Wagner, P., & Carnell, E. (2002). *Effective learning.* London, England: Institute of Education, University of London.

Weinberg, R. S., & Gould, D. (2011). *Foundations of sport and exercise psychology* (5th ed.). Champaign, IL: Human Kinetics.

Weiner, B. (2005). Motivation from an attributional perspective and the social psychology of perceived competence. In A. Elliot and C. S. Dweck (Eds.), *Handbook of competence and motivation* (pp. 73–84). New York, NY: The Guilford Press.

Whitmore, J. (2002). *Coaching for performance: GROWing people, performance and purpose* (3rd ed.). London, England: Nicholas Brealey Publishing.

Wright, P. M., Jacobs, J., Ressler, J., & Jung, J. (2016). Using critical pedagogy to foster transformative educational experience in a sport for development program. *Sport, Education and Society, 21,* 4, 531–548.

Zimmerman, B. J. (2000). Attaining self-regulation: A social-cognitive perspective. In M. Boekaerts, P. Pintrich, & M. Zeidner (Eds.), *Handbook of self-regulation* (pp. 13–39). San Diego, CA: Academic Press.

# 5 The consistent psycho-social development of young footballers

## Implementing the 5C's as a vehicle for interdisciplinary cohesion

*Karl Steptoe, Tom King, and Chris Harwood*

## Abstract

The development of positive psycho-social processes and psychological characteristics in youth athletes has received substantial research attention over the last decade, with a greater understanding gained of the role played by key stakeholders including peers, coaches, parents, sport scientists, and education providers. For the sport psychologist working in the professional football domain, it has become imperative to embed training of psychological skills within the multi- and interdisciplinary context. In this chapter the authors reflect on their combined experiences of working within professional football academies and the implementation of the 5C's (Commitment, Communication, Concentration, Control, Confidence) programme to promote a cohesive message of psychological support and increase engagement from all those involved in player development. The case describes how the flexibility of the 5C's framework fostered collaboration with members of the management team to target and define the most valued behaviours and responses agreed to represent positive psychological performance in training and competition. The initial organisational level work provided an important platform from which bespoke training programmes could be designed and implemented along the development pathway with key messages supported and reinforced by the young players' support network. The case represents the utility of the 5C's framework in aligning approaches to psycho-social skill development and in the consistent assessment, intervention, and evaluation of psychological performance.

The training of positive developmental outcomes of young athletes has received wide attention from researchers within sport psychology over the last decade. More specifically, the psycho-social processes of talent development and the psychological characteristics of elite youth athletes appear central to studies targeting positive youth development (Jones & Lavallee, 2009). Key stakeholders in player development and the wider support network (e.g. coaches, parents, sport scientists, education providers) play an integral role in the effective delivery of sports psychology services. Consequently, a priority for the sport psychologist is to embed any programme within a wider multidisciplinary context.

The general positive youth development literature posits qualities of competence, character, connection, confidence, caring, and contribution, defined as the 6C's, as desired outcomes toward the development of a civilised society (Lerner, Fisher, & Weinberg, 2000).The 5C's of Commitment, Communication, Concentration,

Control, and Confidence (Harwood, 2008; Harwood, Barker, & Anderson, 2015) represent one such framework applicable to the youth sport domain that aims to increase awareness and development of motivational, interpersonal, and self-regulatory skills. This chapter details the implementation of a 5C programme within a premier league football academy to promote a cohesive message regarding the psychological support of young footballers. The chapter considers the challenges associated with delivering consistent sport psychology messages within a multidisciplinary team and details the priorities given to coach, parent, and player intervention. This case details the role played by the sport psychologist in providing psycho-education at the organisational, team, and individual level to ensure corresponding sport psychology messages. These include consistent understanding of assessment and intervention as well as clarity for all, in determining what constitutes enhanced psychological performance.

The chapter begins by outlining the increasing prominence that support in sport psychology provision has been given, following strategic changes to player development in academy football and the specific responsibilities of the sport psychology staff in the case described. The chapter summarises the applied practice of the authors over a four-season period in which challenges to engagement are discussed and working models are adapted to maximise effective service delivery. Specifically, this case details how the flexibility of the 5C's model of psycho-social development has enabled both its implementation across all phases of the academy and increased 'buy in' to the possibility of psychological skill development. Interventions with the academy management team that provided the foundation of this process are described and are posited by the authors as an essential component of work, if consistent messages are to be achieved. The consequence of this underpinning work is then realised in the training programmes designed to support parents and coaches in the shaping, progression, and reinforcement of positive 5C responses and to ultimately equip players with the skills to demonstrate strength and to excel in this area.

## Historical barriers to engagement and the changing landscape

In October 2011 key football stakeholders that included The Premier League, Football League representatives, and The Football Association, agreed to develop a long-term strategy for youth development; the Elite Player Performance Plan (EPPP). With this vision came increased consultancy opportunities for sport and exercise psychology practitioners as football clubs awarded the highest category status (1 highest award to 4 lowest award) could benefit from greater resources to invest in their programmes. An academy's category status is determined by an independent audit of factors that include: productivity rates, training facilities, sport science support and coaching, education and welfare provisions. To satisfy the psychology support criteria necessary to obtain category 1 status, the appointment of an accredited Sport and Exercise Psychologist or practitioner in training with the British Psychological Society (BPS), regulated by the Health and Care Professions Council (HCPC), was required. Initial entry to the academy was, therefore, gained by the first author under the supervision of the third author to meet these objectives.

The initial job description was commensurate with the common perceived role of sport psychology in football and specifically targeted to impact performance enhancement across the development pathway (Gamble, Hill, & Parker, 2013).

There was an incongruity at that time between the perceived importance of the mental side of the game and player/coach engagement in specific psychological training programmes. Psychological narratives permeated match debriefs and player meetings, particularly in attempts to explain suboptimal individual and team performances. When analysing the factors contributing to success, however, psychological attributes often appeared to be subordinate to technical, tactical, and physical assets. Coaching staff have experienced substantial change in their roles and training over the last 20 years, receiving an increased breadth of training in all aspects of sport science, but that has also resulted in a more precise focus of their work, as other specialist practitioners have been brought in to academies to support performance development. The coaches' extensive experience has equipped them with a tacit knowledge with which to identify talent, develop young players, and to influence positive team performance. This expertise has appeared to also contribute to a disconnect between the perceived ability of the coach to 'just know when a player's head isn't right' whilst at the same time not enabling them to operationalise that knowledge in the most meaningful way to improve assessment and to monitor change. As a result, a fixed mindset had developed among staff around psychological performance, with labels ascribed to players (e.g. confidence player, switches off, 'choker') without clear direction as to how these unhelpful perceptions could be altered. This challenge for players was made harder still as isolated incidents of suboptimal performance initiated a confirmation bias that reinforced the coach's negative opinions. In contrast, positive demonstrations of psychological performance would often go unnoticed or would not be perceived as evidence of progression in this area.

These early experiences of work in academy football were compatible with those shared by other practitioners (e.g. Barker, McCarthy, & Harwood, 2011; Gamble et al., 2013; Pain & Harwood, 2004), who have highlighted the misconceptions of sport psychology and its value, as being detrimental to engagement. In contrast to these views, research by Mills, Butt, Maynard, and Harwood (2012) proposed a wide range of multidimensional skill development opportunities within academy football that address factors found to both positively and negatively influence player development. These include: increasing self-awareness, coping with setbacks, developing a professional attitude and emotional competence, competitiveness, and managing the influence of significant others. The findings of Mills et al. resonated with the observations of the first author and with assessment of both organisational and individual stakeholder needs. What had been primarily a reactive role, resourced to provide 'light-touch' support or 'psychological first aid' to those deemed most in need, required greater integration into the player development programme in order to be proactive in developing psychological strengths in young footballers; equipping them with the skills to meet the known demands of academy football and to demonstrate the possible progression in this area.

## Multi and interdisciplinary distinctions

The aims of the Elite Player Performance Plan (EPPP) are to provide a world-class youth development system through the delivery of four core functions: (1) a comprehensive games programme; (2) world class education and innovative teaching; (3) a world-leading coach development programme; and (4) elite performance programmes that strive to find effective ways of increasing the quantity and quality of home-grown players. In line with these aims, sport psychology services were to be delivered within the assembled multidisciplinary performance, coaching, and welfare-oriented environment. Over time, however, subtle differences between multi- and interdisciplinary working practices became apparent, influencing the effectiveness of psychological intervention, leading to renewed priorities of work. It was true that players had access to a wide range of expertise to aid performance that included: strength and conditioning staff, physiotherapists, technical coaches, nutritionists, the social welfare and education officer as well as the sport psychologist, however, work would often be confined to each domain with limited opportunities to share development or for cross-department reinforcement of key objectives. Collins, Moore, Mitchell, and Alpress (1999) have suggested that these environments may in fact be an even greater source of stress than the competitive environment itself; an opinion supported by our practice experiences. Players can reduce disclosure as they are uncertain of the degree of confidentiality that exists between all staff members. They are reluctant for information to be shared with coaches and decision makers as they believe that this may negatively influence progression and/ or playing opportunities.

The first author had time to better understand the historical organisational culture and elite performance department sub-cultures (Cruickshank & Collins, 2012a; Fletcher & Wagstaff, 2009), as well as the implicit and explicit interdepartment pressures that had understandably developed because of a perceived need to demonstrate independent contribution to player development. The challenge in this case was to develop a shared vision, philosophy, and working model of psychological assessment, and intervention and evaluation that all members of the interdisciplinary team would have confidence in and that would satisfy their own interests and beliefs pertaining to psychological performance enhancement. For sport psychology to have a meaningful impact on player development, key messages needed to be reinforced across departments, towards agreed standards demonstrative of excellence. It was felt that such a project would have the potential to not only maximise the efficacy of psychological intervention but could also positively influence the high-performance culture through the creation of shared beliefs, expectations, and practices across departments that persist despite inevitable variation in individual and team performances (Cruickshank & Collins, 2012b).

It became our primary objective to pursue an inter- rather than multidisciplinary approach when integrating the full-time psychology programme within the high-performance team. Specifically, we wanted to ensure: (1) that there was a synergy between practitioners toward player development; (2) there was clear communication, particularly of psychological objectives; (3) that all involved in the player support network were aware of player performance goals, and importantly; (4) that all staff had confidence in the value of both their own services and of other members of the interdisciplinary team. In short it was intended that there be an advancement in sport and performance psychology provision, from being one-of-many performance support services available to young players [a programme, in our opinion, multidisciplinary in nature]; to a discipline embedded in the processes of player identification, training, support, and progression that reinforces the goals and objectives of all tasked with player development. It was felt that this interdisciplinary structure would maximise both performance and well-being outcomes for players as well as increasing the perceived value of sport psychology, as it would be contributing to multiple elite performance solutions through collaboration with other disciplines. To achieve these aims a psycho-social model and framework compatible with the interdisciplinary environment was imperative.

## Getting on the same page: the 5C's

The 5C's framework developed by the third author represented one such model that had already been predominantly integrated into coach and parent education programmes (Harwood, 2008; Harwood et al., 2015). We considered an apposite vehicle for promoting our interdisciplinary approach to psycho-social development. The principles of the applied sport programming (Fraser-Thomas, Côté, & Deakin, 2005) and bio-ecological models of youth development (Bronfenbrenner, 1999) from which the intervention work of Harwood (2008) was formulated, were in direct correspondence with our interdisciplinary objectives. Specifically, these models proposed that dynamic environments influence youth development through the promotion of key internal assets (e.g. commitment to learning, interpersonal competence, restraint, and self-esteem) and that integral to this development are external assets that typify high-quality, reciprocal social relationships between players and members of their development network (e.g. coaches, parents, and teammates). Holt and Dunn (2004) offer support for these assets in their exploration of the parameters associated with successful player progression in academy football. These revealed commitment, resilience, and discipline as psycho-social competencies, and social support as a key environmental condition. Together these internal and external assets in academy football are thought to play protection, enhancement, and resiliency roles (Benson, 1997).

The culmination of research and applied consultancy by Harwood (2008) further advocated for the role of organised youth sport programmes that target the training of psycho-social competence, rather than a sole focus on developing highly skilled athletes. These reflections from field work also highlighted a perceived lack of confidence in coaches' ability to embed psychological development into training sessions and so the intervention targeted increasing efficacy in this area. The resultant 5C's framework focused on the development of observable player responses associated with Commitment, Communication, Concentration, Control, and Confidence. These terms represented the key motivational, interpersonal, and self-regulatory attributes fundamental to core educational interventions in youth sport (e.g. Thelwell, Greenlees, & Weston, 2006) and that also represent the internal assets and psycho-social competencies of positive youth development models. Of equal significance to the present case was simplicity of the 5C's 'user friendly' terminology that we anticipated would unite members of the interdisciplinary team and wider support network in the pursuit of consistent psychological messages.

Each of the 5C's is underpinned by research from associated motivation, interpersonal, and self-regulation theory. A players' *commitment* to train and perform, for example, can be understood from the quality of motivation and definitions of competence striving, detailed by Self-Determination (Deci & Ryan, 1985) and Achievement Goal theories (e.g. Elliot, Murayama & Pekrun, 2011; Nicholls, 1984). For *communication* to develop, contextual and developmental factors need to be considered (DeVito, 1986; Gouran, Wiethoff, & Doelger, 1994); *concentration* within the 5C's is grounded in the principles of attention proposed by Nideffer and Sharpe (1978) and *control* centres on both mental and physical arousal regulation techniques that include breathing and self-talk. Finally, *confidence* is both enhanced by the attainment of the preceding 5C competencies and represents the players' belief in their capacity to execute the behaviours necessary to attain specific performance standards. As such, confidence is reflective of Self-Efficacy Theory (Bandura, 1977).

Research by Harwood (2008) and Harwood et al. (2015) has supported the utility of promoting adaptive training/supportive environments through 5C education programmes in successfully increasing coach efficacy in the development of players' psycho-social competencies and also in positively impacting observable adaptive behaviours defined by the 5C's. The 5C framework provided us with a platform with which to meet four revised department objectives relating to: (1) player profiling; (2) player development; (3) parent education; and (4) coach development. The requirement to provide support across foundation, youth, and professional development phases to players, coaches, and parents still presented a challenge to resources. Successful implementation of the programme, therefore, relied on the realisation of the high-performance culture proposed by Cruickshank and Collins (2012b) and consideration of who would be best positioned to deliver key messages and to shape psycho-social development.

## Implications for players, coaches, and parents

Rather than seek consensus from coaches on the target behaviours and responses that constituted positive psychological performance, we believed that shared values would be best achieved if promoted at the highest level of the coaching hierarchy, therefore intervention was targeted at the organisational level. Over the three seasons, the psychology team had made note of over 130 terms, behaviours, and responses reported by the coaching staff to represent positive psychological performance or a desired player mindset. We approached the academy management team to get an understanding of the perceived importance of these attributes to player development and to work towards agreed standards that all members of the interdisciplinary team could support. The academy manager, technical lead, head of coaching, and head of recruitment were first asked to rate each of the items for importance (0 = not at all important to 100 = extremely important). The responses were averaged and any item scoring below 70 was removed. After this process 44 items remained and the management team were then asked to allocate each of the remaining items to the C (Commitment, Communication, Concentration, Control, Confidence) that they believed the item to most accurately represent. Final 5C standards were determined after agreement on the allocation of a behaviour/ response to a C and following discussion by the authors to satisfy that each standard was representative of the appropriate motivational, interpersonal, or self-regulatory competency (Figure 5.1).

The standards were worded in such a way as to be applicable to multiple contexts within the academy environment (i.e. gym, training ground, match-day, classroom) so that opportunities to both evaluate and acknowledge progression would be possible for all members of the interdisciplinary team. To conclude this process it was important that all staff had confidence that the proposed model would meet their

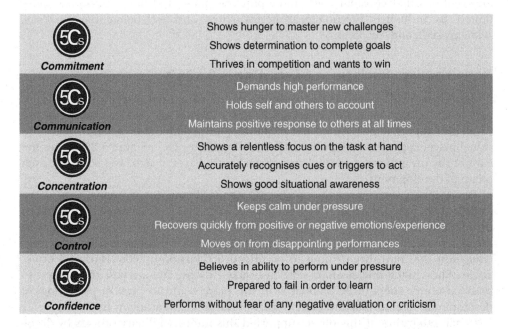

*Figure 5.1* Agreed academy 5C standards.

needs and develop the skills that they believed were important to player development. To achieve this, we agreed upon an academy psychology philosophy that incorporated and highlighted key terms that staff had suggested were important and that detailed how these would be achieved through the development of the 5C's:

> Players who demonstrate consistently high level 5C standards will have **self-belief** and a **hunger to be the best,** they will possess the skills to **positively influence team momentum** at important moments in training, matches, and the season, through **emotional intelligence** and exceptional **interpersonal and self-regulatory skills**. The academy recognises that a players' mental strength is not predetermined or fixed and that they can strengthen psychological performance through both their, and the coaches' **growth mindset**. Collectively these positive psychological behaviours will influence **creativity, courage, bravery,** and **leadership** when facing challenges and the demands of professional football and will ultimately epitomise the player with a **competitive edge**.

The 5C standards provided us with a consistent language with which to discuss psycho-social development at the academy and increased opportunities for key stakeholders to reinforce and shape desired responses. Through this shared 5C lens we were able to achieve four important outcomes: (1) the consistent assessment of players' psychological performance; (2) the ability to provide players with current perceptions of their psychological performance; (3) increased opportunities to work with coaches to set specific 5C actions in player development plans that would lead to progression in perceptions of 5C standards; and (4) the design of bespoke

interventions that consider each developmental phase and target those best positioned to influence psychological performance and well-being (i.e. coaches,
academy staff, and/or parents).

## Demonstrating, developing, and excelling in the 5C's

A phase-specific 5C psychology programme was implemented that prioritised parent
and coach education at the foundation phase, psychological skills training at the
youth development phase, and the promotion of psychological strength and individual player support at the professional development phase. Figure 5.2 outlines the
aims of the programme and the focus of work with player, coach, and parent at each
phase of development.

Developing player awareness of the 5C standards was the principal aim at the
foundation phase, providing the youngest players (8–11 years) with opportunities
throughout the season to demonstrate these positive responses in training and
match contexts. These objectives were primarily achieved through coach and parent
education that have been found to be effective (Harwood, 2008; Harwood et al.,
2015). Short pitch-side sessions were also taken by psychology staff that aimed to
both raise awareness of 5C standards in the players and to present psychological
development as a normal and integral part of training and academy life.

Coach education at this phase supported this interdisciplinary process by developing skills to progress each of the 5C's. The PROGRESS acronym (Harwood &
Anderson, 2015) provided a structure with which to support coaches in embedding
5C development within their training sessions. Through (P) promotion and (R) role
modelling, players gained increased awareness of the importance of the 5C skills to
the academy and performance and to the specific behaviours and responses that are
perceived as being appropriate to the elite environment. Players are central to the
process and as such are given (O) ownership of their learning to enhance motivation for this area. Coaches are encouraged to not only promote the demonstration
of positive 5C standards within sessions but to also apply coaching and pedagogical
principles to psychological development and to offer opportunities for differentiation and progression and specifically for players to (G) grow each C. Positive demonstration is appropriately (R) reinforced and players are actively (E) empowered
to monitor and encourage positive performance in teammates. With this in place,
the coach ensures that they (S) support the supporter during the session and finally
incorporate, into the normal session debrief, the time for (S) self-review, where
levels of 5C standards are assessed and future goals in this area set.

To complete the aims of intervention at this phase, we supported parents
through workshops and the provision of educational materials to highlight how they
can both shape and reinforce desired 5C standards in players. One effective
example of work in this area is use of 5C bingo cards (Figure 5.3). This educational
resource served four complementary purposes: (1) to increase communication
between academy and parents as to the aims of sessions; (2) to detail specific standards that the academy values in young players; (3) to encourage awareness of these
additional measures of success beyond typical performance outcomes (e.g. winning,
goals scored, pass accuracy, clean sheets); and (4) to positively reinforce attainment
of these standards with their child. Parents were invited to take a card at training
that contains a random selection of up to seven 5C standards and make a note of

| Phase | Role | | Commitment | Communication | Concentration | Control | Confidence | Competitive Edge |
|---|---|---|---|---|---|---|---|---|
| **Foundation** DEMONSTRATING PROGRESSING SHAPING A COMPETITIVE EDGE | Player | Intro Profiling | DEMONSTRATING Commitment | DEMONSTRATING Communication | DEMONSTRATING Concentration | DEMONSTRATING Control | DEMONSTRATING Confidence | DEMONSTRATING Competitive Edge |
| | Coach | Intro Profiling | PROGRESSING Commitment | PROGRESSING Communication | PROGRESSING Concentration | PROGRESSING Control | PROGRESSING Confidence | PROGRESSING Competitive Edge |
| | Parent | Intro Profiling | SHAPING Commitment | SHAPING Communication | SHAPING Concentration | SHAPING Control | SHAPING Confidence | SHAPING Competitive Edge |
| **Youth** PREPARING FOR THE KNOWN DEMANDS OF ACADEMY FOOTBALL, PARENTING AND COACHING | Player | Intro Profiling | *TRAINING 1* *1-2-1 – ILP* *Observation* | *TRAINING 2* *1-2-1 – ILP* *Observation* | *TRAINING 3* *1-2-1 – ILP* *Observation* | *TRAINING 4* *1-2-1 – ILP* *Observation* | *TRAINING 5* *1-2-1 – ILP* *Observation* | *TRAINING 6* *1-2-1 – ILP* *Observation* |
| | Coach | Intro Profiling | *DEVELOPING* *Motivation 1* | *DEVELOPING* *Motivation 2* | *DEVELOPING* *Interpersonal Skills 1* | *DEVELOPING* *Interpersonal Skills 2* | *DEVELOPING* *Self Regulation 1* | *DEVELOPING* *Self Regulation 2* |
| | Parent | Intro Profiling | *ASSESSING* *Demands* | *PREPARING* *Demand 1* | *PREPARING* *Demand 2* | *PREPARING* *Demand 3* | *PREPARING* *Demand 4* | *PREPARING* *Demand 5* |
| **Professional** PERFORMING AS AN ELITE PLAYER, TEAM AND COACH | Player | Intro Profiling | *EXCELLING* *1-2-1 – ILP* *Observation* | *EXCELLING* *1-2-1 – ILP* *Observation* | *EXCELLING* *1-2-1 – ILP* *Observation* | *EXCELLING* *1-2-1 – ILP* *Observation* | *EXCELLING* *1-2-1 – ILP* *Observation* | *EXCELLING* *1-2-1 – ILP* *Observation* |
| | Coach | Intro Profiling | *PERFORMING 1* *1-2-1 (COACH)* | *PERFORMING 2* *1-2-1 (COACH)* | *PERFORMING 3* *1-2-1 (COACH)* | *PERFORMING 4* *1-2-1 (COACH)* | *PERFORMING 5* *1-2-1 (COACH)* | *PERFORMING 6* *1-2-1 (COACH)* |
| | Parent | Intro | *INFORMING* | *INFORMING* | *INFORMING* | *INFORMING* | *INFORMING* | *INFORMING* |

*Figure 5.2* Phase-specific 5C psychology programme.

5Cs B I N G O

| | | | | | |
|---|---|---|---|---|---|
| 5Cs | Shows hunger to master new challenges | Shows determination to complete goals | Thrives in competition and wants to win | | |
| 5Cs | | Demands high performance | Holds self and others to account | Maintains positive response to others at all times | |
| 5Cs | | | Shows a relentless focus on the task at hand | Accurately recognises cues or triggers to act | Shows good situational awareness |
| 5Cs | Keeps calm under pressure | | Recovers quickly from positive or negative emotions/ experience | | Moves on from disappointing performances |
| 5Cs | | Believes in ability to perform under pressure | | Prepared to fail in order to learn | Performs without fear of any negative evaluation or criticism |

*Figure 5.3* Parent education materials: example 5C bingo card.

the time that they observed a good example of the 'C'. This enabled the sport psychology staff to then work with members of the performance analysis team to review a video of the session and to further highlight, reinforce, and discuss this positive 5C demonstration.

The experiences of the authors and the reported applied practice of colleagues in academy football have contributed to a number of known demands that are presented at each phase. These include: playing out of position, reduced game time, overcoming injury, managing school and football training workloads, parental pressures, potential release from the academy, and challenges with peers, both within the football and education environments. Consistent with our proactive approach, increased efficacy in 5C competencies were proposed to better equip the young players to meet these anticipated challenges and so these were discussed with players, parents, and coaches in advance. Priorities in the youth development phase (12–16 years) were therefore: to provide players with training that enabled them to sustain motivation during challenging periods and adversity; to value multiple measures of success; develop skills that promote emotion regulation to minimise the impact of stress on performance; enhanced listening and acknowledging skills, the ability to provide constructive feedback and to recognise the influence of non-verbal behaviour; increased capacity to respond to relevant cues and the ability to switch attentional styles; and to maximise a player's full involvement in training and match situations with a diminished fear of making mistakes.

The coach and parent education programmes at this phase continued to champion the impact of the players' environment and the role of the support network in both promoting positive psychological performance (5C standards) and in managing the demands of academy football. In coach sessions, specific strategies for developing motivational, interpersonal, and self-regulatory skill were discussed (see Table 5.1 for example strategies) and the sport psychology staff observed sessions to provide feedback on coach effectiveness in this area. Players in the youth and professional development phases were assessed by the coaches in each Meso (6-week training cycle) for their demonstration of 5C standards and were also asked to rate themselves on this competency. These data enabled the sport psychology staff in interdisciplinary meetings to: (1) highlight discrepancies between player–coach assessments that suggest priorities for education regarding desired standards; and (2) set specific objectives and actions for the player to evidence progression in each standard.

Coach and parent education are key features of both foundation and youth development phases, however, the changing player–parent relationship and role of the parent at the professional development phase were acknowledged in setting the department objective of 'informing' parents of continued psychology messages and academy perceptions of their child's performance in this area. The primary focus at this phase was on demonstrating excellence across the 5C's and has contributed in large part to a positive culture shift regarding the role, purpose, and value of sport psychology intervention. This acknowledges the objective of developing mental strengths and demonstrating psychological assets as opposed to solely assisting those in need.

*Table 5.1* Coach strategies for enhancing 5C standards

| 5C's | Example strategies |
| --- | --- |
| Commitment | Skill-specific feedback and reinforcement, attention to both equality and consistency for acknowledging player achievements, encouragement after making regular mistakes, and reinforcement towards approach behaviours |
| Communication | Demonstrations of specific verbal and non-verbal communication, silent football and non-verbal drills, appointing a communication police team, and reinforcement of players giving and receiving feedback from performance |
| Concentration | Increase player awareness of their role and the importance of concentration, 'good' vs 'bad' demonstration of attentional style, sample drills to practise both internal and external cues, reinforcement of attentional control from role models, maintained attention during distraction, and the use of a 'concentration monitor' to give feedback of use of attention |
| Control | Reinforcement of recovery from mistakes, permitting role playing of different emotions to increase awareness, 'good' vs 'bad' demonstrations of player self-control |
| Confidence | Peer acknowledgement of skill achievement, encouragement of persistence and approach behaviours, allowing players to act in a confident way, and players publicly acknowledging progressive self-accomplishments |

## Conclusions

There has been an increased focus on understanding the psycho-social processes of developing talent and the psychological attributes of young athletes competing at an elite level. Whether the goal of positive youth development is towards enhancing life skills or performance, both are of great relevance to the academy footballer as they attempt to meet the demands of the elite environment. It is important to note that a large percentage of those young players will not ultimately transition to the elite level and, for this reason, consideration must be given at the organisational and coaching levels towards how to maximise development opportunities for young athletes, whilst also maintaining a focus on the competencies associated with optimal performance in football.

The 5C's have provided an effective framework for parent and coach education programmes in academy football and remain so in our work. However, the simplicity and flexibility of the model provides practitioners with an even greater opportunity to impact player psycho-social development and to enhance performance. The 5C's represent a common language for psychology that promotes a consistent and cohesive message regarding psychological assessment, intervention, and evaluation. We believe that the 5C framework can unite multidisciplinary teams and ensure that training toward the attainment of psychological performance objectives is, in fact, interdisciplinary in its delivery.

## References

Bandura, A. (1977). Self-efficacy: Toward a unifying theory of behavioral change. *Psychological Review, 84*(2), 191–215.

Barker, J., McCarthy, P., & Harwood, C. (2011). Reflections on consulting in elite youth male English cricket and soccer academies. *Sport and Exercise Psychology Review, 7*(2), 58–72.

Benson, P. L. (1997). *All kids are our kids: What communities must do to raise caring and responsible children and adolescents.* San Francisco, CA: Jossey-Bass.

Bronfenbrenner, U. (1999). Environments in developmental perspective: Theoretical and operational models. In S. L. Friedman & T. D. Wachs (Eds.), *Measuring environment across the life span: Emerging methods and concepts* (pp. 3–28). Washington, DC: American Psychological Association.

Collins, D., Moore, P., Mitchell, D., & Alpress, F. (1999). Role conflict and confidentiality in multidisciplinary athlete support programs. *British Journal of Sport Medicine, 33*, 208–211.

Cruickshank, A., & Collins, D. (2012a). Change management: The case of the elite sport performance team. *Journal of Change Management, 12*, 209–229.

Cruickshank, A., & Collins, D. (2012b). Culture change in elite sport performance teams: Examining and advancing effectiveness in the new era. *Journal of Applied Sport Psychology, 24*, 338–355. doi:10.1080/10413200.2011.650819.

Deci, E. L., & Ryan, R. M. (1985). *Intrinsic motivation and self-determination in human behavior.* New York, NY: Plenum Press.

DeVito, J. A. (1986). *The communication handbook: A dictionary.* New York, NY: Harper & Row.

Elliot, A. J., Murayama, K., & Pekrun, R. (2011). A 3 × 2 achievement goal model. *Journal of Educational Psychology, 103*(3), 632–648.

Fletcher, D., & Wagstaff, C. R. D. (2009). Organizational psychology in elite sport: Its emergence, application and future. *Psychology of Sport and Exercise, 10*, 427–434.

Fraser-Thomas, J., Côté, J., & Deakin, J. (2005). Youth sport programs: An avenue to foster positive youth development. *Physical Education and Sport Pedagogy, 10*, 19–40.

Gamble, R., Hill, D. M., & Parker, A. (2013). Revs and psychos: Role, impact and interaction of sport chaplains and sport psychologists within English premiership soccer. *Journal of Applied Sport Psychology, 25*(2), 249–264.

Gouran, D. S., Wiethoff, W. E., & Doelger, J. A. (1994). *Mastering communication* (2nd ed.). Boston, MA: Allyn and Bacon.

Harwood, C. (2008). Developmental consulting in a professional football academy: The 5Cs coaching efficacy program. *The Sport Psychologist, 22*(1), 109–133.

Harwood, C. G., & Anderson, R. (2015). *Coaching psychological skills in youth football: Developing the 5Cs.* London, England: Bennion-Kearney.

Harwood, C. G., Barker, J. B., & Anderson, R. (2015). Psycho-social development in youth soccer players: Assessing the effectiveness of the 5Cs intervention program. *The Sport Psychologist, 29*(4), 319–334.

Holt, N. L., & Dunn, J. G. (2004). Toward a grounded theory of the psycho-social competencies and environmental conditions associated with soccer success. *Journal of Applied Sport Psychology, 16*(3), 199–219.

Jones, M. I., & Lavallee, D. (2009). Exploring the life skills needs of British adolescent athletes. *Psychology of Sport and Exercise, 10*(1), 159–167.

Lerner, R. M., Fisher, C. B., & Weinberg, R. A. (2000). Toward a science for and of the people: Promoting civil society through the application of developmental science. *Child Development, 71,* 11–20.

Mills, A., Butt, J., Maynard, I., & Harwood, C. (2012). Identifying factors perceived to influence the development of elite youth football academy players. *Journal of Sports Sciences, 30*(15), 1593–1604.

Nicholls, J. G. (1984). Achievement motivation: Conceptions of ability, subjective experience, task choice, and performance. *Psychological Review, 91*(3), 328–346.

Nideffer, R. M., & Sharpe, R. (1978). *ACT: Attention control training.* New York, NY: Wideview.

Pain, M. A., & Harwood, C. G. (2004). Knowledge and perceptions of sport psychology within English soccer. *Journal of Sports Sciences, 22,* 813–826.

Thelwell, R. C., Greenlees, I. A., & Weston, N. J. (2006). Using psychological skills training to develop soccer performance. *Journal of Applied Sport Psychology, 18*(3), 254–270.

# 6   Decision making and non-verbal intelligence in football

*Itay Basevitch and Erkut Konter*

**Abstract**

The chapter addresses a number of issues related to decision making and non-verbal intelligence in football. Players consistently make non-verbal decisions throughout a game of football. Thus, decision making as non-verbal intelligence seems to be one of the most important skills in football that differentiates between high and low skill players, older and younger players, and successful and less successful performers. Physical challenges, techniques, tactics, and psychological skills of performance in football are mostly non-verbal in nature. In this chapter, conceptual definitions of decision making and related theories are presented from a cognitive perspective including non-verbal intelligence in football. The chapter also dwells on different measurement methods of decision making and non-verbal intelligence. In general, findings indicate that: (a) skills such as anticipation and option generation can be measured and trained; (b) despite growing interest, there are still barriers and concerns in integrating sport psychologists and methods for improving decision making and non-verbal intelligence in football teams; (c) psychological skills necessary to achieve success are still under-developed and rarely used. In addition, researchers in football using Test of Non-verbal Intelligence-2 (TONI-2) suggest that older football players, starters, professionals, footballers in central positions, and, interestingly, female football players have higher TONI-2 scores compared to their respective counterparts. Overall, results indicate the importance of decision-making processes including non-verbal intelligence in football performance.

## Decision making in football

Players consistently make decisions throughout a game of football. On average, per game, each team makes more than 500 actions (e.g. shots, passes, headers, dribbles; Luhtanen, Belinskij, Häyrinen, & Vänttinen, 2001). Each action is a consequence of a decision made by a player (Tenenbaum, 2003). Thus, decision making is one of the most important skills in football and has been studied extensively. Indeed, research has indicated that decision making can differentiate between high and low skill players, older and younger players, and successful and less successful performances (Ward & Williams, 2003).

The majority of research in the area of decision making was conducted in individual sports (e.g. tennis, badminton; Abernethy & Russell, 1987 and Williams,

Ward, Knowles, & Smeeton, 2002) and individual situations in team sports (e.g. penalty taking in football, hockey, cricket, and baseball; Fadde, 2006; Mann, Ho, De Souza, Watson, & Taylor, 2007; Ward et al., 2008; Williams & Burwitz, 1993; Williams, Ward, & Chapman, 2003). Early research focused on the ability to memorise patterns of plays with the assumption that higher-level players are able to recall and recognise players' position in structured patterns of play better than lower-level players (Williams & Davids, 1995). Furthermore, researchers used static pictures earlier and only later moved to dynamic plays to measure these memory recall and recognition skills. As technology and innovative research paradigms developed (e.g. eye–tracking, video-based paradigms, performance analysis), measurement and training of decision-making skills (i.e. anticipation, situational assessment, and choosing the best option) were examined. Findings provided insights to the underlying mechanisms (e.g. more efficient gaze behaviours, ability to extract cues from the environment, advanced knowledge base and memory structures) of successful decisions of high-level athletes in sport.

In football specifically, research on the decision-making process during penalties from both the goalkeeper and penalty taker's perspective has been expansive (Lopes, Araújo, Peres, Davids, & Barreiros, 2008; Savelsbergh, Williams, Kamp, & Ward, 2002). Furthermore, research examining the decision-making process of individual players in other set plays (e.g. Helsen & Pauwels, 1993) and developing plays in the open field have increased in the past 30 years (Ward, Ericsson, & Williams, 2013). Researchers in the past decade have also shifted their attention to examining referees' decision-making skills (Schweizer, Plessner, Kahlert, & Brand, 2011) and provided suggestions of possible frameworks to examine coaches' decision-making processes (Cloes, Bavier, & Piéron, 2001; Ford, Coughlan, & Williams, 2009).

## Definitions

Decision making is a process in which players need to effectively attend and interpret environmental cues while integrating information from stored knowledge (i.e. memory) in order to choose an appropriate response, make a decision, and execute an action (Marteniuk, 1976b; Tenenbaum, 2003). Furthermore, decision making is a complex and multidimensional process that involves several systems (i.e. sensory, perceptual, cognitive, motor), and the surrounding environment (see Figure 6.1) (Mayer, 1983; Tenenbaum & Land, 2009).

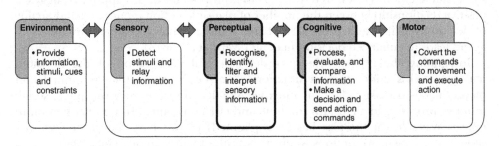

*Figure 6.1* The human performance model with a focus on the decision-making process, including the relevant systems involved and their function.

Sources: Marteniuk, 1976b; Tenenbaum, 2003.

Decision making consists of three important skills: (1) anticipation – the ability to predict what will happen next by integrating information available from the environment with information obtained from past experiences (Poulton, 1957; Tenenbaum, 2003); (2) situational assessment – the ability to generate plausible options and thereafter to prioritise them (Ward, Suss, & Basevitch, 2009); (3) decision making – the ability to choose which action and movement will result in the best outcome, considering various factors and constraints, such as motor skills and other environmental, cognitive, and physiological constraints (Raab, 2003).

## Theories and models

Two main theories that explain the decision-making process from a cognitive perspective have been proposed. The two theories can be viewed as complementing each other and have been examined in a series of studies (see Raab & Johnson, 2007; Ward et al., 2013). The first theory is based on naturalistic decision-making models (e.g. Recognition-Primed Decision (RPD) model, see Klein, 1989), that suggest that 'people can recognize a situation as typical, thereby calling forth typical reactions without having to sift through large sets of alternatives' (Klein, Wolf, Militello, & Zsambok 1995, p. 63). Thus, proponents of this approach claim that experts rely on automatic and serial recognition-based processes and subsequently generate few options when making a decision (Raab, de Oliveira, & Heinen, 2009). Based on RPD, Johnson and Raab (2003) proposed that expert team players use the Take-The-First (TTF) heuristic, in which the first options generated are correspondingly the best options (Raab & Johnson, 2007). The RPD model and TTF heuristic, which assume that anticipation and decision making are based on fast automated recognition-based processes, predict that fewer options are generated as expertise is developed, and that the first option generated is, correspondingly, the best option (Klein et al., 1995; Raab et al., 2009).

However, findings from other studies in various domains such as football (Ward et al., 2013), support a different perspective on the decision-making process. Namely, that experts use detailed representations (i.e. long-term working memory; LTWM) to analyse, evaluate, and assess situations (Ericsson & Kintsch, 1995). Thus, according to the LTWM theory, experts develop the skills to efficiently encode and retrieve information to and from long-term memory (LTM), which enables them to generate situational representations and utilise feed-forward information to achieve successful decisions (Ericsson & Ward, 2007). Proponents of this approach suggest a positive relationship between the number of plausible options generated and quality of decision making, and propose that the ability to analyse a situation and think ahead leads to enhanced decision making (Ward et al., 2013).

Integrating the two theories provides a logical explanation of the decision-making process under various situations. Specifically, when time is limited and players need to make a fast (or unexpected) decision, they rely on quick, serial, intuitive processes to align with the time and task constraints. However, when more time is available (or the play has been planned) players have time to analyse the situation and compare options when making the final decision. Thus, players have the flexibility and skills to adjust their decision-making strategy to the constraints of the situation, leading to efficient and successful processes.

## Measurements

The majority of research examining the decision-making process throughout history made use of the expert–novice paradigm (Fadde, 2006; Vaeyens, Lenoir, Mazyn, Williams, & Philippaerts, 2007). This research design allows differences to be captured between successful and less successful players, which provides explanations about the underlying processes and skills used and needed for consistent superior performance (Ericsson & Ward, 2007).

The presentation of static and dynamic simulations using temporal and spatial occlusion paradigms were applied to compare skill level differences and understand the underlying mechanisms of successful decision making. These methods of study enabled comparison of decision making under conditions varying in temporal and spatial exposure. In the temporal occlusion paradigm, the film is stopped and occluded at varying time periods of a developing play or action, and the participant is asked to predict (e.g. anticipate) the next occurrence. While in the spatial occlusion paradigm, varying parts/sections of the film are masked, and as in the temporal paradigm, the participant's task is to anticipate the opponent's action or the outcome of the developing play (e.g. pass, shot, or dribble) based on the information available. Differences in performance and behavioural characteristics among various temporal and/or occluded conditions are then analysed and examined. These studies consistently support the notion that expert players are not only better in predicting action outcomes, but are able to make successful predictions earlier, while utilising fewer environmental cues than less skilled players (Mann, Ho et al., 2007).

In an attempt to further investigate experts' advanced anticipation skills and decision-making abilities, extensive research was devoted to examine search strategies and gaze behaviours during performance with the use of eye-tracking technology (Williams, Davids, & Williams, 1999). In an example from football, Williams and Davids (1995) used eye-tracking technology to examine the relationship between search strategies and skill level. Experienced and less-experienced players responded by moving to offensive plays shown on a large screen. Results indicated that skilled players were able to change search strategies according to the situation and constraints.

In addition to eye-tracking technology and occlusion paradigms, verbal reports offer a way to examine the thought process of the performer (Ericsson & Simon, 1993). The advantage of this method of data collection is that it provides information regarding the intact process from pre-stimuli presentation (e.g. expectations prior to performance) to post-outcome (e.g. the evaluation of the performance), and as opposed to the eye-tracking and occlusion paradigms, can provide more meaningful insight to the decision-making processes.

For example, analysing data from eye-tracking and occlusion paradigms can shed light on where a player is gazing and the crucial cues needed to anticipate a pass. However, only with the use of verbal reports can it be examined if and how the gaze areas and cues are consciously attended to and used for anticipation and decision making. To date, only a few studies have conducted research with verbal reports whilst exploring the decision-making process (for an example in football see Ward et al., 2013). Findings from these studies provide initial support that verbal report data can provide information (and capture skill-based differences) on how experts use knowledge (e.g. declarative and procedural) to generate action plans, problem representations, and decisions.

## Related research

### Anticipation

Findings from research examining anticipation skills indicated that successful performance was mediated by the ability to predict what will happen next, which itself was mediated by the ability to 'pick up' relevant cues from the environment (Savelsbergh et al., 2002). A mediating factor related to anticipation is the temporal dimension. Successful players can anticipate what will happen next more accurately and earlier, compared to less successful performers (Mann, Williams, Ward, & Janelle, 2007). Thus, an advantage in the amount of time available to process information, make a decision, and perform an action is obtained, which is crucial especially in fast-paced sports where time (and timing) are of utter importance. An example of a relatively early study that examined anticipation skills of football was conducted by Williams and Burwitz (1993). In this particular study, goalkeepers were asked to predict the direction of a penalty shot. Results showed that skilled goalkeepers could anticipate the ball's final location earlier and more accurately than novices. Furthermore, experienced goalkeepers relied on information prior to contact.

### Situational assessment

Situational assessment is defined as the ability to generate and prioritise plausible options. It has been found to be one of the best predictors of expert performance. For example, Ward and Williams (2003) investigated situational assessment skills, among other skills (i.e. anticipation and visual abilities) of football players of different levels (i.e. elite and sub-elite) and different age groups (i.e. U9–U17). Results indicated significant differences between skill level groups and between age groups in the situational assessment measures. Specifically, the elite and more mature players were able to generate relevant options and identify key players better than sub-elite younger players. In accordance with anticipation, the situational assessment skills were the best discriminators between the groups compared to basic visual functions and recall/recognition skills.

### Decision making

Findings from a meta-analysis (Mann, Williams et al., 2007) indicated that decision making significantly differentiated skill level of performers, i.e. skilled performers' decisions were consistently more accurate. In two related studies in football, response accuracy and decision-making time were measured along with other factors (e.g. visual search strategies) to gain a better understanding of the decision-making process (Vaeyens, Lenoir, Mazyn et al., 2007; Vaeyens, Lenoir, Williams, & Philippaerts, 2007).

In the first study, video simulations of developing offensive situations, with variations in the number of offensive and defensive players (e.g. 2 vs 1 and 4 vs 3), were used to examine differences in decision-making skills and search behaviours among various groups (i.e. elite, sub-elite, regional, control). Participants watched videos of developing plays in football on a large screen and were required to either pass the ball to a player on the screen, take a shot, or dribble the ball. Findings indicated that (a) the three football groups (elite, sub-elite, and regional) made faster decisions compared to the non-football group (control) throughout the various scenario conditions, (b) elite and sub-elite players' decision-making time was significantly faster than regional players in all but one condition, and (c) decision-making time increased as a function of the complexity of the situation (e.g. number of players involved, and ratio of offensive to defensive players). Similar findings were found for response accuracy. In addition, findings indicated significant differences in search behaviours; elite players demonstrated different visual search strategies (e.g. fixation location and frequencies) compared to the other players.

In the second study, a similar methodology was applied, however the researchers used a within-task criterion based on the results of a decision-making task to stratify youth players into high and low decision-making groups. Results indicated that the skilled group utilised goal-oriented search strategies, higher fixation frequencies, and longer fixation durations on the player with the ball, as compared with the less-skilled group. Thus, the studies support the notion that decision-making skills are mediated by cue utilisation and anticipation skills.

## Applications

Prevalent in most, if not all, studies in the sport expertise domain, is the conviction that high-skill athletes acquire enhanced perceptual-cognitive skills via practice (Mann, Williams et al., 2007). Furthermore, findings from sport-related studies reveal that expertise is reached through a development process and that deliberate practice is essential to reach expert level performance (Ericsson & Ward, 2007; for football-specific deliberate practice studies see Ford, Ward, Hodges, & Williams, 2009; Ward, Hodges, Starkes, & Williams, 2007).

In the training environment, some of the video-based techniques can be adapted to fit the dynamic and more ecologically valid settings (Shipherd, Basevitch, Filho, & Gershgoren, 2018). For example, training recall of patterns and players can be adapted by using small-sided games. The games can be stopped (e.g. using a whistle) at random points and players need to look down and close their eyes. Then players are asked to point to where certain players are and are marked on how well they were able to recall players' positions. This forces players to look up more and to store patterns of players' positions in efficient ways so that they can retrieve the information quickly and accurately.

## Implications

Although some knowledge has been gained in the area, more research and especially applied research is needed. The next step is to apply the knowledge gained to the field and towards practical applications (Williams & Ward, 2007). There is a positive and encouraging trend towards this next step. Training methods are being developed and empirically tested. Furthermore, there is an increase of interest by coaches and the broader sport community, which consequently has encouraged more research in the area. However, more research is needed to address the many questions that still remain unanswered. For example, in research examining decision-making training using video and film, the angle and perspective of the camera (e.g. player's perspective vs broader perspective), and the skill level of athletes filmed (e.g. same skill level vs higher skill level) must be considered.

Additionally, standardised measurement tools should be developed (Williams & Ward, 2007). It is evident from the vast research in the area, that decision-making skills can be measured and captured. However, just as there are standardised tests that evaluate maths, verbal, physical, and technical skills, there is a need to develop measurement tools that will evaluate decision-making skills, specifically in football. A standardised test that will differentiate between skill levels will benefit coaches, and provide a valuable tool in tracking the development of players.

Furthermore, there is a gap between academia (e.g. researchers and students) and football professionals (e.g. players and coaches) that needs to be addressed. There has been an abundance of research that provides support that these skills can be measured and trained but coaches are not implementing the research findings in training or assessments. Furthermore, some coaches think that decision-making skills are innate and that even if the cognitive skills can be trained, there is a limit to how much a player can improve these skills (Gershgoren et al., 2016).

## Conclusion

The importance of decision-making skills in sports and football specifically, has been established in the past decades indicating that higher-level players have more efficient decision-making processes (e.g. gaze behaviour, anticipation, situational assessment) leading to more successful performance outcomes. Findings indicate that skills such as anticipation and option generation can be measured and initial results show that they can be trained as well. Furthermore, although there is growing awareness within the football community about the importance of the mental aspect of the game, there are still barriers and concerns in integrating sport psychologists in football teams (Pain & Harwood, 2004). However, the psychological skills necessary to achieve success are still under-developed and used compared to other sport science domains (e.g. nutrition, physiology, biomechanics).

## Non-verbal intelligence in football

A related area to decision making is the use of non-verbal intelligence. The decision-making process involves 'game reading' skills which are similar to intelligence skills in other domains (e.g. maths and physics). Footballers in the elite level have often been referred as players with a high game intelligence.

The worldwide influence and daily interest attract ever-increasing attention and intelligent focus into the football (Strudwick, 2016). In addition, football is an international and cross-cultural sport activity, and is a multi-billion-dollar business (Allcorn, 1997; Maças, Claudino, Serodio-Fernandes, & Sampaio, 2007). Moreover, a shift has occurred towards advanced sport science support structures to assist in talent development and player management in professional football clubs (Duncan & Strudwick, 2016). Therefore, it seems very important and a privilege to educate non-verbally intelligent players for most football clubs.

Behaviour can only be as intelligent as the way in which world events are represented in the brain. This is referred to as encoding and it is closely related to perception and attention (Fisher, 1984). Therefore, a player's non-verbal perceptual style is directly responsible for the behaviours exhibited in football, for example: (a) transformation and encoding of environmental stimuli, (b) attention to some stimuli while neglecting others, (c) usage of stimuli to form the internal representation of the external world, (d) symbolisation of events in space and time, and (e) organisation, initiation, and control of movements (Marteniuk, 1976a). In addition, Tenenbaum and Bar-Eli (1995) discussed the intelligence with reference to intellectual capabilities required for successful athletic activity, such as information processing, knowledge, experience, decision making, reaction time, timing, memory and recall, vision, sensorimotor processing, attention, anticipation, cognitive styles, and time and space perception. These all seem to be related to non-verbal intelligence in football.

Fisher (1984) earlier indicated that these assertions point us clearly in the direction of a task demands approach (such as in football). This task demands approach as non-verbal intelligence in football can include many facets; for example, naming and locating features of the environment, searching and detecting task-relevant cues, identifying cue patterns, short- and long-term memory recalls, and decision-making processes seem to be necessary factors related to non-verbal intelligence that footballers face in their environments. Evidence of these facts occurs in many forms in football; for example, when a potential pass receiver attempts to run to control the ball, head the ball, shoot the ball, or pass the ball for another available teammate who has a better position they are demonstrating non-verbal intelligence. In addition, positioning of players in defensive and attacking formats involves non-verbal intelligence. Therefore, it could be put forward that non-verbal intelligence is an interactional construct based on an individual's (a footballer's) non-verbal capacities to handle specific environmental demands (for example, football-specific positions in offence and defence).

Football matches are won by exploiting space. On many occasions this means creating the space to exploit in the first place. Space can be created either by an individual player or a combined play between two or more players (Hughes, 1990). Good football teams use spaces to keep the ball, to advance it, and, ultimately, to score (Mark & Catlin, 1990). In football, two of the most important elements of a successful offence require either skill or tactical sophistication – staying spread out and having a good vision. There is nothing as simple, yet more important, to the success of a football team than good vision. Vision describes the personal habit of constantly scrutinising the football field to get the big picture. Football players should look over the entire field approximately every 5 seconds (Mark & Catlin, 1990). They should note the best place for the ball (usually an area of space) and the location of nearby passing, shooting, and heading opportunities. On defence, players should check the space behind them and plan what to do when they get the ball. Players with vision are distinguished by their apparent ability to perceive events before they happen, and by their ability to influence the play by appropriately redistributing the ball. Therefore, non-verbal problem-solving skills seem important to create and exploit the space and for vision in football. Footballers and teams with poor non-verbal intelligence end up losing opportunities and having problematic team play, physical, technical, tactical, and psychological skills which would be detrimental to development and performance in football.

Similarly, positions, directions, rotations, contiguity, shading, size, length, movement, and figured patterns seem to be vital elements of a successful play in football in relation to the decision-making process and non-verbal intelligence (Konter & Bayansalduz, 2013; Konter & Toros, 2012). These actions in football involve changing the directions, positions, and rotations all the time between defence and offence with the ball and without the ball. All of these seem to be very important for the quality (e.g. taking a good shot at goal or heading) and the quantity (e.g. a number of correct passes and ball stealing) of movements in football to obtain successful results. In addition, combining one player's own skill with the other team players, using appropriate individual, group, and team tactics, and creating the space as an individual, as a group, or as a team, and to the contrary, narrowing the space for the opponents, all involve non-verbal intelligence for successful performance in football. Moreover, a football player who successfully comes out of a crowded and tight-marked area of opponents uses sophisticated non-verbal problem-solving skills.

## Non-verbal intelligence research in football

Limited research in football non-verbal intelligence indicated that practising one-touch play needs players who are creative in reading the game and reacting quickly (Bjurwill, 1993). Konter and Yurdabakan (2010) investigated validity and reliability of the Test of Non-verbal Intelligence-2 (TONI-2: Brown, Shebenou, & Johnsen, 1990) for football in Turkey ($N$=618; 544 males and 74 females). TONI-2 contains 55 multiple choice items arranged in order of difficulty. This is an untimed test which requires 15 minutes to complete. To determine the test, one simply panto-mimes the instructions; no reading, writing, listening, and speaking is involved on the part of the administrator or subject. Non-verbal problem solving is the bases of all the TONI-2 items. Participants (football players) are presented with a set of figures in which one or more figures are missing. The subject then non-verbally answers the items by identifying and pointing the relationship among the figures. Results revealed good validity and reliability results and meaningful differences in relation to age groups in football. Older players have higher TONI-2 scores than the younger ones. In addition, multiple comparisons showed that starters from substitutes, professionals from amateurs, high school players from secondary school players, and central positions from peripheral positions score higher on non-verbal intelligence (Konter, 2009; Konter & Bayansalduz, 2013; Konter & Toros, 2012; Konter & Yurdabakan, 2010). These results could be related to more football experience, age and educational effects, and certain visual demands of specific positions in football. More research is needed for more certain results.

Konter and Toros (2012) researched the non-verbal intelligence of football players in relation to their injury, receiving red and yellow cards as measured by TONI-2 and a personal information form. Data were collected from 310 amateur male football players (age = 14.71 ± 1.38 years, range = 13–17 years) with 5.63 years licensed playing experience ($SD$=4.51). Results indicated that players with higher TONI-2 points have more injuries than players with lower TONI-2 scores. Players with higher non-verbal intelligence might encounter more fouls than others with lower non-verbal intelligence. They might also be more creative problem solvers and conceal their actions better. These could make them more prone to injury as it is difficult for them to be stopped by opponents without close hard tackles and fouls.

Konter and Bayansalduz (2013) investigated the non-verbal intelligence of male football players in relation to their playing positions. Results revealed significant differences ($p < 0.05$) between non-verbal intelligence of football players and their playing positions. Multiple comparisons of mean differences between the TONI-2 scores of football players and their specific playing positions showed that stoppers, full-backs, and centre midfielders have higher TONI-2 points than right and left midfielders and right and left wingers. In addition, centre forward players have higher TONI-2 points than wingers. This result, to some extent, supports the centrality hypothesis except for full-backs in relation to non-verbal intelligence and playing positions in football. It is argued that central positions (such as sweepers or stoppers in football) are more interactive and more task dependent than peripheral positions, and a high proportion of managers and coaches are recruited from players of central positions (Kent, 2006). However, research has been more supportive for the centrality hypothesis regarding racial stereotypes (e.g. blacks are pushed into more non-central positions in football) (Nicholls, McMorris, White, & Carr, 1993; Norris & Jones, 1998). In addition, it is argued that so-called field-independent individuals have excellent vision (in the sense that a good midfielder is said to have good vision). They are the ones who tend to 'ride' the tackles and stay out of trouble. Field-dependent types (for example wingers or peripheral players on the football field) cannot easily focus on relevant visual information (Sanderson, 1996). This result might indicate that players in central positions have higher demands than peripheral positions related to non-verbal problem-solving skills as they are visually attending the wider part and both sides of the football field.

However, positions are affected by the systems of play (e.g. 4–4–2, 3–5–2, 4–3–3, etc.). Each position also has defensive and offensive roles with and without the ball. Each position in football could be of a more defensive or offensive character. Future research could concentrate on more football-specific non-verbal intelligence tests and more sophisticated analyses including personality types, field dependence and independence, defensive and offensive roles, systems of play in relation to non-verbal intelligence, and playing positions in football.

Konter (2009) examined the non-verbal intelligence of male football players in relation to level of play using the adapted version of the TONI-2 which was indicated earlier. Analyses revealed the significant differences between A (U18 and U17 aged group), B (U16 and U15 aged group), and C (U14 and U13 aged group) levels of football players ($p < 0.02$). Results indicated that TONI-2 scores increase with age and level of play. It seems that football itself also develops non-verbal intelligence and it increases with experience and level of football.

Konter and Yurdabakan (2009) investigated the non-verbal intelligence of football players in relation to their age, gender, and level of education ($N=353$, $M_{age}=14.78\pm1.41$, 312 male, 41 female footballers). Data revealed significant differences between age groups, gender, and level of education. Multiple comparisons showed that non-verbal intelligence increases with age from 13 through 17. Results also indicated that female players compared to male players and high school players compared to secondary school players have higher TONI-2 scores in football. Results indicated that not just the age itself but also education and experience play an important role regarding non-verbal intelligence in football. Interestingly, female players have higher scores on the TONI-2 than males. If female players are given more opportunities, special experience, and skill training, they seem to have a great potential regarding non-verbal intelligence in football.

Furthermore, recent neurophysiological studies (Vestberg, Gustafson, Maurex, Ingvar, & Petrovic, 2012) focused on football players' general executive functions including on-line multi-processing such as creativity, response inhibition, and cognitive flexibility. The researchers compared male and female High Division players (HD), Lower Division players (LD), and a standardised norm group. The results showed significantly better scores of executive functions in HD and LD players in comparison to the norm group for both males as well as females. Furthermore, the HD players outperformed the LD players on these tests. In addition, a significant correlation was obtained between the result of the test on executive functioning and measures of performance (e.g. the numbers of goals and assists the players had scored two seasons later). These results seem to be supportive of the non-verbal intelligence research in football.

Slimania et al. (2016) conducted a systematic review and a meta-analysis on the effects of cognitive training strategies on motor and effective psychological skills development in football. They found that cognitive training leads to positive psychological skills development in relation to imagery-cognitive skills and imagery-motivational skills. These skills reduced game-specific stress responses (i.e. decreased muscle tension and increased perceptual abilities) and increased self-confidence. Combining cognitive training strategies (i.e. imagery, goal setting, self-talk, and music) with physical training enhanced positive effects. Psychological skill development was related to improved motor skill performance (Konter, Beckmann, & Mallett, 2019, Chapter 14 in this book).

## Conclusions

Initial research findings highlight the importance of non-verbal intelligence measured by validated TONI-2 and cognitive skills in relation to health (e.g. injury), success (e.g. being starter or substitute, amateur or professional) and performance (e.g. level of play), psychological skills (e.g. imagery, goal-setting, self-talk, relaxation, and increased self-confidence) including various individual variables (e.g. age, gender, education, red and yellow card bookings) in football. Physical educators, managers, coaches, and club administrators look for intelligent players to educate and train them to bring about successful results. Therefore, apart from observations and arbitrary selection procedures, athletes in general and footballers in particular need sound assessment tools related to the different types of decision-making processes including non-verbal intelligence. TONI-2 could be helpful in this regard.

Non-verbal intelligence research in football has generally indicated (Konter, 2009; Konter & Bayansalduz, 2013; Konter & Toros, 2012; Konter & Yurdabakan, 2009, 2010; Slimania et al., 2016; Vestberg et al., 2012) that: (1) comparisons of different age groups from 13 to 17 revealed meaningful differences; the older the football players are the higher their scores on non-verbal intelligence measures. (2) Starters have higher scores than substitute football-players. Coaches spend a lot of time on increasing physical and technical performance of players and asking substitutes to increase these qualities to make the team rather than improving psychological and decision-making processes including non-verbal intelligence. For example, coaches organise special training sessions for the players making passing and shooting mistakes, and having positional problems in defence and offence situations. They simply think that repetition of the skill a number of times would improve the skill instead of specifically focusing on the development of non-verbal intelligence by implementing specific exercises and consulting football psychology experts. (3) Comparisons of amateur and professional players indicated that professional football players have higher scores than the amateur players. Therefore, improving decision-making processes including non-verbal intelligence seems vital to be a professional. (4) Football players that graduated from high school have higher scores than players who graduated from secondary school. It seems that formal education seems to be an important role regarding non-verbal problem-solving skills in football. (5) Results revealed that players in central positions have higher scores than players in peripheral positions. It could be that football players in central positions have higher cognitive demands than players in peripheral positions. They are visually attending the wider part and both sides of the football field. Defending and attacking using central positions are vital as most goals are scored by exploiting the central positions. (6) Interestingly, female players compared to male players have higher TONI-2 scores in football. Female football players should be given more football training opportunities and experiences to achieve their potential of non-verbal intelligence. Limited physical and technical skills and experiences of female football players could prevent them accomplishing their non-verbal intelligence potential. (7) Cognitive training is helpful for the positive psychological skills development of football players. Overall, results indicate the importance of decision-making processes including non-verbal intelligence. Therefore, coaches and managers ought to deal with cognitive factors and be ready to assist their footballers to develop the potential of their sport intelligence (Fisher, 1984). Expert performance by outfield players during primary football activities, competition, or match play involves players successfully executing appropriate perceptual, cognitive, and motor skills, such as decision making and technical actions (Ford, 2016). However, more research is needed in the area to provide further support for the effectiveness of developing these skills.

Future research could concentrate on football-specific factors and items to measure and develop non-verbal intelligence in football. First, items could be organised in offence and defence situations in relation to real playing positions. Second, football games-based activities could be useful for the development of non-verbal problem-solving skills. Third, drill-based activities could be beneficial in which players are active decision makers. Fourth, imagery training would be another opportunity for the development of non-verbal intelligence. Fifth, computer-assisted football simulation training and mental practice could be valuable. Sixth, research could consider the different performance measures (physical, technical, tactical, psychological, social, etc.) related to domain (football) and position-specific (reactive and proactive, central, semi-central, and peripheral) decision-making processes and non-verbal intelligence.

## References

Abernethy, B., & Russell, D. G. (1987). Expert–novice differences in an applied selective attention task. *Journal of Sport Psychology, 9,* 326–345.

Allcorn, E. (1997). Issues management and business arising from the transformation of the football industry. In T. Reilly, J. Bangsbo, & M. Hughes (Eds.), *Science and football III* (pp. 308–313). London, England: E & FN Spon.

Bjurwill, C. (1993). Read and react: The football formula. *Perceptual & Motor Skills, 76*(3), 1383–1386.

Brown, L., Shebenou, R., J., & Johnsen, S. K. (1990). *Test of nonverbal intelligence: A language-free measure of cognitive ability, examiner's manual* (2nd ed.). Austin, TX: Pro-ed.

Cloes, M., Bavier, K., & Piéron, M. (2001). Coaches' thinking process: Analysis of decisions related to tactics during sports games. In M. K. Chin, L. D. Hensley, & Y. K. Liu (Eds.), *Innovation and application of physical education and sports science in the new millennium: An Asia-Pacific perspective* (pp. 329–341). Hong Kong: Hong Kong Institute of Education.

Duncan, C., & Strudwick, T. (2016). National and cultural influences. In T. Strudwick (Ed.), *Soccer science* (pp. 15–35). Champaign, IL: Human Kinetics.

Ericsson, K. A., & Kintsch, W. (1995). Long term working memory. *Psychological Review, 102,* 211–245.

Ericsson, K. A., & Simon, H. A. (1993). *Protocol analysis: Verbal reports as data* (rev. ed.). Cambridge, MA: Bradford Books/MIT Press.

Ericsson, K. A., & Ward, P. (2007). Capturing the naturally-occurring superior performance of experts in the laboratory: Toward a science of expert and exceptional performance. *Current Directions in Psychological Science, 16,* 346–350.

Fadde, P. J. (2006). Interactive video training of perceptual decision making in the sport of baseball. *Technology, Instruction, Cognition, and Learning, 4*(3), 265–285.

Fisher, A. C. (1984). Sport intelligence. In W. F. Straub & J. M. Williams (Eds.), *Cognitive sport psychology* (pp. 42–50). New York, NY: Sport Science Association.

Ford, P. (2016). Skill acquisition and learning through practice and other activities In T. Strudwick (Ed.), *Soccer science* (pp. 75–97). Champaign, IL: Human Kinetics.

Ford, P., Coughlan, E., & Williams, M. (2009). The expert-performance approach as a framework for understanding and enhancing coaching performance, expertise and learning. *International Journal of Sports Science & Coaching, 4*(3), 451–463.

Ford, P., Ward, P., Hodges, N. J., & Williams, A. M. (2009). The role of deliberate practice and play in career progression in sport: The early engagement hypothesis. *High Ability Studies, 20*(1), 65–75.

Gershgoren, L., Basevitch, I., Gershgoren, A., Brill, Y. S., Schinke, R. J., & Tenenbaum, G. (2016). Expertise in soccer teams: A thematic inquiry into the role of Shared Mental Models within team chemistry. *Psychology of Sport and Exercise, 24,* 128–139.

Helsen, W., & Pauwels, J. M. (1993). The relationship between expertise and visual information processing in sport. In J. L. Starkes & F. Allard (Eds.), *Cognitive issues in motor expertise* (pp. 109–134). Amsterdam, The Netherlands: Elsevier.

Hughes, C. (1990). *The winning formula*. London, England: Collins.

Johnson, J. G., & Raab, M. (2003). Take the first: Option-generation and resulting choices. *Organizational Behavior and Human Decision Processes, 91,* 215–229.

Kent, M. (2006). *Oxford dictionary of sports science and medicine*. New York, NY: Oxford University Press.

Klein, G. (1989). Recognition-primed decisions. In W. B. Rouse (Ed.), *Advances in man-machine systems research* (pp. 47–92). Greenwich, CT: JAI Press, Inc.

Klein, G. (1993). A recognition-primed decision making model of rapid decision making. In G. Klein, J. Orasanu, R. Calderwood, & C. Zsambok (Eds.), *Decision making in action: Models and methods* (pp. 138–147). Norwood, NJ: Ablex.

Klein, G., Wolf, S., Militello, L., & Zsambok, C. (1995). Characteristics of skilled option generation in chess. *Organizational Behavior and Human Decision Processes, 62,* 63–69.

Konter, E. (2009). Nonverbal intelligence of football players according to their level of play. *Procedia, Social and Behavioral Sciences,* 1114–1120.

Konter, E., & Bayansalduz, M. (2013). Nonverbal intelligence of football players: Playing positions and lining ups in football. *Energy Education Science and Technology Part B: Social and Educational Studies, 5*(2), 2111–2122.

Konter, E., Beckmann, J., & Mallett, C. (2019). Psychological skills for football players. In E. Konter, J. Beckmann, & T. M. Loughead (Eds.), *Football psychology: From theory to practice*. London, England: Routledge.

Konter, E., & Toros, T. (2012). Nonverbal intelligence of football players according to their injury, received yellow and red cards. *Energy Education Science and Technology Part B: Social and Educational Studies, 4*(4), *1961–1968.*

Konter, E., & Yurdabakan, İ. (2009). Nonverbal intelligence of football players according to their age, gender and educational level. *Procedia, Social and Behavioral Sciences*, 915–921.

Konter, E., & Yurdabakan, İ. (2010). Validity and reliability of the Test of Nonverbal Intelligence-2 (TONI-2) for football players in Turkey. *International Journal of Sport Science and Engineering*, 4(1), 3–14.

Lopes, J. E., Araújo, D., Peres, R., Davids, K., & Barreiros, J. (2008). The dynamics of decision making in penalty kick situations in association football. *The Open Sports Sciences Journal*, 1(1), 24–30.

Luhtanen, P., Belinskij, A., Häyrinen, M., & Vänttinen, T. (2001). A comparative tournament analysis between the EURO 1996 and 2000 in soccer. *International Journal of Performance Analysis in Sport*, 1(1), 74–82.

Maças, V., Claudino, R., Serodio-Fernandes, A., & Sampaio, J. (2007). Sports manager activities in professional and non-professional Portuguese soccer organizations: The VIth World Congress on Science and Football (January). *Antalya: Journal of Sports Science & Medicine*, 6, Supplementum 10.

Mann, D. L., Ho, N. Y., De Souza, N. J., Watson, D. R., & Taylor, S. J. (2007). Is optimal vision required for the successful execution of an interceptive task? *Human Movement Science*, 26, 343–356.

Mann, D., Williams, A. M., Ward, P., & Janelle, C. M. (2007). Perceptual-cognitive expertise in sport: A meta-analysis. *Journal of Sport & Exercise Psychology*, 29, 457–478.

Mark, G., & Catlin, M. D. (1990). *The art of football*. St. Paul, MN: Football Books.

Marteniuk, R. (1976a). Cognitive information processes in motor short-term memory and movement production. In G. E. Stelmach (Ed.), *Motor control: Issues and trends* (pp. 175–199). New York, NY: Academic Press.

Marteniuk, R. (1976b). *Information processing in motor skills*. New York, NY: Holt, Rinehart & Winston.

Mayer, M. (1983). Practice improves adults' sensitivity to diagonals. *Vision Research*, 23, 547–550.

Nicholls, G., McMorris, T., White, A., & Carr, C. (1993). An investigation into the validity of the use of centrality as a criterion for stacking studies in football. In T. Really, J. Clays, & A. Stibble (Eds.), *Science and football II* (pp. 278–284). London, England: E & FN Spon.

Norris, J., & Jones, R. L. (1998). Towards a clearer definition and application of the centrality hypothesis in English professional association football. *Journal of Sport Behavior*, 21(2), 181–195.

Pain, M. A., & Harwood, C. G. (2004). Knowledge and perceptions of sport psychology within English soccer. *Journal of Sports Sciences*, 22(9), 813–826.

Poulton, E. C. (1957). On prediction in skilled movements. *Psychological Bulletin*, 54, 467–478.

Raab, M. (2003). Decision making in sports: Influence of complexity on implicit and explicit learning. *International Journal of Sport and Exercise Psychology*, 1, 310–337.

Raab, M., de Oliveira, R. F., & Heinen, T. (2009). How do people perceive and generate options? *Progress in Brain Research*, 174, 49–59.

Raab, M., & Johnson, J. G. (2007). Expertise-based differences in search and option generation strategies. *Journal of Experimental Psychology: Applied*, 13, 158–170.

Sanderson, F. (1996). Psychology and injury. In T. Reilly (Ed.), *Science and football* (pp. 165–183). London, England: E & FN Spon.

Savelsbergh, G. J., Williams, A. M., Kamp, J. V. D., & Ward, P. (2002). Visual search, anticipation and expertise in soccer goalkeepers. *Journal of Sports Sciences*, 20(3), 279–287.

Schweizer, G., Plessner, H., Kahlert, D., & Brand, R. (2011). A video-based training method for improving soccer referees' intuitive decision making skills. *Journal of Applied Sport Psychology*, 23(4), 429–442.

Shipherd, A. M., Basevitch, I., Filho, E., & Gershgoren, L. (2018). A scientist-practitioner approach to an on-field assessment of mental skills in collegiate soccer student-athletes. *Journal of Sport Psychology in Action*, 1–10.

Slimania, M., Bragazzi, N. L., Tod, D., Dellal, A., Hueg, O., Cheour, F., Taylor, L., & Chamari, K. (2016). Do cognitive training strategies improve motor and positive psychological skills development in soccer players? Insights from a systematic review. *Journal of Sports Science, 34*(24), 2338–2349.

Strudwick, T. (2016). Introduction. In T. Strudwick (Ed.). *Soccer science.* Champaign, IL: Human Kinetics.

Tenenbaum, G. (2003). An integrated approach to decision making. In J. L. Starkes & K. A. Ericsson (Eds.), *Expert performance in sport: Advances in research on sport expertise* (pp. 191–218). Champaign, IL: Human Kinetics.

Tenenbaum, G., & Bar-Eli, M. (1995). Personality and intellectual capabilities in sport psychology. In D. H. Saklofske & M. Zeidner (Eds.), *International handbook of personality and intelligence* (pp. 687–710). New York, NY: Plenum Press.

Tenenbaum, G., & Land, W. (2009). Mental representations as an underlying mechanism for human performance. In M. Raab, J. Johnson, & H. R. Heekeren (Eds.), *Progress in brain research* (pp. 251–266). The Netherlands: Elsevier.

Vaeyens, R., Lenoir, M., Mazyn, L., Williams, M., & Philippaerts, R. (2007). The effects of task constraints on visual search behaviour and decision making skill in youth soccer players. *Journal of Sport and Exercise Psychology, 29*, 147–169.

Vaeyens, R., Lenoir, M., Williams, A., & Philippaerts, R. (2007). Mechanisms underpinning successful decision making in skilled youth soccer players. *Journal of Motor Behavior, 39*, 395–408.

Vestberg, T., Gustafson, R., Maurex, L., Ingvar, M., & Petrovic, P. (2012). Executive functions predict the success of top-soccer players. *PLoS ONE, 7*(4), e34731. doi:10.1371/journal.pone.0034731.

Ward, P., Ericsson, K. A., & Williams, A. M. (2013). Complex perceptual cognitive expertise in a simulated task environment. *Journal of Cognitive Engineering and Decision Making, 7*, 231–254.

Ward, P., Farrow, D., Harris, K. R., Williams, A. M., Eccles, D. W., & Ericsson, K. A. (2008). Training perceptual-cognitive skills: Can sport psychology research inform military decision training? *Military Psychology, 20*, S71–S102.

Ward, P., Hodges, N. J., Starkes, J. L., & Williams, M. A. (2007). The road to excellence: Deliberate practice and the development of expertise. *High Ability Studies, 18*(2), 119–153.

Ward, P., Suss, J., & Basevitch, I. (2009). Expertise and expert performance-based training (ExPerT) in complex domains. *Technology, Instruction, Cognition and Learning, 7*, 121–145.

Ward, P., & Williams, A. M. (2003). Perceptual and cognitive skill development in soccer: The multidimensional nature of expert performance. *Journal of Sport and Exercise Psychology, 25*, 93–111.

Williams, A. M., & Burwitz, L. (1993). Advance cue utilization in soccer. In T. Reilly, J. Clarys, & A. Stibbe (Eds.), *Science and football* (Vol. II, pp. 239–244). London, England: E & FN Spon.

Williams, A. M., & Davids, K. (1995). Declarative knowledge in sport: A by-product of experience or a characteristic of expertise. *Journal of Sport and Exercise Psychology, 7*, 259–275.

Williams, A. M., Davids, K., & Williams, J. G. (1999). *Visual perception and action in sport* (pp. 143–184). London, England: E & FN Spon.

Williams, A. M., & Ward, P. (2007). Perceptual-cognitive expertise in sport: Exploring new horizons. In G. Tenenbaum & R. C. Eklund (Eds.), *Handbook of sport psychology* (pp. 203–223). New York, NY: John Wiley and Sons.

Williams, A. M., Ward, P., & Chapman, C. (2003). Training perceptual skill in field hockey: Is there transfer from the laboratory to the field? *Research Quarterly for Exercise and Sport, 74*, 98–103.

Williams, A. M., Ward, P., Knowles, J., & Smeeton, N. J. (2002). Anticipation skill in a real-world task: Measurement, training, and transfer in tennis. *Journal of Experimental Psychology: Applied, 8*, 259–270.

# Part II
# Coaching essentials in football

# 7 Athlete leadership in football

*Todd M. Loughead, Ashley M. Duguay, and
Matt D. Hoffmann*

**Abstract**

Football players and managers recognize the importance of having strong leadership for team success. Managers believe that strong leadership from their athletes is necessary for teams to function optimally (Bucci, Bloom, Loughead, & Caron, 2012; Gould, Guinan, Greenleaf, & Chung, 2002). This source of leadership is known as athlete leadership and is viewed as an athlete who occupies a formal or informal leadership role within the team and influences team members to achieve a common goal (Loughead, Hardy, & Eys, 2006). This definition highlights two types of leadership roles. The first is a *formal* athlete leadership role, where players are designated to a leadership position by the club (e.g. team captain, vice-captain). The second is an *informal* athlete leadership role where players are perceived by others as being instrumental without being officially appointed by the club as a leader. When leadership on a football team is considered from this perspective, all footballers have the opportunity to engage and provide leadership to their teammates. In fact, research has shown that the responsibility of leading a team does not rest solely on the shoulders of the team captain; rather leadership is shared amongst a group of players. Further research has shown that athlete leadership is related to a host of team dynamic variables including cohesion and collective efficacy. Given these benefits, research has shown the importance of developing athlete leadership and how peer mentoring can be optimally fostered within a team environment.

> Athlete leaders are always needed. Without athlete leaders you cannot have success. But the athlete leaders of today are different from the past. Players like Philipp Lahm, Bastian Schweinsteiger, Miro Klose and Per Mertesacker take responsibility. On the field, but also off the field. Even young players like Manuel Neuer or Sami Khedira want responsibility to be given to them and they are able to see how a team works.
>
> (Joachim Löw, manager of the German national football team, quoted in Lüdeke, 2011)

Within a team environment, both football players and managers recognize the importance of having strong leadership for team success. When we think of leadership in football, some people immediately note the importance of the manager. While this is certainly true, there is another key source of leadership within the team environment: the leadership provided by the football players amongst each other.

Managers believe that strong leadership from athletes is necessary for teams to function optimally (Bucci et al., 2012; Gould et al., 2002). The quote that opens the chapter, from Joachim Löw, the manager of the German men's national football team, highlights this fact and further suggests that leadership is shared amongst several football players on a team. This chapter is divided into four sections. The first section provides an operational definition of athlete leadership. The second section summarizes the athlete leadership research that is pertinent to football. The third section offers some practical implications of athlete leadership and discusses an approach to developing athlete leadership. The fourth section highlights the emerging area of peer athlete mentoring. We conclude the chapter with a summary, highlighting the key aspects of athlete leadership.

## Definition of athlete leadership

Compared to coach leadership, athlete leadership is a relatively new area of research (Loughead, 2017). To foster research in this domain, Loughead et al. (2006) advanced a definition of athlete leadership as an athlete who occupies a formal or informal leadership role within the team and influences team members to achieve a common goal. This definition deliberately highlights two types of leadership roles. The first is a *formal* athlete leadership role, where players are designated to a leadership position by the club (e.g. team captain, vice-captain). The second is an *informal* athlete leadership role where players are perceived by others as being instrumental without being officially appointed by the club as a leader. When leadership on a football team is considered from this perspective, all footballers have the opportunity to engage and provide leadership to their teammates. In other words, athlete leadership can be shared or distributed amongst team members depending on the demands placed upon the team. For instance, athlete leaders can rise to the occasion to deliver leadership and then step back in other moments to allow others to lead. That is, athlete leadership is a shared team process comprised of mutual influence and shared responsibility amongst team members, who lead each other towards the achievement of a common goal.

## Research on athlete leadership

While there is an emerging body of research examining athlete leadership in sport, it is beyond the scope of this chapter to review all of it. Instead, we present research that is of interest to those in football. In particular, this section of the chapter is divided into three parts. In the first part, we present some of the characteristics/ attributes of athlete leaders in football. Second, we provide an overview of the leadership behaviours displayed by these individuals. And third, we briefly highlight the relationships of these leadership behaviours to team dynamics.

As far as the characteristics of athlete leaders go, research has shown that footballers in central positions (e.g. centre-backs, midfielders) are viewed by themselves and their managers, compared to their non-central playing teammates, as having more aptitude in leadership ability (Glenn & Horn, 1993; Lee, Coburn, & Partridge, 1983), and are perceived as being intrinsically motivated and having good morals (Price & Weiss, 2011). Further, Fransen, Vanbeselaere, De Cuyper, Vande Broek, and Boen (2014) sampled coaches and athletes from a variety of sports including football on the distribution of athlete leaders on a team. The results indicated that both formal and informal athlete leaders are key contributors to optimal team functioning. In other words, the responsibility of leading a team does not rest solely on the shoulders of the team captain; rather leadership is shared amongst a group of players. Additional characteristics that have been shown in other sports than football that are also applicable to footballers include being trustworthy (Holmes, McNeil, & Adorna, 2010), possess strong communication skills, lead by example (Bucci et al., 2012; Dupuis, Bloom, & Loughead, 2006), and have a stronger work ethic than teammates (Bucci et al., 2012; Holmes, McNeil, Adorna, & Procaccino, 2008).

Insofar as the athlete leadership behaviours displayed by players are concerned, we present the two most common inventories used to assess a variety of athlete leadership behaviours. The first one, borrowed from the coaching literature, is Chelladurai and Saleh's (1980) Leadership Scale for Sports (LSS), a 40-item questionnaire that measures five different dimensions of leadership behaviours. The five leadership behaviours are Training and Instruction (improve the performance of teammates and instruct them in the skills and tactics of the sport), Democratic Behaviour (include teammates in the decision-making process), Autocratic Behaviour (independence in decision-making), Social Support (engage in satisfying the interpersonal needs of others), and Positive Feedback (praise and encourage teammates for good performance). The second inventory is the Differentiated Transformational Leadership Inventory (DTLI; Callow, Smith, Hardy, Arthur, & Hardy, 2009), which contains 31 items measuring six transformational and one transactional leadership behaviours. The DTLI assesses the transformational leadership dimensions of Individual Consideration (attend to individual teammate's needs and aspirations), Inspirational Motivation (motivate and inspire teammates by stressing goal achievement), Intellectual Stimulation (challenge teammates' assumptions and promote creativity), Fostering Acceptance of Group Goals (promote cooperation and goal setting amongst teammates), High Performance Expectations (expectations for achieving excellence), and Appropriate Role Modeling (set a good example for teammates). The one transactional dimension is Contingent Reward (provide positive reinforcement when teammates perform as expected).

Third, athlete leaders play an important role influencing the team's dynamics. The one team dynamic variable that has been examined in relation to athlete leaders the most in football and in other team sports is cohesion; sometimes commonly known as team chemistry. In brief, cohesion refers to teams sticking together and remaining united in order to achieve their goals and objectives along two major orientations: task and social cohesion (Carron, Brawley, & Widmeyer, 1998). Task cohesion is the similarity, bonding, and closeness around the team's goals and objectives; while social cohesion refers to the similarity, bonding, and closeness around the team as a social unit such as having friends on the team. Taken together, research has shown that there is a positive relationship between using more athlete leadership behaviours and higher perceptions of cohesion. For instance, Vincer and Loughead (2010) in a sample of intercollegiate team sport athletes, including football, found that those athletes who perceived receiving the LSS (Chelladurai & Saleh, 1980) leadership behaviours of Social Support and Positive Feedback from their athlete leaders felt more task cohesion and more socially cohesive with their teammates. Further, Democratic Behaviour was positively associated with task cohesion, while Autocratic Behaviour (as expected) was negatively associated with both task and social cohesion. Similarly, Callow et al. (2009) found that the transformational leadership behaviours, as measured by the DTLI, of Fostering Acceptance of Group Goals and Promoting Team Work, Individual Consideration, and High Performance Expectations were positively associated with task cohesion. The leadership behaviours of Fostering Acceptance of Group Goals and Promoting Team Work were positively related to social cohesion.

Another team dynamic variable associated with athlete leaders in football is collective efficacy. In a sample of adolescent female football players, Price and Weiss (2013) demonstrated that transformational leadership (a composite measure composed of the leadership behaviours of Idealized Influence, Intellectual Stimulation, Inspirational Motivation, Individualized Consideration, and Contingent Reward) was positively associated with collective efficacy. Similarly, in another sample of adolescent female football players, Price and Weiss (2011) found that participants who rated themselves higher in exhibiting leadership behaviours, in turn, rated their team's collective efficacy higher.

## Athlete leadership development

Given the many positive associations between athlete leadership and indicators of effective team functioning (e.g. leadership behaviours, cohesion, collective efficacy), it is vital that those involved in football begin to capitalize on the immense opportunity that this sport offers for players to learn leadership (Gould & Voelker, 2012). The following section provides an overview of athlete leadership development programmes in an effort to provide those involved in football with tangible strategies to proactively employ leadership development efforts with their athletes. As a full review of the leadership programmes is beyond the scope of this chapter, individuals are encouraged to consult these publications to gain a more detailed understanding of the content and methods of delivery.

To our knowledge there are five published articles that have described athlete leadership development programmes. The first two are professional practice articles that detail programmes developed through the Institute for the Study of Youth Sports (ISYS) at Michigan State University. Specifically, Gould and Voelker (2010) outlined a team captain's leadership training programme aimed to help current and future high school team captains learn how to be effective in their leadership role. The content of the programme was delivered through three breakout sessions where athletes explored the responsibilities of being a team captain, how to handle common team problems, and avenues through which they can get their leadership questions answered. To support their learning, athletes also received a self-study captain's workbook.

In the second professional practice article, Blanton, Sturges, and Gould (2014) developed a leadership club for high school athletes designed to encourage participants to take ownership of their learning experiences. Blanton et al. discuss a 2-year programme guided by what the athletes termed the 'four pillars' of leadership: communication, motivation, team cohesion, and positive peer modelling. The culmination of each year focused on a service-learning project chosen by the athletes where they would go out and deliver some type of leadership training (e.g. teach leadership to younger-aged school students).

The next two articles are case studies where athlete leadership development programmes were implemented with elite level athletes. First, Voight (2012) designed a 15-stage (e.g. responsibilities of a leader, follow-ups with captains and coaches) programme that was carried out over the course of a season with two NCAA Division I volleyball teams. The intervention sought to provide leadership development for the leadership group (e.g. team captains), enhance team communication and performance, and assist the leadership group fulfil their daily responsibilities. Second, Cotterill (2017) designed an athlete leadership development programme that targeted three 'levels' of leadership: captaincy development, leadership skill development, and personal growth and leadership development. Participants included 16 male professional cricket players who were identified by their national governing body as being the most talented future players.

Finally, Duguay, Loughead, and Munroe-Chandler (2016) developed and implemented a season-long athlete leadership development programme with two intercollegiate female teams (i.e. basketball and volleyball) that was guided by the theoretical underpinnings of the Multidimensional Model of Leadership (Chelladurai, 1993) and the Full Range Leadership Development (FRLD) process model (Sosik, 2006). Furthermore, in line with shared leadership theory (Pearce, 2004), the programme included all team members and focused on developing leadership capacity at both the individual and team level. Specifically, programme content was delivered through four workshops over the course of the season where participants were given a presentation of leadership principles, a demonstration of the leadership principles, and opportunities to practise the leadership principles. This was accomplished by targeting specific athlete leader behaviours and group dynamics (e.g. cohesion, communication) principles through action learning, reflection exercises, and small group activities. To support their learning, athletes also received a self-study captain's workbook.

Drawing from the programmes described above and in combination with additional literature on athlete leadership, those involved in football should consider the following recommendations to foster athlete leadership development:

- Work with the coaching staff and players to develop a shared understanding of what effective leadership entails. It may be useful to define leadership roles and stress the importance of both formal and informal athlete leader positions. Once this conceptual understanding is established targeting the development of specific skills and behaviours may be more effective (Loughead, Munroe-Chandler, Hoffmann, & Duguay, 2014). Furthermore, allowing the players to partake in this process may help increase their sense of autonomy and acceptance of their leadership responsibilities.
- Deliberately target leadership development with all of your players as each player has the potential to contribute to your team's leadership processes in some capacity throughout the season. A number of scholars have demonstrated the shared nature of athlete leadership (e.g. Fransen et al., 2015; Loughead et al., 2006) and it is likely that many of your players will assume leadership responsibility over the course of a season (e.g. Duguay et al., 2016).
- Deliver leadership development efforts through a number of different learning strategies (e.g. formal education, observation) (Conger, 1992; Gould & Voelker, 2012). Of particular importance is providing players opportunities to lead.

However, coaches must understand that people do not always learn from these experiences (McCall, 2004). Therefore, coaches should facilitate self-reflection and provide feedback. Specifically, incorporating reflection allows players to evaluate the meaning of their experiences through the lens of leadership (Densten & Gray, 2001). This can be done by encouraging players to reflect on the past (retrospective reflection), the future (anticipatory reflection), or in the moment (contemporaneous reflection) (van Manen, 1995). Similarly, providing feedback to players regarding their leadership helps them determine their strengths and weaknesses (Loughead et al., 2014). This information can then be used to guide future personal growth by establishing leadership development goals. Finally, while not a specific component of the leadership development programmes discussed above, mentoring has been suggested in the organizational literature as an important practice in leadership development (Day, 2000). This will be discussed in further detail in the next section.

## Peer athlete mentoring

Thus far in the chapter we have focused on the positives of having strong athlete leadership within teams. An emerging area of research has shown that some athletes also provide another form of leadership to their less experienced peers through individual mentoring relationships (Hoffmann & Loughead, 2016a, 2016b; Hoffmann, Loughead, & Bloom, 2017). Before introducing this body of work, a brief review of the origins of mentoring research from organizational psychology is warranted.

Early research in business indicated that individuals serving as mentors provided instrumental and psycho-social mentoring functions to those they supported (i.e. protégés; Kram, 1980). Instrumental mentoring helped protégés attain their goals and advance in their careers, and comprised of five specific functions including sponsor, coaching, exposure, protect, and challenging assignments. Psycho-social mentoring targeted protégés' personal growth and development within and outside of the organizational setting, and comprised four specific functions including role modelling, acceptance-and-confirmation, counselling, and friendship. An interdisciplinary meta-analysis by Eby et al. (2013) indicated that protégé receipt of instrumental and psycho-social mentoring functions was positively associated to several factors including protégé performance, satisfaction, and sense of affiliation, to name a few. The benefits of being mentored are also evident in the organizational literature comparing protégés to non-mentored individuals. For example, protégés have reported greater organizational commitment (Aryee & Chay, 1994), better organizational socialization (Chao, Walz, & Gardner, 1992), and higher levels of career motivation (Day & Allen, 2004) compared to those who did not have a mentor.

Recent sport research has indicated that mentoring is also relevant within an athlete population (e.g. Benson, Surya, & Eys, 2014; Hoffmann & Loughead, 2016a, 2016b). As such, peer athlete mentoring is defined as:

A dynamic process in which a more experienced and knowledgeable athlete (i.e. mentor) serves as a trusted role model to another athlete (i.e. protégé), assists him/her in their pursuit of goal achievement and advancement in sport, and/or supports his/her personal growth and development. Athletes involved in the process have a nonfamilial and non-romantic relationship.

(Hoffmann et al., 2017, pp. 143–144)

Hoffmann and Loughead (2016a) examined mentored intercollegiate athletes' perceptions of the mentoring functions provided by their best-ever athlete mentor, and how those perceptions related to their personal satisfaction. The results indicated that protégés who received greater levels of psycho-social mentoring also reported greater satisfaction regarding their task performance and contribution to their team. In another study, Hoffmann and Loughead (2016b) explored whether protégés in high quality peer mentoring relationships would report more satisfaction with their athletic experience compared to athletes who were not peer mentored. Indeed, the findings showed that protégés reported higher levels of personal satisfaction, satisfaction with aspects of their team, and satisfaction with facets of their coach's leadership.

Finally, new qualitative research has provided in-depth insight into the experiences of peer mentored athletes competing in elite sport (Hoffmann et al., 2017). The results of interviews with 14 elite athletes (e.g. Olympians) revealed that athlete mentors used specific psycho-social functions that corresponded closely to those advanced by Kram (1980) in organizational psychology (i.e. role modelling, acceptance-and-confirmation, counselling, and friendship). Contrastingly, protégés perceived their mentors used specific instrumental functions that did not correspond with those identified in Kram's research. These new instrumental functions were more relevant to an athlete population and targeted the mental aspect of the protégé's game, their relations with coaches, their task-specific knowledge, and their advancement in their athletic career. Lastly, protégés perceived that their mentoring experiences enhanced their performance and sport confidence, and played a key role in their willingness to serve as peer mentors to other athletes in the future.

Much remains to be learned about peer athlete mentoring relationships. Nonetheless, the research to date suggests these supportive relationships are quite beneficial to protégés. How then do we go about promoting and facilitating mentoring relationships between football players? Beyond recruiting experienced players with the hope they will automatically serve as peer mentors, managers might consider some proactive strategies to encourage closer relations between particular players.

Traditionally, mentoring relationships in sport and organizational contexts develop in one of two ways: informally or formally. Informal relationships develop naturally and without team/organizational assistance; whereas formal relationships occur because individuals are assigned to one another by their team/organization (Ragins, Cotton, & Miller, 2000). Thus, one approach managers could use is to formally assign veteran players to newcomers. For instance, an experienced midfielder could be paired with a rookie midfielder at the beginning of a season. However, evidence from organizational settings indicates that informally mentored individuals often receive greater levels of mentoring functions than those in formal mentoring relationships (e.g. Allen, Day, & Lentz, 2005; Ragins & Cotton, 1999). Unfortunately, while informal relationships may be more beneficial to protégés, they are clearly heavily dependent on luck. However, it has been suggested that well-designed team building activities might serve as prime opportunities for more and less experienced teammates to interact in an informal, natural way (Hoffmann & Loughead,

2016b). That is, activities that require veteran and younger athletes to communicate and work together in dyads or small groups could conceivably lead to the development of mentoring relationships in an organic fashion. Finally, a hybrid approach known as *facilitated mentoring* is a strategy that enables the matching of mentors and protégés within a planned mentoring system (Marshall, 2001). This system includes features such as formal training for individuals in the programme, yet also includes the flexibility of a no-fault termination clause (Marshall, 2001). Managers and their clubs might consider instituting a similar programme with their players.

In sum, we hope football managers will explore some of these suggestions to further enhance the overall leadership within their teams. However, we caution that, to our knowledge, the effectiveness and/or feasibility of these mentoring approaches have yet to be empirically tested with athletes. Future research should aim to examine the plausibility of these mentoring approaches in sport.

## Conclusion

In brief, athlete leadership has a relatively short history compared to sport coaching but nonetheless the research emphasizes the importance of this construct to effective team functioning. The goal of this chapter was to introduce to those interested in football the research conducted in the area of athlete leadership by highlighting the characteristics, leadership behaviours, and the relationship of athlete leadership to team dynamics. Given the benefits of having strong athlete leadership, we provided some suggestions of how those involved in football could enhance athlete leadership within their teams through the use of developmental programmes and peer mentoring.

## References

Allen, T. D., Day, R., & Lentz, E. (2005). The role of interpersonal comfort in mentoring relationships. *Journal of Career Development, 31,* 155–169. doi:10.1007/s10871-004-2224-3.

Aryee, S., & Chay, Y. W. (1994). An examination of the impact of career-oriented mentoring on work commitment attitudes and career satisfaction among professional and managerial employees. *British Journal of Management, 5,* 241–249. doi:10.1111/j.1467-8551.1994.tb00076.x.

Benson, A. J., Surya, M., & Eys, M. A. (2014). The nature and transmission of roles in sport teams. *Sport, Exercise, and Performance Psychology, 3,* 228–240. doi:10.1037/spy0000016.

Blanton, J. E., Sturges, A. J., & Gould, D. (2014). Lessons learned from a leadership development club for high school athletes. *Journal of Sport Psychology in Action, 5,* 1–13. doi:10.1080/21520704.2013.848827.

Bucci, J., Bloom, G. A., Loughead, T. M., & Caron, J. G. (2012). Ice hockey coaches' perceptions of athlete leadership. *Journal of Applied Sport Psychology, 24,* 243–259. doi:10.1080/1041 3200.2011.636416.

Callow, N., Smith, M., Hardy, L., Arthur, C. A., & Hardy, J. (2009). Measurement of transformational leadership and its relationship with team cohesion and performance level. *Journal of Applied Sport Psychology, 21,* 395–412. doi:10.1080/10413200903204754.

Carron, A. V., Brawley, L. R., & Widmeyer, W. N. (1998). The measurement of cohesiveness in groups. In J. L. Duda (Ed.), *Advancements in in sport and exercise psychology measurement* (pp. 213–226). Morgantown, WV: Fitness Information Technology.

Chao, G. T., Walz, P. M., & Gardner, P. D. (1992). Formal and informal mentorships: A comparison on mentoring functions and contrast with nonmentored counterparts. *Personnel Psychology, 45,* 619–636. doi:10.1111/j.1744-6570.1992.tb00863.x.

Chelladurai, P. (1993). Leadership. In R. N. Singer, M. Murphy, & L. K. Tennant (Eds.), *Handbook of research on sport psychology* (pp. 647–671). New York, NY: Macmillan.

Chelladurai, P., & Saleh, S. D. (1980). Dimensions of leader behavior in sports: Development of a leadership scale. *Journal of Sport Psychology, 2*, 34–45.

Conger, J. A. (1992). *Learning to lead.* San Francisco, CA: Jossey-Bass.

Cotterill, S. (2017). Developing leadership skills in sport: A case study of elite cricketers. *Case Studies in Sport and Exercise Psychology, 1*, 16–25. doi:10.1123/cssep.2016-0004.

Day, D. V. (2000). Leadership development: A review in context. *The Leadership Quarterly, 11*, 581–613.

Day, R., & Allen, T. D. (2004). The relationship between career motivation and self-efficacy with protégé career success. *Journal of Vocational Behavior, 64*, 72–91. doi:10.1016/S0001-8791(03)00036-8.

Densten, I. L., & Gray, J. H. (2001). Leadership development and reflection: What is the connection? *International Journal of Education Management, 15*, 119–124.

Duguay, A. M., Loughead, T. M., & Munroe-Chandler, K. J. (2016). The development, implementation, and evaluation of an athlete leadership development program with female varsity athletes. *The Sport Psychologist, 30*, 154–166. doi:10.1123/tsp.2015-0050.

Dupuis, M., Bloom, G. A., & Loughead, T. M. (2006). Team captains' perceptions of athlete leadership. *Journal of Sport Behavior, 29*, 60–78.

Eby, L. T., Allen, T. D., Hoffman, B. J., Baranik, L. E., Sauer, J. B., Baldwin, S., Morrison, M. A., Kinkade, K. M., Maher, C. P., Curtis, S., & Evans, S. C. (2013). An interdisciplinary meta-analysis of the potential antecedents, correlates, and consequences of protégé perceptions of mentoring. *Psychological Bulletin, 139*, 441–476. doi:10.1037/a0029279.

Fransen, K., Vanbeselaere, N., De Cuyper, B., Vande Broek, G., & Boen, F. (2014). The myth of the team captain as principal leader: Extending the athlete leadership classification within sport teams. *Journal of Sports Sciences, 32*, 1389–1397. doi:10.1080/02640414.2014.891291.

Fransen, K., Van Puyenbroeck, S., Loughead, T. M., Vanbeselaere, N., De Cuyper, B, Vande Broek, G., & Boen, F. (2015). Who takes the lead? Social network analysis as a pioneering tool to investigate shared leadership within sports teams. *Social Networks, 43*, 28–38. doi:10.1016/j.socnet.2015.04.003.

Glenn, S. D., & Horn, T. S. (1993). Psychological and personal predictors of leadership behavior in female soccer athletes. *Journal of Applied Sport Psychology, 5*, 17–34. doi:10.1080/10413209308411302.

Gould, D., Guinan, D., Greenleaf, C., & Chung, Y. (2002). A survey of U.S. Olympic Coaches: Variables perceived to have influenced athlete performances and coach effectiveness. *The Sport Psychologist, 16*, 229–250.

Gould, D., & Voelker, D. K. (2010). Youth sport leadership development: Leveraging the sports captaincy experience. *Journal of Sport Psychology in Action, 1*, 1–14. doi:10.1080/21520704.2010.497695.

Gould, D., & Voelker, D. K. (2012). Enhancing youth leadership through sport and physical education. *Journal of Physical Education, Recreation, & Dance, 83*, 38–41. doi:10.1080/07303084.2012.10598828.

Hoffmann, M. D., & Loughead, T. M. (2016a). Investigating athlete mentoring functions and their association with leadership behaviours and protégé satisfaction. *International Journal of Sport and Exercise Psychology, 14*, 85–102. doi:10.1080/1612197X.2014.999348.

Hoffmann, M. D., & Loughead, T. M. (2016b). A comparison of well-peer mentored and non-peer mentored athletes' perceptions of satisfaction. *Journal of Sports Sciences, 34*, 450–458. doi:10.1080/02640414.2015.1057517.

Hoffmann, M. D., Loughead, T. M., & Bloom, G. A. (2017). Examining the experiences of peer mentored athletes competing in elite sport. *The Sport Psychologist, 31*, 134–146. doi:10.1123/tsp.2016-0052.

Holmes, R. M., McNeil, M., & Adorna, P. (2010). Student athletes' perceptions of formal and informal team leaders. *Journal of Sport Behavior, 33*, 442–465.

Holmes, R. M., McNeil, M., Adorna, P., & Procaccino, J. K. (2008). Collegiate student athletes' preferences and perceptions regarding peer relationships. *Journal of Sport Behavior, 31*, 338–351.

Kram, K. E. (1980). *Mentoring processes at work: Developmental relationships in managerial careers* (Unpublished doctoral dissertation). Yale University, New Haven, CT.

Lee, M. J., Coburn, T., & Partridge, R. (1983). The influence of team structure in determining leadership function in association football. *Journal of Sport Behavior, 6*, 59–66.

Loughead, T. M. (2017). Athlete leadership: A review of the theoretical, measurement, and empirical literature. *Current Opinion in Psychology, 16*, 58–61.

Loughead, T. M., Hardy, J., & Eys, M. A. (2006). The nature of athlete leadership. *Journal of Sport Behavior, 29*, 142–158.

Loughead, T. M., Munroe-Chandler, K. J., Hoffmann, M. D., & Duguay, A. M. (2014). Athlete leadership in sport. In M. R. Beauchamp & M. A. Eys (Eds.), *Group dynamics in exercise and sport psychology* (2nd ed., pp. 110–127). London, England: Routledge.

Lüdeke, S. (2011). Löw: Team spirit is above everything for me. Retrieved from www.dfb.de/news/detail/loew-der-teamgedanke-steht-fuer-mich-ueber-allem-30715/.

Marshall, D. (2001). Mentoring as a developmental tool for women coaches. *Canadian Journal for Women in Coaching, 2*(2), 1–10.

McCall, M. W., Jr (2004). Leadership development through experience. *Academy of Management Executive, 18*, 127–130. doi:10.5465/ame.2004.14776183.

Pearce, C. L. (2004). The future of leadership: Combining vertical and shared leadership to transform knowledge work. *Academy of Management Executive, 18*, 47–57. doi:10.5465/AME.2004.12690298.

Price, M. S., & Weiss, M. R. (2011). Peer leadership in sport: Relationships among personal characteristics, leader behaviors, and team outcomes. *Journal of Applied Sport Psychology, 23*, 49–64. doi:10.1080/10412100.2010.520300.

Price, M. S., & Weiss, M. R. (2013). Relationships among coach leadership, peer leadership, and adolescent athletes' psychosocial and team outcomes: A test of transformational leadership theory. *Journal of Applied Sport Psychology, 25*, 265–279. doi:10.1080/10413200.2012.725703.

Ragins, B. R., & Cotton, J. L. (1999). Mentor functions and outcomes: A comparison of men and women in formal and informal mentoring relationships. *Journal of Applied Psychology, 84*, 529–550. doi:10.1037/0021-9010.84.4.529.

Ragins, B. R., Cotton, J. L., & Miller, J. S. (2000). Marginal mentoring: The effects of type of mentor, quality of relationship, and program design on work and career attitudes. *Academy of Management Journal, 43*, 1177–1194. doi:10.2307/1556344.

Sosik, J. J. (2006). Full range leadership: Model, research, extension and training. In C. Cooper & R. Burke (Eds.), *Inspiring leadership* (pp. 33–36). New York, NY: Routledge.

van Manen, M. (1995). On the epistemology of reflective practice. *Teachers and Teaching: Theory and Practice, 1*, 33–50.

Vincer, D. J. E., & Loughead, T. M. (2010). The relationship between athlete leadership behaviors and cohesion in team sports. *The Sport Psychologist, 24*, 448–467.

Voight, M. (2012). A leadership development intervention program: A case study with two elite teams. *The Sport Psychologist, 26*, 604–623. doi:10.1123/tsp.26.4.60.

# 8 Effective coaching in football

*Christine Nash and Clifford J. Mallett*

**Abstract**

Coaches are held totally responsible and accountable for performance outcomes in football. Although this high degree of accountability might seem appropriate to the media and public at large, the reality of understanding effective coaching is more muddied. Effective coaching is complex and multifaceted and occurs within a chaotic, unpredictable, and often uncontrollable environment; that is, it is characterised by an incongruency between intended performance goals and actual results (Jones & Wallace, 2005). The emphasis on winning and the context of football coaching contribute to problematising effective coaching. Therefore, in this chapter, we highlight the problematic nature of judging coaching effectiveness; for example, the varying criteria for assessing coaching effectiveness. Furthermore, we considered the definition of coaching effectiveness in terms of athletes' outcomes, coaches' knowledge, and the saliency of context (Côté & Gilbert, 2009). Coaches have obligations to help players flourish through football and contribute to both professional and personal development. These developmental outcomes are contingent upon the quality of the coaching experience. The discussion on the complexity of coaches' work, the differing tasks and roles of a football coach, will hopefully invite coaches to question and reflect on their current practices, and consider the nature of their impact on players, and what is the evidence of that impact. Finally, effective football coaches should strive to be lifelong learners to provide football players with quality sporting experiences.

Coaches are considered central actors in the coach-athlete-performance relationship (Mallett, 2010; Mallett & Lara-Bercial, 2016). When teams win, coaches are celebrated for their success. In contrast, when teams are losing coaches are typically held totally responsible. A good example of this taken-for-granted role of the head coach is the rise and fall of Claudio Ranieri over a 2-year period. He was the former manager (coach) of Leicester City (English Premier League winners in 2015–2016) and subsequently won *The Best FIFA Men's Coach Award* for 2015–2016 and *BBC Sports Personality of the Year Coach Award* for 2016. On the basis of these public acknowledgements it is reasonable to assume that he is an effective football coach. However, within 12 months he was sacked due to the poor results (losses and subsequent high risk of relegation) of Leicester City. This example, which is not uncommon in football, supports the notion that coaches are held totally responsible for the success of the football team. Nevertheless, it raises some interesting questions, including:

What is the contribution of a coach to a football team? How do we know if a coach has contributed in positive ways to the team performance? What criteria might we use to consider that question? What data (evidence) might be used to assist with a valid and reliable assessment? These are important questions to ponder in thinking about effective coaching in football.

Whilst winning is almost universally considered the single most important criterion for defining success in coaching, Bowes and Jones (2006) highlight the view that coaches are working near or on 'the edge of chaos' (p. 235). For example, as much as coaches attempt to control all factors that underpin successful performance, they have limited influence on some aspects of coaching work in elite sporting contexts (e.g. players' personal issues, injury, illness; Mallett & Côté, 2006). Nonetheless, high-performance (football) coaches are held accountable for producing successful (winning) outcomes (Gillham, Burton, & Gillham, 2013; Kristiansen & Roberts, 2010; Mallett, 2010; Mallett & Côté, 2006) amidst this pathos, chaos, and complexity (Bowes & Jones, 2006; Jones & Wallace, 2005). This over-emphasis on win-loss records (Mallett & Côté, 2006) marginalises the pathos, dynamism, and complexity of coaching in elite football (Bowes & Jones, 2006; Jones & Wallace, 2005) and the ongoing challenges (and opportunities) of working with others in a highly contested setting and context (Mallett, 2007; Rynne & Mallett, 2012) in which there is increasing international investment and competition (Mallett & Lara-Bercial, 2016). To represent high-performance (football) coaching as a series of observable behaviours and knowable processes ignores the complexity of coaches' work and the interplay between personal agency and social context. Any scrutiny of the effectiveness of coaches should consider the many interdependent relationships including (a) nature of coaching tasks; (b) coaches' interpersonal relationships; and (c) the specific coaching setting and broader context (Mallett, 2007; Mallett, Rossi, Rynne, & Tinning, 2016; Rynne & Mallett, 2012).

Coaches are performers in their own right (Mallett & Lara-Bercial, 2016) but making valid judgements about their performance is problematic. Moreover, there is considerable debate around a consensual definition of effectiveness in sport coaching; therefore, in this chapter we will examine some of the scholarly discussions surrounding the notion of effective football coaching. This chapter will highlight key aspects of effectiveness across the performance pathway, from introduction to football to the professional competitive environment. It will also examine the role of coach education and development in facilitating effective coaching behaviours.

## What can we learn from some of the world's most successful coaches?

In a recent international study, Mallett and Lara-Bercial examined the personality, practices, and development of 17 of the world's most successful coaches, known as Serial Winning Coaches (SWC; Lara-Bercial & Mallett, 2016; Mallett & Coulter, 2016; Mallett & Lara-Bercial, 2016). In the recruitment of these participants, coaches who were consistently successful over many years in winning professional league titles or Olympic gold medals (collectively more than 140 medals/titles) were targeted. The participant sample also included gold medal winning athletes ($N=19$) they coached in the past 5 years. These coaches were reported as seeing the 'big picture'; they were optimistic, diligent, emotionally stable, and marginally more extroverted performers, who were visionaries and strategic in delivering on those clearly articulated visions. They were also able to create a strong social identity (Haslam, Reicher, & Platow, 2011) for their team by developing confidence in each other and a sense of 'we' through empathy and collaboration; in other words, they were able to harness the relational power of players and support personnel. The athletes reported that, in comparison to other coaches, these SWC were highly competent in the soft skills (i.e. interpersonal skills such as empathy and intrapersonal skills such as self-awareness). An overarching principle that fuelled the actions of these highly successful coaches was the concept of *driven benevolence* (Lara-Bercial & Mallett, 2016). The SWC were highly driven to pursue excellence, which was underpinned by a coherent and grounded personal philosophy. Central to this philosophy was an 'enduring and balanced desire to considerately support' oneself and others' (Lara-Bercial & Mallett, 2016, p. 123). Indeed, in addition to consistently showing benevolence towards athletes and support staff, a unique finding was the compassion coaches felt towards themselves, which buffered them from the stressors associated with high-performance coaching. Consequently, they created a functional and adaptive work environment that was consistently high performing and innovative.

## Coaching effectiveness?

The notion of effective coaching can be considered from different perspectives that are often contradictory. For example, Arnott and Sparrow (2004) highlighted selection criteria for determining effectiveness or choosing an effective coach, that included previous coaching experience, record of achievements, professional standards, personal style, organisational/cultural fit, systematic approach, costs, knowledge of organisational issues, evidence of ongoing professional development, management experience, experience of the industry, and finally coaching qualifications. From another perspective, the visual and written media and film often tend to portray the coach as something less than effective: 'the coach could be described as either the hapless, comedic character, a figure to be made fun of or the stereotypical coach/instructor who spend his time shouting instructions from the sidelines to 'motivate' his team' (Jolly & Lyle, 2016, p. 43). While these views presented within the media should not be accepted as authentic it does portray a putative view of the sports coach, which undoubtedly demeans the emerging profession of coaching.

Based on a review of literature, Côté and Gilbert (2009) proposed the following integrative definition of coaching effectiveness: 'The consistent application of integrated professional, interpersonal, and intrapersonal knowledge to improve athletes' competence, confidence, connection, and character in specific coaching contexts' (p. 316). According to Côté and Gilbert, any definition of coaching effectiveness should include three essential and foundational components:

1   Athletes' outcomes (e.g. competence, confidence, connection, and character; impact of coaching);
2   Coach's knowledge (e.g. integrated professional, interpersonal, and intrapersonal; coach as learner); and
3   Coaching contexts (e.g. participation, performance; what is coaches' work?).

First, effective coaches should support their players' competence, confidence, connection, and character (4Cs) as key development outcomes. These four Cs are based on the positive youth development (PYD) movement (Larson, 2000) and the work of Lerner and colleagues (2005). Fraser-Thomas and Côté (2009) applied Lerner et al.'s framework to sport. Specifically, Fraser-Thomas and Côté proposed that the focus of sport programmes should be on explicit outcomes that seek to develop positive assets, enhance performance, and foster continued participation in youth sport to thrive through life's experiences. Hamilton, Hamilton, and Pittman (2004) reported the importance of fostering people's strengths to promote adaptive development in youth:

> [it] enables individuals to lead a healthy, satisfying, and productive life as youth, and later as adults, because they gain the competence to earn a living, to engage in civic activities, to nurture others, and to participate in social relations and cultural activities.
>
> (p. 4)

To foster the development of these outcomes (competence, confidence, connectedness, character) from participation in football requires coaches to possess sufficient knowledge. Côté and Gilbert (2009) suggest that coaches' knowledge should be based in three key areas, namely, professional, interpersonal, and intrapersonal. Professional or sport specific knowledge includes knowing the sport (rules, technical, tactical, equipment) and sport science (e.g. development, medicine, recovery). Interpersonal knowledge is important to foster quality player relationships with other actors in the sporting context as well as a knowledge and understanding of sport pedagogy. Intrapersonal knowledge relates to a coach's philosophy, leadership, and importantly ongoing learning and reflection.

Effective coaches not only translate their knowledge to facilitate explicit player outcomes but do so in specific coaching contexts that reflect differences in the roles of coaches (i.e. coaches' work) and player motivations and aspirations, and ability levels. The saliency of the context is central to any consideration of coaching effectiveness. Côté and colleagues (e.g. Côté & Erickson, 2016; Côté, Lidor, & Hackfort, 2009; Côté & Vierimaa, 2014) developed the Developmental Model of Sport Participation with two key pathways for players – participation and performance. In the participation pathway, coaches work with children, adolescents, and/or adults. In the performance pathway, coaches' work is focused on different levels of ability – emerging, performance, and elite players. Furthermore, we might consider that within these contexts there are myriad coaching roles, such as, assistant, coach, senior coach, and head/master coach/manager (International Council for Coaching Excellence (ICCE), 2013). Mallett and Rynne (2015) highlighted that coaches, who are the architects of the sport setting (Mallett, 2005; Nash & Sproule, 2011), should be mindful of the specific needs, motives, and challenges of sport participants across development and for different pathways (participation and performance) to guide the quality of their practice.

What else can we learn from research on successful coaches, cognisant that success is a proxy criterion for coaching effectiveness? Some research studies have presented the developmental trajectories of successful coaches (e.g. Lara-Bercial & Mallett, 2016; Mallett & Côté, 2006; Mallett, Rynne & Billett, 2016; Nash & Sproule,

2009; Rynne, 2014; Rynne & Mallett, 2012; Werthner & Trudel, 2006), motivations (e.g. McLean & Mallett, 2012), perceived needs (e.g. Allen & Shaw, 2009), interactions with others on the coaching/support team (e.g. Nash & Martindale, 2013) and confidantes (e.g. Occhino, Mallett, & Rynne, 2013), their personal qualities and skills, and strategies for coping (e.g. Becker, 2009; Nash & Sproule, 2009; Norman & French, 2013; Olusoga, Maynard, Hays, & Butt, 2012). Studies investigating athletes' perceptions of their coaches' practices have also been conducted (e.g. Purdy & Jones, 2011). This extant literature has revealed some consistent findings (e.g. typically played the sport they coached; hardworking; learn mostly through coaching experience; influenced by more knowledgeable others; influence of sporting experiences to how they coach; short period in transition to elite coaching). However, many studies only consider coaches' perceptions and often through retrospective recall. Other means of data collection, such as observation (Nash & Sproule, 2012) would complement these retrospective studies. Nevertheless, there is limited research examining coaching effectiveness beyond the proxy criterion of coaching success.

In the preceding pages, we have highlighted the problematic nature of judging coaching effectiveness; for example, the varying criteria for assessing coaching effectiveness. Furthermore, we considered the definition of coaching effectiveness in terms of athletes' outcomes, coaches' knowledge, and the saliency of context (Côté & Gilbert, 2009). We now examine what we know and do not know about effective football coaching.

## What is effective football coaching?

In the recruitment of football coaches, there is still an expectation that an effective coach will have been an ex-player who has played the game at the highest level and therefore knows from playing experience how to coach successfully and therefore effectively (Gilbert, Côté, & Mallett, 2006; Rynne, 2014; Trudel & Gilbert, 2006). However, many coaches are appointed without adequate training (Mallett, Rossi et al., 2016).

Research has shown that coach reputation can influence behaviours such as athletes' attention to coach instruction, effort, and persistence in football (Manley, Greenlees, Smith, Batten, & Birch, 2014). Making the transition between player and coach can be a difficult task, which may explain why there are few player-coaches in the professional game of football. Research into the qualities of skilled coaches suggested key differences to those of skilled athletes, examining the perceptual-cognitive abilities of football coaches and players. Findings suggested that with lower levels of information processing, such as the more perceptual tasks, players outperform coaches, while tasks with higher demands on information processing, like strategising or decision making, are more specifically related to coaching skill and therefore the coaches are better than players (Gründel, Schorer, Strauss, & Baker, 2013).

However, there are some ex-players who have become effective coaches but until there is a universally accepted definition of effectiveness within football coaching there will always be debate and discussion around these issues. There are a number of questions that need to be considered around effectiveness in football coaching and there have been attempts using match statistics to identify some key success factors within World Cup campaigns. The performances in three World Cups

(Korea/Japan; Germany; South Africa) were examined with the aim of identifying what made the difference between winning, drawing, and losing teams. Variables were categorised as offensive (goals scored, total shots, shots on target, shots off target, ball possession) and defensive (total shots received, shots on target received, shots off target received, off-sides received, fouls committed, corners against) with the key variables identified as ball possession and the effectiveness of their attacking play (Castellano, Casamichana, & Lago, 2012).

These elements may lead to successful national football teams; however, as mentioned previously in this chapter, effective coaching in football is more complicated than identifying these indicators of success. Effective coaching behaviours are those that result in not only successful team and individual performances but also other positive players' outcomes. These differentiations are important as the effects could impact on the short- and long-term performance of both coach and athlete, and may also determine the quality of the ensuing coach-athlete-performance relationship, central to effective coaching. If football coaches are committed to becoming effective, then the following questions may provide some useful information that coaches can take and apply to their own particular circumstances mentioned earlier, i.e. athletes' outcomes, coach's knowledge, and coaching contexts.

## What is football coaches' work?

Within football there are a number of roles that could essentially involve the same, or similar job. What is the difference between a football manager and a football coach? In some cases, they are very similar but in others they could be markedly different. There are similar semantic and practical differences between assistant coaches, assistant managers, age-group coaches, junior coaches, and player coaches. Some of these positions require a certain level of coach qualification and accreditation; however, in some instances few formal requirements are necessary. This adds to the complexity of the football coaching role and in turn the definition of an effective football coach.

## How do coaches learn their craft? What is the coaching environment?

Football coaches develop their coaching craft using a variety of strategies but key to this development are a supportive club environment, critical thinking skills, and a personal desire to develop their knowledge base in a range of areas (Nash Sproule, & Horton, 2011). Using a social learning theory framework, Occhino et al. (2013) highlighted that high performance football coaches in Australia reported that they learned their craft most through other valued and respected coaches – this was unsurprising; however, a key finding was that who these significant others (confidantes) were changed over time. The primary reason for changing personnel over time was the ongoing development of the coach and the need to seek others who were more knowledgeable in assisting coaches with specific coach-player-performance issues. Hence the authors termed these ever-changing relationships Dynamic Social Networks (DSN) to describe the nature of these interactions.

In another study of Australian coaches, Mallett, Rynne, and Billett (2016) found that these developing high-performance coaches valued an increasing number of sources (e.g. others, study, coaching experience, consultants) to progress their craft over the course of their careers to date as access and self-awareness increased – the importance of multiple sources for learning was underscored. Furthermore, they valued discussions with others and working with consultants to stimulate reflective practices as they progressed in their careers. What was valued at different stages of their coaching careers shifted from what (content) to more about the how and why highlighting the temporal variance in coaching sources. Indeed, beyond access to learning opportunities per se it is important to note the differential engagement of different learning experiences throughout the coaching pathway. It should be noted that in this study, the coaches did not report what they thought was the ideal or preferred way to develop their craft but rather an evaluation of what they had access to. Finally, there was a move away from a reliance on proximal learning sources (e.g. experienced other) for the mentor (experienced) coaches but a shift towards these experienced others for the developing coaches.

Players also learn better in a challenging environment, feeling that a specific activity promotes learning and is developmentally appropriate. So how can effective football coaches influence the practice setting to achieve these objectives? A Finnish football club had success using the Sport Education model to make the environment more player-friendly (Romar, Sarén, & Hastie, 2016). According to Siedentop (1994) the Sport Education model, although primarily developed for physical education, shifts the responsibility to the players and they fulfil a variety of roles, including instructing or coaching their peers.

Sports coaches play a critical role in activating coaching programmes on a daily basis and also the training environment, often known as the motivational climate, within the coaching setting, which can be the athlete's perception of the social environment as created by the coach (MacDonald, Côté, & Deakin, 2010). This motivational climate has a significant influence on participants' motivation, the quality of their involvement, their emotional responses, and the likelihood of their continued participation in or 'drop out' from sport (Duda & Balaguer, 2007). By planning practice sessions, recognising effort and improvement, assessing performance, sharing authority, and ultimately shaping the sport setting, effective coaches create a mastery motivational climate that can have an important and adaptive impact on players' motivation and learning (Morgan & Hassan, 2014). Previous research has identified the positive influences of a mastery climate on participants' motivational responses (e.g. Morgan, Kingston, & Sproule, 2005).

## Are the activities organised?

Many coaching courses emphasise the importance of planning and within the UK the mnemonic, *Plan, Do, Review,* can be repeated as a mantra for coaches. However, this approach can have limitations as well as some benefits for both players and coaches. For example, research findings have consistently shown that the capacity to plan coaching practice is a determining factor of coaching effectiveness (Lyle, 2010). Planning is crucial to the development of a coach since it encourages deep thinking, raises expectations of both coach and player, and provides a template from which thoughtful reflection can occur post-delivery (Abraham & Collins, 2011). Coaches should plan however it can lead to excessive regimentation, with coaches following a plan without any consideration of the players in front of them.

Even with a plan and an extensive background in their particular sport, in this case football, some coaches can struggle to develop a coherent, quality plan for their sessions (Abraham et al., 2014). A quality plan does not mean it has to be followed to the letter but rather provides a fluid guide for the coach with clear objectives, an insistence on quality, and requires some player involvement and interaction.

## Do players have autonomy?

Effective coaching in football is not about shouting instructions from the sidelines or controlling play during practice sessions. Instead, it requires coaches to encourage players to become self-determined (autonomous) on the field of play and confident enough to problem solve and make decisions as to the appropriate actions to take (Larsen et al., 2015; Light, Harvey, & Mouchet, 2014). Unless players are encouraged to think for themselves and evaluate the best course of action during practice they will not be able to make effective decisions during the pressure of competition. Every player on a football team will have some cognitive ability and the coach must be able to plan practice sessions and create a training environment to develop these important footballing abilities (Woods, Raynor, Bruce, & McDonald, 2015). In the modern game of football, coaches and players alike must appreciate and actively promote these decision-making skills, such as what pass to play, what weight of pass, how to create space, and then be able to execute these decisions.

## Is the coach's feedback helpful?

Effective football coaches require skills to identify players' strengths and weaknesses, formulate appropriate corrective and informational feedback and praise, as well as communicating in an accessible language (Januário, Rosado, & Mesquita, 2013). This means the coach has to acquire:

- Observation skills – to watch the players during training and competition and note both individual and team strengths and weaknesses.
- Evaluation skills – to pinpoint the key strengths and weaknesses and understand what is causing these to happen.
- Communication skills – once the coach has observed and evaluated both individual and team performance, they need to provide feedback. Providing meaningful feedback in a way that can be understood and acted upon can be dependent upon the coach's knowledge of both individual players and context.

According to Bortoli and colleagues (2010), experienced coaches tend to give feedback that is more specific in identifying weaknesses, related to previous feedback, and often provided this feedback during the performance. However, as well as coaches requiring to deliver appropriate feedback to their players, effective football coaches need to gain feedback on their own coaching in order to adapt their practice and this is often difficult to access from credible sources (Nash, Sproule, & Horton, 2017).

## Do coaches contribute to players' personal and character development?

Football coaches need to understand their moral obligations to players, especially at the youth and developmental level (Evans, McGuckin, Gainforth, Bruner, & Côté, 2015). The majority of players who start playing football at an early age will not develop into professionals so coaches should adopt a holistic perspective. Players should be engaged in activities that help develop psychomotor, cognitive, and psycho-social abilities that are needed to play football but also encouraged to see the wider implications of participation in a team sport to personal development, including character.

## Assessing/evaluating coach effectiveness

Given the difficulties surrounding a definition of coaching effectiveness it stands to reason that that there are similar problems when measuring or judging effective coaching. For example, there are a number of key stakeholders in the process who would have very different conceptions of effectiveness, namely: performers/teams; coaches; parents; and significant others in current organisations, sporting organisations, and coaching organisations.

Performers, understandably, can have a very self-focused view of the coaching effectiveness (how is the coach helping ME?); whereas, coaches need to view the concept of effectiveness more holistically (how do I develop the team/group to their potential?). Parents, traditionally, view the coach through the lens of their child or children and their particular interests (Is my child getting sufficient playing time?), whereas organisations can have a mixed view (Is the club/team winning?). The current organisation or club should have codes of conduct and professional standards that they need to implement within their particular association and these values should be validated and endorsed by both sporting and coaching organisations. Maintaining a balance between these often opposing views of coaching effectiveness can be a difficult task, necessitating some discussion of values and philosophy amongst *all* key stakeholders so that some agreement and accommodation can be reached. This should preclude disagreements around judgements of coaching effectiveness and also ensure that everyone involved should understand the main principles, how they can be applied, and, importantly, there are nuances, meaning decision making may not be straightforward and vary from situation to situation.

There have been attempts to develop systematic methods of evaluating coaching effectiveness as success in sport, particularly for coaches, has historically been evaluated predominantly through performance outcome measures. The Coach Behavior Scale for Sports (CBS-S; Côté, Yardley, Hay, Sedgwick, & Baker, 1999) was developed to assess the players' perceptions of the coach's behaviours. Further, Mallett and Côté (2006) argued the importance of moving beyond winning and losing to evaluate coach performance using the CBS-S, specifically, arguing for players' voice in any evaluation. This measure has been shown to possess satisfactory ecological validity (Koh, Mallett, & Wang, 2009). Another example of this is the Coaching Success Questionnaire (CSQ-2B), developed by Gillham and colleagues (2013), that can be valuable in determining global elements of effectiveness; however, the authors acknowledge the complexities presented by this type of measurement. Recently, Smith and colleagues (2015) developed a system for assessing the coach-created motivational climate in sport. This means of assessing was based on observing coach behaviours related to self-determination (including basic needs) and achievement motivation theories.

## The performance pathway in football

Many sporting organisations have clearly delineated pathways for the development of players – this is also the case in football. However, not all football clubs and coaches adhere to the principles of talent development by enrolling promising players at a relatively early age aiming to develop players who will be professionals in adulthood. Research has indicated that coaches appear to be relatively ineffective in their selection processes (Nicholls & Worsfold, 2016). This may relate to the emphasis on key principles of nature rather than nurture, physiological issues rather than psychological interventions, and the exclusion of social skills (Miller, Cronin, & Baker, 2015). While player development is of interest to football coaches it is not the purpose of this chapter but serves to highlight the changing nature of effectiveness along the performance pathway.

## How effective is coaching along the performance pathway?

The traditional coaching scenario within football has seen novice coaches working with novice players and, conversely, elite, experienced coaches working with more skilled players. There are a number of issues with this arrangement:

### 1 Where should experienced coaches be deployed?

Within the UK there has been considerable debate around the employment of coaches, which has led to recommendations around minimum standards. A guideline document, *Excellent Coaching Every Time for Everyone* (sportcoachUK, 2010, 2013), has provided five key areas for consideration:

- minimum age
- appropriate qualifications
- appropriate insurance cover
- safeguarding children and vulnerable groups
- policies and procedures.

However well intentioned these guidelines might be, they do provide what are at best minimum standards to comply with health and safety requirements and, as such, have little to do with effective coaching. Research has suggested that rather than experienced coaches working with the more performance end of the playing spectrum, they should be working with beginner players to ensure that they have a positive experience and learn the basics of both movement and football (Nash et al., 2011). In the present system, there appear to be few rewards for experienced coaches working to introduce youngsters to football.

## 2 How should novice coaches be encouraged to learn and develop effective coaching skills?

Often novice coaches can wonder if effective, experienced coaches possess mysterious methods for producing results and consequently often mimic, or copy, the more experienced coaches' skills and drills (Nash & Sproule, 2011). Football coaches need to orchestrate a large number of variables when planning and executing a training session, and their success depends on their coaching knowledge and their skill at contextualising the necessary components for specific situations (Nash et al., 2011). Nevertheless, how do inexperienced coaches gain this understanding (Nash et al., 2011)? Novice coaches should be able to experiment, and use trial and error to work out the most effective ways for them to develop and get the most out of their team. The use of mentoring to provide the often missing link between theory and practice is a recent phenomenon of investigation within sports coaching literature and the ICCE has suggested it as an effective means to encourage and support the ongoing learning and professional development of coaches (ICCE, 2013; McQuade, Davis, & Nash, 2015). Nevertheless, the notion of mentoring within the field of sports coaching is also problematic as it means different things to different people and there is no consensus on what it is and what it is not (Rynne, Crudgington, & Mallett, in press).

## 3 What skills are required at different levels of coaching?

Pain and Harwood (2007) examined the performance environment of the England youth soccer teams. Their finding revealed adhering to a consistent tournament strategy, player understanding, strong team cohesion, organised entertainment activities, detailed knowledge of opposition, an effective physical rest/recovery strategy, and previous tournament experience were major positive influences on performance. However, negative factors perceived were identified as over-coaching, player boredom, player anxiety, physical superiority of the opposition, physical fatigue over the tournament, problems sleeping, and lack of information on the opposition. Research has suggested that there are training behaviours that can act as predictors of team sport success, namely, professionalism, motivation, coping, committed, effort, seeking information to improve, and concentration (Oliver, Hardy, & Markland, 2010).

A so called 'soccer factory' exists in Munich, where effective coaching and development of players along the performance pathway at Bayern Munich, has provided the German national team with a number of key players (Hughes, 2010). However, Grossmann and Lames (2015) suggested that this clear pathway, or route, into the Bundesliga (German professional leagues) is more widespread with over 80% of players progressing through a professional youth academy. Recent research into the successful US women's football coach, Anson Dorrance, has concluded that he believes in eight goals for effective coaching: the leadership style of the coach, creating a positive team environment while retaining discipline, structuring the competitive team environment for success, embedding key psychological principles for elite athletes, acknowledging the challenges of high-performance coaching, realising that elite athletes can establish a great team, the coach being a role model in competition, and finally the long-term development of elite coaching practice (Wang & Straub, 2012).

Much of the published research has concentrated upon the high-performance coaching environment and the coaching required to develop elite performers; however, there is little on the developmental coaching side. According to Condon (2012) many of these coaches struggle to develop the necessary skills due to a combination of circumstances (e.g. money, access, and the transitory nature of coaching engagement).

## Conclusion

In this chapter, we examined the difficulties and challenges surrounding the notion of effective football coaching. The emphasis on winning and the context of football coaching contribute to problematising effective coaching. We hope that the emphasis placed upon the differing roles of a football coach have engendered questioning, reflection on current practice, and a recognition of the complex nature of this topic. Effective football coaches should strive to be lifelong learners, taking advantage of all development opportunities and insist upon quality within their practices.

## References

Abraham, A., & Collins, D. (2011). Effective skill development: How should athletes' skills be developed? In D. Collins, H. Richards, & A. Button (Eds.), *Performance psychology: A guide for the practitioner* (pp. 207–230). London, England: Churchill Livingstone.

Abraham, A., Saiz, A. L. J, Mckeown, S., Morgan, G., Muir, B., North, J., & Till, K. (2014). Planning your coaching: A focus on youth participant development. In C. Nash (Ed.), *Practical sports coaching* (pp. 177–189). London, England: Routledge/Taylor & Francis Group.

Allen, J. B., & Shaw, S. (2009). Women coaches' perceptions of their sport organizations' social environment: Supporting coaches' psychological needs? *The Sport Psychologist, 23,* 346–366.

Arnott, J., & Sparrow, J. (2004). The Coaching Study 2004. University of Central England (UCE), Birmingham, England.

Becker, A. J. (2009). It's not what they do, it's how they do it: Athlete experiences of great coaching. *International Journal of Sports Science & Coaching, 4*(1), 93–114.

Bortoli, L., Bertollo, M., Messina, G., Chiariotti, R., & Robazza, C. (2010). Augmented feedback of experienced and less experienced volleyball coaches: A preliminary investigation. *Social Behavior and Personality: An International Journal, 38*(4), 453–460.

Bowes, I., & Jones, R. L. (2006). Working at the edge of chaos: Understanding coaching as a complex interpersonal system. *The Sports Psychologist, 20,* 235–245.

Castellano, J., Casamichana, D., & Lago, C. (2012). The use of match statistics that discriminate between successful and unsuccessful soccer teams. *Journal of Human Kinetics, 31,* 139–147.

Condon, P. (2012). Grass roots social learning: Guiding young coaches. *Training & Development, 39*(6), 18–19.

Côté, J., & Erickson, K. (2016). Diversification and deliberate play during the sampling years. In J. Baker & D. Farrow (Eds.), *The handbook of sport expertise* (pp. 305–316). London, England: Routledge.

Côté, J., & Gilbert, W. (2009). An integrative definition of coaching effectiveness and expertise. *International Journal of Sport Science and Coaching, 4,* 307–323.

Côté, J., Lidor, R., & Hackfort, D. (2009). ISSP position stand: To sample or to specialize? Seven postulates about youth sport activities that lead to continued participation and elite performance. *International Journal of Sport and Exercise Psychology, 9,* 7–17.

Côté, J., & Vierimaa, M. (2014). The developmental model of sport participation: 15 years after its first conceptualization. *Science and Sports, 29s*, S63–S69.

Côté, J., Yardley, J., Hay, J., Sedgwick, W., & Baker, J. (1999). An exploratory examination of the Coaching Behaviour Scale for Sport. *Avante, 5*, 82–92.

Duda, J. L., & Balaguer, I. (2007). Coach created motivational climate. In S. Jowett & D. Lavallee (Eds.), *Social psychology in sport* (pp. 117–130). Champaign, IL: Human Kinetics.

Evans, M., McGuckin, M., Gainforth, H., Bruner, M., & Côté, J. (2015). Coach development programmes to improve interpersonal coach behaviours: A systematic review using the re-aim framework. *British Journal of Sports Medicine*, 7 May.

Fraser-Thomas, J., & Côté, J. (2009). Understanding adolescents' positive and negative developmental experiences in sport. *The Sport Psychologist, 23*, 3–23.

Gilbert, W., Côté, J., & Mallett, C. (2006). Developmental paths and activities of successful sport coaches. *International Journal of Sports Science and Coaching, 1*, 69–76.

Gillham, A., Burton, D., & Gillham, E. (2013). Going beyond won-loss record to identify successful coaches: Development and preliminary validation of the Coaching Success Questionnaire-2. *International Journal of Sports Science & Coaching, 8*(1), 115–138.

Grossmann, B., & Lames, M. (2015). From talent to professional football-youthism in German football. *International Journal of Sports Science & Coaching, 10*(6), 1103–1113.

Gründel, A., Schorer, J., Strauss, B., & Baker, J. (2013). Does playing experience improve coaching? An exploratory study of perceptual-cognitive skill in soccer coaches. *Frontiers in Psychology, 4*, 129.

Hamilton, S. F., Hamilton, M. A., & Pittman, K. (2004). Principles for youth development. In S. F. Hamilton & M. A. Hamilton (Eds.), *The youth development handbook: Coming of age in American communities* (pp. 3–22). Thousand Oaks, CA: Sage.

Haslam, S. A., Reicher, S. D., & Platow, M. J. (2011). *The new psychology of leadership: Identity, influence and power*. New York, NY: Psychology Press.

Hughes, R. (2010, 23 August). Soccer factory in Munich is building a better Germany. *New York Times*, p. D8.

International Council for Coaching Excellence (2013). *International Sport Coaching Framework* (version 1.2). Champaign, IL: Human Kinetics.

Januário, N., Rosado, A., & Mesquita, I. (2013). Variables affecting athletes' retention of coaches' feedback. *Perceptual and Motor Skills, 117*(2), 389–401.

Jolly, S., & Lyle, J. (2016). The traditional, the ideal and the unexplored: Sport coaches' social identity constructs in film. *Sports Coaching Review*, 41–53.

Jones, R. L., & Wallace, M. (2005). Another bad day at the training ground: Coping with ambiguity in the coaching context. *Sport, Education and Society, 10*(1), 119–134.

Koh, K. T., Mallett, C. J., & Wang, C. K. J. (2009). Examining the ecological validity of the Coaching Behavior Scale (Sports) for basketball. *International Journal of Sport Science & Coaching, 4*, 261–272.

Kristiansen, E., & Roberts, G. C. (2010). Young elite athletes and social support: Coping with competitive and organizational stress in 'Olympic' competition. *Scandinavian Journal of Medicine & Science in Sports, 20*, 686–695.

Lara-Bercial, S., & Mallett, C. J. (2016). The practices and developmental pathways of professional and Olympic serial winning coaches. *International Sport Coaching Journal, 3*, 113–127.

Larsen, T., Van Hoye, A., Tjomsland, H. E., Holsen, I., Wold, B., Heuzé, J. P., & Sarrazin, P. (2015). Creating a supportive environment among youth football players: A qualitative study of French and Norwegian youth grassroots football coaches. *Health Education, 115*(6), 570–586.

Larson, R. W. (2000). Toward a psychology of positive youth development. *American Psychologist, 55*, 170–183.

Lerner, R. M., Lerner, J. V., Almerigi, J., Theokas, C., Naudeau, S., Gestsdottir, S., et al. (2005). Positive youth development, participation in community youth development programs, and community contributions of fifth grade adolescents: Findings from the first wave of the 4-H study of positive youth development. *Journal of Early Adolescence, 25*(1), 17–71.

Light, R. L., Harvey, S., & Mouchet, A. (2014). Improving 'At-Action' decision-making in team sports through a holistic coaching approach. *Sport, Education and Society, 19*(3), 258–275.

Lyle, J. (2010). Planning for team sports. In J. Lyle & C. Cushion (Eds.), *Sports coaching: Professionalism and practice* (pp. 85–98). Edinburgh, Scotland: Churchill Livingstone.

MacDonald, D., Côté, J., & Deakin, J. (2010). The impact of informal coach training on the personal development of youth sport athletes. *International Journal of Sports Science & Coaching, 5*, 363–372.

Mallett, C. J. (2005). Self-determination theory: A case study of evidence-based coaching. *The Sport Psychologist, 19*, 417–429.

Mallett, C. J. (2007). Modelling the complexity of the coaching process: A commentary. *International Journal of Sport Science & Coaching, 2*, 419–421.

Mallett, C. J. (2010). High performance coaches' careers and communities. In J. Lyle & C. Cushion (Eds.), *Sports coaching: Professionalism and practice* (pp. 119–133). Edinburgh, Scotland: Churchill Livingstone.

Mallett, C. J., & Côté, J. (2006). Beyond winning and losing: Guidelines for evaluating high performance coaches. *The Sport Psychologist, 20*, 213–221.

Mallett, C., & Coulter, T. (2016). The anatomy of a successful Olympic coach: Performer, agent, and author. *International Sport Coaching Journal, 3*, 113–127.

Mallett, C. J., & Lara-Bercial, S. (2016). Serial winning coaches: People, vision and environment. In M. Raab, P. Wylleman, R. Seiler, A-M. Elbe, & A. Hatzigeorgiadis (Eds.), *Sport and exercise psychology research: Theory to practice* (pp. 289–322). Amsterdam, The Netherlands: Elsevier.

Mallett, C. J., Rossi, T., Rynne, S., & Tinning, R. (2016). In pursuit of becoming a senior coach: The learning culture for Australian Football League coaches. *Physical Education and Sport Pedagogy, 21*(1), 24–39.

Mallett, C. J., & Rynne, S. B. (2015). Changing role of coaches across development. In J. Baker & D. Farrow (Eds.), *The Routledge handbook of sport expertise* (pp. 394–403). London, England: Routledge.

Mallett, C. J., Rynne, S. B., & Billett, S. (2016). Valued learning experiences of early career and experienced high performance coaches. *Physical Education and Sport Pedagogy, 21*(1), 89–104.

Manley, A. J., Greenlees, I. A., Smith, M. J., Batten, J., & Birch, P. J. (2014). The influence of coach reputation on the behavioral responses of male soccer players. *Scandinavian Journal of Medicine & Science in Sports, 24*(2), e111–e120.

McLean, K., & Mallett, C. J. (2012). What motivates the motivators? *Physical Education and Sport Pedagogy, 17*(1), 21–35.

McQuade, S., Davis, L., & Nash, C. (2015). Positioning mentoring as a coach development tool: Recommendations for future practice and research. *Quest, 67*(3), 317–329.

Miller, P., Cronin, C., & Baker, G. (2015). Nurture, nature and some very dubious social skills: An interpretative phenomenological analysis of talent identification practices in elite English youth soccer. *Qualitative Research in Sport, Exercise and Health*, 1–21.

Morgan, K., & Hassan, M. F. H. (2014). The practice session: Creating a motivational climate. In C. Nash (Ed.), *Practical sports coaching* (pp. 110–126). London, England: Routledge/Taylor & Francis Group.

Morgan, K., Kingston, K., & Sproule, J. (2005). Effects of different teaching styles on the teacher behaviours that influence motivational climate in physical education. *European Physical Education Review, 11*, 257–286.

Nash, C., & Martindale, R. (2013). The relevance of sports science information to coaches of football and rugby league. In H. Nunome, B. Drust, & B. Dawson (Eds.), *Science and football VII: The proceedings of the Seventh World Congress on Science and Football* (pp. 391–397). London, England: Routledge.

Nash, C., & Sproule, J. (2009). Career development of expert coaches. *International Journal of Sports Science & Coaching, 4*(1), 121–138.

Nash, C., & Sproule, J. (2011). Insights into experiences: Reflections of an expert and novice coach. *International Journal of Sports Science & Coaching, 6*, 149–161.

Nash, C., & Sproule, J. (2012). Coaches' perceptions of coach education experiences. *International Journal of Sport Psychology, 43*, 33–52.

Nash, C., Sproule, J., & Horton, P. (2011). Excellence in coaching: The art and skill of elite practitioners. *Research Quarterly in Exercise & Sport, 82*(2), 229–238.

Nash, C., Sproule, J., & Horton, P. (2017). Feedback for coaches: Who coaches the coach? *International Journal of Sports Science & Coaching, 12*(1), 92–102.

Nicholls, S., & Worsfold, P. (2016). The observational analysis of elite coaches within youth soccer: The importance of performance analysis. *International Journal of Sports Science & Coaching, 11*(6), 825–831.

Norman, L., & French, J. (2013). Understanding how high performance women athletes experience the coach–athlete relationship. *International Journal of Coaching Science, 7*(1), 3–24.

Occhino, J., Mallett, C. J., & Rynne, S. (2013). Dynamic social networks in high performance football coaching. *Physical Education and Sport Pedagogy, 18*(1), 90–102.

Oliver, E. J., Hardy, J., & Markland, D. (2010). Identifying important practice behaviors for the development of high-level youth athletes: Exploring the perspectives of elite coaches. *Psychology of Sport & Exercise, 11*(6), 433–443.

Olusoga, P., Maynard, I., Hays, K., & Butt, J. (2012). Coaching under pressure: A study of Olympic coaches. *Journal of Sports Sciences, 30*, 229–239.

Pain, M., & Harwood, C. (2007). The performance environment of the England youth soccer teams. *Journal of Sports Sciences, 25*(12), 1307–1324.

Purdy, L., & Jones, R. (2011). Choppy waters: Elite rowers' perceptions of coaching. *Sociology of Sport Journal, 28*, 329–346.

Romar, J-E., Sarén, J., & Hastie, P. (2016). Athlete-centred coaching using the Sport Education model in youth soccer. *Journal of Physical Education and Sport, 16*(2), 380–391.

Rynne, S. (2014). 'Fast track' and 'traditional path' coaches: Affordances, agency and social capital. *Sport, Education, and Society, 19*, 299–313.

Rynne, S. B., Crudgington, R., & Mallett, C. J. (in press). The coach as mentor. In R. Thelwell & M. Dicks (Eds.), *Professional advances in sports coaching: Research and practice*. London, England: Routledge.

Rynne, S. B., & Mallett, C. J. (2012). Understanding the work and learning of high performance coaches. *Physical Education and Sport Pedagogy, 17*, 507–523.

Siedentop, D. (1994). *Sport education: Quality PE through positive sport experiences*. Champaign, IL: Human Kinetics.

Smith, N., Tessier, D., Tzioumakis, Y., Quested, E., Appleton, P., Sarrazin, P., Papaiannou, A., & Duda, J. L. (2015). Development and validation of the Multidimensional Motivational Climate Observation System. *Journal of Sport & Exercise Psychology, 37*, 4–22.

sportcoachUK (2010). Excellent coaching every time for everyone. sportcoachUK, Leeds, England.

sportcoachUK (2013). Minimum standards for active coaches – Core guidance for organisations. sportcoachUK, Leeds, England.

Trudel, P., & Gilbert, W. (2006). Coaching and coach education. In D. Kirk, D. MacDonald, & M. O'Sullivan (Eds.), *The handbook of physical education* (pp. 516–539). London, England: Sage.

Wang, J., & Straub, W. F. (2012). An investigation into the coaching approach of a successful world class soccer coach: Anson Dorrance. *International Journal of Sports Science & Coaching,* 7(3), 431–444.

Werthner, P., & Trudel, P. (2006). A new theoretical perspective for understanding how coaches learn to coach. *The Sports Psychologist, 20,* 198–212.

Woods, C., Raynor, A., Bruce, L., & McDonald, Z. (2015). Discriminating talent-identified junior Australian football players using a video decision-making task. *Journal of Sports Sciences,* 1–6.

# 9   Collective collapse in football

*Erwin Apitzsch*

**Abstract**

Collective collapse occurs when a majority of the players in a team suddenly perform below expected level in a match, in spite of a satisfactory start, or when a team underperforms right from the start. Research results from a study on 146 male players and 15 coaches in various team sports at the elite level, and a study on a team involved in a collective collapse, and the opposite, a winning turnaround. The behaviour of the players and the coaches accounted for 69.6% of the reasons given for the occurrence of a collective collapse. Lack of communication and lack of role acceptance were given as the main factors. A collective collapse is usually followed by negative emotions, which spread among the team resulting in emotional contagion. In order to avoid a collective collapse or take appropriate action in case it occurs, it is suggested that players focus on the right goal (process goals), use constructive communication (between coach-players, and between players), and execute the expected role performance in their position. In addition, it is suggested that teams appoint 2–3 emotional leaders among the starting players, who are regarded as being expressive, interactive, and contributing to team performance as well as social cohesion. The role of the emotional leader is to implement a positive team atmosphere in times of adversity.

This chapter deals with the phenomenon of collective collapse, or team collapse, emotional contagion, and what can be done to avoid a team collapse or what to do if a team collapse occurs. The recommendations are based on empirical findings, and on my experience of working as a sport psychologist with a variety of sports at differing competition levels.

A key factor for success in team sports is cooperation, and helping each other. In times of adversity, when a football team is facing a possible defeat, it is common to use a derogative language towards teammates, sometimes accompanied by negative body language. This is even more pronounced when the team is facing a collective collapse, that is, having played very well with a victory within reach, when suddenly the team's play deteriorates and results in a loss. This leads to a bad mood, which spreads in the team (emotional contagion), and results in a negative team atmosphere. However, there is a solution to this problem, which will be presented in this chapter.

**Theory, research, and practical implications**

*Collective collapse*

One of the best examples of a collective collapse occurred in the semi-final of the 2014 World Cup where Brazil lost 7–1 to Germany. This was undoubtedly a shocking result, especially since Brazil was playing in its home country. Collective collapses occur not only at the World Cup level but also at the club level. In the first league in Germany, Bundesliga, Borussia Dortmund was in front by 4–0, when Schalke 04 scored their first goal in the second half, followed by three more goals, resulting in a tie 4–4. Dortmund's coach commented: 'If you are leading 4–0, it just cannot happen to lose the game' (Tidningarnas Telegrambyrå (TT), 2017). In a second division football game in Sweden, FC Rosengård lost to Assyriska BK 5–4, after leading 4–1 going into the second half. Rosengård's coach was very disappointed:

> We were struck by a mental collapse in the second half. Such breakthroughs just cannot happen. Our first half is very good, and during the half-time break, we agreed upon not to invite the opponents. But, already during the first five minutes in the second half we had lost the ball three times in our penalty area.
>
> (Jogstad, 2017)

In the qualification group for the 2018 World Cup in Russia, Sweden beat France, and consequently had the chance to finish as the number one ranked team in the group, thereby qualifying directly for the World Cup. However, Sweden then lost unexpectedly to Bulgaria a few months later. A commentator for TV Channel 4 in Sweden reported in his blog (Lundh, 2017) that it was as if the Swedish players thought it would be easier than it was. Unfortunately, uncertainty propagated throughout the Swedish national team, and although one can obviously point to individual player mistakes, their poor performance can be attributed to a collective collapse. For instance, the defence against Bulgaria was not effective. The interaction amongst players was non-existent. The collective performance, where a unit of 11 players does the job, was like it had been blown away. After the match, the national coach said that too many players did not reach their maximum level, as required, but could not point to anything specific. What was most surprising was that Sweden lost to a team that was ranked much lower than them. The above examples show that unexpected drops in performance by football teams are difficult to explain.

According to Apitzsch (2006) a collective collapse occurs when a majority of the players in a team suddenly perform below the expected level in a match, in spite of a satisfactory start (cf. Borussia Dortmund–Schalke 04), or when a team underperforms right from the start of a match (cf. Brazil–Germany). A related term is *choking under pressure* (Beilock & Gray, 2007), which results in poor performance as a response to an individual who faces an important and stressful situation. However, choking may refer to both an individual level and group level. Therefore, the term collective collapse is used here.

Possible theoretical links between collective collapse and related terms can be found in areas including the cognitive approach (Janis, 1982), affective approach (Kelly & Barsade, 2001), behavioural approach (Bion, 1961), and connections between emotions and cognition (Cacioppo & Gardner, 1999; Tickle-Degnan & Puccinelli, 1999; Totterdell, 2000). A study by Apitzsch (2009) on four male coaches, one in football, and all at the elite level, and nine male players from an elite handball team, found the major causes of collective collapses include inappropriate behaviour, failure of the role system to function properly, negative communication within the team, a change in the tactics of the opposing team, and goals being scored by that team. Factors seen as needed to be dealt with to prevent a collective collapse include negative thinking, negative emotions, and negative emotional contagion. The main category of responses perceived as triggering a collective collapse was errors made by members of one's own team (e.g. players failing to carry out their tasks properly or mistakes made by them). All coaches spoke of the importance of understanding (e.g. some players don't do what's expected of them) and accepting (e.g. some players are insecure in their roles). In order to avoid collective collapses, the conclusion was that coaches have to take action, sometimes using drastic measures to alert the players to what needs to be done, and that the players need to accept the tactics and stick to their roles.

To gain a deeper understanding of collective collapse, 146 male players and 15 coaches at the elite level in the team sports floorball, handball, and ice hockey in Sweden, responded to a questionnaire. The results showed that at least one collective collapse per season was reported by 70.8% of the participants, the majority of these collapses (58.0%) occurring in away games. The three factors, behaviour of the players (59.1%), the warm-up (13.2%), and the behaviour of the coach (10.5%) accounted for 82.8% of the reported reasons for a collective collapse. It may be noted that none of the coaches regarded their own behaviour to be the primary reason for a collective collapse. The main effects of a collective collapse can be summarised in the following points: (1) the communication within the team decreases and becomes negative, (2) 90% of what is said is negative, and (3) the bad mood spreads within the team. The negative feelings were Fear of failure (17%), Low self-confidence (10%), Too high expectations (10%), and Stress (8%). The following quotes were stated by the players as to the reason for the collective collapse: 'We behaved as if we had already won', 'We all performed below our normal standard and were afraid of losing', 'Resignation and flight', 'No communication on the court or on the bench', 'We started to blame each other', and 'We waited for somebody else to take action'. Taken together, a lack of communication and lack of role acceptance appear to be the main reasons for the collective collapses. Performing below normal performance level, resignation, and waiting for somebody else to take action, are typical examples of social loafing (see Hanrahan & Gallois, 1993 for a review). Social loafing is a psychological phenomenon stating that individuals in a team exert less than 100% effort due to a loss of motivation. Of the eight conditions, under which social loafing is increased, the one that has the most bearing with regard to football is when players perceive that they are competing against a weaker opponent. Thus, each player should take responsibility for his/her own efforts, and not assume that a teammate will necessarily increase their own effort. Therefore, it is essential for football coaches to continuously address this topic with the aim that the players stay focused and perform their role on the field irrespective of the score during the game.

In matches where collective collapses occur, mainly mental factors were mentioned as being different from other matches, such as the team meeting before the match, not being mentally prepared after a good start of the season, beliefs of being better than the other team, fear of failure, and long-standing losses against the opposing team. Having a meal too close to the match is the only behavioural factor given.

The behaviour of the players and the coaches accounted for 69.6% of the reasons given for the occurrence of a collective collapse. The majority of players (60.5%) and coaches (53.3%) reported that the communication between the coach and the players was the same as usual and not a cause of the team's collapse. The communication between the players was reported as not being different from other matches by 43.6% of the participants. However, when the collective collapse occurred, the communication between the players decreased, negative emotions (anxiety) appeared, and the content of the communication consisted of unspoken expectations (expected somebody else to take action) and got a negative character (started to blame each other).

Resignation, flight, and the expectation that somebody else should take action can be interpreted as signs of chaos. The information from the coach before the match about the opposing team was not as accurate as usual. During the match the communication decreased and at the same time the message from the coach was perceived as wrong, insufficient, or vague.

Sometimes an impending collective collapse may have been avoided one way or another. Slightly more participants (44.7%) reported that they had managed to avoid a collective collapse than those who responded that they had not been able to avoid it (41.0%). The answers to the question of how collective collapses have been avoided previously can be classified into two main categories: (1) No particular action, and (2) Key events.

In the category 'No particular action' answers can be found that indicate that the team continued to play as before but with a little more energy (we showed morale and turned it around; we were able to remain calm and stay focused). However, most answers were found in the category 'Key events', which partly contains conscious actions, for example, change of tactics, partly haphazard actions, for example, a save by the goalkeeper at a critical moment.

It can be noted that increased communication between the coach and the players contributed to an avoidance of a collective collapse, as decreased communication seemed to be an indicator of an impending collapse. Being able to remain calm, combined with concrete actions, is likely to produce a better result when playing below normal standard than waiting for things to happen by chance.

What happens in a team after a collective collapse? In total, analysis of the match after a collective collapse was by far the most common measure (47.7%). Next followed 'Team sessions' (19.9%), and 'Forget the match' (14.5%). Analysis of the match and team sessions accounted for 67.6% of all reported measures and implied communication, which have to be carried out in a non-threatening and constructive way so that the players are open-minded for change.

In sport psychology a distinction is made between different types of goals (Burton, Naylor, & Holliday, 2001). Outcome goals are expressed in the form of winning, for example, the next game, qualifying for the next round in a tournament, finishing on a certain position in the league table. Outcome goals mean comparison with others and cannot be controlled. Process goals focus on what to do during the competition, here and now, to reach the set outcome goal. Outcome goals are what drives elite footballers and constitute an important motivational factor for the occasionally monotonous and boring training, especially during off-season. Performance goals, which the footballer has full control over, are the third type of goal and involve planning and implementing the training needed to achieve the outcome goal.

A football team may be in the situation to win the next game by three goals in order to qualify for the next round in a championship. This may lead to the outcome goal 'We must win the game', which may cause negative thoughts and the risk is then high that the game will not result in a victory. Focusing on outcome goals may increase anxiety and irrelevant thoughts such as worrying too much about the current score of the game instead of focusing on the immediate task at hand. The process goal for each individual footballer in this case would be 'This is what I have to do when our team is in possession of the ball and when the opposing team is in possession of the ball.' This means thinking of the behaviour to be performed and is free from value judgements, which facilitates a positive outcome.

In an experimental study by Filby, Maynard, and Graydon (1999), performance on a football task was measured over a 5-week training period, and then in a competition. Their conclusion was that the superior performance of the groups using multiple-goal strategies provided evidence to support the efficacy of maintaining a balance between the use of outcome, performance, and process goals. Thus, the three types of goals are all important for achieving athletic success, but it is important to use the right goal at the right time.

The practical consequences of handling the collective collapses revealed two main categories, either adherence to the normal routines or taking extraordinary action. In the former case there was general alertness and thoughts about revenge. In the latter case some routines were changed, which had a bearing on the following training sessions, for example, change of tactics, training on weak points, better preparation, and trying to establish a winning mentality. In sum, focusing on the right goal, constructive communication, and executing the expected role performance are key elements to avoid these types of collective collapses. The next question is 'What can be done once a collective collapse has occurred?'

### Emotional contagion

Emotional contagion, defined as 'the tendency to automatically mimic and synchronise *expressions*, vocalisations, postures and movements with those of another person's and, consequently, to converge emotionally' (Hatfield, Cacioppo, & Rapson, 1992, pp. 153–154), is a key issue when it comes to handling a collective collapse in elite team sports. This definition implies that emotional contagion is a social phenomenon (Barsade, 2002) and, thus, may have bearing on the spirit of the team, and ultimately on the outcome of a football game. The social functions of emotions that are most relevant in team sports are the communication of feelings to teammates, and to influence how teammates interact with each other. It should be noted that in contrast to verbal communication, emotional contagion can be regarded as a form of non-verbal communication (Izard, 1989).

To date, only a few studies on emotional contagion have been reported in peer reviewed publications. In sport, Totterdell (1999) found that professional cricket players performed better when they were in a positive mood, expressing happiness, energy, enthusiasm, and being more focused. Moll, Jordet, and Pepping (2010) reported that players who displayed a positive body language in football penalty shootouts were more likely to be on the successful team, implying that emotional contagion is an important process. Sekerka and Fredrickson (2008) highlighted that studies on negative emotions have received significantly more attention than studies on positive emotions, and note that negative emotions narrow an individual's ability to deal with specific actions, whereas positive emotions broaden the individual's possibility to act adequately according to the situational demands. They also reported that positive emotions have been associated with many positive outcomes that include greater persistence, favourable reactions to others, helping others, and motivational factors that help to anticipate success and tackle challenges. However, they also note that people have a strong tendency to consider bad as stronger than good. Cacioppo and Gardner (1999) in summarising the role of positive and negative emotions stated that positive emotions serve as a cue to stay on course, while negative emotions call for some kind of action.

People differ in their expressiveness of experienced emotions. Those who are more extraverted are likely to be better at transferring their non-verbal emotions to others than those who are more introverted (Kelly & Barsade, 2001). Unfortunately, Totterdell (2000) did not find support for this notion with professional cricket players, where only weak evidence was provided, whereby individuals who were more expressive had greater mood linkage with their teammates. One reason for this result is that, unless an individual has a prominent role on the team, it is easier to be influenced by the mood of many teammates than to influence the mood of many teammates. Boss and Kleinert (2015) claim that there still is a lack of explanation for the underlying mechanisms of the concept contagion, and that social contagion, behavioural contagion, and emotional contagion often are used synonymously, although the terms emphasise different aspects of the contagion process. They used the term social contagion in their experimental research since the contagious process takes place in a social context, and found that Heider's Balance Theory as a theoretical approach to this phenomenon is helpful.

In the absence of studies on emotional contagion in football teams, a study of an elite team in handball for men will be referred to. In this study the influence of emotions on players' behaviour and performance was investigated using two match scenarios; a match resulting in a collective collapse, and a match resulting in a victorious turnaround. A victorious turnaround was defined as 'When a majority of the players in a team sport suddenly perform above expected levels in a match of great, often decisive, importance after a bad start to the match'. The coach of the team and the author selected two matches after the end of the season that met this operational definition. The collective collapse occurred at the beginning of March in a league home game against Team X, who were at the bottom of the table. In the case of the victorious condition, Team A would qualify for the playoffs with a win. Team A was leading the match with 28–23 with 11 minutes to play, but lost unexpectedly by two goals. The victorious turnaround occurred in an away playoff game at the end of March against Team Y, known to be a very strong home team. Team A was behind by four goals with 25 minutes to play, but ended up winning the match by two goals.

The collective collapse against Team X was mainly characterised by negative emotions (61.8%). Emotions were measured using Hanin's (2000) Individual Zones of Optimal Functioning (IZOF) that also contained an additional fifth category,

Negative team emotions (T–), based on previous research findings on collective collapse (Apitzsch, 2009). This category contains the following items: Too high expectations, Stressed, Lack of motivation, Overconfident, Low self-confidence, Fear of failure, and Feeling we have already won. The emotions expressed were Irritated, Passive, Angry, Fear of failure, and Feeling of having won the match.

The victorious condition against Team Y was characterised by less negative emotions (49.6%). The dominating emotions were Active, Determined, Intense, Confident, and Brave. The biggest difference between the two matches (i.e. conditions) was for the emotional category P+ (Pleasant and functionally optimal emotions), 13.5% in the collective collapse condition and 32.7% in the victorious condition.

Pleasant and functionally optimal emotions (P+) were viewed as the most important emotions for a successful outcome of a competitive handball match, 64.6% falling into this category in the winning turnaround against Team Y. P+ is also the dominating factor in the loss against Team X (45.7%). It should be highlighted that no emotions belonging to the categories Unpleasant and dysfunctional emotions (N–), and Negative team emotions (T–) were mentioned in the winning turnaround.

The next step was to identify players who could provide leadership in changing a bad mood within the team. The players in Team A had to list five teammates whom they communicated mostly with during the matches against Team X, and Team Y, five teammates who were most important for the performance, and five players who were most important for the social cohesion during the whole season. How the expressed emotions of these players affected the performance of Team A, and their own performance, was indicated on a 4-point scale.

Almost half of the emotions (48.0%) perceived in the defeat against Team X were found in the category T–. The most frequently mentioned emotions were Stressed, Lack of motivation, Fear of failure, and Overconfident. Helpless (N–) and Irritated (N+) were also frequently mentioned. Altogether, these emotions represented 68.0% of all expressed emotions. In the victory against Team Y, the dominating category was N+ (Tense, Worried) 42.9%, followed by N– (Passive, Doubtful) 30.2%, and T– (Stressed, and Fear of failure) 27.0%. These emotions constituted 66.7% of all emotions. The categories P+ and P– were not reported by any of the participants.

The negative categories accounted for 50.9% when playing well against Team X, and 32.6% when playing against Team Y. When playing poorly against these teams, the negative categories accounted for 78.0% and 57.2% respectively.

The results of the Emotional Contagion Scale showed that the players reported being more susceptible to positive emotions (3.2 on a 4-point scale) in comparison to negative emotions (1.6). Further, it should be noted that substitute players were somewhat more susceptible to negative emotions. With regard to positive emotions and general susceptibility, only small mean differences appeared. Generally, the range of the substitute players was larger.

In order, the four players A, E, G, and D emerged as those who were perceived as having the greatest impact on the performance of the other players on the team in both games. Generally, the impact was greater in the victory against Team Y. Player G received the highest rank of the eight teammates, who perceived him as the most influential player.

Players A, E, F, C, and D, were, in that order, rated as those contributing mostly to the performance of the team throughout the season, and players F, D, I, L, and C, in that order, as those contributing mostly to the social cohesion. The two top ranked players on performance were not mentioned as contributing to the social cohesion of the team. Four players, F, C, D, and G, were ranked among the best both with regard to performance and social cohesion.

Only starters were among the top ranked players contributing mostly to the performance of the team. Two substitute players, I (rank 2), and L (rank 5), were among the top ranked players contributing to the social cohesion.

Players G, D, and E were reported to be mostly communicated with by most teammates in both games. Player D received high scores in both games. Player G had the highest score (4.4) in the match against Team X, but dropped to rank four (2.8) against Team Y.

The players were perceived as more susceptible to positive emotions (mean score 3.5 for the five most susceptible players) than negative emotions (mean 2.3). Substitute players were overrepresented with regard to, especially, negative emotions.

When Team A played poorly no positive emotions were listed. Instead team emotions, Stress and Fear of failure, were mentioned as the only ones occurring in both matches. Although the most dominant emotions, when playing poorly, in both matches accounted for almost the same percentage, 68.0% in the collective collapse, and 66.7% in the winning turnaround, only two were common. From these results it can be concluded that teams should focus on evoking positive emotions, and get rid of the negative emotions. The four starting players who were perceived as those contributing mostly to Team A's performance throughout the season, were also those who were perceived as influencing their teammates most in both matches. Player D seemed to be the most consistent player. He had a high ranking on influencing the performance of the team, the social cohesion of the players, and was heavily involved in the interaction with other players in the two matches. However, he was not considered to be susceptible to emotions, either positive or negative. On the other hand, if a key player is an expressive type, he could assume the role of bringing happiness to the team. Player G was highly susceptible to positive emotions (3.6 on a 4-point scale), and considered to be the most influential player (5.0 on a 5-point scale) against Team Y, but ranked only fifth (score 2.8) with regard to interaction during the game. In the game against Team X, he was the one who was rated as having most interactions with his teammates (4.4) and one of the most influential players (3.3). He had about the same amount of playing time and scored twice in both games – why the discrepancy in his interaction with the teammates between these matches is difficult to explain.

Krane and Williams (2010) reported that research has identified several differences in personality characteristics between successful and unsuccessful athletes, and claim that these differences result from more effective thinking and responding in relation to critical situations as well as higher levels of motivation. In particular, successful athletes are characterised, among other factors, by being more self-confident, better able to cope with stress and distractions, better able to control emotions, and better at keeping their focus.

Since emotions are contagious, they can go both ways, spreading a positive or a negative mood. The expression of emotions through body language is by and large an unused possibility. Therefore, it seems justified to advise elite teams to create and maintain a positive spirit, for example, by appointing a starting player, who is regarded as interactive, contributing to team performance as well as social cohesion, and being expressive, the role of communicating positive emotions.

## Practical implications

The areas of collective collapse and emotional contagion in football teams are still under-researched topics. However, the research results from other team sports can be used to prevent collective collapses in football, and provide actions to take to change negative emotional contagion into a constructive, positive mood.

Before the start of the season, the team must agree on a realistic outcome goal, which represents the ambitions of the club and the players. The outcome goal sets the frame for performance goals, which are goals that are required to be completed during training over the course of the season on both a team and individual level. The performance goals must be flexible depending on what happens to the team during the season, for example, change of players and long-term injuries. Finally, each player has a role on the pitch and must stick to his/her role, irrespective of what happens during a specific game. Through process goals the focus is on what to do on the pitch, whereby value judgements, either positive 'We have already won the game' or negative 'We are going to lose', are reduced or eliminated.

If these preventive measures do not materialise, a collective collapse occurs and a negative mood state spreads within the team, resulting in a poor performance. Consequently, the team should have a plan for how to deal with these types of situations. Once the team for the forthcoming season is selected and the players have come to know each other with the team having played a number of preparation games, it is then appropriate to appoint 2–3 players to fulfil the role of implementing a positive team atmosphere in times of adversity.

In addition to these guidelines, there must be a plan to make adjustments in a particular game. In football, the coach can use the time before kick-off and during half-time for instructions. The coach shall communicate in a constructive, encouraging manner, reminding the players of the process goals and the respective role expectations. After the game, especially after an 'unexpected' loss, the analysis should lead to changes in the training programme.

## Conclusion

Collective collapses do occur periodically, resulting in a negative mood which spreads within the team to the detriment of the outcome of the game and the atmosphere in the team. Collective collapses can be avoided or reduced by focusing on process goals and having players fulfil their assigned roles. Appointing leaders who can influence mood within the team should help to produce better team performance and ultimately better results.

## References

Apitzsch, E. (2006). Collective collapse in team sports: A theoretical approach. In F. Boen, B. De Cuyper, & J. Opdenacker (Eds.), *Current research topics in exercise and sport* (pp. 35–46). Leuven, Belgium: LannooCampus.

Apitzsch, E. (2009). Coaches' and elite team players' perception and experiencing of collective collapse. *Athletic Insight: The online journal of sport psychology, 11.*

Barsade, S. G. (2002). The ripple effect: Emotional contagion and its influence on group behavior. *Administrative Science Quarterly, 47,* 644–675.

Beilock, S. I., & Gray, B. (2007). Why do athletes choke under pressure? In G. Tenenbaum & R. C. Eklund (Eds.), *Handbook of sport psychology* (pp. 425–444). Hoboken, NJ: Wiley & Sons.

Bion, W. R. (1961). *Experiences in groups*. London, England: Tavistock/Routledge.

Boss, M., & Kleinert, J. (2015). Explaining social contagion in sport applying Heider's balance theory: First experimental results. *Psychology of Sport and Exercise, 16*, 160–169.

Burton, D., Naylor, S., & Holliday, B. (2001). Goal setting in sport: Investigating the goal effectiveness paradigm. In R. Singer, H. Hausenblas, & C. Janelle (Eds.), *Handbook of sport psychology* (2nd ed., pp. 497–528). New York, NY: Wiley.

Cacioppo, J. T., & Gardner, W. L. (1999). Emotion. *Annual Review of Psychology, 50*, 191–214.

Filby, W., Maynard, I., & Graydon, J. (1999). The effect of multiple-goal strategy on performance outcomes in training and competition. *Journal of Applied Psychology, 1*, 230–246.

Hanin, Y. L. (2000). Individual zones of optimal functioning (IZOF) model. In Y. L. Hanin (Ed.), *Emotions in sport* (pp. 65–89). Champaign, IL: Human Kinetics.

Hanrahan, S., & Gallois, C. (1993). Social interactions. In R. N. Singer, M. Murphy, & L. K. Tennant (Eds.), *Handbook of sport psychology* (pp. 623–646). New York, NY: Macmillan.

Hatfield, E., Cacioppo, J., & Rapson, R. L. (1992). Primitive emotional contagion. In M. S. Clark (Ed.), *Review of personality and social psychology* (pp. 151–177). Newbury Park, CA: Sage.

Izard, C. E. (1989). The structure and functions of emotions: Implications for cognition, motivation, and personality. In I. S. Cohen (Ed.), *The G. Stanley Hall lecture series* (pp. 39–63). Washington, DC: American Psychological Association.

Janis, I. L. (1982). *Victims of group think*. Boston, MA: Houghton Mifflin.

Jogstad, P. (2017, 17 September). Mental kollaps av FCR mot Assyriska [Mental collapse of FCR against Assyriska]. *Sydsvenska Dagbladet*, p. B20.

Kelly, J. R., & Barsade, S. G. (2001). Moods and emotions in small groups and work teams. *Organizational Behavior and Human Decision Processes, 86*, 99–130.

Krane, V., & Williams, J. M. (2010). Psychological characteristics of peak performance. In J. M. Williams (Ed.), *Applied sport psychology: Personal growth to peak performance* (pp. 207–227). Boston, MA: McGraw-Hill Higher Education.

Lundh, O. (2017). Olof Lundh's blog, published 1 September 2017.

Moll, T., Jordet, G., & Pepping, G-J. (2010). Emotional contagion in soccer shootouts: Celebration of individual success is associated with ultimate team success. *Journal of Sports Science*, 1–10.

Sekerka, L. E., & Fredrickson, B. L. (2008). Establishing positive emotional climates to advance organizational transformation. In N. M. Ashkanasy & C. L. Cooper (Eds.), *Research companion to emotion in organizations* (pp. 531–545). Cheltenham, England: Edward Elgar Publishing.

Tickle-Degnan, L., & Puccinelli, N. M. (1999). The nonverbal expression of negative emotions: Peer and supervisor responses to occupational therapy students' emotional attributes. *The Occupational Therapy Journal of Research, 19*, 18–39.

Tidningarnas Telegrambyrå (TT). (2017, 26 November). Dortmund tappade 4–0 till 4–4 i derbyt [Dortmund lost 4–0 to 4–4 in the derby]. *Sydsvenska Dagbladet*, p. B18.

Totterdell, P. (1999). Mood scores: Mood and performance in professional cricketers. *British Journal of Psychology, 90*, 317–332.

Totterdell, P. (2000). Catching moods and hitting runs: Mood linkage and subjective performance in professional sport teams. *Journal of Applied Psychology, 85*, 848–859.

# 10 Leadership power in football

*Erkut Konter, Todd M. Loughead, and Kyle F. Paradis*

## Abstract

The chapter addresses a number of issues related to leadership power in football including conceptual definitions, theoretical approaches, measurement, perceptions, and studies examining leadership power in sport with an emphasis on football. Despite the plethora of research on leadership in sport, an overlooked aspect that forms the nature of leadership is power. There are different sources of power that influence others (e.g. footballers, coaches): expert power, legitimate power, reward power, coercive power, and referent power. Perceptions of power seem to have interactional and dyadic influences that are important in sport (football). In addition, power regulates the nature of the relationship between individuals which has implications for health, fun, development, success, and performance in football. The research would suggest that: (a) football coaches should use the indicated leadership powers for the psychological development of their athletes (e.g. commitment, imagery, peaking under pressure, and coping with stress); (b) coaches' leadership powers have potential to positively influence the team's dynamics (e.g. cohesion) and performance; (c) expert and referent power yield the most positive associations with psychological skills, and individual and team outcomes; and (d) future research should examine the different types of power perceptions in football in relation to personality types (e.g. Big Five, personality of mood states) and other psychological factors (e.g. self-regulation, self-confidence, motivation, mental toughness, courage) in relation to various environmental factors, cultures, and economic conditions.

Leadership has been a key variable of interest for sport psychology researchers and practitioners alike. We know that leadership behaviours and leadership style have a significant influence on performance success of athletes and teams (e.g. Horn, 2008; Weiss & Friedrichs, 1986). In sport like any other contexts, leaders need to make decisions, motivate group members, provide feedback, delegate and direct the group, and foster the group environment through establishing positive interpersonal relationships (Carron & Eys, 2012; Eklund & Tenenbaum, 2014). Early definitions of leadership focused on manipulation, persuasion, and coercion of followers, whereas more recent definitions have shifted to a more positive perception of leadership as a process of assisting, motivating, and directing the achievement of group goals. Thus, recent definitions of leadership reflect this idea and refer to leadership as both an art: 'the art of influencing individuals and groups so that they achieve set goals' (Kent, 2006, p. 314), and a process: 'a process whereby the individual influences a group of individuals to achieve a common goal' (Northouse, 2001, p. 3).

Stemming from the origins of leadership research in sport psychology, Chelladurai (1990) summarized and outlined three different traditional approaches researchers utilized to understand leadership behaviours in sport: (a) the coaching behaviour assessment system (CBAS; Smith, Smoll, & Curtis, 1979; Smith, Smoll, & Hunt, 1977); (b) a normative model of decision styles in coaching (Chelladurai & Haggerty, 1978); and (c) the multidimensional model of leadership (Chelladurai, 2007). These models have been widely adopted to assess coaching behaviours and leadership styles in sport. Studies of leadership in sport have suggested that successful leaders provide technical instruction, clear feedback, and encouragement, focusing more on the positive than the negative (e.g. Chelladurai & Saleh, 1980; Price & Weiss, 2000). More holistic approaches to leadership including transformational (Bass & Riggio, 2006), authentic (Avolio & Gardner, 2005), and servant leadership (Greenleaf, 1977) have also been advanced. These multidimensional and interactional theories of leadership have become increasingly popular, predicated on the notions that: (a) no one set of characteristics can ensure successful leadership; (b) different leadership styles are effective in different situations; and (c) leaders can change their leadership styles over time (Chelladurai, 2007; Eklund & Tenenbaum, 2014). Leader behaviour and leader style have been widely assessed in sport psychology with research findings providing insights and advancements to theory and practice (e.g. Chelladurai, 2007; Loughead & Hardy, 2005; Paradis & Loughead, 2012). Less understood however in the leadership domain is the perceptions of leader power in sport (Konter, 2008a, 2009a; Wann, Metcalf, Brewer, & Whiteside, 2000; Wann & Pack, 2001).

Despite the plethora of research attention on leadership in sport, interestingly an often overlooked but key aspect that forms the nature of leadership is power. In order to further understand the mechanism of power and its influence of leadership in sport, it is fundamental to first obtain insights into the concept of power. Power can be defined as the 'capacity to produce intended and unforeseen effects on others' (Wrong, 1979, p. 21). French and Raven (1959) viewed power as a relational factor, dependent on the relationship between people. Therefore, individuals who possess a certain level of status within a group (e.g. coaches, captains) have the capacity to influence other group members (Carron & Eys, 2012). Thus, the sources of power can be drawn from multiple facets of the group environment leaving individuals who possess such power the ability to influence or change the attitudes or behaviours of others (French & Raven, 1959; Wann et al., 2000).

French and Raven (1959) advanced a theoretical framework of the explanation of power in small-group behaviours that comprise five sources of leadership power. These sources are *reward power* (i.e. the ability to reward others, such as verbal praise, positive body language, and offering more playing time), *coercive power* (i.e. the ability to control others by using punishments, such as verbal reprimands, negative gestures), *legitimate power* (i.e. the ability to use one's position and authority within the organization, group, or team, for example, being an authority figure, possessing official status, and ownership of the organization), *expert power* (i.e. the ability to be knowledgeable, skilful, or talented in a specific domain, for example, being a former star in that sport, having specific education and experience, awarded many titles or medals), and *referent* power (i.e. the ability to be liked and respected by the group members).

This framework has been known as the bases of leadership power (French & Raven, 1959; Frost & Stahelski, 1988; Frost & Moussavi, 2011; Raven, 1992, 2008; Stahelski, Frost, & Patch, 1989). Perceptions of power seem to have interactional importance between sport leaders (e.g. coaches, captains, managers) and their followers (e.g. athletes, staff). Power is therefore a dyadic influence within the group and within the social context of sport. In addition, power regulates the access of individuals to each other and the interaction among them. Thus, status and power are highly related (Jacob & Carron, 1996). In sport, the coach often possesses the greatest status and the greatest power (Carron & Eys, 2012). Moreover, the bases of power can help explain the motivation that influences the use of power, and also addresses issues such as the preference, preparation, implementation, modification/readjustment, and the effectiveness of strategies implemented (Raven, 1992, 2008). Soucie (1994) proposed that French and Raven's framework could be adapted to help understand the social power of sport leadership. A number of studies have supported French and Raven's five interpersonal typologies of power. Compatibility between coaches' and athletes' perception of power was found to influence satisfaction (Horne & Carron, 1985; Riemer & Chelladurai, 1995; Turman, 2006), perceived ability (Summers, 1991), team cohesion (Jacob & Carron, 1998; Turman, 2003; Westre & Weiss, 1991), imagery, coping with stress and controlling competitive anxiety (Konter, 2005), and success and performance (Garland & Barry, 1991). In addition, it was demonstrated that coaches prefer more authoritarian leadership styles (legitimate power and coercive power) than athletes (Chelladurai, Haggerty, & Baxter, 1989). In contrast, coaches who cared about the thoughts and emotions of their athletes (referent power), helped to develop a better coach–athlete relationship with their athletes (Jowett & Ntoumanis, 2004). Consequently, athletes in different age groups (because of their maturity) need different coaching styles and possess different leadership power perceptions (Konter, 2009b). Moreover, recent research indicated that sport leadership power perceptions differed based on individual variables including gender, age, and experience (e.g. Knoppers, Meyer, Ewing, & Forrest, 1990; Shapiro, Ingols, & Blake-Beard, 2011), level of education (e.g. Konter, 2012), level of competition, and football-specific philosophy (e.g. Konter, 2009b).

## Measurement of leadership power in sport

'The horse neighs according to its owner' is a well-known Turkish saying capturing the importance of the leadership quality in relation to power. However, we scientifically need to advance our understanding about the leadership power perceptions in sport through effective measurement tools. The first instrument developed to measure leadership power in sport based on French and Raven's (1959) leadership power framework, is the Power in Sport Questionnaire (PSQ; Wann et al., 2000). There are two versions of PSQ available to measure self-perception (PSQ-S; Power in Sport Questionnaire-Self) and other perception (PSQ-O; Power in Sport Questionnaire-Other) of interpersonal power respectively (Wann et al., 2000).

Konter (2008a, 2009a) initially studied cultural adaptation of both scales PSQ-O and PSQ-S and found that some items of the scales were problematic and implemented follow-up studies to improve the psychometric properties of the scales, and advanced the revised scales (Sport Leadership Power Perception Scale for athletes, SLPS-19 and Instructor Sport Leadership Power Perception Scale, ISLPS-19) with additional new items for a Turkish sample. In addition, a series of studies have been conducted to develop and validate the SLPS-19 and ISLPS-19 for Turkey (Konter, 2008a, 2009a) including initial item development, construct, and criterion validity, as well as reliability and factor analysis with separate samples for Explanatory Factor Analysis (EFA) and Confirmatory Factor Analysis (CFA). The results supported the validity of the ISLPS-19 in a Turkish sample and suggested its applicability in assessing the instructors' sport leadership power perceptions of sport among physical education teachers and coaches including football in Turkey (Konter, 2008a, 2009a). Both scales have five factors and a total of 19 items each with responses provided on a 1–5 Likert-type scale. These validated scales were used in football to answer various research questions elaborated below.

## Research on leadership power in sport

Konter (2017) advanced some initial research findings pertaining to sport leadership power perceptions. When assessing the five different types of power, perceptions of coaching and leadership power yielded some significant gender differences. First, females had higher perceptions of expert power and reward power in relation to their coaches than male athletes, and second, males had higher perceptions of referent power in their coaches than female athletes.

In terms of significant associations between power perceptions and various sport outcomes, referent power was positively related to Determination, Assertiveness, Venturesome, Sacrifice Behaviour, and Total Sport Courage. Second, legitimate power was negatively related to Mastery. Third, coercive power was negatively related to Mastery, Determination, and Total Sport Courage. Fourth, reward power was positively related to Mastery, Determination, and Total Sport Courage.

In terms of power perceptions based on demographic variables, expert power was positively related to age and negatively related to body weight. Lastly, coercive power was negatively related to income and positively related to education.

## Perceptions of leadership power amongst football players

With relevance to the theme of the current book, Konter (2009c) assessed the perceptions of leadership power amongst football players based on their age, gender, sport type, and level of competitive play. In terms of age, football coaches' referent power tended to be more influential to older players (18–23 years old) than to younger players (12–14 years old) (Konter, 2008b, 2009c). As for gender, perceptions of leadership power based on sport type found coercive power and legitimate power were more influential to team sport athletes, whereas expert power had more influence in regards to individual sport athletes (Konter, 2005, 2009c). In terms of competition level, the levels of play that were compared included: A-Level youth players (16–18 years) B-Level youth players (14–16 years), Junior Level players, Amateur players (19 and above aged footballers), Second Division Professional players, and Third Division Professional players. In terms of A-Level youth players, the results showed that this group had higher perceptions of coercive power than the Third Division Professionals. In addition, A-Level youth football players had higher perceptions of expert power than the Junior youth level players, Amateur players, Second Division Professional players, and Third Division Professional players, In terms of B-Level youth players, the results showed that this group had higher perceptions of coercive power than the Junior level players, A-Level youth players, Amateur players, and Second Division Professional players. Moreover, results showed that B-Level youth football players had higher perceptions of expert power than the Junior level players, Amateur players, Third Division Professional players, and Second Division Professional players. These levels and ages appear to be important as a transition period from amateur level to semi-professional and professional level of football. Coercive power and expert power perceptions seem to be critical at the A-Level and B-Level football. We can surmise from these results that A-Level footballers need more expert and coercive power perceptions from their coach.

### Relationship between leadership power and psychological skills

An important consideration when discussing power perceptions of a leader is the influence it might have on psychological skills. Konter (2017) assessed this relationship by collecting data from 236 footballers aged 12–32 years old ($M_{age} = 14.49 \pm 2.63$). Footballers completed the scales of Sport Leadership Power Perception Scale (SLPS-19, Konter, Yang, & Chan, 2015) and the Soccer Psychological Skills Scale-12 (SPSS-12, Konter, 2017). As mentioned above, the SLPS-19 comprises five factors (referent power, legitimate power, expert power, coercive power, and reward power), and the SPSS-12 consists of four factors (imagery, commitment, peaking under pressure, and coping with stress). In terms of the relationships between power and psychological skills, referent power was positively correlated with imagery, and coping with stress. Legitimate power was positively correlated with commitment, and peaking under pressure. Expert power was significantly correlated with imagery, commitment, peaking under pressure, and coping with stress. Reward power was positively correlated with imagery and coping with stress. In contrast, coercive power was negatively correlated with imagery, and peaking under pressure. The implications from these results are the following:

- It is important for footballers to identify with their coaches regarding the benefits of using imagery and coping with stress. However, coaches should remember that players' referent power perceptions could affect their imagery and coping with stress skills. Therefore, coaches who have players struggling with imagery and coping with stress should increase their referent power perceptions (e.g. be more emphatic, improve communication, use reinforcements effectively) to assist their athletes.
- It is important for footballers to have strong perceptions of legitimate power from their coaches to achieve higher commitment and peaking under pressure skills. To increase this type of perception, coaches should have a strong management support, and a solid coaching background.
- It is important for footballers to have strong perceptions of expert power from their coaches to assist with increasing imagery, commitment, peaking under pressure, and coping with stress. Coaches can assist their athletes by having

current knowledge through coach education programmes, and be willing to develop themselves as a coach.

- Coaches need to understand that players' reward power perceptions could affect their imagery and coping with stress skills. Thus, coaches should remember to be fair in delivering rewards and increase their use of intrinsic motivation to aid their players.
- Coercive power could be detrimental for players' imagery and peaking under pressure skills. It is important for coaches to limit this kind of power in relation to developing these psychological skills.

Konter (2017) also assessed the differences of power perceptions of the leader based on their use of psychological skills (imagery, commitment, peaking under pressure, and coping with stress). First, in terms of imagery use, footballers reporting higher imagery use had higher perceptions of leader referent power, expert power, coercive power, and reward power, than football players with lower imagery. However, there was no difference in legitimate power. Imagery as a psychological skill seems to be influential for most of the types of leadership power with the exception of legitimate power (Munroe-Chandler & Guerrero, 2019, Chapter 16 in this book). It seems that effective leadership power perceptions of players are important for the use and development of imagery skill. Referent, expert, coercive, and reward powers of coaches are related more to player imagery than legitimate power.

In terms of commitment, footballers with higher levels of commitment perceived their leaders to be higher in expert power. However, there was no significance related to reward, legitimate, referent, or coercive power. Expert power perceptions seem to be more important than any other power perceptions regarding their commitment. If footballers do not perceive expert power from their coaches this can have commitment issues.

In terms of peaking under pressure, footballers with higher perceptions of this construct have stronger perceptions of referent power, legitimate power, coercive power, expert power, and reward power than football players with lower scores of peaking under pressure. Peaking under pressure as a psychological skill seems to be important for all indicated leadership power perceptions. A number of performance problems arise from stress, anxiety, and not peaking under pressure (Konter, Beckmann, & Mallett (2019), Chapter 14 in this book; Wagstaff, Kenttä, & Thelwell (2019), Chapter 15 in this book).

Finally, in terms of coping with stress, footballers with better coping skills perceived referent power and legitimate power in their leader compared to those with poorer coping skills. Expert power, coercive power, and reward power did not have an association with coping skills. Leaders with referent and legitimate power seem to help athletes cope best. Taken together, these results suggest that referent, legitimate, and expert power are the most influential on athlete psychological skills (please see Chapter 8 on effective football coaching and Chapter 14 on psychological skill in football in this volume).

## Sport leadership power perception of coaches

Gould, Giannini, Krane, and Hodge (1990) and Gould, Tammen, Murphy, and May (1991) argued that seminars and text books have a minimal effect as informational resources for coaches. The research indicated that factors leading to success for coaches consist in learning from their own experience, applying their own style, adapting the changing conditions, and monitoring other successful coaches (expert and referent power). Bloom (1997) argued that athletes working with coaches, who have a strong work ethic (expert power), and better communication skills (referent power) are more satisfied, more successful, have better developed skills, more chance of self-realization and self-actualization. Additionally, Bloom (1997) noted that successful coaches generally seek updated knowledge in their specific field, work hard to continually develop themselves, share and exchange information with their peer coaches, participate in seminars, courses, and conferences, read books, use technology in their sports, and stay constantly in the coaching experience (expert power). Gould, Collins, Lauer, and Chung (2006, 2007) studied the characteristics of high school American football coaches who were recognized for developing character and positive personal characteristics in their players (expert power). They conducted in-depth phone interviews with 10 finalists for the National Football League Charities 'Coach of the Year Program'. Ten of the coaches' former players were also interviewed. They indicated that, while these coaches were highly motivated to win, they made the personal development of their players a top priority (expert and referent power). In addition, these coaches had well-thought-out coaching philosophies and clear expectations relative to rules (expert power), player behaviours, and team needs (referent power). Gould et al. (2006, 2007) concluded that, while common themes and patterns were evident across coaches, each coach focused on a relatively small number of individual specific key principles such as having discipline (legitimate and coercive power), working hard, being totally prepared (expert power), and respecting and putting one's family before other needs (referent power). These findings indicate that leadership power perceptions could be important in relation to different preparation dimensions of sport (i.e. physical, technical, tactical, psychological preparation, and social aspects). These perceptions could also be important for the different motives for competing and participating in sport, including for health, satisfaction, fun, success, and performance.

## Leadership power perceptions of football coaches

Konter (2017) assessed leadership power of coaches in relation to a number of different demographic variables. In terms of age, experience, and education, legitimate power and coercive power were negatively correlated with age, coaching experience, and football coaching education. That is to say that coaches who were younger relied more on coercion and being perceived as legitimate rather than being liked and respected (referent power), acquiring and demonstrating expertise (expert power) or effectively using rewards (reward power) in their coaching. As coaches mature, gain more experience, and further their coaching education, they are less likely to rely on the use of coercion or the nature of their title alone in their coaching. In addition, Konter (2017) found a number of results related to leadership power perceptions and football coaches' philosophical approach, coaches' education, coaches' experience.

*Leadership power perception of football coaches and their philosophy*

Many football coaches adopt or abide by one or more coaching philosophies in their approach to leadership. Interestingly, football coaches who had a philosophy of fun had higher perceptions of expert power than football coaches who focused on development and winning alone. Having fun without the presence of expert power may be problematic for the development and success of footballers.

*Leadership power perception of football coaches and their coaching education*

Football coaches with a university education had significantly higher perceptions of expert power than football coaches with only football coaching courses. In addition, football coaches with a university education combined with other types of university education and football coaching courses had significantly higher perceptions of legitimate power than coaches with only Football Association (FA) football coaching courses. Therefore, the combination of football coaching education seems to be important for perceiving expert power and legitimate power. It seems important for coaches to perceive these powers in themselves first in order to influence their players' fun, performance, and success.

*Leadership power perception of football coaches and their years of experience*

Football coaches with fewer than 10 years of football coaching experience had significantly higher perceptions of legitimate power and coercive power than coaches with more than 10 years of football coaching experience. Ten years of coaching experience appears to be critical for optimizing expert power. The less experienced coaches may tend to apply more coercive power and be in need of more legitimate power. Taken together it seems that experienced coaches with good education are required for effective power to influence fun, performance, and success of players.

## Conclusion

This chapter provides some initial insight on the perception of the different sources of leadership power within football. It seems important for football coaches to view some aspects of leadership power as a positive for the psychological development of their athletes (e.g. commitment, imagery, peaking under pressure, and coping with stress) with the potential to positively influence the team's dynamics (e.g. cohesion), and performance. In general, expert and referent power seem to yield the most positive associations with psychological skills, and individual and team outcomes. As Renaissance philosopher Francis Bacon said, 'knowledge is power'. In addition, from Maslow's (1968) and Alderfer's (1972) basic needs of human beings' theories is that perceptions of psychological connection, love, respect, relatedness, and growth are important concepts for self-actualization and realizing the full potential of interpersonal relationships. Perhaps arguably the greatest football manager of all time, Sir Alex Ferguson sums it up best: 'Build your team around respect, not fear; respect breeds trust – and that's what every leader needs in order to thrive.'

In terms of avenues for future research, researchers could examine the different types of power perceptions in football in relation to personality types (e.g. Big Five, personality of mood states) and other psychological factors (e.g. self-regulation, self-confidence, motivation, mental toughness, courage). Lastly, future research could also consider the different power perceptions in relation to various environmental factors, cultures, and economic conditions in various levels of football.

## References

Alderfer, C. P. (1972). *Existence, relatedness, and growth.* New York, NY: Free Press.

Avolio, B. J., & Gardner, W. L. (2005). Authentic leadership development: Getting to the root of positive forms of leadership. *The Leadership Quarterly, 16*(3), 315–338.

Bass, B. M., & Riggio, R. E. (2006). *Transformational leadership* (2nd ed.). Mahwah, NJ: Lawrence Erlbaum.

Bloom, G. (1997). *Characteristics, knowledge, and strategies of expert team coaches.* Unpublished doctoral dissertation, University of Ottawa, Faculty of Education, Canada.

Carron, A. V., & Eys, M. A. (2012). *Group dynamics in sport* (4th ed.). Morgantown, WV: Fitness Information Technology.

Chelladurai, P. (1990). Leadership in sports: A review. *International Journal of Sport Psychology, 21*, 328–354.

Chelladurai, P. (2007). Leadership in sports. In G. Tenenbaum & R. C. Eklund (Eds.), *The sport psychology handbook* (pp. 113–135). Indianapolis, IN: Wiley.

Chelladurai, P., & Haggerty, T. R. (1978). A normative model of decision styles in coaching. *Athletic Administration, 13*, 6–9.

Chelladurai, P., Haggerty, T. R., & Baxter, P. R. (1989). Decision styles choices of university basketball coaches and players. *Journal of Sport and Exercise Psychology, 11*(2), 201–215.

Chelladurai, P., & Saleh, S. D. (1980). Dimensions of leader behaviour in sports: Development of a leadership scale. *Journal of Sport Psychology, 2*, 34–45.

Eklund, C. R., & Tenenbaum, G. (2014). *Encyclopedia of sport and exercise psychology.* London, England: Sage Publications.

French, J., & Raven, B. H. (1959). The bases of social power. In D. Cartwright (Ed.), *Studies in social power* (pp. 150–167). Ann Arbor, MI: Institute for Social Research.

Frost, D. E., & Stahelski, A. J. (1988). The systematic measurement of French and Raven's bases of social power in workgroups. *Journal of Applied Social Psychology, 18*(5), 375–389.

Frost, T. F., & Moussavi, F. (2011). The relationship between leader power and influence: The moderating role of trust. *Journal of Applied Business Research, 8*(4), 9–14.

Garland, D. J., & Barry, J. R. (1991). Cognitive advantage in sport: The nature of perceptual structures. *The American Journal of Psychology, 104*(2), 211–228.

Gould, D., Collins, K., Lauer, L., & Chung, Y. (2006). Coaching life skills: A working model. *Sport & Exercise Psychology Review, 2*, 10–18.

Gould, D., Collins, K., Lauer, L., & Chung, Y. (2007). Coaching life skills through football: A study of award winning high school coaches. *Journal of Applied Sport Psychology, 19*, 16–37.

Gould, D., Giannini, J., Krane, V., & Hodge, K. (1990). Educational needs of elite U.S. National Team, Pan American, and Olympic coaches. *Journal of Teaching in Physical Education, 9*(4), 332–344.

Gould, D., Tammen, V., Murphy, S., & May, J. (1991). An evaluation of U.S. Olympic sport psychology consultant effectiveness. *The Sport Psychologist, 5*(2), 111–127.

Greenleaf, R. K. (1977). *Servant leadership: A journey into the nature of legitimate power and greatness.* Mahwah, NJ: Paulist Press.

Horn, T. S. (2008). Coaching effectiveness in the sport domain. In T. S. Horn (Ed.), *Advances in sport psychology* (pp. 239–267, 455–459). Champaign, IL: Human Kinetics.

Horne, T., & Carron, A. V. (1985). Compatibility in coach-athlete relationships. *Journal of Sport and Exercise Psychology, 7*(2), 137–149.

Jacob, C. S., & Carron, A. V. (1996). Sources of status in sports teams. *International Journal of Sport Psychology, 27*, 369–382.

Jacob, C. S., & Carron, A. V. (1998). The association between status and cohesion in sport teams. *Journal of Sports Sciences, 16*, 187–198.

Jowett, S., & Ntoumanis, N. (2004). The Coach-Athlete Relationship Questionnaire (CART-Q): Development and initial validation. *Scandinavian Journal of Medicine and Science in Sports, 14*, 245–257.

Kent, M. (2006). *Oxford dictionary of sport science and medicine* (3rd ed.). Oxford, England: Oxford University Press.

Knoppers, A., Meyer, B. B., Ewing, M., & Forrest, L. (1990). Dimensions of power: A question of sport or gender? *Sociology of Sport, 7*, 369–377.

Konter, E. (2005). Perception of leadership power of coaches and athletes according to participation in team and individual sports. *Turkish Journal of Sport Medicine, 40*(2), 43–51.

Konter, E. (2008a). Towards adaptation of self and other versions of leadership Power in Sport Questionnaires for Turkey. *Personality, Motivation, Sport, 13*, 200–211.

Konter, E. (2008b). Leadership power perception of football players according to frequency of playing for the national teams. *Sportmetre, 6*(2), 81–86.

Konter, E. (2009a). Towards adaptation of self and other versions of the revised Power in Football Questionnaire for Turkey. *European Sport Management Quarterly, 9*, 311–332.

Konter, E. (2009b). Perceptions of football players about leadership powers according to their level of play. *Journal of Social Behavior and Personality, 37*(4), 503–512.

Konter, E. (2009c). Leadership perception of coaches and athletes according to their age groups. *Turkish Journal of Counseling Psychology, 4*(31), 61–68.

Konter, E. (2012). Leadership power perception of football coaches and football players according to their education. *Journal of Human Kinetics, 34*, 139–146.

Konter, E. (2017). Psychological skills of soccer players in relation to level of courage, individual and performance variables. International Society of Sport Psychology-ISSP World Congress, 10–14 June, Seville, Spain.

Konter, E., Beckmann, J., & Mallett, C. (2019). Psychological skills for football players. In E. Konter, J. Beckmann, & T. M. Loughead (Eds.), *Football psychology: From theory to practice.* London, England: Routledge.

Konter, E., Yang, X. S., & Chan, K. C. (2015). Sport leadership power perception in Turkey: Scale development and initial validation among children, adolescents, and adults. III International Exercise and Sport Psychology Congress, 23–25 October, İstanbul.

Loughead, T. M., & Hardy, J. (2005). An examination of coach and peer leader behaviours in sport. *Psychology of Sport and Exercise, 6*, 303–312.

Maslow, A. H. (1968). *Toward a psychology of being.* New York, NY: Nostrand.

Munroe-Chandler, K., & Guerrero, M. (2019). Imagery in football. In E. Konter, J. Beckmann, & T. Loughead (Eds.), *Football psychology: From theory to practice.* London, England: Routledge.

Northouse, P. G. (2001). *Leadership: Theory and practice* (2nd ed.). Thousand Oaks, CA: Sage.

Paradis, K. F., & Loughead, T. M. (2012). Examining the mediating role of cohesion between athlete leadership and athlete satisfaction in youth sport. *International Journal of Sport Psychology, 43*(2), 117–136.

Price, M. S., & Weiss, M. R. (2000). Relationships among coach burnout, coach behaviours and athletes' psychological responses. *The Sport Psychologist, 14*, 391–409.

Raven, B. H. (1992). A power/interaction model of interpersonal influence: French and Raven thirty years later. *Journal of Social Behavior & Personality, 7*(2), 217–244.

Raven, B. H. (2008). The bases of power and the power/interaction model of interpersonal influence. *Analyses of Social Issues and Public Policy, 8*(1), 1–22.

Riemer, H. A., & Chelladurai, P. (1995). Leadership and satisfaction in athletics. *Journal of Sport & Exercise Psychology, 17*, 276–293.

Shapiro, M., Ingols, C., & Blake-Beard, S. (2011). Using power to influence outcomes Does gender matter? *Journal of Management Education, 35*(5), 713–748.

Smith, R. E., Smoll, F. L., & Curtis, B. (1979). Coach effectiveness training: A cognitive-behavioral approach to enhancing relationship skills in youth sport coaches. *Journal of Sport Psychology, 1*, 59–75.

Smith, R. E., Smoll, F. L., & Hunt, E. (1977). A system for the behavioral assessment of athletic coaches. *Research Quarterly, 48*, 401–407.

Soucie, D. (1994). Effective managerial leadership in sport organizations. *Journal of Sport Management, 8*, 1–13.

Stahelski, A. J., Frost, D. E., & Patch, M. E. (1989). Use of socially dependent bases of power: French and Raven's theory applied to workgroup leadership. *Journal of Applied Social Psychology, 19*, 283–297.

Summers, R. J. (1991). The association between athletes' perceptions of their abilities on the influence of coach technical instruction. *Journal of Sport Behavior, 14*(1), 30–40.

Turman, P. D. (2003). Coaches and cohesion: The impact of coaching techniques on team cohesion in the small group sport setting. *Journal of Sport Behavior, 26*(1), 86–104.

Turman, P. D. (2006). Athletes' perception of coach power use and the association between playing status and sport satisfaction. *Communication Research Reports, 23*(4), 273–282.

Wagstaff, Kenttä, & Thelwell, R. C. (2019). The use of acceptance and commitment therapy for stress management interventions in football. In E. Konter, J. Beckmann, & T. Loughead (Eds.), *Football psychology: From theory to practice*. London, England: Routledge.

Wann, D. L., Metcalf, L. A., Brewer, K. R., & Whiteside, H. D. (2000). Development of the Power in Sport Questionnaires. *Journal of Sport Behavior, 23*, 423–443.

Wann, D. L., & Pack, M. T. (2001). Perceptions of power in a first-year collegiate varsity program. *Perceptual and Motor Skills, 92(3)*, 834.

Weiss, M. R., & Friedrichs, W. D. (1986). The influence of leader behaviours, coach attributes, and institutional variables on performance and satisfaction of collegiate basketball teams. *Journal of Sport Psychology, 8*, 332–346.

Westre, K. R., & Weiss, M. R. (1991). The relationship between perceived coaching behaviours on group cohesion in high school football teams. *The Sport Psychologist, 5*, 41–54.

Wrong, D. H. (1979). *Power*. New York, NY: Harper.

# 11 Coach justice and competence in football

*Tomás García-Calvo, Francisco M. Leo, and Inmaculada González-Ponce*

**Abstract**

The ability of a coach to be perceived as fair by players when making decisions is important in the functioning of the team. When a coach makes decisions with a consistent criterion and justification, the players can better understand the actions, behaviours, and attitudes of their coach in situations that can become contentious. In this chapter a theoretical explanation of perceived competence and justice in the head coach will be discussed. Further, the importance of the five coach competence dimensions and the four factors of justice will be analysed. In addition, previous research with business and sports groups will be reviewed, which has shown that perceptions of the different facets of perceived justice influence behaviours and attitudes of members of a group. Finally, selected results with professional football players will be presented. This chapter provides evidence about the emergence of disruptive behaviours of the players towards the coach or to his/her teammates since the perception of unfairness in decision-making within the team can generate unrest and discontent by some team members.

Within the study of psychological processes in football, the analysis of coach behaviour has proven to be an essential area due to its importance for the improvement of athlete performance and individual and collective satisfaction of the athletes (Wang & Straub, 2012). This fact has led to an interesting line of research to better understand which variables can optimize players' satisfaction and its derived behavioural benefits, such as higher levels of commitment, effort, or performance (García-Calvo, Leo, González-Ponce, et al., 2014; Myers & Feltz, 2012). In this sense, players' perceptions of how coaches impart justice through their decisions and of the competency level of their work are critical constructs that can help to explain players' satisfaction with their coach and their performance on football teams, as well as cohesion, collective efficacy, or motivation.

In this chapter, we will identify the characteristics of the perception of coaching competency and justice, the existing measures to evaluate them, and the importance of these variables for a new perspective concerning the analysis of coach behaviour in football. Lastly, we will propose some practical implications that could help professionals improve the application of these variables within the football context.

# Theory and research

## Defining coaching justice and competency

The construct of perceived justice was first examined in organizational psychology and is related to employees' perception of their supervisor's fairness. Specifically, perceived justice was conceptualized by Greenberg (1990) as a theory attempting to describe and explain the role of fairness in the workplace.

García-Calvo, Leo, and González-Ponce (2014) explained the characteristics of perceived justice in the context of football using Greenberg's (1990) four dimensions. The first dimension is established from the players' assessment of what they receive from the organization/coach as a result of their efforts (*distributive justice*). The rewards are the tangible aspects that players receive, such as more playing time, being a first-team player, or economic rewards. Distributive justice includes aspects such as equity, rewarding the players according to their contributions, equality, where all players have the chance to earn the rewards, and need, adapting the offer to the player's needs. The second dimension, *procedural justice*, refers to the fairness of the processes to allocate the rewards received from the organization/coach. For example, the coach may consider a player's effort to determine who plays in a match. Similarly, different procedures may be used to determine who is the captain or who should play a certain role within the team. Finally, players may develop cognitions based on their assessment of the quality of interaction with their coach (*interactional justice*), in which two elements play a key role: the quality of the treatment they receive, referring to the dignity and respect with which their coach treats them (*interpersonal justice*), and the clarity of the information they receive from the coach (*informational justice*).

Another concept that is important for satisfaction and performance in football, is coaching competency, that draws on theoretical perspectives related to coaching behaviour (Feltz, Chase, Moritz, & Sullivan, 1999). Coaching competency is defined as athletes' perceptions of their head coach's ability to affect their learning and performance (Myers, Wolfe, Maier, Reckase, & Feltz, 2006, p. 452).

Myers, Wolfe et al. (2006) operationalized this multidimensional and multi-level construct as having four competencies: motivation, game strategy, technique, and character building. Motivation competency (MC) is defined as athletes' evaluations of their head coach's ability to affect their psychological mood and skills. Game strategy competency (GSC) refers to athletes' perception of their head coach's ability to lead during competition. Technique competency (TC) is defined as athletes' ratings of their head coach's instructional and diagnostic abilities. Character building competency (CBC) refers to athletes' assessment of their head coach's ability to influence their personal development and positive attitude toward sport. Subsequently, Myers, Chase, Beauchamp, and Jackson (2010) added a fifth dimension, physical conditioning competency, which refers to athletes' perceptions of their head coach's ability to prepare them physically for sport participation.

## Measures of coaching justice and competency

Perceived justice has been assessed with different instruments which have been based on some of the factors that conceptualize this construct. As an example of this, we can observe the Distributive Justice Index (Price & Mueller, 1981), or the Interactional Justice Scale (Aquino, 1995), which only measures a single factor of perceived justice. To complement these tools, Niehoff and Moorman (1993) conceptualized perceived justice as a three-factor model comprised of distributive, procedural, and interactional justice.

To overcome these limitations, Colquitt (2001) advanced the Organizational Justice Scale, based on the four-factor structure suggested by Greenberg (1990), validating a measure which is currently the most widely used to assess this construct. Therefore, this scale consists of 20 items, grouped into four factors: Distributive, Procedural, Interpersonal, and Informational justice. Colquitt compared multiple a priori factor structures, including one-global-factor, two-factor (with distributive justice as one factor and procedural justice as the other, with procedural subsuming interpersonal and informational justice), three-factor (with distributive, procedural, and interactional justice, formed by interpersonal and informational justice) and four-factor conceptualizations which were explained in the previous section. Confirmatory factor analysis showed that the best fitting model was the four-factor model and the worst one was the one-factor model. Model comparisons using the 90% confidence interval of the Root Mean Square Error of Approximation (RMSEA) illustrated that the four-factor model is significantly better than the three-factor model, this is significantly better than the two-factor model, and this is significantly better than the one-factor model. These results are important since it is corroborated that the concept of perceived justice is multidimensional with four factors. In this sense, coaches who want to be fair in their decisions should attend to these four different dimensions.

With regard to the sports context, most of the works to date have adapted this scale (De Backer et al., 2011; De Backer, Boen, De Cuyper, Høigaard, & Vande Broek, 2015; Ha & Ha, 2015; Nikbin, Hyun, Albooyeh, & Foroughi, 2014; Nikbin, Hyun, Iranmanesh, & Foroughi, 2014). In this way, García-Calvo, Leo, and González-Ponce (2014) adapted this instrument, based on the four factors of justice, which is made up of 12 items: three items to assess Distributive Justice (e.g. 'is consistent and changes the players when they are performing below par'), three items for Procedural Justice (e.g. 'decides who will be part of the first team based on individual talent and physical form'), three items for Interpersonal Justice (e.g. 'treats the players in the training sessions and games respectfully'), and three items to assess Informational Justice (e.g. 'explains and discusses tactical decisions').

Regarding coaching competency, Feltz et al. (1999) developed the Coaching Efficacy Scale (CES), based on the theoretical construct of coach behaviour, which consisted of four factors (motivation, game strategy, technique, and character building). Although this scale was developed to be completed by the coach, Myers, Feltz, Maier, Wolfe, and Reckase (2006) considered that the players should be the ones to assess coaching competency. For this purpose, they defined coaching competency as the players' assessment of their coach's capacity to affect their learning and performance. From this starting point, they developed the Coaching Competency Scale (CCS), that comprises four factors: motivation competence (seven items), game strategy competence (eight items), technique competence (six items), and character building competence (four items). Later, Myers et al. (2010) developed the Athletes' Perceptions of Coaching Competency Scale II-High School Teams (APCCS

II-HST). This scale has all four factors of the CCS, but adds one more factor labelled physical training competency.

Thus, Myers et al. (2010) proposed a multidimensional model composed of five factors: competency for motivating, competency to direct the competition, teaching competency, character-building competency, and physical preparation competency. In this study, the authors found different results with a multi-level analysis. So, the five-factors model was the most adequate when the analysis was intrateam, and a uni-dimensional model was the best fit index when the analysis was interteam. This instrument showed satisfactory reliability coefficients for all the factors of a Spanish version (González-Ponce et al., 2017).

### Summary of the research on justice and competency: latest scientific contributions

It should be pointed out that there are very few research studies that have used perceived justice and coaching competence in the sports context and are practically non-existent in football to our knowledge. In this section we will highlight the studies that used these variables (i.e. justice and competency) and their relationship with other fundamental constructs in football, such as group processes, satisfaction, and performance. First, the main studies developed with these variables will be presented. Second, it will be shown that there are differing results depending on the context and player characteristics. Finally, the most relevant results of a study carried out with perceived justice and coach competence in the context of professional football will be explained.

Among the research that has examined the importance of justice in sports, it would appear players who perceived their coach to be fair in decision-making at different levels (i.e. distributive, procedural, informational, and interactional) had more adaptive attitudes, team identification, and group cohesion (De Backer et al., 2015; Nikbin, Hyun, Albooyeh, & Foroughi, 2014). Results demonstrated that perceived justice was a predictor of the motivational climate and consequently of team identification and team cohesion. De Backer et al. (2015) developed a model that hypothesized that both procedural justice and distributive justice shaped people's social identity within groups, which in turn influences attitudes and behaviours. In support of this assumption, previous research had demonstrated that athletes' perceived justice of the coach positively predicts team identification and team cohesion in elite sport teams (De Backer et al., 2011). In fact, De Backer et al. (2011) noted the importance of players' perceived coaching justice to achieve adequate well-being within the group, to feel united and identified with the group.

In contrast, it has been shown that athletes' perceptions of coaching competency may be associated with group processes such as role ambiguity (Bosselut, Heuzé, Eys, Fontayne, & Sarrazin, 2012), and team cohesion (Turman, 2003). Thus, when athletes perceived their coach to be effective in developing the psychological skills and motivational states of athletes they tended to report greater connection with their coach and team cohesion, and less role conflict. In this sense, González-Ponce et al. (2018), with a multi-level modelling analysis, showed that game strategy and character-building competencies negatively predicted both task and relationship conflicts at the individual level, whereas motivation competency was also added as a significant predictor of task conflict at the team level.

As explained above, in addition to the group processes it is important to analyse other variables such as the players' perception of satisfaction with the coach and performance. In this sense, athletes' perceptions of their coaches being competent (Myers, Beauchamp, & Chase, 2011) and treating their players fairly (Nikbin, Hyun, Albooyeh, & Foroughi, 2014) can be relevant aspects for individual and collective satisfaction and performance. In this way, perceived justice and the competence of the coach will help to achieve an adequate work climate and, therefore, a better team functioning. In addition, this can make the athletes more satisfied with their coach, and therefore improve the perception of individual and collective performance (Kim & Andrew, 2013; Myers et al., 2011; Myers, Wolfe, et al., 2006; Nikbin, Hyun, Iranmanesh, & Foroughi, 2014). For instance, Myers, Wolfe, et al. (2006) found football and ice hockey players' perceptions of their coach's motivation competency positively predicted satisfaction with their coach. Likewise, Myers, Vargas-Tonsing, and Feltz (2005) found that coaching efficacy predicted coaching behaviour, team satisfaction, and winning percentage for men's teams. Total coaching efficacy predicted only coaching behaviour across women teams. Character-building efficacy was negatively related to team satisfaction in women's teams with male coaches. Motivation efficacy was positively related to team satisfaction in women's teams with female coaches.

Another line of research that allows us to advance in the importance of perceived justice and competence over satisfaction with the coach and team performance has been developed by García-Calvo, Leo, González Ponce, Pulido, and Rodríguez (2019). These authors have examined the characteristics of coaches who kept their job throughout the season compared to those coaches who were dismissed during the first (Change 1) or second phase of the season (Change 2). García-Calvo, Leo, et al. (2019) found the differences between these coaches, which emerged mainly at the start of the season, were mostly in perceived justice. As shown in Figure 11.1, coaches who kept their jobs for the entire season were perceived at the beginning of the season by their players as having higher levels of justice, especially in the factors of interpersonal and procedural justice compared to those who lost their coaching job. That is, coaches who received lower ratings of perceived justice from their players at the start of season (after two months of training) were less likely to finish

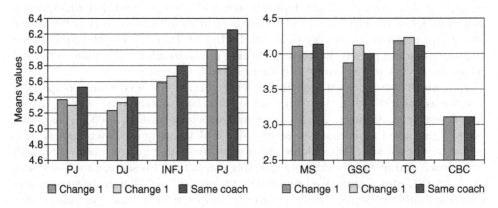

*Figure 11.1* Means values of perception of justice and coach competency at the start of the season on teams that changed or maintained their coach.

the season as the team's head coach. In the case of the coach's competence, no significant differences were found at the beginning of the season in any of its factors, so we could highlight that it has less effect on this variable.

As explained above, the perceptions of competency and justice may not be the same in men and women, or there may be differences between teams, or even players within the same team may grant more relevance to certain aspects as a function of their beliefs and experiences (García-Calvo, Leo, et al., 2019). This fact was contrasted in the study of Myers et al. (2011) because, at the individual athlete level of analysis, the results showed a moderately high and positive relationship between MC and satisfaction with the coach in a sample of intercollegiate teams (Myers, Wolfe, et al., 2006), and a higher positive relationship between MC and TC and satisfaction with the coach in a sample of high school teams (Myers et al., 2011). The results also indicated that coaching competency exerted a large positive effect on satisfaction with the coach at the team/group level of analysis (Myers et al., 2011).

In a study in football, conducted by García-Calvo, González-Ponce, Sánchez-Oliva, Pulido, and Leo (2019) with professional male and female league teams, they found significant differences in the factors of justice and competency that predicted satisfaction with the coach, and, moreover, their evolution throughout the season also varied between the two genders (e.g. Figure 11.2). In general, the results showed that men valued more game strategy competency and procedural and distributive justice, whereas women placed more value on social and relational aspects, such as interpersonal justice and motivational competency. Further, women granted more importance to maintaining adequate interpersonal relations than to the coach's technical and strategic knowledge, as well as to the coach's way of administering justice.

## Practical implications

As indicated throughout this chapter, perceived coaching justice and competency can shed some light on coach behaviour and group processes in the football context. Specifically, considering the influence of these variables on football players'

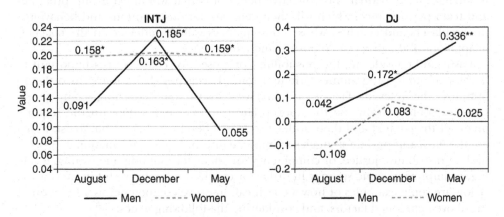

*Figure 11.2* Graphical representation of the interrelationship between perceived justice and satisfaction with the coach for men and women players.

satisfaction and performance as well as on group processes, it is important to advance some priorities in order to initiate appropriate applications in the practice of football.

The first issue to keep in mind is the differentiation of behaviour according to the context in which it occurs. Thus, as shown in diverse studies analysed, players' satisfaction and performance are associated with coaches' behaviours of justice and competency, but they differ as a function of contextual variables, such as athletes' gender, age, or competitive level. Regarding the competitive level, it seems that the higher the competitive demand, the more importance players grant to coaches' competency and their capacity to be fair. Players also rate as higher the aspects related to interpersonal and informational justice.

Hence, coaches must be able to adjust their behaviour accordingly to better adapt to the characteristics of the context and to the needs of their players. Drawing on the idea that the more competent and fairer the coaches' behaviour, the more positive effects they will achieve in the direction of sport teams, it should also be taken into account that a certain kind of justice should be emphasized depending on the context, age, gender, etc., and coaches should focus either on learning- or motivation-related competency.

A second important application of knowing about these variables in the football context is that the perception of coaching justice and competency is dynamic, and this involves constant fluctuations over time (Leo, González-Ponce, Sánchez-Miguel, Ivarsson, & García-Calvo, 2015). These changes are affected by many factors, among which are team performance, achieving individual and collective goals, and the group processes that develop during training and competitions. It is advisable to propose strategies to maintain a good group climate, make the team and players more competitive and efficacious, and have an adequate relationship with the players (García-Calvo, Leo, González-Ponce, et al., 2014; Leo et al., 2015; Leo, Sánchez-Miguel, Sánchez-Oliva, Amado, & García-Calvo, 2014). As can be observed, many of these strategies are related to the behaviours of justice and competency that the players will perceive, so it can be observed that this process is a loop in which coaches' behaviour regarding the way they impart justice and their level of competency will determine how they are perceived by their players. This, in turn, will lead to changes in individual and collective behaviours that will affect group processes and team performance, which will then generate various emotions and behaviours in the players and coaches, whose consequences will be reflected in the coaches' adaptations of the processes of justice and competency.

Lastly and considering the possibilities proposed for coaches, it is important to develop training programmes oriented towards coaches' behaviours, in order to optimize the relevant factors of perceived justice and coaching competency. Coaches could thereby use the appropriate resources depending on the requirements of the context and their athletes' needs. Therefore, it is crucial to ask which are the most appropriate strategies to improve interpersonal, informational, procedural, or distributive justice, or competency for character building, motivating, teaching, or improving game strategy in order for coaches to be successful in their work. Below are some examples of how a coach can improve competency as a function of the above-mentioned factors, and considering the following issues:

*Distributive justice.* Coaches must ensure that all the players have the chance to achieve rewards for their tasks, assigning to each player a relevant role. While not all players will compete in all competitions, coaches should still try to assign some type of role to their players. For instance, players with less playing time can take on a role with more social responsibilities.

*Procedural justice.* In order to improve procedural justice processes, coaches can establish different strategies to make fairer decisions about distributing rewards and imparting justice. The players should participate in the processes and productivity standards to be established for collective functioning, allowing them to set up some of them, which is subsequently approved by all the players. It is important to reach a high degree of collective agreement, so that all the players feel they participated in the behaviour and productivity standards that are to be used. It is equally important for coaches to be consistent in the application of these rules and in their daily compliance, using strategies that engage their players to a greater extent. Lastly, coaches should establish alternative procedures to solve problems or difficulties when applying justice processes such as, for example, exceptions or modifications of the rules for special situations that may emerge during the season. Coaches should also consider the players' views when modifying or applying these issues.

*Informational justice.* The players should be informed about how rewards (first-team player, changes during the game, roles, etc.) are established. For this purpose, besides making them participate in the decision-making process, as noted above, coaches should set up individual meetings with each player to clarify roles, propose individual behaviours that the coach wants the player to perform, and reorient behaviours so that the player will know and follow the productivity standards. It is also recommended to present the main rules and standards that will govern behaviour and team functioning regarding the desired attitudes and values.

*Interpersonal justice.* Coaches should develop social skills that allow them to adapt their relationship with the players. Thus, among the skills to be developed, we underline communication capacity, both to express and to receive information, empathic capacity, to see things from the players' perspective and to understand what they really want to develop, and capacity to relate politely and respectfully to the rest of the team members.

Regarding strategies designed to develop the relevant factors of players' perceived competency, we note the following:

*Game strategy competency.* Coaches should try to improve their capacity to interpret what is going on during the game, in order to make the best decisions possible. For this purpose, they can train this capacity by analysing all the games from a professional perspective, looking for solutions and alternatives to each situation. Moreover, they should develop a plan for each game in advance, establishing guidelines to be followed and decisions to adopt as a function of various aspects and situations that occur during the game.

*Motivational competency.* In order to enhance motivational competency, we can implement strategies based on setting goals that will motivate the players to focus appropriately on training and games. Coaches can also develop communication skills to attract the players' attention and plan their speech adequately to improve motivation in various situations.

*Technical competency.* To improve this competency, coaches should train methodologically, understanding the different existing teaching styles and the possibilities of feedback they can provide, depending on the players' needs and characteristics. The training sessions should also be adequately planned in order to establish in advance the most important moments when the coach must correct or provide guidelines to the players and when this task will be more efficacious.

*Character building.* To develop this competency, coaches should be coherent and honest, using an authentic leadership style to transfer to the players the importance of honesty and effort as the way to achieve success. In this way, coaches seek to transform players' behaviours, beliefs, and attitudes to become better competitors and, at the same time, better people. Likewise, coaches should be behaviour models that serve as a reflection for the players and guide them in this transformational process.

## Conclusions and future research directions

As these constructs are relatively recent in the sphere of psychology applied to football, many very important future lines of research can be developed in the coming years. Hence, one of the first requirements is to establish the characteristics that these variables should have within the context of football in a more contrasted and applied way. For this reason, more studies are needed in different contexts, as male and female teams, competitive or recreational teams, etc. In the same vein, research should establish specific measurement instruments for football, considering the latest postulates of perceived justice differentiated from fairness (Colquitt & Rodell, 2015), and latest competency model (Myers, 2013). It is also necessary to determine the competencies of a football coach, because the competency for physical training is not a determinant in this context, while there may be other competencies that are necessary to be an effective coach.

It would be interesting to specify the strategies that are shown to improve coaching justice and competency from an empirical perspective, carrying out interventions to determine how these strategies affect the players' perception of their coach's behaviour. At the same time, this type of work allows us to know how these strategies will indirectly affect other variables that are essential for football teams' group processes and performance. Thus, by means of this type of research, we could determine what football coaches must develop to work more efficaciously, optimize group processes within their teams, and increase individual and collective performance (see Figure 11.3).

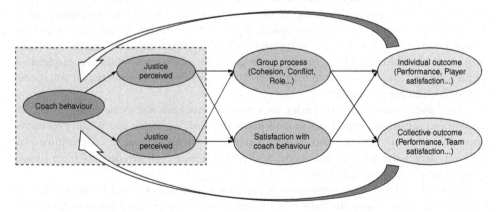

*Figure 11.3* A conceptual framework of coaching effectiveness in sport teams, based on justice and competency variables.

Lastly, it seems essential to carry out longitudinal studies to determine and understand how players' perceptions of coaching justice and competency evolve, and what personal and contextual variables may have an impact on the increase or decrease of their rating of these capacities.

To conclude, we would like to highlight the importance that these variables may achieve in the next few years to explain behaviours and to determine what coaches should do to be successful in their work with a football team.

## References

Aquino, K. (1995). Relationships among pay inequity, perceptions of procedural justice, and organizational citizenship. *Employee Responsibilities and Rights Journal, 8*(1), 21–33. doi. org/10.1007/BF02621253.

Bosselut, G., Heuzé, J. P., Eys, M. A., Fontayne, P., & Sarrazin, P. (2012). Athletes' perceptions of role ambiguity and coaching competency in sport teams: A multilevel analysis. *Journal of Sport & Exercise Psychology, 34*(3), 345–364.

Colquitt, J. A. (2001). On the dimensionality of organizational justice: A construct validation of a measure. *Journal of Applied Psychology, 86*, 386–400. doi.org/10.1037//0021-9010. 86.3.386.

Colquitt, J. A., & Rodell, J. B. (2015). Measuring justice and fairness. In R. S. Cropanzano & M. L. Ambrose (Eds.), *Oxford handbook of justice in the workplace* (pp. 187–202). New York, NY: Oxford University Press. doi.org/10.1093/oxfordhb/9780199981410.013.8.

De Backer, M., Boen, F., Ceux, T., De Cuyper, B., Høigaard, R., Callens, F., ... Vande Broek, G. (2011). Do perceived justice and need support of the coach predict team identification and cohesion? Testing their relative importance among top volleyball and handball players in Belgium and Norway. *Psychology of Sport and Exercise, 12*, 192–201. doi.org/10.1016/j. psychsport.2010.09.009.

De Backer, M., Boen, F., De Cuyper, B., Høigaard, R., & Vande Broek, G. (2015). A team fares well with a fair coach: Predictors of social loafing in interactive female sport teams. *Scandinavian Journal of Medicine and Science in Sports, 25*, 897–908. doi.org/10.1111/sms. 12303.

Feltz, D. L., Chase, M. A., Moritz, S. E., & Sullivan, P. J. (1999). A conceptual model of coaching efficacy: Preliminary investigation and instrument development. *Journal of Educational Psychology, 91*(4), 765–776.

García-Calvo, T., González-Ponce, I., Sánchez-Oliva, D., Pulido, J. J., & Leo, F. M. (2019). What determines coach satisfaction in professional football? Gender differences in a longitudinal study. *Manuscript submitted for publication.*

García-Calvo, T., Leo, F. M., & González-Ponce, I. (2014). Propiedades psicométricas de la escala de justicia percibida en el contexto deportivo [Psychometric properties of the scale of perceived justice in the context of sport]. In *IX Congresso Iberoamericano de Psicologia. Ordem dos Psicologos Portugueses* [Ibero-American Congress of Psychology. Order of Portuguese Psychologists]. Lisbon, Portugal.

García-Calvo, T., Leo, F. M., González Ponce, I., Pulido, J. J., & Rodríguez, M. (2019). What happens when the coach is replaced by another in professional football teams? A group process perspective. *Manuscript submitted for publication.*

García-Calvo, T., Leo, F. M., González-Ponce, I., Sánchez-Miguel, P. A., Mouratidis, A., & Ntoumanis, N. (2014). Perceived coach-created and peer-created motivational climates and their associations with team cohesion and athlete satisfaction: Evidence from a longitudinal study. *Journal of Sports Sciences, 32*, 1738–1750. doi.org/10.1080/02640414.2014.918641.

González-Ponce, I., Jiménez, R., Leo, F. M., Sánchez-Oliva, D., Pulido, J. J., & García-Calvo, T. (2017). Validación al castellano de la escala sobre competencia del entrenador [Validation into Spanish of the athletes' perceptions of coaching competency scale]. *Revista Psicología Del Deporte* [Journal of Sports Psychology], *26*, 95–103.

González-Ponce, I., Leo, F. M., Jiménez, R., Sánchez-Oliva, D., Sarmento, H., Figueiredo, A., & García-Calvo, T. (2018). Athletes' perceptions of coaching competency and team conflict in sport teams: A multilevel analysis. *European Journal of Sport Science, 18*(6), 851–860. doi. org/10.1080/17461391.2018.1461245.

Greenberg, J. (1990). Organizational justice: Yesterday, today, and tomorrow. *Journal of Management, 16*, 399–432.

Ha, J. P., & Ha, J. (2015). Organizational justice-affective commitment relationship in a team sport setting: The moderating effect of group cohesion. *Journal of Management and Organization, 21*, 107–124. doi.org/10.1017/jmo.2014.67.

Kim, S., & Andrew, D. P. S. (2013). Organizational justice in intercollegiate athletics: Perceptions of coaches. *Sport Management Review, 16*(2), 200–210. doi.org/10.1016/j.smr.2012. 08.001.

Leo, F. M., González-Ponce, I., Sánchez-Miguel, P. A., Ivarsson, A., & García-Calvo, T. (2015). Role ambiguity, role conflict, team conflict, cohesion and collective efficacy in sport teams: A multilevel analysis. *Psychology of Sport and Exercise, 20*, 60–66. doi.org/10.1016/j.psych sport.2015.04.009.

Leo, F. M., Sánchez-Miguel, P. A., Sánchez-Oliva, D., Amado, D., & García-Calvo, T. (2014). Análisis de los procesos grupales y el rendimiento en fútbol semiprofesional [Analysis of the group process and the performance in semiprofessional soccer]. *Revista Internacional de Medicina y Ciencias de la Actividad Física y del Deporte* [International Journal of Medicine and Science of Physical Activity and Sport], *14*(53), 153–168.

Myers, N. D. (2013). Coaching competency and (exploratory) structural equation modeling: A substantive-methodological synergy. *Psychology of Sport and Exercise, 14*(5), 709–718. doi. org/10.1016/j.psychsport.2013.04.008.Coaching.

Myers, N. D., Beauchamp, M. R., & Chase, M. A. (2011). Coaching competency and satisfaction with the coach: A multi-level structural equation model. *Journal of Sports Sciences, 29*, 411–422. doi.org/10.1080/02640414.2010.538710.

Myers, N. D., Chase, M. A., Beauchamp, M. R., & Jackson, B. (2010). Athletes' perceptions of coaching competency scale II-high school teams. *Educational and Psychological Measurement, 70*(3), 477–494. doi.org/10.1177/0013164409344520.

Myers, N. D., & Feltz, D. L. (2012). From self-efficacy to collective efficacy in sport: Transitional methodological issues. In G. Tenenbaum & R. Eklund (Eds.), *Handbook of sport psychology* (3rd ed., pp. 799–819). Hoboken, NJ: John Wiley and Sons.

Myers, N. D., Feltz, D. L., Maier, K. S., Wolfe, E. W., & Reckase, M. D. (2006). Athletes' evaluations of their head coach's coaching competency. *Research Quarterly for Exercise and Sport, 77*, 111–121.

Myers, N. D., Vargas-Tonsing, T. M., & Feltz, D. L. (2005). Coaching efficacy in intercollegiate coaches: Sources, coaching behavior, and team variables. *Psychology of Sport and Exercise, 6*(1), 129–143. doi.org/10.1016/j.psychsport.2003.10.007.

Myers, N. D., Wolfe, E. W., Maier, K. S., Reckase, M. D., & Feltz, D. L. (2006). Extending validity evidence for multidimensional measures of coaching competency. *Research Quarterly for Exercise and Sport, 77*(4), 451–463. doi.org/10.1080/02701367.2006.10599380.

Niehoff, B. P., & Moorman, R. H. (1993). Justice as a mediator of the relationship between methods of monitoring and organizational citizenship behavior. *Academy of Management Journal, 36*(3), 527–556.

Nikbin, D., Hyun, S. S., Albooyeh, A., & Foroughi, B. (2014). Effects of perceived justice for coaches on athletes' satisfaction, commitment, effort, and team unity. *International Journal of Sport Psychology, 45*, 100–120. doi.org/10.7352/IJSP2014.45.100.

Nikbin, D., Hyun, S. S., Iranmanesh, M., & Foroughi, B. (2014). Effects of perceived justice for coaches on athletes' trust, commitment, and perceived performance: A study of futsal and volleyball players. *International Journal of Sports Science & Coaching, 9*(4), 561–578. doi. org/10.1260/1747-9541.9.4.561.

Price, J. L., & Mueller, C. W. (1981). A causal model of turnover for nurses. *Academy of Management, 24*(3), 543–565. doi.org/10.2307/255574.

Turman, P. D. (2003). Coaches and cohesion: The impact of coaching techniques on team cohesion in the small group sport setting. *Journal of Sport Behavior, 26*, 86–104. doi. org/10.1177/017084068800900203.

Wang, J., & Straub, W. F. (2012). An investigation into the coaching approach of a successful world class soccer coach: Anson Dorrance. *International Journal of Sports Science & Coaching, 7*, 431–448. doi.org/10.1260/1747-9541.7.3.431.

# 12 Burnout in football coaching

*Zoltán Gáspár and Attila Szabó*

**Abstract**

In this chapter we examine the key determinants and consequences of burnout in football coaching. One purpose is to identify the most common causes of stress in coaching whilst reviewing the studies that have examined stress and burnout in this profession. The extant literature is classified so that the internal and external sources of stress, leading to burnout in football coaches, are integrated into an explanatory model for the better understanding of the phenomenon. Another purpose of the review is to identify the key problems in research in the area of sports coaching, with specific focus on football. It is concluded that whilst the majority of research substantiates the stressful nature of the coaching profession, there are numerous inconsistencies in the current literature that need to be addressed through more systematic research. Coaches may perceive their occupation as stressful and their cognitive appraisal of stress is moderated and/or mediated by a variety of personal and situational variables. By exploring available research on the predictors of burnout two groups of factors emerged consisting of intrapersonal (i.e. demographic, dispositional, cognitive) and situational variables. Coaches' longevity in the profession and their psychological and physical health and well-being is at stake if they neglect stress-induced syndromes, such as burnout. Further research is required to identify key determinants of football coaches' burnout. In view of the lack of such research the genuine health risk of football coaching remains speculative.

Coaching, regardless of sport and the level of competition, has evolved to become a stressful occupation in which people have virtually no control over their professional outlook (Stripe, 1994). Accumulating and continuous stress can lead to burnout, which in turn is a risk for cardiovascular disease and even for overall survival (Ahola, Väänänen, Koskinen, Kouvonen, & Shirom, 2010). This chapter aims to identify the components of stress leading to burnout in football coaching. After conceptualising burnout and internal and external stress as its determinants, the path leading to burnout is examined via representative studies in the field. Subsequently, a brief review of the findings from empirical research is followed by a description of the moderators while some grey areas, subject to future research, are identified.

## Theory and research

### Burnout in football

Burnout in coaches can be conceptualised by Freudenberger's (1974) work on staff burnout in helping professions. The primary symptoms include mental and emotional exhaustion, depersonalisation or cynicism, and decreased personal accomplishment. This theory is further elaborated by Leiter and Maslach (1988) in the context of interpersonal relationships in organisational settings. Their study revealed that the number of pleasant and unpleasant interpersonal relationships with co-workers is related to burnout. However, among the many co-symptoms (i.e. mental or emotional fatigue, depression, inefficiency, loss of motivation, commitment, and performance), emotional exhaustion is considered as the most robust feature of burnout (Maslach, Schaufeli, & Leiter, 2001). Emotional exhaustion stems from chronic life stress, and it is often accompanied by depersonalisation, as a means of defence, through disconnection from others (Maslach et al., 2001). This act reflects avoidance behaviour aimed at easing the burden of stress while making life events more bearable. However, social disconnection takes a toll on interpersonal relationships and, thus, jeopardises personal achievement, which could trigger a vicious circle. Since burnout can persist for up to 15 years (Bakker & Costa, 2014), job loss is often its inevitable outcome in several professions, including professional football coaching.

Kellmann (2002) proposed a model for the better understanding of burnout in athletes. The 'scissor model' or the '*underrecovery* model' purports that burnout results from ongoing life stress accompanied by incomplete recovery. Therefore, burnout is viewed as an imbalance between stress and recovery. Later, Fletcher and Fletcher (2005) proposed a meta-model for burnout in coaches. Their model is primarily based on Lazarus and Folkman's (1984) classical theory on one's cognitive appraisal of stress, mostly its external forms. Cognitive appraisal of stress can lead to either favourable or handicapping reactions, depending on the subjective perception of the stress, self-evaluation of the challenge, and one's means of coping. The whole stress situation is mostly dependent on situational factors and personal characteristics of the individual.

### Internal sources of stress

Internal stressors in football coaching stem from within the individual (Alsentali & Anshel, 2015; Sarafino, 1994). They include self-imposed and perceived pressure to succeed (Mälkki, 2016), handling defeat (Mälkki, 2016), and not reaching personal goals (Hunt & Miller, 1994). Internal stressors may surface in the context of team performance (Roach, 2016) and time constraints (Kellmann, Altfeld, & Mallett, 2016) as well. The limited job security (Kellmann et al., 2016; Ruder, 1991) and lack of control over public scrutiny (Stripe, 1994) comprise other internal sources of stress, over which the coach has no control. Recently the lack of control in one's work environment was associated with an increased risk for suicide (Hemmingsson, 2016).

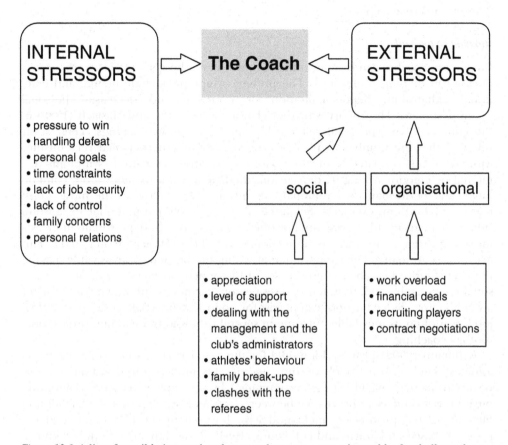

*Figure 12.1* A list of possible internal and external stressors experienced by football coaches.

### External sources of stress

External stressors are those that emerge from the person's interaction with the outside environment (Alsentali & Anshel, 2015; Sarafino, 1994; Schaffran, Altfeld, & Kellmann, 2016). Occupation-related external stressors may have severe adverse effects on health (Pereira & Elfering, 2014). They include two main categories: (1) social stressors, and (2) organisational stressors.

**Social stressors.** Social stressors occur in response to the difficulties which may arise from the coach's negative interaction with other individuals such as the pressure of being unappreciated by athletes, fans, and the media (Kellmann et al., 2016). Other social stressors may stem from the lack of support from upper-level management and deal with meddling administrators (Pereira & Elfering, 2014). Additionally, personality conflicts with assistant coaches, or athletes, as well as confrontations with the referees (Debanne, 2014; Sarafino, 1994) may add to the bulk of social stressors.

**Organisational stressors.** The other group of external stressors stem from a variety of managerial issues reflected in the team's organisational structure (Bentzen, Lemyre, & Kenttä, 2016). Organisational stressors involve the overload in administrative tasks, financial constraints, recruitment of new players, and contract hold-outs (Arnold, Fletcher, & Daniels, 2016; Hunt & Miller, 1994) and they are dependent on social support. However, the assumption that social support predicts the levels of occupational stress in coaching was questioned by Judge et al. (2015), who concluded that the perceived level of social support is only related to specific task-based forms of occupational stress. Apart from the stressors as mentioned above, perceived organisational support appears to mediate coaches' burnout (Kilo & Hassmén, 2016). Consequently, there is a consensus that professional coaches in general, regardless of the type and level of the sport, encounter multiple and reoc-curring stressors in managing their teams.

## Burnout in football coaches

There is relatively little work in the literature that investigates burnout in football coaches (McNeill, Durand-Bush, & Lemyre, 2016). One study that used a qualitative approach (Lundkvist, Gustafsson, Hjälm, & Hassmén, 2012) has identified two primary paths of burnout in football coaches. The first was a *performance* path that was stemming primarily from internal stress while its determinants were related to the self-identity as a coach and the sufficient external pressure to excel in perform-ance. Coaches in this category often exhibited anger, bitterness, cynicism, and even antisocial behaviour. The second path was situational since it was generated mainly by external stressors surfacing in the professional and personal life of the coach. It encompassed work overload, conflict at work, and the struggle to satisfy various obligations in everyday life. As a result, coaches who were on this path of burnout reported depression, exhaustion, and also various physical illnesses. This qualitative work (Lundkvist et al., 2012) underpins the role of both internal and external stres-sors in the aetiology of burnout in football coaches.

Professional football coaches are prime candidates for stress (Costa, Ferreira, Penna, Samulski, & Moraes, 2012). Cook (1996) argued that they are under considerable pressure to perform and their job security is tenuous. Unreasonable expectations from managers, players, fans, and the media often take the toll on the coach's physical and mental health and overall well-being (Omotayo, 1991). Evid-ence indicates that many well-known football coaches have experienced stress-related symptoms, physical and mental illnesses, and, in extreme cases, premature death (Cook, 1996; Omotayo, 1991). However, despite increasing public concern, as well as scholastic attention, over football coaches' job-related stress, and physical and mental health, research is still limited and sporadic in the field. Relatively few studies have examined stress and burnout among professional football coaches (see Table 12.1). These studies can be classified into three groups: (a) studies examining physiological stress, (b) studies investigating psychological stress, and (c) studies examining burnout.

### Physiological stress

Research conducted to investigate the physiological stress in football coaching has focused primarily on measuring coaches' heart rates before, during, and after games. For example, in an early field study, Trzeciak et al. (1981) measured the heart rates of 18 professional football coaches before and during their teams' games.

*Table 12.1* Summary of studies that examined stress and burnout in football coaching

| Author(s) | Participants | Type of sport | Focus of the study | Measurements | Conclusions |
|---|---|---|---|---|---|
| Biener (1986) | 227 male and female coaches | Football | To assess football coaching stress-related problems | Developed own questionnaire | 45% of the coaches felt low to medium levels of stress compared to 11% who felt high level of stress during football matches; various coaching situations were identified as sources of stress |
| Costa et al. (2012) | 217 coaches | Football (141) and futsal (76) | To evaluate the reliability of RESTQ-Coach in a sample of Brazilian futsal and football coaches | Recovery Stress Questionnaire for coaches (RESTQ-Coach) | RESTQ-Coach is a reliable instrument; football coaches had greater physical well-being, self-efficacy, and a greater field of cognitive techniques compared to futsal coaches; futsal coaches felt more stressed by their work activities than football coaches |
| Kellman and Kallus (1994) | 154 male coaches | Football | To examine the interrelation between stress and coaches' behaviour during rest periods | Developed own questionnaire | Highly stressed coaches rated themselves significantly less active, less authoritarian, and less warm-hearted towards their players than low-stressed coaches |
| Kenttä, Hassmén, and Gustafsson (2007) | 47 male coaches | Football | To investigate burnout among elite (male and female players) club level football coaches | Maslach Burnout Inventory (MBI) | More coaches of female players experience moderate to high levels of emotional exhaustion than coaches of male players; due to occupational conditions, leadership demands, time constraints, and size of support staff, female players' coaches are more likely to burnout than male players' coaches |

| Study | Sample | Sport | Aim | Measure | Findings |
|---|---|---|---|---|---|
| Koustelios (2010) | 132 male coaches | Football | To examine the level of burnout among football coaches in Greece | Maslach Burnout Inventory (MBI) | Coaches of this sample were experiencing low level of burnout; age differences were not significant on the burnout subscales |
| Kugler, Reintjes, Tewes, and Schedlowski (1996) | 17 male professional coaches | Football | To examine the effect of acute psychological stress on salivary immunoglobin A and salivary cortisol levels | Coaches' subjective rating of perceived psychological arousal | Football coaches rated themselves as more excited and tense during their teams' games |
| Lundkvist et al. (2012) | 8 coaches previously participated in burnout research and scored 'high' on the burnout measure | Football | To study burnout in elite soccer coaches (factors leading to burnout and its symptoms; stress recovery) | Semi-structured interviews | Revealed a novel conceptualisation of coach burnout with two different profiles (paths: performance environment and life situation) |
| Omotayo (1991) | 40 male professional coaches | Football | To investigate the frequency of burnout among successful and unsuccessful coaches | Maslach Burnout Inventory (MBI) | Success made no difference in frequency of burnout among football coaches |
| Teipel (1993) | Two male professional coaches | Football | To measure heart rate to determine the physiological stress experienced by football coaches | Short-range radio telemetry | There was a close relationship between events on the field, emotional reactions, and heart rate reactivity |
| Teipel (1993) | 28 professional and high amateur coaches | Football | To examine the relationship between specific aspects of psychological stress and football coaching | Developed own questionnaire | Highest evaluations of stress were found in situations of severe threat of relegation and the possibility of a promotion only by a win in the last game of the season |
| Trzeciak, Heck, Satomi, and Hollman (1981) | 18 male professional coaches | Football | To measure heart rate to determine coaches' physiological response to stress | Telemetric device | Coaches' rise in heart rate up to 156b/m was attributed to situations occurring on the field; there is a relationship between individual factors and rise in heart rate |

It was observed that specific game situations and certain individual variables led to changes in the coaches' heart rates. The average heart rate of the football coaches reached 104 beats/minute (bpm) half an hour before the start of the game. However, their heart rates fluctuated between 108 and 156 bpm during the games. The rise in heart rates was attributed to the unfolding of the game, and not to specific actions of the coach. The findings also revealed a non-significant relationship between individual factors and the rise in coaches' heart rates in that younger, or less experienced coaches exhibited slightly higher heart rates than older, or more experienced coaches.

Trzeciak et al.'s (1981) early results were replicated by others who also found that coaches' heart rates in competitive sports (i.e. American football and basketball) may rise as high as 188 bpm in the critical moments of a contest (Kroll & Gundershem, 1982; Ruder, 1991). Additionally, in context of the relationship between age, experience, and stress, similar results were reported by Hunt and Miller (1994), who found that younger, or less experienced coaches were more prone to the stress inherent in the profession than older, or more experienced colleagues.

Teipel (1993) investigated the heart rates of two professional coaches of two opposing second division German teams before, during, and after their respective league game. The study used short-range radio telemetry to measure the coaches' heart rates and video cameras to record their overt behaviours during the game. The design allowed relating the actions of the coaches to their heart rates in specific game situations. The findings revealed that the heart rates of the coaches oscillated between 110 and 160 bpm and rose above 160 bpm when a goal was scored at either side. Therefore, there is an established link between events on the field and coaches' physical-emotional reactions, as reflected by their heart rate responses to the various game situations.

Kugler et al. (1996) examined the effects of mental stress on salivary immunoglobin A (sIgA) and salivary cortisol concentrations in 17 professional football coaches in a real-life situation. The study also assessed the temporal pattern in stress-induced changes in sIgA and cortisol levels. Saliva samples were taken before, during, and after a game from 17 male football coaches. The findings revealed that the football coaches experienced more excitement and tension during the game in contrast to the periods before and after the game. This work shows that beyond heart rate, other physiological and biochemical indices also substantiate the stress experienced by football coaches. Therefore, future studies need to examine a broader range of psychophysiological indices to understand stress in coaching better.

### Psychological stress

Several studies focused on psychological stress in football coaching. Beiner (1986) investigated the sources of stress and coping strategies of 227 professional football coaches. The findings revealed that only 11% of the coaches felt medium to high levels of stress during the contest, while the majority reported low to medium levels of stress. However, more recent studies yielded different outcomes. For example, Kellmann and Kallus (1994) examined the link between stress and football coaches' behaviour during rest and competition season in 154 male and female German football coaches. The results showed that coaches' attitudes toward the players during rest periods were influenced by the stress level experienced in the competition season. Coaches who experienced high levels of stress exhibited less warm-hearted feelings towards their players. Further, coaches who reported high levels of stress during training felt less active and less authoritarian as compared to coaches who experienced low levels of stress.

Teipel (1993) investigated the forms of psychological stress among 28 football coaches from professional and high-amateur German leagues by assessing various stressors, such as coaches' relationship with club officials, fans, media, and opposing team, and other aspects related to the football season. The findings indicated that coaches reported high levels of stress in situations of extreme threat of relegation in the last game, three games before the end of the season, and at mid-season. More-over, high level of stress was associated with a big loss and the probability of promotion only by a win in the last game of the season. The results indicated that football coaches experienced high levels of psycho-physiological stress before, during, and after their team's games. Additionally, it was shown that coaches' fear of losing, and their worry over public scrutiny after a defeat at any stage of the season, was indicative of high levels of psychological stress.

In brief, although only a few studies investigated the psychological stress in football coaching, the results reflect how severe its impact may be on the person and her or his professional activities. Stress has a negative impact that in accord with Stripe (1994) leads to the separation of the professional football coach from her/his profession.

## Burnout

Relatively few studies examined burnout in professional football coaches. Omotayo (1991) studied the frequency of burnout among successful and unsuccessful professional coaches in Nigeria and found that coaches experienced burnout irrespectively of the level of their success. According to the findings, burnout was more closely associated with job-related stress than with winning or losing. In contrast, Koustelios (2010) tested 132 football coaches and found that Greek professional coaches experienced lower levels of burnout compared to the level of burnout of all occupational groups presented by Maslach and Jackson (1986) in the burnout inventory manual. Omotayo's (1991) findings may serve as a starting point in the quest for the better understanding of burnout in football coaches from a cross-cultural perspective. Public scrutiny and expectancy, a significant source of stress in coaching as seen before, differs in various football cultures, which could impact the level of stress experienced by coaches. The generalisation of findings of the above studies should be avoided, due to possible biases stemming from overall cultural and football cultural differences.

Kenttä et al. (2007) investigated burnout among elite club level professional football coaches. They found that coaches of female players were more likely to experience moderate to high levels of emotional exhaustion than coaches of male players. Due to several environmental conditions (i.e. occupational conditions, leadership demands, time constraints, and size of support staff) coaches in the female league were more susceptible to experience symptoms of burnout. Such environmental factors, along with personal and other situational factors, such as the coach's perception of the sport and the meaning of the outcome of the game, need to be examined in future research.

A comparative study by Costa et al. (2012) tested the reliability of the Recovery Stress Questionnaire for Coaches (RESTQ-Coach) between Brazilian football and futsal coaches who differed in three dimensions favouring football coaches: (1) self-efficacy, (2) physical well-being, (3) field of cognitive stress. Futsal coaches reported higher levels of work-related stress. There are several moderator factors in the stress experience of elite football coaches, which may or may not lead to burnout, but only fractions of these factors were studied to date.

## Moderator and mediator factors

### Gender

Some studies found that gender was related to stress appraisal, with women reporting higher levels of stress than men (Kelley, 1994; Kelley & Gill, 1993). However, Malinauskas, Malinauskiene, and Dumciene (2010) examined male and female university coaches and found that both genders were equally prone to burnout.

### Age, experience, and hardiness

Tashman et al. (2010) found that besides gender, experience also affected coaches' appraisal of stress. Other studies corroborated that young, or less experienced coaches reported higher levels of stress as compared to older, or more experienced coaches (Hunt & Miller, 1994; Trzeciak et al., 1981). Similarly, hardiness as a personality construct was linked to stress appraisal. Kobasa (1979) introduced hardiness describing a personality style which enables a person to cope with stressful life events successfully. Later the construct was further elaborated by Maddi (2004) who defined three main attitudes of a hardy person: challenge, control, and commitment. Hardiness comprises all these attitudes to perform well within stressful circumstances. Coaches who reported high levels of hardiness were less likely to perceive various stressors as a threat (Hendrix, Avecedo, & Hebert, 2000; Kelley, 1994). Further, Bawa (2010) found significant correlations between hardiness, burnout, and competition anxiety.

### Personality and social support

The relationship between coaches' personality type and stress appraisal was examined in an early study by Delashmit (1992). Personality types stem from three different behaviour patterns, defined by Friedman and Rosenman (1959). These patterns were named type 'A', 'B', and 'C' personality. Type 'A' personality constitutes a highly competitive, goal-driven, time-restricted, high-speed functioning person. Delashmit's (1992) findings indicated that coaches who exhibit type 'A' personality were more prone to experience stress-related symptoms.

A later study by Tashman et al. (2010) revealed a relationship between perfectionism and burnout in collegiate sports coaches. Perfectionism is a multidimensional construct believed to play an essential role in different psychopathologies. In a study on the dimensions of perfectionism, Frost, Marten, Lahart, and Rosenblate (1990) defined one saliently important dimension: 'excessive concern over making mistakes'. Five further and also significant dimensions were identified in their study: 'high personal standards (1), the perception of high parental expectations (2), the perception of high parental criticism (3), the doubting of the quality of one's actions (4), and a preference for order and organization (5)'. From the aspect of burnout, type 'A' personality and some dimensions of perfectionism show a gripping overlap.

Additionally, Kelley and Gill (1993) concluded that coaches with social support expressed greater satisfaction and reported lower levels of overall stress. This finding supports Taylor's (1992) conjecture that coaches who enjoy support from others are generally healthier than those who have little or no support. Taylor (1992) suggested that social support helps to reduce the effects of stressful situations by modifying the perceived meaning of the stressor.

While research is inconclusive in the context of moderating and mediating factors, it provides a basis for future research aimed at the understanding of the variables that may make some coaches more vulnerable to stress than others. Consequently, more studies are needed to investigate the relationship between coaches' appraisal of job stress and the moderating and mediating variables, including such as win/loss record, task-ego orientation, leadership style, the locus of control, and many others, as well as their interaction with situational factors.

## Conclusions

The academic literature suggests that professional football coaches face significant stress that may lead to different states of burnout that can determine their longevity in the profession and also affect their psychological and physical health and overall well-being. Apart from such a global picture that corresponds to anecdotal claims as well, the following specific conclusions may also be drawn:

### *What we know at this time*

- Professional coaches have limited, or no control over their professional future and lack of control over many situational factors, including performance-outcome; this is a primary source of stress in the profession.
- In any contest, coaches experience significant physiological stress reactions, such as increases in heart rate and salivary cortisol levels.

### *What we need to examine in future research*

- Further investigations are required as supporting evidence is scarce in the following areas: gender, experience, the interaction of psychological factors (i.e. hardiness, personality traits), and situational factors. These factors appear to affect the intensity of stress and, consequently, the likelihood of burnout in football coaches.
- Is there a proportional increase in the stress, experienced by professional coaches, with the level of contest, or level of public scrutiny, and if so, is that related to football culture?
- To what extent are learned cognitive and personality factors determinants of the frequency and intensity of stress experienced by professional football coaches?

- Does the presence (or absence) of close personal relationships, and their quality, affect the predisposition to burnout in coaching, and if yes, how is that moderated by personal and sport-situational factors?

## References

Ahola, K., Väänänen, A., Koskinen, A., Kouvonen, A., & Shirom, A. (2010). Burnout as a predictor of all-cause mortality among industrial employees: A 10-year prospective register-linkage study. *Journal of Psychosomatic Research, 69*(1), 51–57.

Alsentali, A. M., & Anshel, M. H. (2015). Relationship between internal and external acute stressors and coping style. *Journal of Sport Behavior, 38*(4), 357–375.

Arnold, R., Fletcher, D., & Daniels, K. (2016). Demographic differences in sport performers' experiences of organisational stressors. *Scandinavian Journal of Medicine & Science in Sports, 26*(3), 348–358.

Bakker, A. B., & Costa, P. L. (2014). Chronic job burnout and daily functioning: A theoretical analysis. *Burnout Research, 1*(3), 112–119.

Bawa, H. S. (2010). Personality hardiness, burnout and sports competition anxiety among athletics and wrestling coaches. *British Journal of Sports Medicine, 44*(Suppl. 1), i57–i58.

Bentzen, M., Lemyre, P. N., & Kenttä, G. (2016). Changes in motivation and burnout indices in high-performance coaches over the course of a competitive season. *Journal of Applied Sport Psychology, 28*(1), 28–48.

Biener, K. (1986). Stress bei Fussballtrainen. *Deutsche Zeitschrift fuer Sportmedizin, 37*(4), 107–110.

Cook, M. (1996). The science of soccer management. In T. Reilly (Ed.), *Science and soccer* (pp. 259–271). London, England: E&FN Spon.

Costa, V. T., Ferreira, R. M., Penna, E. M., Samulski, D. M., & Moraes, L. C. C. A. (2012). Comparação dos níveis de estresse, recuperação e burnout em treinadores de futsal e futebol brasileiros através do RESTQ-COACH [Comparison of stress, recovery and burnout levels in futsal and soccer Brazilian coaches through RESTQ-COACH]. *Motricidade, 8*(Suppl. 2).

Debanne, T. (2014). Techniques used by coaches to influence referees in professional team handball. *International Journal of Sports Science & Coaching, 9*(3), 433–446.

Delashmit, S. J. (1992). *The effects of game stress situations on the heart rates of selected high school football coaches* (Doctoral dissertation). Retrieved from the elibrary.ru database.

Fletcher, D., & Fletcher, J. (2005). A meta-model of stress, emotions and performance: Conceptual foundations, theoretical framework, and research directions. *Journal of Sports Sciences, 23*(2), 157–158.

Freudenberger, H. J. (1974). Staff burnout. *Journal of Social Issues, 30*(1), 159–165.

Friedman, M., & Rosenman, R. H. (1959). Association of specific overt behaviour pattern with blood and cardiovascular findings: Blood cholesterol level, blood clotting time, incidence of arcus senilis, and clinical coronary artery disease. *Journal of the American Medical Association, 169*(12), 1286–1296.

Frost, R. O., Marten, P., Lahart, C., & Rosenblate, R. (1990). The dimensions of perfectionism. *Cognitive Therapy and Research, 14*(5), 449–468.

Hemmingsson, T. (2016). The association between level of job control and depression and suicide attempt in middle-aged men. *Occupational and Environmental Medicine, 73*(Suppl. 1).

Hendrix, A. E., Acevedo, E. O., & Hebert, E. (2000). An examination of stress and burnout in certified athletic trainers at Division IA universities. *Journal of Athletic Training, 35*(2), 139–144.

Hunt, K. R., & Miller, S. R. (1994). Comparison of levels of perceived stress and burnout among college basketball and tennis coaches. *Applied Research in Coaching and Athletics, 9*, 198–222.

Judge, L. W., Kirkpatrick, K., Bolin, J., Blom, L. C., Dieringer, S., & Bellar, D. (2015). Understanding the occupational stress of collegiate track and field coaches during the championship season. *International Journal of Sports Science & Coaching, 10*(5), 769–782.

Kelley, B. C. (1994). A model of stress and burnout in collegiate coaches: Effects of gender and time of season. *Research Quarterly for Exercise and Sport, 65*(1), 48–58.

Kelley, B. C., & Gill, D. L. (1993). An examination of personal/situational variables, stress appraisal and burnout in collegiate teacher-coaches. *Research Quarterly for Exercise and Sport, 64*(1), 94–102.

Kellmann, M. (2002). Psychological assessment of underrecovery. In M. Kellmann (Ed.), *Enhancing recovery: Preventing underperformance in athletes* (pp. 37–55). Champaign, IL: Human Kinetics.

Kellmann, M., Altfeld, S., & Mallett, C. J. (2016). Recovery–stress imbalance in Australian Football League coaches: A pilot longitudinal study. *International Journal of Sport and Exercise Psychology, 14*(3), 240–249.

Kellmann, M., & Kallus, K. (1994). Interrelation between stress and coaches' behaviour during rest period. *Perceptual and Motor Skills, 79*, 207–210.

Kenttä, G., Hassmén, P., & Gustafsson, H. (2007). Burnout among elite soccer coaches. *Journal of Sport Behavior, 30*(4), 415–427.

Kilo, R. A., & Hassmén, P. (2016). Burnout and turnover intentions in Australian coaches as related to organisational support and perceived control. *International Journal of Sports Science & Coaching, 11*(2), 151–161.

Kobasa, S. C. (1979). Stressful life events, personality, and health: An inquiry into hardiness. *Journal of Personality and Social Psychology, 37*(1), 1–11.

Koustelios, A. (2010). Burnout among football coaches in Greece. *Biology of Exercise, 6*(1), 5–12.

Kroll, W., & Gundershem, J. (1982). Stress factors in coaching. *Coaching Science Up-Date, 83*, 47–49.

Kugler, J., Reintjes, F., Tewes, M., & Schedlowski, M. (1996). Competition stress in soccer coaches increases salivary immunoglobulin A and salivary cortisol concentrations. *Journal of Sports Medicine and Physical Fitness, 36*, 117–120.

Lazarus, R. S., & Folkman, S. (1984). *Stress, appraisal, and coping.* New York, NY: Springer.

Leiter, M. P., & Maslach, C. (1988). The impact of interpersonal environment on burnout and organisational commitment. *Journal of Organizational Behavior, 9*(4), 297–308.

Lundkvist, E., Gustafsson, H., Hjälm, S., & Hassmén, P. (2012). An interpretative phenomenological analysis of burnout and recovery in elite soccer coaches. *Qualitative Research in Sport, Exercise and Health, 4*(3), 400–419.

Maddi, S. R. (2004). Hardiness: An operationalisation of existential courage. *Journal of Humanistic Psychology, 44*(3), 279–298.

Malinauskas, R., Malinauskiene, V., & Dumciene, A. (2010). Burnout and perceived stress among university coaches in Lithuania. *Journal of Occupational Health, 52*(5), 302–307.

Mälkki, K. (2016). *Figure skating coaching in the contemporary sport culture: Finnish figure skating coaches' perceptions about their work* (Master's Thesis in Social Sciences of Sport). The University of Jyvaskyla. Retrieved from: https://jyx.jyu.fi/dspace/bitstream/handle/123456789/50043/URN:NBN:fi:jyu-201606022821.pdf?sequence=1.

Maslach, C., & Jackson, S. E. (1986). *MBI: Maslach Burnout Inventory.* Manual Research Edition. Palo Alto: University of California.

Maslach, C., Schaufeli, W. B., & Leiter, M. P. (2001). Job burnout. *Annual Review of Psychology, 52*(1), 397–422.

McNeill, K., Durand-Bush, N., & Lemyre, P. N. (2016). Understanding coach burnout and underlying emotions: A narrative approach. *Sports Coaching Review*, 1–18.

Omotayo, O. O. (1991). Frequency of burnout among selected soccer coaches. *Asian Journal of Physical Education, 14*(1), 83–88.

Pereira, D., & Elfering, A. (2014). Social stressors at work and sleep during weekends: The mediating role of psychological detachment. *Journal of Occupational Health Psychology, 19*(1), 85–95.

Roach, M. (2016). Does prior NFL head coaching experience improve team performance? *Journal of Sport Management, 30*(3), 298–311.

Ruder, M. K. (1991). How coaches manage stress. *Strategies, 5*(1), 6–10.

Sarafino, E. P. (1994). *Health psychology: Biopsychosocial interactions* (2nd ed.). New York, NY: John Wiles & Sons, Inc.

Schaffran, P., Altfeld, S., & Kellmann, M. (2016). Burnout in sport coaches: A review of correlates, measurement and intervention. *Deutsche Zeitschrift für Sportmedizin, 67*(5), 121–125.

Stripe, C. (1994). Coaching an emotional experience. *SportCare Journal, 1*(1), 35–36.

Tashman, L. S., Tenenbaum, G., & Eklund, R. (2010). The effect of perceived stress on the relationship between perfectionism and burnout in coaches. *Anxiety, Stress, & Coping, 23*(2), 195–212.

Taylor, A. (1992). Coaches are people too. *Journal of Applied Sport Psychology, 4*(1), 27–50.

Teipel, D. (1993). Analysis of stress in soccer coaches. In T. Reilly, J. Clarys, & A. Sibbe (Eds.), *Proceedings of the Second World Congress of Science and Football* (pp. 445–449) London, England: E & FN Spon.

Trzeciak, S., Heck, H., Satomi, H., & Hollman, W. (1981). Heart frequency of Bundesliga football coaches at a competitive match. *Deutsche Zeitschrift fur Sportmedizin, 32*(5), 127–140.

# 13 Recovery in football

*Jahan Heidari, Fabian Loch, and Michael Kellmann*

## Abstract

Modern elite football requires a myriad of different skills from the players encompassing technical, tactical, physical, and psychological capabilities. These demands can exhibit significant stress on the players and need to be balanced by appropriate physiological and psychological recovery in order to maintain a high level of performance. An important prerequisite of recovery interventions consists of the implementation of monitoring routines to assess the specific recovery needs of players and teams. Ideally, a combination of behavioural (e.g. global positioning system), physiological (e.g. blood lactate), and psychological (e.g. questionnaires) instruments for recovery monitoring should be evaluated to enable a detailed picture of the recovery status and the development of individualised recovery interventions. On a physiological level, a recovery protocol entailing rehydration and nutrition, cold water immersion, compression garments, and sufficient sleep should be warranted to promote the physiological recovery process. Psychologically, relaxation techniques can be performed to reduce mental fatigue and should be selected based on the individual preferences. It can be stated that the probability of success in elite football can be significantly increased in case the transfer from scientific knowledge regarding recovery monitoring and interventions can be integrated into practical contexts. The complexity of contemporary elite football suggests an array of different recovery strategies for each player to accomplish optimal functioning. Future research should therefore focus on individual and practice-oriented approaches to both assess and stimulate recovery.

## Introduction

Cristiano Ronaldo uses cryotherapy (i.e. application of very cold temperatures) after football matches or physically demanding training sessions. He has even bought a cryotherapy chamber for his own mansion to be able to access it whenever he wants (Jenson, 2013). Other famous football players also follow this routine on a regular basis within their training facilities (Fleming, 2017). Manchester United has established a partnership with the nutrition company *Science in Sport* to create nutritional products and habits to ensure optimal energy supply and hydration for its football players (Carp, 2018). Swansea City as another Premier League team has recently established so-called 'Snoozy pods'. These inflatable and portable sleep rooms enable players to nap between training sessions and thus provide the possibility to individually design sleeping routines (Edgley, 2017).

*Recovery* is the key term in all these examples. It appears to be considered as some kind of a magic formula which, in recent years, has triggered the attention of sport science research as well as practice in elite sports and football in particular (Nédélec et al., 2012, 2013). Whereas recovery is frequently used in everyday life in different contexts, science agreed on a specified and widely accepted definition of the concept. In science, recovery is labelled as a multi-faceted construct. Accordingly, Kallus (2016) defines recovery as

> an inter- and intraindividual multilevel (e.g. psychological, physiological, social) process in time for the re-establishment of personal resources and their full functional capacity. Recovery includes a broad range of physiological processes like sleep, motivated behaviour (like eating and drinking) and goal-oriented components (like relaxation or meeting friends). Recovery activities can be passive or active and in many instances recovery is achieved indirectly by activities, which stimulate recovery processes like active sports.
>
> (p. 42)

The relationship between stress and recovery can be best described as inter-related and mutually dependent. Stressors (e.g. pressure to perform in competitions) interfere with the homeostatic equilibrium of an organism and evoke a stress reaction in terms of activating resources and bio-psycho-social capacities. Elite athletes are consistently confronted with a variety of stressors and therefore require an adequate amount of recovery to regain their biorhythmic balance. Recovery is highly individual and may consist of either a decrease of, a change of, or a break from stress and can be contemplated as a steady and cumulative process (Kellmann et al., 2018).

High levels of performance in elite sports can only be maintained when athletes are sufficiently recovered. In effect, the exposition to challenging and exhausting activities needs to be followed by appropriate and individualised recovery in order to counterbalance stress and recovery and prevent a downward spiral of health and performance (Heidari et al., 2019; Kellmann et al., 2018). Due to the prevalent success orientation in elite sports, the majority of sports organisations focus on continuous performance enhancement via an increase in training volume and intensity. This intensification of training in terms of overreaching is necessary to initiate a positive adaptation process in athletes. Intensified training leads to a short-term decrement of performance occurring as a result of the calculated and reasonable physical and psychological overload the athlete was exposed to. This process is defined as functional overreaching and is crucial to stimulate and challenge an athlete. Functional overreaching is not accompanied by symptoms of maladaptation in case recovery is provided in a reasonable magnitude (Meeusen et al., 2013). Recovery plays a pivotal role in this process by preventing negative developments and enabling athletes to restore their resources for future performances. If an imbalance of excessive stress (e.g. excessively high training volumes, many matches) without sufficient periods of recovery manifests, this unfavourable ratio may have detrimental effects on athletes' health and performance (Gouttebarge, Aoki, & Kerkhoffs, 2015; Heidari, Hasenbring, Kleinert, & Kellmann, 2017). First, the dysfunctional states of underrecovery and non-functional overreaching (NFO) may establish as a consequence of too much stress and fatigue and too little recovery.

While underrecovery is characterised as a state of insufficient recovery referring to non-sport domains such as the family or the media, NFO is described by training-related endocrinological and psychological changes leading to reduced performance (Kellmann et al., 2018; Meeusen et al., 2013). An increase of underrecovery triggered by daily life demands in combination with long-term sport-specific NFO may result in the overtraining syndrome (OTS). Potential symptoms of the OTS range from muscle soreness to pain sensations and may even cause clinically relevant malfunctions in affected athletes (Meeusen et al., 2013). All of these deleterious conditions can be compensated through adequate recovery but may require a significant amount of time (i.e. weeks to months) and even a cessation of athletic activity (Kellmann et al., 2018). It is therefore recommended to prevent this downward spiral by providing recovery early enough.

Recovery seems to represent an essential element in the schedule of elite football players and teams which was demonstrated by the initially mentioned selection of examples of recovery-related activities. This development is attributable to the nature of modern professional football. Continuous high-level performance in elite football depends on a potpourri of different influences which interact in a multifaceted manner. These influences predominantly stem from training- or competition-related factors but may also consist of non-sport-related factors such as media presence or appointments with sponsors (Harwood & Pain, 2013; Larsen, 2017). All these factors have emerged as a part of the professionalisation of elite football and are accompanied by both advantageous and disadvantageous concomitants. On the positive side, elite football players may access a great variety of resources to constantly improve performance in order to succeed in their career (Akenhead & Nassis, 2016; Rein & Memmert, 2016). On the negative side, stress as a symptom of excessive demands causes negative developments (e.g. injuries) and states of fatigue (Silva et al., 2018; Stubbe et al., 2015) as noted earlier. Fatigue is generally characterised as a state of augmented tiredness due to physical and mental effort (Halson, 2014a; Ranchordas, Dawson, & Russell, 2017). Therefore, recovery is a topic of great importance which needs to be considered to counterbalance stress and fatigue in elite football athletes. Recovery in football differs from other sports due to a number of specific characteristics from both a sport-specific and organisational point of view (e.g. season schedules).

## Specific considerations for recovery in football

The fixture overload in the period from Christmas to New Year in the Premier League may serve as a prominent illustration of the specific need for recovery in elite football. With a closer look at the turn of the year 2017/18, Leicester City had the tightest match schedule with four matches between 23 December and 1 January. The players had to compete in four championship matches (including two away matches) in a time span of just 213 hours between the start of the first and the end of the fourth fixture.

This example demonstrates that the general and sport-specific demands on players are manifold in elite football and have become higher than ever. Particularly the high number of competitive matches per season consisting of national championship matches, domestic (national cup or league cup) and European cup matches (UEFA Champions League or Euro League) appear to have a crucial influence on recovery routines in elite football. Professional European football teams such as Manchester City or FC Barcelona routinely play more than 60 competitive matches over the course of a 45-week season (Ranchordas et al., 2017). Apart from this match schedule within their club, numerous elite players take part in international matches (e.g. international qualifiers, FIFA World Cup 2018, friendly matches) resulting in an extended all-year season with up to 70 competitive matches. Congested training and match schedules are associated with constant travelling, unfamiliar sleeping environments, and interruptions of the circadian rhythms (Laux, Krumm, Diers, & Flor, 2015; Nédélec et al., 2012). Various acute and chronic constraints such as variable wake-up and/or bedtimes as a result of variable match schedules, night soccer matches, consuming alcohol, caffeine, or emotionally stimulating activities can lead to sleep deprivation in football players (Nédélec, Halson, Abaidia, Ahmaidi, & Dupont, 2015). Sleep loss may affect physiological responses to exercise through reduced muscular recovery and immune defence (Fullagar et al., 2015; Kölling, Duffield, Erlacher, Venter, & Halson, 2019). In addition, elite players have to deal with mental stressors such as substantial pressure, heavy performance expectations as well as media presence and increasing public interest. Furthermore, football per se includes both specific physical (e.g. sprinting, change of direction, running speed, jump, technical actions) and psychological (e.g. sustained concentration, perceptual skills, decision-making, information processing in a dynamic environment) demands. The combination of these stressors together with a high number of matches and training sessions performed within a short period of time can result in a multifactorial state of fatigue which requires sufficient recovery (Heidari et al., 2019).

Football-related fatigue can occur during the match after intense short-term periods, towards the end of a match as accumulation of match-related fatigue, or as post-match fatigue after the termination of activity (Dupont, Nédélec, McCall, Berthoin, & Maffiuletti, 2015). The causes of football-related fatigue predominantly comprise physical and psychophysiological parameters, involving mechanisms from the central nervous system to the muscle cell itself in terms of energy production (Smith et al., 2018). In the context of post-match fatigue, dehydration (i.e. negative fluid balance), glycogen depletion in muscle fibres, and muscle damage are described as the main potential causes. Apart from the physiological manifestations of fatigue, elite players may also experience a state of mental fatigue as a consequence of football-specific physical and mental demands (Smith et al., 2018). Recent studies demonstrated that mental fatigue had a negative influence on football-specific running (e.g. intermittent running performance) and is particularly associated with a negative impact on accuracy and speed of football-specific decision-making (Smith, Zeuwts, et al., 2016). Mental fatigue also affects the attentional focus of the players towards irrelevant stimuli and a reduced ability to anticipate the movement of the ball (Smith, Coutts, et al., 2016).

To sum up, players' optimal performance can be hampered since physical and mental fatigue affect an athlete's individual recovery status, well-being, and sleep quantity and quality in a negative way. As mentioned in the introduction, multidimensional recovery is considered as the key to counterbalance multifaceted fatigue in elite football and should be adapted to the specific individual needs of the players. The use of different recovery strategies in practice depends on previous activities as well as the type and the duration of the preceding stress and consequent level of fatigue (Kellmann, 2010; Kellmann et al., 2018). Thus, the parameters of implementation and type of recovery strategy must be adjusted to the specific situation in football and psychophysiological requirements of the players. Therefore, we aim to provide a research overview of physiological and psychological perspectives on recovery and derive football-specific recovery implications such as recovery in half-time or recovery between two training sessions or matches.

## Assessment of recovery in football

In order to stabilise and improve performance and to prevent negative outcomes in elite football, an adequate monitoring of training and competition responses is essential (Heidari et al., 2019; Pelka, Schneider, & Kellmann, 2018). To establish a systematic monitoring regimen, the implementation of a holistic multidimensional monitoring system to quantify the players' training and competition load as well as the individual physiological and psychological consequences of training and competition is warranted (Halson, 2014a; Thorpe et al., 2015). This monitoring system is supposed to provide scientifically based information to refine the training process in order to increase players' performance readiness and to minimise the risk of NFO, injuries, and illnesses (Gabbett et al., 2017; Halson, 2014a). Both objective and subjective standardised instruments measuring fitness and fatigue outcomes should be combined to guarantee for a comprehensive monitoring of players' performance. A holistic monitoring system should include an assessment of both external and internal loads of training and competition (Kellmann et al., 2018; Saw, Kellmann, Main, & Gastin, 2017). An expert team consisting of sport psychologists, sport scientists, doctors, and physiotherapists (amongst others) decides on the systematic collection of monitoring data in football players. This process should also serve a specific purpose which might depend on the team's goals, the time of the season, or the scheduling of future training sessions (Gabbett et al., 2017). In football, a number of different methods can be applied ranging from microtechnologies such as global positioning system for detailed information on the external loads (e.g. power output, speed) to different internal load methods consisting of physiological measures such as oxygen uptake, heart-rate derived assessments, or blood lactate (Buchheit, 2014; Lac & Maso, 2004; McGuigan, 2017).

In addition, Saw, Main, and Gastin (2016) recommend the application of scientifically validated subjective, psychological measures for assessing and monitoring recovery in team sports and football in particular. The Recovery-Stress-Questionnaire for Athletes (RESTQ-Sport; Kellmann & Kallus, 2016) ranks among the most frequently used instruments to monitor stress and recovery in football (Brink et al., 2010; Laux et al., 2015). However, even the shortest version of the RESTQ-Sport requires a minimum of 36 items, which makes it difficult to implement the instrument in tight schedules. To facilitate more applicability in practical settings, a number of short measures for recovery and stress have been recently developed and have already been employed in the monitoring of adolescent football populations for the evaluation of perceived recovery (Pelka et al., 2018; Sawczuk, Jones, Scantlebury, & Till, 2018; Shearer et al., 2017). Namely, the Acute Recovery and Stress Scale (ARSS; Kellmann & Kölling, 2019; Kellmann, Kölling, & Hitzschke, 2016), the Short Recovery and Stress Scale (SRSS; Kellmann & Kölling, 2019; Kellmann et al., 2016), the adapted Brief Assessment of Mood (BAM+; Shearer et al., 2017), and the

Perceived Recovery Status Scale (PRS; Laurent et al., 2011) represent these more economic and time-efficient psychometric instruments. For sleep monitoring, subjective sleep diaries or sleep logs could be combined with objective technical measures (e.g. SenseWear, Actiwatch) to maximise sleep-related recovery output (Kölling et al., 2019; Miller et al., 2017). After the systematic use and analysis of the physiological and psychological monitoring data, interventions can be designed for specific athletes or teams.

## Promotion of physiological recovery in football

The physiological recovery process essentially consists of four steps (the four 'Rs' of recovery). These strategies encompass the factors relax, rehydrate, refuel, and repair which should be applied in a systematic manner. The following realistic but fictional example of an elite football player (Player *D. H.*) should give an impression of fundamental and physiological processes and issues athletes have to deal with:

> *D. H.* is a 25-year-old defender who is playing for an English club in the Premier League in the current season. He steadily developed his talent during his career and after having played for two different German second division teams, he finally became a starter in a top team in the German Bundesliga two years ago. In the last winter break, various clubs became aware of him and he was transferred to an ambitious London football club with the long-term aim to establish the club's position as a Top 5 Premier League club. During the years before playing in the Premier League, he has never had problems with any injuries.
>
> In his first Premier League season, *D. H.* performed well, strengthened the team's defence and helped his team to finish the season in 5th place resulting in the qualification for the UEFA Euro League. Since the start of this season, many players of the team had various problems with injuries. *D. H.* also suffered from various muscular injuries (e.g. torn muscle fibre, pulled hamstrings) in training and matches as well as health-related issues. *D. H.* also struggled with sleeping problems, stronger exhaustion, lack of focus, and the difficulty to perform. These symptoms led to a drop in performance of *D. H.* which was accompanied by a loss of his position in the starting XI.
>
> Despite these problems, the team remained successful and more matches had to be played in the course of the season, which included a lot of travelling. The coaching staff reacted to these circumstances by adapting the training schedule and initiating a collaboration with a team of sport scientists and sport psychologists. These experts aim to establish a monitoring system for recovery and football-specific fatigue to optimise the recovery process of the players.

This case exemplifies a career path consisting of constant fluctuations in performance of a top-level football player. *D. H.* apparently suffered from several minor injuries preventing him from regaining his previous high level of performance. The increase of load in terms of more matches during the season could not be adequately compensated by *D. H.* Such negative outcomes could be prevented through systematic practical protocols of general post-match recovery applicable for entire teams. These protocols should be developed to optimise the recovery response of the players especially in periods with a high number of matches. This systematic post-game recovery process is primarily based on the findings by Dupont et al. (2015) as well as Nédélec et al. (2015). Three basic physiological strategies (i.e. rehydration and nutrition, cold water immersion, and compression garments) are combined in a specific order to enhance recovery as explained below.

Immediately after the match, the players are encouraged to drink a large volume of fluid which should contain a combination of water (150% of body fluid loss) and a high concentration of sodium. Moreover, players should ingest drinks such as chocolate milk in order to restore glycogen, to reduce inflammation, and to stimulate muscle repair. To further accelerate the recovery process, the players are required to take a cold bath at a temperature between 12 and 15 degrees Celsius for 10–20 minutes. The next step in the recovery process consists in the application of compression garments as an easy-to-use strategy until bedtime (Dupont et al., 2015). Regarding their nutrition, the players should eat a meal high in protein and carbohydrate with a high glycaemic index such as white pasta, chicken, or fish within 1 hour after the match, while the 'anabolic window of opportunity' to fully restore carbohydrates and protein lasts up to 4 hours post-exercise (Ranchordas et al., 2017). This systematic recovery protocol ideally ends with a good night's sleep.

Apart from such a generally applicable recovery protocol, individual recovery needs do exist and must be addressed. Specific recovery strategies should be developed and should be tailored to the individual needs of players such as *D. H.* One important strategy suggests that effective sleep is a fundamental determinant of preparation for and recovery from training and competition (Halson, 2014b; Nédélec et al., 2015). Based on the results of specific monitoring analyses (e.g. sleep diaries), sport scientists can aim at optimising sleeping behaviour throughout the training week as well as pre- and post-match day while identifying poor sleeping habits of *D. H.* Efficient and individualised sleep hygiene strategies can be defined to enhance the psychological and physiological sleep functions and to improve quality and quantity of sleep (Fullagar et al., 2015; Nédélec et al., 2015).

Establishing a pre-bed routine with a period of relaxation between the stressors of the day and night-time sleep is considered a very effective strategy for recovery (Halson, 2014b). This relaxation period implies a high level of self-determination by choosing activities adapted to individual needs and preferences (Kellmann et al., 2018). *D. H.* also needs to refrain from caffeine intake post late-afternoon. The environment in his bedroom should be cool, quiet, and dark to contribute to optimal sleep (Fullagar et al., 2015). Furthermore, the players have to make sure that artificial light sources (e.g. TV, standby light, alarm clock) will be removed and that during pre-bed time (mainly 30 minutes prior) the use of smartphones or tablets is avoided. With the help of these illustrative sleep hygiene strategies, players like *D. H.* could benefit from 7–9 hours of sleep at night and may wake up feeling refreshed.

Powernaps can be seen as another useful strategy to reduce daytime sleepiness as well as to restore wakefulness and alertness. Short powernaps appear to be an effective way to foster relaxation and recovery and reduce mental fatigue in elite football, since training sessions are usually scheduled twice a day (Halson, 2014b). Based on recent findings on the effectiveness of powernaps to enhance both physical and mental performance (Pelka et al., 2017; Waterhouse, Atkinson, Edwards, & Reilly, 2007), responsible sport psychologists and sport scientists could initiate a short powernap routine for *D. H.* upon consultation with the coaches. Depending on the training and match agenda, this routine could last between 15 and 25 minutes and could be scheduled during lunchtime or mid-afternoon hours. For the best possible recovery effect, an attainable and functional environment to nap such as portable sleep rooms (Snoozy pods) at the training facilities should be promoted.

A focus on physiological recovery strategies is vital for maintaining the health and performance capacities of elite football players. A combination of universal recovery protocols and flexible elements for individual recovery requirements will ultimately result in productive football players and increase the probability for continuous team and individual success.

## Promotion of psychological recovery in football

In the past, training in football predominantly focused on physical performance factors. Only recently has the impact of psychological determinants been recognised in both research and practice (Nesti, 2017), but a scarcity of scientific evidence characterises the status quo of recovery-specific interventions in football. The following realistic but fictional example of an elite football player (Player *R. K.*) should provide an idea of the psychological processes and difficulties football players are confronted with:

> *R. K.* is 22 years old and has been a professional football player for 4 years. As a midfielder, he has played for three different first division teams so far. *R. K.* was rated as one of the top five nationwide talents in his age group at age 18 and successfully passed the youth national teams of his country until the U-21. Being transferred at age 21 to a struggling team as their saviour, he failed to meet the expectations of the club and fans. At the end of the season, his team was relegated to the second division.
>
> He battled with a number of minor injuries during that time and appeared tired, ponderous, and inattentive during the matches. *R. K.* quarrelled with his performances and even lost his position in the starting XI in the last matches. As a result, he transferred to another team after the disappointing season to start over with a different team and different expectations. The new team was cooperating with a sport psychologist who had established a monitoring routine for recovery and fatigue over the past 2 years. With the help of the sport psychologist, *R. K.*'s performance stabilised. By now he is considerably contributing to the team's success. *R. K.* is now taking better care of his mind and body by focusing more on recovery. He is implementing more breaks into his daily schedule which he uses for powernaps or other restoring activities such as social events or reading. His injury proneness substantially decreased while his overall well-being has significantly increased. *R. K.* is slowly regaining his original level of performance.

This case illustrates how career paths of highly talented football players may proceed. Ups and downs epitomise the world of elite sports where success and continuous high performance constitute the key outcomes. With the above mentioned monitoring instruments, these fluctuations in mental recovery can be quantified and visualised and, most importantly, translated into practical interventions (Gabbett et al., 2017). *R. K.* reports a number of psychological factors affecting his performance, such as dealing with expectations, loss of focus, or reduced motivation. Compared to physiological protocols, the management of subjective psychological issues cannot be realised via a universal routine. Psychological processes in sport are especially prone to inter- and intraindividual fluctuations which may even stem from off-the-field events (e.g. social conflicts). Psychological markers of recovery need to be evaluated and combined with the physiological data. This integrative approach may reveal if psychological issues affect physiological parameters and vice versa. For example, *R. K.*'s tiredness and inattentiveness might have originated from increased media interest towards him. This affected his physical performance capacities and even contributed to the occurrence of injuries (Heidari et al., 2019). This comprehensive methodology allows a detailed picture to be drawn of an athlete's or teams' recovery status as a reaction to external (e.g. training stimuli) or internal (e.g. thoughts) factors. As a consequence of the monitoring process, practical interventions for the football team or individual player need to be designed in cooperation with the coaches and the athletes themselves (Halson, 2014a; Kellmann et al., 2018).

In agreement with all parties, the dosage and content of recovery is decided individually for each player or team (Gabbett et al., 2017; Larsen, 2017). From a psychological point of view, a number of psychological relaxation techniques exist which aim at the enhancement of recovery and thereby implicate an improvement of performance. Among those techniques are, for example, breathing relaxation, progressive muscle relaxation, or biofeedback (Pelka et al., 2016). At least moderate evidence for their effectiveness can be affirmed scientifically but rather on a general sport level, since these techniques have rarely been examined in football-specific contexts (Keilani et al., 2016; Olmedilla-Zafra, Rubio, Ortega, & Garcia-Mas, 2017).

The prevalence of using relevant knowledge of mental recovery strategies for injury preparation and performance enhancement in a variety of team sports including football was examined by Keilani et al. (2016). Mental recovery strategies were evaluated as an effective measure for performance improvement by athletes but the frequency of actual application was rather low. The authors address this discrepancy between knowledge and usage by stating that athletes need guidance to systematically learn the application of these psychological recovery strategies (Keilani et al., 2016). Olmedilla-Zafra et al. (2017) conducted a stress management and muscle relaxation programme to reduce injury incidence in sport in youth football players. A sport psychologist conveyed the programme once a week over a time frame of 3 months. The results not only indicated a decrease in injury incidence in the intervention group, but also demonstrated a high acceptance and commitment among the players and coaches. The design proposed in this study could be adapted to football practical contexts to implement psychological recovery strategies as a daily routine. More exhaustive insights into the acute effectiveness of psychological relaxation techniques are provided by Pelka et al. (2016), while Nédélec et al. (2012, 2013) specifically demonstrate football-related findings for recovery but predominantly on a physiological level.

## Practical implications

One of the bigger issues inherent not only in football consists of the gap between scientific findings regarding recovery and their transfer into practical settings. The examples in the introduction show that recovery routines are prevalent in football but follow a 'personal experience schedule' rather than scientific recommendations. Buchheit (2017) states that scientific evidence needs to find a direct and easily accessible way into the daily routines of sport teams by communicating in a generally comprehensible manner. This could be achieved through the integration of trained sport psychologists and sport scientists who supervise the procedure of recovery monitoring and organise the development of subsequent interventions. The involvement of these experts has been encouraged in recent years within professional teams but their responsibility rarely encompasses recovery. Hence, the next pivotal step would consist of the involvement of sport psychologists into the recovery routines to guide the facet of mental recovery. In line with the recommendations for general sport psychological work, the promotion of commitment and trust via the close interaction with coaches and players remains a crucial aspect. The relationship between sport psychologists and coaches should not be characterised by a rivalry but rather cooperation and the establishment of this relationship can often constitute a delicate task (Larsen, 2017). The integration of recovery as one component of a profound coaching process together with the conception of training as well as technical and tactical analyses needs to be planned and coordinated with the coaching staff. Ideally, an individualised approach to recover can be derived for each player based on the obtained monitoring data (Hecksteden et al., 2017). Content wise, the role of physical recovery has been acknowledged and well addressed in both science and practice (Nédélec et al., 2012, 2013), while the issue of mental recovery represents a relatively new phenomenon with a shortage of underlying scientific evidence. Sleep is the only key recovery strategy with both physical and mental elements that is incorporated in both research (Nédélec et al., 2015) and practice (e.g. Snoozy pods). Considering the fact that modern football players face a plethora of cognitive challenges in training and competition settings (e.g. decision-making, concentration, speed of execution), it is surprising that only a paucity of studies investigated these factors of mental fatigue (Smith, Coutts, et al., 2016; Smith, Zeuwts, et al., 2016) and developed interventions to foster mental recovery and thereby enhance performance (Olmedilla-Zafra et al., 2017). Future research approaches should therefore focus on strategies to increase mental recovery in football and verify their applicability in training sessions or halftime recovery regimens (Russell, West, Harper, Cook, & Kilduff, 2015).

## Conclusion

Recovery entails both physiological and psychological components and can serve multiple purposes. The systematic application of recovery may contribute to injury prevention, rehabilitation after injuries, and to the augmentation of performance. In elite football, congested schedules of training and matches require an optimisation of the recovery process to be effective. While recovery is still primarily considered as a physiological concept in elite football, the importance of psychological interventions to reduce mental fatigue is steadily increasing. Scientific psychological evidence remains scarce but has emerged as a beneficial addition in practical contexts. The profile for a successful football player requires elaborated physiological resources but also a significant mental component which should be addressed adequately through mental recovery and psychological skills training.

The complexity of modern elite football therefore warrants a combination of different recovery strategies for each player to achieve optimal functioning within his football team. In case all pieces of the recovery puzzle are considered and designed towards the needs of each individual football player, an ideal combination of a healthy and efficient player will emerge. Such a player will have the capacity to make efficient use of his abilities and effectively contribute to team success.

## References

Akenhead, R., & Nassis, G. P. (2016). Training load and player monitoring in high-level football: Current practice and perceptions. *International Journal of Sports Physiology and Performance, 11*, 587–593. doi:10.1123/ijspp.2015-0331.

Brink, M. S., Visscher, C., Arends, S., Zwerver, J., Post, W. J., & Lemmink, K. A. (2010). Monitoring stress and recovery: New insights for the prevention of injuries and illnesses in elite youth soccer players. *British Journal of Sports Medicine, 44*, 809–815. doi:10.1136/bjsm.2009.069476.

Buchheit, M. (2014). Monitoring training status with HR measures: Do all roads lead to Rome? *Frontiers in Physiology, 5*, 73. doi:10.3389/fphys.2014.00073.

Buchheit, M. (2017). Houston, we still have a problem. *International Journal of Sports Physiology and Performance, 12*, 1111–1114. doi:10.1123/ijspp.2017-0422.

Carp, S. (2018). Science in sport to fuel Manchester United until 2021. Retrieved from www.sportspromedia.com/news/science-in-sport-to-fuel-manchester-united-until-2021.

Dupont, G., Nédélec, M., McCall, A., Berthoin, S., & Maffiuletti, N. A. (2015). Football recovery strategies: Practical aspects of blending science and reality. *Aspetar Sports Medicine Journal, 4*, 20–27.

Edgley, R. (2017). Football's secret sports science: The power of sleep. Retrieved from http://bleacherreport.com/articles/2720313-footballs-secret-sports-science-the-power-of-sleep.

Fleming, N. (2017). Whole-body cryotherapy: What are the cold hard facts? *Guardian.* Retrieved from www.theguardian.com/lifeandstyle/2017/jul/24/whole-body-cryotherapy-what-are-cold-facts.

Fullagar, H. H., Skorski, S., Duffield, R., Hammes, D., Coutts, A. J., & Meyer, T. (2015). Sleep and athletic performance: The effects of sleep loss on exercise performance, and physiological and cognitive responses to exercise. *Sports Medicine, 45*, 161–186. doi:10.1007/s40279-014-0260-0.

Gabbett, T. J., Nassis, G. P., Oetter, E., Pretorius, J., Johnston, N., Medina, D., … Ryan, A. (2017). The athlete monitoring cycle: A practical guide to interpreting and applying training monitoring data. *British Journal of Sports Medicine, 51*, 1451–1452. doi:10.1136/bjsports-2016-097298.

Gouttebarge, V., Aoki, H., & Kerkhoffs, G. (2015). Symptoms of common mental disorders and adverse health behaviours in male professional soccer players. *Journal of Human Kinetics, 49*, 277–286. doi:10.1515/hukin-2015-0130.

Halson, S. L. (2014a). Monitoring training load to understand fatigue in athletes. *Sports Medicine, 44*, 139–147. doi:10.1007/s40279-014-0253-z.

Halson, S. L. (2014b). Sleep in elite athletes and nutritional interventions to enhance sleep. *Sports Medicine, 44*, 13–23. doi:10.1007/s40279-014-0147-0.

Harwood, C., & Pain, M. (2013). Stress, coping and the mental qualities of elite players. In A. M. Williams (Ed.), *Science and soccer: Developing elite performers* (pp. 154–171). Abingdon, England: Routledge.

Hecksteden, A., Pitsch, W., Julian, R., Pfeiffer, M., Kellmann, M., Ferrauti, A., & Meyer, T. (2017). A new method to individualize monitoring of muscle recovery in athletes. *International Journal of Sports Physiology and Performance, 12*, 1137–1142. doi:10.1123/ijspp.2016-0120.

Heidari, J., Beckmann, J., Bertollo, M., Brink, M. S., Kallus, K. W., Robazza, C., & Kellmann, M. (2019). Multidimensional monitoring of recovery status and implications for performance. *International Journal of Sports Physiology and Performance, 14*(1), 2–8. doi:10.1123/ijspp.2017-0669.

Heidari, J., Hasenbring, M., Kleinert, J., & Kellmann, M. (2017). Stress-related psychological factors for back pain among athletes: Important topic with scarce evidence. *European Journal of Sport Science, 17,* 351–359. doi:10.1080/17461391.2016.1252429.

Jenson, P. (2013). Ice cool Ronaldo: Real Madrid star buys −160C cryotherapy chamber for his house. *Daily Mail.* Retrieved from www.dailymail.co.uk/sport/football/article-2469985/Cristiano-Ronaldo-buys-Cryotherapy-chamber.html.

Kallus, K. W. (2016). Stress and recovery: An overview. In K. W. Kallus & M. Kellmann (Eds.), *The Recovery-Stress Questionnaires: User manual* (pp. 27–48). Frankfurt, Germany: Pearson Assessment & Information GmbH.

Keilani, M., Hasenohrl, T., Gartner, I., Krall, C., Furnhammer, J., Cenik, F., & Crevenna, R. (2016). Use of mental techniques for competition and recovery in professional athletes. *Wiener klinische Wochenschrift, 128,* 315–319. doi:10.1007/s00508-016-0969-x.

Kellmann, M. (2010). Preventing overtraining in athletes in high-intensity sports and stress/recovery monitoring. *Scandinavian Journal of Medicine & Science in Sports, 20,* 95–102. doi:10.1111/j.1600-0838.2010.01192.x.

Kellmann, M., Bertollo, M., Bosquet, L., Brink, M., Coutts, A. J., Duffield, R., ... Beckmann, J. (2018). Recovery and performance in sport: Consensus statement. *International Journal of Sports Physiology and Performance, 13,* 240–245. doi:10.1123/ijspp.2017-0759.

Kellmann, M., & Kallus, K. W. (2016). Recovery-Stress Questionnaire for athletes. In K. W. Kallus & M. Kellmann (Eds.), *The Recovery-Stress Questionnaires: User manual* (pp. 86–127). Frankfurt, Germany: Pearson Assessment & Information GmbH.

Kellmann, M., & Kölling, S. (2019). *Recovery and stress in sport: A manual for testing and assessment.* Abingdon, England: Routledge.

Kellmann, M., Kölling, S., & Hitzschke, B. (2016). *Das Akutmaß und die Kurzskala zur Erfassung von Erholung und Beanspruchung im Sport – Manual* [The acute measure and the short scale of recovery and stress for sports – manual]. Hellenthal, Germany: Sportverlag Strauß.

Kölling, S., Duffield, R., Erlacher, D., Venter, R., & Halson, S. (2019). Sleep-related issues for recovery and performance in athletes. *International Journal of Sports Physiology and Performance, 14,* 144–148. doi:10.1123/ijspp.2017-0746.

Lac, G., & Maso, F. (2004). Biological markers for the follow-up of athletes throughout the training season. *Pathologie Biologie, 52,* 43–49. doi:10.1016/S0369-8114(03)00049-X.

Larsen, C. H. (2017). Bringing a knife to a gunfight: A coherent consulting philosophy might not be enough to be effective in professional soccer. *Journal of Sport Psychology in Action, 8,* 121–130. doi:10.1080/21520704.2017.1287142.

Laurent, C. M., Green, J. M., Bishop, P. A., Sjokvist, J., Schumacker, R. E., Richardson, M. T., & Curtner-Smith, M. (2011). A practical approach to monitoring recovery: Development of a perceived recovery status scale. *Journal of Strength and Conditioning Research, 25,* 620–628. doi:10.1519/JSC.0b013e3181c69ec6.

Laux, P., Krumm, B., Diers, M., & Flor, H. (2015). Recovery-stress balance and injury risk in professional football players: A prospective study. *Journal of Sports Sciences, 33,* 2140–2148. doi:10.1080/02640414.2015.1064538.

McGuigan, M. (2017). *Monitoring training and performance in athletes.* Champaign, IL: Human Kinetics.

Meeusen, R., Duclos, M., Foster, C., Fry, A., Glesson, M., Nieman, D., ... Urhausen, A. (2013). Prevention, diagnosis and treatment of the overtraining syndrome: Joint consensus statement of the European College of Sport Science (ECSS) and the American College of Sports Medicine (ACSM). *Medicine and Science in Sports and Exercise, 45,* 186–205. doi:10.1249/MSS.0b013e318279a10a.

Miller, D. J., Sargent, C., Vincent, G. E., Roach, G. D., Halson, S. L., & Lastella, M. (2017). Sleep/wake behaviours in elite athletes from three different football codes. *Journal of Sports Science & Medicine, 16*, 604–605.

Nédélec, M., Halson, S., Abaidia, A. E., Ahmaidi, S., & Dupont, G. (2015). Stress, sleep and recovery in elite soccer: A critical review of the literature. *Sports Medicine, 45*, 1387–1400. doi:10.1007/s40279-015-0358-z.

Nédélec, M., McCall, A., Carling, C., Legall, F., Berthoin, S., & Dupont, G. (2012). Recovery in soccer: Part I – post-match fatigue and time course of recovery. *Sports Medicine, 42*, 997–1015. doi:10.2165/11635270-000000000-00000.

Nédélec, M., McCall, A., Carling, C., Legall, F., Berthoin, S., & Dupont, G. (2013). Recovery in soccer: Part II – recovery strategies. *Sports Medicine, 43*, 9–22. doi:10.1007/s40279-012-0002-0.

Nesti, M. S. (2017). Working within professional football. In R. J. Schinke & D. Hackfort (Eds.), *Psychology in professional sports and the performing arts: Challenges and strategies* (pp. 192–205). Abingdon, England: Routledge.

Olmedilla-Zafra, A., Rubio, V. J., Ortega, E., & Garcia-Mas, A. (2017). Effectiveness of a stress management pilot program aimed at reducing the incidence of sports injuries in young football (soccer) players. *Physical Therapy in Sport, 24*, 53–59. doi:10.1016/j.ptsp. 2016. 09.003.

Pelka, M., Heidari, J., Ferrauti, A., Meyer, T., Pfeiffer, M., & Kellmann, M. (2016). Relaxation techniques in sports: A systematic review on acute effects on performance. *Performance Enhancement & Health, 5*, 47–59. doi:10.1016/j.peh.2016.05.003.

Pelka, M., Kölling, S., Ferrauti, A., Meyer, T., Pfeiffer, M., & Kellmann, M. (2017). Acute effects of psychological relaxation techniques between two physical tasks. *Journal of Sports Sciences, 35*, 216–223. doi:10.1080/02640414.2016.1161208.

Pelka, M., Schneider, P., & Kellmann, M. (2018). Development of pre- and post-match morning recovery-stress states during in-season weeks in elite youth football. *Science and Medicine in Football, 2*, 127–132. doi:10.1080/24733938.2017.1384560.

Ranchordas, M. K., Dawson, J. T., & Russell, M. (2017). Practical nutritional recovery strategies for elite soccer players when limited time separates repeated matches. *Journal of the International Society of Sports Nutrition, 14*, 35. doi:10.1186/s12970-017-0193-8.

Rein, R., & Memmert, D. (2016). Big data and tactical analysis in elite soccer: Future challenges and opportunities for sports science. *SpringerPlus, 5*, 1410. doi:10.1186/s40064-016-3108-2.

Russell, M., West, D. J., Harper, L. D., Cook, C. J., & Kilduff, L. P. (2015). Half-time strategies to enhance second-half performance in team-sports players: A review and recommendations. *Sports Medicine, 45*, 353–364. doi:10.1007/s40279-014-0297-0.

Saw, A. E., Kellmann, M., Main, L. C., & Gastin, P. B. (2017). Athlete self-report measures in research and practice: Considerations for the discerning reader and fastidious practitioner. *International Journal of Sports Physiology and Performance, 12*, S2127–S2135. doi:10.1123/ijspp.2016-0395.

Saw, A. E., Main, L. C., & Gastin, P. B. (2016). Monitoring the athlete training response: Subjective self-reported measures trump commonly used objective measures: A systematic review. *British Journal of Sports Medicine, 50*, 281–291. doi:10.1136/bjsports-2015-094758.

Sawczuk, T., Jones, B., Scantlebury, S., & Till, K. (2018). Relationships between training load, sleep duration, and daily well-being and recovery measures in youth athletes. *Pediatric Exercise Science, 30*, 345–352. doi:10.1123/pes.2017-0190.

Shearer, D. A., Sparkes, W., Northeast, J., Cunningham, D. J., Cook, C. J., & Kilduff, L. P. (2017). Measuring recovery: An adapted Brief Assessment of Mood (BAM+) compared to biochemical and power output alterations. *Journal of Science and Medicine in Sport, 20*, 512–517. doi:10.1016/j.jsams.2016.09.012.

Silva, J. R., Rumpf, M. C., Hertzog, M., Castagna, C., Farooq, A., Girard, O., & Hader, K. (2018). Acute and residual soccer match-related fatigue: A systematic review and meta-analysis. *Sports Medicine, 48,* 539–583. doi:10.1007/s40279-017-0798-8.

Smith, M. R., Coutts, A. J., Merlini, M., Deprez, D., Lenoir, M., & Marcora, S. M. (2016). Mental fatigue impairs soccer-specific physical and technical performance. *Medicine and Science in Sports and Exercise, 48,* 267–276. doi:10.1249/MSS.0000000000000762.

Smith, M. R., Thompson, C., Marcora, S. M., Skorski, S., Meyer, T., & Coutts, A. J. (2018). Mental fatigue and soccer: Current knowledge and future directions. *Sports Medicine, 48,* 1525–1532. doi:10.1007/s40279-018-0908-2.

Smith, M. R., Zeuwts, L., Lenoir, M., Hens, N., De Jong, L. M., & Coutts, A. J. (2016). Mental fatigue impairs soccer-specific decision-making skill. *Journal of Sports Sciences, 34,* 1297–1304. doi:10.1080/02640414.2016.1156241.

Stubbe, J. H., van Beijsterveldt, A. M., van der Knaap, S., Stege, J., Verhagen, E. A., van Mechelen, W., & Backx, F. J. (2015). Injuries in professional male soccer players in the Netherlands: A prospective cohort study. *Journal of Athletic Training, 50,* 211–216. doi:10.4085/1062-6050-49.3.64.

Thorpe, R. T., Strudwick, A. J., Buchheit, M., Atkinson, G., Drust, B., & Gregson, W. (2015). Monitoring fatigue during the in-season competitive phase in elite soccer players. *International Journal of Sports Physiology and Performance, 10,* 958–964. doi:10.1123/ijspp.2015-0004.

Waterhouse, J., Atkinson, G., Edwards, B., & Reilly, T. (2007). The role of a short post-lunch nap in improving cognitive, motor, and sprint performance in participants with partial sleep deprivation. *Journal of Sports Sciences, 25,* 1557–1566. doi:10.1080/02640410701244983.

# Part III

# Psychological skills for performance development

# 14 Psychological skills for football players

*Erkut Konter, Jürgen Beckmann, and Clifford J. Mallett*

**Abstract**

The chapter addresses a number of issues related to psychological skills and performance in football. Well-developed physical, technical, and tactical competencies are necessary but not sufficient prerequisites for success in modern football. Research indicates that the most successful athletes consistently require and employ psychological skills to enhance performance (e.g. relaxation, imagery, goal setting, self-talk). Thus, psychological skills training should be part of training and practice in football. Despite an increasing acknowledgement of the importance of psychological skills for success in football, a systematic integration of sport psychological services into football still meets resistance. Some of this resistance is due to a lack of knowledge of football staff and coaches. To provide a communicable structure of psychological support, a three-level model of sport psychological support was proposed (Beckmann & Elbe, 2015). The model differentiates basic training (relaxation), psychological skills training, and conflict management. As a basic requirement psychological assessment is integrated into the model to adapt psychological skills training to the needs of the individual player. Psychological skills can be combined and integrated into routines that are also addressed in this chapter. Currently, the numerous psychological skills that have been developed across different sports need to be adapted to the specific demands of football. Promising first attempts to integrate psychological skills into holistic football-specific programmes are presented.

International football, at the highest performance levels, has become increasingly complex over the last few decades (Rampinini, Bishop, Marcora, Bravo, Sassil, & Impellizzeri, 2007). Well-developed physical, technical, and tactical competencies are necessary prerequisites but no longer sufficient to be successful (i.e. win). Arguably, successful performances are dependent upon the execution of advanced psychological skills under pressure in matches. Psychological skills comprise the deliberate use of pre-prepared and structured sequences of specific thoughts and behaviours by athletes and exercisers to regulate their psychological state (Eklund & Tenenbaum, 2014).

Research indicates that the most successful athletes consistently require and employ psychological skills to enhance performance (e.g. Fletcher, Hanton, & Wagstaff, 2012; Gould, Dieffenbach, & Moffett, 2002). These factors include learning processes, and psychological skills, such as goal setting, imagery, self-talk (for an overview see Beckmann & Elbe, 2015). As a consequence, psychological skills training (PST), which is a formalised approach to developing mental skills, has been increasingly accepted as important in modern day football training and practice. Several football clubs and youth academies are employing sport psychology consultants (Nesti, 2010) reflecting the view that it is important to learn and develop these skills and probably as early as possible. According to Johnson, Andersson, and Fallby (2011) about half of the premier league football teams in Sweden contacted a sport psychology consultant during the year 2008. Despite this recognition of the need to develop psychological skills in elite sport, in general, a systematic integration of PST into football training and match routines is considered the exception rather than the rule in many countries.

Despite increasing acknowledgement of the importance of psychological skills for success in football, there remain several challenges in systematically integrating sport psychology services. Johnson and colleagues (2011) found the biggest barriers to using sport psychology were lack of knowledge and/or misconceptions about the field, unclear descriptions of services, and problems integrating sport psychology into practice regimes; e.g. feasible time and positive role models. Often sport psychological support is not seen as a regular and consistent component of training and competitions but only considered when problems arise, such as a series of losses or when the team is already facing relegation. In other words, PST typically is not an integral aspect of player and team development. On an individual level, the provision of sport psychology services is seen as necessary only for problematic athletes (i.e. those who need fixing).

Furthermore, knowledge on the effectiveness of psychological interventions is poor, with assumptions of coaches and players, and especially officials, that psychological skills training lacks effectiveness (e.g. Konter, 2003). Pain and Harwood (2004) examined the knowledge and perceptions of applied sport psychology within English football in a survey with national coaches, youth academy directors, and academy coaches. They found that a lack of finance was the highest rated barrier to the uptake of PST. Other dimensions that emerged from the survey were negative perceptions of psychology or a lack of knowledge on sport psychology. Furthermore, how to integrate sport psychology into the system of players and coaching staff was problematic. Additionally, the coaches reported a lack of clarity regarding the role of sport psychologists and the services they would provide. Heaney (2006) reported that the stigma associated with consulting a psychologist was found to be a barrier to referral. Moreover, in a study by Freitas, Dias, and Fonseca (2013) 13 elite coaches of the Portuguese Premier League acknowledged the importance of PST and the role of sport psychologists but did not feel able to design and apply PST programmes. The researchers suggested that the need to educate football coaches providing more applicable, concrete, and practical PST information is necessary.

## Structuring psychological skills training

In light of the ambiguity regarding sport psychology among coaches and officials in football (Johnson et al., 2011) and other sports, Beckmann and Elbe (2015) proposed a structural model of psychological support. This model consists of three levels: basic training, skills training, and crisis intervention. Basic training consists of psychoregulation techniques such as relaxation. There are no prerequisites for this basic training phase; therefore, it can be introduced from the start of psychological consulting. The second level, skills training, has some prerequisites. One of them can be the use of relaxation techniques. Another prerequisite is knowing what mental resources the athlete possesses for successfully regulating him/herself versus where the athlete lacks such resources. Consequently, the first step in the process of mental coaching consists of identifying the athlete's mental strengths and weaknesses. Beckmann and Elbe (2015) refer to this as 'initial diagnostics'. Based on this assessment, the mental skills training is then tailor-made for each individual athlete.

Additionally, psychological skills training should be periodised like the acquisition and practice of other skills. Balague (2017) addresses the issue of adequately balancing intensity and volume of PST over training periods. For example, how many skills should be taught in one period? For how long should they be practised? What is the ideal difficulty level of the skills? All of these variables still remain without evidence-based answers.

## Foundation of psychological skills training: relaxation

Relaxation training lays the foundation for progressing training in more advanced mental skills. However, relaxation training should not only be understood as foundational to the development of more advanced skills. Knowing how to relax is important for recovery and can support good sleep the night before competition (Kellmann, Pelka, & Beckmann, 2018) and following competition. Additionally, research has shown that relaxation promotes regeneration. It is suggested that regular practice is necessary and can be integrated into training camps as well as over the course of long competitive seasons.

Research findings related to relaxation in football indicate that players perceive relaxation as relevant to performance (Kudlackova, Eccles, & Dieffenbach, 2013). Professional and college athletes considered relaxation to be more important than recreational athletes. Accordingly, professional athletes engaged in more relaxation during a typical week than college and recreational athletes. Kudlackova et al. also found that players moderately used deep breathing, meditation, and imagery relaxation techniques, and applied stretching, compared to autogenic training and progressive muscle relaxation. Players reported coping with competitive anxiety and promoting recovery as the two primary reasons for using relaxation techniques. Moreover, more physical or behavioural techniques (e.g. muscle relaxation) were used in relation to coping with competitive anxiety, whereas more mental or cognitive techniques (e.g. meditation) were used in relation to coping with everyday anxiety.

In general, relaxation training should be a regular part of training, especially in the training of young athletes. Our applied work has shown that relaxation techniques can already be used with younger athletes from the age of 8 years. However, the relaxation training should be embedded in an age-appropriate story (Beckmann & Elbe, 2015).

## Mental skills

Beckmann and Elbe (2015) refer to mental strength as 'the ability to effectively apply self-regulatory skills, which make it possible for individuals to achieve their full performance potential even under unfavourable conditions' (p. 3). Mental skills can be acquired both by individual athletes as well as by teams through mental or psychological skills training (PST). For example, the skill of self-regulation through self-talk is a skill that can be acquired and practised by an individual athlete. Activation, on the other hand, can also affect a team, for instance when concentration needs to be established before a game. Through the preceding diagnostic process, the sport psychologist identifies the strengths and the weaknesses or areas for improvement of an athlete or team. The specific content of the skills training (e.g. self-talk, concentration, or imagery training) should be guided by the diagnosis of their strengths and weaknesses.

PST refers to a systematic and consistent practice of mental or psychological skills for the purpose of enhancing performance, increasing enjoyment, or achieving greater sport or physical activity self-satisfaction (Weinberg & Gould, 2015). Programmes in PST are based on the assumption that thoughts and emotions impact on performance either negatively or positively. Consequently, developing and using psychological skills can help athletes to control or manage thoughts and emotions and contribute to the achievement of peak performance, health, and enjoyment. Slimania et al. (2016) conducted a systematic review and a meta-analysis on the effects of cognitive training strategies on motor and effective psychological skills development in football. They found cognitive training to result in positive psychological skills development in relation to imagery-cognitive skills and imagery-motivational skills. These skills reduced game-specific stress responses (i.e. decreased muscle tension and increased perceptual abilities), and increased self-confidence. Combining cognitive training strategies (i.e. imagery, goal setting, self-talk, and music) with physical training enhanced positive effects. Psychological skill development was related to improved motor skill performance. Furthermore, increasing evidence understanding the mechanisms underlying the effects of psychological skills have been published, including neurophysiological studies. Vestberg et al. (2012) assessed football players' general executive functions including on-line multi-processing such as creativity, response inhibition, and cognitive flexibility. They compared male and female High Division players (HD), Lower Division players (LD), and a standardised norm group. The results showed significantly better scores of executive functions in HD and LD players in comparison to the norm group for both males as well as females. However, the HD players outperformed the LD players on these tests. Furthermore, a significant correlation was obtained between the result of the test of executive functioning and measures of performance (e.g. the numbers of goals and assists the players had scored two seasons later).

Psychological demands for different individuals, different sports, and different positions on a team may differ and therefore these differences should be considered when designing and implementing a PST programme (Beckmann & Trux, 1991). Consequently, it would make sense to develop different psychological skills in players playing different positions in football. Thelwell, Greenlees, and Weston (2006) examined the effects of midfielder-specific psychological skills intervention comprising relaxation, imagery, and self-talk on position-specific performance measures. Three performance subcomponents were assessed over nine competitive matches. The results of this study indicated that the position-specific intervention enabled at least small improvements on the three dependent variables for each participant. All participants perceived the intervention as successful and appropriate to their needs. Kannekens, Elferink-Gemser, and Post (2009) investigated the development of self-assessed tactical skills in youth football players playing different positions. They found that 'Acting in Changing Situations' was assumed to be a crucial tactical skill of defenders. For midfielders 'Positioning and Deciding' were seen as most important, whereas 'Knowing About Ball Actions' was the qualifying factor for attackers. They also found that defenders and midfielders did not improve these tactical skills from ages 14 to 18 years, whereas attackers reported increased tactical skills during this period. In addition, Kannekens, Elferink-Gemser, and Visscher (2011) used the Tactical Skills Inventory for Sports to assess the tactical skills of 105 elite youth football players (mean age = 17.8 years) who participated in a talent development programme. 'Positioning and Deciding' appeared to be the tactical skills that best predicted adult performance. This was especially true for midfielders. For players scoring high on these skills, the odds ratios indicated a 6.60 times greater chance for a player to become a professional than players scoring low on these skills.

However, there still appears to be no general consensus on what the basic psychology skills are in a PST programme (Balague, 2017). Weinberg and Gould (2015) suggested that there might be individual programme differences but coaches and athletes would consider the following psychological skills as essential: arousal regulation, imagery (mental preparation), confidence building, increasing motivation and commitment (goal setting), attention or concentration skills (self-talk, mental plans), and coping with injury.

In a qualitative study by Omar-Fauzee, Jamalis, Ab-Latif, and Cheric (2010) with male university football players (aged 25–36) with an average of 10 years of playing experience four themes emerged from an examination of the most needed psychological skills: imagery, goal setting, self-talk, and relaxation. Similarly, Thelwell, Weston, Greenlees, and Nicholas (2008) found that elite-level coaches reported more frequent use and higher need for self-talk and imagery than relaxation and goal setting in training and competition. Hence, those four skills will be addressed in more detail in the following section. It is noteworthy that often these skills are taught in a more integrated way rather than as discrete skills.

## Goal setting

Goal setting is considered a powerful motivational technique for the enhancement of performance and productivity in sport, business, and personal life. Goals direct behaviour to achieve these important and specific outcomes.

Goal setting is widely used in football (see e.g. Johnson et al., 2011). Some major questions are:

- How clear, detailed, and explicit are these goals?
- Are these goals accepted by all team members?
- What is the level of commitment to these goals?

Goals help to focus and mobilise energy for goal achievement; however, they will only promote maximum effort if they are demanding and within reach. Only specific and hard goals will show the desired effect. In a review of 201 studies mainly in business contexts with more than 40,000 participants, Locke and Latham

(1990) report that in 91% of cases setting challenging and specific goals lead to performance success. A vivid example for the effectiveness of setting specific and challenging goals has been reported in physiotherapy with patients who had limited mobility in their shoulder and elbow joints. One group of patients was asked to: 'Close your eyes and raise your arm as high as possible, … higher, … and even higher.' Another group was asked to set a specific goal: 'Please take the book from the shelf.' Shelf height was adjusted to maximum individual reaching capacity. The group with the hard specific goal demonstrated a performance capability that was approximately 18 degrees higher than the group with 'do your best' instruction.

When setting goals it is important to distinguish between different goals, such as:

- Outcome goals: These involve striving for competition success (norm-referenced); e.g. becoming the highest scoring goalgetter of the season.
- Performance goals: These involve striving for a performance in relation to a standard or reference level set by the athlete or coach which they believe to be applicable for the athlete (self-referenced); e.g. an increase of 10% in the number of passes with the left foot.
- Process goals: These deal with how certain skills or strategies can be implemented; e.g. the fight to recapture the ball after losing it to the opponent.

Research shows most athletes set primarily outcome goals and process-oriented goals (Jones & Hanton, 1996). Outcome-oriented goals, however, can possibly lead to increased levels of fear (Burton, 1989) and even to a withdrawal from competition (Roberts, 1986). A study by Kingston and Hardy (1997) showed that process-oriented goals ('Where am I going to play the ball?') can improve concentration and help to control negative thoughts better than outcome goals. This could be related to the fact that process-oriented goals attract attention and are able to direct and commit the athlete to the goal.

### Team goals

In team sports, such as football, team goals are very important. Together with their coach, players can discuss and determine goals for the coming season. As mentioned above, these goals should be challenging, specific, and positively formulated (e.g. no avoidance goals in the sense of 'We do not want to be relegated'). Finally, particularly in team sports, the setting of group goals appears to be important for athletic performance because it can mobilise team spirit; shared goals promote a 'we-feeling'. In addition, the phenomenon of 'social loafing', the hiding behind team members and letting others do the work can be minimised (Burton, 1993). Furthermore, goals that are set by a person (and not the coach/ parent) and goals that are set jointly by the team should be encouraged because it will promote engagement in pursuing those goals. In relation to the first, there are both individual personal goals as well as individual group goals. To the latter, there is the setting of team goals for an individual member of the team and the setting of team goals for the team as such. At the start of the season we usually ask players to individually write down their goals for themselves and the team. Such goals do not have to be performance goals although those will usually come to mind first. We suggest to players to also think of process goals. For example, a goal with the team could be to be renowned for being the team playing the most attractive football. Individual goals do not have to be egoistic. A player's goal on the team could also be 'I will do everything to support my team, even when I am not playing myself.'

According to the research findings, a multiple goal strategy with a good balance between outcome, performance, and process goals leads to the best results (Filby, Maynard, & Graydon, 1999). Outcome goals are especially important with the motivation to push oneself hard in training. They can lead to one's complete dedication to sport, which is driven by this goal. Overriding, long-term outcome goals are the central source of energy for motivation, dedication, and self-commitment. Such long-term goals can be seen as visions: seeing oneself wearing the jersey of the national team and lining up for a world championship game. From the experience of the authors it appears that some young athletes become more and more afraid of having such visions and rather try to have what they call 'realistic' goals. The function of a vision provided by long-term goals needs to be explained to these athletes including that when you aim high you may not always reach the highest high. It is the pursuit of these lofty goals that encourage effort and commitment and having tried, even if unsuccessfully, can be rewarding.

Fundamentally, goals should be 'SMART', that is to say, specific, measurable, attainable, relevant, and time-based (Bull, Albinson, & Shambrook, 1996). Goal setting should always be combined with the development of strategies for achieving these goals ('path-goal approach'). If a player sets the goal of scoring 10 goals during the season, he should develop specific strategies as to how he could achieve this.

Goal setting may also be different at different ages. McCarthy and Jones (2007) found that improving performance and enjoying sport are the foci of most youth athletes, whereas improving and winning are typically the foci of older athletes (Weinberg, Burke, & Jackson, 1997). Athletes as young as 12 years of age can profit from goal setting.

Feedback on reaching one's goal is very important for effective goal setting. This feedback supports the athletes' goal-directed actions and provides them with information on how they should adapt their goals and/or strategies for achieving a goal in the sense of an optimal fit. One should continuously evaluate whether the goal has been achieved. This should be an integral part of any goal-setting programme. An effective goal-setting programme includes the planning of several different goals and a commitment to these. It includes the development of strategies for achieving these goals, their execution as well as the evaluation of their achievement. This is a continuing process pertaining to short-, middle-, and long-term goals.

Goal setting has proven to be an effective technique. But in the field of sports the results of research on how effective goal-setting training is and what goals are best suited for achieving top performances are inconsistent overall (see e.g. Burton, Naylor, & Holliday, 2001). When practising goal setting it is decisive that goals are accepted and also internalised by the athlete (Erez & Zidon, 1984). It is crucial that the athlete does not only display public compliance, because the coach wants him to set the goal, but shows actual personal acceptance. This becomes especially important when team goals are set where commitment from all team members is required.

Goals might sometimes have negative effects on athletic performance. Defining the hard specific goal is critical. Committing oneself to a goal that is not considered as realistic, because one's own expectancy to reach this goal is not high enough can result in fear of failure (Jones, 1990). However, the problem may not be the goal setting per se (i.e. process) but these individuals' disposition to fear of failure. Before trying to set a realistic goal the belief in the individual's capability of reaching the goal must be supported. Another question often arises: 'What if I set a specific, hard goal and fail?' It is necessary to explain that hard goals are challenging goals because the probability of attaining them is not predictable. Goal setting is a motivational technique that attempts to mobilise all the energy that is needed to reach the goal. All the mobilised energy will never guarantee that the goal is actually reached. Athletes should understand that goal setting is an energy mobilising technique that is extremely useful in performance settings. Failure to achieve a performance goal requires some analysis and evaluation and subsequently the setting of new goals.

Setting a challenging goal may also potentially lead to an increased willingness to take risks and possibly also lead to higher stress levels. One's self-confidence could be undermined if one does not achieve the goals that were set. A clear understanding of goal setting as a motivational technique should be achieved early in the process. Goals may possibly also limit one's attention so that one neglects other areas that are not connected to the specific goal. This narrowed vision can be effective, but can also lead to the loss of important information.

## Imagery

Imagery is a key element of psychological skills training. In imagery, a certain action or sequence of movements is mentally practised through imagination without observable physical activity. From the perspective of cognitive psychology, 'an internal representation of the movement is activated. Its execution – preferably optimal – is repeated and simulated in a selected mental context' (Schack, 2006, p. 255). Studies have shown that many elite athletes consistently utilise imagery (Jones et al., 2002). Through imagery these athletes use all senses to create or re-create an experience during training and competition within their respective sports (Morris, Spittle, & Watt, 2005). The utilisation of imagery was found to improve athletes' performance and regulate motivation, confidence, and anxiety levels (Williams & Cumming, 2012). Imagery can be used to learn skills, refine skills, for rehearsal of tactics, and competition preparation.

Several researchers have investigated whether football players used imagery. In general, it was found that players considered the use of imagery to enhance performance in competition more important than developing physical skills during practice (Barr & Hall, 1992). In addition, Salmon, Hall, and Haslam (1994) found football players to use imagery more for self-motivation than for its cognitive function. Although imagery does not involve the actual execution of a skill it works most effectively in combination with the physical execution of the skill (Feltz, Landers, & Becker, 1988). However, other researchers have analysed the use of imagery in training, especially during and after the practice (e.g. Kerkez, Kulak, & Aktas, 2012; Munroe-Chandler, Hall, Fishburne, & Strachan, 2007). For example, Kerkez et al. (2012) conducted a 14-week study of specific imagery and autogenic relaxation combined with standard physical training on football skill performance in novice boys aged 10–12 years. The research revealed that the mental practice was effective for skill development above and beyond the physical training.

Jordet (2005) instructed midfielders to systematically imagine receiving the ball in game situations and make the appropriate decisions. Over 10–14 weeks each player met the instructor once a week to go through the imagery programme. Two of the three players in the study were found to improve components of perception through ecological imagery training resulting in the development of higher prospective control for attacking players; thereby they improved their performance. Thelwell et al. (2006) instructed five midfielders (19–23 years old) to use a Psychological Skills Training Package over a nine-match period. Imagery was one of the elements in this programme. It contained imagery for enhancing specific aspects of performance, such as successful passes, recovery from a poor first touch or from an incomplete pass, and the completion of a successful tackle. First touch percentage, tackle percentage, and pass percentage were assessed. Unexpectedly, not all the midfielders in the study showed significant enhancement of their performances. Thelwell et al. explained this by pointing out that the involved midfielders had different playing characteristics. Specifically, midfielders can specialise in a number of roles, e.g. more offensive or more defensive. Thus, imagery should be tailored to the specific role of a player within the team.

In order to enhance the development of passing strategies, Seif-Barghi, Kordi, Memari, Mansournia, and Jalali-Ghomi (2012) used a cognitive imagery programme. Players learned a relaxation technique before practising mental imagery: they imagined game scenes and their best performances in these situations. The effects of this intervention were assessed through video analysis. Comparison of performance before and after the imagery-training programme revealed an increase in successful pass rate percentage.

Research provides support for the effectiveness of the PETTLEP (Physical, Environment, Task, Timing, Learning, Emotion, and Perspective) model in designing performance-facilitating imagery interventions. Inclusion of emotional content into imagery practices might be more influential in competitive rather than practice situations (Ramsey, Cumming, Edwards, Williams, & Brunning, 2010). Asynchronous music and Motivational General-Mastery (MG-M) imagery when combined had a facilitative effect on flow and perceived performance. In addition, player comments supported these findings and suggested that the music and imagery intervention strategy have great potential for athletes during pre-competition (Pain, Harwood, & Anderson, 2011). Mental imagery has been found to significantly improve successful pass rates in under 16 (U16) and under 21 (U21) football teams, but not in other categories. It is suggested that in football, successful passing through real competitions as a multidimensional and critical open skill could be enhanced by an ecologically sound method of mental imagery (Seif-Barghi et al., 2012). Goalkeepers use imagery both for motivational and cognitive purposes, but the motivational function, namely its general-mastery component, was slightly more used and with more vivid images. In addition, after competition and when injured, U21 goalkeepers significantly used less imagery than their older counterparts (Ribeiro et al., 2015).

The combination of different types of cognitive imagery training (i.e. cognitive general and cognitive specific) has a positive influence on football performance during training. In addition, motivational imagery (i.e. motivational general-arousal, motivational general-mastery, and motivational specific) has been found to enhance competition performance. Moreover, motivational imagery strategies (i.e. motivational general-arousal, motivational general-mastery, and motivational specific) have efficacy for positively influencing competition-specific indices while the combination of two different types of cognitive imagery training (i.e. cognitive general or cognitive specific) are particularly effective for enhancing football performance during training (Slimania et al., 2016).

Konter and Doğanay (2002) found that players in higher football leagues (professional football divisions in Turkey) showed significantly higher imagery scores than players of lower leagues. In addition, football players with moderate perceptions of their relationship with head coaches have significantly higher use of imagery compared to players with poor or good relationships (Konter, 2002). This could mean that level of relationship between footballers and their head coaches could be influential regarding the use of imagery. Moreover, football players with high scores on football courage (including mastery, determination, assertiveness, venturesome, and sacrificial behaviour in risk circumstances; Konter & Ng, 2012) reported significantly higher use of imagery than football players with low scores on football courage. Finally, footballers with very good and good perceptions of success (i.e. how much does the footballer perceive himself/herself successful in football) have significantly ($p<0.001$) higher use of imagery than footballers with low and moderate levels of success.

Mental imagery can also be used directly before executing a skill in a competition. In this situation it is not used as a method of practice but to prime the activation of relevant processes in the brain. A player could visualise how to get onto the pitch and into the game. He could also use imagery to mentally rehearse playing off an opposition player; this kind of imagery can also be employed to boost self-confidence and courage (Konter, 2017; see Munroe-Chandler & Guerrero, 2019, Chapter 16 in this book, for more detailed information). In general, imagery has been proven to be a very effective psychological skill and athletes show a very positive reaction to the imagery training (Munroe-Chandler & Hall, 2004).

## Self-talk (ST)

Inappropriate or self-defeating inner dialogue is associated with poor performance (i.e. self-fulfilling prophecy). Therefore, an awareness of and then dealing with self-talk are important psychological skills. A key question is to decide whether to focus on developing skills to control thoughts (Cognitive Behavioural Therapy) or to accept them (Acceptance Commitment Therapy).

Self-talk, within a PST package, involves activating mental processes to change or influence existing thought patterns (Theodorakis, Weinberg, Natsis, Douma, & Kazakas, 2000). Hoigaard and Johansen (2004) defined self-talk as an inner conversation, in which the individual explains emotions, approaches, and feelings; estimates, regulates, and changes judgment and assessment; and gives him/herself guidelines and instructions. Hardy, Jones, and Gould (1996) proposed that self-talk can enhance performance through increases in confidence and anxiety management. Self-talk can be broken down into three types: motivational (desire to achieve), mastery-based (to enhance confidence), and instructional (reaffirming competition goals; using other mental skills).

Statements, such as 'I can't make any long passes today' or 'I am just not fast enough for my opponent', are reflective of negative self-talk. Frequently, this internal sceptic dialogue is also characterised by a sense of helplessness: 'I do not know what is wrong', 'I cannot do anything about this situation', or 'Why am I so bad?' These negative and self-defeating thoughts are likely to reduce self-confidence and performance. Even though the overall empirical evidence for the relationship between self-talk and performance is equivocal several studies have in fact shown that negative self-talk results in poorer athletic performance (van Raalte, Brewer, Rivera, & Petitpas, 1994). Additionally, research has shown that the regulation of one's own inner dialogue in terms of staying positive and supportive, results in improved athletic performance (Hatzigeorgiadis, Zourbanos, Mpoumpaki, & Theodorakis, 2009). Numerous investigations also show how positive self-talk affects performance in different critical situations in sports. For example, self-talk can be successfully employed to increase effort (Rushall, 1984), to draw attention to relevant stimuli (Schmid & Peper, 1998), to call forth a change in morale (Hardy & Fazey, 1990), and promote the rehabilitation following an athletic injury (Ievleva & Orlick, 1991).

Self-talk may also consist of neutrally toned, task-specific instructions (Hardy, Gammage, & Hall, 2001). Only a few studies have examined self-talk in football. A study with Iranian elite football players by Daftari, Sofian Omar Fauzee, and Akbari (2010) found negative self-talk to weaken confidence through self-criticism and dwelling on negative thoughts. It also increased the level of perceived stress. Positive self-talk effects were associated with enhanced focus and attention, promoting decision-making (e.g. decreasing reaction time). Also, emotional effects of self-talk, such as motivating players to increase effort, coping with difficult situations, decreasing anxiety, and psyching up were reported as positive effects. At the behavioural level, self-talk was perceived to show benefits for the execution of tasks by increasing attentional focus and creating an awareness of the negative consequences of certain behaviours thereby benefiting the overall performance of the individuals and that of the team. Johnson, Hrycaiko, Johnson, and Halas (2004) used a single-subject multiple baseline design with three female football players to investigate the effectiveness of a 3-month self-talk intervention programme. They found an improvement in shooting performance in two of the three players over the 3 months. All three participants reported enhanced self-confidence compared to baseline.

A key goal of PST is to transform negative into positive thoughts (cognitive restructuring), which is consistent with a cognitive-behavioural approach to behaviour change. For example, replacing thoughts such as 'I hope I don't miss this penalty kick' to 'I am really good at taking penalties.' It is important to create positive inner dialogues, which are most suitable for each athlete. To achieve this, positive self-talk must be formulated by athletes themselves and preferably not by the sport psychologist. The inner dialogues can be reworded in different ways depending on what appears to be most natural to the athlete (Beckmann & Elbe, 2015). A newly created positive self-talk should be practised regularly (similar to physical skills) and should be integrated into athletic practices when possible and appropriate. Furthermore, the efficacy of the inner dialogue can be additionally strengthened by the use of imagery (Cumming, Nordin, Horton, & Reynolds, 2006). Sometimes, controlling thoughts may not be the most appropriate approach. If the motor skill is highly automated, thoughts could disrupt the execution of the skill

(Ehrlenspiel, 2001). Under these conditions it can be useful to stop thoughts as, for example, through the hand-clenching embodiment technique described by Beckmann, Gröpel, and Ehrlenspiel (2013).

## Integrated psychological skills training

Combining different psychological skills to stabilise and improve performance are frequently used in football. Routines, which will be addressed next, consist of such a combination of mental skills. More generally, psychological training in football should be systematic and well structured. Therefore, an integrated approach of psychological skills training is desirable. Psychological skills can be integrated into systematic, larger programmes, some of which will be addressed in the following section.

In a study by Slimania et al. (2016) amateur players were found to utilise the combination of cognitive training strategies/psychological training within precompetitive periods addressing complex and specific football skills. Elite football players (in particular, midfielders) predominantly used goal setting, imagery, and self-talk as opposed to non-elite counterparts demonstrating greater relaxation skill usage. The data also suggested that sport situations (i.e. training, competition), age of players, level of expertise (i.e. elite or otherwise), playing positions (i.e. defenders, forwards, and midfielders), and intervention characteristics moderated the efficacy of cognitive training on the development/refinement of football-specific motor and positive psychological skills.

Thelwell, Greenlees, and Weston (2010) examined the effects of a football-specific combination of psychological skills training comprising self-talk, relaxation, and imagery, on three performance subcomponents specific to midfield players throughout performance. Three participants had three performance subcomponents (passing, first touch, and tackling) assessed across first and second half performances, for a period of eight competitive games. The results showed the intervention to be effective in enhancing performance in the second half for all participants in at least two of the performance subcomponents.

## Routines

Many of the skills described above can be integrated into systematic routines so that they can be applied in the competitive situation (match). A routine is understood as a process, which reflects a consistent pattern of actions or behaviours to promote high performance. Over time, these routines can become habitual requiring little explicit thought. In football, routines can and have been applied in many situations: throw-in, corner, free kick, and penalty kick.

Routines include psychological skills, which are functional for the execution of the impending task; for instance, for eliminating disturbing thoughts and developing concentration and competitive tension. Routines function to stabilise behaviour in regard to certain skills. An 'intentional microcosm' is created, which can be controlled (Schack, Whitmarsh, Pike, & Redden, 2005, p. 145) with the goal of optimising preparations for effective execution of skills and tactics. The player follows a sequence of actions. Currently, one of the world's best players, Cristiano Ronaldo, demonstrates a consistent routine in taking a free kick. He takes a fixed number of steps behind the ball with a consistent length of the strides. He then stands behind the ball in a certain stance: upright body with legs akimbo (hands on the hips and elbows turned outwards). He might also make use of positive self-talk during striding behind the ball and imagery when he is standing behind the ball.

It is essential that athletes develop their own individual routines. The better they understand the functions of their routine and the better it corresponds to their individual needs, the more effective the routine will become (cf. Schack et al., 2005, p. 138). A multitude of investigations confirm the effectiveness of performance routines (cf. Mesagno & Mullane-Grant, 2010). Studies in different sports verify that the best effects on performance are achieved with routines that contain both cognitive elements (focussing of attention, slogans, etc.) as well as physical elements (breathing, movement testing, etc., cf. Mesagno & Mullane-Grant, 2010).

## Integrated programmes of psychological skills training

An integrated approach of psychological skills training is desirable. Psychological skills can be integrated into systematic, larger programmes, some of which will be addressed now. Harwood (2008) developed a 4-month programme in a football academy in Great Britain using the intervention of the '5 Cs' for football, which is centred on commitment, communication, concentration, control, and confidence. Instructions related to the '5 Cs' intervention for football are provided during five 90-minute workshops for coaches. Each workshop is dedicated to one of the skills. Following each workshop, coaches work to integrate strategies in their coaching practice to teach each skill. In a recent paper, Pain (2016) reports English youth teams and many professional academies in England have adapted the '5 Cs' model. The '5 Cs' mental toughness approach in practice also involves one-on-one work with the player off the pitch (e.g. goal setting, rational-emotive behaviour therapy), integration of mental skills on the pitch (e.g. use of process goals, relaxation, self-talk), coaching sessions (e.g. concentration), and interventions linked to parental involvement. Konter and Hankin (2008) proposed a multidimensional-interactional football performance model including psychological skills using the dialectical approach and informed by research findings (see Figure 14.1).

The proposed multidimensional-interactional model of football performance represents an integrated approach for developing football players, which integrates technical, tactical, physical-physiological, and psychological elements or dimensions, within a broader socio-cultural context, and contributes to subsequent performance and other outcomes. Psychological skills are a core element in the model and should be integrated into physical, technical, and tactical training sessions.

The model consists of a four-stage sequence of these four dimensions. The four stages in the model are:

Stage 1: The Fundamental-Primary Conditions includes the situation of the football organisation, historical, and socio-cultural background, management and traditional values, infrastructure and facilities, employed staff and services. These macro forces shape the environment in which the football team operates.

Stage 2: Sport (Football) performance is shaped by physical condition, technical, tactical, and psychological preparation, abilities, characteristics and/or skills (e.g. Strudwick, 2016). Psychological skills training will have an important effect on other training areas (physical-physiological, technical, and tactical training) as illustrated

192   *E. Konter et al.*

1. Fundamental        Historical, Environmental, Socio-economic, Biological,
   Conditions         Cultural, Organizational and Philosophical Conditions
                      (Facilitative-Debilitative / Positive-Negative)
2. Training and Applications

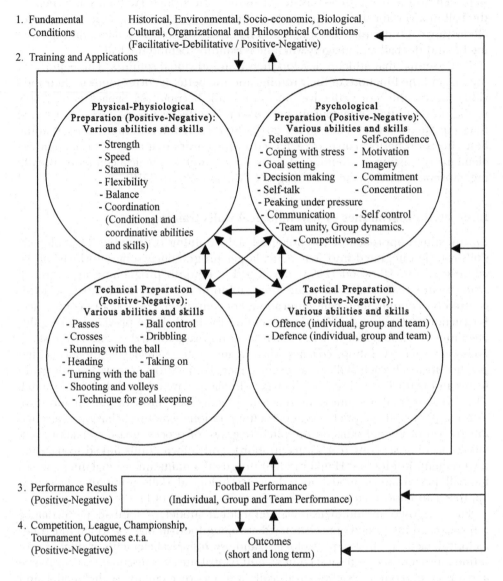

*Figure 14.1* Proposed multidimensional-interactional model of football performance.

in Figure 14.1. Lack of psychological skills will thwart physical, technical, and tactical development. It is noteworthy that the constituent components should be viewed as an overall holistic entity and harmoniously intertwined because they are interdependent. Each aspect of training requires specialist support to obtain the best results; for example, strength and conditioning staff, coaches, assistant coaches, sport psychologist, and the goalkeeper coach (Konter & Hankin, 2008). Many managers, coaches, and players fallaciously believe that they can overcome their performance problems with excessive physical training (Martens, 1987; Weinberg & Gould, 2015) rather than a more holistic and integrated approach.

Stage 3: Performance results are assessed on three levels, such as individual, group (e.g. defenders, midfield), and team performances (i.e. wins and losses or other metrics that might illucidate changes in some element such as tactical awareness) and in terms of short, medium, and long-term goals. The specific nature of football, competition, individual players, and conditions needs to be considered when setting these goals.

Stage 4: Performance outcomes can be affected by and have a very strong effect on the other stages either positively or negatively as they are interdependent (Konter & Hankin, 2008). The arrows in the model show these interdependent relations between components. It is important to note that relationships shown by the arrows do not have similar levels of reciprocity. The quantitative and qualitative effect on each other may vary widely in terms of intensity. The strength of the interdependent relationships can be quite different between the variables. Indeed, all stages could have positive or negative, facilitative or debilitative, or neutral effects on each other (Konter & Hankin, 2008).

Specialists who have a role in the training and applications stage of the proposed model can apply relevant measurements (if appropriate) to shape the development and performance results.

## Conclusions

Even though employing sport psychological interventions in football might be met with some resistance by players, coaches, and officials, the benefits of psychological skills training (PST) is increasingly acknowledged. Resistance might be based on a lack of knowledge on psychological skill training and/or perhaps concerns that others might think they are mentally weak or that others might think that there something wrong with them (Weinberg & Gould, 2015). In comparison to other sports, research on the effectiveness of psychological training in football is relatively scarce. Future developments should include further adjustment of psychological skills to the specific conditions in football and rigorous assessment of its effectiveness in order to provide convincing evidence and increase acceptance. Meanwhile, some national football associations have included sport psychology as a mandatory component in their youth development programmes (e.g. the German Football Association).

## References

Balague, G. (2017). Periodization of psychological skills in sport. *International Society of Sport Psychology-ISSP 14th World Congress*, 10–14 July, Seville, Spain.

Barr, K., & Hall, C. (1992). The use of imagery by rowers. *International Journal of Sport Psychology, 23*, 243–261.

Beckmann, J., & Elbe, A. M. (2015). *Sport psychological interventions in competitive sports.* Newcastle, England: Cambridge Scholars Publishing.

Beckmann, J., Gröpel, P., & Ehrlenspiel, F. (2013). Preventing motor skill failure through hemisphere-specific priming: Cases from choking under pressure. *Journal of Experimental Psychology: General, 142*, 679–691.

Beckmann, J., & Trux, J. (1991). Wen lasse ich wo spielen? Persönlichkeitseigenschaften und die Eignung für bestimmte Positionen in Sportspielmannschaften [Which player will I assign to which position? Personality dispositions and the qualification for certain positions on sport teams]. *Sportpsychologie, 5*(3), 18–21.

Bull, J., S. Albinson, J. G., & Shambrook, C. J. (1996). *The mental game plan: Getting psyched for sport*. Brighton, England: Sports Dynamics.

Burton, D. (1989). Winning isn't everything: Examining the impact of performance goals on collegiate swimmers' cognitions and performance. *The Sport Psychologist, 3*, 105–132.

Burton, D. (1993). Goal setting in sport. In R. N. Singer, M. Murphey, & L. K. Tennant (Eds.), *Handbook of research on sport psychology* (pp. 467–491). New York, NY: Macmillan.

Burton, D., Naylor, S., & Holliday, B. (2001). Goal setting in sport: Investigating the goal effectiveness paradox. In R. Singer, H. A. Hausenblas, & C. M. Janelle (Eds.), *Handbook of research on sport psychology* (2nd ed., pp. 497–528). New York, NY: Wiley.

Cumming, J., Nordin, S. M., Horton, R., & Reynolds, S. (2006). Examining the direction of imagery and self-talk on dart-throwing performance and self-efficacy. *The Sport Psychologist, 20*, 257–274.

Daftari, O., Sofian Omar Fauzee, M., & Akbari, A. (2010). Effects of self-talk on football players' performance in official competitions. *Researchers in Sport Science Quarterly, 1*, 29–37.

Ehrlenspiel, F. (2001). Paralysis by analysis? A functional framework for the effects of attentional focus on the control of motor skills. *European Journal of Sport Science, 1*(5), 1–11.

Eklund, R. C., & Tenenbaum, G. (2014). *Encyclopedia of sport and exercise psychology*. Los Angeles, CA: Sage.

Erez, M., & Zidon, I. (1984). Effects of goal acceptance on the relationship of goal difficulty to performance. *Journal of Applied Psychology, 69*, 69–78.

Feltz, D. L., Landers, D. M., & Becker, B. J. (1988). A revised meta-analysis of the mental practice literature on motor skill learning. In J. Duckmann & J. Swets (Eds.), *Enhancing human performance* (pp. 61–101). Washington, DC: Reiley.

Filby, W. C., Maynard, I. W., & Graydon, J. K. (1999). The effect of multiple-goal strategies on performance outcomes in training and competition. *Journal of Applied Sport Psychology, 11*, 230–246.

Fletcher, D., Hanton, S., & Wagstaff, C. R. D. (2012). Performers' responses to stressors encountered in sport organisations. *Journal of Sports Sciences, 30*(4), 349–358.

Freitas, S., Dias, C., & Fonseca, A. (2013). What do coaches think about psychological skills training in soccer? A study with coaches of elite Portuguese teams. *International Journal of Sports Science, 3*(3), 81–91.

Gould, D., Dieffenbach, K., & Moffett, A. (2002). Psychological characteristics and their development in Olympic champions. *Journal of Applied Sport Psychology, 14*(3), 172–204.

Hardy, J., Gammage, K., & Hall, C. (2001). A descriptive study of athlete self-talk. *The Sport Psychologist, 15*, 306–318.

Hardy, L., & Fazey, J. (1990). *Mental rehearsal: A guide for sports performance*. Leeds, England: National Coaching Foundation.

Hardy, L., Jones, G., & Gould, D. (1996). *Understanding psychological preparation for sport: Theory and practice*. Chichester, England: Wiley.

Harwood, C. (2008). Developmental consulting in a professional football academy: The 5Cs coaching efficacy program. *The Sport Psychologist, 22*(1), 109–133.

Hatzigeorgiadis, A., Zourbanos, N., Mpoumpaki, S., & Theodorakis, Y. (2009). Mechanisms underlying the self-talk–performance relationship. *Psychology of Sport and Exercise, 10*(1), 186–192.

Heaney, C. (2006). Physiotherapists' perceptions of sport psychology interventions in professional soccer. *International Journal of Sport and Exercise Psychology, 1*, 1–18.

Hoigaard, R., & Johansen, B. (2004). The solution-focused approach in sport psychology. *The Sport Psychologist, 18*, 218–228.

Ievleva, L., & Orlick, T. (1991). Mental links to enhanced healing: An exploratory study. *The Sports Psychologist, 5*(1), 25–40.

Johnson, J., Hrycaiko, D., Johnson, G., & Halas, J. (2004). Self-talk and female youth soccer performance. *The Sport Psychologist, 18*(1), 44–59.

Johnson, U., Andersson, K., & Fallby, J. (2011). Sport psychology consulting among Swedish premier soccer coaches. *International Journal of Sport and Exercise Psychology, 9*(4), 308–322.

Jones, G. (1990). A cognitive perspective on the process underlying the relationship between stress and performance in sport. In G. Jones & L. Hardy (Eds.), *Stress and performance in sport* (pp. 17–42). Chichester, England: Wiley.

Jones, G., & Hanton, S. (1996). Interpretation of competitive anxiety symptoms and goal attainment expectancies. *Journal of Sport & Exercise Psychology, 18,* 144–157.

Jones, M. V., Bray, S. R., Mace, R. D., MacRae, A. W., & Stockbridge, C. (2002). The impact of motivational imagery on the emotional state and self-efficacy levels of novice climbers. *Journal of Sport Behavior, 25,* 57–73.

Jordet, G. (2005). Perceptual training in soccer: An imagery intervention study with elite players. *Journal of Applied Sport Psychology, 17,* 140–156.

Kannekens, R., Elferink-Gemser, M. T., & Post, W. J. (2009). Self-assessed tactical skills in elite youth soccer players: A longitudinal study. *Perceptual and Motor Skills, 109*(2), 459–472.

Kannekens, R., Elferink-Gemser, M. T., & Visscher, C. (2011). Positioning and deciding: Key factors for talent development in soccer. *Scandinavian Journal of Medicine and Science in Sports, 21,* 846–851.

Kellmann, M., Pelka, M., & Beckmann, J. (2018). Psychological relaxation techniques to enhance recovery in sports. In M. Kellmann & J. Beckmann (Eds.), *Sport, recovery and performance: Interdisciplinary insights* (pp. 247–259). Abingdon, England: Routledge.

Kerkez, F., Kulak, A., & Aktas, Y. (2012). Effects of specific imagery and autogenic relaxation combined intervention on soccer skill performance of young athletes in Turkey. *Scottish Journal of Arts, Social Sciences and Scientific Studies, 3*(1), 53–67.

Kingston, K., & Hardy, L. (1997). Effects of different types of goals on processes that support performance. *The Sport Psychologist, 11,* 277–293.

Konter, E. (2002). *Investigation of psychological skills according to some variables in professional soccer* (unpublished PhD thesis). Çukurova University, Institute of Social Sciences, Adana, Turkey.

Konter, E. (2003). *Myths and truths in sport psychology applications.* İzmir: Dokuz Eylül Yayıncılık.

Konter, E. (2017). Psychological skills of soccer players in relation to level of courage, individual and performance variables. *International Society of Sport Psychology-ISSP World Congress,* 10–14 June, Seville, Spain.

Konter, E., & Doğanay, A. (2002). Psychological skills of soccer players in relation to being amateur and professional. *Turkish Journal of Sport Medicine, 37*(2), 41–49.

Konter, E., & Hankin, T. (2008). Multi-dimensional-interactional model of sport performance with the soccer example: A dialectical approach. *XIIth Conference of Soccer and Tennis, National Sports Academy* (pp. 34–51). Sofia, Bulgaria.

Konter, E., & Ng, J. (2012). Development of sport courage scale. *Journal of Human Kinetics, 33,* 163–172.

Kudlackova, K., Eccles, D. W., & Dieffenbach, K. (2013). Use of relaxation skills in differentially skilled athletes. *Psychology of Sport and Exercise, 14*(4), 468–475.

Locke, E. L., & Latham, G. P. (1990). *A theory of goal setting and task performance.* Englewood Cliffs, NJ: Prentice Hill.

Martens, R. (1987). *Coaches guide to sport psychology.* Champaign, IL: Human Kinetics.

McCarthy, P. J., & Jones, M. V. (2007). A qualitative study of sport enjoyment in the sampling years. *The Sport Psychologist, 21,* 400–416.

Mesagno, C., & Mullane-Grant, T. (2010). A comparison of different pre-performance routines as possible choking interventions. *Journal of Applied Sport Psychology, 22*(3), 343–360.

Morris, T., Spittle, M., & Watt, A. P. (2005). *Imagery in sport.* Champaign, IL: Human Kinetics.

Munroe-Chandler, K., & Guerrero, M. (2019). Imagery in football. In E. Konter, J. Beckmann, & Loughead (Eds.). *Football psychology: From theory to practice.* London, England: Routledge.

Munroe-Chandler, K. J., & Hall, C. R. (2004). Enhancing the collective efficacy of a soccer team through motivational general-mastery imagery. *Imagination, Cognition and Personality, 24*(1), 51–67.

Munroe-Chandler, K., Hall, C. R., Fishburne, G., & Strachan, L. (2007). Where, when and why young athletes use imagery: An examination of developmental differences. *Research Quarterly for Exercise and Sport, 78*, 103–116.

Nesti, M. (2010). *Psychology in football: Working with elite and professional players*. Abingdon, England: Routledge.

Omar-Fauzee, M., Jamalis, M., Ab-Latif, R., & Cheric, M. C. (2010). The mental skills training of university soccer players. *International Education Studies, 3*(2), 81–90.

Pain, M. A. (2016). Mental interventions. In T. Strudwick (Ed.), *Soccer science* (pp. 389–413). Champaign, IL: Human Kinetics.

Pain, M. A., & Harwood, C. (2004). Knowledge and perceptions of sport psychology within English soccer. *Journal of Sports Sciences, 22*(9), 813–826.

Pain, M. A., Harwood, C., & Anderson, R. (2011). Pre-competition imagery and music: The impact on flow and performance in competitive soccer. *The Sport Psychologist, 25*(2), 212–232.

Rampinini, E., Bishop, D., Marcora, S. M., Bravo, D. F., Sassil, R., & Impellizzeri, F. M. (2007). Validity of simple field tests as indicators of match-related physical performance in top-level professional soccer players. *International Journal of Sports Medicine, 28*, 228–235.

Ramsey, R., Cumming, J., Edwards, M. G., Williams, S., & Brunning, C. (2010). Examining the emotion aspect of PETTLEP-based imagery with penalty taking in soccer. *Journal of Sport Behavior, 33*(3), 295–314.

Ribeiro, J., Madeira, J., Dias, C., Stewart, L. R., Corte-Real, N., & Fonseca, A. (2015). The use of imagery by Portuguese soccer goalkeepers. *Journal of Imagary Research in Sport Physical Activity, 10*(1), 1–9.

Roberts, G. C. (1986). The growing child and the perception of competitive stress in sport. In G. Gleeson (Ed.). *The growing child in competitive sport* (pp. 130–144). London, England: Hodder & Stoughton.

Rushall, B. S. (1984). The content of competition thinking. In W. F. Straub & J. M. Williams (Eds.), *Cognitive sport psychology* (pp. 51–62). Lansing, NY: Sport Science Associates.

Salmon, J., Hall, C., & Haslam, I. (1994). The use of imagery by soccer players. *Journal of Applied Sport Psychology, 6*, 116–133.

Schack, T. (2006). Mentales training [Mental training]. In M. Tietjens & B. Strauss (Eds.), *Handbuch Sportpsychologie* [Handbook of sports psychology] (pp. 254–261). Schorndorf, Germany: Hofmann.

Schack, T., Whitmarsh, B., Pike, R., & Redden, C. (2005). Routines. In J. Taylor & G. Wilson (Eds.), *Applying sport psychology* (pp. 137–150). Champaign, IL: Human Kinetics.

Schmid, A., & Peper, E. (1998). Strategies for training concentration. In J. M. Williams (Ed.), *Applied sport psychology* (3rd ed., pp. 316–328). Champaign, IL: Human Kinetics.

Seif-Barghi, T., Kordi, R., Memari, A., Mansournia, M., & Jalali-Ghomi, M. (2012). The effect of an ecological imagery program on soccer performance of elite players. *Asian Journal of Sports Medicine, 3*(2), 81–89.

Slimania, M., Bragazzi, N. L., Tod, D., Dellal, A., Hueg, O., Cheour, F., Taylor, L., & Chamari, K. (2016). Do cognitive training strategies improve motor and positive psychological skills development in soccer players? Insights from a systematic review. *Journal of Sports Science, 34*(24), 2338–2349.

Strudwick, T. (2016). *Soccer science.* Champaign, IL: Human Kinetics.

Theodorakis, Y., Weinberg, R., Natsis, P., Douma, I., & Kazakas, P. (2000). The effects of motivational versus instructional self-talk on improving motor performance. *The Sport Psychologist, 14*, 253–272.

Thelwell, R. C., Greenlees, I. A., & Weston, N. J. V. (2006). Using psychological skills training to develop soccer performance. *Journal of Applied Sport Psychology, 18*, 254–270.

Thelwell, R. C., Greenlees, I. A., & Weston, N. J. V. (2010). Examining the use of psychological skills throughout soccer performance. *Journal of Sport Behavior, 33*(1), 109–120.

Thelwell, R. C., Weston, N. J. V., Greenlees, I. A., & Nicholas, V. H. (2008). A qualitative exploration of psychological-skills use in coaches. *The Sport Psychologist, 22,* 38–53.

van Raalte, J. L., Brewer, B. W., Rivera, P. M., & Petitpas, A. J. (1994). The relationship between observable self-talk and competitive junior tennis players' match performances. *Journal of Sport & Exercise Psychology, 16,* 400–415.

Vestberg, T., Gustafson, R., Maurex, L., Ingvar, M., & Petrovic, P. (2012). Executive functions predict the success of top-soccer players. *PLoS ONE, 7*(4): e34731. doi:10.1371/journal. pone.0034731.

Weinberg, R. S., Burke, K. L., & Jackson, A. (1997). Coaches' and players' perceptions of goal setting in junior tennis: An exploratory investigation. *The Sport Psychologist, 11,* 426–439.

Weinberg, R. S., & Gould, D. (2015). *Foundations of sport and exercise psychology* (6th ed.). Champaign, IL: Human Kinetics.

Williams, S., & Cumming, J. (2012). Athletes' ease of imaging predicts their imagery and observational learning use. *Psychology of Sport and Exercise, 13,* 363–370.

# 15 The use of acceptance and commitment therapy for stress management interventions in football

*Christopher R. D. Wagstaff, Göran Kenttä, and Richard C. Thelwell*

## Abstract

Stressors have been reported to occur in a wide variety of competitive sports, including football, with numerous positive and negative outcomes. Nevertheless, what is apparent in elite sport is that the demands faced by individuals often require intervention to optimize well-being and performance. The aim of this chapter is to focus on elite-level players' experiences of stress and describe these within the theoretical framework of acceptance commitment therapy (ACT). A brief hypothetical case is presented to showcase some typical performance issues related to stress in a young emerging player at the age of 18 years. This is followed by a brief overview of stress in competitive sport in general and more specifically in football. Subsequently, the theoretical model of ACT is described together with some specific applied interventions aiming to enhance performance and well-being.

## Stress in football through the lens of acceptance commitment therapy

Consider this case ... Terry is an 18-year-old footballer. It is towards the latter stages of a season in which his team, Blackfoot United, have continually performed well and Terry has reinforced his status as one of the rising stars in the league. So far, Terry has been full of confidence and has demonstrated an ability to thrive in high pressure situations. The game in which they are playing is against a rival team for the championship. Going into the final few minutes they are losing 2–1 and have been awarded a penalty. The obvious player to take the penalty is Terry, since he is the regular penalty-taker. In addition, the head coach, Jeff, has confidence in him, and expects Terry to deliver.

The penalty kick ... Prior to taking the kick, Terry becomes aware of his thinking ...

> it's my responsibility ... everyone expects me to score. I must score. I cannot miss. If I miss, I will let everyone down. I can't let everyone down. Why am I thinking this? This is the first time I've felt insecurity and uncomfortable feelings like this. What does it mean? Why am I suddenly thinking about failure as the outcome? Oh xxxx!

Stuck immersed within these anxiety-provoking thoughts and feelings he approaches the ball, and skies it – a major mis-hit.

Consideration 1 – How would you support Terry to deal with this failure and his emotional response to it using your knowledge of stress and emotion, with a specific focus on anxiety?

The after effects … In the following days, Terry started to experience occasional anxiety symptoms due to the increased media scrutiny regarding the penalty miss, his own perceptions of negative feedback from the coach due to the impact of the penalty miss on the match outcome, and non-selection for the national team. In addition, since Terry associates these symptoms with the penalty miss, he has become preoccupied with primary thought of 'I hope that no penalties are awarded in the upcoming game'. 'What if' questions such as 'what if we get a penalty … what if I take another one and I miss again?' become more prominent and Terry makes reference to others taking penalties in order to protect himself and his ego. The negative emotions relating to the penalty miss gradually start to affect other areas of Terry's game and the anxiety experienced when considering penalty kicks, and potential failure, extends to include scoring opportunities from free-kicks. This results in severe performance anxiety and not being able to successfully execute free-kicks with good scoring opportunities.

Terry is now acutely aware of his pre-performance anxiety issues and during this emotional response he also experiences a racing heart, an upset stomach, nausea, and negative cognitions about his ability; all of which make him feel increasingly uncomfortable. While primarily wanting to avoid ruminating about such thoughts and feelings, he tries to distract himself by using thought-stopping approaches. During matches, his emotional and cognitive responses are now reflected in his behaviours where he is less confident with his passing and tackling ability, and general positional play. A single poor pass will quickly lead to self-blaming and pressure for the need to avoid failure with his next pass, consequently the next pass is always extra safe and risk-averse. Mistakes also lead to observable behaviour such as hiding from passes and decisions to not attack opposition players when in possession of the ball, and avoiding commitment to high-risk or 50/50-chance tackles in defence. It is now not only Terry who is aware of his 'safety' behaviour, it is also obvious to the coach, Jeff, who starts to question Terry's enthusiasm and commitment.

Terry is now developing an ongoing fear of failure and he starts to avoid difficult and even normally manageable situations. Greater attention is focused on the increasingly negative newspaper reports about his performances; the media suggest a 'performance slump' and raise questions about his long-term career prospects. Terry's sleep patterns on the nights before matches are increasingly problematic due to expectancy worries. It is at this point that Terry decides to disclose his problems that he has hitherto kept private because of a fear of showing any sign of mental weakness. He speaks with his coach Jeff about the situation and together they discuss the recent performance issues. The outcome of the meeting is that they come to an agreement that Terry might be struggling to cope with recent challenges and they agree that the player will meet with the team's sport psychologist.

## Conceptual framework

Elite football is characterized by highly complex social and organizational environments, which impose numerous demands on sport performers and other personnel that function within them. As a result, it is imperative that multidisciplinary science and medicine teams are aligned with systems, processes, and implementation strategies that assist decision-making. For instance, sport psychologists can help facilitate a balanced approach to training and competition decisions, especially when players are ill, injured, unfit, or out of form. It follows that sport psychologists must continuously monitor and manage health and performance (cf. Dijkstra, Pollock, Chakraverty, & Alonso, 2014; Reid, Stewart, & Thorne, 2004) and consider the best science and medical advice as well as contextual characteristics when supporting individuals in football. In this chapter we aim to provide an outline of the fundamental components of the stress process and delineate between stress-related concepts. After this conceptual introduction, we will return to the case information above and outline a possible intervention based on acceptance commitment therapy (ACT). Specifically, we will reflect on the potential utility of ACT interventions for enhancing performance and well-being in football. It should be noted that the content and focus in this chapter is about the player even though we acknowledge that coaches, managers, and support staff experience a lot of stress as well and that these experiences are often intertwined.

## Defining stress and related concepts

Stress has variously been defined as an environmental stimulus, a person's response, or the result of an interaction between the person and the environment. As the body of knowledge has developed, particularly that surrounding the cognition or appraisal of stimuli and the interpretation of responses, researchers have increasingly considered the nature of the interaction and, most importantly, the psychological processes through which it takes place (Fletcher, Hanton, & Mellalieu, 2006; Jones & Hardy, 1989; Woodman & Hardy, 2001). We define stress as 'an ongoing process that involves individuals transacting with their environments, making appraisals of the situations they find themselves in, and endeavouring to cope with any issues that may arise' (Fletcher et al., 2006, p. 329, adapted from Lazarus, 1999). Several aspects of this 'transactional' definition are particularly noteworthy. First, stress is an ongoing process, and is neither static nor linear. Second, this perspective emphasizes the importance of an individual's appraisals of their environment. Third, 'stress' refers to an umbrella term encapsulating multiple components, which primarily relate to stressors, appraisals, responses, and coping. In terms of stress in football, the transactional conceptualization implies a dynamic relationship between an individual (e.g. footballer, coach, or manager) and the football environment within which he or she is operating (cf. Fletcher et al., 2006). In this transaction, the individual appraises an event (or perceived event) in terms of its meaning for their goals, morals, and values, as well as his or her coping resources. Concurrently, facets of the individual's environment (e.g. personal and organizational history and resources, structure, and climate) influence these appraisals. Depending on the outcomes of these cognitive evaluations, an individual may engage in thoughts and behaviours designed to deal with the situation, strategies which will likely change over time as efforts are reappraised and outcomes evaluated. This ongoing process will affect subsequent appraisals of demands and hence an individual's responses and possible choice of coping strategies. In spite of these general themes, it is important to specifically delineate the components of the stress process.

**Stressors.** The term *stressor* refers to an environmental demand and the term *strain* to an individual's response (Beehr, 1998; Beehr & Franz, 1987). Over the past couple of decades or so, sport psychology researchers have unearthed a wide range of stressors encountered by sport performers (see e.g. Gould, Jackson, & Finch, 1993; McKay, Niven, Lavallee, & White, 2008; Mellalieu, Neil, Hanton, & Fletcher, 2009; Noblet & Gifford, 2002; Scanlan, Stein, & Ravizza, 1991; Thelwell, Weston, & Greenlees, 2007; Weston, Thelwell, Bond, & Hutchings, 2009; Woodman & Hardy, 2001). Collectively, the stressors identified in these studies have been associated with competitive performance, the sport organization within which athletes operate, and personal 'non-sporting' life events (Fletcher et al., 2006).

*Competitive stressors* are defined as 'the environmental demands associated primarily and directly with competitive performance' (Mellalieu, Hanton, & Fletcher, 2006, p. 3). In some of the early exploratory research conducted by sport psychology scholars (e.g. Gould et al., 1993; Holt & Hogg, 2002; James & Collins, 1997) a wide range of performance-related stressors were identified. More recently, researchers (e.g. Hanton, Fletcher, & Coughlan, 2005; Mellalieu et al., 2009; Neil, Hanton, Mellalieu, & Fletcher, 2011) have investigated competitive stressors in a more systematic fashion. Generally, the findings of these studies indicate that the main stressors experienced in relation to competitive performance include injuries, rivalry, underperforming, preparation, pressure, expectations, and self-presentation. To elaborate, demands relating to injuries in athletic populations are commonly reported (see e.g. Gould, Udry, Bridges, & Beck, 1997). Such stressors include the risk of sustaining an injury, the risk of being deliberately injured due to an opponent's actions, the act of getting injured, determining the extent and cause of injury, the inability to train, missing important competitions, loss of fitness, isolation during injury, and maintaining or returning to pre-injury levels of performance and competing whilst injured (see Evans, Wadey, Hanton, & Mitchell, 2012). Athletes have also commonly reported stressors related to the competitive rivalry experience as part of performance and team selection (see e.g. Thelwell et al., 2007; Woods & Thatcher, 2009). Rivalry-related demands include competing against better athletes, deviant opponent behaviour, and competing against up-and-coming opponents.

Another common competitive stressor relates to preparation for competition and is frequently cited by participants in studies exploring the demands experienced by athletes in sport environments (see e.g. Weston et al., 2009). Specifically, sport performers have identified how various aspects of their preparation (e.g. physical, mental, technical, and tactical) have been inadequate, inappropriate, or arduous prior to competition. In addition, athletes have reported experiencing significant pressure to perform well at competition (see e.g. McKay et al., 2008). For example, sport performers have identified the pressurized nature of international competition, performing under pressure, and the pressure to beat others as salient themes. Sport performers from a range of sports have also reported underperforming in competition as a frequently encountered stressor (see e.g. Dugdale, Eklund, & Gordon, 2002). Specifically, the fear of failure, demands related to making errors or mistakes during competition, periods of limited progress, not achieving performance goals, poor personal and team performance, not performing as expected, a loss of form, and performance slumps. One of the most commonly reported types of competitive stressors experienced by athletes relates to performance expectations (see e.g. Gould et al., 1993). Internal expectations

– the pressure that a performer places on themselves as a result of perceived external demands – include wanting to start well during a competition, aspiring to perform to one's ability, and performing well in rankings. External expectations – the pressure placed on a performer by an external source – include being the favourite for a competition, starting well for the benefit of the team, other people expecting you to do well, competing for a better ranking place, and competing on live television. The final type of competitive stressor experienced by sport performers reported in the extant literature is self-presentation issues. Such demands have been repeatedly identified by athletes (see e.g. James & Collins, 1997), and frequently cited themes include the desire to manage the evaluation of performance from coaches and teammates, not wanting to let coaches and teammates down, the demonstration of ability, and seeking recognition. Altogether, being aware of expectations often results in a cognitive drift to possible scenarios and outcomes that lie in the future, i.e. not being in the present moment. This will be addressed in the intervention at the end of the chapter.

*Organizational stressors* are defined as 'the environmental demands associated primarily and directly with the organization within which an individual is operating' (Fletcher et al., 2006, p. 359). In a number of early studies that identified different types of environmental demands, sport psychology researchers unearthed a variety of organizational-related stressors (see e.g. Gould et al., 1993; Scanlan et al., 1991). Subsequently, scholars began to systematically investigate the organizational stressors encountered by athletic performers (see e.g. Fletcher & Hanton, 2003; Fletcher, Hanton, Mellalieu, & Neil, 2012; Hanton et al., 2005; Kristiansen & Roberts, 2010; Woodman & Hardy, 2001). To advance the body of knowledge in this area, Arnold and Fletcher (2012) recently synthesized the research that has identified the organizational stressors encountered by athletes and developed a taxonomic classification of these environmental demands. Using a meta-interpretation method, 34 studies (with a combined sample of 1,809 participants) the authors identified 640 distinct organizational demands. These stressors were then abstracted into 31 subcategories, and four general categories (namely leadership and personal issues, cultural and team issues, logistical and environmental issues, and performance and personal issues). The main leadership and personal issues reported within the extant literature include the coaches' behaviours and interactions, coaches' personality and attitudes, external expectations, support staff, sports officials, spectators, media, performance feedback, and the governing body.

Cultural and team issues typically include communication, team atmosphere and support, roles, cultural norms, goals, and teammate behaviour, personality, and attitudes. Common logistical and environmental issues relate to facilities and equipment, selection, travel, accommodation, competition format, structure of training, weather conditions, rules and regulations, physical safety, and technology. The final type of organizational stressor identified in Arnold and Fletcher's synthesis was performance and personal issues. The main themes within this category include injuries, finances, diet and hydration, and career transitions. Subsequent to this synthesis work, Arnold, Fletcher, and Daniels (2013) developed and validated the Organizational Stressor Indicator for Sport Performers (OSISP). The OSISP measures the frequency, intensity, and duration of demands across five categories of organizational stressors: Goals and Development, Logistics and Operations, Team and Culture, Coaching, and Selection. Via a series of four related studies, the OSISP was shown to display adequate internal consistency and content, factorial, discriminant, and concurrent validity (Arnold et al., 2013).

Beyond the identification of stressors encountered by athletes, researchers in this area have attempted to differentiate the content and quantity of stressors in elite and non-elite sport performers. To elaborate, Hanton et al. (2005) found that elite athletes experienced and recalled more demands associated primarily and directly with the sport organization than with competitive performance. Further, this population appeared more likely to experience similar competitive stressors but varied organizational stressors, perhaps because the former are typically common to most athletes' experiences of performance, whereas the latter are generally disparate and subject to numerous socio-cultural, political, economic, occupational, and technological influences. Recently, Arnold, Fletcher, and Daniels (2016) used the OSISP to observe significant demographic differences for gender, sport type, and competitive level. That is, the authors found that males encounter significantly higher dimensions of logistics and operations organizational stressors than females, and that females encounter significantly higher dimensions of selection organizational stressors than males. For sport type, it was found that performers competing in team-based sports encounter higher dimensions of logistics and operations, team and culture, and selection organizational stressors than those competing in individual-based sports. Finally, when examining competitive level, it was evident that sport performers competing at higher performance levels (e.g. national or international) typically experience organizational stressors more frequently, at a higher intensity, and for a longer duration than those competing at lower levels (e.g. regional or university and county or club).

*Personal stressors* are defined as the environmental demands associated primarily and directly with personal 'non-sporting' life events (Sarkar & Fletcher, 2014). Within this category, stressors encountered by sport performers include the work–life interface, family issues, and the death of a significant other. For instance, the work–life interface has been repeatedly identified as a stressor in the sport psychology literature (see e.g. Gould et al., 1993). Youth athletes at the initial stages of their career have identified difficulties associated with academic commitments, and balancing educational goals with personal relationships (see e.g. McKay et al., 2008). Older athletes in the latter stages of their career have identified demands related to work commitments, specifically the difficulties of balancing personal relationships with a job (see e.g. Noblet & Gifford, 2002). Relocation-related pressures have also been recognized as personal stressors, including problems with finding suitable accommodation, missing family and friends, and adjusting to independent living (see e.g. Giacobbi et al., 2004). Another common personal stressor category relates to those aligned with family issues, which have been a frequent demand encountered by a wide variety of athletes. Specifically, sport performers have faced financial pressures of having to provide for a family (see e.g. Thelwell et al., 2007), relationship problems (see e.g. Gould et al., 1993), family responsibilities (see e.g. Weston et al., 2009) and a volatile family life at home (see e.g. Scanlan et al., 1991). The final personal stressor category identified by sport performers is the death of a significant other. Some athletes report demands aligned with the death of a family member (see e.g. McKay et al., 2008) whereas others have experienced the loss of team members (see e.g. Scanlan et al., 1991).

To conclude, this section has reviewed the stressors encountered by sport performers aligned with the categories of competitive performance (namely preparation, injuries, pressure, underperforming, expectations, self-presentation, and rivalry), the sport organization within which the athletes operate (namely leadership and personal issues, cultural and team issues, logistical and environmental issues, and performance and personal issues), and personal 'non-sporting' life events (namely work–life interface, family issues, and the death of a significant other). By synthesizing the wealth of knowledge on stressors in sport we believe that practitioners working in football will be better prepared to monitor and identify the demands faced by individuals. Nevertheless, according to the transactional stress theory, the central component within the stress process is appraisal.

**Appraisal.** While stressors are clearly a salient feature of sport performers' lives, they only reflect one component of the stress process and say little about how performers cognitively evaluate – or appraise – the demands and resources they perceive. Indeed, the pivotal component of the transactional stress process is that of an individual's appraisal of their environment (see Lazarus & Folkman, 1984). According to Lazarus and Folkman (1984), there are five potential transactional alternatives that may be experienced during the appraisal process: *harm/loss, threat, challenge, irrelevant,* and *benign-positive.* Further, Lazarus and Folkman (1984) proposed that it is an individual's appraisal of the situational relevance to well-being that potentially leads to a stress appraisal rather than the situation itself. Lazarus (1999) asserted that rather than identifying particular stressors, researchers should aim to identify the rules that lead an individual to appraise an event as stressful. Individuals will assess an event according to how relevant it is to their personal welfare and by its situational characteristics. In order for an event to be appraised as stressful it must contain both personal factors and situational factors (Lazarus & Folkman, 1984).

In line with Lazarus and Folkman's (1984) influential work, it is not the situation per se that mediates a stress appraisal. Instead they proposed that eight underlying properties (namely novelty, predictability, event uncertainty, imminence, duration, temporal uncertainty, ambiguity, timing) exist, which underpin all situations perceived as stressful. Thatcher and Day (2008), who interviewed trampolinists regarding their most stressful competitive experiences, support the relevance of these underlying properties in a sporting domain. Other research within the sport context from Neil et al. (2011) indicated that athletes generally respond negatively to organizational stressors, although they do have the potential to interpret these responses as facilitative for their performance. Hanton, Wagstaff, and Fletcher (2012) partially supported these findings by demonstrating that organizational stressors are largely appraised as threatening or harmful, with few coping resources available to sport performers. Didymus and Fletcher (2012), who found that the appraisal (i.e. threat, challenge, harm/loss) experienced was influenced by the situational properties (e.g. imminence, novelty, duration) of the stressors encountered, extended these findings.

**Stress responses.** Strain in sport can relate to psychological, physical, or behavioural reactions, but they are by definition indicators of an individual's negative evaluation of environmental events (i.e. stressors). Evidence shows that the poor management of stressors can in the short term contribute to athletes' underperformance (Gould, Guinan, Greenleaf, Mudbery, & Peterson, 1999), and in the long term be a factor to overtraining syndrome (Kenttä & Hassmén, 1998; Meehan, Bull, Wood, & James, 2004), athletic burnout (Gustafsson, Kenttä, & Hassmén,

2011; Smith, 1986), and poor mental health (Gouttebarge, Aoki, & Kerkhoffs, 2016; Noblet, Rodwell, & McWilliams, 2003). While there has been less research on strain in sport aligned with the transactional stress model, stress response research in sport does provide some insight into their possible implications. Fletcher, Hanton, and Wagstaff (2012) conducted a qualitative study to explore sport performers' responses to stressors encountered in sport organizations. The main emotional responses that were revealed were anger, anxiety, disappointment, distress, happiness, hope, relief, reproach, and resentment. The main attitudinal responses were beliefs, motivation, and satisfaction. The main behavioural responses were categorized as verbal and physical. Focusing on emotional responses, there is some quantitative evidence linking organizational stressor encounters with athletes' anxiety, dejection, anger, excitement, and happiness (Arnold et al., 2013) and a self-report measure to assess sport performers' emotional responses to organizational stressors was recently validated (Arnold & Fletcher, 2015).

## Acceptance commitment therapy (ACT)

Stress-management interventions in sport (see, for a review, Rumbold, Fletcher, & Daniels, 2012) have largely drawn from cognitive behavioural therapy (CBT), which in brief focuses primarily on changing cognitions (i.e. appraisal), emotions, and behaviour to become more adaptive and functional in a specific situation. Collectively, the research on stress interventions in sport indicates that multimodal programmes might be the most effective treatment technique in improving performance. Comparatively, in sport science, far less attention has been devoted to the so-called third wave of CBT methods including various mindfulness-based approaches (Hayes, 2004). Mindfulness is a concept that has grown in popularity over recent years, and refers to a manner of engaging with one's environment (Baltzell, 2016; Gardner & Moore, 2004). Mindfulness has been characterized as paying attention to the present moment and doing so with a non-judgmental attitude (Kabat-Zinn, 2003). A number of interventions and programmes have been designed with varying emphasis on mindfulness and ACT.

In brief, the purpose of ACT work is to increase the psychological flexibility, which simply means the ability to open up and be present and do what is important in life. This is based on the belief that the more aware we can be, the more we can open ourselves to our experience and the more we can act in accordance with our values, the better the quality of our lives and our efficiency.

The ACT model is most often described by six core therapeutic processes. Each of the six core processes is described separately to give a basic understanding of each process. However, in practice it is more fruitful to see the six processes as interdependent of each other.

1   **Flexible attention in the present moment – getting in touch with what is happening here and now:** The easiest is sometimes the hardest – to be fully present, conscious, and to be in touch with what it is happening right now. It's easy to go on autopilot or to get caught up in thoughts and drift away into the future or into the past. This often happens without us noticing and we lose touch with what is happening right now. Training this skill is about consistently paying attention to our experience in the moment and what is happening in the here

and now. In the case provided earlier, Terry should be encouraged to focus on the present that he might experience and accept, rather than on the past mistake, which he cannot influence.

2   **Defusion – to note your thinking:** It's easy to get caught up in our thoughts and being drawn into one thought leading to another with lightning speed. Instead, it is important to learn to separate oneself from our thoughts, mental images, and memories, and to take a step back and notice our thinking. Imagine that you are watching your thoughts like clouds in the sky or think of them as Teflon – they are 'non-stick', they slide away unless you hold onto them. Allow a little distance to observe and notice your thoughts passing without interpretation or hanging on to them. The aim is to understand and relate to *thoughts as just thoughts* and nothing else. In Terry's case, he appears to be unaware of the problematic nature of his rumination. He has not undertaken any meta-cognitive thinking (i.e. thinking about thinking) and might need support to detach himself from the negative thoughts that have overwhelmed him.

3   **Acceptance – opening up:** In order to become fully present in the moment, you need to be willing to accept and open up to what is actually happening right now and that means also allowing unpleasant thoughts, feelings, emotions, and sensations. We often try to avoid or fight discomfort, but with acceptance, rather give up the fight and open up to the undesirable discomfort. Let go of needing it to be different or trying to fix something. It should be carefully emphasized that acceptance in this context does not mean you have to give up or like the discomfort. It simply just means to experience what is actually happening. In our case, Terry desperately wishes to avoid discomfort and takes severe steps to avoid reminders of the mistake and his cognitive and emotional response to it. Opening up is an uncomfortable, but essential step in this process.

4   **Self as a context – the observing ego:** The observing self is sometimes referred to as 'pure consciousness' and refers to the aspect of oneself that is aware of what we are doing, thinking, feeling, and experiencing in the moment. Your thoughts and feelings come and go. Therefore, you are not your thoughts and feelings! Moreover, your body changes throughout life, you change roles, but the self who notices all these things never changes. Just because our case, Terry, feels like a loser, he is not the label he has given himself. His self-worth is intertwined with his thoughts and feelings. He might feel useless, but he is far from it.

5   **Values – knowing what's important:** If anything is possible, what kind of life do you want to live? What do you stand for? What is of greatest significance in your life? Values in this context are a type of compass that provides direction in the journey of life. Unlike traditional goal-setting with a final destination, values provide a desirable direction throughout life. For example, to get married, to have two children, and to be selected for the national team are typical goals that can be achieved and ticked off. In contrast to values, you strive every day to be a loving partner and parent, and to develop as an athlete. For Terry, he appears to have lost sight of any values he has and the 'code' by which he lives his life. He has become fixated on a footballing mistake that he has allowed to define him, and has lost sight of the everyday values that he might work toward that facilitate a meaningful existence.

6   **Committed action – to act in a valued direction:** This process is typically linked to all the traditional behaviour interventions, goal-setting behaviours, exposure,

and skills training. Thus, this part of ACT is explicitly about how one acts and does things in harmony with desired values. Being aware of one's own values is of great importance, but it is only by doing things in harmony with our values that we live fully and meaningfully. To act in a valued direction can involve both pleasant and unpleasant experiences. To do what is desirable and live according to values also means to continue to act in valued direction even if doing so in the present moment would mean discomfort or pain. This is typically true for an athlete during heavy training. For Terry, committing to new behavioural and valued action is important to move beyond his current anxiety-dominated existence. Through committed action, he can experience new meaningful events.

Often the six core therapeutic processes are grouped into three core pillars labelled as *open* (consisting of acceptance and diffusion) and *aware* (consisting of awareness and self as a context) and, finally, *engaged* (consisting of values and committed action) – that fully address functional behaviour with a strong contextual emphasis. These three core pillars of ACT will be applied to the following intervention together with a very brief introduction to behavioural analysis (Tornberg, Gustafsson, & Ekvall, 2019, Chapter 19 in this book).

## Intervention narrative (the 'how to')

A suitably qualified sport psychologist with advanced training in ACT should be sought and employed for this work. At the first meeting, the sport psychologist points out to Terry that demands (i.e. stressors) are common in sport. The practitioner might empathize with the high frequency and intensity of demands Terry faces, attempting to explain that such demands are a normal part of competition (normalizing). They might also self-disclose demands that they have faced or refer to high profile examples. The practitioner might clarify that how one evaluates (i.e. appraises) the demands one faces is potentially more influential than the demands alone, but demonstrate empathy that thinking differently about demands can be difficult. The practitioner could add that when one thinks rigidly about one's stress demands as threats with limited resources to manage these, then one will often experience anxiety. Indeed, it might be noted that anxiety is the most common emotional response to demands (cf. Hanton et al., 2012), and that this emotion is particularly common when one perceives low levels of control or coping resources (cf. Fletcher, Hanton, & Wagstaff, 2012). The practitioner adds that anxiety can become a problem, but that *we* can deal with it. The practitioner validates Terry's experiences, demonstrating empathy and acknowledging the experiences. At first, normalizing and validating the struggles is essential.

Together during the course of their discussion it becomes apparent that Terry's issues began after the penalty miss. It is important to understand what the key problem is, and how it developed over time (i.e. the learning history of the problem). The practitioner undertakes a systematic analysis of Terry's behaviours, including those things he perceives himself to do too much or too little of, each of which are then explored. This is done in a collaborative way in order to understand specific observable behaviours that occur in specific situations (i.e. antecedents) and consequences that follow as a result of the behaviour. The practitioner will also need to consider the clinical significance and mental health issues in each case beyond assessing thoughts, emotions, and behaviours. Therefore, clinical training is fundamental.

When applying the core pillars of ACT – open, aware, and engaged – the practitioner systematically addresses Terry's negative thoughts, emotions, and behaviours based on identified needs. Negative thoughts are not regarded as a problem, but the interpretation, relationship, and how one may act on these may become problematic and unhelpful. Sometimes simply asking an athlete if anything they have done so far to combat and try to get rid of the negative thoughts can be valuable to further spark a motivation for changing behaviour since the answer very often is 'nothing has worked' since the problem still exists. The practitioner can firmly state that the result of trying to 'fix' a psychological problem by avoiding the situation/behaviour associated with the uncomfortable thoughts and emotions usually only perpetuates the problem. Moreover, the discussion might touch on the trappings associated with the pursuit of and perceived 'need' to have control.

In the so-called psycho-education, the player is made aware of their negative thoughts (cognitive anxiety) and this process is often augmented by enhanced awareness of physiological responses (somatic anxiety). It is perhaps not surprising that the negative thought is commonly interpreted by individuals as having some kind of truth. This association becomes further strengthened by subsequent maladaptive behaviours and poor performance.

The practitioner encourages the player to anchor awareness in the present moment and focus on key behaviours that he would like to do more of rather than being caught and fixated in thinking since this will be debilitative to emotions and behaviour. Anchoring awareness in the present moment is a fundamental skill that can be practised both in everyday life and integrated into a sportsperson's skill repertoire. Today, there are several mindfulness applications available that can be downloaded to one's mobile phone or tablet. Engagement with the most basic 10-minute exercises each day will likely benefit one's self-awareness. Moreover, the practitioner might explain that thoughts are just thoughts, they don't come attached with a content that is the absolute truth. The psychologist explains that while the cognitive thoughts are at times important to address, in this case finding 'space' between thoughts, emotions, and being able to execute a flexible repertoire of behaviours is the key. Thoughts and emotions can easily become the major distraction and obstacle to self-awareness in the present moment and lead to a range of behaviours that can negatively impact performance. Interventions that target the problematic relationship to thoughts represent the process of diffusion.

Following diffusion, a more in-depth discussion between the player and the practitioner takes places and reflects on whether one can still perform effectively while experiencing negative thoughts and emotions. The practitioner provides anecdotes and uses metaphors about how other role models and players have been able to achieve under immense pressure and the experience of negative feelings. The practitioner encourages the player to simply open up to the full range of emotions, even the uncomfortable ones, to experience them in the present and try to stay with them, resisting the attempt to change them, avoid them, or fight them – simply pay attention with full awareness to them. Ultimately, when being open and aware the key is then to commit to the desired behaviour.

According to the ACT approach, the form or content of cognition is not directly troublesome, unless contextual features lead this cognitive content to regulate human action in unhelpful ways. The functional contexts that tend to have such deleterious effects are largely sustained by one's language and social transactions. To elaborate, Hayes, Luoma, Bond, Masuda, and Lillis (2006) noted that a context of literality treats symbols (e.g. the thought 'life is hopeless') as one would referents (i.e. a truly hopeless life). A context of experiential control focuses on the manipulation of emotional and cognitive states as a primary goal and metric of successful living.

Hayes et al. (2006) argued that these contexts are interrelated, which helps explain why cognitive fusion supports experiential avoidance – the attempt to alter the form, frequency, or situational sensitivity even when doing so causes behavioural harm (Hayes, Wilson, Gifford, Follette, & Strosahl, 1996). Due to the temporal and comparative relations present in human language, 'negative' emotions are verbally predicted, evaluated, and avoided. Experiential avoidance is based on this natural language process – a pattern that is then amplified by the culture into a general focus on 'feeling good' and avoiding pain. Unfortunately, attempts to avoid uncomfortable private events tend to increase their functional importance – both because they become more salient and because these control efforts are themselves verbally linked to conceptualized negative outcomes – and thus tend to narrow the range of behaviours that are possible since many stimuli might evoke these feared private events.

## Conclusions

In this chapter, we have provided an outline of the fundamental components of the stress process and delineated between stress-related concepts and have contextualized this with the use of a case study of an 18-year-old footballer. In using this case study, we have illustrated how practitioners might incorporate an ACT intervention.

## References

Arnold, R., & Fletcher, D. (2012). A research synthesis and taxonomic classification of the organizational stressors encountered by sport performers. *Journal of Sport and Exercise Psychology, 34*(3), 397–429.

Arnold, R., & Fletcher, D. (2015). Confirmatory factor analysis of the Sport Emotion Questionnaire in organizational environments. *Journal of Sports Sciences, 33,* 169–179.

Arnold, R., Fletcher, D., & Daniels, K. (2013). Development and validation of the Organizational Stressor Indicator for Sport Performers (OSI-SP). *Journal of Sport and Exercise Psychology, 35,* 180–196.

Arnold, R., Fletcher, D., & Daniels, K. (2016). Demographic differences in sport performers' experiences of organizational stressors. *Scandinavian Journal of Medicine & Science in Sports, 26*(3), 348–358.

Baltzell, A. L. (Ed.). (2016). *Mindfulness and performance.* Cambridge, England: Cambridge University Press.

Beehr, T. (1998). An organizational psychology meta-model of occupational stress. In C. L. Cooper (Ed.), *Theories of organizational stress* (pp. 6–27). Oxford, England: Oxford University Press.

Beehr, T. A., & Franz, T. M. (1987). The current debate about the meaning of job stress. *Journal of Organizational Behavior Management, 8*(2), 5–18.

Didymus, F. F., & Fletcher, D. (2012). Getting to the heart of the matter: A diary study of swimmers' appraisals of organizational stressors. *Journal of Sports Sciences, 30,* 1375–1385.

Dijkstra, H. P., Pollock, N., Chakraverty, R., & Alonso, J. M. (2014). Managing the health of the elite athlete: A new integrated performance health management and coaching model. *British Journal of Sports Medicine, 48*(7), 523–531.

Dugdale, J. R., Eklund, R. C., & Gordon, S. (2002). Expected and unexpected stressors in major international competition: Appraisal, coping, and performance. *The Sport Psychologist, 16,* 20–33.

Evans, L., Wadey, R., Hanton, S., & Mitchell, I. (2012). Stressors experienced by injured athletes. *Journal of Sports Sciences, 30,* 917–927.

Fletcher, D., & Hanton, S. (2003). Sources of organizational stress in elite sports performers. *The Sport Psychologist, 17,* 175–195.

Fletcher, D., Hanton, S., & Mellalieu, S. D. (2006). An organizational stress review: Conceptual and theoretical issues in competitive sport. In S. Hanton & S. D. Mellalieu (Eds.), *Literature reviews in sport psychology* (pp. 321–374). Hauppauge, NY: Nova Science.

Fletcher, D., Hanton, S., Mellalieu, S. D., & Neil, R. (2012). A conceptual framework of organizational stressors in sport performers. *Scandinavian Journal of Medicine & Science in Sports, 22,* 545–557.

Fletcher, D., Hanton, S., & Wagstaff, C. R. D. (2012). Performers' responses to stressors encountered in sport organisations. *Journal of Sports Sciences, 30*(4), 349–358.

Gardner, F. L., & Moore, Z. E. (2004). A mindfulness-acceptance-commitment-based approach to athletic performance enhancement: Theoretical considerations. *Behavior Therapy, 35*(4), 707–723.

Giacobbi, P. R., Jr., Lynn, T. K., Wetherington, J. M., Jenkins, J., Bodendorf, M., & Langley, B. (2004). Stress and coping during the transition to university for first-year female athletes. *The Sport Psychologist, 18,* 1–20.

Gould, D., Guinan, D., Greenleaf, C., Mudbery, R., & Peterson, K. (1999). Factors affecting Olympic performance: Perceptions of athletes and coaches from more and less successful teams. *The Sport Psychologist, 13,* 371–394.

Gould, D., Jackson, S. A., & Finch, L. M. (1993). Sources of stress in national champion figure skaters. *Journal of Sport and Exercise Psychology, 15,* 134–159.

Gould, D., Udry, E., Bridges, D., & Beck, L. (1997). Stress sources encountered when rehabilitating from season-ending ski injuries. *The Sport Psychologist, 11,* 361–378.

Gouttebarge, V., Aoki, H., & Kerkhoffs, G. M. (2016). Prevalence and determinants of symptoms related to mental disorders in retired male professional footballers. *The Journal of Sports Medicine and Physical Fitness, 56*(5), 648–654.

Gustafsson, H., Kenttä, G., & Hassmén, P. (2011). Athlete burnout: An integrated model and future research directions. *International Review of Sport and Exercise Psychology, 4*(1), 3–24.

Hanton, S., Fletcher, D., & Coughlan, G. (2005). Stress in elite sport performers: A comparative study of competitive and organizational stressors. *Journal of Sports Sciences, 23,* 1129–1141.

Hanton, S., Wagstaff, C. R. D., & Fletcher, D. (2012). Cognitive appraisals of stressors encountered in sport organizations. *International Journal of Sport and Exercise Psychology, 10,* 276–289.

Hayes, S. C. (2004). Acceptance and commitment therapy, relational frame theory, and the third wave of behavioral and cognitive therapies. *Behavior Therapy, 35*(4), 639–665.

Hayes, S. C., Luoma, J. B., Bond, F. W., Masuda, A., & Lillis, J. (2006). Acceptance and commitment therapy: Model, processes and outcomes. *Behaviour Research and Therapy, 44*(1), 1–25.

Hayes, S. C., Wilson, K. G., Gifford, E. V., Follette, V. M., & Strosahl, K. (1996). Experimental avoidance and behavioral disorders: A functional dimensional approach to diagnosis and treatment. *Journal of Consulting and Clinical Psychology, 64*(6), 1152–1168.

Holt, N. L., & Hogg, J. M. (2002). Perceptions of stress and coping during preparations for the 1999 women's soccer world cup finals. *The Sport Psychologist, 16*(3), 251–271.

James, B., & Collins, D. (1997). Self-presentational sources of competitive stress during performance. *Journal of Sport and Exercise Psychology, 19,* 17–35.

Jones, J. G., & Hardy, L. (1989). Stress and cognitive functioning in sport. *Journal of Sports Sciences, 7*(1), 41–63.

Kabat-Zinn, J. (2003). Mindfulness-based interventions in context: Past, present, and future. *Clinical Psychology: Science and Practice, 10*(2), 144–156.

Kenttä, G., & Hassmén, P. (1998). Overtraining and recovery. *Sports Medicine, 26*(1), 1–16.

Kristiansen, E., & Roberts, G. C. (2010). Young elite athletes and social support: Coping with competitive and organizational stress in 'Olympic' competition. *Scandinavian Journal of Medicine and Science in Sport, 20,* 686–695.

Lazarus, R. S. (1999). *Stress and emotion: A new synthesis.* New York, NY: Springer.

Lazarus, R. S., & Folkman, S. (1984). *Stress, appraisal, and coping.* New York, NY: Springer.

Mackay, C. J., Cousins, R., Kelly, P. J., Lee, S., & McCaig, R. H. (2004). 'Management standards' and work-related stress in the UK: Policy background and science. *Work and Stress, 18,* 91–112.

McKay, J., Niven, A. G., Lavallee, D., & White, A. (2008). Sources of strain among elite UK track athletes. *The Sport Psychologist, 22(2),* 143–163.

Meehan, H. L., Bull, S. J., Wood, D. M., & James, D. V. (2004). The overtraining syndrome: A multicontextual assessment. *The Sport Psychologist, 18*(2), 154–171.

Mellalieu, S. D., Hanton, S., & Fletcher, D. (2006). A competitive anxiety review: Recent directions in sport psychology research. In S. Hanton & S. D. Mellalieu (Eds.), *Literature reviews in sport psychology* (pp. 1–45). Hauppauge, NY: Nova Science.

Mellalieu, S. D., Neil, R., Hanton, S., & Fletcher, D. (2009). Competition stress in sport performers: Stressors experienced in the competition environment. *Journal of Sports Sciences, 27,* 729–744.

Neil, R., Hanton, S., Mellalieu, S. D., & Fletcher, D. (2011). Competition stress and emotions in sport performers: The role of further appraisals. *Psychology of Sport and Exercise, 12,* 460–470.

Noblet, A. J., & Gifford, S. M. (2002). The sources of stress experienced by professional Australian footballers. *Journal of Applied Sport Psychology, 14*(1), 1–13.

Noblet, A. J., Rodwell, J., & McWilliams, J. (2003). Predictors of the strain experienced by professional Australian footballers. *Journal of Applied Sport Psychology, 15,* 184–193.

Reid, C., Stewart, E., & Thorne, G. (2004). Multidisciplinary sport science teams in elite sport: Comprehensive servicing or conflict and confusion?. *The Sport Psychologist, 18*(2), 204–217.

Rumbold, J. L., Fletcher, D., & Daniels, K. (2012). A systematic review of stress management interventions with sport performers. *Sport, Exercise and Performance Psychology, 1,* 173–193.

Sarkar, M., & Fletcher, D. (2014). Psychological resilience in sport performers: A narrative review of stressors and protective factors. *Journal of Sports Sciences, 32,* 1419–1434.

Scanlan, T. K., Stein, G. L., & Ravizza, K. (1991). An in-depth study of former elite figure skaters: III. Sources of stress. *Journal of Sport and Exercise Psychology, 1,* 102–120.

Smith, R. E. (1986). Toward a cognitive-affective model of athletic burnout. *Journal of Sport Psychology, 8*(1), 36–50.

Thatcher, J., & Day, M. C. (2008). Re-appraising stress appraisals: The underlying properties of stress in sport. *Psychology of Sport & Exercise, 9,* 318–335.

Thelwell, R. C., Weston, N. J. V., & Greenlees, I. A. (2007). Batting on a sticky wicket: Identifying sources of stress and associated coping strategies for professional cricket batsmen. *Psychology of Sport and Exercise, 8,* 219–232.

Tornberg, R. Gustafsson, H., & Ekvall, D. (2019). Applied behavioural analysis in top-level football: Theory and application. In E. Konter, J. Beckmann, & Loughead (Eds.). *Football psychology: From theory to practice.* London, England: Routledge.

Weston, N. J. V., Thelwell, R. C., Bond, S., & Hutchings, N. V. (2009). Stress and coping in single-handed round-the-world ocean sailing. *Journal of Applied Sport Psychology, 21,* 460–474.

Woodman, T., & Hardy, L. (2001). A case study of organizational stress in elite sport. *Journal of Applied Sport Psychology, 13,* 207–238.

Woods, B., & Thatcher, J. (2009). A qualitative exploration of substitutes' experiences in soccer. *The Sport Psychologist, 23*(4), 451–469.

# 16 Imagery in football

*Krista Munroe-Chandler and Michelle Guerrero*

**Abstract**

Imagery is a popular mental skill used by athletes. This is evident in the growing popularity of brain-training sport-related apps like Nike Pro Genius – an app designed specifically for football players and dedicated to teaching players various mental skills, including imagery. The purpose of this chapter is to discuss and present theoretical and empirical work of imagery as it pertains to the sport of football. The chapter is divided into six main sections. The first section reviews the conceptualization of imagery and theories and models of imagery. In the second section, popular inventories used to assess imagery ability and imagery frequency are discussed, such as the Movement Imagery Questionnaire-3 (Williams et al., 2012), the Sport Imagery Ability Questionnaire (Williams & Cumming, 2011), and the Sport Imagery Questionnaire (Hall, Mack, Paivio, & Hausenblas, 1998). The third section summarizes the existing body of research on imagery within sport. Specifically, individual characteristics consistently shown to influence imagery ability and imagery use are presented, followed by a brief overview of emerging individual characteristics, namely, narcissism, emotion regulation, and goal orientation. The fourth section highlights empirical evidence on the effectiveness of cognitive and motivational uses of imagery in football. The fifth section outlines applied recommendations for coaches and/or practitioners, and discusses two techniques (i.e. layered stimulus response training and imagery scripts) known to help athletes improve their imagery ability. Finally, the sixth section presents avenues for future research.

In 2014 Nike brought mental training to the masses with the launch of Pro Genius, a brain-training app targeting the psychological aspect of football. Endorsed by football stars such as Cristiano Ronaldo and Mario Goetze, the message behind Nike Pro Genius is simple – 'the world's best train their brain like a muscle'. Visualization, a common term to refer to imagery, is one of several mental skills advocated by Nike Pro Genius. The imagery training component begins with a short YouTube video starring Robert Lewandowski visualizing while sitting on a couch, with a voice-over explaining that the part of the brain used to image an action is the same part that is activated when physically performing the action. The remainder of the video highlights clips of Lewandowski playing football while prompting trainees to mentally rehearse details and scenarios of matches – the pitch, the ground, the weather, the opposition, having control of the ball, kicking the ball into the net, and the crowd applauding.

The recent development of brain-training apps like Nike Pro Genius (and other similar ones) highlights the growing popularity of mental training in sport, and more specifically the use of imagery. Imagery is arguably one of the most popular mental skills used by athletes. The overall objective of the chapter is to present the theoretical and empirical findings of imagery use as it pertains to the sport of football.

We begin the chapter by providing a definition and detailed description of imagery. We then summarize theories and models of imagery and discuss various measures designed to assess imagery ability and frequency. This is followed by a review of the existing empirical research regarding individual characteristics and their impact on imagery effectiveness, and the associated cognitive and motivational benefits of imagery in sport. We highlight practical implications for practitioners seeking to: (a) enhance football players' imagery ability and (b) develop effective imagery scripts. Finally, we conclude with future directions in imagery research.

## Definition, theories, and models

Although often referred to as 'visualization', imagery is so much more in that it can encompass senses other than that of sight. In fact, imagery is most effective when it is multisensory (e.g. auditory, olfactory, tactile, kinaesthetic; Morris, Spittle, & Watt, 2005); and this multisensory component is evident in the widely used sport imagery definition provided by White and Hardy (1998), who define imagery as:

> an experience that mimics real experience. We can be aware of 'seeing' an image, feeling movements as an image, or experiencing an image of smell, tastes, or sounds without actually experiencing the real thing ... It differs from dreams in that we are awake and conscious when we form an image.
>
> (p. 389)

Researchers have long been interested in how imagery works. Over the years, many theories have been proposed (e.g. psychoneuromuscular, bioinformational, triple code) thus providing a deeper understanding of the mechanisms at play. Together these theories provide a foundation that continues to guide the development and refinement of imagery research. The most commonly discussed theories in sport are presented, followed by an overview on the conceptual models of imagery.

Jacobson's (1932) psychoneuromuscular theory notes that the imagery of a skill activates the same neural pathways as those activated when a skill is physically performed. Muscle innervation of the imagined skill, albeit smaller in magnitude than when physically performing the skill, provides feedback to the individual thus allowing for adjustments to be made in motor behaviour. Empirical support for the psychoneuromuscular theory has been found through measurement of electromyographical (EMG) activity (Smith, Collins, & Holmes, 2003).

Lang's (1979) bio-information theory suggests that mental images include both stimulus proposition (i.e. content of the image) and stimulus response (i.e. physiological and affective reaction). For example, a football player may feel butterflies in her stomach due to the anxiety experienced when imagining the penalty kick, or she may neglect external stimuli such as the opposing crowd jeering prior to her taking the penalty kick. The most effective images are those containing both stimulus proposition and response. Although not often recognized, Lang did note the importance of meaning to the image, thus enhancing the significance of the theory. Imagery scripts containing more frequent use of response propositions, compared to stimulus propositions, elicit greater physiological reactions (Bakker, Boschker, & Chung, 1996).

Ahsen (1984), in his triple code theory, clearly outlined not only the image and the stimulus, but also the meaning of the image. Because individuals view their own set of experiences through their own lens, no two people can have the same imagery experience even when provided with the same imagery instructions. In order to enhance performance, Ahsen proposes the most effective images are those that are realistic and vivid, evoke behavioural responses, and impart significance to the individual.

In addition to theories, models are critical to furthering our knowledge and in developing strong research and intervention programmes. In fact, most of the recent sport imagery research has relied on Paivio's (1985) analytic model in which he notes that imagery has both cognitive and motivational functions that operate at a general or specific level. The cognitive general function entails imaging strategies, game plans, or routines (e.g. defending a free kick), whereas the cognitive specific function involves imaging specific skills (e.g. heading the ball). The motivational general function of imagery involves imaging physiological arousal levels and emotions (e.g. staying calm when taking a penalty shot), and the motivational specific function of imagery includes imaging individual goals (e.g. winning the league). In an extension of Paivio's work, Hall et al. (1998) further divided the motivational general function into a motivational general-arousal function, encompassing imagery associated with arousal and stress, and a motivational general-mastery function, representing imagery associated with being mentally tough, in control, and self-confident.

The applied model of imagery use in sport (AMIUS; Martin, Moritz, & Hall, 1999), which follows Paivio's analytic model, provides an explanation for the way in which athletes use imagery to improve performance. According to AMIUS, athletes use imagery in training, competition, and when injured. The sport situation influences the types of imagery used, which are then associated with various cognitive, affective, and behavioural outcomes. Further, the relationship between the imagery type (five functions of imagery as noted above; cognitive specific, cognitive general, motivational specific, motivational general-arousal, motivational general-mastery) and the outcome is moderated by various individual differences, such as imagery ability. Cumming and Williams (2013) proposed a revised model of deliberate imagery use, considering 'who' is imaging (age, gender, competitive level), 'what' is being imaged (the type), and 'why' performers use imagery (the function). The revised model also recognizes the personal meaning as the link between the imagery type and function.

Another imagery model which has received much recent attention is the PETTLEP model (Holmes & Collins, 2001). Because of newer and more sophisticated neuroimaging techniques (e.g. PET and fMRI), it is now known that imagery uses many of the same neural pathways as visual perception; that is, imagery and actual movement are functionally equivalent (Decety, 1996; Jeannerod, 1994). Grounded in neuroscience and based on functional equivalence, the PETTLEP model identifies seven key factors to help guide imagery interventions: physical, environment, task, timing, learning, emotion, and perspective. The *physical* nature of the imagery is dependent upon the task (e.g. does the task call for the athlete to be relaxed prior to imaging?). The image should be as real or as close to the actual *environment* as possible. Depending on the *task*, the athlete's imagery perspective may vary (e.g. skills that rely on form have been found to benefit most from an external imagery perspective). The temporal characteristics or *timing* of the image should be equal to that of the athlete's physical performance (e.g. if a penalty kick takes 10 seconds to physically execute, so too should the imagery). The content of the image should change based on the *learning* of the skill. Images will be more effective if the athlete attaches meaning or *emotion* to them. If imaging winning a match, the athlete can feel the excitement and the joy that is part of it. Consider both *perspectives*, internal (visualizing through your own eyes) and external (visualizing like watching a video), when imaging. Although there have been some studies examining the model's components in isolation (e.g. O & Munroe-Chandler, 2008), more research is needed testing multiple elements of the model (cf. Smith, Wright, Allsopp, & Westhead, 2007) and in different contexts.

## Measurement

In the sport domain, the measurement of an individual's imagery ability and imagery frequency has often been considered. Self-report questionnaires have typically been used given that imagery is an internal mental skill. More research, however, has combined self-report with other indices of imagery experiences such as chronometry or fMRI (Guillot & Collet, 2005).

Imagery ability, which is defined as 'an individual's capability of forming vivid, controllable images and retaining them for sufficient time' (Morris, 1997, p. 37), is an important factor impacting imagery effectiveness. Despite some performers initially being better imagers than others, imagery is a skill that can be improved with practice (Rodgers, Hall, & Buckolz, 1991). The focus will be on the two most common imagery ability measures used in the sport domain due to their inclusion of both movement and visual imagery.

The Movement Imagery Questionnaire (MIQ; Hall & Pongrac, 1983) and the revised MIQ (Hall & Martin, 1997) assesses both visual and kinaesthetic imagery. Visual imagery refers to what the individual sees in one's mind (e.g. size of football net, foot placement on the ball). Kinaesthetic imagery is described as the feelings and sensations associated with the imaged movements (e.g. the force of the kick, arm movement during throw-ins). When completing the questionnaire, individuals are instructed to physically complete the movement sequence (i.e. knee raise, arm movement, waist bend, and jump) and then resume the starting position and recreate the experience using visual imagery, and finally using kinaesthetic imagery. Individuals are then asked to rate the quality of imagery on a Likert scale from 1 (*very easy to picture/feel*) to 7 (*very difficult to picture/feel*). The more recent MIQ-3 (Williams et al., 2012) distinguishes between internal and external visual imagery perspective, thus more fully capturing an individual's imagery ability. Internal visual imagery (first-person perspective) is described as movements that are viewed through one's own eyes. External visual imagery (third-person perspective) is described as movements that are viewed through others' eyes.

The Vividness of Movement Imagery Questionnaire (VMIQ; Isaac, Marks, & Russell, 1986) and the revised VMIQ-2 (Roberts, Callow, Hardy, Markland,

& Bringer, 2008) asks respondents to imagine a variety of motor tasks (e.g. running, kicking a stone) and then rate the image on two perspectives of visual imagery (external and internal), as well as kinaesthetically. All items are measured on a Likert scale ranging from 1 (*perfectly clear and as vivid as normal vision*) to 5 (*no image at all; you only know that you are thinking of the skill*).

An addition to the ability measurement literature has been the Motivational Imagery Ability Measure for Sport (MIAMS; Gregg & Hall, 2006) which assesses motivational imagery abilities. The MIAMS assesses the ability of an athlete to use motivational general-arousal and motivational general-mastery imagery, wherein the participant images the scene and then rates the image on an ease subscale 1 (*not at all easy to form*) to 7 (*very easy to form*) and an emotion subscale 1(*no emotion*) to 7 (*very strong emotion*).

Recently, Williams and Cumming (2011) modified the Sport Imagery Questionnaire (SIQ; Hall et al., 1998) to specifically assess five subscales of imagery ability: skill, strategy, goal, affect, and mastery. The Sport Imagery Ability Questionnaire (SIAQ) is a 15-item measure assessing how easily participants can image the cognitive and motivational functions of imagery. Items are rated on a Likert scale from 1 (*very hard to image*) to 7 (*very easy to image*).

In addition to imagery ability, measuring a performer's use of imagery allows researchers, and practitioners, to determine one's frequency of a specific type of imagery and also allows to see changes from pre- to post-intervention. The various questionnaires assessing the frequency of imagery use in sport will be addressed in the subsequent sections.

The Sport Imagery Questionnaire (SIQ; Hall et al., 1998) is the most widely used measure of imagery frequency in sport (Morris et al., 2005). The self-report questionnaire comprises 30 items assessing the five types of imagery used by adults (cognitive specific, cognitive general, motivational specific, motivational general-arousal, motivational general-mastery). All items are scored on a Likert scale anchored by 1 (*rarely*) and 7 (*often*). The SIQ can be employed with athletes 14 years and older.

There is ample evidence to support young athletes' use of imagery (e.g. Munroe-Chandler, Hall, Fishburne, & Strachan, 2007). Thus, the Sport Imagery Questionnaire for Children (SIQ-C; Hall, Munroe-Chandler, Fishburne, & Hall, 2009) was developed to assess the frequency of imagery use among young (7–14 years) athletes. The SIQ-C includes 21 items measuring the same five types of imagery identified in the adult version. Responses are scored on a Likert scale ranging from 1 (*not at all*) to 5 (*very often*).

## Summary of research in imagery in football

### Individual characteristics

A large body of literature has examined how various individual characteristics influence imagery ability and use. In this section, we first discuss the relationship between imagery ability and imagery use. Next, we describe commonly researched individual characteristics of imagery (i.e. age, image speed, and skill level) and their influence on both an athlete's ability to image and image frequency. The final section outlines emerging individual characteristics of imagery, namely, narcissism, emotion regulation, and goal orientation.

**Imagery ability.** The ability to generate vivid and controllable images is arguably the most studied and well-understood individual characteristic of imagery. Paivio (1986) explained that everyone has the ability to generate images, but that not all generated images are effective. For instance, images may differ in aspects including vividness, controllability, visual representation, kinaesthetic feelings, ease, emotional experiences, and effectiveness of image formation (Hall, 1998). Some researchers have indicated that athletes with higher imagery ability experience more benefits than those with lower imagery ability (Hall, 2001). Athletes can improve the quality of their imagery with practice (Rodgers et al., 1991) and by using layered stimulus response training (Cumming et al., 2017). Furthermore, it has been argued that the relationship between one's ability to image and their imagery frequency is cyclical, such that better imagers are more likely to engage in imagery, and greater imagery use will likely lead to enhanced imagery ability.

An athlete's imagery ability has also been shown to influence the type of imagery used and imagery frequency. Vadocz, Hall, and Moritz (1997) showed that athletes higher in kinaesthetic imagery ability reported using more cognitive specific and motivational general-arousal imagery, whereas athletes higher in visual imagery ability reported using more motivational general-mastery imagery. Other researchers have found that athletes who reported high visual and kinaesthetic imagery abilities also reported a high frequency of cognitive specific imagery (Gregg, Hall, McGowan, & Hall, 2011). Furthermore, a positive relationship has been found between ease of imaging and imagery use, wherein each subscale of the SIAQ most strongly predicted its associated SIQ subscale (Williams & Cumming, 2012). For example, a midfielder who easily generates images of staying focused and confident during a match (i.e. motivational general-mastery imagery ability) will generate more frequent images of mastery (i.e. motivational general-mastery imagery).

**Age.** While there is scant literature examining the impact of age on imagery ability, existing evidence suggests that this individual characteristic should continue to be considered in future imagery studies. Work by Kosslyn, Margolis, Barrett, Goldknopf, and Daly (1990) showed that younger children have a more difficult time scanning, rotating, and generating objects in images compared to older children, yet have similar abilities with respect to maintaining images. Furthermore, younger athletes (12–13 years) have been found to have poorer kinaesthetic imagery ability than older athletes (20–21 years; Parker & Lovell, 2012).

Other research findings have revealed a relationship between age and imagery use, with younger athletes using more cognitive imagery (cognitive specific and cognitive general) than older athletes (Gregg & Hall, 2006). In their qualitative study, Munroe-Chandler et al. (2007) documented various age differences in imagery use. For instance, younger athletes (7–10 years) reported using: (a) less motivational imagery than older athletes (11–14 years), and (b) motivational specific imagery for individual goals only whereas older athletes used motivational specific imagery for both individual and team goals.

**Image speed.** The notion that all images should be imaged in real-time speed is not universally accepted among imagery researchers. While some support the concept of functional equivalence and thereby advocate for real-time image speed (Guillot & Collet, 2008), others argue that athletes could benefit from using different image speeds. Indeed, both recreational and competitive athletes have indicated using three different image speeds (i.e. slow-motion, real-time, and fast-motion; O & Hall, 2009), suggesting that, under certain situations, modifying the speed at which one images may be advantageous (e.g. learning a corner kick for the first time). Shirazipour, Munroe-Chandler, Loughead, and Vander Laan (2016) sought to better understand the potential benefits of varying image speeds and found that athletes used cognitive specific, cognitive general, motivational specific, and motivational general-mastery imagery significantly more during slow-motion and real-time conditions compared to the fast-motion condition.

**Skill level.** It is well-known that skilled athletes use imagery more often than less skilled athletes (Cumming & Hall, 2002). In fact, elite athletes have reported using imagery for cognitive purposes (cognitive specific and cognitive general imagery) more so than less-elite athletes (Arvinen-Barrow, Weigand, Thomas, Hemmings, & Walley, 2007). Several differences in imagery types among senior, junior, and novice athletes have also been noted (Arvinen-Barrow, Weigand, Hemmings, & Walley, 2008). For instance, senior athletes used significantly more cognitive specific, cognitive general, motivational general-arousal, and motivational general-mastery imagery than novice athletes. Some researchers have argued that the underlying reason behind these imagery-frequency differences is that elite athletes are likely more committed and dedicated to their sport and thus spend more time imaging themselves in their sport (Hall, 2001).

**Other individual characteristics.** Several imagery researchers have argued the importance of investigating other, less traditional individual characteristics as they may help to further explain differences in imagery effectiveness. Roberts, Callow, Hardy, Woodman, and Thomas (2010) examined the interactive effects of imagery perspective and narcissism on motor performance. They argued that because narcissists think highly of their abilities, have high levels of confidence, and enjoy looking at themselves from the point of view of others, they are more likely to perform better in environments where self-enhancement opportunities are high and when external visual imagery is used. They found high narcissists using external visual imagery significantly improved performance from the low to high self-enhancement condition.

Emotion regulation is another individual characteristic that has received recent attention within the imagery literature. Anuar, Cumming, and Williams (2017) examined whether two processes of emotion regulation (i.e. reappraisal and suppression) predicted an athlete's ease of imaging skill, strategy, goal, affect, and mastery imagery. They found reappraisal positively predicted and suppression negatively predicted the five types of sport imagery ability.

Gregg, O, and Hall (2016) examined the relationship between athletes' goal orientation and imagery ability. Their results showed that athletes with high task/high ego or high task/low ego goal orientations scored significantly higher on their ability to feel emotions and their ease of generating motivational general-mastery images compared to athletes with low task/high ego or low task/low ego orientations. An implication of this research is that athletes should adopt a task-orientated focus toward their goals if they hope to experience the associated benefits of imagery.

*Cognitive and motivational function of imagery use*

One of the most appealing aspects of imagery use in sport, and specifically football, is its versatility. Although previous research has shown the positive effects of imagery use on football performance (Jordet, 2005; Thelwell, Greenlees, & Weston, 2006), the following section highlights research that has provided support for the cognitive and motivational uses of imagery in football.

Using cognitive imagery to enhance skill acquisition and performance (i.e. cognitive specific imagery) has received the most attention among researchers (Morris et al., 2005). Investigators examining the positive effects of cognitive specific imagery have found significant improvements in young football players' time to complete a football task (Munroe-Chandler, Hall, Fishburne, Murphy, & Hall, 2012) as well as adult football players' execution of a penalty kick (Ramsey, Cumming, Edwards, Williams, & Brunning, 2010).

Evidence for imagery as a means to learn and improve execution of strategies, game plans, and routines (i.e. cognitive general imagery) has been equivocal (see Westlund, Pope, & Tobin, 2012, for review). While studies have shown improvements in strategy execution following a cognitive general imagery intervention in sports other than football (Guillot, Nadrowska, & Collet, 2009), young football players who participated in a 7-week cognitive general imagery intervention showed no improvements in strategy execution (i.e. defending a direct free kick, taking a direct free kick, and defending a corner kick) from baseline to post-intervention (Munroe-Chandler, Hall, Fishburne, & Shannon, 2005). Despite showing no improvements in strategy execution, Munroe-Chandler et al.'s (2005) results did indicate that young football players do use imagery (evident in their increased imagery use scores from pre- to post-intervention). In a more recent study investigating the effects of imagery training on passing improvement in youth and adult elite football players, a cognitive (combined cognitive specific and cognitive general) intervention resulted in significantly better passing when compared to the control group (Seif-Barghi, Kordi, Memari, Mansournia, & Jalali-Ghomi, 2012). Although an often-cited criticism with sport imagery research is the lack of ecological validity, the findings from Seif-Barghi et al. (2012) suggest the effectiveness of imagery use in an open skill, team sport setting.

In addition to cognitive purposes, football players have reported using imagery for motivational purposes (i.e. motivational specific, motivational general-mastery, motivational general-arousal). Much of the motivational research has focused on motivational general-mastery with strong support for its influence on positive outcomes. For example, Munroe-Chandler and Hall (2004–2005) investigated the effects of motivational general-mastery imagery on the collective efficacy of youth female football team (10–12 years). After 13 weeks of an imagery intervention (motivational general-mastery scripts) collective efficacy and imagery use increased. Further, Pain, Harwood, and Anderson (2011), in their study with adult male football players, found that an intervention combining music and motivational general-mastery imagery resulted in increased flow state and imagery use and ultimately perceived performance.

Ramsey et al. (2010) found that an emotion based imagery script (i.e. motivational general-arousal) positively influenced the male and female adult football players' penalty taking performance significantly more than the control group.

And although the emotion based script had no beneficial effects on efficacy or anxiety, its impact on performance is promising. Similarly, researchers (Alwan et al., 2013) found that a guided relaxation imagery intervention (arguably motivational general-arousal although not specified in the study) resulted in reduced cognitive anxiety and elevated self-confidence in college football players prior to a game.

## Applied recommendations

The extent to which imagery is effective often depends on two conditions: athletes' ability to generate clear and vivid images and athletes' correct use and implementation of imagery. In this section, we briefly discuss how a coach or practitioner can help football players improve their imagery ability using a systematic approach, and practical guidelines for developing effective imagery scripts.

### Layered stimulus response training (LSRT)

Imagery ability is a skill that can be improved with practice. The objective of LSRT is to help individuals generate and control their imagery experience more easily (Cumming et al., 2017). This objective is accomplished by breaking down an image into different components and gradually piecing the components together in layers. A LSRT session would begin by having a football player, for example, select a simple image of a targeted scenario such as a corner kick. Next, the player is asked to verbally describe the image in as much detail as possible prior to imaging the scenario. The player then images the entire scenario from start (e.g. standing with the ball in front of them) to finish (e.g. taking the kick). The player is then asked to reflect on their imagery experience by rating the vividness and clarity of their image on a scale. In the next step, the scenario is either re-imagined or developed further by adding/modifying the image's content/characteristics. When the scene is developed further, the player images the scenario as clearly and as vividly as possible while paying close attention to the new element (e.g. sound, touch, thoughts, kinaesthetic, etc.). Once the scenario has been imaged, the player rates and evaluates their scenario by comparing their recent experience to their initial experience. This process is repeated until the player has generated the most realistic image. Several studies have supported the efficacy of LSRT in improving imagery ability (e.g. Weibull, Cumming, Cooley, Williams, & Burns, 2014; Williams, Cooley, & Cumming, 2013).

### Imagery scripts

Scripts are used to ensure that athletes use imagery correctly and gain the most from using imagery. However, until recently, guidelines for creating effective imagery scripts did not exist. Recognizing this gap in the literature, Williams, Cooley, Newell, Weibull, and Cumming (2013) forwarded practical guidelines for how to plan, deliver, and evaluate imagery scripts. They recommended that the 5 Ws should be carefully considered prior to writing an imagery script: Who will use the script (e.g. an individual, group of athletes, type of sport, competitive level)? Where and when will the script be used (e.g. at competition venue, before training, three times/week)? Why is the script being used (e.g. to perfect a specific skill, to increase confidence and mental toughness, to learn a strategy)? What will be imaged (e.g. imaging performing a skill perfectly, imaging bodily sensations, imaging postural changes). Williams et al. also suggested that scripts should be regularly evaluated to ensure coherence between the script and the athlete's goals and preferences. For example, as the football player becomes more comfortable and proficient at imagery, she may want to incorporate more senses into the script, lengthen the duration of the script, or modify the purpose of the script.

## Future directions

Several decades-worth of empirical research has aided researchers' and practitioners' understanding of imagery use in sport. However, there are many research avenues that have not been extensively explored, one of which is athletes' use of various imagery modalities. It is widely noted that the most effective images are multimodal in nature (Hall, 2001; Martin et al., 1999). Research examining imagery in sport has primarily focused on visual and kinaesthetic imagery modalities, with little (if any at all) research examining the other five modalities: auditory, tactile, olfactory, gustatory, and somaesthetic (i.e. bodily sensations). To this end, O, Law, and Rymal (2015) recently wrote a commentary on the auditory sense, providing theoretical and evidence based foundations for the examination of sound in imagery research. While O et al.'s proposed future research direction appears promising, it can be argued that investigating all modalities would provide unique and meaningful contributions to the area of imagery in sport. Researchers interested in this research topic might consider using the Plymouth Sensory Imagery Questionnaire (Psi-Q; Andrade, May, Deeprose, Baugh, & Ganis, 2014), which was designed to assess seven sensory modalities (i.e. visual, auditory, olfactory, taste, touch, bodily sensation, and emotional feeling). The Psi-Q is suitable for use across the breadth of research domains where imagery is a variable of interest.

Another avenue for future research is to examine personality and individual characteristics and their impact on vividness of imagery sensory modalities. For example, are football players with level highs of self-compassion more likely to have vivid body sensation and emotional feeling sensory modalities? Are football players who are more mindful more likely to experience vivid visual and auditory sensory modalities than those who are less mindful? Kharlas and Frewen (2016) examined the associations between mindfulness traits and multisensory imagery and found that individuals who were more mindfully observing also reported greater vividness of visual, auditory, olfactory, gustatory, bodily-kinaesthetic, and emotional imagery. More research examining the associations between personality and individual characteristics and sensory modalities seems warranted.

## Conclusion

Imagery has been, and continues to be, a well-researched psychological skill in the realm of football. Many theories have been proposed to help explain why or how imagery influences performance. Imagery ability as well as imagery frequency are two aspects of imagery that are generally measured with athletes. Additionally, numerous studies have examined the influence imagery has on achieving cognitive and motivational outcomes and, in doing so, have identified factors that can affect imagery effectiveness (e.g. image ability, age, skill level). Future researchers might consider examining the various modalities of imagery as well as the influence of 'non-traditional' individual characteristics such as self-compassion.

## References

Ahsen, A. (1984). ISM: The Triple Code Model for imagery and psychophysiology. *Journal of Mental Imagery, 8*, 15–42.

Alwan, M., Zakaria, A., Rahizam, M., Rahim, A., Hamid, N. A., & Fuad, M. (2013). Comparison between two relaxation methods on competitive state anxiety among college soccer teams during pre-competition stage. *International Journal of Advanced Sport Sciences Research, 1*, 90–104.

Andrade, J., May, J., Deeprose, C., Baugh, S. J., & Ganis, G. (2014). Assessing vividness of mental imagery: The Plymouth Sensory Imagery Questionnaire. *British Journal of Psychology, 105*, 547–563.

Anuar, N., Cumming, J., & Williams, S. (2017). Emotion regulation predicts imagery ability. *Imagination, Cognition and Personality: Consciousness in Theory, Research, and Clinical Practice, 36*, 254–269.

Arvinen-Barrow, M., Weigand, D., Hemmings, B., & Walley, M. (2008). The use of imagery across competitive levels and time of season: A cross sectional study among synchronized skaters in Finland. *European Journal of Sport Science, 8*, 135–142.

Arvinen-Barrow, M., Weigand, D. A., Thomas, S., Hemmings, B., & Walley, M. (2007). Elite and novice athletes' imagery use in open and closed sports. *Journal of Applied Sport Psychology, 19*, 93–104.

Bakker, F. C., Boschker, M. S. J., & Chung, T. (1996). Changes in muscular activity while imagining weightlifting using stimulus or response propositions. *Journal of Sport and Exercise Psychology, 18*, 313–324.

Cumming, J., Cooley, S. J., Anuar, N., Kosteli, M., Quinton, M. L., Weibull, & Williams, S. E. (2017). Developing imagery ability effectively: A guide to layered stimulus response training. *Journal of Sport Psychology in Action, 8*, 23–33.

Cumming, J., & Hall, C. R. (2002). Athletes' use of imagery in the off-season. *The Sport Psychologist, 16*, 160–172.

Cumming, J., & Williams, S. E. (2013). Introducing the revised applied model of deliberate imagery use for sport, dance, exercise, and rehabilitation. *Movement & Sport Sciences, 4*, 69–81.

Decety, J. (1996). Do imagined and executed actions share the same neural substrate? *Cognitive Brain Research, 3*, 87–93.

Gregg, M., & Hall, C. R. (2006). The relationship of skill level and age to the use of imagery by golfers. *Journal of Applied Sport Psychology, 18*, 363–375.

Gregg, M., Hall, C., McGowan, E., & Hall, N. (2011). The relationship between imagery ability and imagery use among athletes. *Journal of Applied Sport Psychology, 23*, 129–141.

Gregg, M., O, J., & Hall, C. R. (2016). Examining the relationship between athletes' achievement goal orientation and ability to employ imagery. *Psychology of Sport and Exercise, 24*, 140–146.

Guillot, A., & Collet, C. (2005). Duration of mentally simulated movement: A review. *Journal of Motor Behavior, 37*, 10–20.

Guillot, A., & Collet, C. (2008). Construction of the motor imagery integrative model in sport: A review and theoretical investigation of motor imagery use. *International Review of Sport and Exercise Psychology, 1*, 31–44.

Guillot, A., Nadrowska, E., & Collet, C. (2009). Using motor imagery to learn tactical movements in basketball. *Journal of Sport Behavior, 32*, 189–206.

Hall, C. R. (1998). Measuring imagery abilities and imagery use. In J. L. Duda (Ed.), *Advances in sport and exercise psychology measurement* (pp. 165–172). Morgantown, WV: Fitness Information Technology.

Hall, C. R. (2001). Imagery in sport and exercise. In R. N. Singer, H. A. Hausenblas, & C. M. Janelle (Eds.), *Handbook of research on sport psychology* (2nd ed., pp. 529–549). New York, NY: Wiley.

Hall, C., Mack, D., Paivio, A., & Hausenblas, H. (1998). Imagery use by athletes: Development of the Sport Imagery Questionnaire. *International Journal of Sport Psychology, 29*, 73–89.

Hall, C. R., & Martin, K. A. (1997). Measuring movement imagery abilities: A revision of the Movement Imagery Questionnaire. *Journal of Mental Imagery, 21*, 143–154.

Hall, C. R., Munroe-Chandler, K. J., Fishburne, G. J., & Hall, N. D. (2009). The Sport Imagery Questionnaire for Children (SIQ-C). *Measurement in Physical Education and Exercise Science, 13*, 93–107.

Hall, C. R., & Pongrac, J. (1983). *Movement Imagery Questionnaire.* University of Western Ontario Faculty of Physical Education.

Holmes, P. S., & Collins, D. J. (2001). The PETTLEP approach to motor imagery: A functional equivalence model for sport psychologists. *Journal of Applied Sport Psychology, 13*, 60–83.

Isaac, A., Marks, D., & Russell, E. (1986). An instrument for assessing imagery of movement: The Vividness of Movement Imagery Questionnaire (VMIQ). *Journal of Mental Imagery, 10*, 23–30.

Jacobson, E. (1932). Electrical measurement of neuromuscular states during mental activities. *American Journal of Physiology, 94*, 24–34.

Jeannerod, M. (1994). The representing brain: Neural correlates of motor intention and imagery. *Behavioral and Brain Sciences, 17*, 187–202.

Jordet, G. (2005). Perceptual training in soccer: An imagery intervention study with elite players. *Journal of Applied Sport Psychology, 17*, 140–156.

Kharlas, D. A., & Frewen, P. (2016). Trait mindfulness correlates with individual differences in multisensory imagery vividness. *Personality and Individual Differences, 93*, 44–50.

Kosslyn, S. M., Margolis, J. A., Barrett, A. M., Goldknopf, E. J., & Daly, P. F. (1990). Age differences in imagery abilities. *Child Development, 61*, 995–1010.

Lang, P. J. (1979). A bio-informational theory of emotional imagery. *Psychophysiology, 16*, 495–512.

Martin, K. A., Moritz, S. E., & Hall, C. R. (1999). Imagery use in sport: A literature review and applied model. *The Sport Psychologist, 13*, 245–268.

Morris, T. (1997). *Psychological skills training in sport: An overview* (2nd ed.). Leeds, England: National Coaching Foundation.

Morris, T., Spittle, M., & Watt, A. P. (2005). *Imagery in sport.* Champaign, IL: Human Kinetics.

Munroe-Chandler, K. J., & Hall, C. R. (2004–2005). Enhancing the collective efficacy of a soccer team through motivational general-mastery imagery. *Imagination, Cognition and Personality, 24*, 51–67.

Munroe-Chandler, K. J., Hall, C. R., Fishburne, G. J., Murphy, L., & Hall, N. D. (2012). Effects of a cognitive specific imagery intervention on the soccer skill performance of young athletes: Age group comparisons. *Psychology of Sport and Exercise, 13*, 324–331.

Munroe-Chandler, K. J., Hall, C. R., Fishburne, G. J., & Shannon, V. (2005). Using cognitive general imagery to improve soccer strategies. *European Journal of Sport Science, 5*, 41–49.

Munroe-Chandler, K. J., Hall, C. R., Fishburne, G. J., & Strachan, L. (2007). Where, when, and why young athletes use imagery: An examination of developmental differences. *Research Quarterly for Exercise and Sport, 78*, 103–116.

O, J., & Hall, C. R. (2009). A quantitative analysis of athletes' voluntary use of slow motion, real time, and fast motion images. *Journal of Applied Sport Psychology, 21*, 15–30.

O., J., Law, B., & Rymal, A. (2015). Now hear this: Auditory sense may be an undervalued component of effective modeling and imagery interventions in sport. *The Open Psychology Journal, 8*, 203–211.

O., J., & Munroe-Chandler, K. J. (2008). The effects of image speed on the performance of a soccer task. *The Sport Psychologist, 22*, 1–17.

Pain, M. A., Harwood, C., & Anderson, R. (2011). Pre-competition imagery and music: The impact on flow and performance in competitive soccer. *The Sport Psychologist, 25*, 212–232.

Paivio, A. (1985). Cognitive and motivational functions of imagery in human performance. *Canadian Journal of Applied Sports Sciences, 10*, 22S–28S.

Paivio, A. (1986). *Mental representations: A dual coding approach.* New York, NY: Oxford University Press.

Parker, J. K., & Lovell, G. P. (2012). Age differences in the vividness of youth sport performers' imagery ability. *Journal of Imagery Research in Sport and Physical Activity, 7*, Article 7.

Ramsey, R., Cumming, J., Edwards, M. G., Williams, S., & Brunning, C. (2010). Examining the emotion aspect of PETTLEP-based imagery with penalty taking in soccer. *Journal of Sport Behavior, 33*, 295–314.

Roberts, R., Callow, N., Hardy, L., Markland, D., & Bringer, J. (2008). Movement imagery ability: Development and assessment of a revised version of the Vividness of Movement Imagery Questionnaire. *Journal of Sport and Exercise Psychology, 30*, 200–221.

Roberts, R., Callow, N., Hardy, L., Woodman, T., & Thomas, L. (2010). Interactive effects of different visual imagery perspectives and narcissism on motor performance. *Journal of Sport and Exercise Psychology, 32*, 499–517.

Rodgers, W., Hall, C., & Buckolz, E. (1991). The effect of an imagery training program on imagery ability, imagery use, and figure skating performance. *Journal of Applied Sport Psychology, 3*, 109–125.

Seif-Barghi, T., Kordi, R., Memari, A. H., Mansournia, M., & Jalali-Ghomi, M. (2012). The effect of an ecological imagery program on soccer performance of elite players. *Asian Journal of Sports Medicine, 3*, 81–89.

Shirazipour, C., Munroe-Chandler, K. J., Loughead, T., & Vander Laan, A. G. (2016). The effect of image speed on novice golfers' performance in a putting task. *Journal of Imagery Research in Sport and Physical Activity, 11*, 13–24.

Smith, D., Collins, D., & Holmes, P. (2003). Impact and mechanism of mental practice effects on strength. *International Journal of Sport and Exercise Psychology, 1*, 293–306.

Smith, D., Wright, C., Allsopp, A., & Westhead, H. (2007). It's all in the mind: PETTLEP-based imagery and sports performance. *Journal of Applied Sport Psychology, 19*, 80–92.

Thelwell, R. C., Greenlees, I. A., & Weston, N. J. (2006). Using psychological skills training to develop soccer performance. *Journal of Applied Sport Psychology, 18*, 254–270.

Vadocz, E. A., Hall, C. R., & Moritz, S. E. (1997). The relationship between competitive anxiety and imagery use. *Journal of Applied Sport Psychology, 9*, 241–253.

Weibull, F., Cumming, J., Cooley, S. J., Williams, S. E., & Burns, V. E. (2014). Walk this way: A brief exercise imagery intervention increases barrier self-efficacy in women. *Current Psychology, 34*, 477–490.

Westlund, N., Pope, J. P., & Tobin, D. (2012). Cognitive general imagery: The forgotten imagery function? *Journal of Imagery Research in Sport and Physical Activity, 7*(1).

White, A., & Hardy, L. (1998). An in-depth analysis of the uses of imagery by high-level slalom canoeists and artistic gymnasts. *The Sport Psychologist, 12*, 387–403.

Williams, S. E., Cooley, S. J., & Cumming, J. (2013). Layered stimulus response training improves motor imagery ability and movement execution. *Journal of Sport and Exercise Psychology, 35*, 60–71.

Williams, S. E., Cooley, S. J., Newell, E., Weibull, F., & Cumming, J. (2013). Seeing the difference: Developing effective imagery scripts for athletes. *Journal of Sport Psychology in Action, 4*, 109–121.

Williams, S. E., & Cumming, J. (2011). Measuring athlete imagery ability: The Sport Imagery Ability Questionnaire. *Journal of Sport and Exercise Psychology, 33,* 416–440.

Williams, S. E., & Cumming, J. (2012). Athletes' ease of imaging predicts their imagery and observational learning use. *Psychology of Sport and Exercise, 13,* 363–370.

Williams, S. E., Cumming, J., Ntoumanis, N., Nordin-Bates, S. M., Ramsey, R., & Hall, C. (2012). Further validation and development of the Change to Movement Imagery Questionnaire. *Journal of Sport and Exercise Psychology, 34,* 621–646.

# 17 Self-confidence and collective efficacy in football

*Edson Filho and Jean Rettig*

## Abstract

Self-confidence is one of the major predictors of performance in football. Collective efficacy is also paramount as high-performing teams show greater group-level confidence compared to lower-performing teams. In this chapter, we review the antecedent, moderator, and outcome variables that influence self-confidence and collective efficacy in football. The first part of the chapter is devoted to self-confidence. We discuss how confidence and self-efficacy beliefs influence athletes' cognitive, affective, and behavioural states and patterns, and elaborate on the linkage between self-confidence and performance in penalty shootouts. In the second part of the chapter, we review the tenets of collective efficacy, as well as measurement guidelines on addressing confidence at the team level. We review empirical evidence on the linkage between self-confidence and collective efficacy and discuss differences in collective efficacy among high- and low-performing football teams. Furthermore, we present research findings suggesting that collective efficacy is dynamically related to myriad team processes, such as cohesion and team mental models. We conclude the chapter with future research recommendations and applied guidelines to enhance self-confidence and collective efficacy in football.

## Self-confidence and collective efficacy in football

> Never give up, and be confident in what you do.
> (Marta da Silva – Five-time FIFA World Player of the Year)

The quote above, from one of the most successful female football players of all time, prompts the question: How do footballers develop confidence in every aspect of their sport domain? Confidence is a complex and multidimensional phenomenon that needs to be considered in light of the human self at large. 'The self' has been used to explain human performance, satisfaction, and relationships with others (Pilarska & Suchańska, 2015). For instance, self-perception, self-esteem, self-worth, and self-regulation are well-studied psychological processes that have been linked to human performance in multiple domains (see Rafaeli-Mor & Steinberg, 2002), including football (Papaioannou et al., 2013). Within this context, this chapter addresses self-confidence and sports performance in general, and football performance in particular. Initially, we cover the conceptual definition of self-confidence and its ubiquitous relationship with anxiety and performance in sports. Subsequently, we discuss the notion of self-efficacy, particularly the key framework by Bandura on the antecedents of task-specific confidence. Special attention is given to self-efficacy in football. Subsequently, given that football is a team sport, we cover the team-level equivalent of self-confidence, commonly referred to as collective efficacy. We conclude by discussing avenues for future research and recommendations for applied work.

## Self-confidence

Stemming from the Latin *con* (for) and *fidere* (trust), confidence pertains to one's trust in one's abilities (see Cashmore, 2002). Within the sport, exercise, and performance psychology literature, confidence has been defined as 'the degree of certainty individuals possess about their ability to be successful in sport' (Vealey, 2001, p. 556). Self-confidence has also been characterized as 'a set of enduring yet malleable positive beliefs that protect against ongoing psychological and environmental challenges associated with performance in sports' (Thomas, Lane, & Kingston, 2011, p. 202). Based on the latter definition, it is clear that confidence includes both a trait-like and state-like component (Weinberg & Gould, 2015). Trait-like confidence is the stable component of someone's confidence beliefs, whereas state-like confidence [...] varies depending on a given situation. In addition to being influenced by personality characteristics and external environmental factors, confidence is also thought to be influenced by the organizational culture at large (see Vealey, 2001).

It follows that self-confidence in sports is viewed as a dynamic psychological process susceptible to great variation depending on one's personality characteristics, situational factors, and broader organizational constraints (see Hays, 2008; Vealey & Chase, 2008). Importantly, these variations in confidence have been found to be associated with different performance standards in sports (see Hays, 2008). In fact, one of the most consistent findings in the peak performance literature is the reciprocal linkage between confidence and performance (Williams, Zinsser, & Bunker, 2015). That is, optimal confidence is linked to optimal performance, which in turn further enhances confidence.

### Self-confidence and performance in sports

The relationship between self-confidence and sport performance falls within a continuum. In practice, athletes may experience *underconfidence, overconfidence,* or *optimal confidence* (Burton & Raedeke, 2008). Underconfidence occurs when athletes lack the appropriate physical or mental preparation, fear failure, and lack the belief that they are able to overcome challenges. When an athlete doubts him/herself, a poor performance is more likely to occur, akin to the "concept of" self-fulfilling prophecy. That is, athletes that expect to underperform tend to underperform, as they are unable to focus their attention on the task at hand, and instead invest attention on task-irrelevant factors. In addition to experiencing negative thought patterns (i.e. negative self-talk), underconfident athletes tend to experience unpleasant and dysfunctional affective states (e.g. anxiety), and exhibit avoidance rather than decisive behaviour (Vealey & Chase, 2008).

Overconfidence occurs when athletes exhibit an inflated belief in their abilities to perform (Cashmore, 2002; Hays, 2008). Thus, the 'too much of a good thing' effect seems to happen when discussing overconfidence. In fact, the risks of overconfidence date back to Greek mythology and the story of Icarus (see *The Icarus Paradox* by Miller, 1992). Icarus received from his father wings made of wax to escape from Crete. His father warned him not to fly too high to avoid having his wings melted by the sun's heat. Icarus disregarded the advice, flew too close to the sun, and succumbed due to this complacency. Icarus's story illustrates some major side effects of overconfidence, including engagement in unnecessary risky behaviour and failure to search for better options (e.g. complacent behaviour), all of which can result in detrimental performance. Some scholars suggest that overconfidence is a fallacy in the sense that athletes cannot be overconfident if their self-confidence beliefs are grounded in realistic expectations (Burton & Raedeke, 2008). Put generally, a realistic and well-founded confidence is what every athlete should aim for.

Optimal confidence is shown by athletes who believe they possess the necessary physical and mental skills to achieve their desired goals (Weinberg & Gould, 2015; Williams et al., 2015). Optimal confidence consists of 'an athlete's realistic belief or expectation about achieving success' (Burton & Raedeke, 2008, p. 188). An athlete with optimal confidence experiences positive cognitive and affective states, and exhibits effective competitive behaviours (Feltz & Lirgg, 2001). In particular, optimally confident athletes exhibit a level of automaticity (*neural efficiency hypothesis*; Babiloni et al., 2010; Bertollo et al., 2016) needed to achieve peak performance experiences. Their thoughts are not hijacked by self-doubt and self-consciousness, and thus attentional resources are directed to do the right thing, at the right time, at the right place. Furthermore, optimally confident athletes tend to exhibit more functional and pleasant affective states, compared to underconfident performers (Hays, Maynard, Thomas, & Bawden, 2007; Hays, Thomas, Maynard, & Bawden, 2005). Finally, athletes with optimal confidence display effective competitive behaviours (e.g. increased levels of effort and persistence), compared to diffident athletes (Hays et al., 2005; 2007).

Self-confidence, as most psychological processes in sports, cannot be understood in isolation (for a review see Filho & Tenenbaum, 2015). In fact, one of the key and most influential theories on the relationship between confidence and performance is the Multidimensional Theory of Anxiety (see Craft, Magyar, Becker, & Feltz, 2003; Martens, Vealey, & Burton, 1990). According to this framework, confidence is inversely related to anxiety. Specifically, when an athlete is highly confident, s/he will experience low anxiety, and vice versa. Anxiety usually manifests through cognitive and somatic symptoms, both having detrimental effects on performance. Cognitive anxiety involves the mental aspect and consists of ruminations, worry, disrupted attention, and negative self-talk that consume mental resources that should be devoted to the task. Somatic anxiety consists of body-related symptoms, such as increased heart and breathing rates, which interfere with the motor output and execution of the task.

It is important to note that the linkage between confidence, anxiety, and performance influences how one thinks, feels, and behaves (i.e. cognitive-affective-behavioural link). Figure 17.1 summarizes the relationship between confidence beliefs and the cognitive-affective-behavioural linkage.

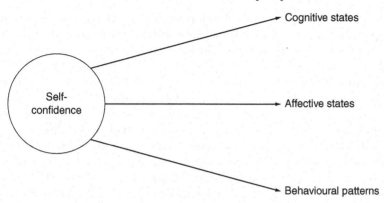

*Figure 17.1* Self-confidence influences behavioural patterns and cognitive and affective states.

From a cognitive standpoint, optimally confident athletes will remain task-focused and engaged in parallel automatic processing rather than regress to serial processing and reinvest attention into irrelevant task factors (see Masters & Maxwell, 2008). High confidence levels in athletes have also been associated with more positive and pleasant affective states (Hays, 2008). Athletes that are more confident also tend to interpret somatic anxiety manifestations as functional rather than dysfunctional to performance (Feltz & Lirgg, 2001). Furthermore, optimally confident athletes exhibit proactive and productive behavioural tendencies, including increased effort and persistence in challenging tasks (Hays et al., 2005; 2007). Finally, it is important to note that athletes' confidence levels vary depending on the task, situation, and domain at large, akin to the notion of self-efficacy put forth by Bandura (1982, 1992, 1997, 2006).

### Self-efficacy in football

Self-efficacy is important in football, as there are many different tasks that must be performed during a game to ensure an optimal performance for the athlete as an individual, and the team as a whole (see FIFA, 2017). In particular, athletes may differ in their self-efficacy levels for the different fundamental techniques in football. Some athletes may be confident in passing but may lack efficacy in dribbling the ball or shooting. Other athletes may not be confident running with the ball, or even controlling the ball when receiving a pass from a teammate. It follows that practitioners working with footballers should assess the efficacy levels of each athlete in the different basic techniques needed to succeed in the beautiful game. Understanding individual capabilities is particularly important in light of evidence that people tend to practise those skills that they know more, rather than engage in tasks that they are less comfortable with (see Baker & Young, 2014; Ericsson, 2003; Toner & Moran, 2015).

In addition to engaging in task-specific training in order to develop task-specific confidence, coaches and practitioners working with footballers should ensure that athletes experience success during practices (i.e. performance accomplishments). Setting goals that are challenging but achievable, while providing specialized instructional feedback, is important in developing efficacy beliefs and expert performance in sports in general, and football in particular. Athletes that reach the highest levels of play experience success and have positive, confident role models during the different stages of their careers (see Côté, Baker, & Abernethy, 2007). Accordingly, task-specific training based on Bandura's self-efficacy theoretical framework can also aid performance in football techniques and challenges, such as penalty kicks (taken during the game) and shootouts (after the regulation match to decide the winner in case of draw; see FIFA law 14: The penalty kick, 2004).

**Self-efficacy in penalty kicks and shootouts.** Although a relatively rare occurrence, a penalty kick is a decisive event in football, especially in the case of a penalty shootout (Jordet, 2009; Lopes, Araújo, Peres, Davids, & Barreiros, 2008). Confidence has been shown to be a primary factor in determining who takes a penalty kick in a football match (Geisler & Leith, 1997). Selection of penalty kick takers is important, as the consequences of failing are considerable, given that the attention of all players and spectators is directed to the player responsible for taking the shot (Jordet, Hartman, & Sigmundstad, 2009). It is noteworthy that confidence and anxiety are among the most frequent affective states experienced by athletes (see Jordet & Elferink-Gemser, 2012). Moreover, low confidence levels and high anxiety are significant factors related to missing a penalty kick (Wilson, Wood, & Jordet, 2013). Fear of failure likely leads to failure itself, as per the self-fulfilling prophecy and the notion that anxiety fosters avoidance-motivation (Weaver, Filson Moses, & Snyder, 2016). Conversely, players that engage in approach-motivation behaviours are more likely to excel when taking a penalty kick (Jordet & Hartman, 2008).

When the stakes are high in penalty shootouts, anxiety tends to increase while confidence decreases, consistent with the Multidimensional Theory of Anxiety discussed earlier. To this extent, Jordet, Hartman, Visscher, and Lemmink (2007) studied over 400 penalties from shootouts at major football tournaments. Their analyses revealed that about 60% of penalty kicks were scored when the outcome resulted in a loss, whereas 92% of penalty kicks were converted when the outcome resulted in a win. Again, confidence influences the cognitive-affective-behavioural patterns of performers. Footballers are more likely to succeed in a penalty kick if they take a longer time to respond to the referee's whistle rather than reacting immediately to it. This behavioural strategy likely allows the kicker extra time to take a deep breath to release feelings of tension (see Jordet et al., 2009) and gaze for longer (i.e. increased quiet eye period; see Wilson et al., 2013; Wood & Wilson, 2012) at the desired target in the goal.

Other behavioural strategies of confident penalty kick takers include adopting a goalkeeper independent-approach, in which the goalkeeper and other environmental stimuli are ignored and attention is mainly directed to the intended targeted; e.g. upper corner of the goal (see Lopes et al., 2008; Wilson et al., 2013). This top-down goal-oriented approach, as opposed to a bottom-up environmental strategy, enhances perception of control, allows for better attentional focus (i.e. focus on core components of action; for a review see Bortoli, Bertollo, Hanin, & Robazza, 2012), and thus leads to functional affective states and better performance.

For the goalkeeper, eye-gazing behaviour has been related to successful performance and confident approach behaviour. Confident and successful goalkeepers gaze at the penalty kick taker for an extended period of time to extract postural information (e.g. angle of approach to the ball; foot and hip position) that might indicate where the ball will be directed (i.e. height and direction) in the goal (Lopes et al., 2008). Successful goalkeepers tend to be more relaxed (e.g. less cognitive and somatic anxiety) and thus are able to wait for longer before committing to one side of the goal, compared to less successful goalkeepers (Savelsbergh, Van der Kamp, Williams, & Ward, 2005). Also noteworthy, goalkeepers try to diminish the penalty kick taker's confidence by looking bigger in the goal (Van der Kamp & Masters, 2008), signalling a greater threat, similar to the notion of deimatic behaviour (e.g. threat display when animals try to look bigger to instil fear in the pray or predator) in biological and evolutionary psychology (see Umbers, Lehtonen, & Mappes, 2015). In other words, by changing their posture and moving patterns in the goal (i.e. jumping, waving their arms), goalkeepers try to intimidate penalty kick takers in an effort to increase the likelihood of a poor shot.

Although a penalty kick is an individual task, it is important to keep in mind that football is a team sport. As renowned footballer Robin van Persie once said, 'To score a goal one has to have confidence in oneself and in that of your partners.' In fact, previous research has shown that individual expression of positive emotions post-successful penalty kick influences team processes, which in turn influence team performance (Moll, Jordet, & Pepping, 2010). Playing at a home venue has also been found to influence the collective sense of confidence shared by athletes in football and other sports (Carron, Loughhead, & Bray, 2005). Overall, although self-confidence beliefs in general are important, the linkage between confidence and performance transcends the individual. As such, we turn our attention next to collective efficacy, which refers to the communal sense of confidence shared by teammates.

## Collective efficacy

We do not feel unbeatable although we feel strong and confident in our style of football.
(Xavi Hernandez – four-time winner of the UEFA Champions League with Barcelona)

The quote by the former Barcelona star player is in line with theory and empirical evidence suggesting that collective efficacy is greater than the sum of individuals' efficacy beliefs (Dithurbide & Feltz, 2012; Feltz & Lirgg, 1998; Feltz, Short, & Sullivan, 2008). That is, collective efficacy is an emergent group-level property (Bandura, 1997). Bandura (1986) first defined collective efficacy as a 'sense of collective competence shared among individuals when allocating, coordinating, and integrating their resources in a successful concerted response to specific situational demands' (p. 309). A decade later, Bandura (1997) defined collective efficacy as a 'group's shared belief in its conjoint capabilities to organize and execute the courses of action required to produce given levels of attainment' (p. 4). Overall, scholars concur that the pervasiveness of under- and over-achieving teams exemplifies the gestalt notion that in team processes such as collective efficacy, 'the whole is greater than the sum of its parts' (see Feltz et al., 2008).

In addition to being a group-level property, collective efficacy is a situation-specific confidence. In fact, Bandura (1997) noted that collective efficacy pertains to the group-level equivalent of self-efficacy. To Bandura (1997), self-efficacy mainly differs from collective efficacy in the unit of agency. Notwithstanding, he argues that both self-efficacy and collective efficacy share similar anteceding factors.

### Unique sources of collective efficacy information in team sports

Theoretically, the sources of self-efficacy and collective efficacy are conceptually equivalent and include past performance accomplishments, vicarious experiences, verbal persuasion, and physiological information (for a review see Bandura, 1997; Feltz & Öncü, 2014; Feltz et al., 2008). The unique sources of collective efficacy information include home-field advantage, leadership, and cohesion.

**Home-field advantage.** Home-field advantage is a well-established phenomenon in the sport sciences and pertains to the fact that teams win more games when playing at home than playing away, given a balanced home and away playing schedule (see Carron et al., 2005). A number of mechanisms (e.g. familiarity with local conditions; territorial dominance; travel effects; crowd influence; referee bias) have been proposed to explain the direct and indirect effects of home-field

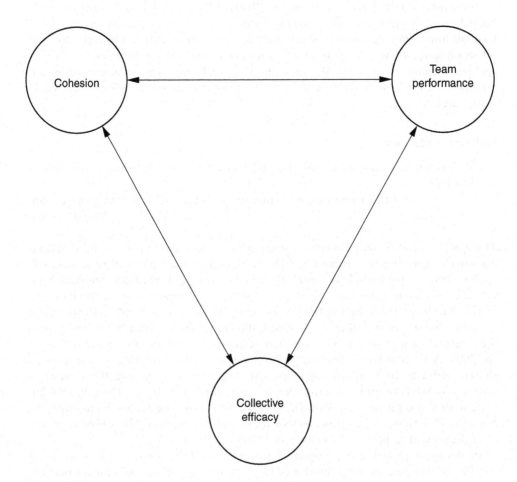

*Figure 17.2* Reciprocal linkage between collective efficacy, cohesion, and team performance.

advantage on individuals' bio-psycho-social states and team performance (Carron et al., 2005). Particular to football, Waters and Lovell (2002) found that professional athletes in England reported significantly higher perceptions of the team's confidence at home games compared to away games.

Although playing at home is oftentimes beneficial to performance, home-field disadvantage may occur as well, especially at the late stages of knockout competitions (Wallace, Baumeister, & Vohs, 2005). As a recent anecdotal example, Brazil was defeated by Germany by six goals (7–1) while playing at home in the 2014 FIFA World Cup semi-finals. To this matter, Wallace and colleagues (2005) observed that home audiences tend to amplify both the costs of failure and the rewards of success. As such, when the stakes are high, playing at home may lead to choking under pressure as the players focus more on avoiding failure rather than on seeking success. Aligned with this notion, Bar-Eli, Tenenbaum, and Levy-Kolker (1992) have long noted that athletes are more susceptible to psychological crisis after unsuccessful performances when performing at home rather than away.

While positive or negative effects of players' self-efficacy and collective efficacy beliefs depend on myriad factors, including the stage of the competition, further research into how mental preparation may contribute to footballers' performance, regardless of crowd factors, is warranted (e.g. Staufenbiel, Riedl, & Strauss, 2016). For instance, it would be beneficial for future research to consider the role of team leaders in promoting efficacy beliefs within the team.

**Leadership.** Team leaders, specifically coaches and peer leaders, such as team captains, are considered to be a major source of collective efficacy in team sports, such as football (Kavussanu, Boardley, Jutkiewicz, Vincent, & Ring, 2008; Loughead & Hardy, 2005; Myers, Feltz, Chase, Reckase, & Hancock, 2008). With respect to coaches, Taggar and Seijts (2003) have shown that leaders' role-efficacy for initiating structure behaviour is positively related to collective efficacy in team settings. More recently, coaches' social support behaviour and players' expectations have also been linked to collective efficacy ratings in a Bayesian network analysis study (Fuster-Parra, García-Mas, Ponseti, & Leo, 2015). High-efficacy coaches positively impact collective efficacy because they tend to exhibit leadership styles that are preferred by athletes, and usually offer more positive reinforcement and instructional feedback (see Feltz, Chase, Moritz, & Sullivan, 1999).

Likewise, high-efficacy team leaders exhibit positive communication patterns, and are sources of confidence during stressful situations both on and off the playing field (see Basevitch & Filho, 2011; Cotterill & Fransen, 2016; Moran & Weiss, 2006). To this extent, previous research suggests that peer leaders communicating social and instrumental support are more likely to be perceived as positive role models by their peers and coaches (Murai & Inomata, 2010). Peer leaders focusing on instrumental goals facilitate mastery experiences, which in turn positively influences collective efficacy. Peer leaders are also able to model confidence while instilling confidence in the team by means of verbal persuasion, hence representing multiple sources of credible efficacy information to their teammates (Filho, Gershgoren, Basevitch, Schinke, & Tenenbaum, 2014). Leaders also influence cohesion within the team, which in turn is positively associated with collective efficacy.

**Cohesion.** Team cohesion is considered to be an antecedent of collective efficacy beliefs (Carron & Hausenblas, 1998; Carron et al., 2005; Feltz et al., 2008). To this extent, Bloom, Stevens, and Wickwire (2003) examined coaches' perception of team cohesion and performance, and concluded that expert sport coaches believe that team cohesion is essential for team performance. Within professional football players, teammates' perceptions of team cohesion and conflict predict changes in collective efficacy (Leo, González-Ponce, Sánchez-Miguel, Ivarsson, & García-Calvo, 2015). In another study with college footballers in the final stages of a knockout tournament, Filho, Tenenbaum, and Yang (2015) concluded that cohesion predicted collective efficacy scores, with more cohesive teams showing higher efficacy levels. Altogether, research findings have consistently shown that cohesion is positively linked to collective efficacy, and scholars have proposed that interventions designed to increase cohesion would possibly impact team members' perceived collective efficacy (Mach, Dolan, & Tzafrir, 2010), as well as team performance at large (Figure 17.2).

### The reciprocal linkage between collective efficacy and team performance in football

Collective efficacy has been found to distinguish performance levels within and between teams in sport contexts in general (Edmonds, Tenenbaum, Kamata, & Johnson, 2009; Feltz & Lirgg, 1998; Myers, Payment, & Feltz, 2004; Ronglan, 2007), and football in particular (Filho et al., 2015; Fransen, Vanbeselaere, De Cuyper, Vande Broek, & Boen, 2015b; Leo, Sánchez-Miguel, Sánchez-Oliva, Amado, & García-Calvo, 2013). For instance, previous research in youth football has suggested that players in high-ranked teams show higher collective efficacy beliefs than members of less successful teams (Leo et al., 2013). Similarly, Filho et al. (2015) observed a positive and moderate relationship between collective efficacy and performance in football among college student-athletes. A qualitative inquiry with elite professional coaches also revealed that efficacy beliefs shared by the players is important in developing high-performing football teams (Gershgoren et al., 2016).

The relationship between collective efficacy and performance is considered bidirectional in nature, akin to the notion of *reciprocal causation* put forth by Bandura (1997) and the notion of a *many-to-many basis relationship* in applied social psychology (see Cacioppo & Berntson, 1992). Importantly, the term causation is used by Bandura to imply 'functional dependence between events' (p. 5), rather than to imply statistical or empirical determinism. Accordingly, reciprocal causation describes the notion that collective efficacy leads to better performance and vice versa. To this matter, Fransen et al. (2015a) observed a reciprocal linkage between players' team confidence and performance in U-17 and U-19 women's football. In another study, Fransen and colleagues (2015b) noted that high-quality performance is a major predictor of collective efficacy.

Overall, collective efficacy is an important team process that has been linked to other team attributes (e.g. home-field advantage, leadership, cohesion), and both objective and subjective team outcomes in football, and other sport and working teams (Goddard, Hoy, & Hoy, 2004; Zaccaro, Blair, Peterson, & Zazanis, 1995). To this extent, Filho et al. (2015) have proposed an integrated view of team dynamics, wherein the reciprocal effects of cohesion, collective efficacy, and team mental models (shared and complementary knowledge held among teammates) on each other, and on performance at large, is taken into account. In addressing collective efficacy in football and team dynamics in general, practitioners and researchers should remember the gestalt saying 'the whole is greater than the sum of its parts'. Scholars should continue to study the reciprocal effects of collective efficacy on other team processes and performance in football. Furthermore, practitioners should develop interventions that impact not only confidence beliefs, but also team processes such as cohesion and team mental models. Additional applied recommendations and avenues for future research are advanced next.

## Future research and applied recommendations

In this section, we provide recommendations for future research and offer suggestions to researchers and practitioners aimed at increasing confidence, self-efficacy, and collective efficacy in the 'football world'.

### Suggestions for future research

Ways forward in applied research include advancing understanding of theory, in line with the adage 'there is nothing more applied than a good theory'. To this, scholars should continue to test the reciprocal linkage among collective efficacy, other team processes, and the performance and well-being of individuals and teams. Testing parsimonious explanatory models, rather than advancing over-parameterized descriptive frameworks, may help practitioners to understand the key mechanisms underlying efficacy beliefs in football. Advancing input-output frameworks on other forms of relational efficacy, so to establish anteceding, moderating, and outcome variables, also seems a fruitful area for future research. To speculate, for instance, such an approach could explain whether collective efficacy is orthogonal or oblique to others' efficacy, coach efficacy, self-efficacy, and relation-inferred self-efficacy.

When addressing collective efficacy, we reiterate the importance of advancing multi-level models of analysis (see Dithurbide & Feltz, 2012; Feltz & Lirgg, 2001). Studies addressing psycho-physiological markers of confidence are also needed, as well as experimental studies, especially studies manipulating mental skills and assessing the influence of such manipulation on confidence and efficacy beliefs. The few existing experimental studies in this arena thus far have shown the benefits of psychological interventions in promoting both self and collective efficacy (Munroe-Chandler & Hall, 2004; Munroe-Chandler, Hall, & Fishburne, 2008), reducing anxiety (see Hazell, Cotterill, & Hill, 2014), and instilling coping skills (Reeves, Nicholls, & McKenna, 2011) among football players.

Furthermore, with the advancement of neuroscience techniques, more research on the neural markers of confidence and its putative neuro-connections with other high-order processes, such as decision-making, is warranted. Longitudinal studies should be considered as well, as confidence, both at the individual and group-level of analysis, is dynamic and thus fluctuates over time. We concede that longitudinal studies are expensive and time-consuming, and coaches and teams are not always willing to participate in these types of studies. Notwithstanding, there are only a handful of longitudinal wave studies on collective efficacy and other team processes in sport, exercise, and performance psychology, and the benefit of conducting such analysis is considerable given that confidence, self-efficacy, and collective efficacy fluctuate over time.

*Practical recommendations*

Practitioners should be prepared to promote performance restoration when efficacy fluctuates down, as well as performance optimization to enhance confidence and efficacy beliefs (see Filho & Tenenbaum, 2015). To restore and optimize confidence, practitioners should help footballers in the establishment of realistic goals that will form the basis for mastery experiences. Modelling and directing athletes to models of confidence, as well as helping them to interpret their bio-psycho-social states as functional rather than dysfunctional to performance, will also boost athletes' self- and collective efficacy beliefs. Positive self-talk is another way to improve efficacy beliefs. Beyond these general, well-established, theory-based guidelines, practitioners should consider the cognitive-affective-behavioural linkage that is influenced by confidence and efficacy beliefs, and that in turn influences these beliefs. Some athletes will respond optimally to cognitive (e.g. self-talk and imagery training), while others respond better to affective (e.g. person-centred intervention), or behavioural approaches (e.g. body language modification, gaze control, trigger cue words).

## Conclusions

In summary, self-confidence, self-efficacy, and collective efficacy are predictors of performance in sports in general, and football in particular. More confident and efficacious players exhibit greater adaptive thinking, feeling, and behavioural states and patterns, while successful teams perform better and develop other team processes, such cohesion and team mental models, more effectively. To conclude, we reiterate that confidence and efficacy beliefs are components of large, complex, and multifaceted selves and team dynamics. Assessing the unique needs of individuals and teams will produce optimal outcomes in light of the notion that confidence and efficacy beliefs vary by person, situation, and team.

## References

Babiloni, C., Marzano, N., Infarinato, F., Iacoboni, M., Rizza, G., Aschieri, P., … Del Percio, C. (2010). 'Neural efficiency' of experts' brain during judgment of actions: A high-resolution EEG study in elite and amateur karate athletes. *Behavioural Brain Research, 207,* 466–475.

Baker, J., & Young, B. (2014). 20 years later: Deliberate practice and the development of expertise in sport. *International Review of Sport and Exercise Psychology, 7,* 135–157.

Bandura, A. (1982). Self-efficacy mechanism in human agency. *American Psychologist, 37,* 122–147.

Bandura, A. (1986). *Social foundations of thought and action: A social cognitive theory.* Englewood Cliffs, NJ: Prentice-Hall.

Bandura, A. (1992). Exercise of personal agency through the self-efficacy mechanism. In R. Schwarzer (Ed.), *Self-efficacy: Thought control of action* (pp. 3–38). Washington, DC: Hemisphere.

Bandura, A. (1997). *Self-efficacy: The exercise of control.* New York, NY: W. H. Freeman.

Bandura, A. (2006). Guide for constructing self-efficacy scales. In F. Pajares & T. Urdan (Eds.), *Self-efficacy beliefs of adolescents* (pp. 307–337). Greenwich, CT: Information Age Publishing.

Bar-Eli, M., Tenenbaum, G., & Levy-Kolker, N. (1992). A crisis-related analysis of perceived spectators' behaviour in competition. *Canadian Journal of Sport Sciences, 17,* 288–298.

Basevitch, I., & Filho, E. (2011). A qualitative examination of college-athlete team captains: On and off field issues. *Performance Excellence Movement Newsletter*, 2–4.

Bertollo, M., di Fronso, S., Filho, E., Conforto, S., Schmid, M., Bortoli, L., & Robazza, C. (2016). Proficient brain for optimal performance: The MAP model perspective. *PeerJ*, 1–26.

Bloom, G. A., Stevens, D. E., & Wickwire, T. L. (2003). Expert coaches' perceptions of team building. *Journal of Applied Sport Psychology, 15*, 129–143. doi:10.1080/10413200305397.

Bortoli, L., Bertollo, M., Hanin, Y., & Robazza, C. (2012). Striving for excellence: A multi-action plan intervention model for shooters. *Psychology of Sport and Exercise, 13*, 693–701.

Burton, D., & Raedeke, T. D. (2008). *Sport psychology for coaches*. Champaign, IL: Human Kinetics.

Cacioppo, J. T., & Berntson, G. G. (1992). Social psychological contributions to the decade of the brain: Doctrine of multilevel analysis. *American Psychologist, 47*, 1019–1028. http://dx.doi.org/10.1037/0003-066X.47.8.1019.

Carron, A. V., & Hausenblas, H. A. (1998). *Group dynamics in sport* (2nd ed.). Morgantown, WV: Fitness Information Technology.

Carron, A. V., Loughhead, T. M., & Bray, S. R. (2005). The home advantage in sport competitions: Courneya and Carron's (1992) conceptual framework a decade later. *Journal of Sports Sciences, 23*, 395–407.

Cashmore, E. (2002). *Sport and exercise psychology: The key concepts*. New York, NY: Routledge.

Côté, J., Baker, J., & Abernethy, B. (2007). Practice and play in the development of sport exercise. In G. Tenenbaum & R. C. Eklund (Eds.), *Handbook of sport psychology* (3rd ed.). Hoboken, NJ: Wiley.

Cotterill, S. T., & Fransen, K. (2016). Athlete leadership in sport teams: Current understanding and future directions. *International Review of Sport and Exercise Psychology, 9*, 116–133.

Craft, L. L., Magyar, T. M., Becker, B. J., & Feltz, D. L. (2003). The relationship between the Competitive State Anxiety Inventory-2 and sport performance: A meta-analysis. *Journal of Sport and Exercise Psychology, 25*, 44–65.

Dithurbide, L., & Feltz, D. L. (2012). Self and collective efficacy. In G. Tenenbaum, R. Eklund, & A. Kamata (Eds.), *Handbook of measurement in sport and exercise psychology* (pp. 251–263). Champaign, IL: Human Kinetics.

Edmonds, W. A., Tenenbaum, G., Kamata, A., & Johnson, M. B. (2009). The role of collective efficacy in adventure racing teams. *Small Group Research, 40*, 163–180. doi:10.1177/1046496408328489.

Ericsson, K. A. (2003). Development of elite performance and deliberate practice. In J. Starkes & K. A. Ericsson (Eds.), *Expert performance in sports: Advances in research on sport expertise* (pp. 49–83). Champaign, IL: Human Kinetics.

Feltz, D. L., Chase, M. A., Moritz, S. E., & Sullivan, P. J. (1999). A conceptual model of coaching efficacy: Preliminary investigation and instrument development. *Journal of Educational Psychology, 91*, 765–776. doi:10.1037/0022-0663.91.4.765.

Feltz, D. L., & Lirgg, C. D. (1998). Perceived team and player efficacy in hockey. *Journal of Applied Psychology, 83*, 557–564. doi:10.1037/0021-9010.83.4.557.

Feltz, D. L., & Lirgg, C. D. (2001). Self-efficacy beliefs of athletes, teams, and coaches. In R. N. Singer, H. A. Hausenblas, & C. M. Janelle (Eds.), *Handbook of sport psychology* (2nd ed., pp. 389–416). New York, NY: Wiley.

Feltz, D. L., & Öncü, E. (2014). Self-confidence and self-efficacy. In A. G. Papaioannou & D. Hackfort (Eds.), *Routledge companion to sport and exercise psychology: Global perspectives and fundamental concepts* (pp. 417–419). New York, NY: Routledge.

Feltz, D. L., Short, S. E., & Sullivan, P. J. (2008). *Self-efficacy in sport*. Champaign, IL: Human Kinetics.

FIFA. (2017). *Welcome to grassroots*. Retrieved from http://grassroots.fifa.com.

FIFA law 14: The penalty kick. (2004). Retrieved from www.fifa.com/mm/document/af developing/refereeing/law_14_the_penalty_kick_en_47369.pdf.

Filho, E., Gershgoren, L., Basevitch, I., Schinke, R., & Tenenbaum, G. (2014). Peer leadership and shared mental models in a college volleyball team: A season long case study. *Journal of Clinical Sport Psychology, 8*, 184–203.

Filho, E., & Tenenbaum, G. (2015). Sports psychology. *Oxford bibliographies*. Oxford, England: Oxford University Press. Retrieved from www.oxfordbibliographies.com/view/document/obo-9780199828340/obo-9780199828340-0175.xml.

Filho, E., Tenenbaum, G., & Yang, Y. (2015). Cohesion, team mental models, and collective efficacy: Towards an integrated framework of team dynamics in sport. *Journal of Sports Sciences, 33*, 641–653. http://dx.doi.org/10.1080/02640414.2014.957714.

Fransen, K., Decroos, S., Vanbeselaere, N., Vande Broek, G., De Cuyper, B., Vanroy, J., & Boen, F. (2015a). Is team confidence the key to success? The reciprocal relation between collective efficacy, team outcome confidence, and perceptions of team performance during soccer games. *Journal of Sports Sciences, 33*, 219–231. http://dx.doi.org/10.1080/02640414.2014.942689.

Fransen, K., Vanbeselaere, N., De Cuyper, B., Vande Broek, G., & Boen, F. (2015b). Perceived sources of team confidence in soccer and basketball. *Medicine & Science in Sports & Exercise, 47*, 1470–1484. doi:10.1249/MSS.0000000000000561.

Fuster-Parra, P., García-Mas, A., Ponseti, F. J., & Leo, F. M. (2015). Team performance and collective efficacy in the dynamic psychology of competitive team: A Bayesian network analysis. *Human Movement Science, 40*, 98–118.

Geisler, G. W. W., & Leith, L. M. (1997). The effects of self-esteem, self-efficacy, and audience presence on soccer penalty shot performance. *Journal of Sport Behavior, 20*, 322–337.

Gershgoren, L., Basevitch, I., Gershgoren, A., Brill, Y. S., Schinke, R. J., & Tenenbaum, G. (2016). Expertise in soccer teams: A thematic inquiry into the role of shared mental models within team chemistry. *Psychology of Sport and Exercise, 24*, 128–139.

Goddard, R. D., Hoy, W. K., & Hoy, A. W. (2004). Collective efficacy beliefs: Theoretical developments, empirical evidence, and future directions. *Educational Researcher, 33*, 3–13.

Hays, K. (2008). Self-confidence in a sporting context. In A. Lane (Ed.), *Sport and exercise psychology: Topics in applied psychology* (pp. 53–70). London, England: Hodder Education.

Hays, K., Maynard, I., Thomas, O., & Bawden, M. (2007). Sources and types of confidence identified by world class sport performers. *Journal of Applied Sport Psychology, 19*, 434–456.

Hays, K., Thomas, O., Maynard, I., & Bawden, M. (2005). Sport confidence in successful and unsuccessful world class performances: A comparison of affect, behaviour and cognition. *Journal of Sports Sciences, 23*, 1289–1290.

Hazell, J., Cotterill, S. T., & Hill, D. M. (2014). An exploration of pre-performance routines, self-efficacy, anxiety and performance in semi-professional soccer. *European Journal of Sport Science, 14*, 603–610. http://dx.doi.org/10.1080/17461391.2014.888484.

Jordet, G. (2009). When superstars flop: Public status and choking under pressure in international soccer penalty shootouts. *Journal of Applied Sport Psychology, 21*, 125–130. doi:10.1080/10413200902777263.

Jordet, G., & Elferink-Gemser, M. T. (2012). Stress, coping, and emotions on the world stage: The experience of participating in a major soccer tournament penalty shootout. *Journal of Applied Sport Psychology, 24*, 73–91.

Jordet, G., & Hartman, E. (2008). Avoidance motivation and choking under pressure in soccer penalty shootouts. *Journal of Sport & Exercise Psychology, 30*, 452–459.

Jordet, G., Hartman, E., & Sigmundstad, E. (2009). Temporal links to performing under pressure in international soccer penalty shootouts. *Psychology of Sport and Exercise, 10*, 621–627.

Jordet, G., Hartman, E., Visscher, C., & Lemmink, K. A. P. M. (2007). Kicks from the penalty mark in soccer: The roles of stress, skill, and fatigue for kick outcomes. *Journal of Sports Sciences, 25*, 121–129.

Kavussanu, M., Boardley, I. D., Jutkiewicz, N., Vincent, S., & Ring, C. (2008). Coaching efficacy and coaching effectiveness: Examining their predictors and comparing coaches and athletes reports. *The Sport Psychologist, 22*, 383–404.

Leo, F. M., González-Ponce, I., Sánchez-Miguel, P. A., Ivarsson, A., & García-Calvo, T. (2015). Role ambiguity, role conflict, team conflict, cohesion and collective efficacy in sport teams: A multilevel analysis. *Psychology of Sport and Exercise, 20*, 60–66. http://dx.doi.org/10.1016/j.psychsport.2015.04.009.

Leo, F. M., Sánchez-Miguel, P. A., Sánchez-Oliva, D., Amado, D., & García-Calvo, T. (2013). Analysis of cohesion and collective efficacy profiles for the performance of soccer players. *Journal of Human Kinetics, 39*, 221–229. doi:10.2478/hukin-2013-0085.

Lopes, J. E., Araújo, D., Peres, R., Davids, K., & Barreiros, J. (2008). The dynamics of decision making in penalty kick situations in association football. *The Open Sports Sciences Journal, 1*, 24–30.

Loughead, T. M., & Hardy, J. (2005). An examination of coach and peer leader behaviors in sport. *Psychology of Sport and Exercise, 6*, 303–312. doi:10.1016/j.psychsport.2004.02.001.

Mach, M., Dolan, S., & Tzafrir, S. (2010). The differential effect of team members trust on team performance: The mediation role of team cohesion. *Journal of Occupational and Organizational Psychology, 83*, 771–794. doi:10.1348/096317909X473903.

Martens, R., Vealey, R. S., & Burton, D. (1990). *Competitive anxiety in sport.* Champaign, IL: Human Kinetics.

Masters, R. S. W., & Maxwell, J. P. (2008). The theory of reinvestment. *International Review of Sport and Exercise Psychology, 1*, 160–183.

Miller, D. (1992). *The Icarus paradox.* New York, NY: HarperCollins.

Moll, T., Jordet, G., & Pepping, G. J. (2010). Emotional contagion in soccer penalty shootouts: Celebration of individual success is associated with ultimate team success. *Journal of Sports Sciences, 28*, 983–992.

Moran, M. M., & Weiss, M. R. (2006). Peer leadership in sport: Links with friendship, peer acceptance, psychological characteristics, and athletic ability. *Journal of Applied Sport Psychology, 18*, 97–113. doi:10.1080/10413200600653501.

Munroe-Chandler, K. J., & Hall, C. R. (2004). Enhancing the collective efficacy of a soccer team through motivational general-mastery imagery. *Imagination, Cognition and Personality, 24*, 51–67.

Munroe-Chandler, K., Hall, C., & Fishburne, G. (2008). Playing with confidence: The relationship between imagery use and self-confidence and self-efficacy in youth soccer players. *Journal of Sports Sciences, 26*, 1539–1546.

Murai, G., & Inomata, K. (2010). Effective leadership of captains of sport teams. *Japanese Journal of Experimental Social Psychology, 50*, 28–36. doi:10.2130/jjesp. 50.28.

Myers, N. D., Feltz, D. L., Chase, M. A., Reckase, M. D., & Hancock, G. R. (2008). The coaching efficacy scale II–high school teams. *Educational and Psychological Measurement, 68*, 1059–1076. doi:10.1177/0013164408318773.

Myers, N. D., Payment, C. A., & Feltz, D. L. (2004). Reciprocal relationships between collective efficacy and team performance in women's ice hockey. *Group Dynamics: Theory, Research, and Practice, 8*, 182–195.

Papaioannou, A. G., Appleton, P. R., Torregrosa, M., Jowett, G. E., Bosselut, G., Gonzalez, L., … & Zourbanos, N. (2013). Moderate-to-vigorous physical activity and personal well-being in European youth soccer players: Invariance of physical activity, global self-esteem and vitality across five countries. *International Journal of Sport and Exercise Psychology, 11*, 351–364.

Pilarska, A., & Suchańska, A. (2015). Self-complexity and self-concept differentiation – What have we been measuring for the past 30 years? *Current Psychology, 34*, 723–743.

Rafaeli-Mor, E., & Steinberg, J. (2002). Self-complexity and well-being: A review and research synthesis. *Personality and Social Psychology Review, 6*, 31–58.

Reeves, C. W., Nicholls, A. R., & McKenna, J. (2011). The effects of a coping intervention on coping self-efficacy, coping effectiveness, and subjective performance among adolescent soccer players. *International Journal of Sport and Exercise Psychology, 9*, 126–142.

Ronglan, L. T. (2007). Building and communicating collective efficacy: A season-long in-depth study of an elite sport team. *Sport Psychologist, 21*, 78–93.

Savelsbergh, G. J. P., Van der Kamp, J., Williams, A. M., & Ward, P. (2005). Anticipation and visual search behavior in expert soccer goalkeepers. *Ergonomics, 48*, 1686–1697.

Staufenbiel, K., Riedl, D., & Strauss, B. (2016). Learning to be advantaged: The development of home advantage in high-level youth soccer. *International Journal of Sport and Exercise Psychology*, 1–15. doi:10.1080/1612197X.2016.1142463.

Taggar, S., & Seijts, G. H. (2003). Leader and staff role-efficacy as antecedents of collective-efficacy and team performance. *Human Performance, 16*, 131–156.

Thomas, O., Lane, A., & Kingston, K. (2011). Defining and contextualizing robust sport-confidence. *Journal of Applied Sport Psychology, 23*, 189–208.

Toner, J., & Moran, A. (2015). Enhancing performance proficiency at the expert level: Considering the role of 'somaesthetic awareness'. *Psychology of Sport and Exercise, 16*, 110–117.

Umbers, K. D., Lehtonen, J., & Mappes, J. (2015). Deimatic displays. *Current Biology, 25*, R58–R59.

Van der Kamp, J., & Masters, R. S. W. (2008). The human Müller-Lyer illusion in goalkeeping. *Perception, 37*, 951–954. doi:10.1068/p6010.

Vealey, R. S. (2001). Understanding and enhancing self-confidence in athletes. In R. N. Singer, H. A. Hausenblas, & C. M. Janelle (Eds.), *Handbook of sport psychology* (pp. 550–565). New York, NY: Wiley.

Vealey, R. S., & Chase, M. A. (2008). Self-confidence in sport: Conceptual and research advances. In T. S. Horn (Ed.), *Advances in sport psychology* (3rd ed.). Champaign, IL: Human Kinetics.

Wallace, H. M., Baumeister, R. F., & Vohs, K. D. (2005). Audience support and choking under pressure: A home disadvantage? *Journal of Sports Sciences, 23*, 429–438.

Waters, A., & Lovell, G. (2002). An examination of the homefield advantage in a professional English soccer team from a psychological standpoint. *Football Studies, 5*, 46–59.

Weaver, J., Filson Moses, J., & Snyder, M. (2016). Self-fulfilling prophecies in ability settings. *The Journal of Social Psychology, 156*, 179–189.

Weinberg, R., & Gould, D. (2015). *Foundations of sport and exercise psychology* (6th ed.). Champaign, IL: Human Kinetics.

Williams, J. M., Zinsser, N., & Bunker, L. (2015). Cognitive techniques for building confidence and enhancing performance. In J. M. Williams & V. Krane (Eds.), *Applied sport psychology: Personal growth to peak performance* (pp. 274–303). New York, NY: McGraw-Hill Education.

Wilson, M., Wood, G., & Jordet, G. (2013). The BASES expert statement on the psychological preparation for football penalty shootouts. *Sport & Exercise Scientist, 38*, 8–9.

Wood, G., & Wilson, M. R. (2012). Quiet-eye training, perceived control and performing under pressure. *Psychology of Sport and Exercise, 13*, 721–728.

Zaccaro, S. J., Blair, V., Peterson, C., & Zazanis, M. (1995). Collective efficacy. In J. E. Maddux (Ed.), *Self-efficacy, adaptation, and adjustment: Theory, research, and application* (pp. 305–328). New York, NY: Plenum.

# 18 Concentration and self-talk in football

*Mirko Farina and Alberto Cei*

## Abstract

Concentration and self-talk are key (often underappreciated) factors underlying elite sport performance. In this chapter we define concentration and self-talk and look at some of their applications. We investigate their relation, their functions, and discuss their contribution to sport performance. We focus on the specific role that concentration and self-talk play in football. So, we analyse how they improve players' performance by, for instance: (i) providing a balanced level of anxiety, (ii) enhancing focus and attention, (iii) promoting decision-making skill and decreasing reaction time, (iv) motivating to increase efforts, (v) improving coordination with teammates and, more generally, deterring behaviours that have negative consequences on the field. We then analyse the peak moment of any football performance (the act of scoring a goal) and look at how to use concentration and self-talk to increase the chances of scoring a goal (or not conceding it). We conclude by providing practitioners with a series of applied coaching strategies that can be used to build more successful coaching programmes (both in team sports and in football). To do so, we first identify some crucial game factors influencing football performance (e.g. game momentum, stress, anxiety, the players' capacity to re-focus on the present) and then look at how coaches can intervene to satisfy some of these game demands.

## Concentration and self-talk in football

Concentration is one of the key factors underlying elite performance.[1] Vernacchia (2003) defined concentration as 'the ability to perform with a clear and present focus' (p. 144). Concentration therefore entails the capacity to focus attention on the task at hand. This means that to be successful in competitive situations athletes must be able to learn how to focus attention and control thoughts.

As former Manchester United goalkeeper Edwin van der Sar noted on the importance of concentration in football: 'Concentration is [a] big part of being a footballer ... Everything you do during the day is centered around being able to focus for those 90 minutes during a game. But the moment you are tired, your concentration levels start to slip.'[2] According to van der Sar then elite performance

---

1 Concentration and attention are, on our view, synonyms. Throughout this chapter we use the word concentration because we believe it better reflects the operative approach we pursue and stand for.
2 www.dailymail.co.uk/sport/football/article-1099048/Van-der-Sar-United-stay-focused-win-Club-World-Cup.html#ixzz4UcvjpbAo (last accessed April 2018).

requires that athletes do not react to potential distractions. These distractions can be external or internal. External distractions can be visual or auditory, and may include other competitors, spectators, and media. Internal distractions may include negative self-talk, fatigue, and emotional arousal.

Elite performance therefore can only meaningfully occur when athletes (at minimum) voluntarily concentrate on the cues in their environment to pursue an action that is within their ability and are at the same time able to avoid potential distractions (Smith, 2003).[3]

However, concentration (and the capacity to voluntarily avoid potential distractions) are not the only crucial factors affecting elite performance. Self-talk is another crucial factor. Hardy, Hall, and Hardy (2005) defined self-talk as a 'multidimensional phenomenon concerned with athletes' verbalizations that are addressed to themselves' (p. 905) and subsequently (Hardy, 2006) as 'verbalizations or statements addressed to the self ... serving at least two functions; instructional and motivational' (p. 82).

More recently, Van Raalte, Vincent, and Brewer (2016) provided a definition that emphasizes the linguistic features of self-talk. According to them, self-talk is 'the syntactically recognizable articulation of an internal position that can be expressed internally or out loud, where the sender of the message is also the intended receiver' (p. 141). The addition of the term 'syntactically recognizable' is of particular importance since it distinguishes self-talk from other verbalizations (such as shouts of frustration like 'aaahhhh!'), self-statements made through gestures, and self-statements made outside of the context of formal language. Defining self-talk as an 'articulation of an internal position' also contributes to anchor its meaning within the individual and places the origin of self-talk in consciousness and information processing.

Self-talk has many potential applications, including breaking bad habits and sustaining efforts in acquiring new skills and is normally categorized in three types: positive, instructional, and negative.

Positive self-talk focuses on increasing energy and efforts but does not carry any task-related clue (e.g. 'I can do it'). Positive self-talk thus shapes our minds with thoughts enabling us to manage difficult situations and stress more effectively. It also increases motivation and it is therefore essential for athletes to attain consistent and optimal performance (Blumenstein & Lidor, 2007). Instructional self-talk helps the performers' understanding of task requirements by facilitating their attendance to task-relevant cues that aid the players' concentration during task execution. As such instructional self-talk can be said to help athletes in focusing on the technical aspects of the performance and in improving their motor skills (Hardy, Begley, & Blanchfield, 2015). Negative self-talk is critical and gets in the way of a person reaching their goals. Negative self-talk thus interferes with a positive mindset, creates a failure mentality, deflates self-confidence, reduces motivation, generates anxiety, and disrupts optimal arousal (Burton & Raedeke 2008).

Unfortunately, coaches in many football academies display a considerable lack of knowledge concerning the training of players' mental skills (Harwood & Anderson, 2015). This crucial lack of knowledge has determined an under-appreciation of the

---

3 It must be noted that it is not coincidence that the performance of anxious athletes is often ineffective. This is because their mind is unable to appropriately focus and is kept busy with thoughts (distractions) that are not pertinent to the action that needs to be performed (Woodman & Hardy, 2003).

contribution of both concentration and self-talk to elite football performance. Concentration and self-talk are nevertheless paramount to footballers attaining top performance in that they allow them, among other things, to work on their technique and enhance movements and executions (Beilock, Carr, MacMahon, & Starkes, 2002).

The objectives of this chapter are two-fold. First, we want to explain the relationship between concentration and self-talk in football. Second, we provide practitioners with a series of applied strategies that can be used to enhance their coaching. Before we turn to these two major goals, however, we briefly review a series of empirical findings on concentration and self-talk and reflect on their relevance to sport performance.

## Concentration and self-talk in sport performance

The role of concentration in sport performance has been extensively analysed (Moran, 1997). Many researchers have attempted to specify the processes underlying this construct. Memmert (2009), for example, has individuated four main sub-processes characterizing concentration in sport performance.

The first of these sub-processes is related to the selection of relevant stimuli. This sub-process has been described as a 'moderator variable', moderating between the acquisition of relevant information and the actions subsequently undertaken by the player. Such actions are usually based on a selective commitment that determines, for instance, a footballer's preference of certain stimuli over others (Memmert, 2009). This sub-process explains how environmental stimulation is selected by players and how this selection is dependent upon their competences, their personal condition, and the specific context arising during the course of a match.

The second sub-process concerns the mechanisms enabling players to focus on two or more sources of information at the same time. This sub-process is usually investigated via the methodological design of dual task conditions, which allows – for example – to measure basic attention performance of a secondary task while performing a primary task, or to quantify the effects of distraction on performance. This sub-process often, but not always, involves forms of inattentional blindness (Simons & Chabris, 1999), whereby if attention is kept on an object (e.g. the trajectory of the ball), the player often fails to notice an action (e.g. a free teammate nearby), even if it is right in front of them.[4]

The third sub-process concerns the relation between performance and activation levels. It is therefore all about individuating how to maintain the right focus when pressure builds up and when athletes get tired. Research has shown that in order for athletes to reach the optimal individual level (or best performance), activation needs to be at a moderate level of arousal (Martens & Landers, 1970).

The fourth sub-process refers to the orientation towards salient stimuli and is described as the capacity to respond, in the shortest amount of time, to a relevant stimulus. This sub-process mainly relates to the players' flexibility to re-orient the focus of their concentration in the visual space. For instance, an experienced footballer may successfully predict the outcome of a future chain of events based on the observation of a single relevant cue and moves accordingly to anticipate that future

---

4 E.g. www.youtube.com/watch?v=IGQmdoK_ZfY (last accessed April 2018).

action. In contrast, less experienced footballers will lack this capacity and instead will need time to think, which is sequential in character and requires them passing through each step in a chain of events. As a result, these less experienced footballers are normally unable to successfully predict future actions from a single isolated cue.

Having described and explained the role of concentration in sport performance we next turn to analyse the functions of self-talk. It has been suggested (Zinsser, Bunker, & Williams, 2001, see also the first section above) that self-talk has two main functions: (i) to help create statements relevant to technical instructions, tactical choices and kinaesthesis (this is known as instructional self-talk), and (ii) to create statements that are instrumental to boost self-confidence, efforts, and the creation of positive mood (this is known as motivational self-talk). A number of studies have explored these two dimensions of self-talk and their potential relations (Zetou, Nikolaos, & Evaggelos, 2014). It is to these studies that we now briefly turn.

Rushall and colleagues demonstrated the importance of using key words related to mood states, task-relevant sentences, and positive statements to increase sport players' performances (Rushall 1989; Rushall, Hall, & Rushall, 1988). Hardy, Jones, and Gould (1996) showed that self-talk is crucial to sport performance because it controls anxiety, increases motivation, and triggers appropriate action. Zinnser, Bunker, and Williams (2006) found that self-talk facilitates learning, improves task performance, boosts self-confidence, and helps achieve optimal arousal. In addition, Gould, Finch, and Jackson (1993) found that the most common technique used by top skating athletes was instructional self-talk. Instructional self-talk has also been reported to be highly beneficial for tennis players' volleying (Landin & Hebert, 1999) as well as for 100 m sprinting (Mallett & Hanrahan, 1997).

Other researchers have looked at the influence of instructional versus motivational self-talk on various motor skills (Theodorakis, Weinberg, Natsis, Douma, & Kazakas, 2000). Instructional self-talk was reported to be more effective than motivational self-talk for fine motor skills, involving small movements that occur in the wrists, hands, fingers, feet, and toes. Both motivational and instructional self-talk were found to be equally effective for motor skills requiring strength and endurance (Theodorakis et al., 2000). All these studies have thus contributed to raise awareness on the importance of self-talk for achieving top sport performance.

Having discussed the role of concentration and self-talk in sport performance we next focus on their specific role in football.

## Concentration in football

According to the attentional style approach originally proposed by Nideffer (1985) and adapted to football by Pain (2016),[5] footballers must be able to broaden or narrow the focus of their attention quickly and appropriately in response to specific match situations. Under conditions of intense psychological pressure footballers have little time to devote to the rational analysis of a situation (e.g. pass the ball rather than shoot). This is because the speed of the game requires them to act fast, formulating thoughts within a few milliseconds. Consequently, high pressure match

5 Pain's model (2016) emphasizes the role played by specific cognitive processes, particularly concentration, in the development of elite performance. This model has been adopted by the Football Association (FA) and by many football academies around the world.

conditions must be extensively practised during training until the players' responses to such situations become fully automated. This is instrumental to allow the players to focus on playing the game without the need of constantly assessing what is best in a specific situation. In practical terms, this means that a decision and therefore a behaviour must be taken and implemented while the ball is in motion and it is in these types of situations that the differences between amateurs and experts is evident. While the amateur typically focuses on the technical execution of the task, the expert is typically more oriented towards the tactical components of his/her actions. The reason is that years of training have prepared the footballer for this situation and the player has mastered the technique which has become fully automatized (Christensen, Sutton, & McIlwain, 2016).

A number of studies have compared novices and expert performances (Lum, Enns, & Pratt 2002). In football (Memmert, 2009; Williams, Davids, Burwitz, & Williams, 1993), research has shown that expert players are typically more oriented to observe other players without the ball (environmental focus), whereas less experienced footballers focus their attention on the ball and on teammates to whom they could pass it (skill focus). Furthermore, highly skilled athletes analyse only a few relevant elements of the game for a longer duration compared to amateurs, who instead attempt to process a large amount of information over a restricted period of time. Thus, it seems it is not just the amount of attention or concentration that is important in achieving top performance (accurately and quickly); but rather the fact that concentration must be complemented by the skill to locate and select the appropriate environmental focus (Williams, Davids, & Williams, 1999). In football, this involves the ability to selectively concentrate (as quickly as possible) on the most significant environmental signals; those that allow the player to 'read the game', that is, to anticipate the opponents' actions.

Before concluding this subsection, it is important to reflect on the influence that emotions may have on selective concentration. One approach at our disposal to try to understand the relationship between emotion and concentration is Hanin's (2000) Individual Zone of Optimal Functioning (IZOF). The IZOF model (Hanin, 2000) asserts that emotion is a key component of the psychobiosocial state characterizing human functioning. The model states that each athlete has an individual zone of optimal activation (IZOF) characterizing his/her best performances and aims to describe the relationship between emotional experiences and relative success in sporting tasks. Five basic dimensions (form, content, intensity, time, and context) are used in this model to describe individually optimal and dysfunctional structure (Robazza, Pellizzari, & Hanin, 2004) and to map the influence of positively/negatively toned emotions, personal metaphors, and physical sensations on performance before during and after sporting events (Ruiz, Raglin, & Hanin, 2017).

Many psychological programmes have used the IZOF model to teach individual players how to enter the zone of optimal activation (for a review see Ruiz et al., 2017). However, to our knowledge, the IZOF model has not been applied to football so far. Nonetheless, we believe that there are potential benefits of using this model among footballers. For example, the IZOF model could be used to create a balanced level of anxiety which would allow the players to concentrate and therefore perform to their best, thereby avoiding the detrimental effect taking place on their performance when they are out of their optimal 'zone' of activation.

## Self-talk in football

Self-talk, as we have seen above, may affect sport performance. A number of studies (e.g. Hatzigeorgiadis, Theodorakis, & Zourbanos, 2004; Zourbanos, Hatzigeorgiadis, Bardas, & Theodorakis, 2013) have found a positive correlation between performance enhancement, positive self-talk (which boosts confidence and belief in one's ability), and instructional self-talk (which diverts the focus of attention on to certain elements of a movement to increase attentional focus, thereby helping execution). However, there is a potential methodological problem affecting many studies on self-talk and sport performance. Many of these studies have not been conducted in real performance contexts; rather they have been conducted in laboratory-based settings examining performances such as specific motor tasks (e.g. vertical jump), aspects of more complex sports (e.g. forehand drive in tennis), or in simulated competitions (e.g. 100 m, 1-mile running) (Theodorakis, Hatzigeorgiadis, & Zourbanos, 2012). Given the lack of research in real performance contexts it is quite difficult to draw clear and definite conclusions on the role that self-talk may play in football.

However, Daftari, Fauzee, and Akbari (2010) in a seminal study (which awaits replication) examined the perceived positive and negative effects of self-talk on football performance on Iranian elite-level football players (members of the national team). The participants of this study were 25 Iranian male professional footballers (mean age 27 years). The footballers were presented with an open-ended questionnaire which solicited information about perceived effects of self-talk in three occasions: before the match, during the match, and after the match. The results demonstrated that the perceived effects of self-talk on professional footballers in real performance contexts can be categorized in two main categories: positive and negative.

Positive effects comprised more than 80% of the perceived effects of self-talk, while negative effects comprised less than 20% of the responses. The three most cited positive effects of self-talk were: 'it enhances coordination with teammates (15.6%)', 'it enhances focus and attention (12.5%)', 'it promotes decision-making skills (11.4%)'. The results indicate that the perceived effects of self-talk among these participants were to: (i) increase players' coordination through mental rehearsal of critical situations; (ii) enhance athletes' concentration and sharpen the accuracy of their movements; (iii) boost their ability to make correct decision with precision in the shortest time.

Data from Table 18.1 were then reorganized (Table 18.2) into three subcategories (*cognitive, emotional,* and *executive*) that the authors thought would more precisely indicate the perceived effects of self-talk at mental and behavioural levels.

These findings, besides confirming the perceived importance of self-talk in football, also provide clarity about the mental skills that may be influenced by self-talk. These results also show that self-talk can be used as a controlling mechanism to prevent negative consequences (such as disputes with referees or conflicts with other players) that can significantly impair performance. In addition, these findings have important implications for both footballers and coaches. Being aware that self-talk can promote efficiency on the field allows both players and coaches to work on self-talk skills to help gain desirable results.

Having reviewed the role of self-talk in football we next focus on the most important moment of any football performance (the act of scoring a goal) and look at what concentration and self-talk can tell us about it.

*Table 18.1* Rank of the players' cited positive and negative effects of self-talk on their performance

| Footballers' perceived effects of self-talk | No. of responses | Percentage for category |
|---|---|---|
| *Positive effects* | | |
| It enhances coordination with teammates | 30 | 15.6 |
| It enhances focus and attention | 24 | 12.5 |
| It promotes decision-making skill | 22 | 11.4 |
| It decreases anxiety and psyches up | 16 | 8.3 |
| It motivates to increase efforts | 15 | 7.8 |
| It reduces behaviours having negative impact | 14 | 7.2 |
| It helps to cope with defeat in post-match time | 12 | 6.2 |
| It decreases reaction time | 11 | 5.7 |
| It helps rehearse match tactics | 9 | 4.6 |
| **TOTAL** | **154** | **80.2** |
| *Negative effects* | | |
| It increases stress level | 16 | 8.3 |
| It can weaken confidence | 13 | 6.7 |
| It discourages by dwelling on significant others' negative thoughts | 9 | 4.6 |
| **TOTAL** | **38** | **19.7** |

Source: adapted from Daftari et al. (2010).

*Table 18.2* Frequency distributions of effects of ST at mental and behavioural levels

| Category | No. of responses | Percentage for category |
|---|---|---|
| *Cognitive effects* | | |
| It enhances focus and attention | 24 | 12.5 |
| It promotes decision-making skill | 22 | 11.4 |
| It decreases reaction time | 18 | 9.3 |
| It helps rehearse match tactics | 9 | 4.6 |
| **TOTAL** | **73** | **38.0** |
| *Emotional effects* | | |
| It motivates to increase efforts | 15 | 7.8 |
| It helps to cope with defeat in post-match time | 12 | 6.2 |
| It decreases anxiety and psyches up | 11 | 5.7 |
| It can weaken confidence | 13 | 6.7 |
| It can increases stress level | 16 | 8.3 |
| It discourages by dwelling on significant others' negative thoughts | 9 | 4.6 |
| **TOTAL** | **76** | **39.5** |
| *Behavioural effects* | | |
| It enhances coordination with teammates | 28 | 14.5 |
| It reduces behaviours having negative impact | 14 | 7.2 |
| **TOTAL** | **42** | **21.8** |

Source: adapted from Daftari et al. (2010).

## Goals as tests of concentration and self-talk

Arguably, one of the most important statistics in a football game concerns the number of goals scored and conceded. Carlo Ancellotti, one of the most successful coaches of all time, claimed that a goal represents the peak of a match and the moment that can have a huge impact on a team's confidence (Higham, Harwood, & Cale, 2005).

Ray Clemence, another football coach, echoed this understanding:

> Just before half-time, just after half-time and depending on where you are in the game, the last 10 minutes of the game as well are key times in a match. Just before the half-time because there might be an element of mental fatigue rather just physical because you've worked so hard maybe for 40 minutes. If you concede a goal just before half-time, you have no time to recover from it. You feel deflated because there's no chance to come back straight away. So, it is a vital time. Just half-time is also important.
>
> (Ray Clemence, in Higham et al., 2005, p. 96)

These comments show that during a football match there seems to be specific phases or key moments that are more crucial or relevant than others and that scoring a goal during these phases may have a huge impact on the team's morale.

In order to test the reliability of these assertions, Cei and D'Ottavio (2009) investigated the distribution of goals in Italy's Serie A football for the 2007–2008 season. The findings show that most of the goals were scored in the last 15 minutes of the game, at the end of the first half-time, and at the beginning of the second half-time. Cei, Tonelli, Pantanella, and D'Ottavio (2011) partially extended these findings. The authors looked at the distributions of goals in four major European championships (Premier League, Serie A, La Liga, and Eredivisie) for three consecutive seasons. The results showed that the goals deciding the outcome were mostly scored (69% for a draw or a win) in the last 30 minutes of the matches (Figure 18.1).

These findings seem to empirically confirm the comments made by Ancellotti and Clemence (that there are certain phases in any football performance than are more crucial than others) and, therefore, highlight the importance of maintaining concentration at these key moments of the match.

In the history of football there have been teams that have performed extraordinarily well under pressure exploiting the capacity to concentrate in key moments of the match (Swann et al., 2016). One of such teams was Manchester United. Under the guidance of Sir Alex Ferguson, the team enjoyed numerous victories and concentration and determination became two of its defining features. In his autobiography, Ferguson (2013) confessed that the team's plan when losing was to avoid negative thoughts, keep a high degree of focus, and wage a high-intensity attack in the last 15 minutes of the match. This strategy often paid off, such as against Bayern Munich of Germany in the 1999 UEFA Champions League Final. Manchester United's approach to the game clearly showed how a great focus on task-related cues and on performance improvement in preference to winning could directly affect the result of a high-profile football match.

Similar considerations can be made with respect to self-talk. Gianluca Vialli, former Italian footballer and Chelsea manager, noted that in negative situations one

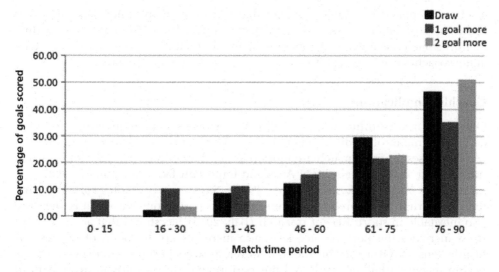

*Figure 18.1* When the goals are scored. Data from three Italian Serie A championships.

Source: reprinted from 'The analysis of the football team through the analysis of the timing goals' by A. Cei, C., Tonelli, L. Pantanella, and S. D'Ottavio 2011. *Movimento*, 27, 7–18. Copyright year 2011, by Edizioni Luigi Pozzi, reprinted with permission.

must remain lucid: 'I never played in a match where, when we had the momentum against us, I thought there's nothing we can do about it. That never happened to me. I have always thought we could turn it around' (Higham et al., 2005, p. 199). The behaviours and mental approaches a player must adopt in these situations are well explained by Mark Hughes, former Manchester United player and Welsh manager, who said: 'If you're are getting stretched you will go back to basics, play tighter, close the lines up, get more compact and reorganize and think steady the ship and then go again once it's calmed down' (Higham et al., 2005, p. 189).

To teach players how to use self-talk to keep a positive approach when difficult circumstances arise, Pain (2016) suggested the adoption of three steps. In the first step, a player writes down in a log instances of negative self-talk that occurred during the match and then discusses these instances with a sport psychology consultant. The goal here is to learn how to move away from these negative thoughts via rational dialogue (e.g. change 'I must win' to 'I really want to win' or 'I must win the approval of others' to 'It is nice but not essential to gain their approval'). Second, the player must write down in his/her log positive affirmations. This approach helps to avoid rumination over negative thoughts (e.g. 'I always make the same errors'). The third step consists in recording a player's pre-match ideal performances and associating them with music that triggers positive thoughts. The successful implementation of this approach requires a minimum of 3 months of practice. Pain (2016) reported a case study where a gifted midfielder, at the end of this psychological training, became less critical and more able to find the positive aspects of his performance by being more rational and balanced. Moreover, this player's negative perfectionism was reduced, allowing him to be more positive in pursuing his goals.

Having analysed the role of concentration and self-talk in football performance we can now move on to the second goal of our chapter: providing practitioners with a series of applied coaching strategies that can be used to build more successful coaching programmes (both in team sports and in football). To do so, we first identify some crucial game factors influencing football performance and then look at how coaches can intervene to satisfy some of these game demands.

## Coaching implications

One of the factors influencing football performance is game momentum. As noted earlier, a number of studies (Cei et al., 2011; Higham et al., 2005) have shown that certain phases during a match are more relevant than others and therefore concentration must always remain high. A second important factor affecting football performance is stress (Yerkes & Dodson, 1908). Stress is a psychological factor that tends to disrupt the homeostasis of our body. It is part of our life and it is therefore also inevitable in sport. Recent research (Bali, 2015) has shown that as the level of stress increases the performance level also increases, to the point of eustress, or healthy tension. Over this threshold, however, as stress becomes overwhelming, the person reaches a fatigue point and her performance levels starts to drop. A third factor influencing football performance is anxiety. Often anxiety is an unpleasant state of mind, which disrupts emotional reactivity and causes nervousness. However, anxiety is also an essential ingredient of any competitive situation (Hanin, 2000). Without a certain level of anxiety (neither too high, nor too low) there cannot be competitive performance. Thus, anxiety is also conductive to elite football performance. A fourth factor affecting football performance is the players' capacity to refocus on the present once the team has scored or has conceded a goal (Redwood-Brown, Sunderland, Minniti, & O'Donoghue, 2017). This fourth factor often depends on a fifth factor, which is the capacity to control and regulate tension and inner aggression (Isberg, 2000).

In order to deal with these factors, and ultimately improve player performance, coaches can intervene with a series of strategies targeting both self-talk and concentration (Swann, Moran, & Piggott, 2015). For instance, coaches can enhance self-talk in terms of process and content. The process refers to the structure of self-talk:[6]

- the sentences must be short and specific,
- proffered in the first person of the present tense,
- their contents must be positive,
- their meanings have to be significant (with a goal),
- the sentences must be planned and repeated often and in advance,
- when negative thoughts arise, they must be substituted with positive affirmations,
- cue words can be learned and practised as reminders to cope with stressful moments.

The content of the statements must also be focused:

- on the actions to perform and not exclusively on the results,
- on players' behaviours (because they are the only things they can control),

---

6 These strategies can be applied to many sport teams. However, they are also effective in football and this is the reason why we discuss them here.

- on motivation or on technical instructions,
- on coach advice,
- on team behaviours (to keep playing high-intensity attacking football),
- on the team's motto (players can identify cue words to boost their morale and cohesiveness).

Concentration can also be improved through self-talk. The use of certain statements and cue words, for instance, allows the players to select the information needed to keep up motivation (maintain high levels of confidence and a sense of control over their performance) and to stay focused (being fully absorbed in the task to the point that they are unaware of the crowd) (Krane & Williams, 2006). This can also be done in the locker room just before the game, where players – through mental repetitions – learn to relax and distinguish between relevant cues and non-relevant stimuli (Williams & Krane, 2015).

It is also fundamental that players – ahead of the match – develop an optimal emotional balance and a heightened self-awareness. This can be achieved through specific meditation exercises, which the coach can present to the players during training (Williams & Krane, 2015). The goal here is to maintain composure, to stop unhelpful thoughts, to keep the adrenaline flow going, and to have a positive mental attitude, which allows the player to be in control of the game and to handle any critical situation that arises (Swann et al., 2016).

## Conclusion

In this chapter we defined concentration and self-talk. We investigated their relation and explored their contribution to sport performance. We focused on the specific role that concentration and self-talk play in football. We analysed the peak moment of any football performance (the act of scoring a goal) and looked at how to use concentration and self-talk to increase the chances of scoring a goal (or not conceding it). We concluded by providing a series of coaching strategies aimed at improving, through concentration and self-talk, performance in footballers.

It is hoped that this chapter will spark new interest in these topics among scholars and practitioners and that it will provide new theoretical grounds for more detailed understandings of the role of concentration and self-talk in football.

## Acknowledgements

The authors acknowledge the editors of this collection, especially Erkut Konter, for the invaluable support throughout the preparation of this chapter. Thanks also to the anonymous reviewers for their sharp and helpful comments and feedback on early drafts of this manuscript. Mirko Farina expresses his appreciation to the British Academy for the Humanities and Social Sciences and to King's College, London for generously financing his research.

# References

Bali, A. (2015). Psychological factors affecting sports performance. *International Journal of Physical Education, Sports and Health, 1*(6), 92–95.

Beilock, S. L., Carr, T. H., MacMahon, C., & Starkes, J. L. (2002). When paying attention becomes counterproductive: Impact of divided versus skill-focused attention on novice and experienced performance of sensorimotor skills. *Journal of Experimental Psychology: Applied, 8*, 6–16.

Blumenstein, B., & Lidor, R. (2007). The road to the Olympic Games: A four-year psychological preparation program. *Athletic Insight, 9*, 15–28.

Burton, D., & Raedeke, T. D. (2008). *Sport psychology for coaches.* Champaign, IL: Human Kinetics.

Cei, A., & D'Ottavio, S. (2009). Abilità di concentrazione sotto stress. *L'allenatore, 5*, 26–32.

Cei, A., Tonelli, C., Pantanella, L., & D'Ottavio, S. (2011). The analysis of the football team through the analysis of the timing goals. *Movimento, 27*, 7–18.

Christensen, W., Sutton, J., & McIlwain, D. J. (2016). Cognition in skilled action: Meshed control and the varieties of skill experience. *Mind & Language, 31*(1), 37–66.

Daftari, O., Fauzee, S. O., & Akbari, A. (2010). Effects of self-talk on football players performance in official competition. *Researcher in Sport Science Quarterly, 1*, 29–37.

Ferguson, A. (2013). *My autobiography.* London, England: Hodder & Stoughton/Hachette.

Gould, D., Finch, L. M., & Jackson, S. A. (1993). Coping strategies used by national champion figure skaters. *Research Quarterly for Exercise and Sport, 64*, 453–468.

Hanin, Y. L. (2000). *Emotions in sport.* Champaign, IL: Human Kinetics.

Hardy, J. (2006). Speaking clearly: A critical review of the self-talk literature. *Psychology of Sport and Exercise, 7*, 81–97.

Hardy, J., Begley, K., & Blanchfield, A. W. (2015). It's good but it's not right: Instructional self-talk and skilled performance. *Journal of Applied Sport Psychology, 27*(2), 132–139.

Hardy, J., Hall, C. R., & Hardy, L. (2005). Quantifying athlete self-talk. *Journal of Sport Sciences, 23*, 905–917.

Hardy, L., Jones, G., & Gould, D. (1996). *Understanding psychological preparation for sport: Theory and practice of elite performers.* New York, NY: Wiley.

Harwood, C., & Anderson, R. (2015). *Coaching psychological skills in youth football: Developing the 5Cs.* Oakamoor, England: Bennion Kearny.

Hatzigeorgiadis, A., Theodorakis, Y., & Zourbanos, N. (2004). Self-talk in the swimming pool: The effects of self-talk on thought content and performance on water polo tasks. *Journal of Applied Sport Psychology, 16*, 138–150.

Higham, A., Harwood, C., & Cale, A. (2005). *Momentum in soccer: Controlling the game.* Leeds, England: Coachwise.

Isberg, L. (2000). Anger, aggressive behavior, and athletic performance. *Emotions in Sport, 1*, 13–33.

Krane, V., & Williams, J. M. (2006). Psychological characteristics of peak performance. In J. M. Williams (Ed.), *Applied sport psychology: Personal growth to peak performance* (5th ed., pp. 207–227). New York, NY: McGraw-Hill.

Landin, D., & Hebert, E. P. (1999). The influence of ST on the performance of skilled female tennis players. *Journal of Applied Sport Psychology, 11*, 263–282.

Lum, J., Enns, J. T., & Pratt, J. (2002). Visual orienting in college athletes: Explorations of athlete type and gender. *Research Quarterly for Exercise and Sport, 73*, 156–167.

Mallett, C. J., & Hanrahan, S. J. (1997). Race modeling: An effective cognitive strategy for the 100 m sprinter? *The Sport Psychologist, 11*, 72–85.

Martens, R., & Landers, D. M. (1970). Motor performance under stress: A test of the inverted-U hypothesis. *Journal of Personality and Social Psychology, 16*, 29–37.

Memmert, D. (2009). Pay attention! A review of visual attentional expertise in sport. *International Review of Sport and Exercise Psychology, 2*, 119–138.

Moran, A. (1997). *The psychology of concentration in sport performers.* London, England: Routledge.

Nideffer, R. M. (1985). *Athletes' guide to mental training.* Champaign, IL: Human Kinetics.

Pain, M. (2016). Mental interventions. In T. Strudwick (Ed.), *Soccer science* (pp. 389–414). Champaign, IL: Human Kinetics.

Redwood-Brown, A. J., Sunderland, C. A., Minniti, A. M., & O'Donoghue, P. G. (2017). Perceptions of psychological momentum of elite soccer players. *International Journal of Sport and Exercise Psychology*, 1–17.

Robazza, C., Pellizzari, M., & Hanin, Y. (2004). Emotion self-regulation and athletic performance: An application of the IZOF model. *Psychology of Sport and Exercise, 5*, 379–404.

Ruiz, M. C., Raglin, J. S., & Hanin, Y. L. (2017). The individual zones of optimal functioning (IZOF) model (1978–2014): Historical overview of its development and use. *International Journal of Sport and Exercise Psychology, 15*, 41–63.

Rushall, B. S. (1989). Sport psychology: The key to sporting excellence. *International Journal of Sport Psychology, 20*, 165–190.

Rushall, B. S., Hall, M., & Rushall, A. (1988). Effects of three types of thought content instructions of skiing performance. *The Sport Psychologist, 2*, 283–297.

Simons, D. J., & Chabris, C. F. (1999). Gorillas in our midst: Sustained inattentional blindness for dynamic events. *Perception, 28*, 1059–1074.

Smith, D. J. (2003). A framework for understanding the training process leading to elite performance. *Sports Medicine, 33*(15), 1103–1126.

Swann, C., Crust, L., Jackman, P., Vella, S. A., Allen, M. S., & Keegan, R. (2016). Performing under pressure: Exploring the psychological state underlying clutch performance in sport. *Journal of Sports Sciences*, 1–9.

Swann, C., Moran, A., & Piggott, D. (2015). Defining elite athletes: Issues in the study of expert performance in sport psychology. *Psychology of Sport and Exercise, 16*, 3–14.

Theodorakis, Y., Hatzigeorgiadis, A., & Zourbanos, N. (2012). Cognitions: Self-talk and performance. In S. Murphy (Ed.), *Oxford handbook of sport and performance psychology* (pp. 191–212). New York, NY: Oxford University Press.

Theodorakis, Y., Weinberg, R., Natsis, P., Douma, I., & Kazakas, P. (2000). The effects of motivational versus instructional self-talk on improving motor performance. *The Sport Psychologist, 14*, 253–272.

Van Raalte, J. L., Vincent, A., & Brewer, B. W. (2016). Self-talk: Review and sport-specific model. *Psychology of Sport and Exercise, 22*, 139–148.

Vernacchia, R. (2003). *Inner strength: The mental dynamics of athletic performance.* Palo Alto, CA: Warde Publishers.

Williams, A. M., Davids, K., Burwitz, L., & Williams, J. G. (1993). Cognitive knowledge and soccer performance. *Perceptual and Motor Skills, 76*, 579–593.

Williams, A. M., Davids, K., & Williams, J. G. (1999). *Visual perception and action in sport.* London, England: Taylor & Francis.

Williams, J. M., & Krane, V. (2015). *Applied sport psychology: Personal growth to peak performance.* New York, NY: McGraw Hill.

Woodman, T., & Hardy, L. (2003). The relative impact of cognitive anxiety and self-confidence upon sport performance: A meta-analysis. *Journal of Sports Sciences, 21*(6), 443–457.

Yerkes, R. M., & Dodson, J. D. (1908). The relation of strength of stimulus to rapidity of habit formation. *Journal of Comparative Neurology and Psychology, 18*, 459–482.

Zetou, E., Nikolaos, V., & Evaggelos, B. (2014). The effect of instructional self-talk on performance and learning the backstroke of young swimmers and on the perceived functions of it. *Journal of Physical Education and Sport, 14*(1), 27–35.

Zinsser, N., Bunker, L., & Williams, J. M. (2001). Cognitive techniques for building confidence and enhancing performance. In J. M. Williams (Ed.), *Applied sport psychology: Personal growth to peak performance* (4th ed., pp. 284–311). Mountain View, CA: Mayfield.

Zinsser, N., Bunker, L., & Williams, J. M. (2006). Cognitive techniques for building confidence and enhancing performance. In J. M. Williams (Ed.), *Applied sport psychology: Personal growth to peak performance* (pp. 349–381). New York, NY: McGraw-Hill.

Zourbanos, N., Hatzigeorgiadis, A., Bardas, B., & Theodorakis, Y. (2013). The effects of self-talk on dominant and non-dominant arm performance on a handball task in primary physical education students. *The Sport Psychologist, 27*, 71–176.

# 19 Applied behavioural analysis in top-level football

## Theory and application

*Rasmus Tornberg, Henrik Gustafsson, and Daniel Ekvall*

**Abstract**

Despite a strong research base and the potential for effective behaviour modification, the application of behavioural sport psychology in team sport is rarely described in the literature. Therefore, drawing on our experiences as sport psychology consultants the aim of this chapter is to provide a description of how applied behaviour analysis (ABA; Baer, Wolf, & Risley, 1968, 1987) can be applied in top-level football. ABA has extensive support from other contexts including behavioural problems in youth and organizational development and we have found it very useful in our work with athletes. First, behavioural sport psychology in relation to cognitive behavioural therapy (CBT) and psychological skills training (PST) will be discussed. Second, the seven dimensions of ABA will be described using examples from the football. Finally, the application of these dimensions is highlighted in a case of an elite football player experiencing anxiety and self-confidence issues. We also summarize the benefits of adopting a behavioural approach in football. With so few descriptions of ABA in sport, we hope this chapter could provide a useful start for practitioners.

Behavioural sport psychology is the use of behavioural analysis principles to enhance the performance and well-being of athletes, coaches, and others (e.g. parents) involved in sport (Martin & Tkachuk, 2000). Since the 1970s, PST in sport has primarily been dominated by a social-cognitive perspective and self-instructional skills developed in the early CBT literature (cf. Gardner & Moore, 2006). CBT has a substantial evidence base supporting the efficacy of its treatments for a number of psychological problems including for example anxiety disorders and anger control problems and is effective across age groups and populations (cf. Hofmann, Asmundson, & Beck, 2013). CBT is an umbrella term for a variety of methods combining principles from both behavioural (e.g. Farmer & Chapman, 2015) and cognitive therapy (e.g. Beck, 1976), in order to achieve changes in individuals' emotions, cognitions, and behaviours (cf. Hofmann et al., 2013). Within the applied field of sport psychology, CBT can be viewed as a form of cognitive behavioural training (Gustafsson & Lundqvist, 2016), with the aim of modifying dysfunctional performance-related behaviours (e.g. avoiding certain anxiety-provoking situations), increasing adaptive behaviours (e.g. following the game plan or taking the penalty kick despite experiences of anxiety), or learning new functional skills (e.g. use the 'weak' foot during competitive matches). By using the term 'training' instead of 'therapy' we avoid the risk of a potentially negative connotation of the term (e.g. therapy being associated with mental illness).

In its infancy, PST was grounded in the CBT literature and subsequently influenced by cognitive theory (Whelan, Mahoney, & Meyers, 1991). Although several methods (e.g. cognitive restructuring, imagery, and goal setting) are included under the CBT umbrella, scholars have argued (Gustafsson, Lundqvist, & Tod, 2017) that relatively little attention has been given to techniques from the behaviour therapy branch of CBT (for an exception see Luiselli & Reed, 2011). Also, critical voices argue that self-control-related techniques are dated, lack evidence for their efficacy, and are incongruent with knowledge obtained in contemporary research (Martin, Vause, & Schwartzman, 2005). As Gardner and Moore (2006, p. 8) argue, 'It appears that the field of sport psychology has simply not noticed the recent advancements in behavioural psychology.' In light of this reasoning, several advantages exist for sport psychologists considering adoption of behavioural theories and CBT applications. A fundamental aspect of behavioural psychology is ABA in which behavioural principles are systematically applied to deal with problematic behaviours and to help individuals reach their potential (Baldwin & Baldwin, 2000). The effectiveness of ABA in various contexts includes organizational effectiveness, problematic youth behaviour, and social skills (Austin & Carr, 2000). ABA is an evidence-based method and although the number of examples from sport is limited (for an exception see Martin & Tkachuk, 2000) it is well suited for working with athletes and teams. This chapter will describe how ABA can be used in top-level football to handle counterproductive behaviours and expand players' behavioural repertoire.

## Applied behaviour analysis

Applied behavioural analysis has been defined as 'the science in which tactics derived from the principles of behaviour are applied systematically to improve socially significant behaviour and experimentation is used to identify the variables responsible for behaviour change' (Cooper, Heron, & Heward, 2014a, p. 40). Baer et al. (1968) stated that ABA should be *applied, behavioural, analytic, technological, conceptually systematic, effective,* and display *generality*. Although these elements were formulated decades ago, they remain pertinent in defining ABA (Cooper et al., 2014a). The seven dimensions are presented briefly below.

According to Baer et al. (1968), the construct *applied* underscores the importance of the behaviour to the context. Applied behaviour analysts are focused on behaviours that enhance and improve people's lives; to meet this criterion analysts select behaviours that are socially significant to the subject (Cooper et al., 2014a). Examples of significant behaviours in top-level football could relate to performance, practice, group dynamics, well-being, and career development domains.

The second dimension, *behavioural*, emphasizes that application concerns the issue of how to encourage individuals to *do* something effectively (Baer et al., 1968). From an applied standpoint, there is little value in telling a player to be 'more responsible'. Rather, the coach should express the feedback in behaviours that can be observed. In the realm of top-level football, significant behaviours might include: giving a teammate advice, or maintaining strength and conditioning regimens during competitive breaks.

An intervention is *analytical, the third dimension,* when the practitioner can demonstrate a functional relation between a certain procedure and the behavioural outcome (Fisher, Groff, & Roane, 2011). A coach that knows exactly how to speak to a furious player in order to calm him down is therefore analytic in this sense; he knows which words to use, when to say them, and why this works.

Furthermore, an intervention is considered *technological* if its methods are sufficiently described so replication is possible (Baer et al., 1968). If the method adopted cannot be replicated, it will be of little value to practitioners. Even if replication in a football environment is hard, due to the complex interaction of individual and situational factors, a thoroughly described approach grounded in well-established behavioural principles would enable coaches to better evaluate and share methods. By doing so, the focus is on the method and not the 'personality' of the coach and/or the players.

A fifth dimension of ABA is that it should be *conceptually systematic,* that is, procedures should stem from basic behavioural principles (Baer et al., 1968). For example, a description of how a midfielder can improve his behaviour when he is furious on the pitch may be good in a technological way, but referring it to '**reinforcement**[1] of replacement behaviours' and '**counter conditioning**' is better. Relating procedures to behavioural principles shows that it stems from a 'discipline rather than a collection of tricks' and thereby facilitates replication (Baer et al., 1968, p. 96).

A sixth dimension of ABA concerns how to influence an individual to do something *effectively* (Baer et al., 1968). When using the term 'effective', Baer and colleagues (1968) emphasize the practical value of an intervention. If a football player reports that she feels more confident after working with a sport psychologist but does not act with confidence, the intervention wouldn't be considered effective if the goal was to improve her performance. According to Baer et al. (1968), it is those who must deal with the behaviour that are ideally positioned to determine whether the behaviour change has been sufficient in relation to the context.

A final dimension of ABA relates to the *generality* of a particular intervention. An intervention is considered to have generality, if it results in behaviour change that: (a) is durable over time, (b) appears in other settings, and (c) spreads to other behaviours (Baer et al., 1968). As the overall goal of ABA is improvement of socially important behaviours, the more general the improvement, the better (Baer et al., 1968). For example, a football player who has struggled with low confidence on the pitch works on his behaviour. After the intervention, he can not only perform the desired behaviours (e.g. challenge an opponent) in practice but also in different games during different circumstances (e.g. not depending on opponent, time in the game and result).

Working from an ABA perspective is a systematic process that proceeds through a series of steps stemming from single-subject research designs. In these designs, the subject acts as his/her own control and the effect of the intervention can be assessed by repeatedly measuring relevant behaviours before (baseline), during, and after the intervention (Luiselli, 2011). According to Roane, Ringdahl, Kelley, and Glover (2011), single-subject designs are well suited for ABA purposes because their goal is to show functional control in which change in the dependent variable (the target behaviour), results from implementation of the intervention. Although various steps

---

1 All words in bold are described in the appendix in the end of the chapter.

in implementing ABA processes have been described (e.g. Farmer & Chapman, 2015; Sundel & Sundel, 2005), several common features can be identified: (1) behaviour assessment, (2) measurement of target behaviours, (3) intervention, and (4) evaluation. In the following section, these steps are described and applied to a case with a top-level football player.

### From theory to practice: a case example of a top-level player with performance anxiety and lack of confidence

William was a 20-year-old midfielder (right wing) in a club in the Swedish Premier League. He held high standards for himself, wanting to perform at a high-level game each and every match. In recent weeks, his performance declined, and according to William, the performance decrement was a consequence of heightened competitive anxiety and lack of confidence. His performance anxiety was particularly evident during situations in which William believed that the consequences of a mistake would be substantial (e.g. cup matches and in the end of a tight match). Large crowds also seemed to trigger apprehensive thoughts such as 'what will my teammates think of me if I make a mistake' or 'I can't let my teammates down'. In addition, intense physiological activation, in the form of increased heart rate, stomach aches, and excessive muscle tension became debilitating for William. In an attempt to address the problem, William tried to avoid mistakes by deliberately avoiding the ball, choosing the simplest solution in various situations (e.g. easy pass instead of challenging an opponent), and failing to take shooting opportunities. On certain occasions, William faked injuries to avoid playing altogether. A negative performance spiral ultimately led William and his coach to contact a behavioural sport psychologist.

### Step 1: behavioural assessment

After listening to William's story, the sport psychologist indicated that he interpreted the case as a behaviour problem: William appeared to change his behaviour when he was anxious and had low confidence. Rather than articulating goals related to the reduction of performance anxiety or improvements in self-confidence, William and the sport psychologist agreed that the goal of the intervention should be the promotion of a more offensive playing style. Data was collected from meetings with William in which the sport psychologist asked questions regarding specific football situations in which he experienced problems and about general life issues which might be influencing his on-field performance (e.g. relationships, spare time). Data was also collected from practice and match observations as well as interviews with coaches to ascertain their perspective on William's behaviour. Finally, the medical staff was consulted to rule out any somatic disorders. A problem list with working issues was created based on the data collection. As it appeared that William's life outside of sport was not adversely affecting his sport performance, the focus of the intervention remained on his competitive anxiety and low sport confidence.

*Topographic analysis*

After gathering information, the sport psychologist summarized data that described Williams's behaviour topographically, that is, its physical characteristics (Cooper, Heron, & Heward, 2014b). In this topographic analysis, behaviour was classified as either behavioural excesses or behavioural deficits (Sundel & Sundel, 2005). Behavioural excess can be described as a high frequency of inappropriate behaviour, while behavioural deficit refers to an absence or low frequency of appropriate behaviour (Sundel & Sundel, 2005). The topographical analysis of William's (motor) behaviours is shown in Table 19.1.

As shown in Table 19.1, almost all the identified behaviours are behaviours that William should have in his repertoire, although William and his coach agreed that he often used his behaviours 'out of context'. For example, sometimes he should choose an easy pass instead of challenging the opponent, depending on the situation, but he used his easy pass excessively and in situations when he should challenge or shoot.

*Functional analysis*

After defining the issues in behavioural terms, functional analysis was used to specify functional relations between the behaviour and controlling antecedents/consequences. This analysis provided a logic for the observed behaviours, as well as valuable information regarding antecedents and consequences that could be used for intervention purposes. To conduct a functional analysis, a sport psychologist must have an intimate knowledge regarding key behavioural concepts, such as operant behaviour.[2] Operant behaviour can be defined as 'any behaviour whose future frequency is determined primarily by its history of consequences' (Cooper et al., 2014b, p. 51). Harvard psychologist B. F. Skinner identified two kinds of consequences that have differing effects on behaviour: reinforcement, that increases the likelihood of occurrence, and **punishment**, decreasing the likelihood of

*Table 19.1* Topographical analysis of William's motor behaviours

| Behavioural excesses | Behavioural deficits |
| --- | --- |
| • Pass the ball to his teammate, often backwards<br>• Make himself 'unavailable' by: (a) not calling for the ball, (b) standing still<br>• Making negative remarks<br>• Excessively detailed routines – e.g. putting socks on in certain order<br>• Claims injury even though no evidence of physical damage is present | • Challenge his opponent with the ball<br>• Taking the ball towards opponent's goal<br>• Shoot at the goal<br>• Hold the ball for an extended time<br>• Run in the space between opponent's defenders<br>• Making himself playable by: (a) calling for the ball verbally, (b) showing that he wants the ball (waving), (c) pointing where he wants the ball, and (d) moving away from opponent to give himself some space. |

2 In this chapter, focus is on operant behaviour even though several other behavioural concepts are relevant for this case in this context. For a comprehensive description of behavioural principles see for example Holt and colleagues (2012).

particular behaviours in the future (Holt et al., 2012). For applied behaviour analysis in football, reinforcement is of particular relevance because it provides information about *why* a player may behave in a certain fashion, and this knowledge can be
used for intervention purposes. Furthermore, two types of reinforcement have been
identified: **positive reinforcement**, which occurs when a behaviour is strengthened
by the subsequent presentation of a stimulus, and **negative reinforcement**, which
takes place when a behaviour is strengthened by the subsequent removal of an aversive stimulus (Holt et al., 2012). An example of positive reinforcement is when a
player's passing behaviour increases after making a couple of successful passes in
the beginning of a match. An example of negative reinforcement is when a player is
passing the ball to a teammate instead of shooting, since he got negative remarks
last time he tried which made him feel bad. In ABA, it is important to demonstrate
not only how a behaviour is linked to its consequences, but also to priori stimuli or
antecedents. In doing so, the behaviour analyst can show the logic of the behaviour
and, based on this logic, suggest strategies for development. This functional relation
can be expressed in a three-term contingency (Cooper et al., 2014b), where antecedents (A), behaviours (B), and consequences (C) are shown.[3]

In William's case, the sport psychologist proposed the hypothesis that William
used avoidant behaviours (i.e. behavioural excesses) when he experienced anxiety
and negative cognitions. This way of handling the problematic situations resulted in
feelings of relief since William did not make mistakes and he continued to avoid
challenges (negative reinforcement). Two examples of these situations are shown
below using the three-term contingency:

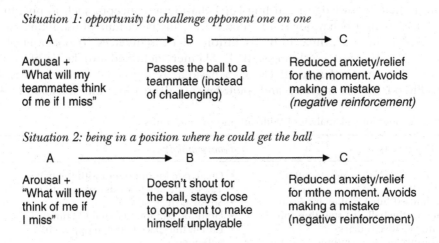

*Situation 1: opportunity to challenge opponent one on one*

A ⟶ B ⟶ C

Arousal +
"What will my
teammates think
of me if I miss"

Passes the ball to a
teammate (instead
of challenging)

Reduced anxiety/relief
for the moment. Avoids
making a mistake
*(negative reinforcement)*

*Situation 2: being in a position where he could get the ball*

A ⟶ B ⟶ C

Arousal +
"What will they
think of me if
I miss"

Doesn't shout for
the ball, stays close
to opponent to make
himself unplayable

Reduced anxiety/relief
for mthe moment. Avoids
making a mistake
*(negative reinforcement)*

In the two examples above, it is evident that the short-term consequence of
reduced anxiety was a positive outcome in the context of the situation (negative
reinforcement). Nonetheless, the behavioural principles highlighted above suggest
the potential for maladaptive outcomes over the long term, in particular a strong
likelihood that William's initial fears and anxiety will likely be maintained and
potentially occur in a variety of competitive situations. Additionally, the maladaptive

---

3 The simplified A-B-C diagram is used in this chapter. For a more comprehensive description of the
  three-term contingency see Sundel and Sundel (2005).

behaviours will likely preclude the possibility that he will attain positive reinforcement such as successful actions (e.g. scoring goals, reach teammate with difficult pass), feelings of joy/pride and praise from coach and teammates. Over time, a lack of positive reinforcement may exacerbate his confidence and anxiety problems.

The sport psychologist also found that certain circumstances intensified William's negative cognitions and emotions. William especially mentioned *important games* and *big crowds* as situations that increased his anxiety. In these situations, he was even more prone to avoid challenges, thus making the 'reward' of not making mistakes even bigger. This value-altering effect of consequences is referred to as *motivating operations* (Michael, 2014).

The sport psychologist provided William and his coach a summary of the topographical and functional analysis, and collectively they decided that the overall behavioural outcome of greatest interest was for William to initiate more offensive play.

### Step 2: measurement of target behaviours

In a complex and ever-changing sport like football, behaviours are often difficult to measure. Hence, a flexible and creative approach is often required to measure target behaviours, even though it is essential to try and reliably measure behaviours despite such challenges. William and the coach agreed to address two behavioural goals: (1) challenging opponents when he had possession of the ball and (2) making himself increasingly 'playable'. These two behaviours were subsequently operationalized in specific behavioural terms. In particular, challenging opponents would be assessed by examining the extent to which William approached his opponent in one-on-one situations, and, when appropriate, try to navigate past him. The behaviour of making himself 'playable' was operationalized by indicating that when the inner midfielder in his team had the ball, William should run into the space between the opponent's left centre-back and wing-back. Although the topographical analysis revealed a wide variety of behaviours, the behaviours just described were selected as a top priority, since it was hypothesized that such behaviours would generalize to other crucial game situations. The coach, William, and the sport psychologist decided that the overall intervention goal was for William to perform the target behaviours in 80% of relevant match situations.

### Baseline measures

In this case, a baseline measure of the target behaviours was difficult to obtain since the subject was aware of the behaviours that would be measured. A baseline was however considered important, since it would make drawing any cause and effect conclusions difficult and limit valuable information that could be used in fostering William's long-term development (e.g. generalization effects). In order to obtain a baseline, video observations were used of William's three latest matches – when he reported high anxiety, low confidence, and a decline in performance. Baseline results showed that in the three matches, William challenged 30, 50, and 30% of possible occasions, and demonstrated 'playability' in 20, 30, and 30% of relevant situations.

*Step 3: intervention*

With a baseline established, the sport psychologist developed an intervention plan based on the topographical and functional analysis previously described. The intervention was as follows:

1   William and the coach were given information (psycho-education) about the functional analysis. The impact of William's avoidant behaviours in intensifying his anxiety and decreasing his confidence over the long term was explained by making reference to principles of **operant and respondent conditioning**. An alternative approach presented to William was to modify his behaviour by playing more offensively, which, it was hoped, would facilitate new learning and foster his long-term development. The sport psychologist discussed the pros and cons of a more offensive approach. William decided that he would like to play more offensively, acknowledging that doing so would entail a greater risk of making mistakes (e.g. losing the ball). He was also aware, however, that adopting a more offensive style was more congruent with his long-term development goals. Assuming a more offensive playing style was deemed important in altering the motivational operations underlining William's willingness to assume risks in situations he previously avoided. By doing so, the fear of making mistakes was hypothesized to decrease due to **habituation, respondent extinction**, and new learning.
2   William was instructed to take every practice and match opportunity to perform the target behaviours, even if he felt anxious or had negative thoughts. The sport psychologist emphasized that to 'play with confidence' was a skill that had to be practised, just like another technical, tactical, or physical skill.
3   William was instructed to *self-register his target behaviours* after practices and matches. The agreed-upon protocol was that William would write down the situations ('challenge'/'playable') he encountered and would indicate whether he performed the target behaviour or not, using his mobile phone. This exercise provided William with self-informed feedback, close in proximity to his actual performances.
4   The coach was instructed to support William's efforts by providing positive feedback as expeditiously as possible following performance of the target behaviours. It was made clear to the coach that the focus of the feedback should be directed towards the behaviours (e.g. the attempt to challenge), rather than the outcome of the behaviour (e.g. whether William won or lost a duel). In addition, the coach provided William with statistics regarding the target behaviours following each match in graphical form, so he could objectively examine his development.
5   During the intervention, the coach and sport psychologist selected video sequences of William performing correct behaviours in specific training or match situations. Doing so helped reinforce William's behaviour modification efforts, and provided opportunities to highlight the performance of effective behaviours. William was also encouraged to watch video sequences on his own and reflect on his efforts.

## Step 4: evaluation

The evaluation was guided by two key questions: (1) To what extent did William reach the goal of performing the target behaviours in at least 80% of relevant situations; and (2) assuming some change occurred, what factors influenced William's behaviour change? Figure 19.1 below presents statistics for each target behaviour.

As shown in Figure 19.1, the goal of 80% was reached after two matches and maintained for an additional three matches. Interviews with William and his coach revealed that William had learned to perform target behaviours in spite of his negative cognitions and emotions. William highlighted the psycho-education component as a central facet of the intervention, which enabled him to see a connection between his thoughts/emotions, behaviours, and short- and long-term consequences. He suggested that such understanding allowed him to act on his long-term values (e.g. skill improvement, high-level performance), rather than allow his negative thoughts and anxiety to preclude him from engaging in desired behaviours. By acting on his long-term values more consistently, William experienced reinforcements more frequently during matches (e.g. passing by his opponent, receiving the ball more often, scoring goals, positive feedback from teammates); reinforcers that were not obtained when William was more passive. William also reported less anxiety, heightened confidence, and a belief that the target behaviours had spread to other 'offensive' behaviours (e.g. take the ball forward instead of passing backwards). It was hypothesized that these positive reinforces would continue to influence William's new behaviour following the intervention.

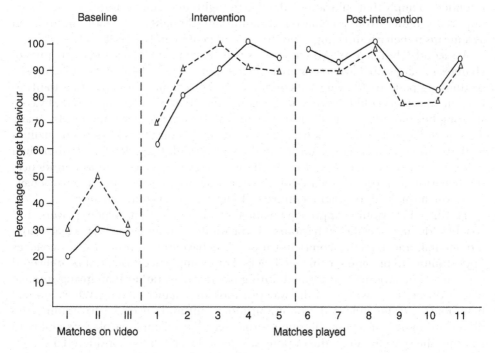

*Figure 19.1* Graph indicating the development of William's target behaviours.

Notes
Circle: challenge opponent; triangle: engage in 'playable' situations.

Both William and his coach indicated that their communication had improved, primarily because the intervention had given them something specific to discuss. The coach reported that he found it easier to provide William with feedback, while William indicated a greater interest in soliciting his coach's assistance in analysing particular situations. The intervention was terminated after William, the coach, and the sport psychologist determined that the goal of the intervention had been achieved. The coach, however, continued to register the target behaviours to gauge William's long-term development. As highlighted in Figure 19.1, William continued to perform the desired behaviours in the intervention aftermath.

## The potential for ABA in top-level football

The definition of behavioural sport psychology provided earlier in this chapter (Martin & Tkachuk, 2000) emphasized the use of behavioural analysis principles in applied sport psychology. The seven dimensions of ABA formulated by Baer and colleagues (1968) provide a basis for these principles. For a sport psychologist working in top-level football, there are several advantages of a behavioural approach, three of which we highlight here. First, ABA interventions focus on what is of primary interest to coaches and players – behaviour change. While interventions focused on altered thoughts or emotions (e.g. cognitive reframing, thought stopping) may be considered successful if athletes report a greater preponderance of positive thoughts or feelings of relaxation, such interventions may not be considered 'effective' unless behavioural changes can also be implemented or observed. This suggestion is not intended to imply that cultivating adaptive thoughts and emotions is not relevant or important; rather, from a behavioural standpoint, thoughts and emotions are seen as a means to behaviour change and not an end goal in and of itself.

A second advantage of ABA is that 'small' changes in behaviours can initiate changes in 'larger' behaviours or areas such as personality ('being more like Messi') or thinking patterns ('having self-confidence'). For example, a player that wants to become 'a leader' could describe target behaviours that a leader engages in, by considering her own ideas and obtaining input from coaches and teammates. By enacting one of the behaviours of a 'leader', the athlete demonstrates leadership qualities in that particular moment, even if she does not 'think like a leader'. Rather than trying to initiate change by addressing 'larger' cognitive issues such as confidence, the behavioural approach focuses on the performance of small, momentary behaviours, which can lead to larger cognitive or long-term behavioural changes.

Third, a behavioural approach facilitates communication. When players and coaches discuss specific behaviours, it provides a foundation for clear, non-judgmental, and effective communication. A behavioural approach gives coaches opportunities to provide specific feedbacks. For example, feedback can be delivered each time a behaviour is performed during or after play, rather than giving summative feedback, such as 'I liked the way you took the chances today'. When football behaviours are the subject of communication, staff and coaches surrounding the player are more apt to use the same vernacular. For example, a player's ability to run into the space between the opponent's defenders could be considered a shared goal of the coaching and performance staff (e.g. head coach, sport psychologist, strength and conditioning coach). Rather than treating a lack of running in the appropriate area as a 'mental problem', the performance staff could discuss the issue with the player as a behavioural one. Despite the aforementioned advantages of ABA, research in the general sport psychology field, and football in particular, is lacking. Therefore, the use of behavioural principles and effective behavioural sport interventions remain an interesting avenue for future research.

## Conclusions

Behavioural sport psychology has not gained too much attention in the sport psychology literature despite strong research base from other settings. The aim of this chapter was therefore to introduce basic behavioural principles and show how ABA can be applied in a football context. We present ABA with a case study of a young football player, and how a behavioural approach can be used to handle counterproductive behaviours and expand a player's behavioural repertoire. By presenting learning principles from behavioural psychology we hope this chapter can inspire sport psychologists and coaches to adopt these principles in practice.

## Glossary
(Holt et al., 2012; Smith, 1993)

**Counter conditioning**   The conditioning of a new response to a particular class of stimuli that is incompatible with the old response.
**Habituation**   A decrease in the strength of response to a repeated stimulus.
**Negative reinforcement**   A response is strengthened by the subsequent removal (or avoidance) of an aversive stimulus.
**Operant conditioning**   A type of learning in which behaviour is influenced by the consequences that follow it.
**Positive reinforcement**   A response is strengthened by the subsequent presentation of a stimuli.
**Punishment**   When a response is weakened by an outcome that follows it.
**Reinforcement**   When a response is strengthened by an outcome that follows it.
**Respondent extinction**   A process in which the conditioned stimuli is permitted repeatedly in the absence of the unconditioned stimuli, causing the conditioned stimuli to weaken and eventually disappear.
**Respondent/classical conditioning**   An organism learns to associate two stimuli such that one stimulus comes to elicit a response that was originally elicited only by the other stimulus.

## References

Austin, J., & Carr, J. (Eds.). (2000). *Handbook of applied behavior analysis*. Oakland, CA: New Harbinger Publications.
Baer, D. M., Wolf, M. M., & Risley, T. R. (1968). Some current dimensions of applied behavior analysis. *Journal of Applied Behavior Analysis, 1*, 91–97.
Baer, D. M., Wolf, M. M., & Risley, T. R. (1987). Some still-current dimensions of applied behavior analysis. *Journal of Applied Behavior Analysis, 20*, 313–327.
Baldwin, J. D., & Baldwin, J. I. (2000). *Behavior principles in everyday life*. Essex, England: Pearson Education Inc.
Beck, A. T. (1976). *Cognitive therapy and the emotional disorders*. New York, NY: International Universities Press.

Cooper, J. O., Heron, T. E., & Heward, W. L. (2014a). Definition and characteristics of applied behavior analysis. In J. O. Cooper, T. E. Heron, & W. L. Heward (Eds.), *Applied behavior analysis* (pp. 22–43). Essex, England: Pearson Education Inc.

Cooper, J. O., Heron, T. E., & Heward, W. L. (2014b). Basic concepts. In J. O. Cooper, T. E. Heron, & W. L. Heward (Eds.), *Applied behavior analysis* (pp. 44–66). Essex, England: Pearson Education Inc.

Farmer, R. F., & Chapman, A. L. (2015). *Behavioral interventions in cognitive behavioral therapy: practical guidance for putting theory into action.* Washington, DC: American Psychological Association.

Fisher, W. W., Groff, R. A., & Roane, H. S. (2011). Applied behavior analysis: History, philosophy, principles and basic methods. In W. W. Fisher, C. C. Piazza, & H. S. Roane (Eds.), *Handbook of applied behavior analysis* (pp. 61–78). New York, NY: The Guilford Press.

Gardner, F., & Moore, Z. (2006). *Clinical sport psychology.* Champaign, IL: Human Kinetics.

Gustafsson, H., & Lundqvist, C. (2016). Working with perfectionism in elite sport: A cognitive behavioral therapy perspective. In A. P. Hill (Ed.), *The psychology of perfectionism in sport, dance, and exercise* (pp. 203–211). London, England: Routledge.

Gustafsson, H., Lundqvist, C., & Tod, D. (2017). Cognitive behavioral intervention in sport psychology: A case illustration of the exposure method with an elite athlete. *Journal of Sport Psychology in Action, 8*(3), 152–162. doi=10.1080/21520704.2016.1235649.

Hofmann, S. G., Asmundson, G. J., & Beck, A. T. (2013). The science of cognitive therapy. *Behavior Therapy, 44,* 199–212. doi.org/10.1016/j.beth.2009.01.007.

Holt, N., Bremner, A., Sutherland, E., Vliek, M., Passer, M., & Smith, R. (2012). *Psychology: The science of mind and behaviour.* New York, NY: McGraw-Hill.

Luiselli, J. K. (2011). Single-case evaluation of behavioral coaching interventions. In J. K. Luiselli & D. D. Reed (Eds.), *Behavioral sport psychology* (pp. 61–78). New York, NY: Springer.

Luiselli, J. K., & Reed, D. D. (Eds.). (2011). *Behavioral sport psychology: Evidence-based approaches to performance enhancement.* New York, NY: Springer.

Martin, G. L., & Tkachuk, G. A. (2000). Behavioral sport psychology. In J. Austin & J. E. Carr (Eds.), *Handbook of applied behavior analysis* (pp. 399–422). Reno, NV: Context Press.

Martin, G. L., Vause, T., & Schwartzman, L. (2005). Experimental studies of psychological interventions with athletes in competitions: Why so few? *Behavior Modification, 29,* 616–641.

Michael, J. (2014). Motivating operations. In J. O. Cooper, T. E. Heron, & W. L. Heward (Eds.), *Applied behavior analysis* (pp. 390–407). Essex, England: Pearson Education Inc.

Roane, H. S., Ringdahl, J. E., Kelley, M. E., & Glover, A, C. (2011). Single-case experimental designs. In W. W. Fisher, C. C. Piazza, & H. S. Roane (Eds.), *Handbook of applied behavior analysis* (pp. 132–147). New York, NY: The Guilford Press.

Smith, R. (1993). *Psychology: The science of mind and behaviour.* New York, NY: McGraw-Hill.

Sundel, M., & Sundel, S. S. (2005). *Behavioral change in the human services. Behavioral and cognitive principles and applications.* Thousand Oaks, CA: Sage Publications.

Whelan, J. P., Mahoney, M. J., & Meyers, A. W. (1991). Performance enhancement in sport: A cognitive behavioral domain. *Behavior Therapy, 22,* 307–327.

# Part IV

# Developing the young player in football

# 20 Parental coaching in football

*Denise Beckmann-Waldenmayer*

## Abstract

It is acknowledged that parents play an essential role in the life of young football players. Therefore, they must be integrated into developmental systems in football. Parents' behaviour is sometimes not appropriate and can even be detrimental to the performance and personality development of young athletes. Most often, this is due to a lack of knowledge on how best to support their child in this context. Parental coaching aims at providing parents with knowledge about children's psychological needs and age-related skill development and how best to support their children. This is addressed from a systemic perspective that attempts to incorporate the different systems interacting in a young player's development such as football, school, and family. Based on current scientific research and practical experience successful parental coaching interventions are described.

## Overview of the chapter's objectives

Practical experience as well as many empirical studies demonstrate the importance of the social environment for the psychological, physical, and social development of children and adolescents. The social environment in football focuses mainly on the development of performance. Therefore, performance demands put on young players are enormous. Social support from parents is essential to counterbalance the pressure from the performance system. For long-term healthy development young athletes require considerate and esteemed support from their parents. A major question is how parents can be effectively integrated into the sport system so that young athletes can benefit from this critical resource. This chapter will explicitly address the influence of parents' behaviour on the development of young athletes, ways of sport psychological consulting for parents, and the necessary prerequisites for the integration of parents into the sport system.

## Anecdotal evidence highlighting the importance of parental coaching

The mother of an 11-year-old athlete once asked for sport psychological coaching. The mother was concerned about conflicts developing between her son and her and sought the help of the sport psychologist to solve this conflict. She reported that her son did not want her to be present at his games. When she drove him home after competitions the boy would put the car window down, turn up the volume on the radio, and turn away from the mother to avoid contact. She found her son's behaviour very hurtful, especially because she just wanted to support him.

Similarly, the father of a 10-year-old athlete phoned to ask for an appointment for sport psychological coaching. He said that his son practised twice a week and competed on weekends. Additionally the son would go to strength and conditioning, physiotherapy, and swimming once a week. In this case, the father complained that his son showed a lack of concentration during games whereas all other players engaged in full concentration. He said that he was very disappointed and that if this continued he would terminate his son's participation in competitive sports.

Football coaches and officials frequently see parents as a nuisance. Coaches complain that parents interfere with their work, insult players on the opposing team, and even yell at their own children in an almost insulting way robbing them of their self-confidence. Several solutions have been proposed by coaches and officials. Some football clubs have drawn lines around the pitch, 10 feet away from the side and end lines, and posted signs saying 'Parents are not allowed beyond this line'. One football coach even suggested building a large fence around the practice ground with a gate and strong lock and a sign to say 'Off-limits to parents'.

These examples from sport psychological practice demonstrate that the interaction between athletic environment, athletes, and parents is often perceived as difficult. In contrast to sport psychological coaching of adult athletes, more complex system interrelations have to be taken into account for junior sports. One reason for this is that young talents find themselves in complex somatic, psychological, and social developmental phases. Additionally, parents play a crucial role in the life of children and adolescents. But instead of seeing the interactions of young players with their parents as sources of problems, a change of view may uncover the huge resources contained in these interactions and the family environment. Adopting a systems perspective takes into account the different interacting systems involved in the development of young players, such as the football academy, school, the parents and so on. This change of perspective could provide an enormous opportunity for the positive, sustained individual development of young talents in football and other sports and shall be described in this chapter.

## Theory and research

### *Summary of studies on parental impact on youth athletes*

Numerous studies deal with parents' impact on junior athletes. These studies indicate that parents can positively as well as negatively impact the development of their children in a variety of ways. Researchers have investigated the influence of parents' verbal communication (Bowker et al., 2009; Holt, Tamminen, Black, Sehn, & Wall, 2008; Omli & LaVoi, 2009), behaviour (Goldstein & Iso-Ahola, 2008), expectations (Gould, Lauer, Rolo, Jannes, & Pennisi, 2006) as well as the timing of communication (Elliott & Drummond, 2015b).

Parents have multiple indispensable roles and functions in the development of their children in sports. They actually play several essential roles. Even when young players live at a football boarding school parents remain extremely significant to their child. Particularly for younger children, parents are the most important role models. According to the social learning approach parents are role models for goal orientation and the development of motivation (Duda & Hom, 1993). Until the age of 10 years, parents are the most important attachment figures (Horn & Weiss, 1991), and continue to play that role alongside peer groups into adolescent years (Ullrich-French & Smith, 2006). Parents are also the primary 'service providers' (bread earner, social and financial support, organisation; Fredricks & Eccles, 2004). They influence the way their children think, the attributions they make, their self-efficacy, values, and competence expectations (Fraser-Thomas & Côté, 2009; Sacks, Tenenbaum, & Pargman, 2006; Sagar & Lavallee, 2010). Consequently, they have a strong impact on children's achievement potential, and children's ability to cope with failure.

Pomerantz, Grolnick, and Price (2005) found that parents influenced their children's experience of competence and autonomy as well as the development of values and, as a consequence, impacted their performance capacity. Van Yperen (1998) showed that parents had a significant effect on children's ability to cope with failure. Parents also influence their children's behaviour and well-being in competitions. They may provide support but can also be perceived as a source of interference by young athletes (Strean, 1995). In their study, Knight, Boden, and Holt (2010) managed to yield a differentiated picture of undesired and desired behaviour of tennis parents. Their sample consisted of 42 young Canadian tennis players ($M_{age}$ = 13.5 years). The junior athletes stated having the following wishes regarding their parents' behaviour:

- No technical and tactical advice
- Remarks concerning attitude and effort – but not regarding performance
- Practical support (e.g. nutrition, clothes)
- Respecting tennis etiquette
- Clear, unambiguous communication (e.g. gestures and facial expressions should be in line with statements made)

Fraser-Thomas, Côté, and Deakin (2008) investigated differences between active swimmers and those who dropped out. They found that drop-outs engaged in less activity outside school, had less structured practice in swimming, and had less individual coaching. Drop-outs were frequently the youngest in their training group and often had no best friend. To a large extent drop-outs had parents who had been athletes themselves. Parents who were former athletes tend to analyse games and competitions to promote the further athletic development and success of their children. Accordingly, these parents also assume an active coaching role. A recent survey conducted on behalf of the Marylebone Cricket Club (MCC, 2015) with 1,002 children aged 8–16 found that 45% of children complained about their parents' bad behaviour, which made them feel like not wanting to take part in sport any more. Interestingly, 84% of parents of those children agreed that negative behaviour discouraged youngsters from sport participation. In the survey, 41% of the children said their parents criticised their performance – 16% saying it happened frequently or all the time. One child reported seeing a mother smash a car window after the opposition scored, another witnessed a dad hit the referee for sending his kid off, whilst one parent recalled police being called when two opposing parents started fighting. If pressure is perceived as too high, this can result in a loss of motivation which in turn can lead to a termination of the young athletes' engagement in sports.

In fact, Weinberg and Gould (2007) showed that high parental pressure is a factor that may even lead to burnout in young athletes. Therefore, it seems extremely important that young talents perceive their parents as caring and supportive.

Most parents believe that they act in the best interest of their children. Many parents believe that the sport context is useful for 'higher' educational goals such as acquiring important values, dealing with criticism, and coping with failure (Elliott & Drummond, 2015a). But there are other parents too who see opportunities for themselves in their child's career. It has been proposed that children may play the role of surrogates for parents who did not achieve their aspired goals in the sport they practised in their youth (e.g. Meân & Kassing, 2008). There are also parents, especially in football, who see their children as a means to make money. For example, the author was consulted by a mother of a 15-year-old member of a foot-ball youth academy who decided school should be a priority over football. The father became furious when he learnt of this as he wanted his son to focus exclu-sively on football. He demolished the son's room and menaced the mother because he held her responsible for their son's intentions.

In contrast to their parents' orientations and expectations, children and adoles-cents are primarily active in competitive sports for fun, being with friends, and experiencing positive emotions (e.g. pride) associated with competitive sports (e.g. Elliott & Drummond, 2015a, 2015b). These diverging perspectives of parents and children entail potential conflict and frequently lead to increased pressure and negative stress for junior athletes (Keegan, Harwood, Spray, & Lavallee, 2009). At worst, physical and mental health can be affected, anxiety symptoms can occur, and ultimately drop-out can result (Fraser-Thomas et al., 2008). Weinberg and Gould (2007) showed parental pressure to be a factor promoting burnout in young athletes.

A caring and supportive family is critical for young athletes. Young athletes are part of their family system with parents and possibly other siblings. Therefore, parents need to be integrated into sport psychological counselling because they play a vital role for children and adolescents as attachment figures as well as legal guard-ians. Sport psychology can support parents to adequately help their children. For example, parental coaching can contribute to an improvement of communication between parents and their children but also between parents and coaches. In paren-tal coaching parents are coached to optimise their interactions with their child, for example after failure in a competition. They should become aware that sibling con-stellations may also be a source of jealousy and conflict because of the high amount of time and resources parents may spend on the athlete at the expense of the other children. Parental coaching emanates from a systemic perspective and indicates the importance of a systematic implementation of parental coaching in football clubs. There are a few models of such an approach in the USA (see Weinberg & Gould, 2007).

Parents should learn which behaviours are most beneficial for their kids and their development. Parental coaching basically involves educating parents about child development, and providing knowledge on what kind of behaviours are most sup-portive. Further, coaches and officials should also better understand and appreciate the role parents play. Ideally coaches and parents should become partners in helping the child achieve his/her full potential. This type of approach would result in an interlocked support system. In order to avoid negative impact and maximise positive effects for the young players, parental coaching should be designed to optimise parents' interactions within the systems. Family therapy provides a good framework for this. In fact, occasionally parent coaching involves conflict resolutions within the family system or between the family and the sport system. A major issue encountered when working with young players can be their parents' divorce. However, most parent coaching will consist of promoting an understanding of child development, improving communication skills, and supporting career planning as holistic life coaching.

In essence, parents should first understand their role in a system that should be designed to support the development of their children not only in sport but also in life. Coaches and football club staff need to understand and acknowledge the indispensable role parents play. Parents should see their primary role in the system as working as a role model, giving emotional support and encouragement. They should represent a growth mindset making completely clear that a failure in sport has nothing to do with personal failure but is something that involves learning and may even motivate the athlete to practise more. At no point should this involve any pressure about winning or losing. Research on personality development has shown that children need the freedom to solve their problems themselves and learn to make their own decisions (Beckmann, Szymanski, Elbe, & Ehrlenspiel, 2006; Kuhl & Kraska, 1989).

The parental coaching I provide mainly consists of: psychological education (e.g. developmental psychology), clarifying parents' expectations regarding the young talent's capacities at a certain age, specific skill training for the parents to support their young child, conflict management, and career consulting. Although parents are motivated to optimally support their children, they often do not know what their children actually expect from them. Research shows that positive parental support leads to higher enjoyment of the sport and higher intrinsic motivation as well as more continuous participation. Parental support can also prevent drop-out.

## Introduction to a systemic view

The systemic approach that can be found in (systemic) family therapy appears to be beneficial for the development of a broader coaching structure in youth football. Core aspects of systemic sport psychological counselling will be presented in the following section (see Beckmann-Waldenmayer, 2012).

The concept of 'systemic counselling' should be considered a generic term encompassing a multitude of models that have been developed since the 1950s (see von Schlippe & Schweitzer, 2007). There are several core assumptions and positions characterising a systemic approach:

### Context specificity

In systemic therapy a symptom is always considered in relation to the context. According to de Shazer (1994) humans are oriented on relationships and their behaviour has to be understood in terms of action and re-action. Each individual is embedded in a context of multiple psycho-social relationships and interaction patterns. This context should be taken into consideration in sport psychological counselling. A football player may be very nervous when he walks onto the pitch to play an important game but may be completely calm and relaxed when giving a presentation in front of a large number of fellow students at university. Therefore, the context determines symptomatic behaviour.

### 'Expanding the space of possibility'

From a systemic perspective explanatory models for a situation or a problem impact the change process. Which data are collected or which questions are asked depends on the particular explanatory model. Systemic thinking assumes that there are several explanatory models. These models are not conceived of as truths but based on the basic concept that the scope as well as the context of observation must be taken into account (see above). According to previous experience, attitude, expectation, and focus of attention, each person will perceive the identical segment of reality differently. Watzlawick's question 'How real is real?!' can be considered a suitable guideline for sport psychologists adopting a systemic perspective (Watzlawick, 1976). This means that different scopes and contexts of observation can imply different explanations of a situation transcending purely linear causal explanatory models (cf. Lang, 2005; Watzlawick, 1976). In this context, systemic sport psychological counselling stands for an expansion of athletes' space of possibility through additional explanatory models and thereby breaks down generalisations and fixed dogmas (von Schlippe & Schweitzer, 2007). Descriptions of athletes and coaches leading to a perpetuation of a problem (e.g. 'you never managed to score against ...', 'player X always has problems understanding the tactics') should be altered and transformed into expanded, more supportive perspectives (Edgette & Rowan, 2007; Lang, 2005).

### Circularity

Behaviours of single individuals are always related to behaviours of others (i.e. every behaviour has a function in the definition of the relationship) as depicted in Figure 20.1.

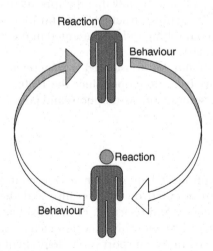

*Figure 20.1* Circularity in relationships (according to Mücke, 2003).

The functions of behaviours are clarified through circular questions. For example, players could be encouraged to express assumptions, wishes, needs of team members, coaches, and parents (Brüggemann, Ehret-Ivankovic, & Klütmann, 2007). This way, problem-relevant dynamics could be detected, convictions of others could be identified, and the total impact of these factors on the shaping of the relationships of all who are involved could be brought home to the players (Bamberger, 2001; von Schlippe & Schweitzer, 2007).

### Systemic Coaching Model for Youth Sport (Beckmann-Waldenmayer, 2012)

Of course, the above-presented core assumptions and stances of systemic counselling are not considered to be an exhaustive list. However, together with the research presented at the beginning of the chapter they constitute a frame for the development of a Systemic Coaching Model for Youth Sport (Figure 20.2). This model shall be presented in more detail for the area of youth football.

Counselling of young athletes is the central aspect of the model. In line with coaching approaches that promote physical development, psychological coaching should also be systematic and periodised. Training models for athletic development frequently transfer adult models to youngsters. But I consider it to be essential that the coaching model is designed in a way that adequately addresses young athletes' age and their current status of physical and psychological development.

The two central performance systems of young players consist of sport and school. They will naturally influence the psychological dynamics of the family system. To promote a smooth and resource-saving flow of activity within the performance system of sport and school, sport psychology should support the balance through workshops, offers of meetings to provide information, or mediation.

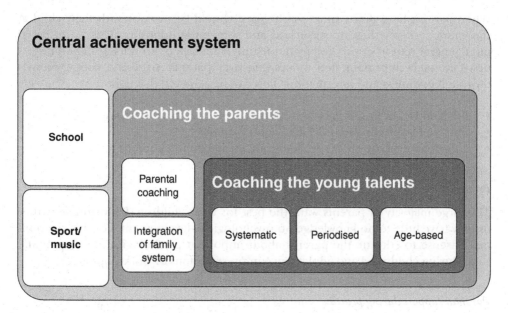

*Figure 20.2* Systemic Coaching Model for Youth Sport.

Source: Beckmann-Waldenmayer, 2012.

## Resulting goals and structure of parental coaching

Based on the systemic counselling model parents' behaviour and communication can be promoted for different practice and game situations. In my experience it is fundamental that parents accept coaching from a sport psychologist and are ready for behavioural change. The first thing to be achieved is for them to develop an idea of what efficient parental support of their children in the football context would look like. Psycho-educational workshops can provide a platform for doing this. Contents of such workshops could first of all involve the presentation of the youth academy's coaching and developmental conception. Parents could be integrated into such a conception as a form of 'coaching units' to arrive at an official and important function within the overall developmental concept. When the parents are treated as esteemed, important partners the definition of specific goals for the parents' behaviour should be facilitated. These behavioural goals could encompass verbal as well as non-verbal behaviour. If these behavioural goals are developed in cooperation with the parents (e.g. at a team day where parents, coaches, and athletes meet and discuss) their commitment to actually implement these goals should increase because they would also reflect the needs of the parents themselves. Different areas for the structuring of the behavioural goals can be developed. Some of these will be described as examples in the following section. Based on the presented theories, scientific results, and my practical experience, I have defined general and specific elements of parental coaching in my work with the youth academy of a professional football club, which will be presented in the following section.

### General debriefing

When parents hear that a sport psychologist should be working with their child at the youth academy they are suspicious and sometimes opposing. This is not based on a general refusal of psychology but mainly on a lack of knowledge. Therefore, a first extremely important step in winning over parents' trust and cooperation is thorough openness and information. This can be achieved through:

- General Debriefing, e.g. information as presentation or workshop
- Personal Debriefing in individual conversations
- Information about sport psychology in a video on the homepage

### Psycho-education

The large majority of parents want the best for their children. Unfortunately, they usually have little to no knowledge on psychological development. For this reason it makes sense to educate the parents about important psychological developmental steps during childhood and adolescence in presentations or workshops.

### Parental support during practice

If young players are not living in residential accommodation at the youth academy parents usually drive their kids to the practice site. Some football clubs have drawn lines around the practice pitches with signs saying that parents are not allowed beyond this line. Some youth academies have special facilities where parents can spend time during practice (such as a cafeteria on top of the youth academy building overlooking the practice grounds). However, as stated earlier, parents could also be seen as an important part in the overall support system of young players. Thus, it makes sense to define clear assignments or duties to the parents during practice. Frequently it can be observed that young players become distracted or even irritated through parents' break-ins or impulsively criticising the coach. In the most adverse case the children will experience a conflict of loyalty – they will neither want to disappoint their coach or team nor their parents. But if they perceive conflicting messages, arriving at a solution acceptable to all parties involved will be difficult if not impossible. Then, of course, the young player's level of experienced stress will become intolerable resulting in various negative reactions (e.g. loss of motivation, drop-out, health problems). Therefore, in an attempt to change this unfavourable situation to something more productive, certain goals could be agreed upon for the practice situation such as:

- no verbal break-ins
- no comments regarding content of practice, technique, tactics, etc.
- no criticism of the coach in public or in front of the players; if considered necessary parents should seek a private conversation with the coach

### Before the game – briefing

Direct briefing immediately before a game should strictly be up to the coaches of the team. However, parents may also consider which message they would like to give their child to take with them into the game. According to research findings (Knight et al., 2010) young athletes do not want to hear anything which conflicts with their coach's role (e.g. advice on technique or tactics). This would lead to the experience of negative emotions, and an increase in experienced stress. Parents' communication should be clear and should not induce additional pressure. What the young athletes would like to hear from their parents are words of esteem, and statements supporting self-confidence. Especially, the inducement of positive, powerful pictures and imaginations is recommended, like that of a tiger skilfully stalking prey and mobilising his power at just the right moment.

### During the game

Meanwhile, research has documented overly aggressive behaviour of parents during competitions, linking sports with war (e.g. Meân & Kassing, 2008). Use of inappropriate or offensive language has become common at games with parents often yelling insults at their own children, the children's coach, the opposing team, and the referee. They also show criticism through facial expression and gestures. This kind of behaviour is likely to result in distraction and demoralisation and may have negative effects on players' well-being and performance. Meân and Kassing (2008) documented examples of parents' communication behaviours that treated a child's lack of success on the field as if it were misbehaviour. In addition to this kind of inappropriate behaviour, parents' attempts at coaching during a game can be frequently observed. In some cases, the parents' shouting may actually support the motivation of the young players. If the players perceive positive support like encouragement this may actually positively affect their performance.

Some youth sport leagues have implemented training programmes to teach more effective and appropriate communication practices. These programmes often involve having parents sign a pledge, with the implication that they could be excluded from games for misbehaviour. However, as mentioned frequently in this chapter it would be preferable to win parents over as supporters rather than excluding them. How to support the children and their team in an appropriate way during games should be part of parent coaching. In line with what was said previously and Meân and Kassing's results (2008), the main message should consist of making only supportive and encouraging comments plus keeping the focus on the kids, and not on parents, coaches, referees, or winning.

### *After the game – debriefing*

As pointed out earlier, especially after losing a game, conflict between parents and their children can occur (Keegan et al., 2009; Meân & Kassing, 2008). These conflicts result from the different needs and expectations of parents and young athletes. In one of the examples provided at the start of this chapter, the young player wanted to come to terms with having lost the game. Maybe he even wanted to postpone a game analysis until he had coped with the frustration and negative emotions. His mother's intent on the other hand was to console him and she may have thought that the best way to do this was to immediately analyse what had happened during the game. Preparations to avoid those conflicts resulting from misunderstanding should already be made before the start of the season. General advice on what would be appropriate parental behaviour in such a situation cannot be given because of the high individuality of needs and the particular parent–athlete relationship. Therefore, before the start of the season young athletes should address what kind of parental behaviour would be most supportive together with their parents. General advice given by Meân and Kassing (2008) based on their research findings is to make the game experience enjoyable for everyone and to keep in mind that winning should be secondary to skill development and enjoyment; and doing fun things like bringing after-game snacks, organising parent cheers, and doing 'the wave'.

## Pre-season workshops for parents

To assimilate parents into an integrated support system for young players, workshops on parental coaching should be organised before the start of the season. In this way parents will be part of the support system from the start. Workshops should not be singular events but be continued during the season on a regular basis to evaluate the outcomes of the measures taken and adjust them if necessary. At minimum, the first workshop would occur at the end of the first leg and a second at the end of the season. For the month in between it might suffice to have a parent newsletter and information available on a special section of the football club's homepage exclusively for parents. Besides providing information on current developments and measures these communications also provide a good opportunity to praise good, constructive parental support. Such a regular exchange increases transparency and in many cases also an emotional bonding to the athletic environment. In addition, given sufficient financial means and qualified staff members, regular sport psychological counselling for parents on an individual basis would ideally be offered.

## Individual coaching sessions

Sometimes individual sessions are necessary to mediate conflict between a young player and his or her parents. The example below will give a brief insight into how individual sport psychological coaching can be implemented:

Diego Meyer[1] is 16 years old and a great talent at the youth academy of a professional football club. Diego's parents have supported his development as a football player since early childhood. Several scouts have attempted to lure him to other clubs. Diego has neglected school to some degree which is not in line with the youth academy's philosophy. His parents are worried because Diego has recently developed a relationship with a slightly older girl. They fear that because of this he will lose his focus on football. They have forbidden him to see the girl and have taken away Diego's mobile phone. At the youth academy, Diego, who had always been cheerful and enthusiastic, became more and more ill-humoured. When I talked to him he mentioned the conflict with his parents, especially his mother. I suggested that we have a meeting with his mother to search for a solution. When the three of us met his mother started to complain about Diego's bad conduct, saying that he had disobeyed her: he tried to get in contact with his girlfriend, and had even lied to his mother about it. I said we would like to exchange the different views on the situation in a friendly respectful atmosphere which would include staying calm, no accusations, no interruptions, rather letting everybody finish what s/he had to say. Then Diego spoke about his perception of the situation. I asked him, 'Do you love your mother and father?' He responded, 'Very much so and that really creates a lot of conflict since at the moment I feel completely exhausted with no energy for anything.' I asked the mother 'How do you feel when you hear this?' She said, 'Well of course, it's nice to hear him say that he loves me but…' I stopped her and said 'I just wanted to know how you feel hearing him say this.' Then I continued, 'We are here because we are all interested in finding a solution for this situation. Is that agreed upon?' The two agreed. It was especially important that the mother eventually conceded that her 16-year-old son was no longer a child and that he needed to be respected. A written contract between Diego and his mother was set up and a copy printed out for each of them. They both signed both of the copies. During the next weeks Diego regained his cheerfulness and enthusiasm. His performance normalised. When I met his mother the next time she also indicated that she was really happy that we managed to solve the conflict and stabilise Diego again.

1 The name has been changed.

## Conclusions

Scientific studies and practical experience show how important and necessary parents are in youth football. Having this in mind, parents should be integrated as part of the sport system. In order to avoid negative impact and maximise positive effects for the talents, parental coaching is designed to optimise parents' interactions within the system. Therefore, the most helpful contributions should be chosen:

- promoting an understanding of child development and education
- promoting an understanding of stress-recovery-balance
- improving communication skills
- goal setting with parents
- supporting career planning
- teaching the coach strategies concerning parental coaching

Furthermore, the most suitable setting should be chosen given the environment. This may vary depending on the existing attitude, the system structure, financial and staff resources. Sometimes, it will involve taking very small steps at the start (e.g. by creating a better understanding about the importance of parental coaching within the management and coaching team). The better the management's support the easier and more effectively can such a programme be implemented.

## References

Bamberger, G. G. (2001). *Lösungsorientierte Beratung* [Solution-oriented counselling]. Weinheim, Germany: PVU.

Beckmann, J., Szymanski, B., Elbe, A., & Ehrlenspiel, F. (2006). *Chancen und Risiken: Vom Leben im Verbundsystem von Schule und Leistungssport* [Chances and risks of living in an integrated system of elite sports and school]. Cologne, Germany: Sportverlag Strauß.

Beckmann-Waldenmayer, D. (2012). Ein systemisches Betreuungsmodell für den Nachwuchsleistungssport [A systemic counselling model for youth sports]. In D. Beckmann-Waldenmayer & J. Beckmann (Eds.), *Handbuch sportpsychologischer Praxis: Mentales Training in den olympischen Sportarten* [Handbook of applied sport psychology: Mental training in Olympic sports] (pp. 70–81). Balingen, Germany: Spitta.

Bowker, A., Boekhoven, B., Nolan, A., Bauhaus, S., Glover, P., Powell, T., & Taylor, S. (2009). Naturalistic observations of spectator behavior at youth hockey games. *The Sport Psychologist, 23*, 301–316.

Brüggemann, H., Ehret-Ivankovic, K., & Klütmann, C. (2007). *Systemische Beratung in fünf Gängen: Ein Leitfaden* [Systemic counselling in five steps: A guideline]. Göttingen, Germany: Vandenhoeck & Ruprecht.

De Shazer, S. (1994). *Words were originally magic.* New York, NY: Norton.

Duda, J. L., & Hom, A. (1993). Interdependencies between the perceived and self-reported goal orientations of young athletes and their parents. *Pediatric Exercise Science, 5*, 234–241.

Edgette, J., & Rowan, T. (2007). *Mental gewinnen: Hypnose im Sport* [Winning mentally: Hypnosis in sports]. Heidelberg, Germany: Carl Auer.

Elliot, S. K., & Drummond, M. J. N. (2015a). The (limited) impact of sport policy on parental behavior in youth sport: A qualitative inquiry in junior Australian football. *International Journal of Sport Policy and Politics, 4*(1), 39–48. doi:10.1080/19406940.2014.971850.

Elliott, S. K., & Drummond, M. J. N. (2015b). Parents in youth sport: What happens after the game?. *Sport, Education and Society, 22*(3), 391–406. doi:10.1080/13573322.2015.1036233.

Fraser-Thomas, J., & Côté, J. (2009). Understanding adolescents' positive and negative developmental experiences in sport. *The Sport Psychologist, 23*, 3–23.

Fraser-Thomas, J., Côté, J., & Deakin, J. (2008). Examining adolescent sport dropout and prolonged engagement from a developmental perspective. *Journal of Applied Sport Psychology, 20*, 318–333.

Fredricks, J. A., & Eccles, J. S. (2004). Parental influences on youth involvement in sports. In M. R. Weiss (Ed.), *Developmental sport and exercise psychology: A lifespan perspective* (pp. 145–164). Morgantown, WV: Fitness Information Technology.

Goldstein, J. D., & Iso-Ahola, S. E. (2008). Determinants of parents' sideline-rage emotions and behaviours at youth soccer games. *Journal of Applied Social Psychology, 38*, 1442–1462. doi:10.1111/j.1559-1816.2008.00355.x.

Gould, D., Lauer, L., Rolo, C., Jannes, C., & Pennisi, N. (2006). Understanding the role parents play in tennis success: A national survey of junior tennis coaches. *British Journal of Sports Medicine, 40*, 632–636. doi:10.1136/bjsm.2005.024927.

Holt, N. L., Tamminen, K. A., Black, D. E., Sehn, Z. L., & Wall, M. P. (2008). Parental involvement in competitive youth sport settings. *Psychology of Sport and Exercise, 9*, 663–685. doi:10.1016/j.psychosport.2007.08.001.

Horn, T. S., & Weiss, M. R. (1991). A developmental analysis of children's self-ability judgements in the physical domain. *Pediatric Exercise Science, 3*, 310–326.

Keegan, R. J., Harwood, C. G., Spray, C. M., & Lavallee, D. E. (2009). A qualitative investigation exploring the motivational climate in early career sport participants: Coach, parent and peer influences on sport motivation. *Psychology of Sport and Exercise, 10*, 361–372. doi:10.1016/j.psychsport.2008.12.003.

Knight, C. J., Boden, C. M., & Holt, N. L. (2010). Junior tennis players' preferences for parental behaviors. *Journal of Applied Sport Psychology, 22*(4), 377–391.

Kuhl, J., & Kraska, K. (1989). Self-regulation and metamotivation: Computational mechanisms, development and assessment. In R. Kaufer, P. L. Ackerman, & R. Cudeck (Eds.), *Abilities, motivation, and methodology: The Minnesota Symposium on learning and individual differences* (pp. 343–374). Hillsdale, NJ: Lawrence Erlbaum Associates Inc.

Lang, A. (2005). Ressourcenorientierte Beratung. Seminarunterlagen zur Ausbildung an der Deutschen Psychologen Akademie [Resource oriented counselling. Seminar brochure of the German Academy of Psychologists]. Bonn, Germany: DPA.

MCC (2015, 17 April). Pushy parents put off pupils from playing sport. Retrieved from www.lords.org/news/2015/april/pushy-parents-put-off-pupils-from-playing-sport.

Meân, L. J., & Kassing, J. W. (2008). Identities at youth sporting events: A critical discourse analysis. *International Journal of Sport Communication, 1*, 42–66.

Mücke, K. (2003). *Probleme sind Lösungen* [Problems are solutions]. Potsdam, Germany: Ökosysteme Verlag.

Omli, J., & LaVoi, N. M. (2009). Background anger in youth sport: A perfect storm? *Journal of Sport Behavior, 32*, 242–260.

Pomerantz, E. M., Grolnick, W. S., & Price, C. E. (2005). The role of parents in how children approach achievement: A dynamic process perspective. In A. J. Elliot & C. S. Dweck (Eds.), *Handbook of competence and motivation* (pp. 259–278). New York, NY: The Guilford Press.

Sacks, D. N., Tenenbaum, G., & Pargman, D. (2006). Providing sport psychology services to families. In J. Dosil (Ed.), *The sport psychologist's handbook: A guide for sport-specific performance enhancement* (pp. 39–61). Chichester, England: John Wiley & Sons Ltd.

Sagar, S., & Lavallee, D. (2010). The developmental origins of fear of failure in adolescent athletes: Examining parental practices. *Psychology of Sport & Exercise, 11*(3), 177–187.

Strean, B. W. (1995). Youth sport contexts: Coaches' perceptions and implications for intervention. *Journal of Applied Sport Psychology, 7*(1), 23–37.

Ullrich-French, S., & Smith, A. L. (2006). Perceptions of relationships with parents and peers in youth sport: Independent and combined prediction of motivational outcomes. *Psychology of Sport and Exercise, 7*(2), 193–214.

Van Yperen, N. W. (1998). Being a sport parent: Buffering the effect of your talented child's poor performance on his or her subjective well-being. *International Journal of Sport Psychology, 29*, 45–56.

Von Schlippe, A., & Schweitzer, J. (2007). *Lehrbuch der systemischen Therapie und Beratung* [Textbook of systemic therapy and counselling]. Göttingen, Germany: Vandenhoeck & Ruprecht.

Watzlawick, P. (1976). *How real is real? Confusion, disinformation, communication.* New York, NY: Random House.

Weinberg, R. S., & Gould, D. (2007). *Foundations of sport and exercise psychology.* Champaign, IL: Human Kinetics.

# 21 Talent development in youth football

*Jürgen Beckmann and Denise Beckmann-Waldenmayer*

## Abstract

Competitive football like many other sports faces the problem that limited resources and a limited number of players on the pitch require selection of players with the highest potential. However, talent is a rather fuzzy concept with no commonly agreed upon definition. Those involved in talent selection should be aware of players' perspectives and pay less attention to the current level of performance. Research shows that current capacity is not a prerequisite for future success; rather psychological factors may be the best predictors of a future career. These factors are basically motivational and volitional. Coachability appears to be another important aspect. In general, a dynamic developmental concept including a growth orientation is needed. From a dynamic perspective, player development should be considered as a concept whose components change over time involving the interplay between multidimensional determinants. The motivational component for instance must not be underestimated because sometimes those who appear to be the most promising drop out. Particularly, the sampling years, until the age of about 14, should mainly consist of motivating deliberate play. But talent development should not merely develop the technical and tactical skills needed on the pitch. Talent development should become 'life coaching' that develops the whole person taking into account the different systems relevant for them in a multidimensional and multifaceted way.

In football, as in most other sports, the early identification and selection of talented players is considered to be of the utmost importance since resources for talent development are limited. Talent development is usually understood as the deliberate advancement of the abilities the selected talent already possesses especially the improvement of strength and physical conditioning. However, the problem is that neither the concept of clearly defining characteristics of a talented player nor the identification and selection is very reliable (e.g. Abbott & Collins, 2004; Vaeyens et al., 2013). Furthermore, a static, innate ability-focused concept marginalises the notion of a growth perspective, which acknowledges the evolution of key qualities given optimally supporting conditions (daily training environment).

Around 1% of players aged 6–8 years selected as members of large football club youth academies will eventually become professional football players (e.g. Calvin, 2017; National Collegiate Athletic Association (NCCA), 2017). In a brutal system boys are successively weeded out – or 'culled', as one pre-academy development centre coach of 6-year-olds put it in Chris Green's book, *Every Boy's Dream* (Green, 2009). According to Green (2009), of the handful of 16-year-olds who make it through the system in England as well as in other countries, half will have left professional football within 2 years, and by the time they are 21, more than 75% will have failed. Besides the ruthless selection system there is yet another important factor: a substantial number of young players drop out not because of insufficient ability but voluntarily in spite of good performance. In a 6-year longitudinal study, Beckmann, Elbe, Szymanski, and Ehrlenspiel (2006) found an attrition rate of up to 44% across different sports. According to Wiese-Bjornstal, LaVoi, and Omli (2009) the major reason for the high attrition rate is 'I was no longer interested' or 'it was no longer fun' (loss of motivation and passion). Moreover, negative behaviours from parents, coaches, and other adults in youth sport contributed to this loss of motivation.

The Beckmann et al. (2006) and the Wiese-Bjornstal et al. (2009) findings also point to the importance of psychological factors in talent development. Kreiner-Phillips and Orlick (1993) found that only psychological factors could distinguish between consistent, top-level performers and those with an inconsistent career. Consequently, Abbott, Button, Pepping, and Collins (2005) maintain that different psychological factors may be more important to talent development at a young age and throughout maturation than the physical qualities desired from adult performances. They claim that both 'psycho-motor' skills (the fundamental motor pathways of skills, such as ball control and kicking) and 'psycho-behavioral' skills (self-motivation, determination, perceived self-confidence, etc.) are the key elements in talent development. According to Morris (2000) the importance of psychological factors in football and their role in talent development has been acknowledged over the past few decades. In fact, most German professional football clubs employ at least one sport psychologist. In particular, sport psychology has become a central element in talent development programmes.

Indeed, there are two different aspects of the role of psychological factors in football. First, mental factors are considered important for success in football (see Konter, Beckmann, & Mallett, 2019, Chapter 14 in this book). Second, factors that promote the successful development of the player (i.e. psychological talent factors) have to be taken into account. Psychological assessment plays a crucial role for both aspects. In consideration of individual players' needs, it is important for coaches to personalise coaching and be focused on the development of talent. As mental training is an essential element in talent development, we will also briefly address how psychological assessment, fundamental training (relaxation techniques), and mental skills training are systematically implemented in youth football from age nine.

The role of personality in athletic success has often been denied (e.g. Vealey, 1992). However, psychological skills associated with individual differences have been found to affect not only performance but also the longevity of a career in sports. For example, Smith and Christensen (1995) found seven psychological characteristics to be good predictors of athletic success. These characteristics are: coping with adversity, coachability, concentration, confidence and achievement motivation, goal setting and mental preparation, peaking under pressure, and freedom of worry.

Furthermore, human beings are always members of more than one social system, which partly determines their values, attitudes, and behaviours. A systems perspective appears to be essential, especially in youth football (see Beckmann-Waldenmayer,

2019, Chapter 20 in this book; Larsen, Henriksen, Alfermann, & Christensen, 2014). The current chapter will incorporate such a perspective, which implies a change in focus: from football coaching to 'life coaching'. Young talented football players might find themselves in tension with other key actors, such as coaches, scouts, and parents, due to conflicting goals and actions. Moreover, players often experience tension between sporting (football) and academic goals. Adults working in talent development should be aware of the different demands in different systems and support the young player in dealing with them.

## Defining talent

There is no commonly agreed upon definition of talent in sport or the academic literature (Gagné, 2000; Howe, Davidson, & Sloboda, 1998). Neither coaches nor researchers agree on how to identify a talented football player (Sæther, 2014; Vrljic & Mallett, 2008; Williams & Reilly, 2000). However, Singer and Janelle's (1999) definition is popular in the literature and covers two dimensions. The static dimension is based on bio-physical and psycho-social aspects, a specific combination of anatomical-physical characteristics, abilities, and personality traits. The dynamic dimension refers to an unfolding of a talent given that specific training and other environmental conditions are provided.

Traditional talent concepts have received criticism over the last decades (e.g. Abbott et al., 2005; Kearney & Hayes, 2018). In relation to these concepts two major shortcomings are critiqued and discussed: (a) the adoption of a static talent concept; and (b) a unidimensional conceptualisation of talent. On the other hand, dynamic concepts including a developmental aspect and the assumption of inherent dynamics have been proposed (Reilly, Williams, Nevill, & Franks, 2000; Simonton, 1999). It is apparent that coaches and researchers are at odds: coaches are interested in the early identification and selection of talented football players, whereas the scientific conceptualisation of a dynamic and nurtured talented player is in opposition to this. Despite the quantum of work that has dealt with developing the concept of talent, it is still not a clearly defined term in football.

Despite this lack of conceptual clarity, talent identification, selection, and development are a major focus in current football youth academies. Generally, it is assumed that performance and physical characteristics in early childhood are good predictors, i.e. talent criteria for future performance (cf. Peltola, 1992). However, early success in juvenile competition performance is merely a first hint of possible potential of a junior athlete but not sufficient for the prediction of outstanding future performance (e.g. Kearney & Hayes, 2018). There are other factors of crucial importance such as psychological factors. Several studies found, for example, cognitive-perceptual skills (perception and anticipation) to be decisive for complex sport performance in many sport disciplines (e.g. Williams, Davids, Burwitz, & Williams, 1993).

There are few elite players who are talented in all aspects of sport. Talent seems to be specific to a particular domain (Hohmann, 2009). In the context of sport talent research, this domain-specific talent should be captured in any talent identification process (Vaeyens, Lenoir, Williams, & Philippaerts, 2008). Elbe, Beckmann, and Szymanski (2003) demonstrated that highly specific assessment of psychological factors (motivation and volition) was a better predictor of future athletic performance than a less specific assessment. These psychological factors were also good predictors of future success. Consequently, football-specific assessment of potential psychological talent predictors may lead to explanations of more of the variance within youth players' behaviours. Simonton (1999) emphasised the importance of a multidimensional approach to understanding the concept of talent implying a multifaceted development process.

## Talent identification and selection

Selection of talented youngsters is considered a key element in competitive sports. However, Williams and Franks (1998) stated that perceptions of talent are diverse and that there is no consensus, nationally or internationally, regarding the theory and practice of talent identification, selection, and development in sport. Thus, fundamental challenges of youth development programmes in football include recognising current participants with the potential to become elite adult players (*talent identification*; Reilly, Williams, & Richardson, 2003) and providing them with the most appropriate learning environment to realise their potential (*talent development*; Vaeyens et al., 2008). Unfortunately, the common understanding of youth development is oriented towards finding young players whose performance characteristics match the requirements of elite adult football. Typically, talent identification and development are regarded as parallel and mutually related procedures (Hohmann, 2009). This model is considered inappropriate and will be argued against in the following section.

A key dilemma is that youth development programmes must select or deselect players from a large population, so that their limited resources can be focused on a smaller number of individuals (Williams & Reilly, 2000). Hence, there is a substantial need to identify the most talented players within the talent identification and development process. To do so, the talent concept is considered necessary (at some stage in the high performance pathway) and often used in many contexts because of the need to legitimise the identification of players ahead of others, often at an early age. Such an understanding indicates the intention to separate the performers on the basis of talent and abilities (current capacity), and to a lesser extent on the development of skills and abilities. The idea of identifying talent at a young age rests on several basic assumptions suggesting that talent is at least (in some camps) partly inherited, is domain-specific, that there are observable early indicators of talent that a 'trained eye' can identify, and that such early indications (current capacity) can predict future success (Durand-Bush & Salmela, 2001).

Sport scientists have tried to identify indicators of talent at an early stage by using different test batteries (Abbott & Collins, 2004). Few of these have managed to describe factors that can be used to identify players who will be more successful than others. At present, many professional football clubs rely on the subjective assessment of scouts or coaches, supported by a 'shopping list' of key criteria. These criteria include acronyms such as TABS (Technique, Attitude, Balance, Speed), SUPS (Speed, Understanding, Personality, Skill) (Stratton, Reilly, Williams, & Richardson, 2004), and TIPS (Talent, Intelligence, Personality, Speed) (Brown, 2001). In recent decades, several extensive models have been presented and an increasing number of researchers are using a more complex model in the attempt to predict what is required to reach a high performance level (Baker, Horton, Robertson-Wilson, & Wall, 2003).

Identifying talents at an early age based on physical abilities is not reliably predictive of future success and involves another problem. A relative age effect (RAE; birth month) phenomenon has been found in many sports, including football. Barnsley, Thompson, and Legault (1992) conducted the first study examining RAE in football, among under-20 and under-17 players who participated in the 1990 Football World Cup. Results showed that players born in the first months (quarters) of the year were over-represented, while those born in the last months of the same year were under-represented. At England's Football Association's School of Excellence at Lilleshall more than 50% of the pupils were born during the first quarter of their year of birth relevant for the selection (Simmons & Paull, 2001). This means that the players who are perceived as talented have an advantage over other athletes in their cohort as a result of differences in maturation and development, which take place at different speeds (Gagné, 2000). The RAE in football is also related to players' position. RAE is more pronounced in several positions than in others. According to Salinero, Pérez, Burillo, and Lesma (2013) forwards and defenders seem to be the positions most affected by RAE, presumably because of the physical size and strength demanded of the players. Even though this effect has been known since 1985, it is still observed today (Wiium, Lie, Ommundsen, & Enksen, 2010). Consequently, many potentially good players may have been lost to the system.

As described above, many researchers have examined the different criteria to identify talent in football (e.g. Helson, Hodges, Van Winckel, & Starkes, 2000; Reilly et al., 2000; Williams & Reilly, 2000). However, a crucial agent has largely been neglected: the role of coaches and their understanding of the identification process, and which criteria they use in their identification. Some studies have shown that many coaches focus on a rather small number of factors when identifying and selecting talent (Williams & Reilly, 2000). One of the few studies concerning coaches' understanding and criteria for identifying talented football players is a Danish study of national youth team coaches. In her study, Christensen (2009) found that coaches use their practical sense and their visual experience to identify talented players. The coaches largely focused on specific skills and the importance of attitudes, and described game intelligence as a vital factor. However, only a few of the coaches could clearly name what criteria they used to identify the most talented players.

A static conceptualisation of talent underpins many problems with talent identification and selection. Therefore, talent identification has been considered from a more dynamic perspective (Reilly et al., 2000; Simonton, 1999) over the last few decades. Instead of focusing on selection of talented players on the basis of early performance and physical characteristics, a process-oriented conceptualisation of talent development was envisioned. Talent identification can be viewed as both 'the start of' and an 'element within' the talent development process, which consequently involves the prediction of success at different stages (Vaeyens et al., 2013). However, as has been pointed out, talent identification and development in football is extremely difficult because clearly defined and objectively measurable characteristics that may indicate an individual's potential to succeed at the elite adult level are lacking (Abbott & Collins, 2004). Consequently, a shift in emphasis from talent identification to development has been suggested (Durand-Bush & Salmela, 2001).

## Developing talents

From a dynamic perspective, talent development should be considered as a concept whose components change as a function of time involving the interplay between multidimensional determinants (e.g. Reilly et al., 2000; Simonton, 1999). Some of these factors may even show unstable, non-linear development (Williams & Reilly, 2000). In fact, some components that could promote a successful, enduring career may not develop until long after the talent identification and selection process, which if not taken into account, will result in poorer selection choices. Furthermore, in a multidimensional conception of talent, disadvantages in one component could be compensated with strengths in other components (Durand-Bush & Salmela, 2001). What is needed is appropriate monitoring of the development of young players and a system supporting sustained development of the whole person. In this system, coaches are central figures. A systems approach also takes into account the role of the parents and school as other influences on the performance system. At the youth academy of FC Augsburg, for example, there is an emphasis on practice that reflects a holistic talent development philosophy. Furthermore, personality assessment is an essential element providing Augsburg coaches with the information they need to become true environmental catalysts in the development of their players.

## A systems approach

Talent development should profit very much from including a systems approach, which consists of different social influences (cf. Williams & Franks, 1998). The social system of the young talented players usually goes beyond the central performance systems of sport and school with family members, friends, or the peer group. In particular, parents play an important role as attachment figures, role models, and legal guardians (Beckmann-Waldenmayer, 2019, Chapter 20 in this book; Goldstein & Iso-Ahola, 2008). They spend a huge amount of time supporting young sport talents. Neely and Holt (2014) suggest that strong parental support is beneficial for young athletes. Indeed, Bremer (2012) found a positive relationship between parental support and positive sport experiences of children. Adequate parental support includes providing emotional support, financial support, and transportation (Jowett & Timson-Katchis, 2005). Additionally, during adolescence peer group contacts are of particular importance and should therefore be taken into account. The central performance systems of children and adolescents consisting of sport and school will influence the psychological dynamics of the family system and friendships (Beckmann-Waldenmayer, 2012). To promote a smooth and resource-saving flow of activity within the performance system of sport and school, it is important to support the balance through relevant approaches (e.g. sport psychological support). This implies strengthening the young players' personality development and thereby increasing their resilience. In line with a dynamic concept of talent development this involves a growth orientation (Dweck, 2016) which will be addressed in the following.

## Error culture and personal growth orientation

Rudi Völler, the national German football coach at the time (pre-2006), frequently criticised the players for playing badly and making mistakes. German football legend

Franz Beckenbauer even called them 'a troop of cucumbers' meaning total losers. Unsurprisingly, the team was indeed very unsuccessful. Then Jürgen Klinsmann took over as national coach. In addition to high-speed offensive play, he introduced a culture in which errors were considered part of the learning process. In preparation for the upcoming FIFA World Cup he even encouraged his players to make errors. One reason for this was that he wanted his players to become less risk aversive. The other goal was that they should learn from their mistakes and thereby build more confidence. At first his team actually performed poorly. With a 1–4 loss against Italy in the year of the World Cup they reached 'rock bottom' and received devastating criticism from the public. Nevertheless, Klinsmann continued with his approach. Eventually, during the World Cup the team played outstandingly. Players who before had been accused of not knowing how to control the ball now advanced to being highly regarded team members. Even though they did not win the World Cup, finishing in third place, the team was now highly praised. And the World Cup was later referred to as Germany's summer fairy tale.

Many successful people view failures as learning experiences that help them to succeed eventually. In line with this, we consider a famous quote from Winston Churchill: 'Success is walking from failure to failure with no loss of enthusiasm.' Michael Jordan, undoubtedly one of the most successful basketball players, said: 'I have missed more than 9000 shots in my career.... 26 times, I have been trusted to take the game-winning shot and missed. I have failed over and over and over again in my life. And that's why I succeeded.' These quotes are very characteristic of what Carol Dweck (2016) calls a 'growth mindset'.

The summer fairy tale of the German football team very well describes what a difference it can make to change from a fixed mindset to a growth mindset. The fixed mindset is associated with the assumption of stable abilities or static talent. Failure and thus making a mistake is perceived as showing a lack of ability. Failure is transformed from an action that went awry to an identity: I am a failure. In contrast, according to Dweck (2016, p. 32) Michael Jordan, proclaimed to be 'the greatest basketball player of all time', has a growth mindset. Jordan knew he had worked hard to develop his abilities. He had experienced struggles and setbacks but always continued to work to become better.

Children's beliefs or views about talent development in sport are influenced by significant others such as parents, peers, and coaches in sport settings. These views influence child development. According to Dweck (2016) if the view is a fixed mindset with the underlying assumption that qualities are carved in stone, which represents the traditional way of looking at talent, there will be a constant urge to prove oneself. From this perspective, errors demonstrate a lack of ability. As a consequence, a learning process, like in learning a new technique, becomes threatening because failing is interpreted as lack of talent.

A fixed mindset appears to be related to win or ego orientation (Gill & Deeter, 1988). A high ego orientation (norm-referenced) is associated with the attitude that winning is all that counts and personal identity is bound to winning in sports: you are only somebody when you are successful (self-worth). Dweck (2016) speaks of 'the loss of one's self to failure' (p. 34). Several studies have shown that such an orientation is detrimental to the development of young talents. In fact, a high win orientation in junior athletes was found to be highly correlated with drop-out (Hellandsig, 1998; Neely & Holt, 2014).

In contrast, in a growth mindset, failure may also be painful but is not seen as defining a person's worth. Instead, failure is associated with learning and development. In this case challenge and interest in learning go hand-in-hand. More challenging goals are set and failure just indicates that one has to try harder. A growth mindset is not about immediate perfection but about learning, developing, growing over time: confronting challenges and making progress.

## Personality assessment to determine strengths and weaknesses to personalise development

A range of psychological factors appears to underlie a young player's potential for growth. Research has dealt with creative potential, mental stability, individualism, egoism, ambition, and trainability (Güllich, 2014; Sæther, 2014; Williams & Reilly, 2000). The seven psychological predictors of athletic success identified by Smith and Christensen (1995) could be reduced to more general concepts like the achievement motive, action versus state orientation, and volitional components. These personality characteristics are assessed annually at FC Augsburg's youth academy to determine players' strengths and weaknesses. The information is used to individually develop players in the areas where they show weaknesses. The personality measures can be considered as a long-term measure of talent development. Additionally, coaches can use the personality assessment information to support their players in coaching at an individual level.

A longitudinal study on psychological talent characteristics with a large sample of players in German youth academies included the Achievement Motive Scale (AMS) and the Volitional Components Questionnaire (VCQ) (Feichtinger & Höner, 2015). An increase in motivational, volitional, and self-regulation capacities was found in young football players between 12 and 14 years over a period of several years. These findings show that some psychological tests are able to identify important developmental characteristics of players. The assessment also helps to recognise individual differences relevant for competition and performance.

Feichtinger and Höner (2015) did not include the Action Control Scale (Action Control Scale-Sport, Beckmann & Wenhold, 2009) in their study. This scale, however, provides very useful information for coaches. A low score on the failure-related ACS indicates failure-related state orientation which is associated with the danger of rumination and a blockage of self-regulation. But this personality disposition has a number of positive aspects as well. Players with this disposition are highly coachable; anecdotally, they are grateful for being given direction. Most importantly, if they are in a balanced mood (relaxed with largely positive affect) they can have a larger creative potential than action-oriented players (cf. Beckmann & Kazen, 1994). Therefore, in a study by Beckmann and Trux (1991) the majority of play makers on German first and second league teams in basketball and volleyball were found to be failure-related state-oriented. Of course, these players are likely to show a performance collapse after a severe mistake or a series of failures, but mental skills training can help them to better cope with such experiences and maintain a good performance level.

In line with Simonton's (1999) approach, recent analysis of personality assessment data reveals an interplay of multidimensional determinants (Beckmann & Schua, 2017). This means that a single score as for example on the SOQ cannot be interpreted as independent of other characteristics of the player. Typically, the pattern rather than a single score yields reliable information. For example, a low score of SOQ competitiveness is found for a player. Considered alone, one might conclude that the player is not suited for competitive football because he does not seem to enjoy competitions and is hence not motivated by competing. Closer inspection of the whole assessment data reveals a pattern that consists of high fear of failure, high failure-related state orientation, and low competitiveness. The major problem in this pattern is actually the high fear of failure. It results in unpleasant ruminations about failing and not meeting expectations (failure-related state orientation). This leads to an anticipation of negative experiences, especially negative emotions when playing in a competition. Of course, this will undermine motivation to compete. Thus, high fear of failure needs to be dealt with in the first instance. If a reduction of fear of failure is achieved the player could come to enjoy competitions and become highly competitive.

The information obtained through the personality assessment is useful for coaches to personalise their coaching. Based on the assessment information the coach may communicate differently with a player high in fear of failure than with a player high in hope for success. Their communications should, for example, emphasise improvements of the player and reduce the player's self-doubt of his own ability. Additionally, whereas state-orientated players require some support to perform well, action-orientated players feel quickly restricted by too many rules and instructions. This is illustrated by a case at a Youth Academy. David is an action-oriented left forward player. He played exceptionally well on the U 19 team but rather poorly on the U 23 team. The U 23 coach, who coached in a very controlling way, complained that he often lost concentration during the game. The U 19 coach, who used very personalised coaching, giving the left forward individual space, could not confirm the U 23 coach's evaluation. In a different context, Antoni and Beckmann (1989) found that action-oriented safety inspectors of a chemical company who were given explicit goals by their superiors showed reactance and performed poorer than without the external goal setting. In the case of the left forward it was assumed that the reactance would result in a reduction of concentration. This was explained to the U 23 coach with the suggestion to give the player more individual free space for decisions on the pitch. The coach implemented this approach in the next games and the 'problem' player became one of the most successful players on his team.

Personality dispositions may also be relevant for the playing position on the pitch. Certain personality dispositions have been suggested in relation to different functions in the team. Positions on the pitch have different tasks and therefore different personality characteristics could be advantageous for the different positions. Daskal (2011) identifies a central midfielder for example as a playmaker, who leads the team and requires a big amount of creative potential to find solutions for every possible situation a team can get in. So it can be expected that coaches rank a midfielder, especially the playmaker, with a higher creative potential than a goalkeeper. This was actually supported in a study by Hartmann, Schua, and Beckmann (2017) with the central midfield players being attributed the highest creative potential by the coaches. State-oriented people tend to deliberate different options and should therefore have more ideas for solutions of play situations on the pitch; i.e. play more creatively than action-oriented players. In fact, Beckmann and Trux (1991) found state-oriented players excelled in playmaker positions whereas action-oriented players appeared to be best suited for striker positions.

Individualism or originality describes the idea that each person should think and act independently rather than depending on others. In the context of playing positions in football, the different situations require different amounts of individualism like wingers, who need to think more individualistically and try to enter one-on-one situations to perform their best game (Daskal, 2011). Egoism is closely related to individualism, but relates more to the selfishness of a person. There may be contrasts between a striker, who when he or she has the ball is mostly only focused on him-/herself and is even in need of this egoism to execute his or her goals. A central midfielder on the other hand needs to play for the whole team and organise the game. Therefore, a central midfielder should have a lower degree of egoism (Daskal, 2011). Hartmann et al. (2017) found individualism and egoism to be mainly attributed by their coaches to strikers whereas defenders were in general seen as less individualistic and egoistic. Thus, the data obtained through personality assessment could also be important for finding a talent's best position on the pitch.

## Mental skills training

Talent development involves personality development and the training of mental skills to improve self-regulation capacities. In the first author's own work with FC Augsburg, the mental skills training programme is based on the personality assessment taking into account strengths and weaknesses. At FC Augsburg we start with basic relaxation training in the team of under 9 year olds (U 9). The relaxation training consists of age-appropriate imaginary journeys, e.g. accompanying Captain Nemo on an underwater excursion meeting dolphins, etc. Step-by-step further concepts are introduced in the older teams: from relaxation breathing to Progressive Muscle Relaxation (PMR) to Autogenous Training (AT) (see Beckmann & Elbe, 2015 for more detailed descriptions).

Gradually, more mental skills are introduced and practised including, for example, imagery and positive self-talk (Beckmann & Elbe, 2015; Konter et al., 2019, Chapter 14 in this book). Special emphasis is put on embodiment techniques and routines. The players learn how controlling their body (posture, gait) can influence their own psychological reactions as well as the perceptions of the opposition players (if your posture reveals a loss of confidence you may build up confidence in your opponent). Special techniques are included in practice like somatic markers, or clenching of the left hand as a reset technique to avoid choking under pressure when, for example, shooting a penalty (see Beckmann & Elbe, 2015 for details). Routines for standard situations are developed and personalised for each player.

An overall goal of the mental skills programme is achieving mental stability, i.e. the ability to cope with stress in daily situations. As young football players progress to become professionals, their level of stress from different sources increases. To prevent burnout and depression, coping skills to deal with stress are developed in addition to relaxation techniques (see e.g. Nixdorf, Beckmann, & Nixdorf, 2019, Chapter 25 in this book).

## Conclusions

Player selection appears to be unavoidable because of limited training facilities, coaches, players on a team, and financial resources in a sport such as football. Therefore, talent identification is seen as a vital part of talent development. But there is almost no systematic and verified knowledge on criteria to identify the most talented players. Coaches usually select players according to immediate needs (winning) during the season, not taking into account the process of development of the athlete. The probability of not selecting a player with potential is high. Also, given a dynamic concept of talent, selection at one point is likely to result in a loss of a number of talented players to the game. According to findings by Güllich (2014) it would be more effective to repeat the procedures of selection and de-selection at all ages yearly to enhance talent identification instead of picking talent only in the early stages.

Regarding the dynamic nature of talent, the developmental process is described as the transformation of an individual's potential into performance in a particular area. From this perspective talent promotion is to develop individual potential for elite performance in the future. Those involved in this process should be aware of players' perspectives and pay less attention to the current level of performance. In fact, contrary to popular assumptions, research shows that current capacity is no prerequisite for future success (Kearney & Hayes, 2018). It appears to be crucial for sustained talent development to not merely develop the technical and tactical skills needed on the pitch. Rather, talent development should become 'life coaching' that develops the whole person taking into account the different systems relevant to them in a multidimensional and multifaceted way (cf. Simonton, 1999).

## References

Abbott, A., Button, B., Pepping, G. J., & Collins, C. (2005). Unnatural selection: Talent identi-fication and development in sport. *Nonlinear Dynamics, Psychology, and Life Sciences, 9*, 61–88.

Abbott, A., & Collins, D. (2004). Eliminating the dichotomy between theory and practice in talent identification and development: Considering the role of psychology. *Journal of Sports Sciences, 22*, 395–408.

Antoni, C., & Beckmann, J. (1989). An action control conceptualization of goal setting and feedback effects. In U. E. Kleinbeck, H. H. Quast, H. Thierry, & H. Häcker (Eds.), *Work motivation* (pp. 41–52). Englewood Cliffs, NJ: Erlbaum.

Baker, J., Horton, S., Robertson-Wilson, J., & Wall, M. (2003). Nurturing sport expertise: Factors influencing the development of elite athlete. *Journal of Sports Science and Medicine, 2*, 1–9.

Barnsley, R. H., Thompson, A. H., & Legault, P. (1992). Family planning: Football style. The relative age effect in football. *International Review of Sport Sociology, 27*, 77–86.

Beckmann, J., & Elbe, A. (2015). *Sport psychological interventions in competitive sports*. Newcastle, England: Cambridge Scholars Publishing.

Beckmann, J., Elbe, A.-M., Szymanski, B., & Ehrlenspiel, F. (2006). *Chancen und Risiken vom Leben im Verbundsystem von Schule und Leistungssport: Psychologische, soziologische und Leistungs-aspekte* [Chances and risks of living in an integrated elite system of sport and school]. Cologne, Germany: Sport und Buch Strauß.

Beckmann, J., & Kazen, M. (1994). Action and state orientation and the performance of top athletes. A differentiated picture. In J. Kuhl & J. Beckmann (Eds.), *Volition and personality: Action and state orientation* (pp. 439–451). Seattle, WA: Hogrefe.

Beckmann, J., & Schua, T. (2017). *Diagnostic pattern analysis.* Manuscript, Technical University Munich.

Beckmann, J., & Trux, J. (1991). Wen lasse ich wo spielen? Persönlichkeitseigenschaften und die Eignung für bestimmte Positionen in Sportspielmannschaften [Who should play which position? Personality characteristics and their relation to playing different positions in sport games]. *Sportpsychologie, 5*(3), 18–21.

Beckmann, J., & Wenhold, F. (2009). *Handlungsorientierung im Sport: Manual zur Handlungsorientierung im Sport (HOSP)* [Action orientation in sports: Manual]. Bonn, Germany: Bundesinstitut für Sportwissenschaft.

Beckmann-Waldenmayer, D. (2012). Ein systemisches Betreuungsmodell für den Nachwuchsleistungssport [A systemic model for counselling in youth sports]. In D. Beckmann-Waldenmayer & J. Beckmann (Eds.), *Handbuch sportpsychologischer Praxis: Mentales Training in den olympischen Sportarten* [Handbook of applied sport psychology: Mental training in Olympic sports] (pp. 70–81). Balingen, Germany: Spitta.

Beckmann-Waldenmayer, D. (2019). Parental coaching. In E. Konter, J. Beckmann, & T. Loughead (Eds.), *Football psychology: From theory to practice.* London, England: Routledge.

Bremer, K. L. (2012). Parental involvement, pressure, and support in youth sport: A narrative literature review. *Journal of Family Theory & Review, 4,* 235–248.

Brown, J. (2001). *Sports talent: How to identify and develop outstanding athletes.* Champaign, IL: Human Kinetics.

Calvin, M. (2017). *No hunger in paradise: The players. The journey. The dream.* London, England: Cornerstone.

Christensen, M. K. (2009). 'An eye for talent': Talent identification and the 'practical sense' of top-level soccer coaches. *Sociology of Sport Journal, 26,* 365–382.

Daskal, O. (2011). *Personality test – What virtues are needed to play a certain position in football.* Retrieved from www.soccerissue.com/2011/04/02/personality-test/.

Durand-Bush, N., & Salmela, J. (2001). The development of talent in sport. In R. H. Singer, H. A. Hausenblas, & C. Janette (Eds.), *Handbook of sport psychology* (pp. 269–289). New York, NY: Wiley.

Dweck, C. S. (2016). *Mindset: The new psychology of success.* New York, NY: Ballantine Books.

Elbe, A.-M., Beckmann, J., & Szymanski, B. (2003). Die Entwicklung des allgemeinen und sportspezifischen Leistungsmotivs von Sportinternatsschüler/innen [Development of general and sport-specific achievement motive in sport boarding school pupils]. *Psychologie und Sport, 10,* 134–143.

Feichtinger, P., & Höner, O. (2015). Talented football players' development of achievement motives, volitional components, and self-referential cognitions: A longitudinal study. *European Journal of Sport Science, 15,* 1–9. doi:10.1080/17461391.2015.1051134.

Gagné, F. (2000). Understanding the complex choreography of talent development through DGMT-based analysis. In K. Heller, F. J. Mönks, R. J. Sternberg, & R. Subotnik (Eds.), *International handbook for research on giftedness and talent* (2nd ed., pp. 67–79). Oxford, England: Pergamon Press.

Gill, D. L., & Deeter, T. E. (1988). Development of the Sport Orientation Questionnaire. *Research Quarterly for Exercise and Sport, 59,* 191–202.

Goldstein, J. D., & Iso-Ahola, S. E. (2008). Determinants of parents' sideline-rage emotions and behaviours at youth soccer games. *Journal of Applied Social Psychology, 38,* 1442–1462. doi:10.1111/j.1559-1816.2008.00355.x.

Green, C. (2009). *Every boy's dream: England's football future on the line.* London, England: A & C Publishers.

Güllich, A. (2014). Selection, de-selection and progression in German football talent promotion. *European Journal of Sport Science, 14,* 530–537. doi:10.1080/17461391.2013.858371.

Hartmann, M., Schua, T., & Beckmann, J. (2017). *Personality characteristics and positions in football.* Manuscript, Technical University Munich.

Hellandsig, E. T. (1998). Motivational predictors of high performance and discontinuation in different types of sports among talented teenage athletes. *International Journal of Sport Psychology, 29*, 27–44.

Helson, W. F., Hodges, N. J., Van Winckel, J., & Starkes, J. L. (2000). The role of talent, physical precocity and practice in the development of soccer expertise. *Journal of Sports Sciences, 18*, 727–736.

Hohmann, A. (2009). *Entwicklung sportlicher Talente an sportbetonten Schulen. Schwimmen. Leichtathletik. Handball* [Development of sport talents in sport schools: Swimming, track and field, handball]. Petersberg, Germany: Michael Imhof.

Howe, M. J. A., Davidson, J. W., & Sloboda, J. A. (1998). Innate talents: Reality or myth? *Behavioral and Brain Sciences, 21*, 399–407.

Jowett, S., & Timson-Katchis, M. (2005). Social networks in sport: Parental influence on the coach-athlete relationship. *The Sport Psychologist, 19*, 267–287.

Kearney, P. E., & Hayes, P. R. (2018). Excelling at youth level in competitive track and field athletics is not a prerequisite for later success. *Journal of Sports Sciences*, doi:10.1080/026404 14.2018.1465724.

Konter, E., Beckmann, J., & Mallett, C. (2019). Psychological skills in football. In E. Konter, J. Beckmann, & T. Loughead (Eds.), *Football psychology: From theory to practice*. London, England: Routledge.

Kreiner-Phillips, K., & Orlick, T. (1993). Winning after winning: The psychology of ongoing excellence. *The Sport Psychologist, 7*, 31–48.

Larsen, C. H., Henriksen, K., Alfermann, D., & Christensen, M. K. (2014). Preparing footballers for the next step: An intervention program from an ecological perspective. *The Sport Psychologist, 28*(1), 91–102.

Morris, T. (2000). Psychological characteristics and talent identification in soccer. *Journal of Sports Sciences, 18*, 715–726.

National Collegiate Athletic Association (NCCA). (2017, 10 March). Estimated probability of competing in professional athletics. Retrieved from www.ncaa.org/about/resources/ research/estimated-probability-competing-professional-athletics.

Neely, K. C., & Holt, N. L. (2014). Parents' perspectives on the benefits of sport participation for young children. *The Sport Psychologist, 28*, 255–268.

Nixdorf, I., Beckmann, J., & Nixdorf, R. (2019). Preventing burnout and depression in youth football. In E. Konter, J. Beckmann, & T. Loughead (Eds.), *Football psychology: From theory to practice*. London, England: Routledge.

Peltola, E. (1992). Talent identification. *New Studies in Athletics, 7*(3), 7–12.

Reilly, T., Williams, A. M., Nevill, A., & Franks, A. (2000). A multidisciplinary approach to talent identification in soccer. *Journal of Sports Sciences, 18*, 695–702.

Reilly, T., Williams, A. M., & Richardson, D. (2003). Identifying talented players. In T. Reilly & A. M. Williams (Eds.), *Science and soccer* (2nd ed., pp. 307–326). London, England: Routledge.

Sæther, S. A. (2014, 19 March). Identification of talent in soccer – What do coaches look for? Retrieved from www.idrottsforum.org/saether140319/.

Salinero, J. J., Pérez, B., Burillo, P., & Lesma, M. L. (2013). Relative age effect in European professional football: Analysis by position. *Journal of Human Sport and Exercise, 8*, 966–973.

Simmons, C., & Paull, G. C. (2001). Season-of-birth bias in association football. *Journal of Sports Sciences, 19*, 677–686.

Simonton, D. K. (1999). Talent and its development: An epigenetic and emergenic model. *Psychological Review, 106*, 435–457.

Singer, R. N., & Janelle, C. M. (1999). Determining sport expertise: From genes to supremes. *International Journal of Sport Psychology, 30*, 117–150.

Smith, R. E., & Christensen, D. S. (1995). Psychological skills as predictors of performance and survival in professional baseball. *Journal of Sport & Exercise Psychology, 17*, 399–415.

Stratton, G., Reilly, T., Williams, A. M., & Richardson, D. (2004). *Youth soccer: From science to performance.* London, England: Routledge.

Vaeyens, R., Coelho E Silva, M. J., Visscher, C., Philippaerts, R. M., & Williams, A. M. (2013). Identifying young players. In A. M. Williams (Ed.), *Science and soccer: Developing elite performers* (3rd ed., pp. 289–306). Milton Park, England: Routledge.

Vaeyens, R., Lenoir, M., Williams, A. M., & Philippaerts, R. M. (2008). Talent identification and development programmes in sport: Current models and future directions. *Sports Medicine, 38,* 703–714.

Vealey, R. S. (1992). Personality and sport: A comprehensive view. In T. S. Horn (Ed.), *Advances in sport psychology* (pp. 25–59). Champaign, IL: Human Kinetics.

Vrljic, K., & Mallett, C. J. (2008). The knowledge of youth performance soccer coaches in identifying talented young soccer players. *International Journal of Coaching Science, 2*(1), 63–81.

Wiese-Bjornstal, D. M., LaVoi, N. M., & Omli, J. (2009). Child and adolescent development and sport participation. In B. Brewer (Ed.), *International Olympic Committee (IOC) medical commission handbook of sports medicine and science: Sport psychology volume* (pp. 97–112). Chichester, England: Blackwell Publishing.

Wiium, N., Lie, S. A., Ommundsen, Y., & Enksen, H. R. (2010). Does relative age effect exist among Norwegian professional soccer players? *International Journal of Applied Sports Sciences, 22*(2), 66–76.

Williams, A. M., Davids, K., Burwitz, L., & Williams, J. G. (1993). Visual search and sports performance. *Australian Journal of Science and Medicine in Sport, 25,* 55–65.

Williams, A. M., & Franks, A. (1998). Talent identification in soccer. *Sports, Exercise and Injury, 4,* 159–165.

Williams, A. M., & Reilly, T. (2000). Talent identification and development in soccer. *Journal of Sports Sciences, 18,* 657–667.

# 22 How youth football players learn to succeed

*Laura Jonker, Barbara C. H. Huijgen, Bart Heuvingh, Marije T. Elferink-Gemser, and Chris Visscher*

## Abstract

Elite youth football players need to develop multiple performance characteristics to be successful, such as physical, technical, tactical, and psychological skills. To become a professional football player, young players need to invest large numbers of training hours over a prolonged period of time to increase their chance of developing a successful career. In this context, self-regulation of learning is supposed to favour learning efficiency. Previous research states that young players with good self-regulatory skills were found to excel over those with poor self-regulatory skills during career development. Self-regulation of learning refers to the extent to which individuals are metacognitively, motivationally, and behaviourally proactive participants in their own learning process. Skills such as reflection and planning (i.e. metacognitive skills), but also effort and self-efficacy (i.e. motivational aspects) are part of the self-regulatory process. In this chapter, we give an insight into the career pathway of 525 elite youth football players in Dutch football academies and relate their chances of becoming professional football players to their development of self-regulatory skills.

## Association football in modern society

The game of football has evolved immensely over the last years. Not only has it become a multi-billion-dollar market, but the characteristics of the game and the players have changed as well. For example, the game has become faster and players spend increasing numbers of training hours to meet the physical demands that go along with a faster game (Barnes, Archer, Hogg, Bush, & Bradley, 2014; Elferink-Gemser, Huijgen, Coelho-E-Silva, Lemmink, & Visscher, 2012; FIFA, 2016; Jonker, Elferink-Gemser, & Visscher, 2009). One might, for example, think of improved agility and technical characteristics to execute the increased number of explosive sprints, high intensity runs, and successful passes when compared to the 2006/2007 season (Barnes et al., 2014). However, not only are the physical and technical demands of importance and may have risen, but also the need for good psychological skills may have been increased. One might think of psychological skills such as mental toughness, decision-making skills, concentration, self-talk, and/or self-regulatory skills (see also related chapters in this book).

Amongst the importance of various psychological skills, recent scientific work addressed the importance of self-regulatory skills in elite football (Huijgen,

Leemhuis, Kok, Verburgh, Oosterlaan, Elferink-Gemser, & Visscher, 2015; Pesce, Tessitore, Casella, Pirritano, & Capranica, 2007; Verburgh, Scherder, van Lange, & Oosterlaan, 2014; Vestberg, Gustafson, Maurex, Ingvar, & Petrovic, 2012) and also football academies and federations have started to pay attention to these skills. Teaching players how to take responsibility for their own learning by means of self-regulation of learning has, for example, become part of the masterplan of the Dutch Football Association (KNVB; Goes et al., 2016).

## Football academies in the Netherlands

Of the 255,000 Dutch football players between 12 and 20 years, approximately 1.5% are selected for a football academy (Jonker, 2015). Young players who have been selected can play in one of 28 football academies in the Netherlands (Goes et al., 2016). The players in these football academies are provided with extra training facilities and training sessions and are supervised by highly certified trainers. This means that they are given the best opportunities to improve towards senior level and are seen as elite youth football players (Baker, Horton, Robertson-Wilson, & Wall, 2003). Presently, Dutch football academies scout their youth players within grassroot clubs mainly on technical, tactical, and physical aspects. However, today's coaches also become more and more convinced by the idea that skills such as leadership, mental toughness, self-determination, and learning efficiency should be part of the scouting and training protocol. They feel that young football players often don't fulfil their potential due to their mindset and/or not taking responsibility for their own careers (Goes et al., 2016).

Several Dutch professional football academies (i.e. PSV, FC Utrecht, AZ, Vitesse, NAC Breda, and FC Groningen amongst others) address the use of self-regulatory skills and the type of mindset in their elite youth football players (Goes et al., 2016). Two popular theories are Dweck's approach of a growth versus a fixed mindset (Dweck, 2006; Dweck & Master, 2009) and Zimmerman's theory of self-regulation (Zimmerman, 2000). It is believed that the development of players should profit from a growth mindset (i.e. players' beliefs that they have influence on their success and that talent and hard work go hand in hand with that success) and the use of self-regulatory strategies (i.e. the extent to which individuals are metacognitively, motivationally, and behaviourally proactive participants in their own learning process) to make the most out of the time spend on training (Dweck, 2006; Zimmerman, 2002).

## Selecting players for the first senior team

By selecting players for a football academy and providing them with the best facilities and coaches, football academies are hoping that youth players will develop their football-related skills towards the level needed for playing in their first senior team. Skills are considered to develop in a dynamical system and do not develop in a linear way over time (see Beckmann & Beckmann-Waldenmayer, Chapter 21 in this book). Only a few players are so-called early bloomers and show the capacities to make their debut in the Premier League of their country at a very young age when compared to the mean age of that competition and the age at which most players make a debut (i.e. Clarence Seedorf, Arjen Robben, and Wayne Rooney at age 16 and more recently Matthijs de Ligt, Justin Kluivert, Mario Götze, and Julian Draxler at age 17; CIES Football Observatory, 2018). In the Netherlands, most players seem to make their debut between 19 and 21 years of age at senior professional level (personal communication, Dutch FA). When participating in senior professional competitions, players are faced with increased pressure, an increased focus on winning, and more numbers of training hours (Goes et al., 2016; MacNamara & Collins, 2010). The development of psychological skills (e.g. motivation, determination, self-regulation; see Konter, Beckmann, & Mallett, Chapter 14 in this book) to meet these increased standards seems to be helpful as most athletes struggle with the standards after making the transition to professional football (MacNamara, Button, & Collins, 2010; MacNamara & Collins, 2010).

## The purpose of this book chapter

The authors conducted a longitudinal study investigating the career pathways of elite youth football players (i.e. players selected as part of a football academy). The attained performance level in adulthood (i.e. professional level vs semi- or non-professional level) was related to their self-regulatory skills, their mean number of training hours per season, years of football experience, and their football academy during adolescence. A player is referred to as professional when he is playing football for pay on a full-time basis. A player is referred to as semi- or non-professional when his main activities and income are not a consequence of his investments in football. Professional and semi- or non-professional players are distinguished on the basis of the number of ECI-points (i.e. 1,400 points, see 'determining attained performance level' for an elaboration). We know that other characteristics such as technical, physical, and other psychological skills are of importance as well, but decided to focus on the before-mentioned aspects first. As such, in this chapter we give insight into the career pathway of elite youth football players and relate their chances of becoming professional football players to their self-regulatory skills.

## Number of training hours

A substantial body of research showed the importance of training hours in the attainment of senior competitive level in sports (Ericsson, Krampe, & Tesch-Römer, 1993; Ford, Ward, Hodges, & Williams, 2009; Helsen, Starkes, & Hodges, 1998 amongst others). The most popular theory underpinning the relationship between performance and hours of training is Ericsson's deliberate practice theory (Ericsson et al., 1993). This theory is well known by its 10,000 hours rule, but also underlines the need to be metacognitively involved, i.e. practice deliberately (Ericsson, 2003; Ericsson et al., 1993). This means that football players need to invest maximal effort and concentration in activities that are not inherently motivating to improve their performance (Ericsson et al., 1993). In recent years, the deliberate practice approach has been criticised as well; especially related to the number of hours spent on training and the importance of deliberate practice and play activities (Macnamara, Moreau, & Hambrick, 2016; Ward, Hodges, Starkes, & Williams, 2007 amongst others). Nevertheless, the importance of assessing critically on which aspects of performance improvement players need to spend their training time on and the notion that one cannot train 'mindlessly' if progression is to be made seem to hold. When it comes to this metacognitive involvement, an emerging body of evidence suggests that a measure of this involvement is related to football players' ability to regulate their own learning (Jonker, Elferink-Gemser, Toering, Lyons, & Visscher, 2010; Toering, Elferink-Gemser, Jordet, & Visscher, 2009). In other words, to their self-regulatory skills. Self-regulated learning is related to someone's capability to maintain optimal levels of emotional, motivational, and cognitive arousal (Diamond, 2013; Zimmerman, 2000).

## Self-regulatory skills and their development

Metacognitive strategies can be defined as the use of strategies that are thoughtfully brought to mind as one prepares to solve a problem (Pesce et al., 2007). Skills such as reflection (i.e. the extent to which players reappraise what they have learned and adapt past knowledge and experience to improve performance), planning (i.e. the awareness of task demands before execution of the task and the capacity to act accordingly), self-monitoring (i.e. the awareness of actions during execution), and evaluation (i.e. the ability to assess both the process employed and the end product achieved after execution) are considered important (Herl et al., 1999; Hong & O'Neil Jr, 2001; Howard, McGee, Shia, & Hong, 2000; Peltier, Hay, & Drago, 2006). For example, Jonker and colleagues (2010) and Toering and colleagues (2009) amongst others, showed that elite youth football players outperform their sub-elite and non-elite peers on metacognitive skills such as reflective thinking.

The importance of motivational aspects has been underpinned as well (Cleary & Zimmerman, 2001; Jonker et al., 2010; Toering et al., 2009 amongst others). Although motivation research has a long tradition resulting in several aspects and definitions of motivation, motivation in this study is defined as the degree to which learners are self-efficaciously, autonomously, and intrinsically motivated to achieve a specific goal (Hong & O'Neil Jr, 2001). This means that elite youth players need to have confidence in their skills, feel a span of freedom to make their own choices, and intrinsically want to be a football player over possible external rewards. Prior studies showed that elite youth football players outperform their non-elite peers on the motivational aspects of effort (i.e. willingness to attain the task goal) and self-efficacy (i.e. how players judge their own capabilities to organise and execute the required actions; Bandura, 1997; Herl et al., 1999; Hong & O'Neil Jr, 2001; Schwarzer & Jerusalem, 1995; Toering et al., 2009).

Developmental studies have shown that people develop self-regulatory skills naturally to some extent. Self-regulatory skills in general are considered to develop from the early age of 2–6 years and these skills increase with age (Alexander, Carr, & Schwanenflugel, 1995; Zelazo & Müller, 2002). When children are approximately 12 years of age, the brain is supposed to have matured enough to be able to use these skills from a more domain-specific repertoire to a general set that can be applied more flexibly between learning tasks (Van der Stel & Veenman, 2008). This means that for young children the brain is only capable to use knowledge learned in one domain for the sake of that domain. For example, the use of planning skills to learn for an exam will only be used to finish the learning of the school task on time. Nevertheless, planning skills can also be used to make a plan on how to train your free kick. It is the same type of strategy, but used for a purpose in another domain. The capacity to use self-regulatory skills within and between domains increases during adolescence (Sebastian, Burnett, & Blakemore, 2008; Zelazo & Müller, 2002).

In addition to natural development, challenging environments are suggested to stimulate the development of self-regulatory skills (Boekaerts, 1997; Boekaerts & Corno, 2005). Challenging environments are those which are rich with goal-setting and feedback. A football environment is such an environment as football players are constantly challenged to set short-term goals such as giving a good pass, to overtake an opponent or score. While executing these actions, players will naturally receive feedback. For example, by missing a penalty and failing to score, the ball is giving feedback, the coach will give feedback, and teammates will react and give information as to how the player can do better next time. Most likely, feedback is also provided by the opponents and the audience.

## Examples of self-regulatory skill use in professional football

A good example of using self-regulatory skills in football is related to the development of the pass between defensive lines of Wim Jonk. Wim Jonk is a former Dutch professional football player who used to play at Ajax with Dennis Bergkamp. With his pass he was able to cross the defence and put Bergkamp in the position to score. After a while all defenders were familiar with his speciality and became capable of defending these passes across the field. For Jonk, this was the moment when he started reflecting on keeping this speciality. So, to be able to unmark Bergkamp, he decided to start practising how to kick the ball with different parts of the foot to hide his intentional action for the defenders (reflection). He decided to come earlier to training (planning) to practise this. During his practice, he was looking back whether he was still on track to improving his pass (self-monitoring) and afterwards he was evaluating whether practising his pass resulted in improved performance. When doing this, it was important for him to put forth effort by coming earlier to practice, but also to believe that practising his pass would lead to unmark Bergkamp (self-efficacy). This is one example of great self-regulatory skills, but there are numerous others. Also, Pierre van Hooijdonk decided to focus on his free kick as he believed that this would make him an important man for Feyenoord and the Dutch squad. He stayed for about 15–30 minutes after each training session to practise his free kick, to count how many goals he scored, and evaluated whether practising his free kick was the best strategy to become more valuable as a player. Because of his practising, his free kick became his speciality and he ended up scoring the decisive goal in the 2002 Europa League final.

## The use of self-regulatory skills for the attainment of professional football

Although much research has already shown the importance of self-regulatory skills by comparing elite with sub-elite players cross-sectionally (Cleary & Zimmerman, 2001; Jonker et al., 2010; Toering et al., 2009), less is known about the importance of self-regulatory skills to increase one's chances of becoming a professional football player. The Groningen talent studies are among the first to have gathered longitudinal data on different important variables that might be able to predict attained performance level in football (Huijgen, Elferink-Gemser, Post, & Visscher, 2009;

Roescher, Elferink-Gemser, Huijgen, & Visscher, 2010). For this chapter, we used a longitudinal design on self-regulatory skills (i.e. reflection, planning, monitoring, evaluation, effort, and self-efficacy), number of training hours, years of football experience, and youth performance level (i.e. measured by the level of the football academy) to determine the important predictors for the career pathway of players in Dutch football academies. Measurements took place when the players ($N$=525; all males) were between 13 and 20 years and in the competitive seasons 2006/2007 through 2009/2010. These characteristics were measured with a self-report questionnaire (SRL-SRS) that was especially conducted for these types of research and found to be valid and reliable (Toering, Elferink-Gemser, Jonker, Heuvelen, & Visscher, 2012). This questionnaire measures the six self-regulatory aspects on a Likert-type scale and measures to what extent players say they use self-regulatory skills. As we followed the players within the football academies between the 2006/2007 and 2009/2010 competitive seasons, we were able to collect longitudinal data (i.e. up to four measurements per player). To investigate whether the players attained a senior professional football level, we determined the attained performance level of the football players, 9 years after the competitive season 2009/2010, based on their club in the 2015/2016 competitive season.

### Determining attained performance level

Measuring performance level in a complex sport such as football is not easy, especially not when you want to compare between players. We decided to determine youth and attained performance level by using the Euro Club Index (ECI). The ECI is a ranking of all football teams in the highest leagues of Europe expressed in ECI points. This means that the higher the number of points, the stronger the team is expected to be. For example, Barcelona had about 4,500 points at the moment of writing and is the strongest team in Europe, whereas the top three teams in the Netherlands (i.e. PSV, Ajax, and Feyenoord) have between 2,250 and 3,250 points.

The advantage of using the ECI is that it enables to compare the relative playing strengths of teams between competitions in Europe at a given point of time. The disadvantage of using this statistic is related to the fact that it does not generate individual player strength. This means that all players of the same team receive a similar ECI value. As no further reliable measurement of player strength is available between country competitions, using team strength to determine player strength is considered sufficient for the purposes of the present study: (1) to get insight in how self-regulatory skills develop in youth football players in Dutch football academies, and (2) to determine important predictive variables.

### How is the ECI determined?

The number of ECI points is derived from actual and historical match results in league matches, in national cup matches, and in UEFA Champions and Europa League or Super Cup matches. Based on historical data the chance that team A wins over team B is predicted and compared to the actual result in which home advantage is taken into account. The impact of recent matches is higher than that of older matches (Gracenote & Hypercube Business Innovation, 2015; for more information see www.euroclubindex.com). For the current study, the ECI points at the start of the 2015/2016 competitive season were used for attained performance level. As the strength of football academies cannot be expressed in ECI points, the ECI value of the first team was used for youth players within the football academies.

## Method and analyses

We used descriptive analyses to determine the percentage of elite youth players making it towards professional football. To draw conclusions on the development of self-regulatory skills, multilevel modelling (MLWin 2.02; Rasbash et al., 1999) was used. Multilevel modelling is a regression analysis that is appropriate for hierarchically structured data. The model describes underlying population trends and models variation related to the time of measurement and individual differences of the players (Peugh & Enders, 2005; Snijders & Bosker, 2000). The procedure described in Snijders and Bosker (2000) was followed to determine the consecutive steps in our model. First, a satisfactory variance structure was established using age. Based on testing each variable against the model including age, we determined the order of the variables entering the model. All six self-regulatory skills were entered separately. We then first modelled the most significant result of all the variables tested against the model with solely age. As youth performance level was most significant, this variable was entered first followed by years of sporting experience and reflective thinking. Number of training hours per week and the other five self-regulatory skills were then added and tested on their significance. During this step-forward method, significance of previous variables was repeatedly checked. Variables that were not significant were excluded from the model ($p < 0.05$). By comparing the deviance of the empty model (i.e. model without prediction variables) and the subsequent models, the model fit was evaluated.

## Results of our analyses

### *10% become a professional football player*

In Table 22.1, information of the 525 elite youth football players in this research is presented. When it comes to the percentage of elite youth players signing a professional contract in football, 10% of them reached professional football. A total of 6% ($n=21$) signed a professional contract at their own football academy, and 3% ($n=11$) as a player of one of the top three clubs in the Netherlands (i.e. PSV, Ajax, or Feyenoord). Only 1% ($n=4$) became a professional player in one of the top competitions abroad (i.e. France, England, or Italy). Of the 90% that became semi-professional football players, non-professional players, or even dropped out of football, most of them were deselected for the first squad either a year before transition to senior competition (17%) or at the moment of their age-related transition (44%).

### *Getting selected for higher youth academies has the highest predictive value*

The multilevel model shows that the football academy that the elite youth football players during adolescence played for has the highest predictive value for the attained performance level ($p < 0.001$). The higher the number of ECI points of the football academy, the higher the chance of signing a contract at a professional football club (i.e. > 1,400 ECI points) 9 years later. Although it is expected that the best elite youth players at a young age choose to play at the highest football academies when they get the choice, these results underline the predictive value of youth performance level related to attained performance level later.

### Predictive value of reflective thinking

Also high scores on reflective thinking (as a self-regulatory skill) is positively related to the chance of reaching professional football ($p=0.04$). This means that reflecting more frequently as an elite youth player increases your chance of becoming a professional football player later. The other self-regulatory skills (i.e. planning, self-monitoring, evaluation, effort, and self-efficacy) did not yield significant results. Reflection involves making sense of previous learning experiences and using this information when setting new goals and making plans for future performance (Ertmer & Newby, 1996). It shapes learning thereby affecting subsequent learning experiences and determining the consecutive steps of the self-regulatory cycle (Mezirow, 1991, 2003). Reflective players are aware of their kind of reasoning, their way of reasoning, and why they need to reason. They are eager to challenge established behavioural patterns and search for strategies to make the most out of their learning.

The use of reflective thinking not only seems to increase the chance of attaining senior professional level in football in general, but our results showed that elite youth football players who attained senior professional level increased in their levels of reflection towards the moment of age-related transition, while the levels of reflective thinking of semi- and non-professional players showed stability. This might suggest that reflective thinking seems to become even more important towards the moment of transition which is in line with earlier research (MacNamara & Collins, 2010). Successful players say that they make more use of this skill.

### Training experience and training volume

No significant predictive value on number of training hours per week has been found in our analyses. As all players were part of a football academy, they all spent large and relatively equal numbers of hours in training. This does not necessarily mean that number of training hours is not important. It seems from Table 22.1 that players from higher football academies (expressed in ECI points larger than 1,400) spend more time on training (mean=7.81; $SD$=2.33) when compared to players from lower football academies (lower than 1,400 points; mean=6.39; $SD$=1.64) for all age categories respectively and that their numbers of hours spent on training per week increase towards the age-related moment of transition. Additionally, elite youth players who reached professional level had more years of football experience ($p<0.001$) specifically as being selected for a football academy (i.e. ages 11–14; Table 22.1) when compared to counterparts who did not reach professional football.

Table 22.1 Means and standard deviations for years of football experience, reflection, and number of training hours per week per attained performance level (i.e., professional players vs semi- or non-professional players)

| | Football experience (yrs) | | | | Reflection (mean score) | | | | Training hours (no. per wk). | | | |
|---|---|---|---|---|---|---|---|---|---|---|---|---|
| | Professional players | | Semi- or non-professional players | | Professional players | | Semi- or non-professional players | | Professional players | | Semi- or non-professional players | |
| | Mean | SD | Mean | SD | Mean | SD | Mean | SD | Mean | SD | Mean | SD |
| 11 and 12 years | 7.29 | 1.05 | 7.00 | 1.16 | 3.95 | 0.81 | 4.18 | 0.37 | 6.75 | 1.94 | 6.41 | 1.13 |
| 13 years | 8.28 | 0.78 | 7.58 | 1.13 | 4.13 | 0.50 | 4.06 | 0.54 | 7.05 | 1.40 | 6.72 | 1.69 |
| 14 years | 8.64 | 1.16 | 8.18 | 1.57 | 4.14 | 0.57 | 4.02 | 0.70 | 7.35 | 2.36 | 7.35 | 3.12 |
| 15 years | 9.22 | 1.60 | 9.38 | 1.38 | 4.22 | 0.41 | 4.07 | 0.53 | 8.46 | 2.39 | 7.27 | 1.67 |
| 16 years | 10.18 | 1.70 | 9.92 | 1.50 | 4.25 | 0.69 | 4.02 | 0.69 | 9.04 | 2.44 | 8.34 | 1.92 |
| 17+ years | 11.63 | 2.22 | 11.65 | 2.04 | 4.36 | 0.42 | 4.12 | 0.59 | 9.53 | 3.16 | 8.16 | 2.19 |

Note
Professional players: 11 and 12 years (n=19), 13 years (n=44), 14 years (n=36), 15 years (n=32), 16 years (n=17), 17+ years (n=16). Semi- or non-professional players:11 & 12 years (n=54), 13 years (n=149), 14 years (n=140), 15 years (n=129), 16 years (n=81), 17+ years (n=73). The n refers to the number of measurements in each age category.

*Early versus late specialisation*

This last result should be interpreted with caution. It would be easy to conclude that having more years of football experience and starting earlier in a football academy favours the discussion of early specialisation in football (i.e. focusing solely on football already at a young age). However, prior work has already addressed that different developmental pathways, including specialising relatively late during development (i.e. a player focuses on a range of different sports and passes through various stages of development), may lead to a successful career in football (Gulbin, Oldenziel, Weissensteiner, & Gagné, 2010; Vaeyens, Güllich, War, & Philippaerts, 2009). This means that players start playing different sports until the age of approximately 12 years (i.e. sampling years), continue by choosing only two or three sports in their years as a teenager (i.e. specialising years), and decide what sport to deliberately focus on at approximately 16 years of age (i.e. Bloom, 1985; Côté, 1999; Côté, Baker, & Abernethy, 2003). The results from the present study should not be interpreted favouring early specialisation as we did not ask the players whether they were, besides of being selected for a football academy, also playing other sports. In addition, the context determines to a high extent what the possibilities of choice are for youth athletes. In the Netherlands, children start playing football from as young as 5 years of age and youth selection already starts before their teenage years. As such, the system seems to stimulate early specialisation. However, in line with Fransen and colleagues (2012), we suggest that from a player's perspective it seems beneficial to be at least part of the football system already during their sampling or specialising years (see the practical implications section below for a discussion regarding this system), but that it would be favourable if they participated in more sports than just football, at least up to the age of around 12.

## Self-regulatory learning or just doing more outside training

The value of frequent use of self-regulatory skills has been underlined by the above-mentioned research. However, what we do not know is what they reflect upon. Therefore, we asked the 2007/2008 and 2008/2009 cohort ($N$=333), within the population used for the study above, about their extra time expenditure outside training to improve performance as part of the SRL-SRS. Amongst extra training, support by additional training, street football, reading about performance improvement, and talking about performance improvement, those who reached professional football spend about twice as much time on thinking about performance improvement per week (i.e. mean=2.8 hours; $SD$=6.3) compared to those who did not reach professional football (i.e. mean=1.5 hours; $SD$=2.6). For example, these football players spent time on watching video clips of themselves and their role models, specifying their own strong and weak points, thinking back on their actions to learn from them, and evolve in self-talk and strategies to be optimally prepared for certain situations.

**An example of reflective thinking in practice**

A reflective strategy can be related to the use of self-talk. In 2003 van Nistelrooy was struggling with his penalties, but had to take the decisive one for Manchester United against Arsenal.

> At that moment I was thinking: Oh no, I have to take it, I felt insecure and I missed. I started working on my anxiety by using self-talk and concentrating on how I am feeling. The coincidence occurred that the same event happened a year later. In the dying seconds of the match, I was the one who had to take the decisive penalty. I was very excited and in my head, I went through the steps I had practised: be aware of where you are, regulate your excitement and score!
>
> (Jonker, Willems, & Lankhout, 2017, p. 47)

When it comes to self-talk as a reflective thinking skill, it is important to distinguish between self-talk as spontaneous and relatively unconscious thoughts and self-talk as a mental strategy with the use of specific cues to improve. Only the second type of self-talk (i.e. self-talk as a mental strategy) seems to be related to reflective behaviour (Hatzigeorgiadis & Biddle, 2008; Mezirow, 1991, 2003; Peltier et al., 2006; Theodorakis, Hatzigeorgiadis, & Zourbanos, 2012).

**Limitations and future research perspectives**

In the present study, we decided to focus on the frequency of using self-regulatory skills in elite youth football players. Although examples of players with good reflective skills are presented, it is not said that these types of strategies are solely based on reflective thinking. The example of van Nistelrooy's anxiety can be considered as a conscious decision to focus on anxiety, but may also be related to stress-regulating strategies. About the same is the case for the example used of Pierre van Hooijdonk. Deciding to focus on his free kick is based on reflective thinking, however, staying after training to practise might also be related to good planning and willingness to put forth effort. In other words, with respect to our research findings, also other psychological skills or mental strategies may be of significant importance.

Other limitations are related to the age of our data. The elite youth football players included in our study were measured approximately 10 years ago when relatively little attention was paid to self-regulatory skills within football academies. This means that the predictive value underpins the importance of reflective thinking in football, but that reflective mean scores of this sample may not be comparable to today's elite youth players. Nevertheless, this study is considered valuable as it may be used to further talent development in football by supporting performance improvement by using self-regulatory skills. Based on this 10-year time gap, but also on the predictive value of reflective thinking, the risk of using solely reflection as a scouting factor should be addressed. The risk exists that football academies start measuring potential players on reflection; however, reflection seems to be something that can be developed (see development of self-regulatory skills and practical implications in this chapter).

Another limitation might be related to age differences between players when determining their future performance. Players reach their peak performance at

25–27 years of age (Dendir, 2016). So, age-related differences in the 2015/2016 competitive season may have led to different performance outcomes. This suggests that it would have been better to determine the performance level at age 25–27. However, drawing conclusions on the future performance level of players when they were at this age, would have resulted in weakened analyses because of little data. Analyses of the Dutch FA showed that only very few players can increase in competitive level between the second and Premier League after the age of 21 (personal communication with the Dutch FA). Although some players used the Dutch second division as a stepping stone towards the Dutch Premier League, almost all of them were picked up for the Dutch Premier League when they were no older than 21 years of age (personal communication with the Dutch FA). Most recent examples are Kevin Strootman (Dutch international), Vincent Janssen (Dutch international), Bas Dost (Dutch international), Demy de Zeeuw (Dutch international), and Dries Mertens (Belgian international). They all started their career in the second division, but were about 21 years of age when making a transfer to the Dutch Premier League.

## Men's versus women's football

During this study we decided to focus solely on men's football. Although women's football in the Netherlands is rising, and the Dutch team even won the 2017 European Championship for women, the career pathway of men and women in football differs largely. Male youth players have the possibility to get selected for a football academy at young age, female youth players on the contrary are most frequently part of male grassroots teams until approximately 16 years and can be selected for extra training facilities from the age of 10 years at the Dutch FA (KNVB, 2017a). After the age of 16, most of them are expected to have developed their skills enough to make their debut in a professional women's football competition that was established in 2012 and has been in its current format since 2015/2016 (KNVB, 2017b). As women's football has reached professional status quite recently in the Netherlands (i.e. 2012), it may be interesting for future studies to assess the role of self-regulatory skills in women's football.

## Conclusions and practical implications

We recommend coaches to assess the history of players before selecting them for their football academy. The significant predictive value of football experience, specifically at a younger age (Table 22.1) may refer to the phenomenon that scouts and coaches frequently struggle with distinguishing between 'real talent' and just more experience at a young age (Ankersen, 2015). Coaches should be aware of this phenomenon as getting selected for football academies, especially academies of higher level, predicts your future career chances. More specifically, this sheds light on the discussion whether early selection is a good or a bad thing by knowing that for many performance characteristics we are not able to predict future performance level already at a young age. On the other hand, football academies are afraid of missing future professionals and have optimised their talent developmental programmes to such an extent that not getting selected decreases the chance of becoming a professional player. We do not consider solving this ethical discussion as part of this book chapter; however, we are delighted to know that the Dutch FA has started a scientific study on the selection process in very young players in cooperation with football academies, coaches, and scientists in the 2017/2018 competitive season.

Furthermore, we recommend coaches involve their football players in the process of goal-setting and feedback from a young age and develop their reflective thinking. Nowadays many coaches try to impose their performance standards on the players, but their job is to make players aware that skills need to be developed and to stimulate their learning by goal-setting, feedback, and reflection. In this perspective, we recommend football federations, such as the Dutch FA, to develop courses and training sessions for coaches and scouts in which they start developing their own self-regulatory skills and how to develop the self-regulatory skills of their players. Specifically, self-regulatory skills may help elite youth players heading towards the age-related transition to professional football (MacNamara & Collins, 2010). One way of stimulating the self-regulatory skills of elite youth players is by making expectations and progress visible. As a coach you can also rely on an 'asking type' of coaching to make players aware of their reflective behaviour and progress. Intervention studies showed that questions like 'How do you think you can develop your skills? What do you need from me and your teammates?' and 'Think of what you want to develop. How do you think you can establish it? What are the hard parts and with what should we start?' are helpful in the development and use of self-regulatory skills (Jonker, 2017; Peters & Kitsantas, 2010; Veenman, Kok, & Blöte, 2005). Furthermore, it is important to make them aware of the fact that learning and improving, even after making your debut, is a necessity and that even the greatest players need to keep on improving their performance.

## References

Alexander, J. M., Carr, M., & Schwanenflugel, P. J. (1995). Development of metacognition in gifted children: Directions for future research. *Developmental Review, 15*, 1–37.

Ankersen, R. (2015). *The goldmine effect: Crack the secrets of high performance.* London, England: Icon Books Ltd.

Baker, J., Horton, S., Robertson-Wilson, J., & Wall, M. (2003). Nurturing sport expertise: Factors influencing the development of elite athlete. *Journal of Sports Science and Medicine, 2*, 1–9.

Bandura, A. (1997). The nature and structure of self-efficacy. In A. Bandura (Ed.), *Self-efficacy: The exercise of control* (pp. 36–78). New York, NY: Freeman.

Barnes, C., Archer, D. T., Hogg, B., Bush, M., & Bradley, P. S. (2014). The evolution of physical and technical performance parameters in the English Premier League. *International Journal of Sports Medicine, 35*, 1095–1100.

Bloom, B. S. (1985). *Developing talent in young people.* New York, NY: Ballantine.

Boekaerts, M. (1997). Self-regulated learning: A new concept embraced by researchers, policy makers, educators, teachers, and students. *Learning and Instruction, 7*, 161–186.

Boekaerts, M., & Corno, L. (2005). Self-regulation in the classroom: A perspective on assessment and intervention. *Applied Psychology: An International Review, 54*, 199–231.

CIES Football Observatory. (2018). Age: Average age on the pitch, current domestic league season. *CIES Football Observatory Digital Atlas.* Retrieved from www.football-observatory.com/IMG/sites/atlas/en/.

Cleary, T. J., & Zimmerman, B. J. (2001). Self-regulation differences during athletic practice by experts, non-experts, and novices. *Journal of Applied Sport Psychology, 13*, 185–206.

Côté, J. (1999). The influence of the family in the development of talent in sports. *The Sports Psychologist, 13*, 395–417.

Côté, J., Baker, J., & Abernethy, B. (2003). From play to practice: A developmental framework for the acquisition of expertise in team sports. In J. L. Starkes & K. A. Ericsson (Eds.), *Expert performance in sports: Advances in research on sport expertise* (pp. 89–113). Champaign, IL: Human Kinetics.

Dendir, S. (2016). When do soccer players peak? A note. *Journal of Sports Analytics, 2*, 89–105.

Diamond, A. (2013). Executive functions. *Annual Review of Psychology, 64*, 135–168.

Dweck, C. S. (2006). *Mindset: The new psychology of success.* New York, NY: Random House.

Dweck, C. S., & Master, A. (2009). Self-theories and motivation. Students' beliefs about intelligence. In K. R. Wentzel & A. Wigfield (Eds.), *Handbook of motivation at school* (pp. 123–140). New York, NY and London, England: Routledge.

Elferink-Gemser, M. T., Huijgen, B. C., Coelho-E-Silva, M., Lemmink, K. A., & Visscher, C. (2012). The changing characteristics of talented football players: A decade of work in Groningen. *Journal of Sports Sciences, 30*, 1581–1591.

Ericsson, K. A. (2003). Development of elite performance and deliberate practice: An update from the perspective of the expert performance approach. In J. L. Starkes & K. A. Ericsson (Eds.), *Expert performance in sports: Advances in research expertise* (pp. 49–87). Champaign, IL: Human Kinetics.

Ericsson, K. A., Krampe, R. T., & Tesch-Römer, C. (1993). The role of deliberate practice in the acquisition of expert performance. *Psychological Review, 100*, 363–406.

Ertmer, P. A., & Newby, T. J. (1996). The expert learner: Strategic, self-regulated, and reflective. *Instructional Science, 24*, 1–24.

FIFA. (2016). *Global football development Vol. 1 – Comparing youth football worldwide: Lessons and proposals for the regular organisation of youth football competitions.* Neuchatel, Switzerland: CIES International Centre for Sports Studies. Retrieved from http://resources.fifa.com/mm/document/footballdevelopment/football/02/84/68/74/globalfootballdevelopmentvol.1_neutral.pdf.

Ford, P. R., Ward, P., Hodges, N. J., & Williams, A. M. (2009). The role of deliberate practice and play in career progression in sport: The early engagement hypothesis. *High Ability Studies, 20*, 65–75.

Fransen, J., Pion, J., Vandendriessche, J., Vandorpe, B., Vaeyens, R., Lenoir, M., & Philippaerts, R. M. (2012). Differences in physical fitness and gross motor coordination in boys aged 6–12 years specializing in one versus sampling more than one sport. *Journal of Sports Sciences, 30*, 379–386.

Goes, J., Jacobs, T., van Ruiven, L., Stekelenburg, M., Brinkhof, S., Verbeek, J., Jonker, L., & van der Zande, R. (2016). *Tomorrow's winners: Developing talent together.* Nieuwegein, The Netherlands: Arko Sports Media.

Gracenote & Hypercube Business Innovation. (2015). Euro Club index. Retrieved from http://euroclubindex.com/asp/Methodology.asp.

Gulbin, J. P., Oldenziel, K. E., Weissensteiner, J. R., & Gagné, F. (2010). A look through the rear view mirror: Developmental experiences and insights of high performance athletes. *Talent Development & Excellence, 2*, 149–164.

Hatzigeorgiadis, A., & Biddle, S. J. H. (2008). Negative thoughts during sport performance: Relationships with pre-competition anxiety and goal-performance discrepancies. *Journal of Sport Behavior, 31*, 237–253.

Helsen, W. F., Starkes, J. L., & Hodges, N. J. (1998). Team sports and the theory of deliberate practice. *Journal of Sport and Exercise Psychology, 20*, 12–34.

Herl, H. E., O'Neil Jr, H. F., Chung, G. K. W. K., Bianchi, C., Wang, S. L., Mayer, R. ... & Suen, T. (1999, March). *Final report for validation of problem-solving measures* (CSE Technical Report #501). Center for the Study of Evaluation and National Center for Research in Evaluation, Standards, and Student Testing, Los Angeles.

Hong, E., & O'Neill, Jr., H. F. (2001). Construct validation of a trait self-regulation model. *International Journal of Psychology, 36*, 186–194.

Howard, B. C., McGee, S., Shia, R., & Hong, N. S. (2000). *Metacognitive self-regulation and problem-solving: Expanding the theory base through factor analysis.* Paper presented at the Annual Meeting of the American Educational Research Association, New Orleans, LA.

Huijgen, B. C. H., Elferink-Gemser, M. T., Post, W. J., & Visscher, C. (2009). Soccer skill development in professionals. *International Journal of Sports Medicine, 30*, 585–591.

Huijgen, B. C. H., Leemhuis, S., Kok, N. M., Verburgh, L., Oosterlaan, J., Elferink-Gemser, M. T., & Visscher, C. (2015). Cognitive functions in elite and sub-elite youth soccer players aged 13 to 17 years. *PLoS One, 10*, e0144580.

Jonker, L. (2015). Competities benchmark [Performance dashboard Dutch national football teams and competitions]. Retrieved from http://bin617.website-voetbal.nl/sites/dash board/knvb_cp/#welkom.

Jonker, L. (2017). *Van aanleg naar intelligentie. Het sporttalent in ontwikkeling* [From physical talent to intelligence: Talented athletes in development]. Nieuwegein, The Netherlands: Arko Sports Media.

Jonker, L., Elferink-Gemser, M. T., Toering, T. T., Lyons, J., & Visscher, C. (2010). Academic performance and self-regulatory skills in elite youth soccer players. *Journal of Sports Sciences, 28*, 1605–1614.

Jonker, L., Elferink-Gemser, M. T., & Visscher, C. (2009). Talented athletes and academic achievements: A comparison over 14 years. *High Ability Studies, 20*, 55–64.

Jonker, L., Willems, L., & Lankhout, M. (2017). *Doelgericht coachen, scoren door contact. Inspiratie behorend bij de training* [Goal-directed coaching, scoring by making connection. Inspiration by our education]. Amsterdam, The Netherlands: Rijser and Ruud van Nistelrooy Foundation.

KNVB (2017a). Talentontwikkeling [Talent development]. Retrieved from www.jpnmeisjes. nl/Soccer/Knvb/KnvbJpn.aspx?Param=1mcMAc3PC1H2oa3LAAnU8w==.

KNVB (2017b). Eredivisie Vrouwen [Women's Premier League]. Retrieved from www.knvb. nl/competities/eredivisie-vrouwen.

MacNamara, A., Button, A., & Collins, D. (2010). The role of psychological characteristics in facilitating the pathway to elite performance. *The Sport Psychologist, 24*, 74–96.

MacNamara, A., & Collins, D. (2010). The role of psychological characteristics in managing the transition to university. *Psychology of Sport and Exercise, 11*, 353–362.

Macnamara, B. N., Moreau, D., & Hambrick, D. Z. (2016). The relationship between deliberate practice and performance in sports. A meta-analysis. *Perspectives on Psychological Science, 11*, 333–350.

Mezirow, J. (1991). *Transformative dimensions of adult learning.* San Francisco, CA: Jossey-Bass.

Mezirow, J. (2003). Transformative learning as discourse. *Journal of Transformative Education, 1*, 58–63.

Peltier, J. W., Hay, A., & Drago, W. (2006). Reflecting on self-reflection: Scale extension and a comparison of undergraduate business students in the United States and the United Kingdom. *Journal of Marketing Education, 28*, 5–16.

Pesce, C., Tessitore, A., Casella, R., Pirritano, M., & Capranica, L. (2007). Focusing of visual attention at rest and during physical exercise in soccer players. *Journal of Sports Sciences, 25*, 1259–1270.

Peters, E. E., & Kitsantas, A. (2010). Self-regulation of student epistemic thinking in science: The role of metacognitive prompts. *Educational Psychology, 30*, 27–52.

Peugh, J. L., & Enders, C. K. (2005). Using the SPSS mixed model procedure to the cross-sectional and longitudinal multilevel models. *Educational and Psychological Measurement, 65*, 811–835.

Rasbash, J., Browne, W., Goldstein, H., Yang, M., Plewis, I., Draper, D., … Lewis, T. (1999). *A user's guide to MLWin.* London, England: Institute of Education.

Roescher, C. R., Elferink-Gemser, M. T., Huijgen, B. C., & Visscher, C. (2010). Soccer endurance development in professionals. *International Journal of Sports Medicine, 31,* 174–179.

Schwarzer, R., & Jerusalem, M. (1995). Generalized self-efficacy scale. In J. Weinman, S. Wright, & M. Johnston (Eds.), *Measures in health psychology: A user's portfolio. Causal and control beliefs* (pp. 35–37). Windsor, England: NFER-NELSON.

Sebastian, C., Burnett, S., & Blakemore, S. J. (2008). Development of the self-concept during adolescence. *Trends in Cognitive Sciences, 12,* 441–446.

Snijders, T. A. B., & Bosker, R. J. (2000). *Multilevel analysis: An introduction to basic and advanced multilevel modeling.* London, England: Sage Publications.

Theodorakis, Y., Hatzigeorgiadis, A., & Zourbanos, N. (2012). Cognitions: Self-talk and performance. In S. M. Murphy (Ed.), *The Oxford handbook of sport and performance psychology* (pp. 191–212). New York, NY: Oxford University Press.

Toering, T. T., Elferink-Gemser, M. T., Jonker, L., Heuvelen, M., & Visscher, C. (2012). Measuring self-regulation in a learning context: Reliability and validity of the Self-Regulation of Learning Self-Report Scale (SRL-SRS). *International Journal of Sport and Exercise Psychology, 26,* 224–242.

Toering, T. T., Elferink-Gemser, M. T., Jordet, G., & Visscher, C. (2009). Self-regulation and performance level of elite and non-elite youth soccer players. *Journal of Sports Sciences, 27,* 1509–1517.

Vaeyens, R., Güllich, A., Warr, C. R., & Philippaerts, R. (2009). Talent identification and promotion programmes of Olympic athletes. *Journal of Sports Sciences, 27,* 1367–1380.

Van der Stel, M., & Veenman, M. V. J. (2008). Relation between intellectual ability and metacognitive skillfulness as predictors of learning performance of young students performing tasks in different domains. *Learning and Individual Differences, 18,* 128–134.

Veenman, M. V. J., Kok, R., & Blöte, A. W. (2005). The relation between intellectual and metacognitive skills in early adolescence. *Instructional Science, 33,* 193–211.

Verburgh, L., Scherder, E. J., van Lange, A., & Oosterlaan, J. (2014). Executive functioning in highly talented soccer players. *PLoS One, 9,* e91254.

Vestberg, T., Gustafson, R., Maurex, L., Ingvar, M., & Petrovic, P. (2012). Executive functions predict: The success of top-soccer players. *PLoS One, 7,* e34731.

Ward, P., Hodges, N. J., Starkes, J. L., & Williams, A. M. (2007). The road to excellence: Deliberate practice and the development of expertise. *High Ability Studies, 2,* 119–153.

Zelazo, P. D., & Müller, U. (2002). Executive function and atypical development. In U. Goswami (Ed.), *Blackwell handbook of cognitive development* (pp. 445–469). Malden, MA: Blackwell Publishers Ltd.

Zimmerman, B. J. (2000). Attaining self-regulation: A social cognitive perspective. In M. Boekarts, P. R. Pintrich, & M. Zeidner (Eds.), *Handbook of self-regulation* (pp. 13–39). San Diego, CA: Academic Press.

# 23 Helping players develop life skills in football

*Daniel Gould and Lucas S. Capalbo*

## Abstract

It is often assumed that participation in football will enhance participant psychological and social growth. Implicit in this assumption is that by playing the beautiful game players will develop such characteristics as teamwork, work ethic, communication skills, integrity, and emotional regulation. It is also assumed that these psychological skills will transfer to off-the-field life situations. This chapter will address how football can be used to develop life skills in participants. We will begin by summarizing the research on life skills development through sport participation in general and football in particular. This literature shows that under the 'right' conditions life skills can be developed through football participation. We will then discuss the steps that can be used to help players develop life skills through football participation. These include: (1) creating an environment conducive for life skills development; (2) emphasizing the intentional teaching and fostering of life skills; (3) selecting coaches with the right philosophy and coaching competencies; (4) fostering strong coach–athlete relationships; (5) coordinating life skills development efforts with other community agencies/individuals in athletes' lives; and (6) teaching for transfer (Gould & Westfall, 2014).

Christina had a great stint with the National team in native Colombia and feels her football experience changed her life. She wants other girls, and not just the ones who were as physically gifted as she was, to gain the confidence, leadership, and teamwork skills that she developed through football. She starts an NGO that focuses on providing football opportunities for young girls but is not quite sure how to structure the programme to maximize the psychological development of her players.

Jose coaches a team in the First Division. His team is struggling as most of the players are selfish ball hogs and don't seem to care about their teammates. His players are better known for their bar fights, womanizing, and run-ins with the law than their play on the pitch. To keep his job Jose needs to turn this around – his players need to develop the mental skills that characterize champions both on and off the field.

Dan has just been hired as the varsity coach in a prestigious high school in the United States. His Athletic Director makes it very clear that his charge is to field a team that competes for the Championship while at the same time making sure the players do well in the classroom and keep up with their academically gifted peers.

While all Dan's players are interested in winning on the pitch some just don't have much interest in their academics.

While these stories involve very different football contexts the one thing they have in common is that the coaches need to develop their players psychologically, not only so they play well on the pitch but off of it as well. In essence, the coaches are all charged with helping their players develop life skills – social and psychological skills that can be fostered through football and transferred beyond the pitch. This is an important task of today's football coach at all levels of play.

Football is undisputedly the most played sport around the world. FIFA (2006) estimated that over 265 million people play football across all four corners of the globe. Knowing that millions of people enjoy the beautiful game in different shapes and forms, more and more people both inside and outside of football recognize that the game can be a great platform to holistically develop young people and allow them to have a positive impact in their communities and on society. Football participation, then, has the capability to teach youth not only technical and tactical aspects of the game, but skills that can be applied on and off the pitch. To help achieve this goal, this chapter will address how football participation can be used to develop life skills in participants. This will be accomplished by defining the basic concepts of positive youth development and life skills, summarizing the important research in the area, and outlining implications for guiding professional practice.

## Understanding positive youth and life skills development

A challenge faced by those wishing to understand life skills development through football is the many terms used to describe the area being studied. Sport for development, psycho-social development through sport, life skills development through sport, and sport for peace, for instance, have all been used to describe the phenomena that is the focus of this review.

At the most general level is positive youth development (PYD) defined as the 'promotion of any number of desirable competencies or outcomes in young people' (Gould & Carson, 2008b, p. 59). Such competencies when promoted through football might include becoming more confident, being physically fit, learning how to strategize and achieve goals, staying in school, and having positive attitudes toward adversities in life (Peacock-Villada, De Celles, & Banda, 2007). PYD programmes through sports, including those using football, are thought to be 'fertile ground for youth to develop skills and attitudes that have considerable value in adult life' (Petitpas, Cornelius, Van Raalte, & Jones, 2005, p. 63) and in their current life as well (Gould & Carson, 2008b).

While PYD refers to a wide variety of skills and competencies ranging from health-related skills to personality dispositions like optimism, life skills are viewed more narrowly. Life skills development in the sport has been defined as 'those internal personal assets, characteristics and skills such as goal setting, emotional control, self-esteem, and hard work ethic that can be facilitated or developed in sport and are transferred for use in non-sport settings' (Gould & Carson, 2008a, p. 60). Hodge, Danish, and Martin (2013) emphasize that the definition of life skills considers psycho-social characteristics rather than isolated behaviours (e.g. money management or cooking skills) which could be considered PYD outcomes. It is also important to recognize that the promotion of life skills can only be considered successful if youth are able to transfer them to non-sport contexts. Life skills transfer is defined as the belief and confidence that the acquired skills and qualities can be applied in other settings (Pierce, Gould, & Camiré, 2016). The focus of this chapter is on life skills development through football.

## Research on life skills

### *General life skills through sport research*

Helping sport participants develop life skills is not a new topic. The Greeks talked about how sport can contribute to the total development of the person, and the founder of the modern Olympic Games, Pierre de Coubertin, wrote extensively about the role of sport in shaping a person's development and ultimate contribution to society (Gould & Voelker, 2014). While researchers have been interested in the topic for some time, a tremendous growth in the area has occurred over the last several decades by researchers from a number of fields (see Gould & Carson, 2008b).

This research on life skills development through sport has employed both quantitative and qualitative methods and has examined a range of topics including what life skills are most important to develop in youth (e.g. Jones & Lavallee, 2009), factors influencing life skills development (e.g. Gould, Flett, & Lauer, 2012), the success of life skills development efforts and tests of interventions designed to foster life skills development (e.g. Weiss, Stuntz, Bhalla, Bolter, & Price, 2013). Reviewing all of this research is beyond the scope of this chapter. However, several reviews of the literature (e.g. Camiré, 2014; Gould & Carson, 2008b; Gould & Westfall, 2014) have been written on the topic and what was found will now be briefly summarized.

Research in this area reveals that sport participation is associated with a wide variety of developmental gains for young people. Specifically, youth sport participants report that they have learned life skills like self-control, stress management and coping strategies, and communication skills (Camiré, Trudel, & Forneris, 2009; Kendellen & Camiré, 2015). Participation in sport is also linked to the development of initiative, enhanced competence-confidence, and team work and social skills (Gould, Cowburn, & Shields, 2014). In addition to positive outcomes some negative outcomes such as negative peer interactions, alcohol use, lost motivation, stress-burnout, and lower morality have been identified (Eccles & Barber, 1999; Gould et al., 2014). Taken together, the evidence supporting the benefits of participation outweigh the evidence supporting negative outcomes (Gould et al., 2014).

Having established sport participation and a desirable psycho-social outcomes link, researchers have identified what factors influence this relationship. Studies have shown that sport environments characterized by caring and welcoming climates and task-oriented motivational climates (where participants are encouraged to make self-comparisons versus socially comparing with others) are associated with enhanced positive life skill outcomes (Gould et al., 2012). Life skills are also enhanced when coaches have philosophies that place primary importance on life skills development (Camiré, Trudel, & Forneris, 2012; Gould, Collins, Lauer, & Chung, 2007), are intentional and proactive about teaching life skills (Bean & Forneris, 2016; Gould et al., 2007), form strong coach–player relationships, focus more on teaching skills like mental preparation, goal setting and competitive strategies, emphasize sportspersonship, and emphasize the importance of transferring life skills to settings beyond sport (Gould et al., 2012). Taking a lead role, greater athlete programme doses, high ratios of adult leaders to youth, and athletes experiencing greater task interdependence are other factors that have been associated with life skills development (Hansen & Larson, 2007).

In recent years investigators have begun evaluating the effectiveness of life skills through sport interventions (e.g. Weiss et al., 2013). The current research demonstrates that life skills interventions can be effective at helping young athletes develop life skills, although more research is certainly needed.

Finally, more is being written about how life skills learned in sport, such as goal setting, potentially transfer to non-sport settings (Pierce et al., 2016; Turnnidge, Côté, & Hancock, 2014). One view is that this is an implicit process where athletes learn life skills while playing sport and then on their own transfer these psychosocial skills to other contexts in their lives. Another view holds that for life skills transfer to take place coaches must explicitly help athletes link and transfer life skills lessons learned in sport to non-sport settings. At the present time, there is some evidence supporting both views, although most life skill development scholars emphasize the importance of taking an intentional approach to both life skill development and transfer, a conclusion that received recent empirical support in a study conducted by Bean and Forneris (2016).

## Developing life skills through football

Football is the most studied sport when it comes to life skill development. Some studies have looked at how life skills organically develop in football (Holt, Tink, Mandigo, & Fox, 2008), others how particular life skills, like goal setting (e.g. Gillham & Weiler, 2013) or sportsmanship (Lamoneda Prieto, Huertas Delgado, Córdoba Caro, & García Preciado, 2015) can be developed, and still others have examined factors thought to influence life skills development in players (Mills, Butt, Maynard, & Harwood, 2012) as well as evaluations of football-based life skills development programmes (e.g. Draper, Forbes, Taylor, & Lambert, 2012; Peacock-Villada et al., 2007). Because of space limitations we will only focus on studies evaluating life skills interventions and those that have focused on the most studied life skills.

An example of the kind of intervention study being conducted was one carried out by Harwood, Barker, and Anderson (2015). The study focused on how coaches facilitate the psycho-social growth of football players. It was a follow-up to Harwood's original research focused on a coaching intervention designed to teach football coaches behavioural strategies they could use to develop the 5Cs of positive youth development originally proposed by Lerner, Fisher, and Weinberg (2000). These Cs included: commitment, communication, concentration, control, and confidence. Harwood's (2008) original work showed that coaches can be taught to facilitate the development of the 5Cs by using strategies like being intentional, increasing player awareness of the Cs, modelling the skills, and reinforcing their use. Most importantly, Harwood and colleagues' (2015) latest research showed that players and their parents reported changes in the 5Cs when the players' coach intentionally used strategies for facilitating them. For example, the striker who participated reported changes in all 5Cs while players' parents made comments like 'I saw a definite improvement in my son's use of the 5Cs' (p. 329). Most interesting were reports by players and parents that the 5Cs were not just used on the pitch but off the field in other areas of players' lives (e.g. parents reporting players being more confident speaking in front of others at school or getting their homework done on time). Hence, some evidence existed to show the 5Cs taught by the coaches were true life skills as they were not only used on the field but in the player's life in general.

In a more focused intervention, Maro and Roberts (2012) assessed the effectiveness of an HIV aids education programme aimed at street male and female children participating in a football programme. They were also interested in examining whether a mastery motivational climate (a climate where the focus is one of self-improvement and comparison versus winning and competitive outcomes) influenced the programme's effectiveness. One intervention group of children received HIV aids and safe sex education from peers, while the second group received the same programme with the addition of an emphasis on a mastery motivation climate. Children in intervention groups differed from control children, who did not participate in the programme, in that they had significantly greater HIV knowledge and positive attitudes and safe-sex behavioural intentions. It was also concluded that the mastery motivational climate further enhanced the programme's effects.

In summary, while more investigations are certainly needed these initial intervention studies show that targeted interventions focused on life skill development through football can be effective in enhancing player life skills. Furthermore, their effectiveness can be amplified by implementing a mastery motivational climate and support from the team management and coaches. Keeping these findings in mind, we will now focus on summarizing studies on the most commonly fostered life skills in football. It is important that these life skills are introduced to players early in life so they have the chance to apply them throughout their careers (Draper et al., 2012).

**Goal setting.** Cultivating goal-setting skills is extremely important in helping individuals identify and achieve both large and small outcomes. Completed goals have also been linked to enhanced self-esteem in athletes (Gould & Carson, 2008b). So, it is not surprising that those in football have been interested in the efficacy of goal-setting programmes for players. Gillham and Weiler (2013), for example, conducted a goal-setting intervention during the pre-season of a female college football team. This intervention taught players how to better set goals in three areas: (1) individual goals, (2) position-group goals, and (3) team goals. In the first week of the pre-season, players watched a presentation about goal-setting strategies (e.g. SMART goals – specific, measurable, attainable, realistic, and timely) and later engaged in a discussion about process, performance, and outcome goals as suggested in Weinberg (2010). Players then set football-related goals for themselves individually (e.g. percentage of successful attempts in certain skills or goals scored) that later were examined by the consultant and the head coach who also provided individualized feedback to every player. In the second step players set goals for their position-group (i.e. defenders, midfielders, and strikers) such as number of goals against for the defence and possession time for the midfielders. Lastly, players set three goals for the team to seek during the entire season (corners earned, shots on target, and being the first to score at every game). All goals were realistically adjusted according to the opponent in order to enhance the team's chance of achieving them. Moreover, substitute players were encouraged to keep track of the team goals during games in order to keep them motivated, focused, and allow them to learn by observation. After the season was over, players reported being more focused, responsive to the coach's feedback, and having more sense of purpose. Learning how to set goals and becoming more focused helped players transition from school activities during the day to football practices in the evening. A limitation of these studies is the failure to specifically assess if the improved goal setting in football transferred to other areas of the players' lives.

**Communication.** Communication is part of the 5Cs of football. Communication skills can be manifested in the beautiful game by players 'asking questions to coaches about a drill or skill, sharing information with coaches and accepting feedback, and encouraging, praising, and instructing teammates clearly and confidently' (Harwood, 2008, p. 115). As part of an intervention developed to foster life skills for young South African and Zambian participants of a football programme, Peacock-Villada et al. (2007) included the teaching of constructive praise, vocabulary development, and positive outlook in order to allow players to identify their strengths. Additionally, coaches created an activity called a 'praise circle' in which players were encouraged to praise each other and be praised by the coach. Peacock-Villada et al. (2007) identified that their initiative helped players become good listeners, engaging, effective, inclusive, well organized, and team players. Thus, male players, before the initiative, tended to try solving problems on their own, but after participating in this initiative, they learned how to ask for help.

**Personal responsibility.** Considered an important psycho-social skill for youth to develop, personal responsibility is often underserved in their repertoire (Gould & Carson, 2008a). Football programmes have used Hellison's (1995) model for developing social and personal responsibility through sports (Cecchini, Montero, Alonso, Izquierdo, & Contreras, 2007; Cecchini, Montero, & Peña, 2003). This model argues that responsibility is developed when youth move up through five stages of personal responsibility: (1) self-control and respect for others, (2) effort and participation, (3) self-direction, (4) caring for others, and (5) applying these goals outside the pitch.

Cecchini and colleagues (2003) applied Hellison's model to a group of school-aged youth in Spain using football. As suggested by the model, the authors organized the daily practices by starting with an open practice to facilitate coach–player interaction, followed by a chat about the values to be worked in the session. Later, coaches conducted a regular football practice that would end with a debriefing session to evaluate and reflect upon what was learned in that session. Additionally, other complementary strategies were used to reinforce the values being taught (e.g. short debates, posters to be displayed in their schools to remind them of the lessons learned, direct instructions of rules and game techniques). Lastly, participants were encouraged to adopt a new attitude (e.g. participant reflects on negative conduct, apologizes, and is accepted back into practice), placed in leadership positions to help others less skilled (academically and in football), allowed to adapt the drills according to their learning pace, and encouraged to reflect about their own actions (Cecchini et al., 2003). After 20 hours of intervention sessions over 2 months, participants in the intervention group were characterized by a significant improvement in feedback, delayed gratification, self-control, and fair play (indicators of personal responsibility). Thus, negative aspects such as rough play and poor sportsmanship behaviours decreased in comparison to the control group that participated in regular football practices. Similar results were obtained in a later study by Cecchini and colleagues (2003) that employed comparable conditions.

**Leadership.** It is thought that football is a great platform to shape leaders. Leadership is seen as a fundamental piece in optimizing team performance and should be deliberately developed and encouraged among players (Pain & Harwood, 2008). However, not all players have the opportunity to take in leadership roles and consequently develop the skills to become effective leaders (Gould & Carson, 2008a). Therefore, coaches should create more leadership opportunities within the team beyond team captains and assistant captains so more players can experience the role and possibly develop the necessary skills to perform it. Research suggests that players who feel confident, valued, and who are allowed to make some meaningful decisions by their coaches have increased chances of showing leadership or taking responsibility when it is needed (Taylor & Bruner, 2012).

Hubball and Robertson (2004) suggested a problem-based learning approach to developing leadership in football among other life skills. The problem-based learning approach provides players with experiential and collaboration learning. Based on this approach, coaches begin by assessing the team and players' characteristics (e.g. motives for participation, goals with football, strengths and weaknesses in the game). Once the initial assessment is done, small-sided competitive games are conducted and coaches should allow players to give inputs on the initial planning (e.g. specific roles, strategies). Consecutively, coaches facilitate peer coaching by providing periodic opportunities for players to conduct team and individual observations using performance-analysis worksheets during practices and games. The peer-coaching role also includes providing feedback to players and encouraging them to think as coaches. Players can mentor their teammates or players from younger age groups. Wright and Côté (2003) stated that younger players are also likely to develop leadership skills as they interact with older teammates.

## Implications for guiding practice

In a recent review of the research and best practice literature on developing life skills through sport participation, Gould and Westfall (2014) outlined a series of steps guiding practice. Some of the more important steps are discussed below.

### Create an environment conducive for life skills development

Considerable research shows that life skills are more likely to be fostered in sport participants when certain types of environments are created. Specifically, when coaches create caring climates where all athletes feel welcomed and included (Fry et al., 2011). In addition, life skills are more likely to be developed in motivational climates that are more task or mastery versus ego-oriented (Duda & Balaguer, 2007). Hence, when those in the sport environment focus on personal development and self-referenced improvement versus competitive outcomes and social comparisons between players, life skills are more likely to be fostered. Lastly, Hodge and colleagues (2013) also suggest that life skills are more likely learned in environments where athletes' basic needs of autonomy, competence, and relatedness are met.

### Emphasize the intentional teaching and fostering of life skills

While athletes can certainly learn life skills from their own trial and error experiences in sport, a more consistent approach to their development occurs when coaches are intentional in fostering life skills development. Specifically, coaches are intentional when they identify the specific life skills (e.g. team work, goal setting) they hope to develop and then foster the development of these skills and attributes by directly teaching and reinforcing them or by creating environments that will lead to teachable life skill moments.

### Select coaches with the right philosophy and coaching competencies

Studies have shown that life skills are more likely to be fostered in athletes when coaches adopt philosophies that place primary importance on their development (Collins, Gould, Lauer, & Chung, 2009). In other words, the development of life skills is not a secondary objective of the coach. They are a primary objective. This does not mean coaches who are effective at developing life skills in their players do not care about winning. These coaches often view life skills as helping one's team be successful. However, what they do not do is emphasize winning over the personal development of their players.

### Foster strong coach–athlete relationships

Life skills development in athletes has been linked to strong coach–athlete relationships (Gould et al., 2012). That is, when a strong coach–athlete relationship is established life skills are more likely to be developed. Establishing a strong coach–athlete relationship, then, is essential if a coach is to foster life skills in his or her players.

### Coordinate life skills development efforts with other community agencies/individuals

The old adage that 'it takes a village to raise a child' applies to life skills through football development efforts. A coach is more likely to be successful in developing life skills in his or her players if he or she involves other people and institutions within that player's life. For instance, if a coach is working to develop goal-setting skills in his or her players it would be wise to inform the players' parents and teachers of his efforts. That way, these individuals can support the player's effort and/or assist in transferring goal setting from the playing field to school or home situations.

### Teach for transfer

Studies have found evidence that life skills do not transfer automatically from one domain to the other (Danish, Fazio, Nellen, & Owens, 2002; Petitpas, Danish, McKelvain, & Murphy, 1992). Players are not always aware of the life application of these skills and they may lack the necessary confidence to employ them in other domains (Petitpas et al., 1992). Therefore, programmes should provide explicit support for youth to apply life skills successfully in non-sport situations (Petitpas et al., 2005). Gould and Carson (2008a) suggested that transferability of life skills can be achieved by highlighting the similarity of situations on and off the field, creating awareness, using previous transfer experiences, and having support and reinforcement of transfer. Programme leaders can use open transfer by encouraging participants to apply certain skills into any situation of their lives or closed transfer by giving participants a problem scenario based on their reality and encouraging them to solve it using what they have learned.

## Conclusions

Participation in football not only can be an enjoyable and productive experience in itself but under the right conditions can teach players life skills that prepare them for a more productive and worthwhile life. This will more occur when coaches and other leaders in the game intentionally prioritize and foster these skills. It is imperative, therefore, that those in football leadership positions help players develop life skills through the game. With that being said, football associations should provide specific coaching courses in this area and clubs should adopt the teaching of life skills to their philosophy while encouraging and supporting coaches to be intentional when teaching these skills. Coaches and leaders must be aware of their importance in the overall development of young players and in supporting adult players, professionals or not, in making good decisions on and off the field. Future research in this area should include cross-sectional studies comparing the personal development of players intentionally coached for life skills versus those who were not, longitudinal studies assessing the long-term retention of life skills learned in football, studies designed to determine whether life skills learned in football are successfully transferred to non-football settings, and case studies of winning football coaches who intentionally foster life skills in their programmes.

## References

Bean, C. N., & Forneris, T. (2016). Examining the importance of intentionally structuring the youth sport context to facilitate psychosocial development. *Journal of Applied Sport Psychology, 28*, 410–425. doi:10.1080/10413200.2016.1164764.

Camiré, M. (2014). Youth development in North American high school sport: Review and recommendations. *Quest, 66*(4), 495–511.

Camiré, M., Trudel, P., & Forneris, T. (2009). High school athletes' perspectives on support, communication, negotiation and life skill development. *Qualitative Research in Sport and Exercise, 1*, 72–88. doi:10.1080/19398440802673275.

Camiré, M., Trudel, P., & Forneris, T. (2012). Coaching and transferring life skills: Philosophies and strategies used by model high school coaches. *The Sport Psychologist, 26*(2), 243–260.

Cecchini, J. A., Montero, J., Alonso, A., Izquierdo, M., & Contreras, O. (2007). Effects of personal and social responsibility on fair play in sports and self-control in school-aged youths. *European Journal of Sport Science, 7*(4), 203–211.

Cecchini, J. A., Montero, J., & Peña, J. V. (2003). Repercusiones del programa de intervención para desarollar resposabilidad personal y social de Hellison sobre los comportamientos de fair-play y auto-control [Outcomes of Hellison's program for personal and social development on fair play and self-control]. *Psychothema, 15*(4), 631–637.

Collins, K., Gould, D., Lauer, L., & Chung, Y. (2009). Coaching life skills through football: Philosophical beliefs of outstanding high school football coaches. *International Journal of Coaching Science, 3*(1), 1–26.

Danish, S. J., Fazio, R. J., Nellen, V. C., & Owens, S. S. (2002). Teaching life skills through sport: Community-based programs to enhance adolescent development. In J. L. Van Raalte & B. W. Brewer (Eds.), *Exploring sport and exercise psychology* (2nd ed., pp. 269–288). Washington, DC: American Psychological Association.

Draper, C. E., Forbes, J., Taylor, G., & Lambert, M. I. (2012). Empowering professional soccer players in South Africa: Evaluation of Project Ithuseng. *International Journal of Sport Science and Coaching, 7*(3), 579–591.

Duda, J. L., & Balaguer, I. (2007). Coach-created motivational climate. In S. Jowett & D. Lavallee (Eds.), *Social psychology of sport* (pp. 117–130). Champaign, IL: Human Kinetics.

Eccles, J. S., & Barber, B. L. (1999). Student council, volunteering, basketball, or marching band: What kind of extracurricular involvement matters? *Journal of Adolescent Research, 14,* 10–43.

FIFA. (2006). The big count 2006. Retrieved from www.fifa.com/mm/document/fifafacts/bcoffsurv/bigcount.statspackage_7024.pdf.

Fry, M. D., Guivernau, M., Kim, M., Newton, M., Gano-Overway, L. A., & Magyar, T. M. (2011). Youth perspectives of a caring climate, emotional regulation, and psychological well-being. *Sport, Exercise & Performance Psychology, 9*(1), 44–57.

Gillham, A., & Weiler, D. (2013). Goal setting with a college soccer team: What went right, and less-than-right. *Journal of Sport Psychology in Action, 4*(2), 97–108.

Gould, D., & Carson, S. (2008a). Personal development through sport. In O. Bar-Or & H. Hebestreit (Eds.), *The encyclopedia of sports medicine: The child and adolescent athlete* (pp. 287–301). Oxford, England: Blackwell Science.

Gould, D., & Carson, S. (2008b). Life skills development through sport: Current stands and future directions. *International Review of Sport and Exercise Psychology, 1*(1), 58–78.

Gould, D., Collins, K., Lauer, L., & Chung, Y. (2007). Coaching life skills through football: A study of award winning high school coaches. *Journal of Applied Sport Psychology, 19*(1), 16–37.

Gould, D., Cowburn, I., & Shields, A. (2014). 'Sports for all' – a summary of the evidence of psychological and social outcomes of participation. *Elevate Health Series, 15*(3). Presidents' Council on Fitness, Sports, and Nutrition Science Board, Rockville, MD.

Gould, D., Flett, M. R., & Lauer, L. (2012). The relationship between psychosocial developmental and the sports climate experienced by underserved youth. *Psychology of Sport & Exercise, 13*(1), 80–87.

Gould, D., & Voelker, D. K. (2014). The history of sport psychology. In R. C. Eklund & G. Tenenbaum (Eds.), *Encyclopedia of sport and exercise psychology* (pp. 346–351). Thousand Oaks, CA: Sage Publications.

Gould, D., & Westfall, S. (2014). Promoting life skills in children and youth: Applications to sport contexts. In A. Rui Gomes, R. Resende, & A. Albuquerque (Eds.), *Positive human functioning from a multidimensional perspective. Vol. 2: Promoting healthy lifestyles* (pp. 53–77). New York, NY: Nova.

Hansen, D. M., & Larson, R. (2007). Amplifiers of developmental and negative experiences in organized activities: Dosage, motivation, lead roles, and adult-youth ratios. *Journal of Applied Developmental Psychology, 28,* 360–374.

Harwood, C. (2008). Developmental consulting in a professional football academy: The 5Cs coaching efficacy program. *The Sport Psychologist, 22,* 109–133.

Harwood, C. G., Barker, J. B., & Anderson, R. (2015). Developmental consulting in a professional football academy: The 5Cs coaching efficacy program. *The Sport Psychologist, 29,* 319–334. http://dx.doi.org/10.1123/tsp. 2014-0161.

Hellison, D. R. (1995). *Teaching personal and social responsibility through physical activity.* Champaign, IL: Human Kinetics.

Hodge, K., Danish, S., & Martin, J. (2013). Developing a conceptual framework for life skills interventions. *The Counseling Psychologist, 41*(8), 1125–1152.

Holt, N. L., Tink, L. N., Mandigo, J. L., & Fox, K. R. (2008). Do youth learn life skills through their involvement in high school sport? A case study. *Canadian Journal of Education, 31*(2), 281–304.

Hubball, H., & Robertson, S. (2004). Using problem-based learning to enhance team and player development. *Journal of Physical Education, Recreation, & Dance, 75*(4), 38–43.

Jones, M. I., & Lavallee, D. (2009). Exploring the life skills needs of British adolescent athletes. *Psychology of Sport and Exercise, 10*(1), 159–167.

Kendellen, K., & Camiré, M. (2015). Examining former athletes' developmental experiences in high school sport. *SAGE Open, 5*(4). doi:10.1177/2158244015614379.

Lamoneda Prieto, J., Huertas Delgado, F. J., Córdoba Caro, L. G., & García Preciado, A. V. (2015). Development of sportsmanship social components in juvenile players. *Cuadernos de Psicología del Deporte, 15*(2), 113–123.

Lerner, R. M., Fisher, C. B., & Weinberg, R. A. (2000). Toward a science for and of the people: Promoting civil society through the application of developmental science. *Child Development, 71*, 11–20. doi:10.1111/1467-8624.00113.

Maro, C. N., & Roberts, G. C. (2012). Combating HIV/AIDS in Sub-Saharan Africa: Effect of introducing a mastery motivational climate in a community based sport programme. *Journal of Applied Psychology, International Review, 61*, 699–722. doi:10.1111/j.1464-0597.2011.00482.x.

Mills, A., Butt, J., Maynard, I. W., & Harwood, C. (2012). Identifying factors perceived to influence the development of elite football academy scholars. *Journal of Sport Sciences, 30*, 1593–1604.

Pain, M. A., & Harwood, C. (2008). The performance environment of the England youth soccer teams: A quantitative investigation. *Journal of Sport Sciences, 26*(11), 1157–1169.

Peacock-Villada, P., DeCelles, J., & Banda, P. S. (2007). Grassroots soccer resiliency pilot program: Building resiliency through sport-based education in Zambia and South Africa. *New Directions for Youth Development, 116*, 141–154.

Petitpas, A. J., Cornelius, A. E., Van Raalte, J. L., & Jones, T. (2005). A framework for planning youth sport programs that foster psychosocial development. *The Sport Psychologist, 19*, 63–80.

Petitpas, A., Danish, S., McKelvain, R., & Murphy, S. (1992). A career assistance program for elite athletes. *Journal of Counseling and Development, 13*, 344–357.

Pierce, S., Gould, D., & Camiré, M. (2016). Definition and model of life skills transfer. *International Review of Sport and Exercise Psychology, 10*(1), 186–211.

Taylor, I. M., & Bruner, M. W. (2012). The social environment and developmental experiences in elite youth soccer. *Psychology of Sport and Exercise, 13*, 390–369.

Turnnidge, J., Côté, J., & Hancock, D. J. (2014). Positive youth development from sport to life: Explicit or implicit transfer? *Quest, 66*, 203–217. doi:10.1080/00336297.2013.867275.

Weinberg, R. (2010). Making goals effective: A primer for coaches. *Journal of Sport Psychology in Action, 1*, 57–65.

Weiss, M. R., Stuntz, C. P., Bhalla, J. A., Bolter, N. D., & Price, M. S. (2013). 'More than a game': Impact of The First Tee life skills programme on positive youth development: Project introduction and Year 1 findings. *Qualitative Research in Sport, Exercise and Health, 5*(2), 214–244.

Wright, A. D., & Côté, J. (2003). A retrospective analysis of leadership development through sport. *The Sport Psychologist, 17*, 268–291.

# 24 The critical transition from junior to elite football

## Resources and barriers

*José L. Chamorro, David Sánchez-Oliva, and Juan J. Pulido*

**Abstract**

The popular idea that it is quite difficult to become a professional soccer player is well known by all persons involved in any way in the world of soccer. According to the Fédération Internationale de Football Association (FIFA), more than 265 million people play football around the world. With these numbers we can imagine the quantity of children that play soccer, slowly moving up in categories with the dream of making the transition into the elite of this sport one day. In the last decade, researchers have developed theoretical models and studies about how to understand the athlete in this transition and to explore what factors have influence in the process of adaptation to professional sport. This chapter will review the different theoretical frameworks used to explore this transition to professional sport through three different categories (Alfermann & Stambulova, 2007): (a) career development descriptive models, (b) career transitions explanation models, and (c) career transitions intervention models. In addition, we will discuss the main conclusions reached by the works that have studied this transition and those factors that influence the performance and well-being of young elite athletes following the suggestion of Bruner, Munroe-Chandler, and Spink (2008), which classified barriers and resources transition on and off the field, with particular emphasis on soccer. Finally, we will discuss the practical implications of these results accompanied by recommendations for young soccer players, coaches, families, and clubs on how to act to try to make the adjustment to professional soccer as successful as possible.

More than 10 years ago, in 2006, the Fédération Internationale de Football Association (FIFA; International Federation of Football Association) carried out a large survey (called the *big count*; FIFA, 2006) in which it was estimated that more than 265 million people worldwide directly participated in football. That number comprises 4% of the world population. With these figures, it is not difficult to imagine the number of boys and girls who play every weekend, dreaming of someday becoming professionals in this sport, but only a very few of them will ever get there.

In the world of football, coaches, managers, and journalists habitually talk about young players who stood out at an early age and later could not adapt to professional football; and the reverse, young players who did not stand out early but eventually became professional football players. The transition from youth football to professional football is one of the most critical phases in the career of football players. According to Stambulova (2009), athletes perceive this transition as the most difficult of all the ones they must cope with during their sport career, and many of them fail. An example of how difficult it is for football players to successfully make this transition is shown in the data provided by Haugaasen and Jordet (2012). According to these authors, out of the 265 million people who regularly play football, only 0.04% play in a professional league. Another example of how difficult it is to go through this transition successfully and become a professional player is illustrated by data collected by Green (2009) in English football. The study shows that, out of 10,000 youngsters who play in the lower categories of professional clubs each season, less than 1% will become professional players.

This chapter will scientifically explore from a holistic perspective the aspects that are relevant and that influence the transition from junior to elite football. This will be done by reviewing studies conducted in football as well as the sport transition literature from all sports. Conclusions and recommendations about how to prepare young players for the transition from junior to senior football with a greater likelihood of success are discussed.

## Holistic view of the transition to being a professional player

Transition was defined by Schlossberg (1981) as 'an event or non-event that leads to a change in the assumptions about oneself and the world, which requires a corresponding change in one's behaviors and relationships' (p. 5). The scientific community's interest in studying sport transitions reveals their importance in sports and in athletes' lives because, as proposed by Stambulova, Alfermann, Statler, and Côté (2009), successfully overcoming the transitions both in and outside of sports provides the athlete with a better opportunity to live a long and successful career, whereas failing the transition could lead to negative consequences such as premature dropout of the sport and becoming vulnerable to drug/alcohol abuse. Therefore, helping athletes to prepare for transition from junior to elite football should be a concern for coaches, managers, parents, and sport psychologists.

Historically, the pioneering studies of sport transition focused on athletes' retirement, which was considered analogous to retirement from an occupational career (e.g. Park, Tod, & Lavallee, 2012). However, sports careers include other types of transitions besides retirement (Stambulova, 1994; Wylleman & Lavallee, 2004), such as the transition to elite sport. Transitions can be normative (events that occur as a rule in a sportsperson's career) or non-normative (events that may or may not occur in a sportsperson's career). A normative transition, like sports initiation, turning professional, or retirement, is determined by age or by an organizational characteristic of the sport (Wylleman & Lavallee, 2004). Athletes who manage to attain a sports career must undergo it. In contrast, a non-normative transition is less predictable, and includes, for example, changing clubs, injuries, dismissal of the coach, or other unexpected events (Stambulova et al., 2009). In contrast to normative transitions, athletes may or may not experience the non-normative ones. The main feature of normative transitions is that they are predictable. Therefore, prevention measures can be taken to prepare the player for the transition. Non-normative transitions are less predictable and often coping with the possible negative consequences is required.

As interest in this research topic has grown, studies of the transition to elite sports have increased (Alge, 2008; Bruner et al., 2008; Jorlén, 2007; Pummell, Harwood, &

Lavallee, 2008). The difficulty involved in successfully coping with this transition puts athletes onto two uneven paths. Most of them fail and go on to recreational levels or else they quit, whereas only a small group goes on to become elite sportspersons (Stambulova et al., 2009). An example of the inequalities of these two paths is found in the study of Vanden Auweele, Martelaer, Rzewnicki, De Knop, and Wylleman (2004) in which they explored the sport careers of 167 Belgian champions from a variety of sports 5 years after they had been proclaimed champions at ages 14–18 (e.g. they were 19–23 years old at the time of the study). They observed that only 17% of them were at an elite level, 31% had remained at the amateur level, 28% had ups and downs, and 24% had quit.

When exploring the causes of such a low level of success, it can be seen that a lack of sport talent itself is not the cause of many athletes' failure or quitting (for the problems of identifying a talent in sports see Beckmann & Beckmann-Waldenmayer, 2019, Chapter 21 in this book). This is why models are needed that take into account the athlete as a whole, seen both as a person and as an athlete. Within the transitional descriptive models more frequently used in research and at the applied level is that of Wylleman and Lavallee (2004), who propose a model of the stages faced by athletes throughout their sport career, which has been updated by Wylleman, Reints, and De Knop (2013; Figure 24.1), who included a new dimension. The model specifies that, throughout athletes' sports career, five levels of development must be taken into account, each one of them with different stages and the transitions that occur between them. The five levels are: (1) the athletic level, which describes the stages from sports initiation until retiring from the sport; (2) the psychological level, which describes the experiences throughout individual development during childhood, adolescence, and adulthood; (3) the psycho-social level, which indicates the people from the athletes' environment who were important at each stage of his/her personal and sports life, such as parents, siblings, coaches, teammates, partner; (4) the academic/vocational level, which examines experiences from the academic sphere (school, institute, university, etc.) and the work setting; and (5) the financial level, which describes the different economic supports received by athletes throughout their career. The model conceives and views athletes as persons in all their aspects at the global level. Many studies on transitions have chosen a holistic perspective to understand the athlete; that is, the elite sportsperson, besides being considered as an athlete, must also be considered and treated as a multidimensional and integral person (Bruner et al., 2008; Pummell et al., 2008; Stambulova & Alfermann, 2009; Torregrosa, Boixadós, Valiente, & Cruz, 2004; Wylleman & Lavallee, 2004).

Evidence in favour of the holistic approach to career development comes from different investigations that have shown the interactions between the diverse levels proposed. For example, Wuerth, Lee, and Alfermann (2004) reported that the parents of athletes who made a successful transition from initiation to the improvement stage participated more in their child's athletic pursuits than the parents of athletes who did not achieve this transition. Also, Bruner et al. (2008) described the difficulties in and out of the rink caused by the transition to elite ice hockey in young players, such as demonstrating that they were competent to perform at an elite level or the difficult situation of living far from their families. Therefore, successful transition from junior to senior is largely accompanied by young athletes' capacity to adapt to changes at the sport, psychological, psycho-social, and

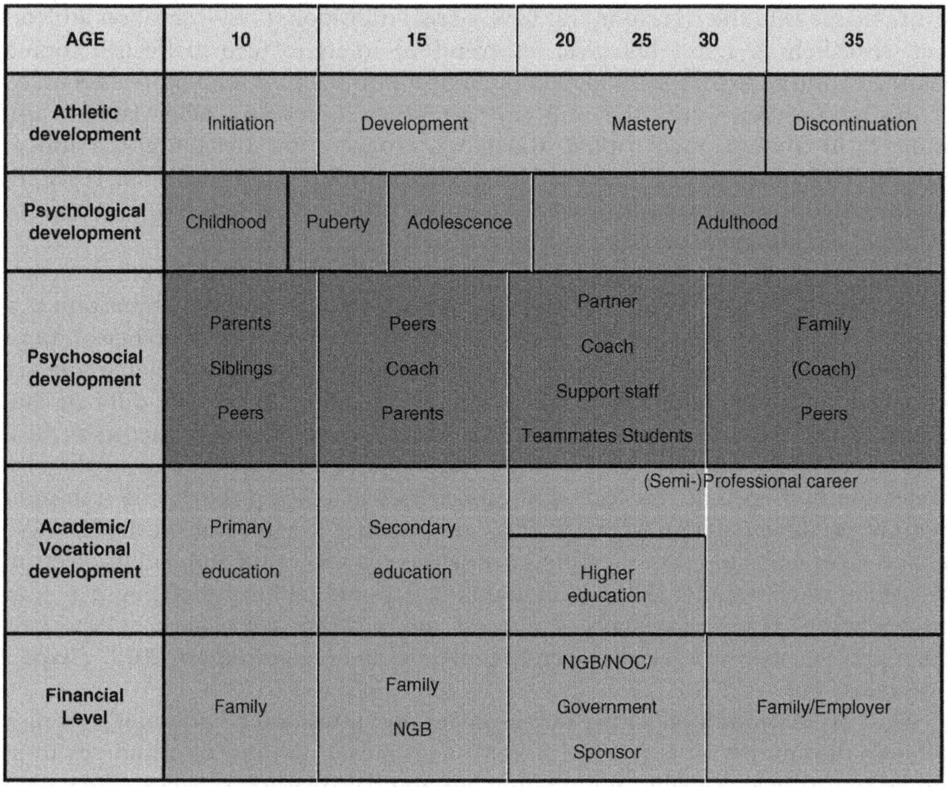

| AGE | 10 | 15 | 20 | 25 | 30 | 35 |
|---|---|---|---|---|---|---|
| Athletic development | Initiation | Development | Mastery | | | Discontinuation |
| Psychological development | Childhood | Puberty | Adolescence | Adulthood | | |
| Psychosocial development | Parents Siblings Peers | Peers Coach Parents | Partner Coach Support staff Teammates Students | | | Family (Coach) Peers |
| Academic/ Vocational development | Primary education | Secondary education | (Semi-)Professional career Higher education | | | |
| Financial Level | Family | Family NGB | NGB/NOC/ Government Sponsor | | | Family/Employer |

*Figure 24.1* The Holistic Athletic Career Model.

Source: adapted from Wylleman et al., 2013.

academic/work levels they encounter in the new stage, as shown by the above-mentioned studies, and their success in making these transitions has a direct influence on the future of their sports careers.

Taking a different approach, Stambulova (2003) proposed a transitional inter-vention model called the Athletic Career Transitions Model. According to this model, a series of demands during transition creates a developmental conflict between 'what the athlete is' and 'what the athlete wants to be or should be'. This stimulates athletes to mobilize resources and find ways of dealing with the barriers or obstacles that arise. The athlete's effectiveness in the face of the transition depends on the balance between the resources or coping strategies and the barriers during transition. The resources and obstacles may be internal (stemming from the athlete him- or herself) or external (from the athlete's environment). Resources and strategies in transition have a positive effect on the coping process, whereas obstacles or barriers have a negative effect. These resources and barriers in young football players will be discussed later.

According to the Athletic Career Transitions Model (Stambulova, 2003), the process of coping has two main results: successful transition and crisis transition. Athletes who mobilize and develop the necessary resources to effectively cope with the demands of transition will have a successful transition, whereas athletes who cannot cope with the transition will have a crisis transition. Crisis-transition athletes may seek help (e.g. psychological intervention) to try to turn ineffective coping strategies into strategies that will help them deal with the transition more effectively. If this intervention works, they will have a positive successful – albeit late – transition. If, in contrast, their coping strategies are once again ineffective, the athlete will probably have to face the 'cost' of a failed transition. Among these costs are undesired sports outcomes such as over-training, premature dropout from the sport, injuries, psychosomatic distress, etc.

Thus, according to the above theoretical models, when a football player makes the transition to the professional stage, he or she is mainly making a transition at a sports level. But at the same time, athletes may be making the psychological transition from adolescence to youth or even the academic transition from secondary education to higher education. These multiple transitions can create difficult situations in the lives of athletes. Football players seek resources or strategies to deal with the different situations that they are experiencing and try to overcome the obstacles and barriers that arise. Stressful experiences that take place during transition require personal coping resources. Thus, the capacity to effectively deal with these experiences may represent the difference between a successful and an unsuccessful transition to elite sports (Finn & McKenna, 2010) and ineffective coping may lead to psychological problems such as burnout and depression that have an especially high prevalence in youth sports (see Nixdorf, Beckmann, & Nixdorf, 2019, Chapter 25 in this book).

Most of the studies on career development and transition from junior to senior athletes did not particularly address football. However, the research findings from other sports yield valuable information for football players, coaches, clubs, and other agents who are involved in the development of young professionals. This research also provides a framework for future research in the area of football. Accordingly, we will subsequently present the main investigations both in football and in other sport settings following the proposal of Bruner et al. (2008) for a differentiation of factors that affect the transition to senior in 'on the field' and 'off the field' factors. This differentiation was subsequently adopted by Chamorro, Torregrosa, Sánchez-Oliva, and Amado (2016) with Spanish football players.

## The transition to professional football on the field

The development of high-level football players is a complex process (Mills, Butt, Maynard, & Harwood, 2012). As we can see in the Holistic Athletic Career Model (Wylleman et al., 2013), the main transition experienced by potential elite athletes occurs at the sports level. Thus, athletes must first face changes in training and competition conditions (Bruner et al., 2008; Chamorro, Torregrosa, Sánchez-Oliva, & Amado, 2016; Finn & McKenna, 2010; McNamara & Collins, 2010; Pummell et al., 2008). Specifically, in football, young players who enter a professional team encounter an increased level of physical demands, intensity of the game, tactical complexity, and level of competitiveness. In order to deal with these changes, the younger football players improve their sports qualities and the more adaption resources they have, the more likely it is that they will be able to adapt to these changes. But Chamorro, Torregrosa, Sánchez-Miguel, Sánchez-Oliva, and Amado (2015) indicate that following a lifestyle based on healthy habits is another resource to deal with strictly sport demands. According to Pisarek, Guszkowska, Zagorska, and Lenartow-icz (2011), the concept of a healthy lifestyle is considered essential by great athletes. Hence, educating young football players in these aspects will be very useful in equipping them to face the challenges that arise as they transition to elite football.

These changes at the sport level promote a series of challenges for the participants at other levels. For example, the increased physical, tactical, and strategic demands, and rhythm and speed of the game lead young football players to question their competence when comparing themselves with their more experienced teammates (Chamorro, Torregrosa, Sánchez-Oliva, & Amado, 2016). Football players who stood out and who perceived themselves as having a better performance level than their teammates frequently become more modest once they reach the professional world. According to the study of Pummell et al. (2008) with equestrian riders, when these athletes did not feel sufficiently prepared for the level of competence demanded, they felt uncertain, and their sense of control decreased. This situation seems to be the key to the transition to being a professional. Morley, Morgan, McKenna, and Nicholls (2014) have shown that football coaches and young players both recognize that feeling competent and self-assured is a crucial aspect of the competition and training context and, by extension, of adaptation to the professional world.

Participants also suffer from various pressures and their psychological consequences. When reaching the elite level, high pressure originates from the club demanding results, the weekly matches, as well as from the competition among the players. Moreover, the players demand a high performance of themselves, which translates into pressure to reach this level and to show that they can fulfil the goals (Finn & McKenna, 2010). According to Chamorro, Torregrosa, Sánchez-Oliva, and Amado (2016), these situations become a source of stress that lead to negative feelings and thoughts during training and competition, such as a high level of tension, insecurity, concern about mistakes, frustration about undesirable results, and somatic and cognitive anxiety (Morris, Tod, & Eubank, 2016). According to Palazzolo and Arnaud (2013), this type of stress is frequently based on the athlete's interpretation of a concrete situation because external situations rarely cause this stress (cf. Lazarus & Folkman, 1984). It is the player's interpretation of the situation that is key. Moreover, in a review on personality in sports, Allen, Greenless, and Jones (2013) reported that research has historically considered these feelings and forms of assessing the environment as being negatively related to performance.

These findings clearly show that football players must mobilize psychological resources that help them perform. Among the psychological skills most frequently used by football players to face the above-mentioned challenges are self-confidence, high self-esteem, and positive self-talk to offset failures (Chamorro, Torregrosa, Sánchez-Oliva, & Amado, 2016). Mateo-March et al. (2013) indicated that, among other psychological skills, self-esteem improved the performance of motorcyclists. The systematic review of the effects of self-talk by Tod, Hardy, and Oliver (2011) concludes that there is a positive relation between this skill and performance (see Konter, Beckmann, & Mallett, 2019, Chapter 14 in this book). Moreover, there are a number of personal values and variables at the psychological level that help young players cope with transitional demands. The football players in the study of Chamorro, Torregrosa, Sánchez-Oliva, and Amado (2016) identified sacrifice, work, enthusiasm, perseverance, and the desire to improve as key aspects. Humility emerged as an aspect considered essential. In the words of one of the participants, 'humility is essential, if you think that now you're Maradona, you neglect the work and constancy needed to achieve your best' (p. 84). Although these resources depend on oneself to carry them out, they can be trained throughout the football player's development. Coaches and policy-makers of junior football frequently leave these resources to chance. Developing and training them at early ages can be crucial so that, when the time comes, the players can adapt to elite football.

Therefore, these results suggest that the technical and psychological aspects of sports should accompany young football players during this difficult transition, with special attention paid to the players' self-perceptions of competence, their self-demands (especially excessive demands), and the experienced pressure to perform well. Focusing and addressing these issues will enhance the athletes' development as football players and their performance on the field.

## The transition to professional football off the field

In addition to on-the-field transitions there is also a transition to the professional world off the field. For example, economic and social interests must be addressed by the transitioning player. These interests directly influence the development of football players, distorting their natural development. Many youth players experience pressures from their families to achieve an elite sports level in order to attain a certain social or economic status. According to Sagar and Lavallee (2010), parents can thereby contribute to developing fear of failure in their children through three categories: punitive behaviours of their children's actions, controlling behaviours, and high achievement expectations. At the same time, one of the resources that is most appreciated by young football players and that seems to play a relevant role in helping them cope more successfully with the transition process is family and social support (e.g. Chamorro, Torregrosa, Sánchez-Oliva, & Amado, 2016; Morris, Tod, & Oliver, 2015; Morris, Tod, & Oliver, 2016). Frequently, young elite players must leave their homes because they are recruited by clubs far away. Thus, they undergo a sudden change when leaving their immediate family and friends and starting a new life in a new place, and the experience of this situation can be a barrier to dealing with the process of transition to professional level. Therefore, family involvement can be paradoxical with social support/family involvement either becoming a resource for young football players or, in the form of pressure, it becomes a barrier for them. Pummell et al. (2008) suggest that the social support of the close environment (family, friends, etc.) should be limited to providing emotional support and, in this way, prevent it from becoming counterproductive for the football player. As a result, it is crucial to train the athlete and their significant others in these aspects (see Farina & Cei, 2019, Chapter 18 in this book). Clubs should implement concrete strategies accordingly.

The social impact of the players' performances and how they are evaluated by fans and the mass media can add additional pressure to the transitioning player. Young elite football players already appear on the front pages of magazines and newspapers, and they are often faced with assessments and criticisms from various sectors of society. These situations, which do not depend on the football players' characteristics, trigger reactions of stress in the youngsters seeking to adapt to professional football (Nixdorf, Beckmann, & Nixdorf, 2019, Chapter 25 in this book). Reducing the impact of these situations on young players should be of vital importance to all those who have a close relationship with them, such as coaches, families, clubs, and sport psychologists. By the same token, teaching the young players skills how to use social networks and how to interact with the media should be addressed by football education institutions.

## Academic level and dual careers

The model of Wylleman et al. (2013) advocates the existence of an academic life parallel to the sports life. Many parents of young football players are concerned about their children's academic vocational/training during the training stages as football players, mostly, so that their children have other career options in case they do not become professional football players. There are even some elite football clubs that grant considerable importance to academic/vocational training of players, assigning resources so that the athletes can combine their sports training with their academic training. However, when young football players become young elite football players, both their family environment and their sports environment develop an attitude that becoming a professional is guaranteed, and their educational training seems to fade into the background (Chamorro, Torregrosa, Sánchez-Oliva, & Amado, 2016). Accordingly, Cosh and Tully (2014) state that athletes frequently place their sport career before their academic achievements. In principle, it seems extremely important to have an academic education parallel to the education in sport as an alternative because the chances of reaching the goal of becoming a professional are small. In addition, some authors and institutions have identified the advantages of combining sport and education/vocation training (Torregrosa & González, 2013).

A relatively recent concept that has captured the attention of researchers, sporting organizations (e.g. United States Olympic Committee (USOC), 2012) and political institutions (EU Expert Group, 2012) is the concept of dual careers (DC). The development of DC is a preventive proposal so that athletes who do not manage to become elite players will find professional alternatives outside of sports, and athletes who do achieve it will have an easier transition to an alternative professional career when they retire from high competition sports (Torregrosa, Chamorro, & Ramis, 2016; Torregrosa, Ramis, Pallarés, Azocar, & Selva, 2015; Tshube & Feltz, 2015) and, also, following a dual career could help to manage their finances in a more productive way.

Torregrosa et al. (2016) have stimulated a debate about the benefits of DC for athletes. According to these authors, when we refer to elite athletes, or athletes who wish to become elites, we mean people who seek an outcome within the activity they perform, in this case, at the sports level. Therefore, if the development of the player as a footballer is dissociated from the academic/occupational level, political or federal institutions and other sports professionals' determination to promote DC could lose impetus for the athletes or clubs. Studies such as that of Gledhill and Harwood (2015) or Hollings, Mallett, and Hume (2014) suggest that the development of a unique sport identity that does not conflict with other identities would be a resource for athletes who want to achieve sports success. However, there is another stream that includes the benefits that an academic/occupational career would have on the development of sports. For example, Aquilina (2013) suggests that encouraging athletes to focus on aspects other than sports achievements (e.g. academic achievements) helps to lower tensions related to the pressure to compete. Moreover, the athletes can learn skills in other activities, such as academic ones (e.g. intellectual stimulation), which can subsequently be used in their life in sport. For example, studying technical drawing could improve the field vision skills of young football players. Chamorro, Torregrosa, Sánchez-Oliva, García-Calvo, and León (2016), suggest that granting more importance to achievements in other life spheres (including the academic sphere) than the sports sphere is related to a more adaptive motivational pattern in the transition from junior to senior (motivation was identified as a key aspect in this transition in the studies of Morris et al., 2015; Morris et al., 2016; Pummell et al., 2008; Stambulova et al., 2012). Moreover, the model of Wylleman et al. (2013) proposes an interaction between the different levels of their model and the influence among these levels. For example, just as the psycho-social level can influence the sports level either positively or negatively, the academic/work level might behave similarly. In this way, the studies of Gledhill and Harwood (2015) and Hollings et al. (2014) describe the consequences of poor management of identities, but studies are lacking that evaluate their good management and their influence at the sports level.

## Conclusions and practical implications

The need for a global view of the young football player, who is considered not just an athlete but a person, when dealing with the transition from junior to professional football was discussed. Moreover, knowledge on this transition offers opportunities in the preparation of players to successfully cope with it. Being a normative transition, it is known that every football player who turns professional will have to deal with this transition process at some point in their careers. For this reason, we believe that the sooner we provide young football players with coping and career development strategies, the earlier they will be internalized, and athletes will be more effective at putting them into practice. This makes the clubs directly responsible for this training. For these reasons, we encourage clubs to create programmes considering all the variables presented in this chapter because this will not only influence young athletes' personal and psychological well-being but can influence their performance as well.

One of the consequences derived from the fact that football players' useful coping strategies come both from the sports level (e.g. physical, technical, and tactical strategies) and from the psycho-social level is the key role played by the sport psychologist in the preparation of young football players who wish to become professionals. Therefore, a football or team psychologist should conduct intervention programmes that support and strengthen both the athlete's skills and environmental resources that he or she can use to more effectively cope with and move smoothly through career transitions. An example of what the sport psychologist could contribute to this transition is the holistic intervention proposal of Larsen, Henriksen, Alfermann, and Christensen (2014) who work with young players from a well-known Danish football club. These authors recommend taking into account six main points when performing this kind of intervention: (a) the practitioner should acknowledge that the athlete is embedded in an environment; (b) the intervention should be built on a thorough assessment of the environment from a holistic perspective; (c) the practitioner should not only work with the individual players, but also aim to optimize the entire environment around the athlete or team; (d) an intervention should take into consideration that an environment is always situated in a larger cultural setting of, for example, a national culture and a sport-specific culture, and plan accordingly; and (e) and (f) the intervention should aim to create and maintain a strong and coherent organizational culture and treat the athletes as whole human beings by supporting the development of a holistic package of psychosocial skills that will be of use for the athletes not only in their sport, but other life spheres as well (see Farina & Cei, 2019, Chapter 18 in this book).

To conclude this chapter, below we offer some general guidelines to take into account when preparing young football players to master the transition to professional football:

- Educate football players during the training phases about the importance of a healthy lifestyle. Besides the benefits of this lifestyle for physical and psychological health, it will be very useful to meet the challenges at the sports and competitive levels that will arise when players start the process of transition to elite sports.
- Raise the awareness of the football staff (e.g. coaches, sport psychologists, physical trainers etc.) about the importance and consequences for young football players of feeling competent within the team. Moreover, help them achieve a real perception of what they must do to regulate the pressures to perform so that, ultimately, these will not negatively influence their development as football players and their performance on the field.
- Clubs should implement strategies and programmes to try to remove young football players from the economic interests that surround them (i.e. representatives, advertising contracts etc.) as well as to relativize and manage their presence in mass media.
- Implement strategies and programmes to raise awareness and coach the players' families, with a special emphasis on aspects that support the player and those that turn into pressure for the player.
- Educate young football players about the benefits of academic education not only for the future, but as an aid to cope with the potential problems in football career transition, at the sports level and the psychological and social levels. If necessary, help them to manage their time to carry out a DC.

## References

Alfermann, D., & Stambulova, N. B. (2007). Career transitions and career termination. In G. Tenenbaum & R. C. Eklund (Eds.), *Handbook of sport psychology* (pp. 712–733). Hoboken, NJ: John Wiley & Sons.

Alge, E. (2008). *Successful career transition from Young Rider to senior in equestrian sport* (unpublished doctoral thesis). Halmstad University, Halmstad, Sweden.

Allen, M. S., Greenless, L., & Jones, M. (2013). Personality in sport: A comprehensive review. *International Reviews of Sport Psychology, 6*(1), 184–208.

Aquilina, D. (2013). A study of the relationship between elite athletes' educational development and sporting performance. *The International Journal of the History of Sport, 30*(4), 374–392. doi:10.1080/09523367.2013.765723.

Beckmann, J., & Beckmann-Waldenmayer, D. (2019). Talent development in football. In E. Konter, J. Beckmann, & T. Loughead (Eds.), *Football psychology: From theory to practice.* London, England: Routledge.

Bruner, M. W., Munroe-Chandler, K. J., & Spink, K. S. (2008). Entry to elite sport: A preliminary investigation into the transition experiences of rookie athletes. *Journal of Applied Sport Psychology, 20*(2), 236–252.

Chamorro, J. L., Torregrosa, M., Sánchez-Miguel, P. A., Sánchez-Oliva, D., & Amado, D. (2015). Challenges in the transition to elite football: Coping resources in males and females. *Revista Iberoamericana de Psicología del Ejercicio y el deporte, 10*(1), 113–119.

Chamorro, J. L., Torregrosa, M., Sánchez-Oliva, D., & Amado, D. (2016). Football on and off the field: Challenges in transition from junior to elite. *Revista de Psicología del Deporte, 25*(1), 81–89.

Chamorro, J. L., Torregrosa, M., Sánchez-Oliva, D., García-Calvo, T., & León, B. (2016). Future achievements, passion and motivation in the transition from junior-to-senior sport in Spanish young elite soccer players. *The Spanish Journal of Psychology, 19,* e69. doi:10.1017/sjp. 2016.71.

Cosh, S., & Tully, P. J. (2014). 'All I have to do is pass': A discursive analysis of student athletes' talk about prioritising sport to the detriment of education to overcome stressors encountered in combining elite sport and tertiary education. *Psychology of Sport and Exercise, 15,* 180–189. doi:10.1016/j.psychsport.2013.10.015.

EU Expert Group. (2012). *EU guidelines on dual careers of athletes.* Brussels.

Farina, M. & Cei, A. (2019). Concentration and self-talk in football. In E. Konter, J. Beckmann, & T. Loughead (Eds.), *Football psychology:. From theory to practice.* London, England: Routledge.

Fédération Internationale de Football Association. (2006). Big count. Retrieved from http://es.fifa.com/aboutfifa/media/newsid=529409.html.

Finn, J., & McKenna, J. (2010). Coping with academy-to-first-team transitions in elite English male team sports: The coaches' perspective. *International Journal of Sports Sciences & Coaching, 5*(2), 257–279.

Gledhill, A., & Harwood, C. (2015). A holistic perspective on career development in UK female soccer players: A negative case analysis. *Psychology of Sport and Exercise, 21,* 65–77. http://dx. doi.org/10.1016/j.psychsport.2015.04.003.

Green, C. (2009). *Every boy's dream: England's football future on the line.* London, England: A & C Black Publishers Ltd.

Haugaasen, M., & Jordet, G. (2012). Developing football expertise: A football-specific research review. *International Review of Sport and Exercise Psychology, 5*(2), 177–201. doi:10.1080/1750984X.2012.677951.

Hollings, S. C., Mallett, C. J., & Hume, P. A. (2014). The transition from elite junior track-and-field athlete to successful senior athlete: Why some do, why others don't. *International Journal of Sports Science & Coaching, 9,* 457–472. http://dx.doi. org/10.1260/1747-9541. 9.3.457.

Konter, E., Beckmann, J., & Mallett, C. (2019). Psychological skills in football. In E. Konter, J. Beckmann, & T. Loughead (Eds.), *Football psychology: From theory to practice.* London, England: Routledge.

Jorlén, D. (2007). *Career transitions for Swedish golf juniors – from regional to national junior elite competitions* (unpublished doctoral thesis). Halmstad University, Halmstad, Sweden.

Larsen, C. H., Henriksen, K., Alfermann, D., & Christensen, M. K. (2014). Preparing footballers for the next step: An intervention program from an ecological perspective. *The Sport Psychologist, 28,* 91–102. http://dx.doi.org/10.1123/pes.2013-0015.

Lazarus, R. S., & Folkman, S. (1984). *Stress, appraisal, and coping.* New York, NY: Springer.

Mateo-March, M., Rodriguez-Perez, M. A., Costa, R., Sanchez-Munoz, C., Casimiro-Andujar, A. J., & Zabala, M. (2013). Effect of an intervention program on perceived stress, self-esteem and performance in youth elite motorcyclist. *Revista de Psicología del Deporte*, *22*(1), 125–133.

McNamara, A., & Collins, D. (2010). The role of psychological characteristics in managing the transition to university. *Psychology of Sport and Exercise*, *11*, 353–362.

Mills, A., Butt, J., Maynard, I., & Harwood. C. (2012). Identifying factors perceived to influence the development of elite English football academy players. *Journal of Sport Sciences*, *30*, 1–12.

Morley, D., Morgan, G., McKenna, J., & Nicholls, A. R. (2014). Developmental contexts and features of elite academy football players: Coach and player perspectives. *International Journal of Sport Sciences & Coaching*, *9*(1), 217–232.

Morris, R., Tod, D., & Eubank, M. (2016). From youth team to first team: An investigation into the transition experiences of young professional athletes in soccer. *International Journal of Sport and Exercise Psychology*, *15*(5), 523–539. doi:10.1080/1612197X.2016.1152992.

Morris, R., Tod, D., & Oliver, E. (2015). An analysis of organizational structure and transition outcomes in the youth-to-senior professional soccer transition. *Journal of Applied Sport Psychology*, *27*(2), 216–234. doi:10.1080/10413200.2 014.980015.

Morris, R., Tod, D., & Oliver, E. (2016). An investigation into stakeholders' perceptions of the youth-to-senior transition in sport. *Journal of Applied Sport Psychology*, *28*(4), 375–391. doi:10.1080/10413200.2016.1162222.

Nixdorf, I., Beckmann, J., & Nixdorf, R. (2019). Preventing burnout and depression in youth football. In E. Konter, J. Beckmann, & T. Loughead (Eds.), *Football psychology: From theory to practice*. London, England: Routledge.

Palazzolo, J., & Arnaud, J. (2013). Anxieté et performance: de la théorie à la pratique. *Annales Médico-Psychologiques*, *171*, 382–388.

Park, S., Tod, D., & Lavallee, D. (2012). Athletes' career transition out of sport: A systematic review. *International Review for Sport and Exercise Psychology*, *13*, 444–453.

Pisarek, A., Guszkowska, M., Zagorska. A., & Lenartowicz, M. (2011). Characteristics of athletes' approach to the question of physical health and health behaviors: Do athletes lead healthy lifestyles?. *Journal of Applied Sport Psychology*, *23*(4), 459–473.

Pummell, B., Harwood, C., & Lavallee, D. (2008). Jumping to the next level: A qualitative examination of within-career transition in adolescent event riders. *Psychology of Sport and Exercise*, *9*, 427–447.

Sagar, S., & Lavallee, D. (2010). The developmental origins of fear of failure in adolescent athletes: Examining parental practices. *Psychology of Sport and Exercise*, *11*(3), 177–187. doi:10.1016/j.psychsport.2010.01.004.

Schlossberg, N. K. (1981). A model for analyzing human adaptation to transition. *The Counseling Psychologist*, *9*(2), 2–18.

Stambulova, N. (1994). Developmental sports career investigations in Russia: A post-perestroika analysis. *The Sport Psychologist*, *8*, 221–237.

Stambulova, N. (2003). Symptoms of a crisis-transition: A grounded theory study. In N. Hassmén (Ed.), *SIPF yearbook 2003* (pp. 97–109). Örebro, Sweden: Örebro University.

Stambulova, N. (2009). Talent development in sport: The perspective of career transitions. In E. Tsung-Min Hung, R. Lidor, & D. Hackfort (Eds.), *Psychology of sport excellence* (pp. 63–74). Morgantown, WV: Fitness Information Technology.

Stambulova, N., & Alfermann, D. (2009). Putting culture into context: Cultural and cross-cultural perspectives in career development and transition research and practice. *International Society of Sport Psychology*, *7*, 292–308.

Stambulova, N., Alfermann, D., Statler, T., & Côté, J. (2009). ISSP positions stand: Career development and transition of athletes. *International Society of Sport Psychology*, *7*, 395–412.

Stambulova, N., Franck, A., & Weibull, F. (2012). Assessment of the transition from junior-to-senior sports in Swedish athletes. *International Journal of Sport and Exercise Psychology*, *10*(2), 79–95.

Tod, D., Hardy, J., & Oliver, E. (2011). Effects of self-talk: A systematic review. *Journal of Sport & Exercise Psychology, 33*(5), 666–687.

Torregrosa, M., Boixadós, M., Valiente, L., & Cruz, J. (2004). Elite athletes' image of retirement: The way to relocation in sport. *Psychology of Sport and Exercise, 5*(1), 35–43.

Torregrosa, M., Chamorro, J. L., & Ramis, Y. (2016). Transition from junior to senior and promoting dual careers in sport: An interpretative review. *Revista de Psicología Aplicada al Deporte y al Ejercicio Físico, 1*(1), e6.

Torregrosa, M., & González, M. (2013). Athletes' in Spain: Professionalization and developmental consequences. In N. Stambulova & T. Ryba (Eds.), *Athletes' careers across cultures* (pp. 185–196). London, England: Routledge.

Torregrosa, M., Ramis, Y., Pallarés, S., Azocar, F., & Selva, C. (2015). Olympic athletes back to retirement: A qualitative longitudinal study. *Psychology of Sport & Exercise, 21*, 50–56. http://dx.doi.org/10.1016/j.psychsport.2015.03.003.

Tshube, T., & Feltz, D. L. (2015). The relationship between dual-career and post-sport career transition among elite athletes in South Africa, Botswana, Namibia and Zimbabwe. *Psychology of Sport and Exercise, 21*, 109–114. http://dx.doi.org/10.1016/j. psychsport.2015.05.005.

United States Olympic Committee (USOC). (2012). Athlete Career, Education and Life Skills Working Group. Retrieved from www.teamusa.org/~/media/TeamUSA/USOC/Working-Group-Report-FINAL-12-5-12.pdf?la=en.

Vanden Auweele, Y., De Martelaer, K., Rzewnicki, R., De Knop, P., & Wylleman, P. (2004). Parents and coaches: A help or harm? Affective outcomes for children in sport. In Y. Vanden Auweele (Ed.), *Ethics in youth sport.* Leuven, Belgium: LannooCampus.

Wuerth, S., Lee, M. J., & Alfermann, D. (2004). Parental involvement and athletes' career in youth sport. *Psychology of Sport and Exercise, 5*(1), 21–33.

Wylleman, P., & Lavallee, D. (2004). A developmental perspective on transitions faced by athletes. In M. Weiss (Ed.), *Developmental sport and exercise psychology: A lifespan perspective* (pp. 503–523). Morgantown, WV: Fitness Information Technology.

Wylleman, P., Reints, A., & De Knop, P. (2013). Athletes' careers in Belgium: A holistic perspective to understand and alleviate challenges occurring throughout the athletic and post-sport career. In N. B. Stambulova & T. V. Ryba (Eds.), *Athletes' careers across cultures* (pp. 31–42). New York, NY: Routledge.

# 25 Preventing depression and burnout in youth football

*Insa Nixdorf, Jürgen Beckmann, and Raphael Nixdorf*

## Abstract

Until 2009 burnout and depression had been widely ignored in German football. In 2007 one of Germany's greatest talents, Sebastian Deisler, ended his career aged 27 due to depression. But only after Germany's national goalkeeper, Robert Enke, committed suicide in 2009, did official football declare that steps needed to be taken against burnout and depression. The following chapter will give you an overview of the definition, classifications, and theoretical assumptions about burnout and depression in elite athletes. We present current research and findings on sport specifics and football-related aspects (such as cognition and attitude, coping with stress and motivation) regarding these two syndromes, summarizing research and highlighting the most important aspects for young football athletes. The chapter continues with a section regarding practical implications. Here, a strong focus on prevention among young athletes is presented highlighting structural aspects and recommending content of prevention in youth football players. Concluding, the chapter will offer future research directions and deductions for applied sport psychologists active within football.

Sebastian Deisler was seen as the one-in-a-century talent in German football. In 2007 he ended his career at the age of 27. He had had several knee and groin surgeries. But he ended his career because of depression.

> So much madness was staged around me. Every day they were focusing on me, but they never asked me how I felt about it ... I tried to deal with all the attention I got in Berlin by partying like the other football professionals did, buying fancy watches, expensive glasses, clothing ... I only wanted to play football, talk about football. But all of a sudden my whole life was in the spotlight, football had so many side effects. My life was pocketed. Sometimes I lay in bed and prayed, 'Oh my God, I'm not going to make it.' I even cursed my talent ... Everybody knew me. I was on top in football, a big car was parked outside. But none of it made me happy. I asked myself: Is this what my goal is? I was sick at heart. I lived against my nature.
>
> (Sußebach & Willeke, 2009)

Sebastian Deisler had good social support and psychotherapy. He survived but never returned to football (Rosentritt, 2009). Robert Enke, Germany's national team goalie, could not manage his depression and committed suicide in 2009 aged 32 (Reng, 2011). After this and reports of more cases of burnout and depression in German football the issue could no longer be swept under the carpet. Andi Biermann, another professional football player, had thought that after all the statements given by football officials at the memorial service for Robert Enke depression had become an accepted disease. But, after confessing that he suffered from depression his contract was not prolonged. He wrote a book entitled *Red Card Depression* (Biermann & Schäfer, 2011). In 2014 Andi Biermann committed suicide.

Apart from Germany, there are also many cases in football with athletes suffering from depression and burnout. Stan Collymore, for example, revealed his suffering in social media and an autobiographic book illustrating his personal struggles. Mental health issues have increasingly become a mainstream concern in British politics, but they are rarely, if ever, discussed as an aspect of the nation's most loved sport. Football has a hugely influential role in the formative years of young men (the group least likely to reach out for mental health support), and yet most of us are unaware of what is being done to tackle issues in the sport and give no thought to the impact of our own punditry.

It might come as a surprise to learn that every year around 200 players and ex-players reach out to mental health services provided by the Professional Footballers' Association (PFA) via the charity Sporting Chance. For confidentiality reasons, figures on how many players from the Premier League seek support are unavailable, but since the ever-growing network of counsellors and psychotherapists currently stands at 82 we can assume the service is a success.

Since several before-mentioned cases of prominent elite athletes affected by depression have become publicly known, psychological well-being and mental disorders have become topics of increasing public and scientific interest. However, few empirical data are available on this specific topic with elite athletes. Although depression among elite athletes seems to be a topic of interest, empirical data on prevalence rates and research on mechanisms in this regard is still rare. However, recent results on depression prevalence in elite athlete samples are noteworthy and range between 4% (Schaal et al., 2011), 24% (Wolanin, Hong, Marks, Panchoo, & Gross, 2016), 27% (Gulliver, Griffiths, Mackinnon, Batterham, & Stanimirovic, 2015), and in some cases even up to 68% in the last 36 months (Hammond, Gialloreto, Kubas, & Davis, 2013). Obviously, there is variability in prevalence estimates, which might be due to different assessment methods (questionnaire vs interview), different assessment times (period of heavy exercise, recovery, or championship), or samples (different sport disciplines, gender, etc.). Especially junior athletes were found to have relatively high levels of depressive symptoms (Nixdorf, Frank, Hautzinger, & Beckmann, 2013). In fact, recent reviews on this matter (Frank, Nixdorf, & Beckmann, 2013; Wolanin et al., 2014) suggest depression in elite athletes to be connected to sport-specific mechanisms and factors such as injuries, overtraining, or exceeding stress.

The following chapter will give an overview of current knowledge primarily on depression but also on the related topic of burnout in elite sports and football in particular, important correlating variables, and the role of prevention within this context.

# Theory and research

## Classification and definition of depression and burnout

Burnout and depression can be considered as important aspects in the context of psychological well-being in athletes (e.g. Gouttebarge, Frings-Dresen, & Sluiter, 2015; Gulliver et al., 2015). Both syndromes affect athletes on physical and emotional dimensions and have the potential to have negative outcomes such as chronic mental suffering, dropout, or even suicidal ideation (Doherty, Hannigan, & Campbell, 2016). Depression is a concept that is deeply rooted in the history of medical science and therefore is an obligatory part of the *Diagnostic and Statistical Manual of Mental Disorders* in its current fifth edition (DSM V; American Psychiatric Association, 2013) as well as in the International Classification of Diseases (ICD 10; Dilling, Mombour, Schmidt, Schulte-Markwort, & Remschmidt, 2015). Therefore, clear diagnostic criteria for several depressive disorders are provided. For example, symptoms of depressed mood, anhedonia, fatigue, feelings of guilt, or suicidal ideation can be associated with depression. Furthermore, depression can be regarded as a multisystem disorder with affective, cognitive, and physiological manifestations (Insel & Charney, 2003; Lee, Jeong, Kwak, & Park, 2010).

In contrast, burnout is a younger concept with the first findings in the 1970s (Freudenberger, 1974). Burnout is mainly described as a three-dimensional syndrome involving emotional exhaustion, cynicism, and lack of professional efficacy in response to occupational stress (Maslach & Jackson, 1981; Maslach, Schaufeli, & Leiter, 2001). Although research is concerned with defining and exploring burnout (Maslach, 2001) its medical recognition as a discrete diagnosis has been discussed without consensus. Still, burnout is often considered as a part or a sub-category of depression and therefore included in this chapter (for review see Bianchi, Schonfeld, & Laurent, 2015).

## Depression and burnout in sports

Research on depression in elite athletes is only recently evolving. At first, articles on depression were more theoretical and pointed to overlaps with overtraining and the physical demands in elite sports (Armstrong & Van Heest, 2002; Puffer & McShane, 1992). These assumptions based on findings from Morgan and colleagues (Raglin, Morgan, & O'Connor, 1991) pointed to an association between overtraining and depressed mood. The first empirical data with clinical relevant measurements among college athletes (Armstrong & Oomen-Early, 2009; Storch, Storch, Killiany, & Roberti, 2005; Yang et al., 2007) and recent research on this matter recognize the relevance and in some cases the severity of depressive syndromes in athletes (Gulliver et al., 2015; Nixdorf et al., 2013; Wolanin et al., 2016). For assessing depression in elite athletes, different measurements are used (for discussion see Frank, Nixdorf, & Beckmann, 2013). In order to diagnose a depressive disorder, a structured interview is performed by a clinical expert. However, in research clinical questionnaires for assessing depressive symptoms are most often used, which also highlights the severity of depressive symptoms. Therefore, the Center for Epidemiologic Studies Depression Scale (CES-D) from the National Institute of Mental Health (Radloff, 1977) is widely used. The CES-D is a short self-report scale designed to measure depressive symptomatology in the general population. It has also repeatedly been used to assess depressive symptoms among elite athletes (e.g. Armstrong & Oomen-Early, 2009; Junge & Feddermann-Demont, 2016; Yang et al., 2007).

In contrast, research on burnout rapidly increased since 1984 (Caccese & Mayerberg, 1984) and many reviews followed (Dale & Weinberg, 1990; Eklund & DeFreese, 2015; Fender, 1989; Goodger, Gorely, Lavallee, & Harwood, 2007). In addition, the concept of burnout was adapted and specified for the domain of sports and was called *athlete burnout* (Smith, 1986). This adaption promoted a scientific examination and vivid discussion on burnout in regards to the domain of sports including athletes and coaches (Goodger et al., 2007). Athlete burnout is characterized with three core dimensions, which are (a) physical and emotional exhaustion, (b) sport devaluation, and (c) reduced sense of accomplishment (Raedeke & Smith, 2001). This is also reflected in the most common measurement for athlete burnout: the Athlete Burnout Questionnaire (ABQ; Raedeke & Smith, 2001). This questionnaire is most often used to assess burnout with its three core dimensions with 15 items and thus represents a brief but reliable measurement.

### Theory and concepts of depression and burnout in sports

Taking a look at the theoretical framework, athlete burnout and depression are often conceptualized in a stress-based model. The development of depression is most often described by a vulnerability-stress model (e.g. Alloy et al., 2006; Haffel et al., 2005; Hyde, Mezulis, & Abramson, 2008). Here, certain vulnerabilities (genetics, social aspects, cognitive distortions, etc.) in combination with a stressor (chronic or acute) can lead to depression (Lee et al., 2010). Findings among athletes also illustrate the relation to stress (Nixdorf et al., 2013) and certain stressors such as training loads or pressure to perform well (Nixdorf, Frank, & Beckmann, 2015). Regarding theories on athlete burnout we find three different starting points: (1) A stress-based model with emphasis on personality factors (Smith, 1986), (2) on the social context (Coakley, 1992) and (3) on an integrated burnout model based on both (Gustafsson, Kenttä, & Hassmén, 2011). Smith (1986) saw burnout as a potential outcome from the inability of coping with the chronic psychological stress athletes are facing in elite levels. Coakley (1992) assumed that burnout arose due to the structure and conditions of sport environments, assuming young athletes lost autonomy and developed narrow, sport-centred identities, which led to burnout. More recently, Gustafsson et al. (2011) suggested an integrated burnout model which includes many of the antecedents (perceived sport stress, one-dimensional athletic identity, less adaptive forms of sport motivation, etc.).

### Current research findings on depression and burnout in sports

In order to successfully develop and conduct prevention programmes, the consideration of important factors linked to depression and burnout is necessary. Therefore, the shared stress-based conceptualization provides useful information as stress is a central factor for depression and burnout. Findings indicating connections between stress and depression (Nixdorf et al., 2015; Nixdorf et al., 2013) as well as with stress and burnout (De Francisco, Arce, Vílchez, & Vales, 2016; Raedeke, 1997) highlight this importance. However, stress itself can be considered as an outcome of stressors interacting with the ability to successfully cope with these stressors (Lazarus, 1991, 2006; Lazarus & Folkman, 1987).

Regarding important stressors, findings illustrate injuries as a major stressor for affected athletes (Gouttebarge, Frings-Dresen, & Sluiter, 2015; Grylls & Spittle, 2008; Junge & Feddermann-Demont, 2016). Athletes with current or past injuries are at higher risk for depressive symptoms and burnout. Especially the connection to concussions is at interest here (Hutchison, Mainwaring, Comper, Richards, & Bisschop, 2009; Mainwaring, Hutchison, Bisschop, Comper, & Richards, 2010). American football is of special concern due to the sport-specific high chance of concussions and impacts in the area of head and shoulders. However, European football should be also taken into consideration due to the impacts in performing headers. Additionally, there is a relatively high likelihood of injuries compared to no-contact sports such as badminton, swimming, or snooker. Results in football samples highlight this stressor (Gouttebarge, Aoki, & Kerkhoffs, 2015; Junge & Feddermann-Demont, 2016). Further stressors with relation to depression and burnout are competition and especially failure during important competitions (Hammond, Gialloreto, Kubas, & Davis, 2013) and overtraining due to periods of intensified training (Armstrong & Van Heest, 2002; Lemyre, Roberts, & Stray-Gundersen, 2007; Nixdorf et al., 2013). Tabei, Fletcher, and Goodger (2012) explored organizational stressors, specifically for football players and found various stressors to be connected with athlete burnout. Major stressors in this regard were 'training and competition load, training and competition environment, travel arrangements, nutritional issues, risk of injury, leadership style, lack of social support, career and performance development, inadequate communication channels, and role overload' (Tabei et al., 2012, p. 160). The authors further conclude that the experience of burnout is influenced by the psycho-social dynamics within sport organizations. This is in line with findings from Nixdorf et al. (2015) illustrating stressors with close relation to the sport environment (e.g. training loads, pressure to perform) to show the strongest connection to depressive symptoms, chronic stress, and dropout intentions.

Recent research on depression showed differences between sport disciplines (Schaal et al., 2011). Results repeatedly showed that athletes in individual sport disciplines report higher levels of depression (Nixdorf et al., 2013; Wolanin et al., 2016). This was also replicated in a study with a large football sample on the team sports side (Nixdorf, Frank, & Beckmann, 2016). However, to conclude that football players should be at lower risk might be misleading. The authors also pointed out, that psychological mechanisms (attribution after failure in this case) might explain such differences. Results showed also higher levels of perceived pressure from outside in team sports, which might highlight another important factor for football players (Nixdorf et al., 2016). The more professional a football player becomes the higher the media attention and therefore the pressure to succeed. Pressure from outside to perform well is considered to be a part of perfectionism and will be further elaborated in the following.

### Cognition and attitudes

Perfectionism can be considered a personal disposition characterized by striving for flawlessness and setting exceedingly high standards, which is accompanied by tendencies for overly critical evaluations of one's behaviour (see Flett & Hewitt, 2002; Frost, Marten, Lahart, & Rosenblate, 1990; Hewitt & Flett, 1991b). Aspects of perfectionism can be regarded as maladaptive or adaptive (Stoeber & Otto, 2006). This is discussed particularly in sports, where striving can be considered as adaptive on first sight (Gotwals, Stoeber, Dunn, & Stoll, 2012). However, maladaptive aspects have been linked to depression (Hewitt & Flett, 1991a). In athletes, perfectionistic concerns have been repeatedly linked to burnout (e.g. Hill, Hall, Appleton, & Kozub, 2008; Madigan, Stoeber, & Passfield, 2015). Especially in football samples the negative outcomes of perfectionism have been examined. Althoug some positive aspects could be found, the general implication is for perfectionism to be a potential vulnerabiliy for experiencing burnout (Stoeber & Becker, 2008). Maladaptive aspects such as perfectionistic concerns appeared to be the highest risk factor for young football players (Hill, 2013). Moreover, research has also demonstrated longitudinal links highlighting the importance of perfectionism in developing burnout in athletes (Madigan et al., 2015). A recent study including a large sample of youth football players also found prospective connections between cognitive factors and both burnout and depression (Frank, Nixdorf, & Beckmann, 2017). In this study many possible factors were assessed in the beginning of a sporting season and their predictive value for increase of symptoms in depression and burnout over the season was analysed. Results revealed for dysfunctional attitudes, a related maladaptive pattern of rigid and overly critical attitudes (Haffel et al., 2005) to be a valuable predictor for increased levels of depressive symptoms and burnout as well.

*Motivation*

Besides the importance of cognition and attitudes another often discussed factor is related to motivation. For instance, motivational aspects from the self-determination theory (Ryan & Deci, 2000) have often been utilized and showed valuable aspects in explaining athlete burnout (Madigan, Stoeber, & Passfield, 2016). In terms of self-determination theory, controlled motivation appears to be positively associated with burnout whereas autonomous motivation was found to be negatively connected with athlete burnout (Appleton & Hill, 2012). Such motivational aspects were also shown in football, whereas self-determined motivation was protective in terms of athlete burnout (Curran, Appleton, Hill, & Hall, 2011). Also longitudinal investigations showed autonomous environments (perceived coaching behaviour) to prevent burnout in football players (Adie, Duda, & Ntoumanis, 2012). However, motivation seems also connected to other constructs such as perfectionism and long-term effects and relations are just at the beginning of being understood (Madigan et al., 2016).

*Coping*

Coping is considered to be a personal skill or a group of strategies used to handle stress and deal with negative events. With regards to the before mentioned relation to stress it has been postulated that coping strategies might be important in order to successfully cope with the various stressors (Lazarus, 2006). Lending support to this hypothesis, Nixdorf et al. (2013) as well as Crocker and Graham (1995) show correlations between coping strategies and depressive symptomatology. Nixdorf et al.

(2013) more specifically showed that the frequent use of negative coping strategies (escape, resignation, and self-pity) correlated with high levels of depressive symptomatology and positive strategies (situation control and addressing oneself in encouraging tones) showed correlations with low levels of depression. With regards to burnout there are numerous studies illustrating coping to be important for athlete burnout. Raedeke and Smith (2004) for example showed that coping was mediating the stress–burnout association.

## Practical implications

### Definition of prevention and its relevance

Few would disagree that it is better to prevent a problem than to correct it. Romano and Hage (2000) define prevention as including one or more of the following: (1) stopping a problem behaviour from ever occurring; (2) delaying the onset of a problem behaviour, especially for those at risk for the problem; (3) reducing the impact of a problem behaviour; (4) strengthening knowledge, attitudes, and behaviours that promote emotional and physical well-being; and (5) promoting institutional, community, and government policies that further physical, social, and emotional well-being of the larger community. This conceptualization is consistent with Caplan (1964) who identified prevention interventions as primary, secondary, and tertiary prevention, and with the alternative definition by Gordon (1983) that identified prevention interventions as universal, selected, and indicated for those not at risk, at risk, and experiencing early signs of problems. Romano and Hage (2000) also mention that although dimensions 1, 2, and 3 can be conceptualized in traditional primary, secondary, and tertiary terms and refer to the individual, dimensions 4 and 5 are conceptualized within a 'risk-reduction' framework. Regarding the community of elite football this definition, including possible prevention of mental disorders, such as depression and burnout, on an institutional level seems adequate and necessary.

Taking into account the before mentioned characteristics of elite football and its football academies (e.g. strong competition, media presence, high pressure to perform, accumulated stress) and remembering the theoretical framework of the development of burnout and depression one can argue a strong need for prevention programmes within youth football.

### Prevention of mental health in youth football

#### Organizational aspects of prevention

Mental disorders are often stigmatized in elite sports (Bauman, 2016; Steinfeldt & Steinfeldt, 2012). Athletes often perceive themselves in a specific role. Not fulfilling this role would go along with certain possible implications in terms of contracts (organizational or medial). This appears to be highly relevant for football as media attention is tremendous and implications for athletes' careers and financial rewards are huge. In response to research inquiries, German football officials responded in a very reserved way in the past decade. Illustrative examples of rejections argued with 'general exclusion of research related to personal topics of footballers', 'negative testing of antidepressants in the past', or 'resentments of broaching the topic in the team'. These arguments themselves might illustrate lack of information and underlying fear of constructively approaching the challenge of mental health in footballers. Fortunately, some clubs and important officials recognized the relevance of this topic and are cooperating, which is illustrated by recent research findings on this matter (Junge & Feddermann-Demont, 2016; Nixdorf et al., 2016). To overcome this issue on a larger scale, changes in social climate might be necessary. However, first steps might root in solid information and support offers for athletes and coaches; leading to a general prevention of mental disorders. Providing information on the relevance (e.g. prevalence rates), the syndrome itself, and the possibilities for further information and help is therefore important. These steps would fall into dimensions 4 and 5 of the above mentioned definition by Romano and Hage (2000). However, it might be even more important to not just inform on mental health but to provide information where players and other affected persons can seek help. It would be misleading to induce feelings of responsibility in coaches and officials with no expertise in this field. Providing access to practitioners or initiatives with expertise in prevention and treatment of burnout and depression however is an important task for coaches and supporting people with close relation to athletes. Findings on depression in athletes showed lower levels of depression for athletes experienced with sport psychological coaching (Nixdorf et al., 2013). Therefore, it would be preferable to have sport psychologists in place. In addition, sport psychologists integrated in a support team can help fight the stigma of mental health. In the case that the sport psychologist has a clinical background (bearing in mind that the training and requirements for sport psychologists is different in every country) the before mentioned vulnerabilities (e.g. attribution, coping strategies) can be trained and improved within a concept of primary and secondary prevention. Though it should be considered that a mere additional workshop on 'coping with stress' for example should never be obligatory for all players since the idea of broadly distributing different interventions on all athletes can be considered an added stressor itself, if a player has in fact good strategies to begin with. Keeping this in mind, a broad spectrum of primary prevention workshops might not be the way to go. Especially, if vulnerabilities are known through multiple research (e.g. negative coping strategies or attributional style) and screening instruments are developed, a secondary prevention of topics being of major importance for the individual player seems more reasonable.

*Content of prevention*

Table 25.1 gives an overview of general prevention on mental health subdivided on an individual and an organizational level regarding the before mentioned three types of prevention. A general goal on an organizational level would be the implementation of a sport psychologist as part of the training staff. The content of prevention on an individual level should always be done by a skilled sport psychologist and in this matter regarding the clinical issues of burnout and depression, a clinical training would be an advisable background. This will most likely help fight the stigma and will offer a direct connection to educating coaches and officials regarding mental health. Since, as mentioned before, the idea of broadly distributing different interventions on all athletes can be considered an added stressor

*Table 25.1* Overview of prevention content

|  | Organizational level | Individual level |
|---|---|---|
| **Primary prevention** | Implementing a sport psychologist<br>• Fighting the stigma<br>• Providing a network of support and an exchange with practitioners and initiatives outside the club | Educating about symptoms, vulnerabilities, and developmental factors |
| **Secondary prevention** | Implementing a regular screening | Discussing screening results with the athlete and training possible vulnerabilities |
| **Tertiary prevention** | Quick reintegration of athletes in the team (e.g. after an injury or treatment) | Relapse prevention and support in reintegration in the training and the team |

itself, we highly emphasize implementing a screening in order to assess vulnerabilities to burnout or depression (e.g. attribution style, perfectionism).

Athletes should be educated about (early) symptoms of depression and burnout and possible vulnerabilities in this regard. Keeping in mind the developmental factors of depression and burnout a screening as regular as every 3–5 months is advisable. If a screening within a football club is implemented and conducted a secondary prevention should be to discuss the screening results with the players and then using established and evaluated intervention (e.g. gathered from behavioural therapy) to improve possible vulnerabilities. These trainings can be done in groups, since there is a stigma and a strong need for anonymity is in need we recommend individual coaching on these issues. In case an athlete developed symptoms of depression or burnout or fulfils a diagnosis, after treatment, relapse prevention and support in reintegration in the training and the team would be considered a tertiary prevention.

## Future research directions and conclusions for applied sport psychologists active within football

Mental health in elite sports especially in football has been largely neglected in the past. Recently it has increasingly started to be taken seriously by professional football. To date, few scientific studies address mental health problems in football up to now, due to a reluctance of officials to grant researchers access to the population of professional football players. However, the resistance is fading as the full range and impact of the problem goes public. Especially, unions of professional football have their share in this development. The 2015 study commissioned by the FIFPro World Players' Union was a milestone in this respect (Gouttebarge, Aoki, & Kerkhoffs, 2015). The present chapter mainly focused on depression and burnout as one of the most researched areas of psychological disorders in elite sports. Even here there still is a lack of football-specific studies. Besides a need for differentiating the two constructs, there is definitely a need for discovering football-specific factors for burnout and depression among football players. As Sebastian Deisler states in his biography (Rosentritt, 2009) especially the extraordinarily well-paid football stars may be faced with stress factors that can lead to depression. The media plays an important role in this context but also fans have little understanding of players' experiences. According to Martyn Heather, Head of Welfare and Education at the Premier League, 'Dealing with injuries or loss of form can be really tough and if you are susceptible to mental health issues these can easily be a trigger. It is hard for fans to understand that someone playing a sport they love, and being paid a lot of money, can experience mental health issues.' Michael Bennett, Head of Player Welfare at the PFA, agrees. 'The public perception is: why should these players have any problems when they are earning a large amount of money?' (quotes from Keble, 2016). The present chapter shows that not only players who are already stars are susceptible to burnout and depression but young players may be at even higher risk given the many uncertainties on their career path. As the Gouttebarge, Aoki, and Kerkhoffs (2015) study indicates, burnout, depression, and drug addiction are serious problems in football. But currently we know almost nothing about other psychological disorders in football as in other sports.

To prevent mental health problems in football, psychological resilience should be promoted in young players early on. In a number of European countries mental health counselling has meanwhile been introduced (since 2013 in the UK). In Germany, psychology has become an integral part in the development of players in youth academies (see Beckmann-Waldenmayer, 2019, Chapter 20 in this book). Jean Cote's youth coaching model is becoming more and more accepted (Fraser-Thomas, Côté, & Deakin, 2005). Life coaching instead of pure football coaching is a fundamental change in perspective adopted by many of these academies (Beckmann & Nash, 2017).

Additionally, better understanding the mental health issues in elite sports and especially in football could help make the subject more approachable for people across society, notably for males who still tend to avoid it more than females. Discussing mental health issues in football might encourage more people to seek help.

## Conclusion

The chapter gives an overview on issues of depression and burnout in elite football and summarizes the current state of research in this field. Depression and burnout in elite football has raised public awareness. Empirical data on this issue are just evolving. The prevalence rates for depression are just as high in elite sports compared to the general population. Studies revealed correlated factors (e.g. chronic stress, recovery, injury, perfectionism, coping strategies) and first prospective connections have been uncovered (e.g. dysfunctional attitudes, rigid and overly critic attitudes), which have been a valuable predictor for increased levels of depressive symptoms and burnout. The chapter further gives an overview of prevention strategies and content and its importance in youth football.

## References

Adie, J. W., Duda, J. L., & Ntoumanis, N. (2012). Perceived coach-autonomy support, basic need satisfaction and the well- and ill-being of elite youth soccer players: A longitudinal investigation. *Psychology of Sport and Exercise, 13*(1), 51–59. doi:10.1016/j.psychsport.2011.07.008.

Alloy, L. B., Abramson, L. Y., Whitehouse, W. G., Hogan, M. E., Panzarella, C., & Rose, D. T. (2006). Prospective incidence of first onsets and recurrences of depression in individuals at high and low cognitive risk for depression. *J Abnorm Psychol, 115*(1), 145–156. doi:10. 1037/0021-843X.115.1.145.

American Psychiatric Association. (2013). *Diagnostic and statistical manual of mental disorders* (5th ed.). Washington, DC: APA.

Appleton, P. R., & Hill, A. P. (2012). Perfectionism and athlete burnout in junior elite athletes: The mediating role of motivation regulations. *Journal of Clinical Sport Psychology, 6*(2), 129–145.

Armstrong, L. E., & Van Heest, J. L. (2002). The unknown mechanism of the overtraining syndrome: Clues from depression and psychoneuroimmunology. *Sports Med, 32*(3), 185–209.

Armstrong, S., & Oomen-Early, J. (2009). Social connectedness, self-esteem, and depression symptomatology among collegiate athletes versus nonathletes. *Journal of American College Health, 57*(5), 521–526. doi:10.3200/JACH.57.5.521-526.

Bauman, N. J. (2016). The stigma of mental health in athletes: Are mental toughness and mental health seen as contradictory in elite sport? *Br J Sports Med, 50*(3), 135–136. doi:10.1136/bjsports-2015-095570.

Beckmann, J., & Nash, C. (2017). *From sport coaching to life coaching.* Manuscript, Technical University of Munich.

Beckmann-Waldenmayer, D. (2019). Parental coaching in football. In E. Konter, J. Beckmann, & T. M. Loughead (Eds.), *Football psychology: From theory to practice.* London, England: Routledge.

Bianchi, R., Schonfeld, I. S., & Laurent, E. (2015). Burnout-depression overlap: A review. *Clin Psychol Rev, 36*, 28–41. doi:10.1016/j.cpr.2015.01.004.

Biermann, A., & Schäfer, R. (2011). *Rote Karte Depression. Das Ende einer Karriere im Profifußball* [Red card depression: The end of a professional football career]. Gütersloh, Germany: Gütersloher Verlagshaus.

Caccese, T. M., & Mayerberg, C. K. (1984). Gender differences in perceived burnout of college coaches. *Journal of Sport Psychology, 6*(3), 279–288.

Caplan, G. (1964). *Principles of preventive psychiatry.* New York, NY: Basic Books.

Coakley, J. (1992). Burnout among adolescent athletes – a personal failure or social-problem. *Sociology of Sport Journal, 9*(3), 271–285.

Crocker, P. R., & Graham, T. R. (1995). Coping by competitive athletes with performance stress: Gender differences and relationships with affect. *The Sport Psychologist, 9*(3), 325–338.

Curran, T., Appleton, P. R., Hill, A. P., & Hall, H. K. (2011). Passion and burnout in elite junior soccer players: The mediating role of self-determined motivation. *Psychology of Sport and Exercise, 12*(6), 655–661. doi:10.1016/j.psychsport.2011.06.004.

Dale, J., & Weinberg, R. (1990). Burnout in sport: A review and critique. *Journal of Applied Sport Psychology, 2*(1), 67–83. doi:10.1080/10413209008406421.

De Francisco, C., Arce, C., Vílchez, M. d. P., & Vales, Á. (2016). Antecedents and consequences of burnout in athletes: Perceived stress and depression. *International Journal of Clinical and Health Psychology, 16*(3), 239–246. doi:10.1016/j.ijchp. 2016.04.001.

Dilling, H., Mombour, W., Schmidt, M. H., Schulte-Markwort, E., & Remschmidt, H. (2015). *Internationale Klassifikation psychischer Störungen: ICD-10 Kapitel V (F) klinisch-diagnostische Leitlinien* (10. Auflage) [International classification of mental disorders: ICD-10 chapter V (F) clinical diagnostic guidelines (10th ed.)]. Bern, Switzerland: Hogrefe Verlag.

Doherty, S., Hannigan, B., & Campbell, M. J. (2016). The experience of depression during the careers of elite male athletes. *Front Psychol, 7*, 1069. doi:10.3389/fpsyg.2016.01069.

Eklund, R. C., & DeFreese, J. (2015). Athlete burnout: What we know, what we could know, and how we can find out more. *International Journal of Applied Sports Sciences, 27*(2), 63–75.

Fender, L. K. (1989). Athlete burnout: Potential for research and intervention strategies. *The Sport Psychologist, 3*(1), 63–71.

Flett, G. L., & Hewitt, P. L. (2002). Perfectionism and maladjustment: An overview of theoretical, definitional, and treatment issues. In P. L. Hewitt & G. L. Flett (Eds.), *Perfectionism: Theory, research, and treatment* (pp. 5–31). Washington, DC: American Psychological Association.

Frank, R., Nixdorf, I., & Beckmann, J. (2013). Depressionen im Hochleistungssport: Prävalenzen und psychologische Einflüsse [Depression in elite athletes: Prevalence and psychological factors]. *Deutsche Zeitschrift fuer Sportmedizin, 64*(11), 320–326. doi:10.5960/dzsm.2013.088.

Frank, R., Nixdorf, I., & Beckmann, J. (2017). Analyzing the relationship between burnout and depression in junior elite athletes. *Journal of Clinical Sport Psychology, 11*(4), 287–303.

Fraser-Thomas, J. L., Côté, J., & Deakin, J. (2005). Youth sport programs: An avenue to foster positive youth development. *Physical Education and Sport Pedagogy, 10*, 19–40.

Freudenberger, H. J. (1974). Staff burn-out. *Journal of Social Issues, 30*(1), 159–165.

Frost, R. O., Marten, P., Lahart, C., & Rosenblate, R. (1990). The dimensions of perfectionism. *Cognit Ther Res, 14*(5), 449–468.

Goodger, K., Gorely, T., Lavallee, D., & Harwood, C. (2007). Burnout in sport: A systematic review. *The Sport Psychologist, 21*, 127–151.

Gordon, R. S. (1983). An operational classification of disease prevention. *Public Health Reports, 98*(2), 107–109.

Gotwals, J. K., Stoeber, J., Dunn, J. G. H., & Stoll, O. (2012). Are perfectionistic strivings in sport adaptive? A systematic review of confirmatory, contradictory, and mixed evidence. *Canadian Psychology/Psychologie canadienne, 53*(4), 263–279. doi:10.1037/a0030288.

Gouttebarge, V., Aoki, H., & Kerkhoffs, G. (2015). Symptoms of common mental disorders and adverse health behaviours in male professional soccer players. *Journal of Human Kinetics, 49*(1), 277–286. doi:10.1515/hukin-2015-0130.

Gouttebarge, V., Frings-Dresen, M. H., & Sluiter, J. K. (2015). Mental and psychosocial health among current and former professional footballers. *Occup Med (Lond), 65*(3), 190–196. doi:10.1093/occmed/kqu202.

Grylls, E., & Spittle, M. (2008). Injury and burnout in Australian athletes. *Percept Mot Skills, 107*(3), 873–880. doi:10.2466/pms.107.3.873-880.

Gulliver, A., Griffiths, K. M., Mackinnon, A., Batterham, P. J., & Stanimirovic, R. (2015). The mental health of Australian elite athletes. *Journal of Science and Medicine in Sport, 18*(3), 255–261. doi:10.1016/j.jsams.2014.04.006.

Gustafsson, H., Kenttä, G., & Hassmén, P. (2011). Athlete burnout: An integrated model and future research directions. *International Review of Sport and Exercise Psychology, 4*(1), 3–24. doi:10.1080/1750984x.2010.541927.

Haffel, G. J., Abramson, L. Y., Voelz, Z. R., Metalsky, G. I., Halberstadt, L., Dykman, B. M., … Alloy, L. B. (2005). Negative cognitive styles, dysfunctional attitudes, and the remitted depression paradigm: A search for the elusive cognitive vulnerability to depression factor among remitted depressives. *Emotion, 5*(3), 343–348. doi:10.1037/1528-3542.5.3.343.

Hammond, T., Gialloreto, C., Kubas, H., & Davis, H. (2013). The prevalence of failure-based depression among elite athletes. *Clinical Journal of Sport Medicine, 23*(4), 273–277. doi:10.1097/JSM.0b013e318287b870.

Hewitt, P. L., & Flett, G. L. (1991a). Dimensions of perfectionism in unipolar depression. *J Abnorm Psychol, 100*(1), 98–101.

Hewitt, P. L., & Flett, G. L. (1991b). Perfectionism in the self and social contexts: Conceptualization, assessment, and association with psychopathology. *J Pers Soc Psychol, 60*(3), 456–470.

Hill, A. P. (2013). Perfectionism and burnout in junior soccer players: A test of the 2×2 model of dispositional perfectionism. *J Sport Exerc Psychol, 35*(1), 18–29.

Hill, A. P., Hall, H. K., Appleton, P. R., & Kozub, S. A. (2008). Perfectionism and burnout in junior elite soccer players: The mediating influence of unconditional self-acceptance. *Psychology of Sport and Exercise, 9*(5), 630–644. doi:10.1016/j.psychsport.2007.09.004.

Hutchison, M., Mainwaring, L. M., Comper, P., Richards, D. W., & Bisschop, S. M. (2009). Differential emotional responses of varsity athletes to concussion and musculoskeletal injuries. *Clin J Sport Med, 19*(1), 13–19. doi:10.1097/JSM.0b013e318190ba06.

Hyde, J. S., Mezulis, A. H., & Abramson, L. Y. (2008). The ABCs of depression: Integrating affective, biological, and cognitive models to explain the emergence of the gender difference in depression. *Psychol Rev, 115*(2), 291–313. doi:10.1037/0033-295X.115.2.291.

Insel, T. R., & Charney, D. S. (2003). Research on major depression: Strategies and priorities. *Jama, 289*(23), 3167–3168.

Junge, A., & Feddermann-Demont, N. (2016). Prevalence of depression and anxiety in top-level male and female football players. *BMJ Open Sport and Exercise Medicine, 2*(1), e000087. doi:10.1136/bmjsem-2015-000087.

Keble, A. (2016, 5 December). Overcoming the empathy barrier: Mental health in the Premier League. *VICE Sports*. Retrieved from https://sports.vice.com/en_au/article/xybgbn/overcoming-the-empathy-barrier-mental-health-in-the-premier-league.

Lazarus, R. S. (1991). *Emotion and adaptation*. New York, NY: Oxford University Press.

Lazarus, R. S. (2006). *Stress and emotion: A new synthesis*. New York, NY: Springer Publishing Company.

Lazarus, R. S., & Folkman, S. (1987). Transactional theory and research on emotions and coping. *European Journal of Personality, 1*(3), 141–169.

Lee, S., Jeong, J., Kwak, Y., & Park, S. K. (2010). Depression research: Where are we now? *Mol Brain, 3:8*. doi:10.1186/1756-6606-3-8.

Lemyre, P.-N., Roberts, G. C., & Stray-Gundersen, J. (2007). Motivation, overtraining, and burnout: Can self-determined motivation predict overtraining and burnout in elite athletes? *European Journal of Sport Science, 7*(2), 115–126. doi:10.1080/17461390701302607.

Madigan, D. J., Stoeber, J., & Passfield, L. (2015). Perfectionism and burnout in junior athletes: A three-month longitudinal study. *J Sport Exerc Psychol, 37*(3), 305–315. doi:10.1123/jsep. 2014-0266.

Madigan, D. J., Stoeber, J., & Passfield, L. (2016). Motivation mediates the perfectionism-burnout relationship: A three-wave longitudinal study with junior athletes. *J Sport Exerc Psychol*, 1–39. doi:10.1123/jsep.2015-0238.

Mainwaring, L. M., Hutchison, M., Bisschop, S. M., Comper, P., & Richards, D. W. (2010). Emotional response to sport concussion compared to ACL injury. *Brain Inj, 24*(4), 589–597. doi:10.3109/02699051003610508.

Maslach, C. (2001). What have we learned about burnout and health? *Psychology & Health, 16*(5), 607–611.

Maslach, C., & Jackson, S. E. (1981). The measurement of experienced burnout. *Journal of Organizational Behavior, 2*(2), 99–113.

Maslach, C., Schaufeli, W. B., & Leiter, M. P. (2001). Job burnout. *Annual Review of Psychology, 52*(1), 397–422.

Nixdorf, I., Frank, R., & Beckmann, J. (2015). An explorative study on major stressors and its connection to depression and chronic stress among German elite athletes. *Advances in Physical Education, 05*(04), 255–262. doi:10.4236/ape.2015.54030.

Nixdorf, I., Frank, R., & Beckmann, J. (2016). Comparison of athletes' proneness to depressive symptoms in individual and team sports: Research on psychological mediators in junior elite athletes. *Front Psychol, 7:893*. doi:10.3389/fpsyg.2016.00893.

Nixdorf, I., Frank, R., Hautzinger, M., & Beckmann, J. (2013). Prevalence of depressive symptoms and correlating variables among German elite athletes. *Journal of Clinical Sport Psychology, 7*(4), 313–326.

Puffer, J. C., & McShane, J. M. (1992). Depression and chronic fatigue in athletes. *Clin Sports Med, 11*(2), 327–338.

Radloff, L. S. (1977). The CES-D scale: A self-report depression scale for research in the general population. *Applied Psychological Measurement, 1*(3), 385–401. doi:10.1177/01466216 7700100306.

Raedeke, T. D. (1997). Is athlete burnout more than just stress? A sport commitment perspective. *Journal of Sport & Exercise Psychology, 19*(4), 396–417.

Raedeke, T. D., & Smith, A. L. (2001). Development and preliminary validation of an athlete burnout measure. *Journal of Sport and Exercise Psychology, 23*(4), 281–306.

Raedeke, T. D., & Smith, A. L. (2004). Coping resources and athlete burnout: A examination of stress mediated and moderation hypotheses. *Journal of Sport & Exercise Psychology, 26*(4), 525–541.

Raglin, J. S., Morgan, W. P., & O'Connor, P. J. (1991). Changes in mood states during training in female and male college swimmers. *Int J Sports Med, 12*(6), 585–589. doi:10.1055/s-2007-1024739.

Reng, R. (2011). *A life too short: The tragedy of Robert Enke.* London, England: Yellow Jersey Press.

Romano, J. L., & Hage, S. M. (2000). Prevention and counseling psychology revitalizing commitments for the 21st century. *The Counseling Psychologist, 28*(6), 733–763.

Rosentritt, M. (2009). *Sebastian Deisler. Zurück ins Leben* [Sebastian Deisler: Back to life]. Duisburg, Germany: Edel.

Ryan, R. M., & Deci, E. L. (2000). Intrinsic and extrinsic motivations: Classic definitions and new directions. *Contemp Educ Psychol, 25*(1), 54–67. doi:10.1006/ceps.1999.1020.

Schaal, K., Tafflet, M., Nassif, H., Thibault, V., Pichard, C., Alcotte, M., … Toussaint, J. F. (2011). Psychological balance in high level athletes: Gender-based differences and sport-specific patterns. *PLoS One, 6*(5), e19007. doi:10.1371/journal.pone.0019007.

Smith, R. E. (1986). Toward a cognitive-affective model of athletic burnout. *Journal of Sport Psychology, 8*(1), 36–50.

Steinfeldt, J. A., & Steinfeldt, M. C. (2012). Profile of masculine norms and help-seeking stigma in college football. *Sport, Exercise, and Performance Psychology, 1*(1), 58–71.

Stoeber, J., & Becker, C. (2008). Perfectionism, achievement motives, and attribution of success and failure in female soccer players. *Int J Psychol, 43*(6), 980–987. doi:10.1080/00207590701403850.

Stoeber, J., & Otto, K. (2006). Positive conceptions of perfectionism: Approaches, evidence, challenges. *Personality and Social Psychology Review, 10*(4), 295–319. doi:10.1207/s15327957 pspr1004_2.

Storch, E. A., Storch, J. B., Killiany, E. M., & Roberti, J. W. (2005). Self-reported psychopathology in athletes: A comparison of intercollegiate student-athletes and non-athletes. *Journal of Sport Behavior, 28*(1), 86–98.

Sußebach, H., & Willeke, S. (2009). Man muss härter sein als ich. Interview with Sebastian Deisler. *Die Zeit, 41.* Retrieved from www.zeit.de/2009/41/DOS-Deisler.

Tabei, Y., Fletcher, D., & Goodger, K. (2012). The relationship between organizational stressors and athlete burnout in soccer players. *Journal of Clinical Sport Psychology, 6*(2), 146–165.

Wolanin, A., Hong, E., Marks, D., Panchoo, K., & Gross, M. (2016). Prevalence of clinically elevated depressive symptoms in college athletes and differences by gender and sport. *Br J Sports Med, 50*(3), 167–171. doi:10.1136/bjsports-2015-095756.

Yang, J., Peek-Asa, C., Corlette, J. D., Cheng, G., Foster, D. T., & Albright, J. (2007). Prevalence of and risk factors associated with symptoms of depression in competitive collegiate student athletes. *Clinical Journal of Sport Medicine, 17*(6), 481–487. doi:10.1097/JSM.0b013e 31815aed6b.

# Index

Page numbers in **bold** denote tables, those in *italics* denote figures.